INTERNATIONAL
FINANCIAL
ACCOUNTING

A COMPARATIVE APPROACH

INTERNATIONAL FINANCIAL ACCOUNTING

A COMPARATIVE APPROACH

Clare Roberts

Pauline Weetman

Paul Gordon

FINANCIAL TIMES
PITMAN PUBLISHING

FINANCIAL TIMES

MANAGEMENT

LONDON · SAN FRANCISCO
KUALA LUMPUR · JOHANNESBURG

Financial Times Management delivers the knowledge,
skills and understanding that enable students,
managers and organisations to achieve their ambitions,
whatever their needs, wherever they are.

London Office:
128 Long Acre, London WC2E 9AN
Tel: +44 (0)171 447 2000
Fax: +44 (0)171 240 5771
Website: www.ftmanagement.com

A Division of Financial Times Professional Limited

First published in Great Britain 1998

ISBN 0 273 62376 1

British Library Cataloguing in Publication Data
A CIP catalogue record for this book can be obtained from the British Library

10 9 8 7 6 5 4 3 2 1

Typeset by Pantek Arts, Maidstone, Kent
Printed and bound in Great Britain by William Clowes Ltd, Beccles

The Publishers' policy is to use paper manufactured from sustainable forests.

Contents

Part 2
COUNTRY STUDIES

Part 3
REACTIONS TO INTERNATIONAL DIVERSITY IN FINANCIAL REPORTING SYSTEMS

Preface

Introduction

International accounting is an enigma. There is no universal practice of account-ing – each country has its own set of rules and guidance for financial reporting by corporate enterprises. At the same time there are companies which provide infor-mation to investors, lenders or other groups in more than one country. The study of international accounting involves documenting and measuring similarities and differences in financial reporting practices; identifying factors which may have caused the similarities and differences to occur; classifying systems of accounting on the basis of common characteristics; and observing organisations whose role it is to encourage greater similarity of international accounting practice. Having a working knowledge of similarities and differences in accounting practices inter-nationally is essential for all companies involved in any form of international business and for investors and their advisers who seek a cross-border portfolio of shares. International accounting offers a challenge to the researcher in overcoming barriers of culture and language.

Aim of the book

This text aims to bring to undergraduate and postgraduate courses in accounting and finance an awareness of similarities and differences in accounting practices and an ability to analyse the causes and consequences of those similarities and dif-ferences. There is a strong emphasis placed on International Accounting Standards as the focus of comparison, because of the growing importance and increasing acceptance of IASs.

The book aims also to familiarise students with the growing body of research into international accounting practices, giving detailed explanation of research methods which may encourage students to apply such techniques in project work.

Structure of the book

Part 1, containing the first seven chapters of the book, sets the analytical framework for the study of accounting practice. The institutional framework is described in Chapter 1, covering in general terms the influence of the political system, the eco-nomic system, the legal system, the tax system, the financing system and the accounting profession. Cultural influences on accounting rules and practice are explained in Chapter 2 using well-known academic sources. Practical approaches to measuring international differences in accounting rules and practices are presented in Chapter 3, drawing on methods established in the research literature that are suitable for student project applications. Classification of accounting systems, as presented in Chapter 4, provides a framework indicating international similarities and differences.

Chapters 5 to 7 provide the basis of International Accounting Standards (IASs) and European Union practice against which specific countries may be compared. Chapters 5 and 7 describe the institutions while Chapter 6 explains key aspects of each IAS and sets out the controversial issues which have been explored in establishing the standard.

Part 2 contains Chapters 8 to 17, setting out separate country studies. The Introduction to Part 2 sets out the structure of each chapter and the learning outcomes, which are consistent for each country studied. There is strong emphasis, in the content of each country chapter, on the institutional environment within which accounting practice operates. An academic framework based on perceived cultural differences and accounting values allows initial classification against which practice can be measured and evaluated.

The countries have been selected to cover aspects of European accounting (France, Germany, The Netherlands and the UK), English-speaking countries (Australia and the US), an Eastern European country (Hungary), an established Far East country (Japan), a command economy introducing elements of market forces (China) and a developing capital market (Egypt). Taken as a whole, this set of country-specific studies provides a range of insight into how accounting has developed under varying influences. Each chapter is linked to Chapters 1 to 7 in the framework of construction of the chapter.

Chapters 18 and 19 return to the global picture. Stock market listing behaviour (Chapter 18) is one factor which indicates a company's attitude to globalisation. Corporate reporting policies (Chapter 19) consider the extent to which a company must pay attention to the needs of those using financial statements.

Particular features

In particular, students and lecturers will find the following features helpful:

- *there is a strong emphasis on International Accounting Standards* as a basis for comparison of international similarities and differences, at a time when the IASs are receiving careful and serious attention from standard-setting authorities in many countries;

- *consistent structure of chapters* dealing with national accounting in the context of an institutional framework, a cultural perspective and a comparison with IASs;

- *examples of accounting practices* which are drawn from published accounts;

- *names of major companies* in each country are given as a guide to students intending to investigate further;

- *case studies* are drawn from practice and from research studies to illustrate the general points of principle contained in early chapters;

- *end-of-chapter questions* encourage students to analyse and compare the information within and between chapters;

- *experienced researchers* show how the methods used in research papers may be understood and applied in undergraduate honours and postgraduate courses;
- *an accompanying Lecturer's Guide* assists students and lecturers in the practical exploration of the wealth of material available for study of aspects of international accounting. (This Guide is available free to lecturers adopting this text.)

Flexible course design

There was a time when the academic year comprised three terms of around 10 weeks each. Now there are increasingly semesters of around 15 weeks each. The material in this book is sufficient for a 15-week semester; it may require more selective treatment for the 10-week term. For those seeking to plan a shorter course, Chapters 1 to 4 are a self-contained unit describing the academic literature. Chapters 5 to 7 set a practical framework. Thereafter each country chapter is self-contained but it is not essential to use every one of them. A short course (such as a half-semester) could comprise Chapters 1 to 4 plus one EU and one non-EU country. A term of 10 weeks might draw on Chapters 1 to 7, plus two or three national chapters, and Chapter 19 on corporate reporting policies.

Target readership

This book is targeted at final year undergraduate students on degree courses in accounting or business studies. It is also appropriate for use in a core module of a specialist postgraduate MSc taught course or an MBA. It has an international perspective, in its basis of International Accounting Standards, and so is not restricted to study within a particular country.

The book should also be of interest to professional readers and general management because a comparative analysis is provided which links to much of the intuitive work carried out.

Acknowledgments

The authors have used much of the material of this text in their respective teaching assignments with final year and postgraduate students and are appreciative of feedback from students in several universities.

They are grateful to the following reviewers of the international chapters:

Australia
Chris Kelly
Senior Lecturer
Deakin University
Geelong
Victoria 3217

China
Professor Zhengfei Lu
School of International Business
Nanjing University
22 Hankou Road
Nanjing
Jiangsu 210008

France
Professor Jean-Claude Scheid
Conservatoire National des Arts et Métiers
Institut National des Techniques Économiques et Comptables (INTEC)
292 Rue St Martin
Paris 75141

Germany
Professor Dr Wolfgang Ballwieser
Ludwig-Maximilians-Universität
Seminar für Rechnungswesen und Prüfung
Ludwigstrasse 28/RG
Munich 80539

Hungary
Professor Derek Bailey
Thames Valley University
St Mary's Road
London W5 5RF

Japan
Professor Kazuo Hiramatsu
School of Business Administration
Kwansei Gakuin University
1-1-155 Uegahara Nishinomiya
Hyogo 662

The Netherlands
D H van Offeren
Assistant Professor of Accounting
University of Amsterdam
Roetersstraat 11
1018 WB Amsterdam

USA
Professor James A Schweikart
Dept of Accounting
E. Claiborn Robins School of Business
University of Richmond
Virginia 23173

Particular thanks for encouragement and support must go to Pat Bond, Sadie McClelland and Annette McFadyen at Financial Times Pitman Publishing.

The authors also acknowledge with thanks the following organisations and individuals who have given them permission to use material in this book:

Omneya H Abd Elsalam
Accounting Books, The Institute of Chartered Accountants in England and Wales
American Accounting Association
Blackwell Publishers
David Cairns
Cambridge University Press
The European Accounting Review
Garland Publishing
Gower Publishing
The International Accounting Standards Committee
The Journal of International Business Studies
Macmillan Press
RD Nair and WG Frank
Sage Productions
The University of Texas at Dallas, Center for International Accounting Development

Plan of the book

Part 1

THE EXTENT OF INTERNATIONAL DIVERSITY IN FINANCIAL REPORTING SYSTEMS

International harmonisation: standardisation and the IASC

Harmonisation is a process of moving away from diversity towards harmony. Harmony is achieved where clusters of very similar practices are identified. Standardisation is a process of moving by regulatory means to a state of uniformity where all participants apply the same practices. The academic research described in Chapter 3 is largely concerned with harmonisation. Harmonisation is achieved by a gradual process of mutual understanding and adaptation. For those who seek a more clearly defined route to international similarity in accounting, the route of standardisation may be attractive. This requires an international regulatory body or guidance from a body which is in a position to influence the national regulators.

There is a variety of bodies seeking to promote harmonisation on a world stage or in larger groupings of countries. Their work is outlined in Chapter 5. Standardisation, however, has been seen most effectively in the work of the International Accounting Standards Committee (IASC). This work is fundamental to an understanding of accounting similarities and differences. Chapter 5 explains the operation of the IASC as a regulatory body, its approach to setting International Accounting Standards (lASs) and the conceptual basis on which it sets those standards.

A key to the success of the IASs internationally is the acceptance by leading stock exchanges of financial statements prepared on the basis of IASs. Chapter 6 explains, for each IAS, the accounting issue covered, the points of contention and the steps taken in recent years to achieve standardisation. The key element of the work of the IASC in the 1990s has been acceptance by the leading stock exchanges, through their organisation IOSCO (International Organization of Securities Commissions), of financial statements prepared according to IASs. Each of the country chapters (8 to 17) contains a section setting out the areas where the accounting practice of that country differs from or resembles the relevant IAS.

Learning outcomes

Specific learning outcome are set at the start of each chapter of Part 1. Overall, the learning outcomes are that on completion of Part 1 the student should be able to:

- set out a framework of institutional and external influences which should be applied to any country-specific study
- set out a framework of cultural factors and accounting values to be applied to any country-specific study
- carry out a simple measurement of international differences in accounting practices using data provided for the purpose
- explain the various approaches to accounting classification
- explain the work of the International Accounting Standards Committee
- use the relevant IAS as a basis for comparison with country-specific information provided for the purpose.

Chapter 1

Institutional and external influences on accounting rules and practices

1.1 **PURPOSE OF THE CHAPTER**

This chapter explores some of the reasons why financial accounting rules and practices differ across countries. Many factors have influenced the development of accounting and there are many reasons why countries have developed different accounting systems.[1] This chapter explores some of the ways in which a society can organise itself and how this affects the way in which accounting is undertaken. Five different features of a country are explored in this chapter, namely:

- the political and economic system
- the legal system
- the taxation system
- the corporate financing system
- the accounting profession.

Accounting rules and practices are not only developed inside a country, they may also be imported into the country. This chapter therefore concludes by looking at the process of importing and exporting accounting rules and practices.

Learning objectives

After reading this chapter you should be able to:

- Understand how various aspects of a country's political and economic system influence its accounting system.
- Distinguish between common and code law systems and describe how the legal system typically influences the system of accounting regulation.

---

[1] While accounting includes not only financial reporting but also management accounting, auditing and public sector accounting, the term 'accounting system' is used in this book unless otherwise stated, to mean the financial reporting system. This includes both the rules or regulations and the actual practices of profit-orientated limited liability companies.

- Describe the ways in which the tax system can influence accounting rules and practices.
- Identify possible differences in the financing of companies internationally and describe how these differences may help to explain differences in accounting rules and practices.
- Understand how the way in which the accounting profession is organised can influence accounting rules and practices.
- Understand how a country might import or export accounting rules and practices.

The chapter proceeds by introducing a general model that explains the types of factors that influence accounting. It then carries on to look at two of these, namely institutional factors and external factors. Chapter 2 then explores what is meant by 'culture', and looks at how the culture of a country can influence its accounting system.

1.2 FACTORS INFLUENCING THE DEVELOPMENT OF ACCOUNTING SYSTEMS

No two countries have identical accounting systems. In a few cases – such as that of the UK and Ireland, or the USA and Canada – the differences are relatively few and relatively minor. In other instances – such as, for example, the UK and France, or the USA and Mexico – the differences are much greater and include some quite fundamental differences. (*See* Case study 1.1 at the end of the chapter for more on the differences between accounting practices in the USA, Canada and Mexico.) Differences can exist at all levels of the accounting system. For example, if the treatment of assets is considered, a wide range of different rules and practices are found. Countries can adopt different valuation methods, ranging from strict historical cost to full current cost systems. Countries can also adopt quite different definitions of an asset – using either legal ownership- or economic control-based definitions. Differences in the relative importance accorded to different accounting principles – in particular the matching or accruals principle and the prudence or conservatism principle – will also influence the accounting methods used.

Both measurement and disclosure rules vary across countries. Differences in disclosure regulations include differences in the scope of the financial statements. For example, the USA requires only group financial statements, but individual financial statements have traditionally been more important in countries such as Italy or Japan.

Many reasons have been given to explain why accounting systems vary so much. Exhibit 1.1 illustrates the range of possible influences.

The accounting system is the outcome of a complex process. It is influenced by and it also influences a number of factors. These include ecological or environmental and institutional factors relating to the country in question, with its governmental or political, economic, legal, tax, educational and financial systems all being important. Factors originating from outside the country can also be important, and its past trading and colonial links and current patterns of foreign investment can influence accounting. The culture of a country is also important,

Exhibit 1.1   THE INFLUENCES ON AN ACCOUNTING SYSTEM

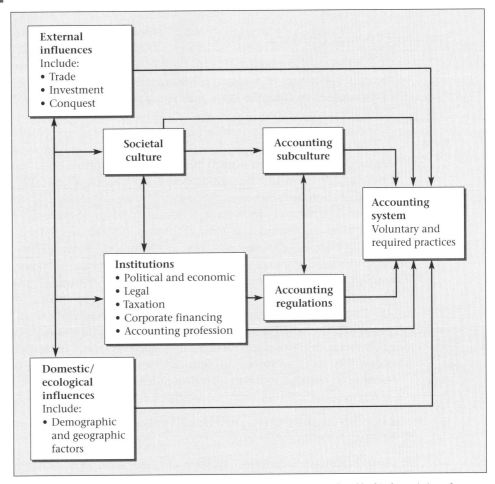

Source: Adapted from Gray (1988). Copyright Accounting Foundation. Reproduced by kind permission of Blackwell Publishers

and culture can be seen as a moderating influence that either reinforces or reduces the influence of the other factors. All of these help to explain the accounting regulations of a country – the objectives of accounting, whether to meet the needs of investors, creditors, the government or other users; the mode of regulation, whether by government, the profession or other group(s); and the extent and strictness of regulation. However, accounting practices are not simply the result of regulations. Voluntary practices are also important. As can be seen in Exhibit 1.1, voluntary practices are also the outcome of a complex process, being influenced by a wide range of ecological, institutional, external and cultural factors.[2]

While all of these factors are important, in most developed western countries the most important influences on the accounting system are the institutions of the country – in particular how it organises its political and economic, legal, financial and professional systems.[3] It is to these factors that we now turn our attention.

---

[2] Radebaugh (1975)
[3] Puxty *et al.* (1987)

1.3 THE POLITICAL AND ECONOMIC SYSTEM

1.3.1 Types of political system

One of the most important determinants of accounting regulations and practices is the political system of a country. Differences in political systems will be reflected in differences in how the economy is organised and controlled. This will then influence the objectives or role of accounting.

The most common system in place in Western Europe, North America, Japan and Australasia is the *liberal–democratic* system. A second important system is the *egalitarian–authoritarian* political system. China, North Korea, Vietnam and Cuba would all fall into this category, as would the Soviet Union and East Europe before the fall of communism.[4]

What is particularly important to accounting is how each system organises economic relations. Egalitarian–authoritarian political systems tend to co-exist with centrally planned economic systems. In the extreme form, all the processes of production would be jointly owned and controlled by the workers; prices, outputs, demand and supply would all be determined by centralised plans. Accounting would serve two roles – to help in centralised planning and to help in controlling the economy. Accounting need then be concerned only with physical units; 'profit' would have no meaning or significance. One example of an accounting system with many of these features, until recently, was China. The Chinese system is described in Chapter 16, and illustrates an accounting system that was very different from any that exists in liberal–democratic societies.

1.3.2 Liberal–democratic political systems and state control of the economy

Liberal–democratic political systems are associated with capitalist economic systems. In its most extreme form prices, output, demand and supply are all determined in the market place, the government does not interfere. In practice, no country has gone this far, and government regulates and controls at least some aspects of the market place and corporate behaviour.

Government control can be manifested in a number of ways. In most capitalist countries, the government has owned industrial organisations – in France, Italy and Spain, for example, the state has traditionally owned a range of commercial companies, including large manufacturing enterprises. However, state ownership is not the same as state control of business. The state may own commercial companies, but not play an active role in managing them, alternatively, it may not own any businesses, but may play an active role in managing or controlling business. State control of the economy can take different forms. The government may manage consumer demand with relatively little contact with or regulation of business, alternatively, it may manage supply, being actively involved in management and control.

---

[4] Blondel (1995)

There are also differences between countries with respect to the predominant attitude towards business. Business–government relations may be seen mainly in terms of co-operation: business may be seen as a 'good thing', operating in the interests of society by generating wealth and employment. Alternatively, business–government relations may be viewed in adversarial terms: large profits will be seen as the outcome of exploitation of workers, customers or other groups. Government will then be required to protect these less powerful groups, whether labour, customers or society in general.

1.3.3 Liberal–democratic political systems and the regulation of accounting

The extent to which the government actively controls the economy, and the means it uses, will influence its willingness to control or regulate accounting, the regulatory structures used and the types of regulation.

If government believes in a 'hands-off' approach with minimal regulation of companies, accounting is less likely to be heavily regulated. Companies will tend to be left to decide what to report and how to report it. Uniform accounting methods and the reporting of strictly comparable information will be relatively unimportant and accounting regulation will probably be delegated to the profession or other independent bodies.

If, instead, the government believes in a 'hands-on' approach to controlling the economy, it will be much more likely to regulate accounting. Accounting information will now be needed by the government so that it can actively plan and manage corporate behaviour. There is more likely to be a uniform or rigid system of financial reporting imposed upon all companies.

1.3.4 Liberal–democratic political systems and corporate attitudes towards accounting

The ways in which government–business relations are organised and the government's attitude towards business will affect the attitudes of business managers. If big business is viewed with suspicion, managers are likely to use financial statements to manage business–society and business–government relationships. Managers are more likely to favour measurement rules and practices that reduce reported earnings. Similarly, extra disclosures may be seen as a way of demonstrating that the company is acting in socially desirable ways – disclosure may thus be seen as a way of legitimating the actions and activities of business.

If, on the other hand, business–government relations are generally co-operative and profits are seen as a measure of success, companies will generally be less concerned with justifying themselves. There may be less voluntary disclosure of information, especially social information. Companies are also less likely to favour conservative income measurement rules and will tend to attempt to maximise rather than minimise their reported earnings (assuming, of course, that this has no adverse impact on the company's tax bill).

1.3.5 Types of business organisation

An important economic feature influencing accounting is the type of business organisation that dominates the economy. Two features of business organisations are particularly important in helping to explain accounting rules and practices:

- the complexity of business organisations
- the industrial structure of the country.

1.3.5.1 The complexity of business organisations

The way in which businesses are organised obviously has a major impact on the internal accounting information system and management accounting in general. As a company increases in size and complexity, the need for sophisticated management accounting systems increases – problems of control, performance evaluation and decision making all increase. While less obvious, differences in business complexity also affect the financial accounting system. If companies are generally small or family owned there is little need for external reporting and there should be relatively few accounting regulations. As companies increase in size, the need for external finance, whether by debt or equity, is also likely to increase. This means that there is a greater need for external information and the amount of accounting regulation will increase in response. As companies increase in size they are also likely to become more complex. Typically, companies will start to arrange themselves into groups, with subsidiaries, associates and/or joint ventures all becoming more important. Again, accounting regulations will tend to reflect these changes. For example, greater emphasis will be placed upon the regulation of group financial statements and extra disclosure requirements in areas such as segment reporting will be more likely.

1.3.5.2 The industrial structure of a country

Some accounting issues are industry-specific. Whether or not a country regulates a particular industry-specific issue will obviously depend upon the relative importance of that industry to the economy. For example, if a country is highly dependent upon foreign trade and investment, with many of its companies being multinational, it is more likely to be concerned with the issue of foreign currency transactions and translation and is more likely to issue accounting regulations in this area. Other issues are even more industry-specific. For example, accounting for the oil and gas industry has been an important and contentious issue in the USA. Issues of how to account for other extractive industries and agriculture are generally more important in developing countries than in developed countries. The International Accounting Standards Committee (IASC) has recently begun a project on accounting for agricultural projects, as a result of pressure from a number of developing countries.

The importance of certain types of industry may also influence wider accounting regulations. For example, the UK standard on research and development was strongly influenced by the potential impact of alternative accounting methods on the behaviour of companies in the aero-engineering and other research and development-dependent industries.[5] Likewise, one of the very few times when

---

[5] Hope and Gray (1982)

the US Congress directly regulated accounting was over the issue of investment tax credits: Congress was concerned that the accounting rules should not adversely affect the investment behaviour of capital-intensive businesses and so impede the economic recovery of the USA.[6]

The importance or relevance of other accounting issues depends upon how the economy of a country is structured. For example, accounting for pensions is an important issue in the USA, which has a very complex and detailed pension standard. This reflects the particular institutional arrangements of the USA, where many companies run employee pension schemes. In other countries, pensions are run entirely by the state or through private arrangements, and accounting for pensions is then less important. Likewise, the importance of issues such as leases, off-balance sheet finance and financial instruments depends upon the ways in which banks and other financial institutions work and the types of financing they provide.

1.3.6 The importance of inflation

Another important economic influence on accounting is inflation. As inflation rates increase the problems of historical cost accounting also increase. Developed western countries have seldom suffered from high inflation and have tended to view inflation accounting with suspicion, and as a result a system of strict historical accounting is found in much of continental Europe and North America.

Inflation continues to be a serious problem in some countries, though. Mexico, Chile and Brazil, for example, have all had annual inflation rates of over 100% in recent years. Obviously, when inflation is running at such levels, the historical cost of an asset soon becomes irrelevant. Thus, various forms of inflation accounting are or have been found in these countries. One interesting example of this is Brazil.[7] A

Exhibit 1.2 ENAP (CHILE): PRICE-LEVEL STATEMENTS AND ACCOUNTING POLICY

Basis of presentation of the financial statements
These consolidated financial statements expressed in Chilean pesos have been prepared in accordance with accounting principles generally accepted in Chile and the accounting regulations established by the Chilean Superintendency of Securities and Insurance.

Price-level restatement
In order to reflect in the financial statements the effects of price-level changes on the purchasing power of Chilean currency during the year, non-monetary assets and liabilities, equity and income, cost and expense accounts have been restated in accordance with the Income Tax Law and with accounting principles generally accepted in Chile. The variation in Consumer Price Index (IPC) considered as a basis for these restatements, with a one-month time lag, amounted to 8.2% for the year ended December 1995.

Source: Taken from the financial statements, year ended 31 December 1995

---

[6] Zeff (1972)
[7] Doupnik (1987)

new Corporation Law was introduced in 1976 which was designed to strengthen the stock market. One of its major concerns was the protection of minority shareholders, so it introduced rules making the payment of dividends obligatory. Therefore, income had to be clearly defined and this was done using a system of monetary corrections: official monthly price indexes were used to update the values of assets, depreciation, cost of sales and owners' equity. These regulations were withdrawn in 1986 as part of a series of anti-inflationary economic measures. Other Central and South American countries continue to use various forms of current cost accounting. An example can be seen in Exhibit 1.2 which reproduces part of the accounting policy statement of the state-owned Chilean oil company, ENAP.

1.4 THE LEGAL SYSTEM

1.4.1 Types of legal system

Two types of legal systems are found in liberal–democratic countries, namely Romano-Germanic (or code law) and common law legal systems.

The countries of continental Europe, Latin America and much of Asia have various forms of code law. Laws are generally codified (often using a similar organisational framework to that of the French Napoleonic codes of 1804–11). The philosophy behind the laws in these countries may be described as one where the role of law is to describe and mandate acceptable behaviour. Laws consist of rules and procedures that have to be followed. Typically, Commercial Codes regulate the behaviour of all commercial organisations, this includes the regulation of accounting.

The alternative to code law is common law. Here, the philosophy is one where the role of law is to prohibit undesirable behaviour rather than to prescribe or codify desirable behaviour. This system has its origin in England from where it was exported to the USA and the British Commonwealth, where it takes various forms. In common law countries much of the law is developed by judges or the courts who set case law during the resolution of specific disputes. Statute law does exist, but it tends to be less detailed and more flexible than its equivalent in code law countries.

1.4.2 Accounting and code law legal systems

In code law countries governments have generally regulated accounting as one part of their measures to ensure orderly business conduct. Accounting regulations are one part of a complete system of commercial regulations that apply to all business organisations. Regulations are designed to protect all the parties to any commercial transaction and to ensure orderly business conduct, emphasis is placed upon the protection of outsiders – in particular, creditors. Creditors have been seen as one – and very often the most – important user of financial statements. The tax authorities are often also an important user, and accounting regulations have often been set with their needs in mind. Shareholders have generally not been seen as so important. (This is not surprising when it is realised that most businesses are not listed and do not have many external shareholders.) The financial statements of individual companies are often more highly regulated than are consolidated statements. This is because the tax authorities are interested in the individual company not the group, and most legal contracts with creditors, suppliers or customers also occur at the individual company level.

In most code law countries accounting is regulated primarily through an accounting code which is typically prescriptive, detailed and procedural. Thus, the accounting regulations include not only detailed disclosure rules but also measurement and book-keeping rules. It is quite common for countries to also have industry-specific regulations or plans.

1.4.3 Accounting and common law legal systems

England is a good example of a common law country. Companies Acts have been concerned mainly with disclosure of information for the protection of the owners of limited liability companies, that is, the shareholders. Not only have companies to follow the specific provisions of the Companies Acts but they also have a general duty to present financial statements that are 'true and fair'. The courts interpret this legal requirement to mean that, unless a company can demonstrate otherwise, it must also follow accounting standards as set by the private sector body, the Accounting Standards Board (ASB). The standards set by the Accounting Standards Council (ASC) and the ASB are an example of piecemeal regulations – each standard covers one particular issue. There are many standards in force at any one time and they are issued in an *ad hoc* manner (*see* Chapter 11).

The legislature has a less important direct role in accounting regulation in some other common law countries. For example, in the USA while the legislature in the form of the Congress has ultimate authority for the federal regulation of accounting, it has used this in very few cases. Instead, it has delegated authority to the Securities and Exchange Commission (SEC) which in turn has delegated authority for accounting standard setting to an independent body, the Financial Accounting Standards Board (FASB) (*see* Chapter 13).

In contrast to code law countries, the main reason for accounting regulation in common law countries has been the need to protect the owners of companies. Thus, accounting regulations have tended to grow in a piecemeal fashion alongside the growth of limited liability companies and the separation of owners and managers. Accounting has often been regulated only because the free market system has been seen to break down and has not provided sufficient information of an adequate quality. The emphasis is on accounting and reporting at the group level. Finally, because the emphasis is on equity providers rather than creditors or taxation authorities, the measurement rules tend to be less conservative than those of code law countries.

1.5 THE TAXATION SYSTEM

1.5.1 The relationship between tax rules and financial reporting rules

In some countries, the taxation system is an important influence on accounting. In others it has little or no influence on reporting rules and practices. Code law countries tend to have common tax and financial reporting regulations, while common law countries tend instead to keep the tax and financial reporting regulations separate from each other. However, the precise relationship between the two varies across countries and there are always exceptions to these generalisations.

Three types of tax systems can be identified. These are systems where:

- the tax rules and the financial reporting rules are kept entirely, or very largely, independent of each other
- there is a common system, with many of the financial reporting rules also being used by the tax authorities
- there is a common system, with many of the tax rules also being used for financial reporting purposes.

1.5.2 Independent tax and financial reporting regulations

One of the best examples of this type of system is the UK. Here, the tax and financial reporting rules are kept separate with the two being set by different bodies. For example, depreciation in the financial statements is based upon a Statement of Standard Accounting Practice (SSAP), here SSAP12, which requires companies to select the depreciation methods that are 'the most appropriate having regard to the types of asset and their use in the business' (para. 15). In contrast, the tax charge is based upon a system of predetermined tax-depreciation allowances. Not only is tax depreciation uniform, but the rates often serve economic policy objectives providing investment incentives.

While many other countries also have largely independent tax and reporting rules, there are often some issues where the tax and accounting rules are not independent of each other. For example, in the USA the tax rules do not affect the financial reporting rules or practices with the one exception of stock or inventory valuation. Thus, the 'last in, first out' (LIFO) system can be used for tax purposes only if it is also used for financial reporting.

1.5.3 The use of financial reporting rules by the tax authorities

Many of the countries of the British Commonwealth follow the example of the UK in having independent tax and financial reporting systems. (Not only did the UK often export its English common law legal system, it also exported its taxation system.) However, the tax system in many developing British Commonwealth countries is not as sophisticated and the rules are not as well developed as they are in the UK. This has meant that the tax authorities have not set detailed and all-embracing rules for the calculation of taxable income. Instead, they have tended to rely wholly or largely upon reported earnings as the basis for calculating tax liabilities. The accounting regulations are therefore by default also the tax regulations.

This has important implications for accounting. It means that where there are no accounting regulations, or the regulations permit some choice, there will be a very strong incentive for managers to choose methods that minimise their tax liability. They will not choose the method that is most informative or the method that best reflects the 'true and fair' position of the company if it leads to a higher tax bill. It also means that companies will be more resistant to new accounting regulations that increase their tax liability, thus making it more difficult to introduce such regulations and, if they are introduced, increasing the problems of non-compliance.

1.5.4 The use of tax rules for financial reporting

The third alternative is where the tax authorities set detailed rules for the calculation of taxable earnings and these rules have to be followed not only in the tax returns but also in the external financial statements. There are variations in exactly how the system works, but this approach can be found in most of the countries of Western Europe. The systems in place in France and Germany will be discussed in Chapters 8 and 9 respectively. Another example is that of Austria.[8] Commercial law regulates financial reporting. Here, there are several tax allowances that can be claimed only if they are also disclosed in the financial reports, this applies even if the resultant values would not otherwise be allowed by the Commercial law. For these items, the tax rules take precedence. Most companies attempt to provide information of most use to external report readers. They therefore show the tax allowances as a separate item in untaxed reserves in the balance sheet rather than treating them as changes in the value of the relevant assets. In other areas the Commercial law allows companies to choose between alternative accounting treatments while the tax authorities do not prescribe a particular treatment (e.g. LIFO or FIFO for inventory). For these items, whichever method is used for financial reporting purposes will also be used by the tax authorities. Finally, there are other items (such as goodwill and depreciation) where the tax rules, while independent of the financial reporting rules, are the more prescriptive, allowing fewer choices. Companies will want to minimise their book-keeping costs. So, for these items, most companies use the tax rules for reporting purposes rather than using different methods in the two reports.

Tax is calculated at the individual company rather than at the group level. This is one reason why accounting for the individual company has traditionally been considered more important than group accounting in much of Western Europe. It also means that companies are often far more restricted in their choice of methods of accounting at the individual company level than at the group level. Thus, the tax rules have been largely responsible for a two-tier system of regulation and reporting in many EU countries, with accounting at the group level showing more signs of converging towards an international norm.

1.6 THE CORPORATE FINANCING SYSTEM

Companies are financed in a variety of different ways. Both debt and equity can take many different forms and can be provided by many different types of individuals and institutions. The way in which a company is financed affects accounting in a number of ways. For example, if equity finance is relatively more important than debt finance, accounting regulations are more likely to be designed to

---

[8] Wagenhofer (1995)

provide forward looking information useful for investment decision-making purposes. If debt financing is relatively more important, accounting measurement rules should be relatively more conservative, being designed to protect creditors. The sophistication of finance providers and the extent to which they have to rely upon financial statements will also impact significantly upon accounting disclosures – both mandatory and voluntary.

1.6.1 Corporate financing patterns

Average debt–equity ratios provide an indication of differences in financing across countries.[9] One study of financing patterns in 11 European countries[10] found very different average debt–equity ratios. The UK showed the least reliance on debt, clearly favouring equity financing instead. The UK had the lowest ratio of debt to debt *plus* equity at 20%, followed by Spain at 25% and the Netherlands at 26%. In contrast, debt financing was more popular than equity finance in Belgium (51%) and Switzerland (55%).

Differences in corporate financing will also be reflected in differences in stock market activity. Exhibit 1.3 provides some information on the major stock markets.[11] The stock exchanges from countries discussed in Part 2 of the text are highlighted.

Looking first at the number of companies listed, the most important market is clearly the USA, in the form of NASDAQ[12] and New York (NYSE) while London (LSE) has nearly as many domestic companies listed on it than does the NYSE and considerably more than Tokyo, markets in countries that are both much larger than the UK. The size of the LSE is even more remarkable when compared to the rest of Europe. It has nearly four times as many domestic companies listed than either Paris or the combined German markets. Reflecting the long history of foreign trading and financing in the UK, the LSE has more foreign listings than does any other market, including NASDAQ. However, it is not only the number of companies listing that is important, the size of the companies listed is also relevant. One measure of size is the market value of a company's shares or its stock market capitalisation. If we look at the stock market capitalisation of domestic companies only, then the NYSE is clearly the most important stock market followed by Tokyo with a market capitalisation of less than one-half of the NYSE, followed by the slightly smaller LSE.

Exhibit 1.4 provides details of the relative capitalisation of the major equity markets in the period 1982–94. From this, it can be seen that the NYSE has been the largest market in most of this period, although it was briefly overtaken by Tokyo in the late 1980s. Given differences in the size of the countries, a more appropriate measure of size might be stock market capitalisation compared to gross

---

[9] Average debt–equity ratios only provide an indication of differences. They will be affected by differences in the samples chosen and by differences in the accounting rules used in different countries.

[10] Tucker (1994)

[11] London Stock Exchange (1997). Again, a word of warning is in order. Differences in market structures and differences in the methods of data collection mean that these figures are not strictly comparable, although they do indicate important differences.

[12] NASDAQ or the National Association of Securities Dealers Automated Quotation System is a computerised quotation system which allows potential buyers and sellers of securities traded on the Over-the-Counter (OTC) market to locate the market makers who will buy and sell OTC securities.

Exhibit 1.3 MAJOR EQUITY MARKETS, 1996

Exchange	Dom.[1] market value (£m.)	Turnover value (£m.) Dom.	Int.[1]	No. Cos listed Dom.	Int.
EU					
Amsterdam	266,766	108,637	472	217	216
Brussels	78,942	14,381	2,346	146	146
Copenhagen	43,739	4,851	112	237	12
Dublin	20,494	3,619	n/a	76	11
Germany	392,095	449,325	13,620	681	n/a
Helsinki	36,284	12,897	–	71	–
Italian	150,894	60,331	14	244	4
London	1,016,971	370,810	519,581	2,423	533
Luxembourg	19,170	442	10	54	224
Madrid	120,738	46,689	14	353	4
Paris	345,276	161,267	3,602	686	187
Stockholm	141,360	75,896	3,643	217	12
Vienna	19,861	11,821	399	106	36
OTHER					
Australian	185,001	91,892	822	1,135	55
Hong Kong	269,866	108,115	117	561	22
Johannesburg	134,768	14,070	919	599	27
Korea	82,194	99,892	–	760	–
Mexico	62,788	25,630	–	193	–
NASDAQ	840,341	1,868,274	78,330	5,140	416
New York	4,085,095	2,192,585	197,097	2,602	305
Oslo	34,243	21,633	566	158	14
Singapore	90,917	35,434	–	223	43
Switzerland	176,368	243,049	14,562	213	223
Taiwan	186,704	281,303	–	382	–
Tokyo	1,764,801	517,328	848	1,766	67
Toronto	313,177	141,041	529	1,265	58

[1] Dom. = domestic, Int. = international

domestic product (GDP). On this basis, only LSE and Luxembourg (an important international financial centre) have a stock market domestic capitalisation that exceeds GDP.

Exhibit 1.4 shows some interesting changes in relative capitalisation since 1982. In particular, moves to increase the importance of the Paris Bourse appear to have been successful, while stock market investment also increased significantly in countries such as Taiwan, Malaysia and Korea, which were, until recently, all rapidly expanding economies.

From an accounting perspective, what is important is not only the size of the equity market but also its micro-structure. The amount of active trading that occurs, and the types of traders that exist, affect the level of demand for both

Exhibit 1.4	STOCK MARKET CAPITALISATION: SHARE OF WORLD MARKET, 1982–94

	1982 %	1984 %	1986 %	1988 %	1990 %	1992 %	1994 %
USA	53.37	51.95	38.23	27.92	33.24	39.84	42.89
Japan	16.69	20.29	30.33	43.20	33.15	25.14	20.52
UK	7.45	6.92	7.61	8.08	10.42	9.96	7.74
Canada	4.24	3.89	2.93	2.53	2.58	2.51	4.34
Germany	2.83	2.56	4.29	2.72	4.07	3.48	3.20
France	1.83	1.33	2.63	2.53	3.47	3.48	3.06
Switzerland	1.70	1.88	2.34	1.65	1.89	2.03	2.59
Hong Kong	0.00	0.00	0.88	0.88	0.99	1.84	1.82
Taiwan	0.00	0.00	0.00	1.28	0.84	0.82	1.71
South Africa	3.95	2.25	1.76	1.34	1.17	1.22	1.48
Netherlands	2.06	2.10	2.04	1.47	0.92	1.10	1.36
Australia	1.70	1.71	1.37	1.56	1.29	1.35	1.29
Korea	0.22	0.26	0.24	1.01	0.94	0.89	1.28
Malaysia	0.69	0.81	0.25	0.25	0.41	0.75	1.25
Italy	0.85	0.76	2.44	1.56	1.79	1.26	1.23
Other	2.52	3.29	2.66	2.02	2.83	4.33	4.24

Source: Fédération Internationale des Bourses de Valeurs, as reported in Pagano and Steil (1996), p. 55

financial information in general and for particular types of information. For example, if individual small shareholders are active investors then there will be more demand for financial statements orientated to relatively unsophisticated shareholders. If most shares are owned by a small number of pension funds or investments trusts more emphasis will probably be placed on investor–corporate relationships. Important concerns may then be the protection of private shareholders and the prevention of insider trading.

1.6.2 Market liquidity and financial institutions

There are differences not only in the size of the various stock markets but also in their liquidity or depth. In particular, there are differences in the proportion of listed companies that are actively traded. For example, three stocks (Deutsche Bank, Daimler–Benz and Siemens) accounted for roughly one-third of the turnover on the German exchanges in 1994, while approximately 400 of the listed companies on these exchanges are regarded as illiquid (with annual turnover of less than DM 15 million).[13]

There are a number of reasons why some markets are more liquid than others. Cultural factors may affect individuals' saving habits and attitudes to stock market trading. Historical factors affecting the growth of stock markets and the relationships between banks and industrial companies are obviously also important, as are current institutional arrangements. Particularly important here are the costs and

---

[13] Pagano and Steil (1996), p. 16

ease of trading, the ways in which pensions are organised and the range of financial intermediaries that exist. For example, pension premiums of current employees may be used to finance existing pension commitments; alternatively, they may be held and invested in the stock market until used to finance the future pensions of current employees. Investment trusts and unit trusts are important in some countries, both of these are designed to allow individuals to invest cheaply and efficiently in the stock market.

At the risk of too much simplification, two models may be identified. In the UK model there is a long history of an active stock market. A wide range of financial intermediaries exists, with pensions being increasingly financed through insurance companies, and investment and unit trusts being important depositories of personal savings. Complementing this is the role of banks, which have traditionally provided only short-term or medium-term financing to industry. This contrasts sharply with what might be termed the 'German model'. Here, the financial system is dominated by approximately 4,000 banks, although commercial banking is dominated by the 'Big Three' of Deutsche Bank, Dresdner Bank and Commerzbank. The banks tend to be less specialised than in the UK, with no distinction between commercial and investment banks, and they increasingly offer life insurance and pension products. While other types of financial institutions do exist, they are far less important than in the UK. The banks are the repository of most personal savings and have tended to have close relationships with industrial companies. They offer more long-term loans than do UK banks, and they often also hold shares in industrial companies as well as acting as proxy shareholders for their private customers. They are also more likely to have representatives on the Boards of companies than do their equivalent in the UK.

1.6.3 Equity ownership patterns

These differences are reflected in differences in the ownership structure of industry. Exhibit 1.5 provides some information on ownership patterns in seven European countries, the USA and Japan.

The relative importance of individual investors has fallen in all these countries over the last 25 years, despite major privatisation programmes in some of them. The fall is smallest in the USA, and here 48% of all shares are still held by private shareholders. But the most important difference lies in the relative importance of financial institutions and non-financial corporations. Thus, for example, non-financial institutions hold 42% of German shares but they hold only 9% of all shares in the USA and 2% in the UK. In contrast, 62% of all shares are held by financial institutions in the UK.

Reflecting the importance of non-financial corporate ownership of shares, many large European companies are closely held. If 'closely held' is defined as a company where the major shareholder owns at least 25% of the equity, then fully 85% of German and 79% of French listed companies are closely held in comparison to only 16% in the UK.[14] This has implications for the demand for information about corporate activities and the importance of published financial statements. When banks are major providers of long-term funds or where companies are closely held,

---

[14] Franks, Mayer and Rennebog (1995)

| Exhibit 1.5 | OWNERSHIP OF LISTED STOCKS IN MAJOR STOCK MARKETS, 1969–94 |

	Year	Households %	Non-financial corporations %	Government institutions %	Financial institutions %	Foreign owners %
France	1977	41	20	3	24	12
	1994	32	16	6	23	22
Germany	1970	28	41	11	11	8
	1994	17	42	6	19	17
Italy	1994	26	22	24	22	7
Japan	1970	40	23	0	35	3
	1993	20	28	1	42	8
Norway	1994	10	26	19	15	31
Spain	1994	32	10	16	18	23
Sweden	1994	17	24	8	31	21
UK	1969	50	5	3	36	7
	1994	18	2	1	62	16
USA	1981	51	15	0	28	6
	1993	48	9	0	37	6

Note: 'Care should be taken before reading too much into the data. Due to the different market structure in each of the surveyed countries, the organisations which collected the data used different methodologies, sample rates and time periods' (Stock Exchange Quarterly, p. 11)

Source: Berglof (1996), p. 153; *Stock Exchange Quarterly*, Summer 1995

then the most important fund providers have a direct and close link to the company. They may be actively involved in its management and, even if they are not, they can demand information from the company. In contrast, when equity financing is important but ownership is dispersed, the financial statements will be the most – and often the only – important source of information available to a company's finance providers. Not only will they demand information, but their interests have to be protected by accounting regulations.

1.7 THE ACCOUNTING PROFESSION

A further important influence on the regulation and practice of accounting may be the accounting profession itself. The size, role, organisation of and importance of the accounting profession all result from the interplay of the various factors discussed earlier in this chapter. For example, the role of the auditor and the way in which the profession is regulated (whether by government or self-regulation) both depend upon the type of legal system in place. Likewise, the importance of the profession – in terms of who it audits and how many audits are conducted – depends upon the types and numbers of companies that exist.

The profession in turn influences the institutions of a country and its accounting system. The way in which the profession is organised and society's attitude towards accountants and auditors will tend to affect auditors' ability to influence or control the behaviour of companies and their reporting systems. The extent to which auditors are independent and their power relative to the companies which they audit are important here. Whether auditors are seen as being independent, powerful professionals or instead are seen as being under the control or influence of the companies they audit will affect the perceived value of financial statements, and this will happen even if these perceptions are wrong.

1.7.1 Size of the accounting profession

Some idea of the size of the accounting profession in the countries looked at in Part 2 can be seen from the data given in Exhibit 1.6. This illustrates some very large differences. The most extreme difference emerges between the UK and Germany: there are approximately 150,000 financial accountants in the UK and Ireland and only 8,000 in Germany. While this example is commonly discussed, it is somewhat misleading. The UK figures are overstated when compared to most other countries. It is common for people to retain membership of an accounting body even if they have moved into industry or commerce – or, indeed, even retired – and this accounts for at least one-half of the UK and Ireland figures. Movement from accounting into industry or commerce on qualification or relatively soon after gaining full membership of an accounting body is common in the UK. In contrast, the German figure is considerably understated compared to most other countries. There are many more tax experts (Steuerberater) than Wirtschaftsprüfer. Also excluded from these figures are a second tier of auditors who can audit only private companies. However, while some of the differences in the size of the profession are explicable by methods of definition, large differences still remain. In particular, it remains true that the profession tends to be larger in the British Commonwealth and the USA than it is in Western Europe or Japan.

Not only are there major variations in the size of the profession, but there are also a number of other important differences. There are differences in the degree of the profession's independence – in most of the common law countries the profession is largely self-regulating, it is responsible for the licensing of accountants or auditors, including setting entry requirements, training and examinations. In contrast, in the code law countries many of these roles are carried out by the state. Similar differences exist with respect to control of the audit – who determines auditing guidelines or standards, and under what authority auditors act.

1.7.2 Accountants' role in regulation

Accounting regulations may or may not be set by the profession. As discussed above, in code law countries accounting regulations are generally set by the government. However, even here the profession often plays a role. It may act as an advisor to the government, providing input into the regulatory process. It may issue standards or recommendations in areas where there are no legal regulations.

Exhibit 1.6	THE ACCOUNTANCY PROFESSION IN SELECTED COUNTRIES

Country	Professional body	Major functions	Year start	Size m.	Pop. m.
Australia	Institute of Chartered Accountants of Australia (ICAA)	Accountant	1885	27,000	17.8
	Australian Society of Certified Public Accountants (ASCPA)	Accountant	1886	62,000	
China	Chinese Institute of Certified Public Accountants	Auditor	1984	58,000	1,220.2
France	Compagnie Nationale des Commissaires aux Comptes (CNCC)	Legal auditor	1936	9,000	58.1
	Ordre des Experts-Comptables (OEC)	Accountant	1952	12,000	
Germany	Institut der Wirschaftsprüfer (IdW)	Auditor	1931	6,000	81.6
Hungary	Hungarian Chamber of Auditors	Statutory auditor	1932		10.1
Japan	Japanese Institute of Certified Public Accountants	Auditor/Accountant	1927	11,000	125.1
Netherlands	Nederlands Instituut van Registeraccountants (NIVRA)	Auditor/Accountant	1895	8,000	15.5
UK & Ireland	Institute of Chartered Accountants in England & Wales (ICAEW)	Auditor/Accountant	1880	97,000	61.6
	Institute of CA of Scotland (ICAS)	Auditor/Accountant	1854	13,000	
	Institute of CA of Ireland (ICAI)	Auditor/Accountant	1888	8,000	
	Chartered Association of Certified Accountants (CACA)	Auditor/Accountant	1891	38,000	
USA	American Institute of Certified Public Accountants (AICPA)	Auditor/Accountant	1927	301,000	267.1

It may issue pronouncements that explain or expand government regulations. The French profession in the form of the OEC and the CNCC provides a good example of this approach (as discussed in Chapter 8).

In common law countries, the regulation of accounting tends to be delegated by the government to an independent body. Thus, in the UK (as discussed in Chapter 11), standard setting was, until recently, largely left to the ASC. The ASC comprised part-time representatives, mainly from the accounting profession. While it has been replaced by the ASB, the accounting profession plays an important role in the ASB's work.

1.8 OTHER INFLUENCES

There are a number of other factors which have affected various accounting rules and practices in one or more countries. Particularly important are:

- accidents of history
- the exporting or imposition of accounting rules or practices by a more powerful or sophisticated society
- the importing of accounting rules or practices from other country(ies).

1.8.1 Accidents of history

There are numerous examples of accounting rules or practices originating from shocks to the system or accidents of history. For example, much of the early UK company law legislation, including accounting regulations, was the result of financial crises or collapse of companies. Other more significant examples of major economic shocks include the collapse of the US and German stock markets in the 1920s. Similar events in the two countries resulted in very different institutions and regulations. In the USA the collapse of the stock market led to the creation of the SEC and increased accounting regulations to protect and encourage share ownership (*see* Chapter 13). In Germany, the collapse of the stock market and the resulting increase in debt financing led to regulations which were focused upon creditor protection (*see* Chapter 9).

1.8.2 The exporting/imposition of accounting

Accounting regulations and practices have always been exported and imported from the earliest days of double entry bookkeeping. Exporting occurs for a number of reasons.[15] The profession itself has always been one source. For example, Price Waterhouse started in London in 1849, but then opened offices in New York and Chicago before it opened its second UK office in Liverpool in 1904. Several US accounting firms were set up by UK trained accountants. This movement of accountants led to many early similarities between accounting in the UK and the USA. International trade in accountants and accounting firms continues to the present time, with the larger firms being active worldwide. This means that they often export their accounting and auditing standards and these are then used where there are no local regulations.

A second major factor in the export of accounting has been colonialism.[16] The UK and France exported many of their legal and administrative structures and their educational systems to their colonies. Following independence, local factors have become more important and the influence of the former colonial powers has declined. But many institutions have not changed very much. For example, all of the Caribbean Economic Community (CARICOM) members (which are English-speaking, former British colonies), with the one exception of Barbados, have

---

[15] Parker (1989)
[16] Cooke and Wallace (1990)

Company Acts based upon various UK Companies Acts ranging from the 1829 Act to the 1948 Act.[17] Similar influences can also be seen in the former French colonies of Africa which use accounting codes based upon the French code.[18]

Depending upon the history of a country, the accounting system may show evidence of many different influences. For example, as will be discussed in Chapter 15, Japanese accounting regulations reflect the exporting of both German and US regulations. (One particularly interesting example of a country being influenced by a large number of other countries is Turkey. *See* Case study 1.2 for a description of the various external influences on the Turkish accounting system.)

1.8.3 The importing of accounting

Countries may also seek actively to import accounting regulations or practices. This may be done because developing accounting rules is both expensive and time-consuming. It is much less costly to see what other countries have done and to select those rules that most suit your own needs. Thus countries may import an entire set of rules, or specific rules only. The countries of Eastern Europe are a good example of the current importation of accounting. Having overthrown communism they are seeking links with the EU, and they are faced with the task of completely overhauling their accounting systems. One example of this is Hungary, as discussed in Chapter 14.

In a similar way, individual companies may also import accounting practices. Fletcher Challenge, a New Zealand forestry company, for example, describes its accounting policies as follows:

Accounting convention
The financial statements are based on the general principles of historical cost accounting, including the going concern concept and the accrual basis of accounting . . . These financial statements are presented in accordance with the Companies Act 1993 and have been prepared in accordance with the Financial Reporting Act 1993 and *comply with US GAAP [generally accepted accounting principles] where this does not conflict with New Zealand law.*
(Annual Report, 30 June 1997, italics added)

PetroFina, a Belgian petroleum company, also uses US standards:

These financial statements were developed using the guidelines of the Royal Decree of November 25, 1991, concerning the annual accounts of industrial holding companies. However, *for accounting practices specific to the petroleum industry or those not yet implemented under Belgium accounting law, the Group has followed statement of 'Financial Accounting Standards' (SFAS).*
Accordingly, since 1991 PetroFina has applied SFAS19 to account for its oil and gas exploration and production expenditures using the Successful Efforts method. Likewise, since 1992 the Group has applied SFAS109 to value the provision for deferred taxes.
(Annual Review, 31 December 1996, italics added)

1.9 SUMMARY AND CONCLUSIONS

This chapter has provided an overview of many of the factors that influence accounting. It is always dangerous to generalise too much; there will always be

---

[17] Chaderton and Taylor (1993)
[18] United Nations (1991)

exceptions to any generalisations, and there will always be countries that do not follow the typical pattern. As long as this is recognised, there are enough similarities across countries to make generalisations possible. Therefore, in this chapter we have seen how accounting rules and practices are influenced by a large number of quite different factors. Particularly important are the following:

- political and economic system
- legal system
- taxation system
- corporate financing system
- the accounting profession.

Finally, we also saw how a country may import and export accounting rules and practices.

As we saw in Exhibit 1.1, there is no simple universal relationship between any particular institution and the accounting system. All the factors identified are important. Also important are the interactions between the factors identified. Accounting and accountants are influenced by the institutions of a country and by external influences and they in turn can also influence a country's institutions in many complex and changing ways.

Despite these complexities, we can still discern some general patterns which tend to hold true, and this chapter identified some of these. In particular, we saw how the political and economic system, the taxation system and the corporate financing system all tend to influence the demand for accounting information and the objectives served by the financial reporting system. As we saw, the most important users of financial statements may be shareholders or they may be creditors or taxation authorities. The type of legal system a country has and the strength of the accounting profession tend to influence who regulates accounting, and the rigidity of the regulations. The regulatory structures and the users both tend in turn to influence the specific measurement rules adopted and the extent of disclosures made, whether mandatory or voluntary.

Chapter 2 looks not at institutions but instead at the people involved in accounting and the influence of culture on accounting. Chapters 3 and 4 then look at ways of describing and measuring accounting differences and similarities internationally. In Chapters 5 and 6 we turn our attention to moves towards international harmonisation. The work of the International Accounting Standards Committee (IASC) is examined in some depth while work of other bodies is also briefly looked at and the International Accounting Standards (IASs) are described.

Having set the international scene in Part 1, Part 2 of the book goes on to look at the accounting systems of specific countries. It is always difficult to decide which countries should be examined. Two criteria guided our choices – the countries should either be important in the sense that they are influential, being successful in exporting aspects of their accounting systems, or they should be interesting – in the sense of being a good example of a particular kind of accounting system. Four EU countries are examined: France, Germany, Netherlands and the UK. Chapters 12 and 13 look at two developed English-speaking countries:

Australia and the USA. The former command economies of eastern Europe are illustrated by the example of Hungary in Chapter 14, Chapters 15 and 16 look at the two Far East countries of Japan and China, while Chapter 17 looks at Egypt.

Finally, the two chapters of Part 3 look at the impacts of international diversity in accounting. Chapter 18 looks at stock exchanges, listing behaviour and shareholder investment strategies. Chapter 19 concludes by looking at corporate disclosure strategies.

Case study 1.1

ACCOUNTING IN NAFTA: DIFFERENCES IN REPORTING PRACTICES

The North American Free Trade Association (NAFTA) is made up of Mexico, the USA and Canada. On almost any measure of similarity, such as language, economic performance, institutions or culture, the USA is far more similar to Canada than it is to Mexico. This is also true of accounting. For example, one recent study looked at 100 measurement and disclosure practices in the USA, Canada and Mexico.[19] Data was collected from 'Big-6' audit partners in each country regarding the proportions of their major clients utilising each possible alternative.

Few significant differences were found between practices in the USA and Canada. Of 44 measurement issues, only two differed significantly. First, Canadian companies were less likely to use last in, first out (LIFO) for stock or inventory valuation, a feature probably due to differences in the tax rules. While LIFO is allowed for financial reporting in both the USA and Canada, Canada does not allow it for tax purposes but the USA does. Indeed, the American tax authorities accept LIFO for tax purposes only if it is also used in financial reporting. Secondly, Canadian companies tended to capitalise at least some research and development (R&D) costs, while in the USA all R&D must be expensed immediately. Of the 56 disclosure issues covered, the only significant differences found between Canada and the USA related to the breakdown of inventory costs (into finished goods, work-in-progress and raw materials or other similar categories) and disclosure of the amount of R&D costs charged to income in the period (in both cases, disclosure was more common in the USA).

There were seven measurement issues where there were significant differences between the USA and Mexico and a further 19 items with significant differences in the level of disclosure. (*See* below for the full list of the differences between Mexico and the USA.) As can be seen, some of these differences reflect quite fundamental differences in the accounting systems in place. In particular, several differences appear to have resulted from Mexico's long experience of severe inflation, which has led to a system of accounting that revalues fixed assets and does not demand the use of the 'lower of cost or market' rule for inventory valuation. This can be compared with the US adherence to strict historical costs.

---

[19] Salter, Kantor and Roberts (1994)

■ *Case study 1.1 continued*

Accounting practices that differ between the USA and Mexico

Measurement rules

- fixed assets stated at revalued amounts
- fixed assets stated at cost *less* accumulated depreciation
- inventories stated at the lower of cost or market value
- marketable securities which are long-term assets, stated at the lower of cost or market value
- under equity accounting for investments, adjust for inter-company profits and similar
- in defined benefit plan pension schemes, compute costs and liabilities for all covered employees
- record deferred taxes.

Disclosure rules
Disclose:

- effects of changes in the general price level
- effects of changes in prices of inventory or fixed assets
- amount and period of commitments for long-term (finance) leases
- market value of quoted investments, if different from carrying amounts
- receivables from officers
- details of stock options exercised and outstanding
- details of significant acquisitions, divestitures or discontinued operations
- interim reports
- amount of pension fund liability or deferred charge and funding approach adopted
- assets and liabilities or net assets of enterprise's pension fund
- unusual or extraordinary gains and losses
- basic or primary earnings per share
- separate disclosure of impact of enterprise's operations, investments and financing activities
- consolidated and parent company statements
- revenue from foreign operations
- results of significant industry segments
- assets of significant industry segments
- results of significant geographical segments
- assets of significant geographical segments.

Case study 1.2

ACCOUNTING IN TURKEY: EXTERNAL INFLUENCES

Legal requirements that affected accounting entered Turkish business life for the first time with the adoption of the Commercial Code (Law on Commerce) in 1850, which was a translation of the first and third books of the French Commercial Code. By 1864, translation of the whole of the French Commercial Code had been completed.

From 1850 until about 1925, the impact of French accounting on Turkish accounting practice was significant. This was because most of the instructors or authors on accounting and tax in Turkey had received their accounting education in France. Since Italian accounting principles were largely adopted by the French, the so-called Italian System of Accounting practised in Turkey was first introduced through French publications . . .

In 1926 a new Commercial Code was introduced based mainly on the Commercial Codes of Italy and Germany. However, sections of the new code were taken from the Commercial Codes of Belgium, France, Austria, Hungary, Chile, Argentina, Spain, Romania, Britain and Japan as well as Italy and Germany. The copying of elements of foreign law led to the Turkish Code being piecemeal, and it was therefore not as effective as planned.

During the period 1926–60, Turkish accounting practice was considerably influenced by German accounting. This influence became more pronounced after several well known German management and accounting professionals emigrated to Turkey in the early 1930s, fleeing the Nazi regime in Germany. In this period, most of the students going abroad went to Germany for accounting education and many Turkish state economic enterprises employed German consultants for the reorganisation of their accounting systems. Another German influence on the Turkish accounting system was the introduction of income tax based on the 1950 German model.

After the defeat of Germany in the Second World War the USA emerged as the main influence. Of particular importance was the Marshall Plan of economic help which marked the beginning of US business involvement on Turkey. More and more students were sent to the USA for business education and special institutions and programmes were established in Turkey to introduce American management theories and practice. The impact of American accounting practice has been even more pronounced over the last three decades.

Source: Cooke and Curuk (1996), p. 341

QUESTIONS

Institutional influences (1.2)

1 What are the main institutional influences on accounting practices in general?

2 Which of the influences identified above are most important in your country?

3 Why might the importance of the various influences identified differ across countries and over time?

4 To what extent has the importance of the influences identified above varied over time in your country?

Political and economic factors (1.3)

1 How does the political and economic system of your country fit into the classification described in the chapter?

2 How might the type of political and economic system of a country influence the accounting regulatory system?

3 How might the type of political and economic system of a country influence the types of accounting measurement rules adopted?

4 How might the type of political and economic system of a country influence the type of accounting disclosure rules adopted?

5 How might the type of political and economic system of a country influence the type of accounting measurement and disclosure practices voluntarily adopted by companies?

The legal system (1.4)

1 How does the legal system of your country fit into the classification described in the chapter?

2 How might the type of legal system of a country influence the accounting regulatory system?

3 How might the type of legal system of a country influence the types of accounting measurement rules adopted?

4 How might the type of legal system of a country influence the type of accounting disclosure rules adopted?

5 How might the type of legal system of a country influence the type of accounting measurement and disclosure practices voluntarily adopted by companies?

The taxation system (1.5)

1 How does the taxation system of your country compare to the description given in the chapter?

2 How might the type of taxation system of a country influence the accounting regulatory system?

3 How might the type of taxation system of a country influence the types of accounting measurement rules adopted?

4 How might the type of taxation system of a country influence the type of accounting disclosure rules adopted?

5 How might the type of taxation system of a country influence the type of accounting measurement and disclosure practices voluntarily adopted by companies?

The corporate financing system (1.6)

1 How does the corporate financing system of your country compare to the description given in the chapter?

2 How might the type of corporate financing system of a country influence the accounting regulatory system?

3 How might the type of corporate financing system of a country influence the types of accounting measurement rules adopted?

4 How might the type of corporate financing system of a country influence the type of accounting disclosure rules adopted?

5 How might the type of corporate financing system of a country influence the type of accounting measurement and disclosure practices voluntarily adopted by companies?

The accounting profession (1.7)

1 How does the accounting profession in your country compare to the description given in the chapter?

2 How might the type of accounting profession of a country influence the accounting regulatory system?

3 How might the type of accounting profession of a country influence the types of accounting measurement rules adopted?

4 How might the type of accounting profession of a country influence the type of accounting disclosure rules adopted?

5 How might the type of accounting profession of a country influence the type of accounting measurement and disclosure practices voluntarily adopted by companies?

External influences (1.8)

1 How do the external influences on accounting practice in your country compare to those described in the chapter?

2 How might external influences on a country influence the accounting regulatory system?

3 How might external influences on a country influence the types of accounting measurement rules adopted?

4 How might external influences on a country influence the type of accounting disclosure rules adopted?

5 How might external influences on a country influence the type of accounting measurement and disclosure practices voluntarily adopted by companies?

REFERENCES

Berglof, E. (1996) 'Equity trading – the evolution of European trading systems', in European Capital Markets Institute, in *The European Equity Markets: The State of the Union and an Agenda for the Millennium*. London: Royal Institute of International Affairs, 1–58.

Blondel, J. (1995) *Comparative Government: An Introduction*, 2nd edn. London: Prentice Hall.

Chaderton, R. and Taylor, P.J. (1993) 'Accounting systems of the Caribbean: Their evolution and role in economic growth and development', *Research in Third World Accounting*, 2, 45–66.

Cooke, T.E. and Curuk, T. (1996) 'Accounting in Turkey with reference to the particular problems of lease transactions', *European Accounting Review*, 5(2), 339–59.

Cooke, T.E. and Wallace, R.S.O. (1990) 'Financial disclosure regulation and its environment: A review and further analysis'. *Journal of Accounting and Public Policy*, 9, 79–110.

Doupnik, T.S. (1987) 'The Brazilian system of monetary correction', *Advances in International Accounting*, 1, 111–35.

Franks J., Mayer C. and Rennebog, L. (1995) *The Role of Take-overs in Corporate Governance*. London: London Business School.

Gray, S.J. (1988) 'Towards a theory of cultural influence on the development of accounting systems internationally', *Abacus*, 24(1), 1–15.

Hope, T. and Gray, R. (1982), 'Power and policy making: the development of an R&D standard', *Journal of Business Finance and Accounting*, 9(4), 531–58.

London Stock Exchange (1997) *Fact File 1997*.

Meek, G.K. and Saudagaran, S.M. (1990) 'A survey of research on financial reporting in a transnational context', *Journal of Accounting Literature*, 9, 145–82.

Pagano, M. and Steil, B. (1996) 'Equity trading: The evolution of European trading systems', in Steil, B. (ed.), *The European Equity Markets*. London: Royal Institute of International Affairs, 1–58.

Parker, R.H. (1989) 'Importing and exporting accounting: The British experience', in Hopwood, A.G. (ed.), *International Pressures for Accounting Change*. London: Prentice Hall/ ICAEW, 7–29.

Puxty, A.G., Willmott, H.C., Cooper, D.J. and Lowe, T. (1987) 'Modes of regulation in advanced capitalism: Locating accountancy in four countries', *Accounting, Organisations and Society*, 12(3), 273–91.

Radebaugh, L.H. (1975) 'Environmental factors influencing the development of accounting objectives, standards and practices in Peru', *International Journal of Accounting*, Fall, 39–56.

Salter, S.B., Kantor, J. and Roberts, C.B. (1994) 'Free trade and financial reporting: an examination of reporting practices in Canada, the United States and Mexico', *Journal of International Accounting, Auditing and Taxation*, 3(2), 237–50.

Tucker, J. (1994) 'Capital structure: An econometric perspective on Europe', in Pointon, J., *Issues in Business Taxation*. London: Avebury, 139–80.

United Nations (1991) *Accountancy Developments in Africa: Challenge of the 1990s*. New York: United Nations CTC.

Wagenhofer, A. (1995) 'Austria – Individual accounts', in Ordelheide, D. and KPMG (eds), *Transnational Accounting*. London: Macmillan, 231–314.

Zeff, S.A. (1972) *Forging Accounting Principles in Five Countries*. Champaign, IL: Stipes Publishing.

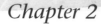

Chapter 2

Cultural influences on accounting rules and practices

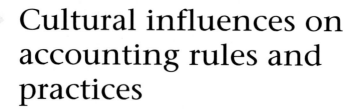

2.1 PURPOSE OF THE CHAPTER

In Chapter 1 we looked at a range of institutions that influence accounting rules and practices, and saw how they help to explain why accounting differs across countries. However, this is not the whole story. This chapter continues to look at the influences on accounting systems. It looks at the influence of culture, both the culture of a country and the culture or subculture of accountants.

Learning objectives

After reading this chapter you should be able to:

- Understand what is meant by the term 'culture', and describe the cultural dimensions identified by Hofstede.
- Describe the relationship between culture and organisational structures.
- Describe the accounting values identified by Gray, and explain how they might be related to culture.
- Evaluate research which has used these accounting values and assess their significance for those seeking international harmonisation.

The institutions of a country are set up and run by people. Accounting regulations are similarly set by people and accounting is carried out by people. Both will be influenced by the people who create them, the people who maintain them and the people who use them. Obviously, different people think and act in different ways. They have different tastes, different beliefs and different attitudes. However, these are not completely random: people often share many similar tastes, beliefs and attitudes. While we will define 'culture' more fully below, we can think of these common attributes as the 'common culture' of a group. The group which shares such a common culture may be the country or society as a whole, or it may be a smaller group of people such as accountants!

If we return to our model of the influences on an accounting system, as reproduced in Exhibit 2.1, we can see how accounting is affected or influenced by societal culture and accounting culture. Differences in the culture of a society are reflected in the ways in which society organises itself. The ways in which the economic system is organised, the ways in which companies are set up, controlled and financed, the legal system and the organisation of professions are all influenced by culture. But culture also has a more direct influence on accounting. It influences account preparers, regulators, auditors and users, and so influences the types of rules that are promulgated and the practices followed.

This chapter goes on to explain more fully what is meant by 'culture'. It then looks at some of the evidence on cultural differences across societies, exploring ways in which culture can affect business – in particular how it affects the ways in which businesses are organised, who makes decisions in organisations and what motivates employees. Finally, the cultural values of accountants are discussed and the link between accounting and culture is explored.

Exhibit 2.1 **THE INFLUENCES ON AN ACCOUNTING SYSTEM**

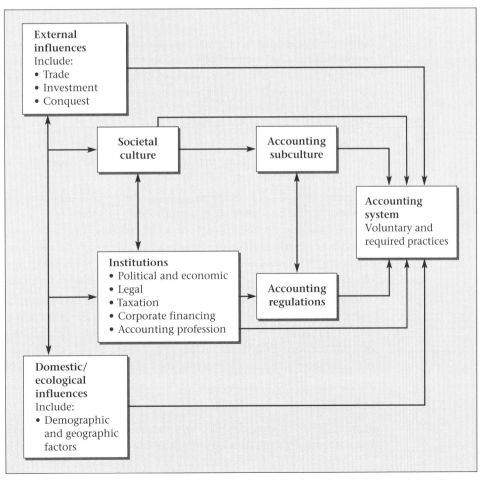

Source: Adapted from Gray (1988). Copyright Accounting Foundation. Reproduced by kind permission of Blackwell Publishers

2.2 DEFINING CULTURE

2.2.1 The culture of a country

'Culture' in the sense that it is used here refers to the set of common ideas, beliefs and values that are shared by the members of a group of individuals. One of the simplest working definitions of this is given by Hofstede (1984), who defined culture as 'the collective programming of the mind which distinguishes the members of one human group from another'.

This definition highlights three important points about culture.[1]

- culture is collective, rather than being a characteristic of any one individual
- it is not directly observable, but it can be inferred from people's behaviour
- it is of interest only to the extent that it helps to differentiate between groups – due to cultural differences, groups will behave in different and definable ways.

Cultural differences exist at a number of different levels. Hofstede identified four: symbols; heroes; rituals; and values:

1 *Symbols* are the most superficial of the four: they comprise words, gestures, pictures or objects that have particular meanings for a cultural group. An example might be the meaning that different societies tend to attach to Coca-Cola. Coca-Cola can be seen as the most obvious thing to drink on a hot day, or it may be seen as a drink only suitable for the young. It may be seen as being desirable, indicating sophistication and affluence, or it may be seen as an unwelcome example of US international dominance.

2 *Heroes* are individuals (whether real or imaginary) who embody those characteristics that are particularly prized by a society (for example, Superman in the USA, Asterix in France or Tintin in Belgium).

3 At the next level are *rituals* or activities that, of themselves, have little or no extrinsic value but have an essential social or intrinsic value. They range from simple rituals, such as different forms of greeting, through to more complex and formalised rituals such as the Japanese tea ceremony, through to apparently purposive activities such as the ways in which business meetings are conducted. (Indeed, it has been argued[2] that much of accounting is a ritual.)

4 The final core level of culture is *values*. This may be thought of as preferences for particular states of being. Examples include views about what is good or evil, natural or unnatural, desirable or undesirable and honest or dishonest. This does not, of course, mean that everyone acts on these beliefs or that they describe everyone's personal preferences. Instead, they describe general beliefs or social norms.

2.2.2 Subcultures

Culture in terms of shared beliefs and values exists at many levels. There is societal culture or the culture of a country. Inside any country there are a number of

---

[1] Hofstede (1991)
[2] Gambling (1987)

distinct, although often overlapping, groups with their own culture (usually referred to as 'subcultures' to distinguish them from the culture of the society as a whole). Different regional areas, ethnic or religious groups may share distinct sub-cultures. At the level of the company there will also be an organisational or corporate subculture. Indeed, one way that a company can successfully manage uncertainty or instability is by developing a well defined corporate culture: every-one in the organisation should then know and internalise the company's aims, will know what is expected of them and how they should react. This reduces the need for written rules, regulations and procedures and it helps employees to make better decisions in new or unusual circumstances.[3] In addition, each work group and profession, including accountants and the accounting profession, will have its own subculture.

2.2.3 The dimensions of culture

Culture is a complex phenomenon, too complex to be easily described or measured. However, it can be unbundled into a number of underlying dimensions, each of which is less complex. Each dimension covers one aspect of culture which can then be described, measured and quantified. Different cultural or subcultural groups can then be measured on each dimension and so compared with each other. There have been a number of attempts at doing this. Two of the more interesting examples are by Trompenaars (1993) and Hofstede (1984, pp. 83–4). We will look briefly at both of these studies.

Trompenaars surveyed the employees of 50 companies in 30 countries in the late 1980s and early 1990s and came up with a list of seven cultural dimensions. Exhibit 2.2 reproduces his description of these dimensions. The first five are con-cerned with how people relate to each other. These have obvious implications for the ways in which businesses should be run, as one key factor in the design of any business organisation is its employees and their attitudes, beliefs, values and behaviour. These dimensions affect, for example, what motivates an individual, how people think about and measure success and whether or not personal and business relationships are kept independent of each other. The other two dimen-sions are concerned with attitudes towards time and towards the environment. Again, these have implications for how business relationships are organised.

In a similar, but older, study of the employees of IBM,[4] Hofstede developed four cultural dimensions, as reproduced in Exhibit 2.3. These are not identical to those suggested by Trompenaars, but they describe a similar series of basic beliefs and attitudes towards other individuals and society. A fifth construct, termed 'Confucian dynamism' which is concerned with the long-term or short-term orien-tation of a society, was found to be more relevant than uncertainty avoidance when a similar analysis was later conducted based upon Chinese values.[5]

Hofstede has, rightly, been criticised for his choice of terminology, and in particu-lar the use of the terms 'masculinity versus femininity'. It has been argued by many

---

[3] Balaga and Jaeger (1984)
[4] Hofstede (1984)
[5] Hofstede and Bond (1988)

Exhibit 2.2   CULTURAL DIMENSIONS IDENTIFIED BY TROMPENAARS (1993)

Universalism versus particularism

The universalist approach is roughly: 'What is good and right can be defined and always applies.' In particularist cultures far greater attention is given to the obligations of relationships and unique circumstances. For example, instead of assuming that one good way must always be followed, the particularist reasoning is that friendship has special obligations and hence may come first. Less attention is given to abstract societal codes.

Individualism versus collectivism

Do people regard themselves primarily as individuals or primarily as part of a group? Furthermore, is it more important to focus on individuals so that they can contribute to the collective as and if they wish, or is it more important to consider the collective first since that is shared by many individuals?

Neutral versus emotional

Should the nature of our interactions be objective and detached, or is expressing emotion acceptable? . . . [Either] business relationships are typically instrumental and all about achieving objectives. The brain checks emotions because these are believed to confuse the issues. The assumption is that we should resemble our machines in order to operate them more efficiently . . . or business is a human affair and the whole gamut of emotions deemed appropriate.

Specific versus diffuse

When the whole person is involved in a business relationship there is a real and personal contact, instead of the specific relationship specified in the contract. In many countries a diffuse relationship is not preferred, but necessary before business can proceed.

Achievement versus ascription

Achievement means that you are judged on what you have recently accomplished and on your record. Ascription means that status is attributed to you, by birth, kinship, gender or age, but also by your connections . . . and your educational record.

Attitudes to time

In some societies what someone has achieved in the past is not that important. It is more important to know what plan they have developed for the future. In other societies you can make more of an impression with your past accomplishments than those of today. In certain cultures time is perceived as passing in a straight line, a sequence of disparate events. Other cultures think of time more as moving in a circle, the past and present together with future possibilities.

Attitudes to the environment

Some cultures see the major focus affecting their lives and the origin of vice and virtue as residing within the person. Here, motivations and values are derived from within. Other cultures see the world as more powerful than individuals. They see nature as something to be feared or emulated.

Exhibit 2.3   CULTURAL DIMENSIONS IDENTIFIED BY HOFSTEDE (1984)

Individualism versus collectivism
Individualism stands for a preference for a loosely knit social framework in society wherein individuals are supposed to take care of themselves and their immediate families only. Its opposite, Collectivism, stands for a preference for a tightly knit social framework in which individuals can expect their relatives, clan, or other in-group to look after them in exchange for unquestioning loyalty . . . The fundamental issue addressed by this dimension is the degree of interdependence a society maintains among individuals. It relates to people's self-concept: 'I' or 'we'.

Large versus small power distance
Power Distance is the extent to which the members of a society accept that power in institutions is distributed unequally. This affects the behaviour of the less powerful as well as of the more powerful members of society. People in Large Power Distance societies accept a hierarchical order in which everybody has a place which needs no further justification. People in Small Power Distance societies strive for power equalisation and demand justification for power inequalities. The fundamental issue addressed by this dimension is how a society handles inequalities among people when they occur.

Strong versus weak uncertainty avoidance
Uncertainty avoidance is the degree to which the members of a society feel uncomfortable with uncertainty and ambiguity. This feeling leads to beliefs promising certainty and to maintaining institutions protecting conformity. Strong Uncertainty Avoidance societies maintain rigid codes of belief and behaviour and are intolerant towards deviant persons and ideas. Weak Uncertainty Avoidance societies maintain a more relaxed atmosphere in which practice counts more than principles and deviance is easily tolerated. The fundamental issue addressed by this dimension is how a society reacts to the fact that time runs only one way and that the future is unknown: whether it tries to control the future or to let it happen.

Masculinity versus femininity (Low *versus* high nurturing)
Masculinity stands for a preference in society for achievement, heroism, assertiveness, and material success. Its opposite, Femininity, stands for a preference for relationships, modesty, caring for the weak and the quality of life. The fundamental issue addressed by this dimension is the way in which a society allocates social (as opposed to biological) roles to the sexes.

writers that this terminology reinforces notions of gender differences that may, at best, be considered suspect. Later writers have instead used various terms such as 'human heartedness' and 'nurturing'. Of the alternatives proposed, nurturing best describes the same set of characteristics without ascribing either gender or sex differences to them. We will also use this term instead of masculinity/femininity.

Hofstede measured his four dimensions for each of a range of 50 countries and three geographical groupings of countries.[6] The results obtained by Hofstede for the countries discussed in Part 2 of this book, are reproduced in Exhibit 2.4 (note that Hofstede did not look at Hungary, China or Egypt).

---

[6] Hofstede (1991)

Exhibit 2.4 SCORES AND RANKINGS FOR INDIVIDUAL COUNTRIES FROM HOFSTEDE'S (1984) CULTURAL DIMENSION RESEARCH

	Individualism versus collectivism		Large power distance versus small power distance		Strong uncertainty avoidance versus weak uncertainty avoidance		Low nurture versus high nurture (masculinity versus femininity in Hofstede)	
	Score	Rank	Score	Rank	Score	Rank	Score	Rank
Australia	90	2	36	41	51	37	61	16
France	71	10/11	68	15/16	86	10/15	43	35/36
Germany	67	15	35	42/44	65	29	66	9/10
Japan	46	22/23	54	33	92	7	95	1
Netherlands	80	4/5	38	40	53	35	14	51
UK	89	3	35	42/44	35	47/48	66	9/10
USA	91	1	40	38	46	43	62	15
Arab countries	38	26/27	80	7	68	27	53	23

The interpretation of these scores and rankings is set out in Exhibit 2.5. Hofstede used cluster analysis to identify groupings of countries and from his clusters proposed dividing lines separating one of the pairs of characteristics from the other. Exhibit 2.5 also sets out the dividing points specified by Hofstede. For example, any country scoring more than 50 on the Individualism/collectivism dimension could be described as being individualistic. Countries scoring less than 50 would instead be described as being collectivist.

Exhibit 2.5 INTERPRETATION OF HOFSTEDE'S SCORES

Characteristics	Score	Rank	Country
Greatest individualism		91	1	USA
Dividing point	50			
Greatest collectivism		6	53	Guatemala
Largest power distance		104	1	Malaysia
Dividing point	44			
Smallest power distance		11	53	Austria
Strongest uncertainty avoidance		112	1	Greece
Dividing point	56			
Weakest uncertainty avoidance		8	53	Singapore
Low nurturing (masculinity)		95	1	Japan
Dividing point	50			
High nurturing (femininity)		5	53	Sweden

2.3 CULTURE AND BUSINESS

2.3.1 Culture and leadership style

Culture affects how a society organises itself. It will affect businesses and accounting in a variety of ways. If we look first at the relationship between business and culture, Hofstede (1991) suggests that culture influences both the preference for particular leadership styles and organisational structures and the motivation of employers and employees. Hofstede went on to describe how the cultural dimensions he had identified were linked to various organisational characteristics. For example, he argued that leadership styles would be particularly affected by individualism and power distance. If a country is highly individualistic, then leadership styles and structures would tend to be based upon the satisfaction of personal needs. Individual self-interest would feature strongly and personal relationships and loyalties would have relatively little relevance. In collectivist societies leadership would be more of a group phenomenon. Leaders would be successful only if they emphasise the group. Employee welfare would be relatively more important. Culture would also affect the degree of participation – whether extensive and real; consultative; symbolic; or non-existent.

While these differences have little direct impact upon financial accounting, they have obvious implications for management accounting. Leadership style affects who makes what decisions in the company. This affects the accounting information system, which must be designed to ensure that decision-makers receive the relevant information. The performance evaluation system must be designed so that performance measures reflect decision-making authority.

2.3.2 Culture and motivation

Motivation is similarly affected by culture. Individualism versus collectivism and high versus low nurturing are particularly important. The importance of theories of motivation for financial accounting can be seen, for example, in agency theory. This is one of the most important theories to emerge in accounting in recent years and it has implications for the design of corporate governance systems and the regulation of auditing and financial reporting. The theory seeks to explain the behaviour of corporate managers. Agency theory assumes that managers are motivated by self-interest (high individualism), in particular by their remuneration including perks (low nurturing). Given these assumptions, it follows that managers will maximise their own income even at the expense of the owners of the company. Controls have to be put in place to prevent this happening. These include auditing and financial reporting, both of which monitor the behaviour of managers. However, monitoring by itself is not sufficient to ensure that managers act in the best interests of owners. Other contracts such as debt covenants are also important in limiting managers' freedom of action. Share options and profit-based performance bonuses may, for example, act to bring managers' interests into harmony with those of the external shareholders. Thus, financial reporting and auditing regulations, other contractual arrangements and managers' preferences for particular measurement and reporting practices are all premised upon certain, usually implicit, assumptions about the behaviour of managers.[7]

If the culture of a country is very different from that assumed by agency theory with, in particular, higher scores on both collectivism and nurturing, agency theory may not provide a good explanation of managers' behaviour. This means that the optimal amount and type of regulatory structures and rules may also be very different.[8] One example of an obvious and striking cultural difference may be seen in the case of Tanzania. This society is more collectivist than are any of the developed Anglo-American countries, with the extended family being particularly important. Thus, one of the earliest Tanzanian accounting standards (TSSAP 2 issued in 1983) includes extensive disclosure requirements with respect to related parties transactions.[9] What is striking about TSSAP 2 is the relative prominence given to related parties' disclosures and the way in which 'related parties' is defined primarily in personal terms, being mainly seen as family members. In contrast, in the UK related parties are defined primarily in business terms.[10] While 'members of the close family' fall under the UK definition of related parties, far more emphasis is placed upon business associates and other parties with direct or indirect control or influence (*see* Case study 2.1 for extracts from the requirements in both countries).

2.3.3 Culture and organisational structures

Finally, culture also affects organisational structures. This has obvious implications for both management and financial accounting. One example is Japanese companies, as will be discussed in more detail in Chapter 15. Japanese corporate groups are often not based on majority share ownership. Instead, group membership is often based upon a multitude of relationships such as supplier, customer and debt relationships and common directorships. Rather than there being majority share-ownership by a clearly defined parent company there are often relatively small share cross-holdings throughout the group. This affects the usefulness of consolidated or group statements which are based upon the assumption that a group is made up of a parent company, subsidiaries and subsubsidiaries, all organised in a hierarchical structure.

Hofstede argued that the two cultural constructs that most affect how organisations are structured are power distance (which primarily influences superior–subordinate relationships) and uncertainty avoidance (which primarily influences the amount and type of rules in place). Hofstede also identified the types of business organisations which should be most common in particular countries, as illustrated in Exhibit 2.6 below.[11] (*Note*: This brief and simple description offers only an extremely simplified picture. As with any generalisation, many organisations will be structured very differently, and what Hofstede describes may be best thought of as a tendency towards preferring particular styles of organisation.)

---

[7] Jensen and Meckling (1976)
[8] Kaplan and Ruland (1991); Ogden (1993)
[9] National Board of Acountants and Auditors (1983)
[10] Accounting Standards Board (1995)
[11] Hofstede (1984), p. 216

Exhibit 2.6 ORGANISATIONAL TYPES AS IDENTIFIED BY HOFSTEDE (1984)

	A	*B*	*C*	*D*
Power distance	Low	High	Low	High
Uncertainty avoidance	Weak	Weak	Strong	Strong
Organisation type	Implicitly structured	Personnel bureaucracy	Workflow bureaucracy	Full bureaucracy
Implicit model of the organisation	Market	Family	Well oiled machine	Pyramid
Countries	Anglo/US Scandinavian Netherlands	South East Asian	Germany Finland Israel	Latin Med. Islamic Japan

Exhibit 2.6 shows us that, for example, countries characterised by relatively high power distance and strong uncertainty avoidance should tend to favour organisations run on fully bureaucratic lines. Here, explicit formal rules are more likely to prescribe behaviour. Power and authority tends to depend upon the position held rather than upon personal characteristics. In contrast, in countries such as the UK, USA or Australia, which can be characterised by relatively small power distance and weak uncertainty avoidance, organisations should tend to be at least implicitly modelled upon the market place.

Thus, relatively less emphasis tends to be placed upon formal rules. Personal attributes and performance are both important in determining an individual's power and authority, while performance measures will be based upon the outcomes achieved rather than the actions undertaken.

2.4 CULTURE AND ACCOUNTING

2.4.1 Accounting subculture

We have seen how societal culture influences the organisational structures and decision-making processes of companies. These, in turn, will influence the accounting system. But culture also has a more direct impact upon financial accounting. The financial accounting system is set up and run by and for various groups of people, in particular auditors, management accountants or other statement preparers, accounting regulators (who may or may not also be accountants) and statement users.

Each of these groups may be thought of as a distinct subcultural group with their own subcultures. Some of these groups are not very homogeneous and will not have a well defined subculture. For example, shareholders range from private individuals to companies holding shares in associates and subsidiaries, to investment trusts and pension schemes. They have little in common beyond perhaps sharing a belief in private ownership of industry, profit maximisation by companies and personal wealth maximisation. In contrast, accountants are a relatively homogeneous group – they share a common professional education and tend to have common working experiences. They have a relatively well defined subculture distinct from the culture of the wider society.

If we return to our model of the influences on accounting rules and practices (Exhibit 2.1) we can see that ecological or environmental and external factors both directly influence the institutions and culture of a country. Societal culture also itself influences the institutions of a country, with the two reinforcing each other. When it comes to accounting, the subculture of accountants is influenced by the culture of the wider society while it influences the accounting rules and practices. The system is a dynamic one in the sense that the accounting system provides feedback, influencing society's institutions and culture.

The unique factors influencing accountants will not normally be strong enough to completely override or obliterate societywide cultural differences. Thus, for example, the culture of the UK is different from the culture of (say) Japan, Germany or Korea and the subculture of UK accountants should therefore also be different from the subculture of accountants from Japan, Germany or Korea. The fact that all these accountants perform similar, although not identical jobs, should not be enough to obliterate all cultural differences, although it will obviously reduce them. We would expect to find that Hofstede's 'cultural dimensions' are systematically linked to a number of similar 'subcultural dimensions' or 'accounting values'.

2.4.2 Accounting values

If we return to Hofstede's cultural dimensions or values, the two that will have the most influence on accounting are 'uncertainty avoidance' and 'individualism'. In a high uncertainty avoidance country, institutions will be organised in ways that minimise uncertainty. Rules and regulations will tend to be explicit and prescriptive, they will tend to be detailed, all-embracing and rigid. Individualism, on the other hand, affects motivation. It will therefore affect preferences for particular earnings measurement rules and disclosure practices. It will also influence the extent to which people are happy to accept rules and controls imposed from above or will be willing to use their personal or professional initiative and be prepard to take risks. This affects their willingness to accept uniform accounting rules in preference to a more permissive system involving the use of professional discretion.

The work of Hofstede was extended by Gray (1988) who identified four 'accounting values' or 'subcultural dimensions'. '*Professionalism* versus *statutory control*' and '*uniformity* versus *flexibility*' both describe attitudes towards regulation, in particular attitudes towards the type of control system and the level or extent of control that is preferred. '*Conservatism* versus *optimism*' is concerned with attitudes towards measurement. Attitudes towards uncertainty are particularly important here. The final value, '*secrecy* versus *transparency*', is concerned with attitudes towards disclosure. Exhibit 2.7 reproduces Gray's definition of each of these four accounting values.

| Exhibit 2.7 | ACCOUNTING VALUES IDENTIFIED BY GRAY (1988) |

Professionalism versus statutory control

A preference for the exercise of individual professional judgement and the maintenance of professional self-regulation, as opposed to compliance with prescriptive legal requirements and statutory control.

Uniformity versus flexibility

A preference for the enforcement of uniform accounting practices between companies and the consistent use of such practices over time, as opposed to flexibility in accordance with the perceived circumstances of individual companies.

Conservatism versus optimism

A preference for a cautious approach to measurement so as to cope with the uncertainty of future events, as opposed to a more optimistic, *laissez-faire*, risk-taking approach.

Secrecy versus transparency

A preference for confidentiality and the restriction of disclosure of information about the business only to those who are closely involved with its management and financing, as opposed to a more transparent, open and publicly accountable approach.

Gray also argued that Hofstede's societal cultural values will be systematically linked to his accounting values. The hypothesised relationships between the two are illustrated in Exhibit 2.8, which describes which of Hofstede's cultural dimensions are most strongly associated with each of Gray's four accounting values.

The relationships described in Exhibit 2.8 can instead be shown in a diagrammatic way, *see* Exhibit 2.9.

2.4.3 Applying cultural analysis to accounting

There have been a number of attempts to test these hypothesised relationships. However, this is not an easy task. There are problems with using Hofstede's scores, since he based his work on employees of IBM in the period 1968–73, and the scores may not be valid for other groups in the 1990s.[12] For example, he ignored religion which can also affect attitudes towards business and accounting.[13] There are also problems with measuring Gray's accounting values. Auditors or other accountants can be asked their views on various issues, but this is not easy. A more common approach is to look instead directly at the accounting system. Thus, for example, rather than looking at attitudes towards conservatism, studies have looked at the importance of conservatism in the measurement rules and practices of countries. They have then tested the hypothesis that, for example, countries that are more uncertainty avoidant and more collectivist will have relatively more conservative measurement rules. This approach implicitly assumes that there is a

---

[12] Trompenaar's work may be more appropriate as it is more up to date and is based on many companies. However, unlike Hofstede, he has not disclosed the full scores of each country. One reason why so many studies use Hofstede's work is because he has disclosed all the relevant scores.

[13] Hamid *et al.* (1993)

Exhibit 2.8 ASSOCIATION BETWEEN HOFSTEDE'S CULTURAL DIMENSIONS AND GRAY'S ACCOUNTING VALUES

Gray's accounting values	Cultural dimensions affecting the country's accounting values	
Professionalism *versus* Statutory control	Professionalism tends to be associated with: ● individualism ● weak uncertainty avoidance ● small power distance.	Statutory Control tends to be associated with: ● collectivism ● strong uncertainty avoidance ● large power distance.
Uniformity *versus* Flexibility	Uniformity tends to be associated with: ● strong uncertainty avoidance ● large power distance ● collectivism.	Flexibility tends to be associated with: ● weak uncertainty avoidance ● small power distance ● individualism.
Conservatism *versus* Optimism	Conservatism tends to be associated with: ● strong uncertainty avoidance ● collectivism ● high nurture.	Optimism tends to be associated with: ● weak uncertainty avoidance ● individualism ● low nurture.
Secrecy *versus* Transparency	Secrecy tends to be associated with: ● strong uncertainty avoidance ● large power distance ● collectivism ● high nurture.	Transparency tends to be associated with: ● weak uncertainty avoidance ● small power distance ● individualism ● low nurture.

Exhibit 2.9 THE RELATIONSHIP BETWEEN CULTURAL DIMENSIONS AND ACCOUNTING VALUES

Cultural dimension	Relationship to accounting values			
	Professionalism	Uniformity	Conservatism	Secrecy
Individualism	+	−	−	−
Uncertainty avoidance	−	+	+	+
Power distance	−	+	NR	+
Nurturing	NR	NR	+	+
Accounting practice mainly influenced	Authority	Application	Measurement	Disclosure

Key: + Positive relationship. For example, the *higher* is individualism, the *higher* will be professionalism
    − Negative relationship. For example, the *lower* uncertainty avoidance, the *higher* will be professionalism
    NR No relationship.

direct relationship between accounting values and accounting systems. However, as we have seen, accounting systems are influenced by many factors. There may be a relationship between Hofstede's values and accounting systems but the reasons for this may not be correctly specified. Thus, there may be no relationship between Hofstede's dimensions and Gray's accounting values.

2.4.4 An example of a study using accounting values

A number of studies have attempted to measure Gray's accounting values to see whether or not they are linked to Hofstede's cultural values in the ways hypothesised. One of these studies will be described, that by Salter and Niswander (1995). Gray's accounting values are concerned with values and beliefs of accountants. It is an immense task to measure these directly, especially in the international area. Salter and Niswander instead used indirect measures of accounting values. They assumed that, for example, differences in attitudes towards secrecy or transparency will be reflected in differences in disclosure, while differences in attitudes towards conservatism will be reflected in differences in measurement rules.

The ways in which they measured the four accounting values are described in Exhibit 2.10.

Exhibit 2.10 THE MEASUREMENT OF ACCOUNTING VALUES

Accounting value	*Measurement used*	
Professionalism	Score for audit perspective + professional structure, where:	
	Audit perspective	1 Conform with legal requirements
		2 Fairly, consistently present, in conformity with
		3 True and fair, in conformity with
		4 True and fair
	Professional structure	0 Law/legislated
		1 Practitioner body
Uniformity	*De jure:*	0 Common law system
		1 Code law system
	De facto	Number of practices with high level of uniformity (less than 25% or greater than 75% compliance rate)
Conservatism	Conservatism 1	Use of various practices that reduce assets or income
	Conservatism 2	Use of various practices that increase assets or income
Secrecy	Disclosure index	Two used, each designed to measure the level of disclosure

Source: Salter and Niswander (1995), p. 385. Used with the permission of the *Journal of International Business Studies*

This study provides some support for Gray's arguments. As discussed above, Gray argued that the two cultural dimensions most important for accounting are individualism and uncertainty avoidance. Using the scores provided by Hofstede and applying the analysis to 29 countries, Salter and Niswander found that uncertainty avoidance was related to all four of Gray's accounting values. In contrast, individualism helped to explain only one of the four accounting values, namely secrecy: the more individualistic countries tend to disclose the most. There was also little support for the expected relationships between accounting values and either power distance or nurturing.

There have been a number of other studies that have looked at the relationship between Hofstede's work and accounting. For example, culture has been used to help explain some of the differences in the accounting regulatory systems of the Anglo countries of the UK, the USA, Australia and Canada in comparison to the Asian countries of Singapore, Hong Kong and Taiwan.[14] These two groups of countries are culturally quite dissimilar. The study looked in very general terms at regulatory systems, and was fairly successful in doing this. In contrast, another study, on the contrary, argued that culture fails to explain many of the accounting differences between France and Germany.[15] These two countries are culturally more alike than are the two groups of countries in the former study. It was also concerned with more detailed features of the accounting systems.

2.5 IS CULTURE AN IMPORTANT INFLUENCE ON ACCOUNTING?

There are many supporters of the view that culture has a significant influence on accounting. Indeed, this is fairly incontrovertible: culture, in the sense of how people think and feel and their values, beliefs and attitudes affects their behaviour. Accounting regulations and practices are an outcome of human behaviour.

The models linking accounting and culture suggest that culture acts as an intervening factor. Culture modifies the influence of ecological or environmental and external factors. It also influences the values or subculture of accountants and the institutions of a society. These in turn both influence accounting systems. Given the complexity of these relationships, it would not be too surprising to find that some countries have similar cultures but dissimilar accounting systems, while other countries have similar accounting systems but dissimilar cultures. It is the complex combination or interaction of all these factors that is important.

Even if there is a clear and consistent connection between culture and accounting, researchers may have failed to uncover it. Most studies of accounting rely upon the work of Hofstede (not least because he provides quantified measures for a range of countries). Hofstede has reduced a very complex phenomenon down to four dimensions. Unfortunately, all we have are the raw or mean scores for each country. We really need more information than this. For example, how typical or representative are the scores for each cultural dimension? Do most people have very similar beliefs, attitudes and values or not? If the people of a society are culturally very similar, culture is more likely to help to explain their accounting

---

[14] Kirsch (1994)
[15] Fechner and Kilgore (1994)

system. If, instead, a country is culturally heterogeneous with people holding very different views or values, then it is far less likely that a measure of 'average culture' will help to explain the accounting system.

While there are many supporters of Hofstede who argue that his work helps us to understand differences in accounting internationally, there is far from universal support for this. Some of the arguments used by opponents of this approach are summarised by Most (1995), when he argued that:

> he [i.e. Hofstede] used questionnaires to elicit responses designed to identify national groups with attitudes; on the basis of these responses, he found national patterns that led to a classification of organisations and, by inference, of accounting practices.
>
> First, why was this process chosen? The established classification of civilisation allocates each culture to one of these eight classes: Occidental, Muslim, Japanese, Hindu, Confucian, Slavic, African and Latin American. A researcher seeking to identify national patterns of accounting would first attempt to map empirical observations into these classes, investigating any differences that arose. It would be found that modern communications have broken down the strict separations that the categories imply . . . It would doubtless be found that culture is too complex a concept to be analysed using a simple model.
>
> We also find Hofstede's model suspect on other grounds. Power distance and uncertainty avoidance are not unequivocal measures of human characteristics. An individual might accept the uneven distribution of power on the national level but not on the regional, on the regional but not on the tribal, or on the tribal but not within the family. Any society that is based on agriculture, or has a sizeable cultivation sector, must be characterised as one with a low level of 'anxiety . . . in the face of unstructured or ambiguous situations'. Although Hofstede did not make much use of the other 'values', similar criticisms can be levelled at them – individualism versus collectivism has lost much of its significance since his research was done; as for the distinction between masculinity and femininity, the less said, the better. It would appear that the values selected by Hofstede were not found by a process of observation and measurement but simply invented in order to initiate a series of exploratory observations.
>
> The conclusion drawn by Hofstede and his followers, that culture 'dictates' the accounting environment and accounting and auditing judgements, must be rejected as not proven.

While we would not go as far as Most (and we would certainly not agree with his attack on the lack of observation and measurement), the evidence linking societal culture to accounting is far from conclusive. Even if the theory is correct, and there is a significant relationship between societal cultures and accounting systems, it may not be easy to empirically prove such a relationship. Not only are there problems in defining and measuring 'culture', but similar problems exist with respect to the definition and measurement of 'accounting values' and 'accounting systems'. Given these problems, it is not surprising that empirical studies have not found a perfect match between culture and accounting. What is perhaps more important is the fact that, while far from perfect, they have found some empirical support for a relationship between accounting systems and cultural values.

2.6 SUMMARY AND CONCLUSIONS

This chapter has looked at the influence of culture on accounting. We followed Hofstede in defining culture as 'the collective programming of the mind that distinguishes the members of one human group from another'. This was then broken down into the four dimensions of:

- individualism versus collectivism
- large versus small power distance
- strong versus weak uncertainty avoidance
- high versus low nurturing.

The chapter then went on to show how culture can affect business, in particular how it can influence leadership styles, the motivation of employers and employees and organisational structures. Culture can also more directly influence accounting by influencing the subculture of accountants. Four 'accounting values' were described:

- professionalism versus statutory control
- uniformity versus flexibility
- conservatism versus optimism
- secrecy versus transparency.

Finally, the chapter concluded by reviewing a number of empirical studies. From these, and other similar studies, it can be concluded that culture appears to provide a useful first step in understanding or explaining differences between the accounting systems of many countries. However, it provides a far from complete explanation of either the differences between all countries or the differences in specific detailed rules and practices.

Case study 2.1

ACCOUNTING FOR RELATED PARTIES IN THE UK AND TANZANIA

Tanzania: TSSAP 2

'Related party' transactions
The term 'related party' shall include:

(a) the chief executive of the enterprise, his [sic] spouse and children;
(b) every member of the board of directors or their equivalent, however designated along with each member's spouse and children;
(c) the parents, brothers and sisters of those mentioned in (a) and (b) above, and
(d) any body corporate which has an influence over the composition of the board of directors of the enterprise.

There shall be a full disclosure of loans of every description made during the accounting period or outstanding at any time during the accounting period to or from any person coming within the definition of 'related party' with particulars of:

(a) nature and conditions of such loans;
(b) identity of the party;

■ *Case study 2.1 continued*

(c) maximum amount outstanding at any time during the accounting period;
(d) rate of interest, if any, applicable to the loan;
(e) details of any guarantee or securities available.

There shall be a disclosure of safari [i.e. holiday] and other imprests and all forms of temporary borrowings outstanding on the Balance Sheet date from any person falling within the definition of the 'related party' provided the amount outstanding exceeds five thousand shillings, stating particulars of:

(a) amount outstanding;
(b) purpose of the imprest or other form of temporary accommodation;
(c) how long the amount has been outstanding;
(d) steps taken for the recovery of the amount.

There shall be a disclosure also of the interest of 'related parties' in:

(a) shares and debentures of the enterprise;
(b) contracts in force at any given time during the accounting period or any transaction in which any of the 'related parties' has or had an interest which is of significance to the enterprise.

UK: FRS 8

Guidance on the definition of a related party:
(a) Two or more parties are related parties when at any time during the financial period:

  (i)   one party has direct or indirect control of the other party; or
  (ii) the parties are subject to common control from the same source; or
  (iii) one party has influence over the financial and operating policies of the other party to an extent that the other party might be inhibited from pursuing at all times its own separate interests; or
  (iv) the parties, in entering a transaction, are subject to influence from the same source to such an extent that one of the parties to the transaction has subordinated its own separate interests.

(b) For the avoidance of doubt, the following are related parties of the reporting entity:

  (i)   its ultimate and intermediate parent undertakings, subsidiary undertakings, and fellow subsidiary undertakings;
  (ii) its associates and joint ventures;
  (iii) the investor or venturer in respect of which the reporting entity is an associate or a joint venture;
  (iv) directors of the reporting entity and the directors of its ultimate and intermediate parent undertakings; and
  (v)   pension funds for the benefits of employees of the reporting entity or of any entity that is a related party of the reporting entity;

■ *Case study 2.1 continued*

(c) and the following are presumed to be related parties of the reporting entity unless it can be demonstrated that neither party has influenced the financial and operating policies of the other in such a way as to inhibit the pursuit of separate interests:

(i) the key management of the reporting entity and the key management of its parent undertaking or undertakings;

(ii) a person owning or able to exercise control over 20 per cent or more of the voting rights of the reporting entity, whether directly or through nominees;

(iii) each person acting in concert in such a way as to be able to exercise control or influence over the reporting entity; and

(iv) an entity managing or managed by the reporting entity under a management contract.

(d) Additionally, because of their relationship with certain parties that are, or are presumed to be, related parties of the reporting entity, the following are also presumed to be related parties of the reporting entity:

(i) members of the close family of any individual falling under parties mentioned in (a)–(c) above; and

(ii) partnerships, companies, trusts or other entities in which any individual or member of the close family of (a)–(c) above has a controlling interest.

Disclosure of transactions and balances

Financial statements should disclose material transactions undertaken . . . with a related party. Disclosure should be made irrespective of whether a price is charged. The disclosure should include:

(a) the names of the transacting related parties;

(b) a description of the relationship between the parties;

(c) a description of the transactions;

(d) the amounts involved;

(e) any other elements of the transactions necessary for an understanding of the financial statements;

(f) the amounts due to or from related parties at the balance sheet date and provisions for doubtful debts due from such parties at that date; and

(g) amounts written off in the period in respect of debts due to or from related parties.

Source: TSSAP 2, *Information Required to be Disclosed in Financial Statements* (National Board of Accountants and Auditors, 1983); FRS 8, *Related Party Disclosures* (ASB, October 1995).

QUESTIONS

Describing culture (2.2)

1 What is meant by the terms 'culture' and 'subculture', and why are the two different?

2 Why might accountants have a particularly strong subculture?

3 Describe what you think this accounting subculture might be like.

4 Describe your country in terms of the seven cultural dimensions described by Trompenaars.

5 Describe your country in terms of the four cultural dimensions described by Hofstede.

6 Using the data on Hofstede's scores and rankings provided in Exhibits 2.4 and 2.5, describe each of the countries listed in Exhibit 2.4 and place them each into relevant groups.

Effects of culture (2.3)

1 How might each of Hofstede's cultural dimensions affect corporate leadership styles?

2 How might each of Hofstede's cultural dimensions affect organisational structures?

3 How might each of Hofstede's cultural dimensions affect what factors motivate employees?

4 Why does Most criticise Hofstede's work?

Accounting and culture (2.4)

1 Describe Gray's four accounting values and describe how they are linked to Hofstede's cultural dimensions.

2 Describe your country in terms of Gray's four accounting values.

3 Does your description of your country's accounting values and cultural dimensions, as defined by Hofstede, support the hypothesised link between the two as described in Exhibit 2.9?

4 How are Gray's accounting values linked to the system of accounting regulation?

5 How are Gray's accounting values linked to accounting measurement rules and practices?

6 How are Gray's accounting values linked to accounting disclosure rules and practices?

7 What are the main problems involved in measuring accounting values?

REFERENCES

ASB (1995) *FRS 8, Related Party Transactions*. London: Accounting Standards Board.

Balaga, B.R. and Jaeger, A.M. (1984) 'Multinational corporations: control systems and delegation issues', *Journal of International Business Studies*, Fall, 25–40.

Fechner, H.H.E and Kilgore, A. (1994) 'The influence of cultural factors on accounting practice', *International Journal of Accounting*, 29(4), 265–77.

Gambling, T. (1987) 'Accounting for rituals', *Accounting, Organisations and Society*, 12(4), 319–29.

Gray, S.J. (1988) 'Towards a theory of cultural influence on the development of accounting systems internationally', *Abacus*, 24(1), 1–15.

Hamid, S., Craig, R. and Clark, F. (1993) 'Religion: a confounding cultural element in the international harmonisation of accounting?', *Abacus*, 29(2), 131–48.

Hofstede, G. (1984) *Culture's Consequences: International Differences in Work-related Values*. Beverly Hills, CA: Sage Publications.

Hofstede, G. (1991) *Cultures and Organisations: Software of the Mind*. London: McGraw-Hill.

Hofstede, G. and Bond, M.H. (1988) 'The Confucius connection: From cultural roots to economic growth', *Organizational Dynamics*, 16(1), 5–21.

Jensen, M.C. and Meckling, W.H. (1976) 'Theory of the firm: Managerial behaviour, agency costs and ownership structure', *Journal of Financial Economics*, 3, 305–60.

Kaplin, S.E. and Ruland, R.G. (1991) 'Positive theory, rationality and accounting regulation', *Critical Perspectives on Accounting*, 2, 361–74.

Kirsch, R.J. (1994) 'Towards a global reporting model: Culture and disclosure in selected capital markets', *Research in Accounting Regulation*, 8, 71–110.

Most, K. (1995) 'A critique of international accounting theory', *Advances in International Accounting*, 7, 3–11.

National Board of Accountants and Auditors (1983) *Tanzanian Statement of Standard Accounting Practice No.2: Information Required to be Disclosed in Financial Statements*. Dar Es Salaam: NBAA, June.

Ogden, S.G. (1993) 'The limitations of agency theory: The case of accounting-based profit sharing schemes. *Critical Perspectives on Accounting*, 4, 179–206.

Salter, S.B. and Niswander, F. (1995) 'Cultural influence on the development of accounting systems internationally: A test of Gray's [1988] theory', *Journal of International Business Studies*, 26(2), 379–98.

Trompenaars F. (1993) *Riding the Waves of Culture: Understanding Cultural Diversity in Business*. London: Nicholas Brealey Publishing, 8–10.

Chapter 3

Measuring international differences in accounting rules and practices

3.1 ## PURPOSE OF THE CHAPTER

Chapters 1 and 2 looked at reasons why countries have adopted different accounting systems. This chapter looks at the impact of these differences. The ways in which differences in accounting systems can be measured are explained and some of the empirical studies using these techniques are examined.

Learning objectives

After reading this chapter you should be able to:

● Understand how Comparability Indexes are used to measure differences in reported figures.

● Understand how Concentration Indexes are used to measure differences in accounting methods.

● Measure the comparability of profits and the level of harmonisation, using simple examples.

● Evaluate published research which has used these techniques and assess the significance of this research for those seeking international harmonisation.

Differences in the accounting practices of countries are of two types. First, similar events can be reported in different ways in different countries. One reason for this might be, for example, differences in the valuation rules for various assets and liabilities. Second, different events may be reported in different countries. For example, companies may provide only group or consolidated accounts or they may also provide full parent company financial statements. Differences in accounting rules or practices can impose significant direct and indirect costs on providers and users of financial statements. Direct costs include extra preparation or analysis costs, indirect costs arise because different information leads to different decisions.

This chapter begins by looking at the types of differences that exist between the accounting systems of countries. It then explores briefly the impact of these differences on the preparers and users of financial accounts.

Finally, it looks at the techniques that can be used to quantify or measure the differences between accounting systems and it explores some of the empirical studies that have tried to do this.

3.2 SOURCES OF DIFFERENCES BETWEEN ACCOUNTING SYSTEMS

The differences between the accounting systems of companies located in different countries fall into three categories:

- differences in the rules of different countries
- differences in the ways in which the rules are interpreted or implemented
- differences in preferred practices (including voluntary disclosure practices).

Each of these types of differences will be briefly explored below.

3.2.1 Differences in accounting rules

The most obvious reason why companies from different countries use different accounting methods or report different information is because the rules or regulations call for different treatments. To illustrate this, we can look at some of the rules in the UK and the USA. For example, in the UK, investment properties have to be measured at current values while in the USA they can be shown only at historical costs. Similarly, deferred tax is calculated using the full liability method in the USA, while in the UK companies must defer only the potential or likely liability.

The case where the rules in one country are stricter or allow less choice than do the rules in the other country is also common. For example, the UK allows fixed assets to be shown at either historical or current values, while only historical costs are allowed in the USA. In this example, a UK company could choose to use those accounting methods that are also allowed in the USA, in which case there will be no differences in the accounting methods used by the UK company and US companies. Alternatively, it could choose methods that are not allowed in the USA. Then its statements will not be comparable to those produced by similar US companies. (Eventually a new UK standard will bring amortisation in the UK, also.)

Finally, one country may have rules while another country does not. For example, the USA has many industry-specific rules or standards that do not exist in the UK. Again, depending upon the accounting methods actually used by UK companies, the statements of companies from the two countries may or may not be comparable.

3.2.2 Differences in the interpretation of accounting rules

Even where the rules of two countries are identical, they may be interpreted or applied in consistently different ways by companies in the two countries.[1] Many areas of accounting entail the use of estimates, forecasts or judgements. For ex-

---

[1] Davidson and Chrisman (1993)

ample, to calculate economic depreciation rates you must first decide on the most suitable allocation basis, the useful life of the asset and its residual value. All of these involve the use of estimates, forecasts and judgement. Other accounting rules, by contrast, include ambiguous terms. For example, when deciding whether or not to disclose information on contingencies, a company must decide on exactly what is meant by terms such as 'probable' (does this mean, for example, 95% certain, or is an event with a 85% chance of occurring still probable) and 'remote' (is this an event with a 10% chance or a 5% chance of occurring)?

The use of estimates and the interpretation of ambiguous terminology mean that identical events may be measured and reported in different ways by different companies. Obviously, there may be differences inside a country, but the differences will often be much greater in an international setting.

We saw in Chapter 1 how accounting rules and practices were influenced by a wide variety of factors, while in Chapter 2 we saw how culture affects accounting. We saw, for example, how the link between taxation and financial reporting and the creditor versus shareholder orientation of the financial statements could affect attitudes towards income measurement. Where reported earnings form the basis for the calculation of taxable earnings and where the main users of the financial statements are creditors, companies will probably interpret and implement accounting rules in ways that minimise rather than maximise reported earnings. Similarly, culture tends to affect how people interpret ambiguous terms such as 'probable' and 'remote'. A person coming from a society that is relatively unhappy with uncertainty may interpret 'probable' in a more restrictive way than will someone coming from a society that is more comfortable with uncertainty.

3.2.3 Differences in preferred accounting practices

A distinction must be made between accounting regulations, or *de jure* issues, and actual practices, or *de facto* issues. Accounting regulations often contain a number of options. There may also be a large number of issues which are not covered by accounting regulations at all, giving companies even more choice.

While it is relatively straightforward (although not necessarily easy) to compare the accounting regulations of two countries, this may tell us relatively little about how similar the accounting practices of companies actually are. *De facto* practices may differ considerably across countries, even if there are few *de jure* differences. Alternatively, if all companies, irrespective of country of domicile, choose wherever possible to use similar methods, *de facto* differences may be less than the *de jure* differences. Therefore, the actual practices of real companies must be compared if you want to gain a full picture of international accounting differences. As discussed later in this chapter, this is a far from easy task.

3.3 THE IMPORTANCE OF DIFFERENCES IN ACCOUNTING SYSTEMS

3.3.1 Companies as preparers and users of financial statements

Many companies will be affected by international accounting differences. A company that engages in any form of international trade may have to use foreign financial statements or prepare financial statements using the rules of other countries. A company that exports or imports goods may want to assess the creditworthiness of its trading partners. A company that wants to borrow money from foreign bankers or other lenders may have to produce financial data using the rules that these potential lenders are familiar with. However, it is multinational companies that will be most affected by international accounting differences.

Local accounting rules will usually have to be used in the financial statements of foreign subsidiaries. These statements may be required by local tax authorities, shareholders or debt providers. However, most countries require companies to produce group accounts using consistent accounting methods across all subsidiaries. This may mean that the company has to produce two sets of financial statements for some of its subsidiaries – one using local generally accepted accounting principles (GAAP) for local reporting purposes and one using parent company GAAP for consolidation. If the rules applicable to external financial statements are different from the rules used by tax authorities, the company may have to produce even more different financial statements for the same subsidiary.

These multiple reporting requirements may involve substantial extra direct costs – there may be additional data collection, collation and auditing costs. There may also be extra indirect costs due to differences in reporting requirements. The existence of different accounting systems may result in the same event being reported in two, or more, very different ways. This may create confusion and dysfunctional behaviour inside the company. If there are two set of figures each apparently measuring the same events, which is 'correct'?; which one should local management seek to maximise?; what should they do if the two accounting systems conflict, so that actions that increase reported earnings under one system reduce earnings reported under the alternative set of rules?

Rather than having different measurement rules, a country may have extra or different disclosure rules. However, companies may be unwilling to provide this extra information. Extra disclosure requirements may involve considerable extra collection, collation, auditing and dissemination costs. Companies may also fear the consequences of disclosing extra information that could be of use to their competitors (usually called 'competitive disadvantage'). Alternatively, the extra information may affect the views or decisions taken by other users, such as governments, trade unions or employees, customers and suppliers.

If the additional costs are substantial they may affect the decisions taken by a company. Indeed, as discussed in Chapter 7, one of the reasons why the EU has regulated accounting is that it believed that accounting rules could influence corporate investment decisions. If the disclosure requirements are very different in the various member states, companies from outside the EU may invest in those countries with the least onerous requirements. Differences in disclosure requirements may also affect companies' financing decisions. As discussed in Chapter 5, this is one of the main reasons why stock exchanges have been pressing for stricter international accounting standards. Chapter 18 reviews empirical evidence which shows that companies appear to be more likely to list on those foreign stock markets which do not require any extra information.

3.3.2 Investors

Shareholders are increasingly investing in foreign companies. Just as in a domestic setting investors can reduce their risk by investing in a diversified portfolio of companies, they can further reduce their risks by investing in an international portfolio of companies. However, if companies from different countries produce figures using different methods or provide different information, then their statements will not be comparable with each other. Normally, not enough information is given to allow the user to convert the reported figures to those that would have been produced under a different set of accounting rules. The reader of foreign financial statements may thus have great difficulty in understanding what the figures mean.

For example, if a German investor is interested in a UK company, she may compare its financial statements with a similar German company and find that the UK company appears to be more profitable. This may be because the German company really is less efficient than the UK one. Alternatively, the German company may be more efficient than the UK company, but uses accounting methods that reduce its reported earnings. If the German investor knows that German accounting rules are different, but she cannot measure or quantify the impact of these differences, she may decide not to invest in the UK at all or she may decide to invest in British companies only if they appear to be very much more profitable than their German alternatives. Whatever investment decision she finally makes, she will have made a different decision from that which she would have made had the German and UK companies used the same accounting methods. (This issue is explored further in Chapter 18.)

3.3.3 Other groups affected by international differences

If companies or shareholders make different decisions because of international differences in accounting, other groups will also be affected. If differences in disclosure rules affect a company's foreign location decision, then local communities, actual and potential employees and governments will be affected. Similarly, stock market listing decisions affect the stock market(s) themselves, other stock market participants and the balance of payments of countries. Shareholders' investment decisions have secondary impacts or implications for other companies that are not invested in, and for the economy as a whole.

It is not only companies and shareholders that use financial statements. Employees of foreign owned subsidiaries and their trade unions representatives may use financial statements in negotiations on pay or conditions. Host governments may use financial statements to help them in economic planning. Customers, suppliers and lenders may want to gauge the creditworthiness or future prospects of foreign owned companies. They may not have the power to demand information produced under local rules and they will have to rely upon financial statements produced under unfamiliar foreign rules. This may mean that they have to spend extra resources in learning about the accounting differences and in calculating their impact on the reported figures. Alternatively, they may be unable or unwilling to do this. In this case they are likely to be misled by the financial statements and may make quite different decisions.

Finally, accountants have to audit the statements of multinational groups, including foreign subsidiaries. The problems and additional expenses involved in having to understand and audit figures produced under multiple accounting jurisdictions may be considerable.

3.4 MEASUREMENT OF DIFFERENCES IN REPORTED FIGURES

One way of comparing companies' financial statements is to measure the extent of the differences between them. If we can measure and quantify the extent of the differences, we can see which statements are most alike and which are most different. We can measure changes over time to see if moves towards harmonisation are working and we can assess whether or not the differences are important.

There are a number of different ways to measure the extent of differences or the extent of similarities across different financial statements. One approach is to measure the difference in reported earnings and shareholders' funds that are caused by differences in the accounting methods used. Here, we would produce one set of financial statements under local rules and another set for the same company using a different set of rules. An alternative approach is to look instead at the methods or rules used by two companies. Here we would count the number of rules that are the same and the number that are different. Each of these two alternatives will give us some idea of how similar or dissimilar the financial statements are. However, they can often give very different results.

There may be a lot of accounting rules that are different between two companies or two countries, but the overall impact of these difference on reported profits and shareholders' funds may be very small. Some of the accounting differences may result in higher profits or shareholders' funds in one country while other differences result in lower figures. The effects may thus cancel each other out. Alternatively, none of the differences in methods or rules may be very important, in that none cause material differences in the figures reported. In other cases there may be very few rules that are different, but each of these different rules may have a material impact on profits and shareholders' funds.

When looking at ways of measuring differences in accounting systems we must therefore look at both the differences in the figures reported and the differences in the methods used. The rest of section 3.4 looks at how to measure differences in reported figures, while section 3.5 looks at how to measure differences in the accounting methods used.

3.4.1 Foreign GAAP financial statements

To measure the impact on reported figures of accounting differences you need two sets of figures – one set produced using domestic reporting methods or generally accepted accounting principles (domestic GAAP) and the other set reporting the same events but using an alternative set of principles based upon the GAAP of a second country.

A number of companies do this, and report two sets of figures, one using domestic GAAP and a second set using the GAAP of a foreign country. As explored further in Part 3 of this book, the main reason for providing foreign GAAP statements is the existence of foreign shareholders and foreign stock market listings. For example, the London stock exchange requires companies to produce annual accounts of an 'international quality'. If a company wishes to list on the London Stock Exchange and its domestic GAAP statements do not meet these quality criteria, the company may be required to produce a second set of financial statements. Statements following UK or US GAAP, IASC standards or EU Directives would all be acceptable.

More common than two complete sets of financial statements under different GAAP is the situation where a company provides a complete set of financial statements under domestic GAAP and a reconciliation statement using foreign GAAP. Foreign companies listing on American stock exchanges have to provide a reconciliation statement in their annual report filed with the SEC (Form 20-F) and it is also often reproduced in their annual report. The reconciliation statements provided by British Telecom (BT) are reproduced in Exhibit 3.1. As can be seen, these statements start with domestic GAAP profit or net income and shareholders' equity. They then list all the significant differences in accounting rules in the UK and USA. For each of these issues BT discloses the size of the adjustment or the difference between the figures that would be reported under domestic and US rules. The statements then end up by disclosing net income or profits and shareholders' equity under US GAAP. BT also provides a statement describing the main differences between the two GAAP (not reproduced here).

If we look at the reconciliation statement of BT we can see that, for 1997, earnings based upon UK GAAP were £2,077 million, while using US GAAP they were instead £2,149 million. The largest difference between the two was due to differences in the treatment of employee severance costs. (In the UK severance costs are charged to income in the period when the employee leaves, while in the USA they are charged in the period in which the termination conditions are agreed.) This meant that UK GAAP-based profits were £156 million lower in 1997 but were £152 million higher in 1996. Other important differences were deferred tax (lowering US-based earnings by £148 million) and pension costs (increasing US-based earnings by £83 million).

As regards shareholders' equity, the two items resulting in the largest differences were again deferred tax (making US GAAP-based equity £1,942 million smaller than UK GAAP-based equity) and goodwill (making US GAAP-based equity £2,146 million larger than UK GAAP-based equity).

3.4.2 The comparability index

In the BT example in Exhibit 3.1 we saw that earnings were £72 million more under US GAAP than UK GAAP. However, this figure by itself tells us relatively little. We need a measure of the difference in the reported figures that takes into account its significance – in the context of UK earnings of £2,077 million, is a difference of £72 million significant or not? We also need a measure of differences that we can use to compare companies or countries. Finally, it would be helpful if our measure of difference yielded figures that made some intuitive sense, so we could understand what the measure meant without having to go back to the original financial statements.

Exhibit 3.1   RECONCILIATION STATEMENT, BRITISH TELECOM: 1997

UNITED STATES GENERALLY ACCEPTED ACCOUNTING PRINCIPLES RECONCILIATIONS

Net income and shareholders' equity reconciliation statements

The following statements summarise the material estimated adjustments, gross of their tax effect, which reconcile net income and shareholders' equity from that reported under UK GAAP to that which would have been reported had US GAAP been applied.

Net income YEAR ENDED 31 MARCH

	1995 £m	1996 £m	1997 £m	1997 $m(a)
Net income applicable to shareholders under UK GAAP	1,731	1,986	2,077	3,406
Adjustments for:				
Pension costs	(392)	18	83	136
Early release schemes	125	(152)	156	256
Capitalisation of interest, net of related depreciation	(18)	(22)	(23)	(38)
Goodwill	85(b)	(74)	(73)	(119)
Mobile cellular telephone and broadcasting licences amortisation	130(b)	–	–	–
Software and other intangible asset capitalisation and amortisation, net	21	38	77	126
Deferred taxation	56	14	(148)	(243)
Other items	6	(2)	–	–
Net income as adjusted for US GAAP	1,744	1,806	2,149	3,524
Earnings per American Depositary Share as adjusted for US GAAP *(c)*	£2.80	£2.87	£3.39	$5.56

Shareholders' equity AT 31 MARCH

	1996 £m	1997 £m	1997 $m(a)
Shareholders' equity under UK GAAP	12,678	11,116	18,230
Adjustments for:			
Pension costs	(1,140)	(1,057)	(1,733)
Early release schemes	(168)	(12)	(20)
Capitalisation of interest, net of related depreciation	366	337	553
Goodwill, net of accumulated amortisation	2,174	2,146	3,519
Software and other intangible asset capitalisation and amortisation	196	260	426
Deferred taxation	(1,802)	(1,942)	(3,185)
Dividend declared after the financial year end	715	764	1,253
Other items	(9)	(24)	(39)
Shareholders' equity as adjusted for US GAAP	13,010	11,588	19,004

(a) Translated at US$1.64 to £1.00, the Noon Buying Rate in New York in effect on 31 March 1997.

(b) The disposal of the group's interest in AT&T Corporation shares which had been exchanged for shares in McCaw Cellular Communications, Inc., during the year ended 31 March 1995 gave rise to adjustments, increasing net income, of £125 million to goodwill and £137 million to mobile cellular telephone and broadcasting licence amortisation.

(c) Each American Depositary Share is equivalent to 10 ordinary shares of 25p each.

Source: British Telecom, annual report, 1997, p. 68

One measure which meets these criteria was suggested by Gray,[2] who developed what he called a conservatism index. If we use US GAAP earnings (or shareholders' equity) as a benchmark and look at the impact of moving from US GAAP-based figures to those produced under UK GAAP, the index takes the form:

$$1 - \frac{(\text{Earnings}_{USA} - \text{Earnings}_{UK})}{|\ \text{Earnings}_{USA}\ |}$$

We do not want an index that is negative simply because the company is making a loss. Therefore the denominator, being absolute earnings, ignores the sign of the earnings figures. The index will take the value of 1.0 if the two earnings figures are the same, it will be greater than 1.0 if UK GAAP-based earnings are larger than are US GAAP-based earnings, while an index of less than 1.0 means that UK GAAP-based earnings are smaller than are US GAAP-based earnings.

While this index was originally called the 'conservatism index', this term is misleading as accounting methods that result in a lower earnings figure are not always more conservative. For example, the revaluation of fixed assets is not generally thought of as a conservative valuation rule. However, any revaluation will result in higher depreciation charges, and therefore lower earnings. Many other accounting rules are concerned with the question of when costs or revenues are recognised in the income statement rather than being concerned with the amount recognised. Development costs, for example, can be charged to income in the period incurred or capitalised and charged over a number of future periods. These rules therefore result in differences in the pattern of earnings recognition over time but do not affect the total earnings of the entity over its life. They will thus result in lower earnings in some period(s) but in other period(s) they will result in higher earnings figures. The index is therefore better thought of as an index of how similar or dissimilar the figures are, or how comparable they are. We will therefore instead refer to this index as the 'comparability index'.

Just as, in Exhibit 3.1, the difference between US and UK GAAP-based earnings and equity was broken down into its constituent parts, the comparability index can also be broken down into partial indexes, each one measuring the impact of one accounting issue. For example, if we want to calculate the partial index due to differences in deferred tax we would calculate the index as follows:

$$1 - \frac{\text{Difference due to deferred tax}}{|\ \text{Earnings}_{USA}\ |}$$

An example of the calculation of the index for earnings and shareholders' equity is given in Exhibit 3.2.

Note that the overall index is equal to the sum of the two partial indexes *less* 1.0, or if there were *N* partial indexes, it would be equal to the sum of all *N* partial indexes *less* (*N* − 1).

In a later study, Weetman and Gray[3] applied this technique to 42 UK companies who provided reconciliations of reported earnings to US GAAP-based earnings. The

---

[2] Gray (1980)
[3] Weetman and Gray (1990)

Exhibit 3.2   AN ILLUSTRATION OF THE CALCULATION OF COMPARABILITY INDEXES

	£m.
Profit attributable to shareholders – UK GAAP	110
Adjustments due to differences in the treatment of:	
Pension costs	10
Deferred tax	(20)
Net income in accordance with US GAAP	100
Shareholders' equity – UK GAAP	800
Adjustments due to differences in the treatment of:	
Goodwill	300
Deferred tax	(100)
Shareholders' equity in accordance with US GAAP	1,000

Comparability index calculations

Earnings:

Total
$$1 - (\text{Profit}_{USA} - \text{Profit}_{UK})/|\,\text{Profit}_{USA}\,|$$
$$1 - (100 - 110)/100 = 1 - (-0.10) \qquad = 1.10$$

Partial:

Pension costs	$1 - (10/100) = 1 - 0.10$	$= 0.90$
Deferred tax	$1 - (-20/100) = 1 - (-0.20)$	$= 1.20$

Shareholders' equity:

Total $\qquad 1 - (1000 - 800)/1000 = 1 - 0.20 \qquad = 0.80$

Partial:

Goodwill	$1 - (300/1000)$	$= 0.70$
Deferred tax	$1 - (-100/1000)$	$= 1.10$

total indexes and the partial indexes for deferred tax and goodwill are reproduced in Exhibit 3.3.

The indexes shows that earnings were less under US GAAP in all three years, and that, for two of the three years, the differences were significant at the 5% level. They were also quite large (on average, 25% in 1987 and 17% in 1985). Especially important were the differences in treatment of goodwill, being significant for all three years. Goodwill differences were, on average, equivalent to as much as 18% of US earnings in 1987. This was a period of relatively high takeover activity. Goodwill on acquisitions was therefore large and this led to significant amortisation charges in the income statements of many companies when using US rules. The 'practice' shows the statistical significance of the result. Where the 'p value' is 0.05 or less, the result is highly significant.

Exhibit 3.3 COMPARISON OF UK AND US GAAP-BASED EARNINGS OF UK COMPANIES

	Year	Number of cos	Mean index	Standard deviation	T-test p value	Lowest index	Highest index
Total index							
	1985	35	1.1659	0.340	0.003	0.506	5.093
	1986	35	1.0913	0.352	0.060	0.180	2.875
	1987	34	1.2523	0.466	0.002	0.586	11.313
Partial indexes:							
Deferred tax							
	1985	34	1.0345	0.117	0.047	0.784	2.372
	1986	33	1.0117	0.087	0.220	0.062	1.298
	1987	32	1.0446	0.074	0.001	0.694	1.313
Goodwill							
	1985	32	1.1033	0.161	0.000	1.000	1.554
	1986	32	1.0968	0.136	0.000	0.994	2.804
	1987	31	1.1812	0.060	0.003	0.998	3.693

3.4.3 The use of reconciliation statements

The comparability index has also been used in a number of other studies that have looked at the differences in reported figures under various GAAP.[4] However, the index is not without its problems. If the reported earnings figure is very small, the index will often be extremely large, which may be misleading. (This is because the change in earnings is being compared to a very small denominator – the benchmark GAAP-based earnings – and, in these cases, it is probably better to compare the change in earnings to a different measure of significance, such as turnover.) More important than this, though, are the problems involved in using reconciliation statements as the source of data on the impact of GAAP differences.

Reconciliation statements are becoming increasingly common, but they are still produced by relatively few companies. These companies are generally among the largest and most international companies. They may not therefore be typical or representative of other smaller or less international companies. Where alternative methods can be used, these companies may not make the same choices as are made by other companies. No company will want to produce two sets of accounts with very different earnings or equity figures unless they have to. This is because many users of the accounts know very little about accounting and will view the figures – and therefore also the company – with suspicion if it apparently cannot

---

[4] *See*, for example, Emenyonu and Gray (1992); Weetman and Gray (1991)

decide how much money it really made. Companies which have to produce reconciliation statements are therefore likely, where possible, to select accounting methods that are acceptable under both domestic and foreign GAAP.

Even if this is not the case, it is always dangerous to make generalisations based upon a few cases. The first German company to list on the New York Stock Exchange (NYSE) was Daimler–Benz, and this example is often quoted to illustrate how large the differences in earnings can be under different GAAP. On listing for the first time, Daimler–Benz's reported earnings fell from a profit of DM615 million under German GAAP to a loss of DM1,839 million under US GAAP (giving a comparability index of 2.33). However, to quote only this one year and this company is misleading. As can be seen in Case study 3.1 at the end of this chapter, much of the difference was due to a one-off adjustment. In other years the differences in reported figures under the two GAAP were very much less. In 1995, for example, the difference was only DM5 million on a German GAAP-based loss of DM5,734 million.

Finally, nearly all of the reconciliation statements provided reconcile domestic GAAP figures to US GAAP figures. Thus, it might be relatively easy, for example, to compare UK and US practices or German and US practices, but it is much more difficult to compare UK and German practices.

3.4.4 Simulation studies

Given the problems involved in using reconciliation statements, we need to find an alternative way to measure GAAP differences. One possibility is to use simulations. Real companies can be used, or a company can be created using artificial data. The figures can then be recalculated under a number of different GAAP. If real companies are used, then the samples used can be large enough to be statistically representative of the entire population of companies. If an artificial company is created, we can use average figures derived from all companies or from particular sectors, so creating a typical or average company. Alternatively, we could create an atypical company that illustrates particularly interesting or problematic issues.

A number of simulation studies have been carried out and one of these will be looked at to get an idea of how they work. Walton[5] compared accounting in the UK and France (more information on this study, including the figures generated can be found in Case study 3.2, at the end of this chapter). Walton created an artificial construction company that, among other things, had some foreign operations, extraordinary items and leased assets. The case was presented to a number of accountants in the two countries, who produced balance sheets and income statements for the foreign subsidiary and the parent company. While there were some very significant differences between the average figures generated by the UK and French respondents, for anyone interested in international harmonisation, the most important and interesting result (p. 198) was that:

> Variations in treatment within each jurisdiction are quite clear from the results, and it is by no means obvious that a user would obtain a greater consensus by comparing two reports from the same country with each other than by comparing one report from each country.

---

[5] Walton (1992)

3.5 MEASUREMENT OF DIFFERENCES IN THE ACCOUNTING METHODS USED

3.5.1 The H-index

So far we have looked at differences in the reported figures of companies that are caused by using different accounting methods. We could instead ignore the actual figures produced and look at the accounting methods used. We would then look at the number of accounting methods that are the same and the number that are different across companies and use this to calculate a measure of how comparable the financial statements are. This method is usually applied only to *de facto* practices because the accounting rules in most countries contain options. However, it could be adapted to measure *de jure* methods. To measure *de jure* methods, where countries allow different ranges of alternatives, we could calculate two concentration measures. The maximum possible level of comparability can be measured using, wherever possible, those alternatives that are the same in both countries. Likewise, the minimum possible comparability level can be measured using, wherever permitted, different alternatives.

The comparability or similarity in the accounting methods used by a group of companies increases as fewer alternative methods are used or as the methods used become more concentrated around one alternative. We can use this idea of 'concentration' to measure comparability. In economics, an industry is said to be more concentrated if a small number of companies accounts for most of the sales of that industry. In the same way, financial statements may be said to be more comparable if a small number of alternative accounting methods is used and most companies use the same alternative. There are many different ways in which industrial concentration can be measured, but one in common research use is the Herfindahl or H-index. The H-index can also be used to measure the comparability of accounting methods.

The H-index takes the form:

$$\sum_{i=1}^{n} p_i^2$$

where: p_i is the proportion of companies using accounting method i
n is the maximum number of possible methods that can be used.

Exhibit 3.4, panel A, gives a numerical illustration of how to calculate the H-index. This is a simple example of accounting issues 1–3. For each issue two alternative treatments, *A* and *B*, are allowed. For issue 1, half of the companies choose method *A* and the other half use method *B*, giving an index of 0.50. In contrast, for issue 2 method *A* is far more popular, being used by 90% of the companies. There is therefore much more consensus and the H-index increases to 0.82. For issue 3 method *B* is now the more popular, being used by 90% of the companies, so the H-index is again 0.82.

Panel B of Exhibit 3.4 gives information on accounting issues 1–4. For each of these issues four possible alternatives, *A–D*, exist, although not all are always used in practice. Now, the lowest-value H-index is 0.25. This is for issue 1, where there

Exhibit 3.4 CALCULATION OF THE HERFINDAHL INDEX

Panel A

Proportion of companies using method:	A	B	Calculation	H-index
Accounting issue				
1	0.50	0.50	$0.5^2 + 0.5^2$	0.5
2	0.90	0.10	$0.9^2 + 0.1^2$	0.82
3	0.10	0.90	$0.1^2 + 0.9^2$	0.82

Panel B

Proportion of companies using method:	A	B	C	D	H-index
Accounting issue					
1	0.25	0.25	0.25	0.25	0.25
2	0.05	0.25	0.25	0.45	0.33
3	0	0.33	0.33	0.33	0.33
4	0	0	0	1.00	1.00

is no consensus regarding the best treatment and all four alternatives are equally popular. The highest H-index is 1.0 for issue 4. Here all the companies use method *D*.

We can see from this that the H-index varies from a low of $1/n$ (where n is the maximum number of treatments permitted, in this case 4) to a high of 1.00, when all companies use the same method.

3.5.2 The C-index

The H-index offers a fairly simple way of measuring comparability. However, it is not a perfect measure. There is no one-to-one relationship between the relative popularity of alternative methods and the resultant values of the H-index so that the index value cannot be interpreted in an unambiguous way. For example, in Exhibit 3.4, Panel B accounting issue 2 gives an index of 0.33. The H-index is also 0.33 for issue 3 although the distribution of companies across the alternatives is very different. More seriously, the H-index cannot cope with multiple reporting. As discussed above, companies may provide a reconciliation statement or other infor-mation which allows the user to see the effects of more than one accounting method. In these cases the H-index would be based upon the method used in the main financial statements and would ignore the supplementary disclosures. This will have the effect of underestimating the comparability of the financial state-ments. The existence of such multiple reporting led van der Tas[6] to develop what he calls the compatible or C-index. This is a similar type of index but it can cope with multiple reporting.

---

[6] van der Tas (1988, 1992)

Rather than looking at the proportion of companies that uses each accounting method, the C-index instead looks at the number of financial statements that are compatible with each other. It measures the number of pairs of statements that apply either the same accounting method or provide enough additional information to allow users to make comparisons themselves (that is, the number of compatible reports). The pairs of compatible reports are then compared to the maximum number of possible pairs of reports.

Using a slightly different version of the C-index, one that is slightly easier to use, as developed by Archer *et al.*,[7] the C-index takes the form:

$$\frac{\sum (n_i \times (n_i - 1))}{(N \times (N - 1))}$$

where: n_i is the number of companies using method i
    N is the total number of companies.

An example of how to calculate the C-index is given in Exhibit 3.5.

Exhibit 3.5 CALCULATION OF THE C-INDEX

Number of companies using method:					
	A	*B*	*C*	*Calculation*	*C-index*
Accounting issue					
1	15	1	4	$[(15 \times 14) + (1 \times 0) + (4 \times 3)/(20 \times 19)]$	0.584
2	7	5	8	$[(7 \times 6) + (5 \times 4) + (8 \times 7)/(20 \times 19)]$	0.311

In this example there are two accounting issues being considered and there are three alternative ways of accounting for each issue. Data is provided on the practices used by 20 companies. There is more consensus over the acceptable treatment for issue 1, where 15 of the 20 companies used method *A*. For issue 2 no single treatment is particularly popular. The C-index reflects this, being 0.584 for issue 1, but falling to only 0.311 for issue 2. As with the H-index, the C-index will vary from a minimum of 0.0 (where each company uses a different method) to 1.0 (where all companies use the same method). The actual values taken by the H- and C-indexes will be different (except at these two extremes of 0.0 and 1.0), although they converge towards each other as number of companies considered increases.

3.5.3 Measurement of international harmony

The H- and C-indexes both measure harmony or compatibility inside a single country. However, we need a measure of international harmony. There are two ways to think about international harmony and each can be used to develop a compatibility measure. One approach is to take the perspective of an international investor who wants to choose potential investments from a group of companies

---

[7] Archer *et al.* (1995)

from a number of countries. To this investor, the country of domicile of the companies may not be particularly important. All she wants is to invest in those companies which will provide the best return, irrespective of their country of domicile. To do this, she wants to know the extent to which the financial statements of the group of companies being considered are compatible. Others, such as standard setters, may instead want to compare the practices found in different countries, so that the country of domicile of the companies being considered is of vital importance. The alternative approach therefore does not ignore the countries the companies come from, but instead seeks to measure the level of harmonisation between typical practices in one country and typical practices in one or more others. For a complete picture of international harmonisation, each perspective is valuable and indexes measuring each type of harmonisation – within a group of companies irrespective of country, and between the 'typical' company from different countries – would be helpful.

Archer *et al.*[8] suggested that the C-index could be used to measure both types of harmonisation by breaking it down into its component parts: a within-country index and a between-country index. Exhibit 3.6 provides a two-country illustration of how this is done (exactly the same type of analysis would apply if there were more than two countries).

The overall C-index takes exactly the same form as it did in our earlier example of one country in Exhibit 3.5. To calculate the C-index in a multi-country setting you ignore the fact that the companies come from different countries and calculate the C-index for the entire sample of companies. Thus, in Exhibit 3.6, the overall index is based upon the total sample of 25 companies, four of which use method 1, eight of which use method 2 while the remaining 13 companies use the final alternative, method 3. Thus, the total number of pairs of companies that uses the same accounting method, irrespective of whether they come from country 1 or country 2, is 112, out of a total of 300 pairs of companies, giving an overall index of 0.373.

The within-country C-index is formed by combining the C-indexes of each separate country. In other words, it is an average of their C-indexes. It effectively treats each country as if it had a completely different set of accounting methods – thus, in Exhibit 3.6, it looks across each of the two-country rows. It is calculated by adding together the number of compatible pairs in country 1 (2 + 20 + 6)/2 and the number of pairs in country 2 (2 + 6 + 90)/2 to give us 63 compatible pairs of companies out of a maximum of 150 pairs, resulting in a value of 0.420. (In this example, we have added together the pairs from each of the six cells, thus forming a weighted average of the two countries. If the size of each sample was not important, we could instead take a simple average by calculating a separate C-index for each country and averaging these two C-indexes, which would have given a value of 0.389.)

The between-country index instead looks at the compatibility of pairs or vectors of companies, one company from each country – thus, in Exhibit 3.6, we are now looking down each of the three columns. The index is formed by calculating the number of pairs of companies, one from each country that both use method 1 (2×2), the number of pairs using method 2 (5×3) and the number using method 3 (3×10). This is then compared to the maximum possible number of comparable pairs (10×15) to give an index of 0.327.

---

[8] Archer *et al.* (1995)

Exhibit 3.6	CALCULATION OF BETWEEN-COUNTRY AND WITHIN-COUNTRY C-INDEXES

Country	Method			Number of companies
	1	*2*	*3*	
1	2	5	3	10
2	2	3	10	15
Total	4	8	13	25

	Number of comparable pairs	*Total number of possible pairs*	*Index*
Overall Index	$((4 \times 3) + (8 \times 7) + (13 \times 12))/2$ 112	$(25 \times 24)/2$ 300	0.373
Within-country Index	$((2 \times 1) + (5 \times 4) + (3 \times 2) +$ $(2 \times 1) + (3 \times 2) + (10 \times 9))/2$ 63	$((10 \times 9) +$ $(15 \times 14))/2$ 150	0.420
Between-country Index	$(2 \times 2) + (5 \times 3) + (3 \times 10)$ 49	(10×15) 150	0.327

3.5.4 Measurement of EU harmonisation

There have been a few studies that have measured the compatibility of financial statements.[9] However, they have used different indexes, different countries, different accounting issues and different types of companies. This means that it is difficult to draw any conclusions from them. Therefore, only one of these, the study by Archer *et al.* (1995), will be described to give an idea of how C-indexes can be used to measure international – or in this case EU – compatibility.

The C-index and its two components were used to measure changes in harmony across Europe between 1986/7 and 1990/1. This is a period during which the EU attempted to increase accounting harmonisation. If this was successful, the level of harmony achieved, as measured by the C-indices, should have increased. A sample of 89 internationally traded companies from eight countries was used, and data was collected from annual reports. This has the advantage that it means that actual practices were considered; however, financial statements often do not provide much detailed information on exactly which accounting methods have been used.

---

[9] *See*, for example, Hellman (1993); Herrman and Thomas (1995); Tay and Parker (1990)

This means that the only issues that can be studied are those where companies usually disclose their exact accounting methods: many potentially important issues cannot be examined.

The two areas chosen by this study were deferred tax and goodwill, and five alternative treatments were identified for each (*see* Exhibit 3.7). The study found that the overall level of compatibility was low especially for deferred taxation, where the C-index was only 0.149 in 1986/7 and 0.216 in 1990/1. However, the between-country compatibility had increased quite substantially over the period, from 0.108 to 0.186. This was mainly due to a number of Swedish companies

Exhibit 3.7 COMPATIBILITY OF EUROPEAN FINANCIAL REPORTING PRACTICES

Deferred taxation

Possible treatments
A Nil provision or taxes payable approach
B Full provision
C Partial provision
D Deferred tax recognised, method unspecified or recognised for some companies only
E No recognition and not known if deferred tax applicable or not

C-indices

	1986/7	1990/1
Within-country	0.371	0.379
Between-country	0.108	0.186
Total index	0.149	0.216

Goodwill

Possible treatments
A Written-off against profit and loss in year of acquisition
B Written-off against reserves in year of acquisition
C Shown as asset and not amortised
D Shown as asset and amortised over period exceeding one year
E Other or unspecified treatment

C-indices

	1986/7	1990/1
Within-country	0.582	0.539
Between-country	0.347	0.377
Total index	0.383	0.403

changing their practices, coupled with increasing disclosures by the German and Swiss samples. Particularly striking differences emerged between the practices of companies from France, the Netherlands and Sweden, which tended to use the full provision method, and companies from the UK and Ireland, which instead used the partial provision method. For goodwill, the level of compatibility was considerably higher, at 0.383 in 1986/7 and 0.403 in 1990/1, although major differences still existed. Within-country compatibility actually decreased over the period while between-country compatibility increased, due mainly to a number of German companies changing their methods. The main reason that between-country compatibility was not higher was that capitalisation and amortisation was the almost universal treatment in Belgium and France while immediate write-off to reserves was instead more common in the Netherlands and the UK. Little consensus existed within the samples from Germany, Sweden and Switzerland.

3.6 MEASUREMENT OF DIFFERENCES IN INFORMATION DISCLOSURE

The comparability index and the H- and C-indices are all concerned with differences in the accounting techniques used – or, in other words, differences in the measurement system. To gain a complete picture of an accounting system we must also look at disclosure practices, including voluntary disclosure practices. There have been a great number of studies that have looked at disclosure practices inside particular countries. Many of these have tried to model the voluntary disclosure decision by measuring the association between the amount of voluntary disclosure and various company-specific factors. Countries looked at include: Japan,[10] Mexico,[11] New Zealand,[12] Nigeria,[13] Sweden,[14] Tanzania,[15] the UK[16] and the USA.[17] There is general support for the proposition that disclosure levels increase as companies get larger. Very often, the listing status of the company and the industry it operates in are also important. Profitability and leverage, in contrast, generally appear not to be important.

Far less interest has been shown in the question of whether or not disclosure practices differ across countries. Given our discussion in Chapters 1 and 2, we would expect this to be the case. Mandatory disclosure requirements should vary across countries, just as do mandatory measurement rules. Voluntary disclosure levels will also tend to vary across countries. Both rules and practices will be affected by cultural values. We saw in Chapter 2 that one of Gray's (1988) four accounting values was secrecy versus transparency. We also saw that this accounting value was related to Hofstede's (1984) four cultural dimensions. Gray hypothesised that high transparency or high disclosure levels should be positively related to weak uncertainty avoidance; small power distance; high individualism; and low nurturing. Disclosure practices will also be influenced by the institutions of a country.

[10] Cooke (1991)
[11] Chow and Wong-Boren (1987)
[12] Hossain *et al.* (1995)
[13] Wallace (1988)
[14] Cooke (1989)
[15] Abayo *et al.* (1993)
[16] Firth (1979)
[17] Buzby (1975)

Particularly important for voluntary disclosures will be the corporate financing system. It would be expected that the more dependent companies are upon equity rather than debt financing, and the more dispersed is that share ownership, then the more the company is likely to disclose in its annual report to shareholders.

Voluntary disclosure practices may also be a function of the level of mandatory rules. If mandatory disclosure levels are set very high there is obviously less scope for voluntary disclosure. However, if mandatory levels are high because of cultural or institutional factors in a country, companies may be willing, as discussed above, to voluntarily disclose more. Thus it is not really clear if high mandatory disclosure levels imply high or low voluntary disclosure levels. However, it is not only the absolute amount of voluntary disclosures that will tend to vary across countries. There will often also be significant differences in the types of disclosure made.

There are a number of ways of measuring the amount of voluntary disclosure made. One of the simplest approaches is to use a scorecard of likely disclosures. If a company discloses the information then it is scored '1', if it has not disclosed the information, but it could have been provided, it is scored '0', while if the item is not relevant for that company then it is not scored but is ignored. Companies can then be compared on the basis of the proportion or percentage of relevant items they each disclose:

$$\frac{\text{Number of items disclosed}}{\text{Maximum number of items that could have been disclosed}}$$

The scores for each company examined from any one country can then be averaged to obtain the country's disclosure score. One of the biggest problems with this approach is deciding what items to include: items that are voluntary in one country or one time period may be required in another, and thus, the items used in surveys in one country and one time period may not be applicable in another. This is a particular problem for cross-national studies of voluntary disclosures. The items included must be voluntary in all countries; however, if the levels of mandatory disclosure are very different, companies in some countries may be disclosing much information voluntarily. But this would not be picked up by the research instrument if they are mandatory in some of the other countries being examined.

This is less of a problem in some areas than in others. It is not a major problem, for example, when looking at social or environmental disclosures, as most countries have few or even no disclosure requirements in this area.

3.6.1 The measurement of environmental and social disclosure

There have been a number of studies that have looked at the disclosure of social and environmental information across different countries.[18] One of the earliest of these was by Roberts (1991), who looked at the disclosures made by large companies in five European countries (France, Germany, the Netherlands, Sweden and Switzerland). Roberts used a simple check-list of 54 items covering nine areas concerned with either the environment or employee-related matters (*see* Exhibit 3.8).

---

[18] *See*, for example, Adams *et al.* (1995); Roberts (1990)

Exhibit 3.8   ENVIRONMENTAL- AND EMPLOYEE-RELATED DISCLOSURE CHECK-LIST
USED BY ROBERTS (1991)

Environment protection statement
1 Policies
2 General descriptive statements
3 Types of controls employed
4 Costs incurred
5 Outputs/achievements

Process-related information
1 Policies
2 Description of specific examples
3 Costs incurred
4 Outputs/achievements – qualitative statements
5 Outputs/achievements – quantitative measures

Product-related information
1 Policies
2 Description of specific examples
3 Outputs/achievements – qualitative statements
4 Outputs/achievements – quantitative measures

Environment-related investments
1 Policies
2 Description of specific examples
3 Costs incurred
4 Outputs/achievements – qualitative statements
5 Outputs/achievements – quantitative measures

Research and development activities
1 Policies
2 Description of specific examples
3 Overview of all environment related activities
4 Costs incurred

Energy usage information
1 Policies
2 Energy sources used – qualitative statements

3 Energy sources used – quantitative statements
4 Energy sources used – costs
5 Improvements achieved – qualitative statements
6 Improvements achieved – quantitative statements
7 Improvements achieved – costs

Political statements
1 Views on legislation
2 Views on environmental demands
3 Actions undertaken (lobbying, etc.) – specific
  examples
4 Actions undertaken – policies

Employment information
1 Disabled employees – numbers/costs/policies
2 Trainee policies
3 Trainee costs
4 Trainee numbers
5 Trainee hours
6 Pay awards
7 Maternity/paternity leave
8 Share/profit schemes
9 Hours worked
10 Absenteeism
11 Labour turnover
12 Pensioners – numbers/benefits

Health and Safety
1 Policies
2 Description actions undertaken – qualitative
3 Description actions undertaken – financial
4 Training activities – qualitative
5 Training activities – quantitative
6 Accidents – qualitative information
7 Accidents – quantitative
8 Illness – time lost

Using the 1988 or 1989 annual report, Roberts found that there were significant differences across the five countries in terms of the total amount of information disclosed and the amount of employee-related information disclosed. However, there were relatively few differences with respect to the amount of environmental disclosures.

More recent studies of environmental disclosures have become much more sophisticated, and have used various forms of content analysis. Content analysis-based disclosure check-lists are designed to measure whether or not an item is disclosed and also to record the form that disclosure takes. Part of one such content analysis form used to measure environmental disclosures is reproduced in Exhibit 3.9.

Exhibit 3.9   EXTRACT FROM A CONTENT ANALYSIS FORM USED TO RECORD ENVIRONMENTAL DISCLOSURES

	Type	Time	Area	Extent	Non-narrative
Description of:					
● emission targets					
● other targets					
● external standards					
● legislation					
Achievements re:					
● emission targets					
● other targets					
● external standards					
● legislation					
Non-compliance with:					
● emission targets					
● other targets					
● external standards					
● legislation					
Impacts re:					
● emission levels					
● waste					
● inputs used					
● energy used					
● recycling					
● noise abatement					

As can be seen, this is not simply a yes/no check-list of items that may or may not be disclosed. Instead, for each item that might be disclosed, five questions have to be answered, as explained in Exhibit 3.10.

The use of this type of content analysis check-list form means that different types of disclosures can be examined. For example, researchers might be interested in comparing the level of disclosure of financial and non-financial information. Alternatively, it can be used as the basis of a scoring system which rates or scores the disclosures made on the basis of their extensiveness or the quality of the information provided. Thus a company that discloses only qualitative examples of activities for parts of the company might be scored '1'. A company that discloses information about the same activities but provides quantitative data for all of the company might be scored '3', while financial data covering several years might be scored '5'. Again, the score received by a company would be compared to the maximum possible score it could have got, to produce a measure of the relative level of disclosure.

This type of scoring system is often accused of being too subjective. Certainly, it is not always easy to design a good weighting system and different people may have different views on how items should be weighted. However, the problem of how to measure disclosure quality does not go away if it is ignored, and the decision to score all disclosures equally is also a subjective decision. A more valid reason not to try to measure disclosure quality is the argument that often the extra sophistication is simply not necessary. If we are looking at a fairly large number of items of information, a company that scores relatively highly on an equally weighted scoring system will also usually score relatively highly on any other type of weighted scoring system.

Exhibit 3.10   EXPLANATION OF CONTENT ANALYSIS CHECK-LIST FORM

Type	Qualitative Quantitative or Financial information
Time	Time period covered by disclosures
Area	Information given for: All of company Specific geographical area(s) or Specific line(s) of business only
Extent	Describe all relevant activities of the area or give examples of activities carried out only
Non-narrative	Disclose pictures/diagrams/graphs

This type of research instrument was used in a later study[19] that replicated and extended Roberts' work. Using annual reports from four years later (i.e. 1992 or 1993) and looking at the same five countries plus the UK, this study came to a somewhat different conclusion. It looked at environmental, employee and ethical information and measured the amount of space devoted to a number of issues in each of these three areas. It also measured the number of items that were disclosed in total and the number of items that were disclosed in quantified or financial terms.

The results of this study were interesting in that it not only found that the six countries disclosed significantly different amounts of information across each of the three areas and three types of disclosure, but it also found that the two countries disclosing the most were Germany followed by the UK. If we consider these two countries then it obvious that they are very different. Germany has a long history of worker participation in corporate management, with works' councils being common. It also has a very active and vociferous Green Party. The UK, in contrast, has a relatively small Green movement, the Green Party has not been very important in domestic politics and the UK has no history of works' councils, while the trade union movement has substantially decreased in power and influence over the last decade or so. The authors of this work thus conclude that what motivates the voluntary disclosure of social and environmental information in the two countries is probably very different. In Germany, information may well be disclosed as a reaction to external pressures. In the UK, it is more probable that it is disclosed proactively in an attempt to pre-empt such external pressures – if companies can demonstrate that they are acting in socially acceptable ways then perhaps there will be less demand for more regulations and government control of their activities.

3.6.2 The measurement of other types of disclosure

There have been a number of studies which have been wider in scope, looking at all or most types of voluntary disclosure. It is difficult to compare these studies or to describe their findings in general terms. They have looked at different countries, different time periods and different types of companies, and have used different disclosure check-lists. This section will therefore not attempt to draw generalisations but will instead look at just two of these studies by Meek *et al.* (1995) and Gray *et al.* (1995). These two studies looked at a wide range of information of three types – strategic, non-financial and financial – all items being voluntary in both the UK and the USA at that time (see Exhibit 3.11). This breakdown of disclosures into three types was necessary as different factors may influence the voluntary disclosure of the different types of information. For example, the disclosure of financial information is likely to be most influenced by corporate financing needs and forms of financing employed. In contrast, disclosure of non-financial information or employee and social information is most likely to be influenced by political and societal pressures for additional disclosures. Thus, companies in one country may tend to disclose relatively large amounts of financial information while companies from another country may instead disclose relatively large amounts of non-financial information.

---

[19] Adams *et al.* (1997)

Exhibit 3.11 VOLUNTARY DISCLOSURE CHECK-LIST AS USED BY MEEK *ET AL.* (1995)

Strategic information

1 General corporate information
   1 Brief history of company
   2 Organisational structure

2 Corporate strategy
   3 Statement of strategy and objectives – general
   4 Statement of strategy and objectives – financial
   5 Statement of strategy and objectives – marketing
   6 Statement of strategy and objectives – social
   7 Impact of strategy on current results
   8 Impact of strategy on future results

3 Acquisitions and disposals
   9 Reasons for the acquisitions
   10 Reasons for the disposals

4 Research and development
   11 Corporate policy on R&D
   12 Location of R&D activities
   13 Number employed in R&D

5 Future prospects
   14 Qualitative forecast of sales
   15 Quantitative forecast of sales
   16 Qualitative forecast of profits
   17 Quantitative forecast of profits
   18 Qualitative forecast of cash flows
   19 Quantitative forecast of cash flows
   20 Assumptions underlying the forecasts
   21 Current period trading results – qualitative
   22 Current period trading results – quantitative
   23 Order book or back-log information

Non-financial information

6 Information about directors
   24 Age of directors
   25 Educational qualifications
   26 Commercial experience of executive directors
   27 Other directorships held by executive directors

7 Employee information
   28 Geographical distribution of employees
   29 Line-of-business distribution of employees
   30 Categories of employees, by gender
   31 Identification of senior management and their functions
   32 Number of employees for two or more years
   33 Reasons for changes in employee numbers or categories
   34 Amount spent on training
   35 Nature of training
   36 Categories of employees trained
   37 Number of employees trained
   38 Data on accidents
   39 Cost of safety measures
   40 Redundancy information (general)
   41 Equal opportunity policy statement
   42 Recruitment problems and related policy

8 Social policy and value added information
   43 Safety of products (general)

44 Environmental protection programmes – quantitative
45 Amount of charitable donations
46 Community programmes – general
47 Value added statement
48 Value added data
49 Value added ratios
50 Qualitative value added information

Financial information

9 Segmental information
   51 Geographical capital expenditure – quantitative
   52 Geographical production – quantitative
   53 Line-of-business production – quantitative
   54 Competitor analysis – qualitative
   55 Competitor analysis – quantitative
   56 Market share analysis – qualitative
   57 Market share analysis – quantitative

10 Financial review
   58 Profitability ratios
   59 Cash flow ratios
   60 Liquidity ratios
   61 Gearing ratios
   62 Intangible valuations – except goodwill and brands
   63 Dividend pay-out policy
   64 Financial summary – for at least six years
   65 Restatement of financial information to non-UK/US GAAP
   66 Off-balance sheet financing information
   67 Advertising information – qualitative
   68 Advertising information – quantitative
   69 Effects of inflation on future operations – qualitative
   70 Effects of inflation on results – qualitative
   71 Effects of inflation on results – quantitative
   72 Effects of inflation on assets – qualitative
   73 Effects of inflation on assets – quantitative
   74 Effects of interest rates on results
   75 Effects of interest rates on future operations

11 Foreign currency information
   76 Effects of foreign currency fluctuations on future operations – qualitative
   77 Effects of foreign currency fluctuations on current results – qualitative
   78 Major exchange rates used in the accounts
   79 Long-term debt, by currency
   80 Short-term debt, by currency
   81 Description of foreign currency exposure management

12 Share price information
   82 Market capitalisation at year end
   83 Market capitalisation trend
   84 Size of shareholders
   85 Types of shareholders

Source: Meek *et al.* (1995), pp. 569–70. Used with the permission of the *Journal for International Business Studies*

Gray *et al.* (1995) looked at large UK and US multinational companies and compared those that were listed only on their domestic stock exchange with those that were internationally listed (i.e. listed on both the London and New York stock exchanges). They were interested in the questions of whether internationally listed companies disclosed more information and disclosed more harmonised information than did domestically listed companies.

For the US sample, they found that internationally listed companies disclosed significantly more information than did domestically listed companies, including significantly more strategic and non-financial information. (This was true after controlling for the possible effect of sample differences with respect to size and multinationality, as measured by the proportion of foreign sales.) For the UK sample, the results were somewhat different, with internationally listed companies disclosing significantly more financial information. They then compared the UK and US samples. For the domestically listed companies, the UK companies disclosed significantly more non-financial information while the US companies disclosed significantly more financial information. For the international group, significant differences also existed, but there was less of a difference between the two countries. Now, the only significant difference was with respect to non-financial information. These results clearly suggest that international listing does not eliminate all country-specific differences in voluntary disclosures. However, it appears to moderate or reduce national differences by, in particular, reducing the difference between the amount of financial information disclosed.

The second study, by Meek *et al.* (1995) looked at the same companies plus a sample of internationally listed European companies from France, Germany and the Netherlands ('internationally listed European companies' were defined as those that listed on either the London or New York stock exchange). Using the same disclosure check-list they modelled the voluntary disclosure decision through four regression equations (the four dependent variables being: all disclosures; strategic; non-financial; financial information). Exhibit 3.12 reports their findings regarding the amount of disclosure made by the sample companies.

The regression analysis failed to support the hypothesis that disclosure decisions were a function of either profitability or multinationality. All the other independent variables (size, country, industry, leverage and listing status) were significant in at least one of the four regressions. However, none was significant across all four equations (for example, size was not a significant explanator of the amount of strategic information disclosed). The listing status was significant in explaining the overall level of disclosure and the amount of strategic and financial information. It was not important in explaining the level of disclosure of non-financial information. This, again, supports the assertion that stock market pressures and financing needs are most likely to influence the decision to disclose financial information and other information about the financial and future prospects of the company. In contrast, stock market and financing needs are far less likely to influence decisions regarding the voluntary disclosure of employee and social information.

Exhibit 3.12 THE DISCLOSURE OF VOLUNTARY INFORMATION AS FOUND BY
MEEK *ET AL.* (1995)

Info:	Strategic		Non-financial		Financial		Total	
	Mean %	Std dev.	Mean %	Std dev.	Mean %	Std dev.	Mean %	Std dev.
All cos	21.03	13.8	18.06	11.0	16.62	8.9	18.23	7.5
All USA	17.22	10.5	11.89	7.1	16.54	6.8	15.20	5.4
Int. USA	20.03	11.0	14.50	7.4	17.27	7.1	17.09	5.5
Dom. USA	14.43	9.3	9.27	5.7	15.81	6.5	13.32	4.6
All UK	16.83	8.5	25.70	9.1	14.58	9.3	18.73	6.8
Int. UK	17.41	9.7	25.71	10.3	16.92	10.4	19.87	8.0
Dom. UK	16.24	7.3	25.69	8.0	12.24	7.4	17.60	5.2
All Eur	36.52	16.6	23.01	12.4	19.67	11.8	25.16	8.3
Int. Eur	36.51	17.5	21.87	13.3	23.19	9.3	26.23	8.4
Dom. Eur	36.53	15.1	24.16	11.6	16.15	13.2	20.09	8.3

3.7 SUMMARY AND CONCLUSIONS

This chapter has looked at the techniques that can be used to measure differences in accounting systems. It showed how the comparability index can be used to measure the impact of GAAP differences on the reported figures. The comparability index can be used to measure differences in both reported earnings and shareholders' equity and it can also be broken down into partial indices used to measure the impact of differences in the treatment of specific issues. However, it is not only the difference in reported figures that is important.

Standard setters and others interested in international harmonisation may also want to measure the degree of difference or similarity in the accounting methods used. This chapter therefore also looked at concentration indices, in particular the H-index and the C-index, which both measure differences in the accounting methods used by companies. Taking the idea of international harmonisation slightly further, the C-index was also broken down into two constituent indices which measure rather different aspects of harmonisation. The chapter also looked at a number of empirical studies that have quantified international harmonisation by using either the comparability index or the C-index and concluded that there were still some substantial differences across companies both within and across different countries. Particularly important, at least as regards their impacts upon the reported figures, are a relatively small number of items including goodwill and other intangibles, deferred tax and pensions

Finally, the chapter looked at the disclosure of voluntary information. The various ways of measuring voluntary disclosure were looked at and a number of studies reviewed. While it is difficult to generalise across studies, the studies discussed clearly show that the level of voluntary disclosure varies across countries.

Perhaps more important than this, though, is the conclusion that we should not simply talk of 'voluntary information'. Instead, the types of disclosure being considered are important. Different considerations appear important in determining the level of disclosure of different types of information, and companies in some countries tend to disclose relatively more financial information while companies in other countries tend instead to disclose relatively high levels of social information, including employee and environmental information

Case study 3.1

DAIMLER–BENZ: RECONCILIATION OF EARNINGS FROM GERMAN TO US GAAP

Daimler–Benz was the first German company to list on the New York Stock Exchange (NYSE) when it listed in 1993. A number of reasons have been suggested. The company had a mismatch between the importance of its foreign operations and the foreign ownership of its equity. With 40% of its sales coming from outside Germany, only 7.2% of its shares were owned by non-Germans. The company also had a number of significant shareholders, such as

	1995	1994	1993 (DM m.)	1992	1991	1990
Net income (loss) as reported under German GAAP:	(5,734)	895	615	1,451	1,942	1,795
Add changes in appropriated retained earnings – provisions, reserves and valuation differences	(640)	409	(4,262)	774	64	738
Other adjustments:						
Goodwill and business acquisitions	(2,241)	(350)	(287)	(76)	(270)	(251)
Business dispositions and deconsolidations	369	(652)	–	337	(490)	–
Consolidation of non-consolidated subsidiaries	–	–	–	–	636	(512)
Pensions and other retirement benefits	(219)	(432)	(524)	96	(66)	(153)
Financial instruments	49	633	(225)	(438)	86	35
Securities	238	(388)	–	–	–	–
Deferred taxes	2,621	496	2,627	(646)	(126)	(758)
Other	Various balancing items					
Net income (loss) in accordance with US GAAP	(5,729)	1,052	(1,839)	1,350	1,886	884

Source: Daimler–Benz, Form 20-F 1995; Radebaugh *et al.* (1995)

■ *Case study 3.1 continued*

Deutsche Bank and the Emirate of Kuwait. If any of these decided to sell a large block of their shares on the German exchanges it could have caused a major fall in the company's share price. Any substantial sale could be better absorbed in the far larger NYSE.

On listing, the first year's figures based upon US GAAP showed a loss of DM1839 million rather than a profit of DM615 million. Much of this change was caused by the write-back of provisions. German law allowed a company to set up provisions to cover the cost of future internal business operations. Under US regulations such provisions are not allowed as there was no external party involved. The massive size of the reconciliation required ensured that Daimler–Benz received a tremendous amount of publicity when it issued these reconciliation statements. The general impression given by this publicity was that German and US accounting regulations were very different, and German requirements were far more conservative. However, many of the differences were one-off adjustments. As can be seen from the figures reproduced opposite, the year of listing, 1993, was something of an atypical year, although the US GAAP-based profits were lower than the German GAAP-based earnings in all years except 1995, when they were virtually identical.

Case study 3.2

A SIMULATION STUDY OF UK AND FRENCH ACCOUNTING

Walton (1992) explored the impact on the reported figures of differences in the accounting methods used in the UK and France. To do this, he chose a number of accounting issues – some where there are differences in terms of the prescribed rules in the two countries and others where companies have a choice of which methods to use.

The company modelled was a construction company. Specifically, there was a domestic parent company whose premises were compulsory purchased at a loss and whose new premises were partially financed by a government grant and partially financed by a US-denominated long-term loan. In addition, the parent sold and leased back some plant giving the possibility of showing a profit on the disposal. Finally, an overseas subsidiary was set up to carry out a long-term construction contract. Thus, the case included extraordinary items, long-term foreign currency transactions, the capitalisation of interest charges, government grants, leased assets and long-term contracts.

The case study was then presented to a number of auditors and account preparers in both the UK and France. This is not a real company so the results may not apply in practice, but they do provide valuable insights into the types of differences that can exist. The differences in the figures generated by the

▶

participants were often very large, especially for the accounts of the subsidiary, as shown below. However, the most noticeable, and surprising, conclusion is that for the subsidiary the average responses of the UK participants were more conservative than were the French responses. As shown in the average figures for turnover, profit both before and after interest, net assets and net equity were all less for the UK respondents and often very much less. For example, the average profit before interest calculated by the French sample was 12,793 while for the UK sample it was instead a loss of 12,014.

In contrast, for the parent company, there was little difference in the average figures generated by the UK and French samples – but, this time, the French responses tended to be slightly more conservative and they showed considerably more variability than did the UK responses.

| | British sample | | French sample | | Conservatism |
	Mean	Std dev.	Mean	Std dev.	index
Overseas subsidiary					
Turnover	136,644	83,407	185,930	36,432	0.735
Profit before interest	(12,014)	50,759	12,793	23,357	–0.939
Interest	(4,675)	5,619	(4,031)	1,654	0.841
Profit after interest	(16,689)	51,344	8,763	22,812	–1.904
Total net assets	168,711	51,670	208,938	23,091	0.807
Net equity	2,911	51,256	28,763	22,812	0.101
Parent company					
Turnover	1,331,733	44,577	1,345,000	76,572	0.990
Profit before interest	340,340	28,012	352,598	78,076	0.965
Interest	19,478	10,374	33,692	19,950	0.578
Profit after interest	320,862	30,012	318,906	86,169	1.006
Extraordinary items	33,770	24,538	58,182	14,444	0.580
Profit after extraordinary	287,092	19,003	260,724	77,221	1.101
Total net assets	865,802	28,802	860,227	86,214	1.006
Net equity	551,862	18,339	538,895	102,203	1.024

QUESTIONS

Differences between accounting systems (3.2)

1 What are the three types of differences that can exist between different accounting systems?

2 What are the possible reasons for the existence of each of the differences identified above.

3 If you had to quantify the extent of differences between two countries, how might you go about collecting the required information on each of the three types of differences?

4 What problems might you encounter when collecting this information?

Impact of differences in accounting systems (3.3)

1 When might a multinational company be affected by the three types of differences identified above?

2 What will be the likely impacts on a multinational company of these differences?

3 When might an investor be affected by the three types of differences identified above?

4 What will be the likely impact on an investor of these differences?

5 What other users might be affected by these three types of differences, and what are the likely impacts of these differences on them?

The comparability index (3.4)

1 What is a comparability index and how are partial comparability indices prepared?

2 How are the comparability and partial comparability indices calculated?

3 Use the information provided in Case study 3.1 on Daimler–Benz and calculate the comparability index and the three most important partial comparability indices for the years 1995, 1993 and 1991.

4 What do your findings tell you about the comparability of German and US GAAP?

5 What were the main findings of Weetman and Gray (1990) when they compared the UK and US GAAP-based earnings of UK companies?

6 Given the discussion in Chapters 1 and 2 on why accounting differs across countries, are the results of Weetman and Gray (1990) what you would have expected or not? Explain your answer.

7 If you were asked to do a similar study to measure the comparability of French and US companies, how would you set about doing it? What problems do you think you would encounter?

The H-index and the C-index (3.5)

1 What is the H- or Herfindahl index, and how is it calculated?

2 What is the C-index, and how is it calculated?

3 What is the difference between the H- and the C-index? Which do you think is more useful? Explain your answer.

4 How can the C-index be disaggregated into two indices when used on companies from different countries?

5 Which of the two C-index subindices identified above is likely to be of more interest to international investors? Explain your answer.

6 Which of the two C-index subindices is likely to be of more interest to international standard setters? Explain your answer.

7 If you were asked to measure the comparability of UK and US financial statements using the C-index, how would you set about doing it? What problems do you think that you would encounter?

Voluntary information disclosure (3.6)

1 Why do the amount and type of voluntary disclosure made vary across countries?

2 How could you measure and compare the voluntary disclosure made by companies in different countries? What problems might you encounter when attempting to do this?

3 What were the main findings of Gray, Meek and Roberts (1995), and Meek, Roberts and Gray (1995)? Do you find their results surprising or not? Explain your answer.

REFERENCES

Abayo, A.G., Adams, C.A. and Roberts, C.B. (1993) 'Measuring the quality of corporate disclosure in less developed countries: The case of Tanzania', *Journal of International Accounting Auditing and Taxation*, 2(2), 145–58.

Adams, C.A., Hill, W.Y. and Roberts, C.B. (1995) 'Environmental, employee and ethical reporting in Europe', *Research Report,* 41. London: Chartered Association of Certified Accountants.

Adams, C.A., Hill, W.Y. and Roberts, C.B. (1997) 'Corporate social reporting practices in Western Europe: Legitimating corporate activities?', *British Accounting Review*, 30(1).

Archer, S., Delvaille, P. and McLeay, S. (1995) 'The measurement of harmonisation and the comparability of financial statement items: Within-country and between-country effects', *Accounting and Business Research*, 25(98), 67–80.

Buzby, S.L. (1975) 'Company size, listed vs unlisted stocks, and extent of financial disclosure', *Journal of Accounting Research*, 13(1), 16–37.

Chow, C.W. and Wong-Boren, A. (1987) 'Voluntary financial disclosure by Mexican corporations', *The Accounting Review*, 62(3), 533–41.

Cooke, T.E. (1989) 'Voluntary corporate disclosure by Swedish companies', *Journal of International Financial Management and Accounting*, 1(2), 1–25.

Cooke, T.E. (1991) 'An assessment of voluntary disclosure in the annual reports of Japanese corporations', *International Journal of Accounting*, 26(3), 174–89.

Davidson, R.A. and Chrisman, H.H. (1993) 'Interlinguistic comparison of international accounting standards: The case of uncertainty expressions', *International Journal Accountancy*, 28(1), 1–16.

Emenyonu, E.N. and Gray, S.J. (1992) 'EC accounting harmonisation: An empirical study of measurement practices in France, Germany and the UK', *Accounting and Business Research*, Winter, 49–58.

Firth, M.A. (1979) 'The impact of size, stock market listing and auditors on voluntary disclosure in corporate annual reports', *Accounting and Business Research*, 9(36), 272–80.

Gray, S.J. (1980) 'The impact of international accounting differences from a security-analysis perspective: Some European evidence', *Journal of Accounting Research*, 18(1), 64–76.

Gray, S.J. (1988) 'Towards a theory of cultural influence on the development of accounting systems internationally', *Abacus*, 24(1), 1–15.

Gray, S.J, Meek, G.K. and Roberts, C.B. (1995) 'International capital market pressures and voluntary annual report disclosures by US and UK multinationals', *Journal of International Financial Management and Accounting*, 6(1), 43–68.

Hellman, N. (1993) 'A comparative analysis of the impact of accounting differences on profits and return on equity: Differences between Swedish practice and US GAAP', *European Accounting Review*, 2(3), 495–530.

Herrman, D. and Thomas, W. (1995) 'Harmonisation of accounting measurement practices in the European Community', *Accounting and Business Research*, 25(100), 253–65.

Hofstede, G. (1984) *Culture's Consequences: International Differences in Work-Related Values.* Beverly Hills, CA: Sage Publications.

Hossain, M., Perera, M.H.B. and Rahman, A.R. (1995) 'Voluntary disclosure in the annual reports of New Zealand companies', *Journal of International Financial Management and Accounting*, 6(1), 69–85.

Meek, G.K., Roberts, C.B. and Gray, S.J. (1995) 'Factors influencing voluntary annual report disclosures by US, UK and continental European multinational corporations', *Journal of International Business Studies*, Third Quarter, 555–72.

Radebaugh, L.H., Gebhardt, G. and Gray, S.J. (1995) 'Foreign stock exchange listings: A case study of Daimler–Benz', *Journal of International Financial Management and Accounting*, 6(2), 158–92.

Roberts, C.B. (1990) 'International trends in social and employee reporting', *Occasional Research Paper*, 6. London: Chartered Association of Certified Accountants.

Roberts, C.B. (1991) 'Environmental disclosures: A note on reporting practices in mainland Europe'. *Accounting, Auditing and Accountability Journal*, 4(3), 62–71.

Tas, L.G. van der (1988) 'Measuring harmonisation of financial reporting practices', *Accounting and Business Research*, 18(70), 157–69.

Tas, L.G. van der (1992) 'Evidence of EC financial reporting harmonisation: The case of deferred tax', *European Accounting Review*, 1(1) 69–104.

Tay, J.S.W. and Parker, R.H. (1990) 'Measuring harmonisation and standardisation', *Abacus*, 26(1), 71–88.

Wallace, R.S.O. (1988) 'Corporate financial reporting in Nigeria', *Accounting and Business Research*, 18(72), 352–62.

Walton P. (1992) 'Harmonization of accounting in France and Britain: Some evidence', *Abacus*, 28(2), 186–99.

Weetman, P. and Gray, S.J. (1990) 'International financial analysis and comparative corporate performance: The impact of UK versus US accounting principles on earnings', *Journal of International Financial Management and Accounting*, 2(2/3), 111–29.

Weetman P. and Gray, S.J. (1991) 'A comparative international analysis of the impact of accounting principles on profits: The USA versus the UK, Sweden and the Netherlands', *Accounting and Business Research*, 21(84), 363–79.

*Chapter 4*

The classification of accounting systems

PURPOSE OF THE CHAPTER

Chapter 3 looked at ways of measuring differences or similarities in accounting systems. This chapter looks at a very different way of comparing accounting systems, namely by classifying or placing them into groups of similar systems. The chapter will describe the main types of accounting classification systems that exist, and evaluate their usefulness. Chapters 3 and 4 therefore provide a number of benchmarks which can be used to compare the individual country studies of Part 2 of this text.

Learning objectives

After reading this chapter you should be able to:

● Explain why it is important to classify accounting systems.

● Distinguish deductive from inductive approaches to classification.

● Distinguish simple from complex classification systems.

● Explain the advantages and limitations of the different types of classification systems.

● Evaluate published research which develops or uses classification systems.

In Chapter 3 we looked at ways of measuring the level of harmonisation between different national accounting systems. Harmonisation measures are a useful way to quantify differences – both with respect to the figures reported and the accounting methods used. However this is not the only way in which accounting systems can be compared. Harmonisation measures treat all accounting issues in the same way, irrespective of whether or not they are important. Some differences in the accounting methods used can have a large impact on reported figures, but still not be very important because they are transitory differences or because they can be changed relatively easily without affecting any other aspects of the accounting system. The use of straight line or accelerated depreciation, for example, may have a large impact on reported profits but the difference is not significant from a theoretical viewpoint. Both are methods of allocating the cost of an asset to the periods that benefit from its use and, as such, are in harmony with each other. Other differences may have relatively little impact upon the reported figures but still be important. Whether or not a company capitalises leased assets, for example, may have little effect on its reported profits, but it is very important from a theoretical perspective. The alternative treatments of leased assets reflect very different views on what an asset is, and they are not compatible or in harmony with each other: non-capitalisation is based upon a legal definition of assets while capitalisation takes an economic perspective instead.

If we want to gain a complete picture of an accounting system or of differences across accounting systems, we must differentiate between significant or fundamental differences and non-significant or non-fundamental differences. Looking only at the impact of differences upon reported figures or only at the number of techniques that are different is not enough.

Classifying accounting systems contributes to this aim. Classifications attempt to place cases (here, the accounting systems of countries) into systematic categories or groups. A good classification system is one where each country's accounting system can be placed in one, and only one, group. The accounting systems of countries in any one group should share the same important or underlying features while also being quite distinct from the accounting systems in the other groups. Differences in unimportant features or transitory differences should not affect the classification system – indeed, the number of differences between countries placed in the same category might be quite large.

4.2 REASONS FOR CLASSIFYING ACCOUNTING SYSTEMS

There are several reasons for classifying accounting systems. A good classification system should provide a simple way of describing and analysing complex phenomena. In the absence of a classification system, anyone who wants to know about accounting in Italy, for example, must list and describe all the main accounting rules and practices in Italy, such as the methods used to value fixed assets, inventory, intangibles and leases and the rules for consolidation, deferred taxation, foreign currency translation, etc. If the same person then wants to know about accounting in Spain, a similarly long list will be required. A simpler approach would be to turn to classification studies which might show that Italy and Spain are in the same group as France, having government-imposed systems based upon Romanic law with tax rules also influencing the reported figures. While this does not tell us the specific accounting rules of Italy or Spain, we would now have a set of expectations regarding the specific rules and practices of each country. Time and effort can then be concentrated on learning about those rules or practices that are different from what is expected – hopefully a very much smaller list of items.

Classification therefore offers a way to simplify a complex world. Classifications not only help students, accountants, investors or anyone else who wishes to understand or compare different accounting systems; they also help domestic and international standard setters. At the level of the individual country, standard setters will be able to look at other countries in the same group for guidance on how they have solved similar problems. This should help them to see which solutions are most likely to be successful, having worked in other countries in the same group, and which will probably be unsuccessful, having failed in other group members. In an international setting, regional or international standard setters can see which countries should be relatively easy to harmonise (those countries in the same group) and which will probably be the hardest (countries in the most widely separated groups). They can also see which issues should be easy to harmonise (issues that are not fundamental) and which issues will probably be far more difficult (fundamental issues).

4.3 TYPES OF CLASSIFICATION SCHEMES

There have been many attempts at classifying accounting systems and many different types of classification schemes have been used. They differ in terms of the type of reasoning used, whether inductive or deductive. They also differ in degree of complexity. Both inductive and deductive classifications vary from the very simple to the complex. The simplest schemes are those which use discrete yes/no categories. More complex schemes may use several different classificatory features or variables, while the most complex involve several layers (or hierarchies).

This chapter will continue by describing the main features of each of these different types of classifications. Once the main types of classification systems have been introduced, some of the more important classification studies will be looked at.

4.3.1 Deductive classifications

Deductive classification schemes (sometimes instead called intuitive or *a priori* classifications) decide upon the relevant categories on the basis of the knowledge or beliefs of the classifier. They start with statements such as 'I believe that . . . ' or 'I think that the most important features or factors are . . . '. Examples might be to classify accounting systems on the basis of the valuation system used (for example, all strict historical cost systems would be placed into one category, systems using a modified historical cost system would be placed into a second category and fully-fledged inflation accounting systems would be allocated to the third group) or the extent of professional discretion allowed (e.g. accounting systems where the financial statements must comply with all laws and regulations versus those where the statements present information fairly and in conformity with laws and regulations, so that they have to disclose extra information if this is required for 'fair' presentation, versus those where the statements must give a true and fair view even if this means that not all rules or regulations are always fully followed).

These two examples are both classifications that use certain features of the accounting system itself to group countries. However, it is more common to find deductive classifications that instead classify countries on the basis of various business or cultural environmental features. Examples include classifications based upon the type of legal system; cultural values; or the main users of financial statements. These classifications are based upon the argument that the accounting system of a country is the outcome of specific business or cultural features. If we choose the correct or relevant features or descriptors, the resulting groups of countries should have accounting rules or practices that are substantially similar inside each group and substantially different across the groups.

Many of the proposed deductive classification schemes have not been tested to check whether or not the accounting systems inside each group are indeed similar to each other while also being dissimilar to those in the other group(s). However, the validity of these classifications can be tested. To do this, countries would be assigned to the hypothesised categories using deductive reasoning. Various statistical tests would then be applied to the accounting rules or practices of the countries in each category to see whether or not the hypothesised or suggested classifications are indeed valid.

4.3.2 Inductive classifications

Inductive classifications do not rely upon a theory of accounting to develop categories. Unlike deductive classifications they are data-driven rather than theory-driven. They start with data in the form of the specific accounting rules or practices of a number of countries. Typically, they use a large number of countries and an even larger number of accounting rules and/or practices. Groups or categories of countries are then generated by a variety of statistical techniques. Some studies have also gone a stage further and tried to explain the resultant categories by reference to the business, economic or cultural features of each country. Typically, data on a range of features such as those discussed in Chapter 1, that might help explain accounting rules or practices, would also be collected for each country. Various statistical tests would then be run to see which features could be used to generate the same country groupings – or, in other words, which features appeared to 'explain' the groups initially found.

4.3.3 Discrete classifications

The simplest classifications are those that categorise or place accounting systems into discrete or mutually exclusive groups. Categorising countries into two groups on a yes/no basis, for example. Some countries use common law while others use code law, so accounting systems could be classified on the basis of whether the country uses one or other type of legal system. While this is a very simple classification it is intuitively appealing and several deductive classifications have used the legal system as the classification factor, as discussed below. Empirical studies also support the usefulness of this classificatory variable.[1]

The type of legal system is a binary variable – code versus common law – and so it provides a basis for two groups of countries. The advantage of such binary classifications is that they are very simple and easy to use: it is generally clear to which category each accounting system belongs. Other classificatory variables may be used which lead to three or more groups. At least in theory, a classification exercise could result in an infinite number of groups. However, the most useful classifications contain a limited number of groups, since as the classification scheme becomes more complex and the number of groups increases, the problem of deciding which countries fit into which groups also increases.

---

[1] Salter and Doupnik (1992)

4.3.4 Classifications using continuous variables

An alternative approach to using discrete or categorical variables is to classify countries using continuous classificatory variables. For example, we might use the influence of tax rules as a classificatory variable. Countries could then be placed along a continuum ranging from the complete independence of tax rules and financial reporting rules to complete dependence, where external financial statements are identical to those used for taxation. Even where a continuous grouping or classification factor is used, countries can still be classified into two or more discrete groups. But now a second decision must also be made – namely, where along the continuum do we place the break point(s), or what are the critical value(s) of the grouping variable that differentiates between the groups? If we have chosen a sensible grouping factor, this should be fairly obvious. For example, if countries tend to cluster at the two extremes of 'little or no influence of tax rules' and 'heavy dependence on tax rules', then there are two groups of countries, and it will be fairly obvious which countries fit into which group.

4.3.5 Multidimensional mapping

A slightly more complex way of classifying accounting systems is to use 'multidimensional mapping'. Rather than classifying on the basis of one grouping factor only, this method groups accounting systems on the basis of a number of factors or features, n, where n can range from 2 to infinity. In effect, an n-dimensional picture or map is produced and countries are located on each dimension depending upon the specific values of each grouping factor. The simplest of these are two-dimensional maps, as illustrated by Exhibit 4.1. Two-dimensional classifications are fairly easy to understand and easy to represent graphically; however, there is no reason why more complex classifications cannot be developed using more dimensions or factors.

The advantage of multidimensional mapping is that it can be used to classify more complex phenomena. For example, a two-dimensional classification might be based upon (1) the independence or interdependence of tax and financial reporting rules and (2) the use of historical or current costs. While we are using two continuous classification variables we can still place accounting systems into discrete groups. As can be seen in Exhibit 4.1, each accounting system or country is initially placed onto what may be thought of as a map of accounting systems. Countries where tax and financial accounting are kept separate, with the latter based upon historical costs, would be placed in sector A. Those where tax and financial accounting are kept separate, but the latter uses current costs, would be placed in sector B, etc. The exact location of each country in each quadrant would depend upon the strictness of historical cost rules and the extent to which tax rules impact upon financial reporting. Let us assume that the eight countries, a–h, have been correctly placed onto the map. As a second stage we can group these countries into discrete categories. From their positions on the map, as shown in Exhibit 4.1 we appear to have three groups or categories. Category or group 1 contains the four countries a, b, d and f, group 2 contains the two countries c and g, while group 3 contains the remaining two countries, e and h.

Exhibit 4.1   A PROPOSED TWO-DIMENSIONAL CLASSIFICATION

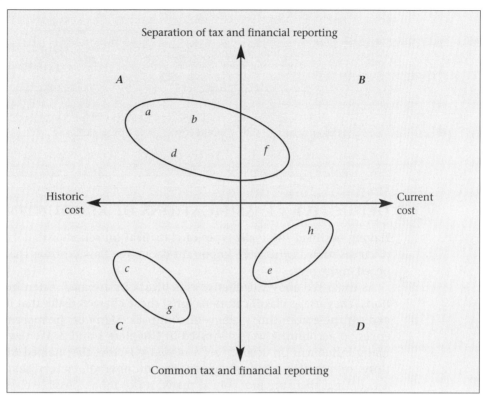

4.3.6 Hierarchical classifications

All of the classification schemes looked at so far place countries' accounting systems into discrete categories or groups. For example, in Exhibit 4.1 we have three groups of countries. Anyone interested in comparing the countries classified might want to know whether an accounting system placed in group 1 was more similar to those in group 2 or those in group 3. They might hypothesise, for example, that groups 2 and 3 are the two groups that are most alike. However, the classification scheme does not tell us this, we have to hypothesise it for ourselves.

Hierarchical classifications attempt to answer this type of question. The use of hierarchical classification systems in accounting was first proposed by Nobes (1984), although similar classifications have a long history in the natural sciences. A hierarchical classification using the same two factors as before is presented in Exhibit 4.2. While countries are placed in one of four groups, *A–D*, we can now see the relationship between the groups and understand the linkages between the countries. In particular, this classification tells us that the more important or fundamental classificatory factor is the importance of tax regulations. Countries that are placed in either of groups *A* or *B*, both common tax and reporting, should have more similar accounting systems than would countries that are placed, for example in groups *A* and *C*, both historical cost systems.

Exhibit 4.2 A PROPOSED HIERARCHICAL CLASSIFICATION

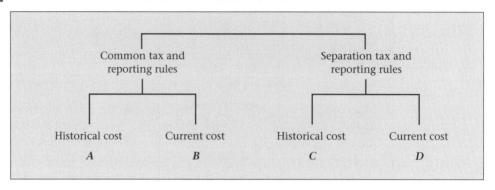

4.4 DEDUCTIVE CLASSIFICATIONS OF ACCOUNTING SYSTEMS

Having outlined the main types of classification schemes that exist, this section discusses some of the more important deductive classifications that have been proposed in the past.

As discussed above, deductive classifications are most often indirect classifications. They use as classificatory factor(s) those characteristics that influence or help explain the accounting systems of countries. Many of the more important influences on accounting were discussed in Chapters 1 and 2. We saw that there were many influences on accounting and many factors that helped to explain regulations or practices. Indeed, given the number of factors that can influence accounting, there are probably as many, if not more, possible classificatory factors than there are countries to classify. We therefore need to select the most important factors. Fortunately, this is not quite as difficult as it might at first seem.

Many of the factors that influence accounting are closely related to each other. For example, the legal and tax systems tend to be highly related. Code law countries tend to have far less of a separation between tax and accounting regulations than do common law countries. The same countries will tend to be classified in the same ways whichever of these two factors is used. Therefore, when classifying countries we could choose to use either the legal system or the tax system as a basis for classification, but we would not need to use both. We can also make our task easier by ignoring some countries. Obviously, we would like a classification system that correctly groups all countries and if we cannot correctly classify all countries we should try to refine and improve our analysis. But at this stage in our understanding of comparative accounting systems, we can ignore any special or unusual cases or countries and still develop useful classification schemes. Most of the classifications in the literature, for example, have ignored or excluded communist and less developed countries.

Various deductive categorical classifications have been proposed in the past with authors concentrating upon very different country characteristics. Three types of factors have been used as classificatory variables, namely: (1) the objectives of accounting, (2) the political, economic or cultural environments of countries and (3) external influences on countries. Examples of classifications using each of these types of factors will now be explored.

4.4.1 Mueller's classifications

Accounting classifications can be traced back to the early work of Hatfield (1966), first published in 1911, who noted similarities between the USA and the UK and between France and Germany. The modern work instead really began with Mueller (1967) who, using casual observation, divided accounting systems into four types – largely, but not exclusively, based upon the objectives of accounting:

1 **Macroeconomic systems**, such as Sweden where the most important function of accounting is to provide data to facilitate governmental direction of the economy. (*Note*: Since this work was done, the Swedish accounting system has undergone some major changes. Following Sweden's entry into the EU, the accounting system is now less influenced by macroeconomic considerations.)

2 **Microeconomic systems**, such as the Netherlands, where accounting is seen as a branch of business economics, and is aimed primarily at aiding the objectives of the individual business.

3 **Independent discipline systems**, such as the USA and the UK, where accounting is seen as a service function derived from business practices and is characterised by the use of professional judgement.

4 **Uniform systems**, such as France or Germany, where accounting is seen as a means of government administration and control.

The grouping variable is fairly complex, involving as it does the ways in which accounting has developed and the ways in which it is viewed in a country. Although Mueller offered typical examples of countries in each category it was often not clear where other countries fit – or, indeed, if they fit at all – into any of the four groups.

While Mueller treated the four groups as distinct categories, placing each country into only one of the four groups, later writers have used his ideas but modified the analysis. Rather than using these concepts to classify countries into four separate groups, they have been used to develop a 2×2 classification which combines the characteristics into pairs. One axis is the micro/macro orientation of the accounting system – whether the primary objective of accounting statements is seen as the provision of information useful for the economy as a whole or information useful to the individual company or corporate stakeholder. The other axis measures the way in which regulations are set – whether a uniform system or a system of independent and flexible rules. For example, Oldham (1987) proposed such a classification, as illustrated in Exhibit 4.3. This useful classification, concentrating as it does upon Europe, highlights a limitation of all classification studies. Accounting is not static and a classification that is useful at one point in time may not be useful at a later date. Oldham recognised this problem and produced two different classifications, the one reproduced in Exhibit 4.3, which illustrates the position in the mid-1980s and a second classification, reproduced in Exhibit 4.4, which refers to the position a decade earlier, in the mid-1970s.

In a later study, Mueller (1968) developed an alternative classification based upon four characteristics of the economic and cultural environments of countries. The important features identified were:

Exhibit 4.3 OLDHAM'S PROPOSED CLASSIFICATION USING MUELLER'S
ACCOUNTING VARIABLES: THE MID-1980s

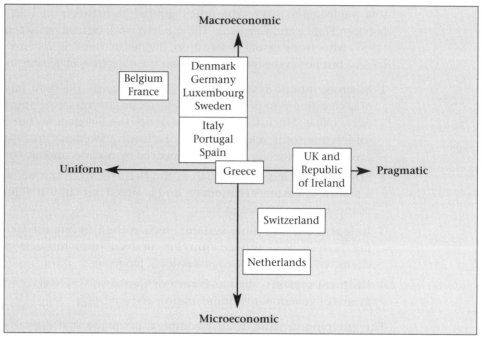

Source: Oldham (1987)

Exhibit 4.4 OLDHAM'S PROPOSED CLASSIFICATION USING MUELLER'S
ACCOUNTING VARIABLES: THE MID-1970s

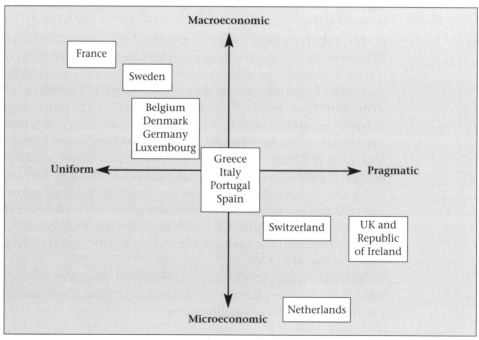

Source: Oldham (1987)

- stage of economic development
- business complexity
- political persuasion
- legal system.

A far more exhaustive classification system was then developed which could cope with a wider range of national accounting systems. Ten business environments were identified, each of which, it was argued, represented a different type of accounting system. The ten groups were labelled by Mueller as follows:

- North America
- South America
- Mexico and Israel
- British Commonwealth (excluding Canada)
- Germany and Japan
- Continental Europe (excluding Germany, the Netherlands and Scandinavia)
- Scandinavia
- Developing nations of the Near and Far East
- Africa (excluding South Africa)
- Communist.

4.4.2 Spheres of influence

Mueller's two classifications were both based upon features of the domestic institutional or cultural environment of a country. However as discussed earlier, the accounting rules and practices of countries are typically influenced also by external factors. In some countries most of the rules and practices have been imported from elsewhere, with little or no local adaptation. Therefore they bear little or no relationship to specific features of that country, such as the stage of business development or business complexity. Such a mismatch between the internal business or cultural environment and accounting is likely to be particularly common in developing countries. Cooke and Wallace (1990), for example, provide evidence suggesting that developed and developing countries should be categorised separately. They looked at the financial disclosure regulations of a number of countries and tried to match these with a variety of economic and cultural features. They found that the relationship between disclosure regulations and features internal to the country were stronger for developed countries than it was for developing countries. Interestingly, and somewhat surprisingly, they also found that the stage of economic development does not help to explain the extent of regulation. This provides clear evidence that, at least for developing countries, we cannot successfully classify if we use only factors that are internal to the country. As discussed in Chapter 1 but not examined by Cooke and Wallace, the accounting regulation of developing countries will often be highly influenced by trade partners or past colonial or other links to particular developed countries.

This idea of exporting or importing accounting rules and practices leads to an alternative type of classification system, which is best illustrated by the work of Seidler (1967). He discussed what he termed 'spheres of influence' and identified three systems:

- **British:** The UK and countries influenced by the UK including the British Commonwealth
- **American:** The USA and areas influenced by the USA such as Israel, Mexico and parts of South America
- **Continental:** Led by France, and including those parts of Southern Europe and South America which base their legal system on the Code Napoléon.

This is a very simple classification system that, in terms of how it is derived, is almost the complete opposite of Mueller's two classification schemes in that it ignores all internal factors. Instead it looks only at external influences and identifies three countries that Seidler argues have had the greatest success in exporting their accounting systems.

While it might appear to be relatively easy to group countries on the basis of external influences, even here a more complex classification is required. Seidler's three categories are clearly not exhaustive and so the proposed classification does not meet one of the requirements of a good classification system. For example, it excludes Scandinavia; also excluded is Africa, which includes former Portuguese colonies which appear to have a quite distinct accounting system mirroring their former colonial partner.[2] Another group or sphere that could have been included are the former communist states of Eastern Europe, all of which were strongly influenced by the USSR (and, in some cases, such as Poland and the then East Germany also by Germany).

However, more important than these omissions is the fact that the end-product of this type of classification, in terms of the groups developed, will be different depending upon the initial starting point. If we look at what happened in the period from the Second World War until the mid-1960s, when Seidler developed his classification, then it is probably correct to classify US and UK spheres of influence as separate groups. However, if we go back further into history, it can be argued that the UK and US systems are not distinct. The USA was originally very influenced by the UK, with many of the leaders of the US profession in its early days being UK-trained.

If we look at what is happening to accounting in the 1990s, then a far more complex classification scheme would have to be developed. Now EU Directives and European countries would be shown as influencing the UK, while the UK has in turn influenced the EU. Therefore the UK has also influenced accounting in other European countries. The increasing international influence of US accounting, both through direct pressures or influences and through its indirect influence via the IASC and international stock markets, would also have to be shown. Indeed, it is not at all clear that Seidler's classification helps at all to explain **current** changes in accounting systems. Although these moves towards increasing regional and international har-

---

[2] United Nations (1991)

monisation are far from complete, a late 1990s' version of the spheres of influence model would have to be far more complex than the model suggested by Seidler.

4.4.3 Gray's classification

Slightly more complex than any of the categorical classifications looked at so far are classifications using multidimensional mapping. As discussed earlier, any number of dimensions is possible although the simplest forms are those that use only two dimensions or classificatory factors. One example of a two-dimensional classification was developed by Gray (1988). As discussed in Chapter 2, Gray described four accounting values which he hypothesised were linked to the culture of the country. Using these four accounting values, he went on to suggest two two-dimensional maps of accounting systems. One of the most interesting and important things about this work is how Gray defined an 'accounting system'. Rather than trying to classify accounting systems in their entirety he argued that we need to differentiate between two types of systems. First, he classified countries on the basis of their system of regulation. Two dimensions were considered – who regulates accounting (statutory control versus the profession) and how flexible are the rules that they set (uniform versus flexible). He also produced a second classification based upon the measurement and disclosure rules themselves. The two dimensions used here were the importance of conservatism or prudence and the openness or transparency of the disclosure rules. Countries were then placed on the maps on the basis of judgement, as shown in Exhibit 4.5.

Gray did not use the maps to develop discrete categories or a classification of countries, being content to place countries into the relevant quadrants. However the work could be extended fairly easily and countries could be classified or placed into discrete groups on the basis of their location on the maps. If we look at the map of measurement and disclosure systems, for example, we could argue that there are two groups of countries. Those countries placed in the quadrant of relatively high secrecy and conservatism fall into one group, while those countries placed in the quadrant of relatively high optimism and transparency form a second.

4.4.4 AAA's morphology of accounting systems

This idea of multidimensional mapping was also used by the American Accounting Association (AAA) to produce what they called a morphology of accounting systems.[3] This morphology is a systematic attempt to list and describe all of the most important features that influence accounting systems. The AAA's proposed morphology is illustrated in Exhibit 4.6. As can be seen, they identified eight influences on accounting systems, or what they termed 'parameters'. Each of these parameters was then described in terms of a limited number of 'states of nature'. For example, the AAA argued that a country's economic system had an important influence on the accounting system. In addition, the economic system of a country could take one of four possible forms or states of nature: it could be a traditional economy, a market economy, a planned market economy or a planned economy.

---

[3] American Accounting Association (1977)

Exhibit 4.5 TWO-DIMENSIONAL CLASSIFICATIONS PROPOSED BY GRAY

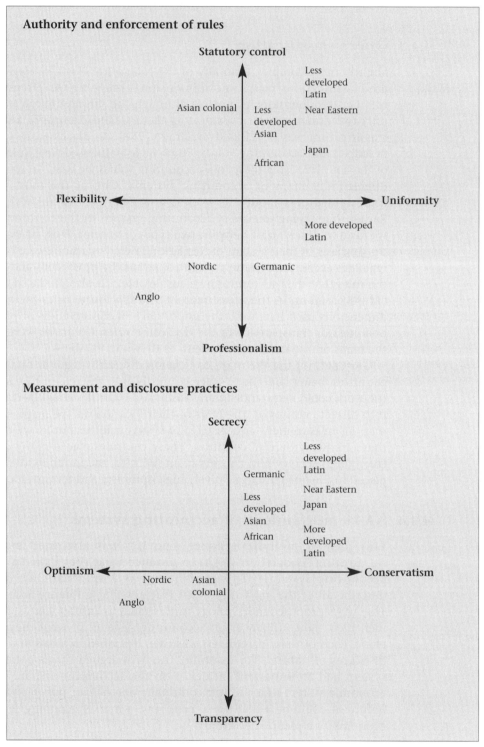

Source: Gray (1988), pp. 12–13. Copyright Accounting Foundation. Reproduced by kind permission of Blackwell Publishers

| Exhibit 4.6 | AAA's PROPOSED MORPHOLOGY OF ACCOUNTING SYSTEMS |

Parameter	States of nature				
	1	2	3	4	5
P_1 Political system	Traditional oligarchy	Totalitarian oligarchy	Modernising oligarchy	Tutelary democracy	Political democracy
P_2 Economic system	Traditional	Market	Planned market	Plan	–
P_3 Stage of economic development	Traditional society	Pre take-off	Take-off	Drive to maturity	Mass consumption
P_4 Objectives of financial reporting	Investment decisions	Management performance	Social measurement	Sector planning and control	National policy objectives
P_5 Sources of/authority for standards	Executive decree	Legislative action	Government administrative unit	Public–private consortium	Private
P_6 Education training and licensing	Public informal	Public formal	Private informal	Private formal	–
P_7 Enforcement of ethics and standards	Executive	Government administrative unit	Judicial	Private	–
P_8 Client	Government	Public	Public enterprises	Private enterprises	–

Source: American Accounting Association (1977), p. 99. Reproduced with permission

Again, this is an indirect way of describing accounting systems in that the parameters identified are not aspects of the accounting system itself. Instead, they are features of the business and economic environment of countries. The main advantage of this approach is that it is a way of describing a very complex construct – the accounting system – in a very much simpler way. Instead of having to describe an almost infinite number of accounting rules and practices we can instead describe a small number of parameters. Accounting systems with the same values for each parameter would be classified as being in the same category. For example, the UK could be described as P_1^5, P_2^2, P_3^5, P_4^1, P_5^4, P_6^4, P_7^4, P_8^4. Any other countries which have the same combination of parameter values would also be members of the same group as the UK, and it is hypothesised that they will have an accounting system that is essentially similar to that of the UK.

At first sight, this morphology results in an extremely complex and large classification scheme. With eight parameters all with four or five states of nature there are fully 160,000 different possible combinations. In practice, it is not as bad as this, as many of these combinations are not feasible – for example, a country will not have a traditional economic system and a mass consumption stage of economic development. However, the morphology remains untested and no one has calculated how many combinations of the various states of nature exist in practice, or how many different accounting groups would actually emerge from the morphology.

4.4.5 Hierarchical classifications

As briefly discussed above, all the classification schemes looked at so far are categorical classifications. They all place countries into discrete, non-overlapping and, hopefully exhaustive, categories. As such, they assume that all the countries in any one category share similar characteristics while also being significantly different from the countries in the other categories. In practice, of course, it is not quite as simple as this. Instead, differences between countries are a matter of degree and some countries placed in the same group will be more alike than are other countries in the same group. In addition, countries in different groups will share some common characteristics. We therefore want to know which countries or groups of countries are most similar or dissimilar and how similar or dissimilar they are. Answers to these types of questions can be provided by the most complex deductive classifications, which are hierarchical classifications, as best illustrated by the work of Nobes (1984). He proposed a classification that sought to classify the measurement practices of listed companies in developed western countries in 1980 – that is, before corporate practices might have changed due to EU harmonisation moves. The proposed hierarchy was used to classify 14 countries, as illustrated in Exhibit 4.7, and data on these countries was also collected to test the proposed classification.

As can be seen, this classification has certain similarities with some of the earlier deductive classifications. At the most fundamental level Nobes again argues for two classes of accounting systems, microeconomic- and macroeconomic-based. In the micro class, accounting is seen as serving the needs of the company itself or its specific stakeholders, while in the macro class the orientation is more towards the needs of society as a whole. Each of these two classes splits into two families, with the resultant four families very largely equating with the four groups proposed by Mueller. Similarly, the two species of UK- and US-influenced countries are similar to two of the groups proposed by Seidler.

This classification was tested by Nobes and the results strongly supported the two classes, although there was relatively little support for the finer categories. The classification was also tested by Doupnik and Salter (1993). They produced an inductive classification applying statistical analysis to data on actual accounting practices. They then assessed whether or not their classification and the categories of countries developed were similar or dissimilar to those suggested by Nobes. While Nobes's original classification scheme was designed to explain measurement practices, Doupnik and Salter tested it using data on both measurement and disclosure practices. In addition, they used data for 1990 rather than 1980 (when the

Exhibit 4.7 NOBES'S PROPOSED HIERARCHICAL CLASSIFICATION OF ACCOUNTING SYSTEMS

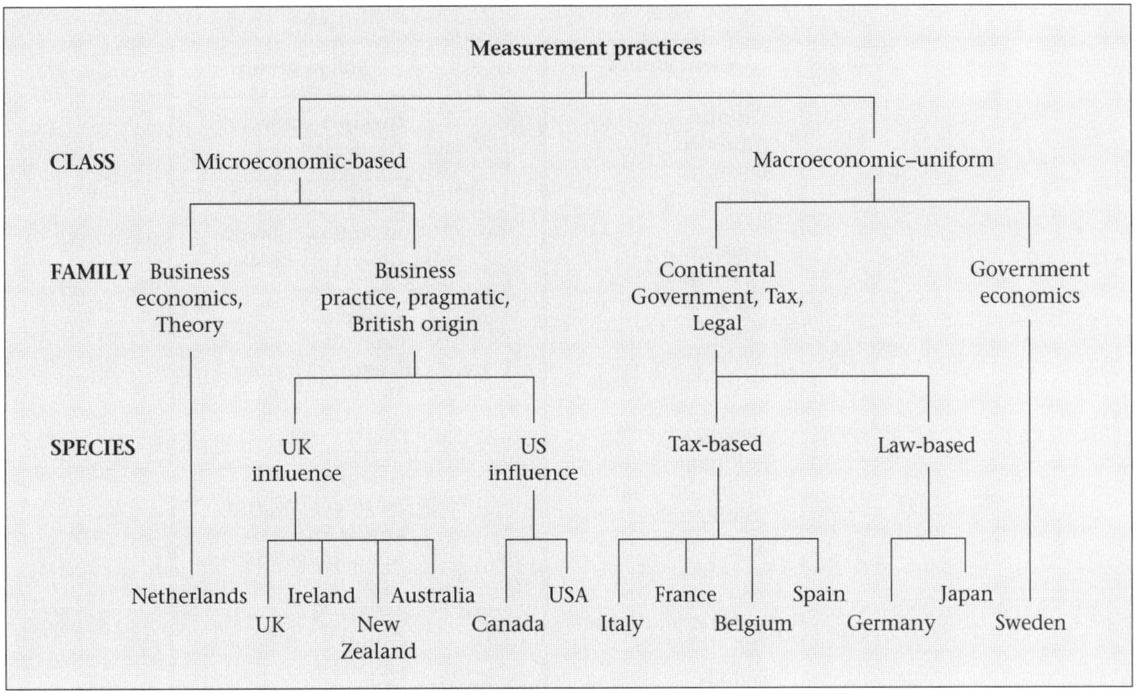

Source: Nobes (1984), p. 94. Reproduced with kind permission of Croom Helm

classification was first proposed) and more countries. This is an example of a study that uses cluster analysis as a means of grouping countries. There are many different ways of doing a cluster analysis, but they typically start by placing all the countries into one large group or cluster. This is then split into two groups of countries that are most dissimilar from each other. Each of these two new clusters is then broken down further into dissimilar groups and the process continues until the maximum number of clusters or groups is reached.

Despite using very different data from that originally employed by Nobes, Doupnik and Salter's results provide some quite strong support for Nobes's classification. They found two solutions, one with two groups and one with nine groups. At the two-group level, the results clearly support the micro/macro split with the classification being identical to that proposed by Nobes. The nine-group solution, as reproduced in Exhibit 4.8, also tends to support Nobes's classification. While more groups were found, this is mainly because more countries were tested, with Latin American (group 4) and Arab (group 6) groups emerging. One of the main differences from Nobes is the finding that the Netherlands is now part of the UK group (group 1). This may reflect the effects of EU harmonisation attempts. In addition, Germany and Japan are now both classified as single-country groups (group 8 and 9 – Japan has always proved extremely difficult to classify, due to its distinct history and culture).

103

Exhibit 4.8 GROUPS OF ACCOUNTING SYSTEMS DERIVED BY DOUPNIK AND SALTER

Micro groups	Macro groups
Group 1 Australia Botswana Hong Kong Ireland Jamaica Luxembourg Malaysia Namibia Netherlands Netherlands Antilles New Zealand Nigeria Philippines Papua New Guinea South Africa Singapore Sri Lanka Taiwan Trinidad and Tobago UK Zambia Zimbabwe	**Group 3** Costa Rica
	Group 4 Argentina Brazil Chile Mexico
	Group 5 Colombia Denmark France Italy Norway Portugal Spain
	Group 6 Belgium Egypt Liberia Panama Saudi Arabia Thailand UAE
	Group 7 Finland Sweden
Group 2 Bermuda Canada Israel USA	**Group 8** Germany
	Group 9 Japan

Source: Doupnik and Salter (1993), p. 53

4.5 INDUCTIVE CLASSIFICATIONS OF ACCOUNTING SYSTEMS

Instead of developing a deductive or hypothesised classification based upon a theory of what factors influence accounting or what are the important similarities and differences across various accounting systems, inductive studies use a variety of statistical methods to develop classifications. While there are important differences across the various inductive classifications, they all follow a similar approach. The primary data source is most often a survey of lots of quite detailed accounting rules or practices, or both. Countries are then allocated to specific groups or categories using various types of statistical analysis.

4.5.1 Use of Price Waterhouse surveys

Many of these studies, especially the earlier ones, used Price Waterhouse (PW) survey data. PW undertook three surveys in 1973, 1975 and 1979 covering from 38 countries in 1973 to 64 companies in 1979. In each study, PW partners from each country were asked about the use of a variety of accounting practices. The issues covered included both measurement and disclosure issues, varying from a total of 233 items in 1973 to 267 items in 1979. A number of later studies have instead used other data sources, including specially developed surveys of accountants[4] and surveys of actual financial statements.[5]

Two of the studies using the PW data will be described here. The study by Da Costa, Bourgeois and Lawson (1978) is of interest not only because it was the first to use the PW data but, more importantly, because it highlights some of the problems that can occur with this type of classification. Da Costa *et al.* adopted what appears to be a sensible method of classifying accounting systems, but the conclusions reached are very different from what might have been expected. There are several reasons why this study failed to reach what might be termed 'sensible results', and some of these problems were overcome in a later study by Nair and Frank (1980). Despite the fact that this study uses data that is now 20 years old, many of its conclusions still hold and it remains perhaps the most important inductive classification study.

4.5.2 Da Costa *et al.*'s study

Da Costa *et al.* (1978) used the subset of the 1973 PW data (100 questions in all). They input this data into a factor analysis computer program. (Factor analysis is a statistical method that summarises large data sets; it reduces and replaces the underlying data with a much smaller set of factors all of which are linear combinations of original data.) The Da Costa *et al.* study reduced the 100 PW questions to seven factors. These factors were then each labelled or described as follows:

- **Factor 1**: A measure of financial disclosure
- **Factor 2**: The influence of company law on accounting practice
- **Factor 3**: The importance of income measurement
- **Factor 4**: Conservatism as a guideline policy
- **Factor 5**: The influence of tax law on accounting practice
- **Factor 6**: The importance of inflation
- **Factor 7**: The orientation of information to capital market users.

Many of these factors (and especially factors 2, 4, 6 and 7) are very similar to those identified in various deductive studies. For example, factor 2 (influence of company law) is similar to the code/common law classification, while as we saw earlier, factor 4 (conservatism) was used by Gray (1988). The values for each of these seven factors were then used as inputs into a cluster analysis. However, the results of this analysis were different from what might have been expected. Two groups or clusters emerged – a British Commonwealth group and a non-Commonwealth group. The British Commonwealth group makes intuitive sense. The problem lies with the second group, which consisted of the USA as well as much of South America

---

[4] *See*, for example, Doupnik and Salter (1993)
[5] *See*, for example, Choi and Bavishi (1980)

and Europe. This group therefore classifies countries such as Switzerland and Brazil (both code-based but one strict historical costs and the other an inflation adjusted system) with the USA (a common law system).

There are several possible reasons for these odd results. First, there are problems with the method of data analysis. (If cluster analysis is used it should really be used with the original data. If factor analysis is used, then countries should be categorised on the basis of their most important factor or the factor scores should be used as inputs into a discriminant analysis. A discriminant analysis is similar to a regression analysis but the independent variable is not continuous but is a 0/1 variable of membership/non-membership of the category.)

Second, there may be problems with the data. A limited set of PW data was used. Only 100 of the 233 practices contained in the PW survey were included and different classifications might have been generated if a different subset of questions had been considered.

4.5.3 Some problems of using survey data

There are several problems with the PW data set. The questions asked related to several different types of accounting issues. Exhibit 4.9 lists a few of the questions contained in the 1979 survey.[6]

From this, it can be seen that the PW surveys include questions on broad concepts and underlying principles as well as questions on specific issues inside each

---

Exhibit 4.9 SOME QUESTIONS ASKED IN THE PRICE WATERHOUSE (1979) SURVEY

> **Question 2**
> Financial statements are drawn up on the premise that the business will continue in operation indefinitely.
>
> **Question 10**
> Departures from the going concern concept are disclosed.
>
> **Question 29**
> Fixed assets are stated at cost of acquisition or construction, *less* accumulated depreciation.
>
> **Question 47**
> In historical cost statements, revaluation reserves that arise when fixed assets are stated at an amount in excess of cost are available for charges arising on subsequent downward revaluation of fixed assets.
>
> **Question 27**
> The basis on which fixed assets are stated is disclosed.
>
> **Question 185**
> The amount written-off deferred development costs is disclosed.

---

[6] Fitzgerald *et al.* (1979)

of the financial statements – both measurement and disclosure issues. If all of these questions are input into a statistical analysis they are accorded equal importance. Some of the questions asked are very important, others are trivial and others cover issues that are of importance to only a few companies. If the survey includes all of these types of questions the statistical analysis cannot differentiate between important and unimportant ones and will treat all questions in the same way. Therefore, unimportant ones may swamp important issues so that the resultant classifications may either be very unstable or incorrect.

If we were to design a data base of accounting issues to be used as the basis for developing an inductive classification scheme we would have to decide which issues are important and which are unimportant. We would also have to decide whether to include both regulations and practices or whether instead to limit the data base to just regulations or just practices. A classification based upon regulations or *de jure* issues might be quite different from one that was based upon practices or *de facto* issues. As we have seen earlier, in some countries the accounting regulations are set with the needs of the tax authorities or creditors in mind. Discretionary accounting practices and disclosures may instead be designed to meet the needs of stock market participants. Unfortunately, the PW surveys all include both *de jure* and *de facto* issues.

We would also have to consider the question of which types of organisation should be covered by our data base of accounting issues. In the UK, this is not really a problem. All but the very smallest UK limited liability companies have to follow the same Companies Acts and accounting standards while the stock market requires very few additional disclosures. In other countries, such as the USA, there are very different requirements for listed companies (regulated by the Securities and Exchange Commission or SEC) and non-listed companies (regulated at the state rather than the federal or countrywide level). In much of Europe the important distinction is instead between the individual company and the group. In France, for example, group financial statements have been heavily regulated by the stock market. The regulations are mainly aimed at providing information useful for investors and the rules often contain a wide range of choices. In contrast, the financial statements of individual companies have been mainly regulated by the government. The rules are mainly designed to meet the needs of the government, the tax authorities and creditors. They tend not only to result in relatively conservative profit measures but they are also highly uniform, giving companies little discretion or choice in what methods to use. Therefore, if our data base of accounting issues was restricted to issues that applied to group financial statements we might find that France, the UK and the USA were all placed in the same group. If instead our data base was limited to issues applying to individual company financial statements we would probably find that the UK and France were placed into different groups. (The USA might even be totally excluded from our data base as listed companies have to report only group financial statements.)

4.5.4 Nair and Frank's study

Nair and Frank (1980) argued in a similar way that we should not use all accounting issues to categorise countries. In particular they argued that a classification based upon disclosure issues might be quite different from a classification based upon measurement issues. This is because disclosure and measurement rules are often set by different bodies (for example, the stock market and the government in France or the SEC and the FASB in the USA). Also, the two sets of rules may be set with different considerations in mind (shareholder information needs versus tax or economic planning needs).

They therefore split the 1973 and 1975 PW data into measurement issues and disclosure issues and developed two classifications – one based upon measurement issues and the other based upon disclosure issues. The data was fed into a factor analysis programme and groups were formed by allocating countries to categories based upon their highest factor loadings.

To see how this is done, assume that we are classifying three countries 1–3 and, having used factor analysis we find that the underlying data can be described by three factors, *A–C*. The factor weightings for the countries are as follows:

Factor	*A*	*B*	*C*
1	0.9	0.05	0.05
2	0.4	0.3	0.3
3	0.3	0.4	0.3

If we classify on the basis of the highest factor weightings, as done by Nair and Frank, we would allocate countries 1 and 2 to one group as they each have the highest weighting on factor *A*, and country 3 to the other group. However, if we use discriminant analysis instead we would allocate on the basis of their factor loadings on all three factors. Now, country 1 would be allocated to one group and countries 2 and 3 would be allocated to the other group, a result that is more appropriate.

Looking first at Nair and Frank's results for measurement issues, the groups generated are reported in Exhibit 4.10.

Five factors were extracted from the 1973 measurement data. No country had their highest loading on the fifth factor, so four groups were formed. These groups generally appear to make sense. They may be thought of as being:

Group 1: British Commonwealth group
Group 2: Latin American group
Group 3: Continental European group
Group 4: United States-led group.

The analysis was just as successful when the 1975 data was used, although now six factors were extracted. Five groups were formed, four being quite similar to those found using the 1973 data plus group 5, which contained only one country, Chile. When the 1973 and 1975 groups are compared it can be seen that groups 1 and 4 are both very stable. Group 1, the British Commonwealth group, has lost Pakistan which instead joined group 2. Group 4, the US-led group, lost two countries, with Panama moving to group 2 and Venezuela moving to group 3. Rather more movement is shown in the other two groups. Group 2, the Latin American group, gained Italy and Spain from group 3 (plus Greece which was not included in the earlier survey). Group 2 is now better thought of as a group of Latin American and South European countries. Group 3, originally a Continental European group, having lost Italy and Spain is now more appropriately thought of as a North European group.

Exhibit 4.10 NAIR AND FRANK'S GROUPS BASED UPON MEASUREMENT ISSUES

1973 data

1	2	3	4
Australia	Argentina	Belgium	Canada
Bahamas	Bolivia	France	Japan
Fiji	Brazil	Germany	Mexico
Ireland	Chile	Italy	Panama
Jamaica	Colombia	Spain	Philippines
Kenya	Ethiopia	Sweden	USA
Netherlands	India	Switzerland	
New Zealand	Paraguay	Venezuela	
Pakistan	Peru		
Singapore	Uruguay		
South Africa			
Trinidad and Tobago			
UK			
Zimbabwe			

1975 data

1	2	3	4	5
Australia	Argentina	Belgium	Bermuda	Chile
Bahamas	Bolivia	Denmark	Canada	
Fiji	Brazil	France	Japan	
Iran	Colombia	Germany	Mexico	
Ireland	Ethiopia	Norway	Philippines	
Jamaica	Greece	Sweden	USA	
Malaysia	India	Switzerland	Venezuela	
Netherlands	Italy	Zaire		
Singapore	Pakistan			
South Africa	Panama			
Trinidad and Tobago	Spain			
UK	Uruguay			
Zimbabwe				

Source: Nair and Frank (1980). Reproduced with kind permission of the American Accounting Association

The disclosure-based groups are generally less easy to characterise (although from a purely statistical point of view the classifications are just as successful). As shown in Exhibit 4.11, seven groups were derived from the 1973 disclosure data.

Exhibit 4.11 NAIR AND FRANK'S GROUPS BASED UPON DISCLOSURE ISSUES

1973 data

1	2	3	4	5	6	7
Australia	Bolivia	Belgium	Canada	Argentina	Sweden	Switzerland
Bahamas	Germany	Brazil	Mexico	Chile		
Fiji	India	Colombia	Netherlands	Ethiopia		
Ireland	Japan	France	Panama	Uruguay		
Jamaica	Pakistan	Italy	Philippines			
Kenya	Peru	Paraguay	USA			
New Zealand		Spain				
Singapore		Venezuela				
South Africa						
Trinidad and						
Tobago						
UK						
Zimbabwe						

1975 data

1	2	3	4	5	6	7
Belgium	Australia	Bahamas	Bermuda	Argentina	Denmark	Italy
Bolivia	Ethiopia	Germany	Canada	India	Norway	Switzerland
Brazil	Fiji	Japan	Ireland	Iran	Sweden	
Chile	Kenya	Mexico	Jamaica	Pakistan		
Colombia	Malaysia	Panama	Netherlands	Peru		
France	New Zealand	Philippines	UK			
Greece	Nigeria	USA	Zimbabwe			
Paraguay	Singapore	Venezuela				
Spain	South Africa					
Uruguay	Trinidad and					
Zaire	Tobago					

Source: Nair and Frank (1980). Reproduced with kind permission of the American Accounting Association

Group 1 is again a British Commonwealth group which, with the exception of the omission of the Netherlands, is identical to the 1973 measurement group. Group 4, the US-led group, is again very similar to that found using 1973 measurement data, with the only differences being the addition of the Netherlands and the omission of Japan, which is instead placed in group 2. The other four groups are difficult to explain, in particular there is no clear rationale or explanation for group 2 which contains Japan, two British Commonwealth Asian countries (Pakistan and India), two South American countries (Bolivia and Peru) and Germany, a result that has no intuitive appeal. The disclosure groups are generally not very stable, with many countries changing groups between 1973 and 1975 suggesting that the classification is not too successful. Sweden now forms part of a Scandinavian group, due to the addition of data from Norway and Denmark, the US-led group remains fairly stable while the British Commonwealth group has fractured into two.

Nair and Frank also attempted to seek explanations for the groups obtained by using 14 cultural and economic variables to discriminate among the 1975 groups of countries. The variables chosen included language variables, which they argued acted as proxies for cultural and historical links, various GNP-based variables reflecting the stage of economic development and a series of trading bloc variables. The analysis met with some success with two trading bloc variables, the use of French and *per capita* income being important in explaining the measurement groups and the use of German and English, the importance of the agricultural sector and three trading bloc variables helping to explain the disclosure results. However, these explanations of group membership are far from conclusive. Indeed, they had little success when using these variables to predict rather than to explain group membership.

There are several ways in which we can assess the success of these inductive classifications. Statistical analysis is obviously important, and this suggests that Nair and Frank have been at least moderately successful. But more important, we need to ask ourselves: 'Do the groups appear to make sense?' Again, it would appear that the classifications are reasonably successful, but not a total success. Some of the groups found by Nair and Frank make intuitive sense, but others do not. Likewise, some of the groups are fairly stable, but others are not.

There are a number of possible explanations for why the analysis was not more successful. The analysis was based upon the PW data which has been strongly criticised, especially by Nobes (1982). He highlights four problems with these surveys. That they contain a number of mistakes; other answers, while correct, give a misleading picture; the questions chosen tend to exaggerate UK/US differences; and, most importantly, the data was not developed for this purpose. As Nobes (1982, p. 63) argues:

> When classifying plants or animals, biologists largely ignore the most obvious characteristics. That is, they do not carry out factor analysis on animals by weight, colour, number of legs, nature of body covering, length of life, etc. This would merely lead to a classification of that data. It would group man with ostriches, dolphins with sharks, bats with owls, and so on.

4.6 WHAT CONCLUSIONS CAN BE DRAWN?

As we have seen in this chapter, classifications have been developed using a variety of different approaches and there often appears to be little in common between many of the studies. The deductive studies classify on the basis of a wide range of different economic and cultural factors. However, many of these factors are highly correlated so that the resultant groups of countries identified by the various studies are often very similar. These studies suggest, in particular, that there are leading countries in each group. Other countries, often less developed and with historical political and economic links to the leading countries, are influenced by and follow them. When it comes to explaining these groups, the most obvious result is that there are at least two types of accounting systems: a law-based, standardised, macro-based system and a more pragmatic, professionally orientated, micro-based system.

Perhaps the main contribution of the deductive studies is not so much to offer classifications of particular countries, but rather to offer descriptions of the key features of national accounting systems and to suggest which factors are influential in their development.

The inductive studies offer a quite different way of developing a classification. Rather than relying upon deductive or *a priori* arguments they use statistical tests to analyse a large amount of detailed information on accounting rules and/or practices. These studies have a number of weaknesses, particularly the misuse of statistical tests and unthinking use of large data sets. They have also used different types of data and included different countries and different time periods. It is not too surprising, therefore, that the results of the many different classification studies are not always consistent. What is perhaps more surprising is the extent of agreement that there is across the various studies.

Some groups and subgroups clearly emerge from many of the classification studies. In particular, there appears to be:

1 A large Commonwealth group, which may split into two sub-groups of:
   – Developed Commonwealth and
   – Developing Commonwealth;

2 A US-influenced group;

3 A South European group;

4 A South American group;

5 A Central or North European group.

There is also evidence to support the view that no single classification can successfully include all accounting systems, especially when an 'accounting system' is defined to include all aspects of accounting. Disclosure and measurement systems are often sufficiently different to mean that countries need to be classified on the basis of either their disclosure system or their measurement system. While more work needs to be done in this area, different groups will probably also emerge if we consider the practices of different types of companies. For example, countries might be classified quite differently if we looked only at the accounting practices of large listed groups rather than, for example, the practices of individual companies or smaller non-listed groups. In particular, the larger and more international a company is, then the more likely it is to follow internationally accepted practices and the fewer differences there should be across companies from different countries.

There are several possible ways forward. We could use increasingly sophisticated statistical methods alongside data bases that have been specifically developed for the purpose of classification. This would undoubtedly lead to better classifications as many of the problems of the existing classifications could be avoided. However, the new classifications will probably not be significantly better or very different from those discussed above. Before we can develop new and significantly improved or more useful data sets of accounting rules and practices we need to decide which rules and practices are important and vary in a consistent and predictable manner across countries, and which occur randomly or are temporary or trivial. The most useful way forward is therefore not to carry on replicating past studies using improved data sets or statistical tests, but instead to concentrate upon detailed individual country case studies. We will turn our attention to such detailed case studies in Part 2 of this book.

4.7 SUMMARY AND CONCLUSIONS

This chapter has looked at attempts to classify the accounting systems of various countries. All of these classifications attempt to place accounting systems into distinct or non-overlapping groups or categories. The accounting systems inside any one group should share similar characteristics while also being different from the systems placed in the other groups.

The chapter provided an overview of the different types of classifications which are all based upon one or other of two types of reasoning. We saw how deductive or *a priori* classifications start with a theory of accounting or accounting differences which is used to develop the categories. Key features of the accounting system or the economic, institutional or cultural environment of countries are identified on the basis of prior knowledge and theoretical arguments and these are used to guide the classification of accounting systems. Inductive classifications, in contrast, start with the accounting rules or practices themselves and use various statistical techniques to uncover the underlying groups.

Having discussed the different ways in which classifications can be developed the chapter went on to describe examples of each of the main types of classification. Several of the more important and more influential empirical studies were discussed. These empirical studies cover a range of different countries, use data from very different time periods and even define an 'accounting system' in quite different ways. As such, they have also come to some quite different conclusions regarding the resultant groups of countries. However, they do share a number of common results and this chapter finished by drawing out conclusions regarding the different types of accounting systems that appear to exist internationally.

QUESTIONS

An overview (4.2 and 4.3)

1 What are the main reasons for wanting to classify accounting systems?

2 What are the main types of classification systems that have been used to classify accounting systems? Give an example of each type.

3 Which do you think are the most useful? Explain your answer.

Deductive classifications (4.4)

1 What types of factors have been used as classificatory variables in deductive classifications? Give an example of the use of each type of factor.

2 What are the strengths and weaknesses of the deductive approach to classification?

3 Of the deductive classification studies described in this chapter, which do you think is the best? Explain your answer.

4 If you were to develop a deductive classification, how would you go about doing it? What are the main problems that you think you would encounter?

Inductive classifications (4.5)

1 What are the strengths and weaknesses of the inductive approach to classification?

2 Of the inductive classification studies described in this chapter, which do you think is the best? Explain your answer.

3 If you were to develop an inductive classification, how would you go about doing it? What are the main problems that you think you would encounter?

Classification and the definition of an 'accounting system' (4.3–4.6)

1 The term 'accounting system' can be taken to mean *de jure* or *de facto* measurement or reporting practices of all companies or certain types of companies. To what extent have the classification studies described in this chapter differentiated between different concepts of an accounting system?

2 What evidence is there that the results of classifying countries will be different if different concepts of an accounting system are considered? (For example, to what extent might the groups be different if all companies were considered or if only listed group companies were considered?)

3 Which concepts or definitions of an accounting system are likely to be the easiest to empirically classify? Explain your answer.

4 Which concepts or definitions of an accounting system are likely to be the hardest to empirically classify? Explain your answer.

REFERENCES

AAA (1977) 'Committee on international accounting operations and education', *Accounting Review*, Supplement, 65–132. New York: American Accounting Association.

Choi, F.D.S. and Bavishi, V.B. (1980) 'International accounting standards: Issues needing attention', *Journal of Accounting*, March, 62–8.

Cooke, T.E. and Wallace, R.S.O. (1990) 'Financial disclosure regulation and its environment: A review and further analysis', *Journal of Accounting and Public Policy*, 9, 79–110.

Da Costa, R.C., Bourgeois, J.C. and Lawson, W.M. (1978) 'A classification of international financial accounting practices', *International Journal of Accounting*, Spring, 73–86.

Doupnik, T.S. and Salter, S.B. (1993) 'An empirical test of a judgmental international classification of financial reporting practices', *Journal of International Business Studies*, 24(1), 41–60.

Fitzgerald, R.D., Stickler, A.D. and Watts, T.R. (1979) *International Survey of Accounting Principles and Reporting Practices*. London: Price Waterhouse International/Butterworths.

Gray, S.J. (1988) 'Towards a theory of cultural influence on the development of accounting systems internationally', *Abacus*, 24(1), 1–15.

Hatfield, H.R. (1966) 'Some variations in practices in England, France, Germany and the US', *Journal of Accounting Research*, Fall, 169–82.

Mueller, G.G. (1967) *International Accounting*. London: Macmillan.

Mueller, G.G. (1968) 'Accounting principles generally accepted in the US versus those generally accepted elsewhere', *International Journal of Accounting*, Spring, 91–104.

Nair, R.D. and Frank, W.G. (1980) 'The impact of disclosure and measurement practices on international accounting classifications', *Accounting Review*, July, 426–50.

Nobes, C.W. (1982) 'A typology of international accounting principles and policies: A comment', *AUTU Review*, Spring, 62–5.

Nobes, C.W. (1984) *International Classification of Financial Reporting*. London: Croom Helm.

Oldham, K.M. (1987) *Accounting Systems and Practice in Europe*, 3rd edn. London: Gower.

Salter, S.B. and Doupnik, T.S. (1992) 'The relationship between legal systems and accounting practices: A classification exercise', *Advances in International Accounting*, 5, 3–22.

Seidler, L.J. (1967) 'International accounting – The ultimate theory course', *Accounting Review*, October, 775–81.

United Nations (1991) *Accounting Developments in Africa: Challenge of the 1990s*. New York: United Nations CTC.

Chapter 5

International harmonisation and standardisation

5.1 PURPOSE OF THE CHAPTER

The purpose of this chapter is to establish a comprehensive knowledge and understanding of the international accounting standard setting process, with particular reference to the International Accounting Standards Committee (IASC) and its work programme aimed at having core standards in place to the satisfaction of the International Organization of Securities Commissions (IOSCO) by 1998.

Learning objectives

After reading this chapter you should be able to:

- Describe the main international organisations seeking harmonisation or standardisation.
- Explain the nature and operations of the International Accounting Standards Committee.
- Understand the challenges facing the IASC in its work.
- Describe the main features of the Framework for the Preparation and Presentation of Financial Statements.
- Understand how multinational companies benefit from the availability of International Accounting Standards.

5.2 WORKING TOWARDS INTERNATIONAL CO-OPERATION

Harmonisation is a process by which accounting moves away from total diversity of practice. The end result is the state of harmony where all participants in the process cluster around one of the available methods of accounting, or around a limited number of very closely related methods. **Standardisation** is a process by which all participants agree to follow the same or very similar accounting practices. The end result is a state of uniformity.

A definition of 'harmony' takes a liberal view of what is meant by similarity of accounting method. It may be achieved as a result of natural forces such as changes in culture, growth of economic groupings, international trade, political dependency, or evolution of new securities markets. Such forces cause enterprises, accounting organisations or national regulators to learn from and imitate each others' practices.

A definition of 'uniformity' takes a much stricter view of what is meant by the same or very similar accounting practices. Achievement of uniformity within a defined period of time requires the intervention of a regulator or facilitator. The actions of international regulatory organisations seeking to achieve uniformity may provide one of the factors in the wider process of harmonisation.

There are organisations around the world which are seeking to harmonise aspects of international accounting practice or at least to foster understanding. Some are private sector federations of interested bodies, some are governmental or intergovernmental organisations, and some others rely on committed individuals for their continuity.

The following sections explain a variety of leading international accountancy organisations. Some operate at a regional level defined by geographic linking of more than one country or state. Others have a worldwide level of operation, although membership and geographical coverage may vary from one to the next.

5.2.1 Regional accountancy bodies

Regional accountancy bodies are in the main non-governmental organisations (NGOs). Although at the outset a number of these bodies had ambitions to develop accounting standards, little real success has been achieved. Most of these regional professional organisations have concentrated their energies on educational matters, organisation of conferences and the general dissemination of information to their members and the wider business community. Some have acted as effective pressure groups at global level, ensuring that their distinctive regional voice is heard in the international accounting standard setting process. The leading regional accountancy bodies are listed in Exhibit 5.1.

The lack of any significant progress in standard setting by regional bodies is partly due to the problem of enforcement. Non-governmental bodies generally lack the power to insist on compliance with their rules. For a regional accounting standard setting body to be effective one of the following methods of enforcement would be required:

- the professional accountancy bodies or auditing authorities of each member state of the region agree to apply or approve the regional standards rather than national variations
- those who govern companies (management or regulators) in each member state agree to apply or approve the regional standards rather than national variations
- national legislators or standard setters agree on the use of common regional standards
- national stock exchanges agree to accept the standards defined on a regional basis.

The first two of these conditions have not generally been achieved, probably because business which crosses national boundaries is international in nature rather than being contained to a specific region linking a group of companies or states. Standardisation has required the intervention of wider groupings of accountancy bodies and interested persons; intergovernmental organisations; and action by securities markets at an international level.

Exhibit 5.1 THE LEADING REGIONAL ACCOUNTANCY BODIES, 1997

ECSAFA **East, Central and Southern African Federation of Accountants**
This is a body which represents professional accountancy bodies in the region.

AAC **African Accounting Council**
Standardisation at an all-Africa level has been attempted through the AAC but with limited success. This has been due in part to the conflicting accountancy traditions of the former French and British colonial influences across Africa.

AFA **Association of Southeast Asian Nations (ASEAN) Federation of Accountants**
The economic linkages fostered by ASEAN led naturally to the linking of professional accountants. Brunei, Indonesia, Malaysia, the Philippines, Singapore and Thailand are the member nations.

CAPA **Confederation of Asian and Pacific Accountants**
Established by professional accountancy bodies as a forum for discussion of accounting problems met by accountants in Asia and Pacific countries.

FEE **Fédération des Experts Comptables Européens (Federation of European Accountants)**
Brings together professional bodies from European countries, including but not restricted to the EU, to work towards enhancing European harmonisation.

NFA **Nordic Federation of Public Accountants**
The NFA is a member of the IASC Board. It includes Denmark, Finland, Iceland, Norway and Sweden.

ASCA **Arab Society of Certified Accountants**

IAAA **InterAmerican Accounting Association**
Membership covers accountancy bodies in countries of Central and South America. Activities include translation of International Accounting Standards.

CCA **Caribbean Conference of Accountants**

5.2.2 Wider groupings of accountancy bodies and interested persons

There are organisations which have formed to link accountancy bodies and interested persons across national boundaries (*see* Exhibit 5.2). These have all formed as a result of various voluntary initiatives. They are not driven by national governments.

Central to international co-operation in accounting is the International Federation of Accountants (IFAC). Formed in 1977, its membership consists of professional accountancy bodies in 85 countries. Its objective is the development and enhancement of a co-ordinated worldwide accountancy profession and harmonised standards. IFAC is organised through a general assembly of all member associations; a Council of 15 members, elected by the general assembly; and a committee structure, membership of which is appointed by the Council.

Exhibit 5.2 ORGANISATIONS OF ACCOUNTANCY BODIES AND INTERESTED PERSONS LINKING ACROSS NATIONAL BOUNDARIES

IFAC	**International Federation of Accountants** Membership is similar to IASC but responsibilities are more diverse. Contributes to IASC budget. Important work in the area of auditing is done by IAPC (*see* below). IFAC also has committees dealing with Education, Ethics, Financial and management accounting, and the Public sector. Organises World Congress of Accountants every five years.
IAPC	**International Auditing Practices Committee** A committee of IFAC (*see* above). Issues exposure drafts and auditing guidelines, in order to improve uniformity of auditing practices. Members of IFAC undertake to promote national observance of IAPC guidelines where possible.
IASC	**International Accounting Standards Committee** Founded by private sector professional accountancy bodies with the purpose of issuing International Accounting Standards.
G4	**Group of Four (G4)** Accountancy bodies in the USA, Canada, the UK, Australia (G4) and New Zealand (G4+1) are working together to provide joint input to the development of the work of IASC and to influence international developments.
EAA	**European Accounting Association** International organisation bringing together institutional and individual membership from around the world. Organises annual conference and publishes an academic journal.
IAAER	**International Association for Accounting Education and Research** Academic community members concerned with issues in financial reporting.

Each committee is given responsibility in particular technical areas of IFAC work as diverse as education, ethics and the public sector. From the perspective of published financial information perhaps the most important of these committees is the International Auditing Practices Committee (IAPC). The IAPC issues International Auditing Guidelines (IAGs) under its own authority, setting down internationally recognised methods of conducting an independent examination of financial statements.

IFAC encourages international accountancy co-operation on a subglobal basis. To this end it recognises four regional accountancy bodies (*see* Exhibit 5.1) whose views are actively sought by IFAC committees as representing the distinctive views and interests of their members.

CAPA	Confederation of Asian and Pacific Accountants
ECSAFA	East, Central and Southern African Federation of Accountants
FEE	Fédération des Experts Comptables Européens (Federation of European Accountants)
IAAA	InterAmerican Accounting Association

119

Neither IFAC nor its recognised regional bodies have attempted directly to develop accounting standards at an international level. Instead IFAC accepts that the IASC is the major source of authoritative guidance on standardisation of international accounting practices.

5.2.3 Intergovernmental organisations

IASC works closely with a number of intergovernmental bodies. These are shown in Exhibit 5.3. These bodies co-operate with each other and with IASC.

Chapter 7 considers the work of the European Commission in more detail.

5.2.4 Organisations of securities markets and analysts

Exhibit 5.4 lists some of the co-ordinating organisations for securities markets, analysts and fund managers.

Securities markets regulators are particularly interested in the presentation of accounting information as a means of ensuring an efficient market. They have the power to accept or refuse a company's access to the market. The regulators seek to apply strict accounting requirements but also want to avoid undue restrictions which will inhibit growth of the market. They are able to enforce regulations on those companies which seek to raise finance through the stock market.

Analysts who are writing reports on companies need some reassurance about comparability and need to be aware of the usefulness of a standard approach to accounting practice when making international comparisons.

| **Exhibit 5.3** | INTERGOVERNMENTAL ORGANISATIONS, 1997 |

EU	**European Union** European Commission issues Directives which form a basis for national law within each member country. Accounting Directives (Fourth and Seventh) are largely concerned with harmonisation of presentation in financial statements.
OECD	**Organization for Economic Cooperation and Development** Established by 24 of the world's 'developed' countries to promote world trade and global economic growth. Is concerned with financial reporting by multinational companies. OECD has a Working Group on Accounting Standards. Issues guidelines for multinational companies, carries out surveys and publishes reports. Work extends to Central and Eastern Europe, e.g. the Coordinating Council on Accounting Methodology in the CIS.
ISAR	**Intergovernmental Working Group of Experts on International Standards of Accounting and Reporting** Operates within the United Nations, with a particular interest in accounting and reporting issues of the developing countries. Carries out surveys and publishes reports. Makes recommendations with regard to transnational companies.

Exhibit 5.4 ORGANISATIONS OF SECURITIES MARKETS AND ANALYSTS, 1997

IOSCO   International Organization of Securities Commissions

EASDAQ European Association of Securities Dealers Automatic Quotation system
A pan-European over-the-counter (OTC) securities market, requiring issuers to publish annual audited, and unaudited quarterly, financial statements, prepared under IASs, or using accepted national accounting standards with a reconciliation to IASs, or US GAAP.

AIMR   Association of Investment Management and Research
A US body which produced a report 'Financial Reporting in the 1990s and Beyond' containing forward-looking proposals.

EFFAS   European Federation of Financial Analysts' Societies
Has developed the European method of financial analysis. This involves a standardised approach to the classification and presentation of financial statements.

FEAS   Federation of Euro-Asian Stock Exchanges
20 member exchanges from 18 countries in Europe (outside EU and EFTA), Central and South Asia and the Middle East.

ICCFAA International Co-ordinating Committee of Financial Analysts' Associations
Has made a contribution by supporting progress in the direction of harmonisation.

5.3 OBJECTIVES OF THE IASC

The IASC is an independent body, not controlled by any particular government or professional organisation. Its main purpose is the achievement of uniformity in the accounting principles which are used by businesses and other organisations around the world concerned with financial reporting.

The IASC was formed in 1973 through an agreement made by professional accountancy bodies from Australia, Canada, France, Germany, Ireland, Japan, Mexico, the Netherlands, the UK and the USA.

The objectives of the IASC are stated in its Constitution as:

● to formulate and publish in the public interest accounting standards to be observed in the presentation of financial statements and to promote their worldwide acceptance and observance, and

● to work generally for the improvement and harmonisation of regulations, accounting standards and procedures relating to the presentation of financial statements.

The operations of the IASC are delegated to a Board appointed from the membership of the organisation. The Board benefits from receiving advice from an Advisory Council and a Consultative Group.

5.4 ORGANISATION OF THE IASC

5.4.1 Membership

Since 1983 the membership of IASC has included all the professional accountancy bodies that are members of IFAC (*see* Exhibit 5.5). A joint meeting of all members takes place every two and a half years. Although IASC is older than IFAC by four years, the creation of IFAC brought into being a global structure from which IASC

Exhibit 5.5 INTERNATIONAL DISTRIBUTION OF IASC MEMBERSHIP, 1996

Professional accountancy bodies in the following countries are members of IASC:

Argentina	Iceland	Philippines
Australia	India*	Poland
Austria	Indonesia	Portugal
Bahamas	Iraq	Romania
Bahrain*	Ireland	Saudi Arabia
Bangladesh	Israel	Sierra Leone
Barbados*	Italy	Singapore
Belgium	Jamaica*	Slovenia
Bolivia	Japan	South Africa
Botswana*	Jordan*	Spain
Brazil	Kenya*	Sri Lanka*
Bulgaria	Korea	Sudan
Canada	Kuwait*	Swaziland
Chile	Lebanon*	Sweden
Colombia	Lesotho	Switzerland
Croatia	Liberia	Syria
Cyprus*	Libya	Taiwan
Czech Republic	Luxembourg	Tanzania
Denmark	Malawi*	Thailand*
Dominican Republic	Malaysia*	Trinidad and Tobago*
Ecuador	Malta	Tunisia
Egypt	Mexico	Turkey
Fiji	Netherlands	Uganda*
Finland	New Zealand	UK
France	Nigeria*	USA
Germany	Norway	Uruguay
Ghana	Pakistan	Zambia
Greece	Panama	Zimbabwe*
Hong Kong	Paraguay	
Hungary	Peru	

* Standard setting bodies of these countries use IASs as the basis for their national requirements; also Brunei, the CIS, Mauritius, Mongolia, Oman, Papua New Guinea, the United Arab Emirates.

Source: *IASC Annual Review 1996*. Copyright © International Accounting Standards Committee (IASC), 166 Fleet Street, London EC4A 2DY, United Kingdom.

could obtain wider authority. IASC retains its independence from IFAC by having its own constitution that can be altered only by a meeting of members. However, the council of IFAC is responsible for electing the professional accountancy association members of the IASC board.

5.4.2 The Board of the IASC

Under the IASC constitution, the members of the IASC delegate responsibility for the activities of IASC to the Board. The Board has direct responsibility for all the technical work of IASC, including the approval of exposure drafts and IASs.

The Board includes representatives of the professional accountancy bodies in 13 countries. There are also financial analysts from Europe and North America and representatives of organisations representing preparers of financial statements. The European Commission, the Financial Accounting Standards Board (FASB), IOSCO and the Public Sector Committee of IFAC each sends observers.

In 1995 the IASC Board was restructured to provide greater representation for developing countries, preparers of financial statements and national standard setting bodies. Two new members representing business were the Federation of Swiss Industrial Holding Companies and the International Association of Financial Executives Institutes (IAFEI). A list of Board members is published in the IASC *Annual Report*.

5.4.3 Advisory Council

The Advisory Council was established on the recommendation of a working party reviewing the structure of the IASC. Council members are outstanding individuals in senior positions from backgrounds such as the accountancy profession, business and other users of financial statements. There are three stated functions of the Advisory Council.

1 **Set direction**

Review and comment on the strategy of the IASC Board, to ensure that the needs of its constituencies are being met

2 **Promotion and fund raising**
   – Promote participation in and acceptance of the work of the IASC by all interested parties
   – Assist with the raising of finance to enable IASC to carry out its activities, while ensuring IASC's independence

3 **Review and reporting**
   – Review IASC's budget and financial statements
   – Prepare an annual report for publication in the IASC Annual Review on the effectiveness of the Board.

The council is required to ensure that the independence and objectivity of the Board in making technical decisions on proposed IASs is not impaired. The Council should not participate in, or seek to influence, those decisions.

5.4.4 Consultative Group

The Consultative Group, established in 1981, advises the Board on all aspects of its work programme, plans and priorities. The Group plays an important role in the process of gaining acceptance for IASs. It includes representatives of international organisations of preparers and users of financial statements, intergovernmental organisations, development agencies, the academic community, and standard setting bodies. IASC works with members of the consultative group in gaining acceptance for standards and in meeting significant concerns.

5.4.5 Financing the IASC

The IASC has described itself as a 'low budget organisation', relying a great deal on help from persons around the world who are willing to give time to support its activities. Professional accountancy bodies make contributions, international organisations may give grants for specific projects. Sales of publications also make a contribution. In order to complete the core standards programme under the agreement with IOSCO, the Advisory Council undertook to help IASC increase its funding from 1995 onwards. Contributions from multinational companies are a potentially valuable source of finance and showed an almost fourfold increase in 1996 (*see* Exhibit 5.6). The Advisory Council attaches great importance to raising funds in a balanced way from many countries so that different countries can be seen to be making fair contributions.

Exhibit 5.6 SOURCES OF GROSS REVENUE AND MAJOR COSTS, 1996

Gross revenue	%	£000
Board Members and IFAC	29	701
Sales of publications	25	617
International accounting firms, companies and others in various countries	38	932
World Bank for project on agriculture	5	122
Miscellaneous	3	67
	100	2,439
Major costs		
Secretariat	61	1,258
Travel costs for Board and Committee members and promotions	28	565
Distribution of publications	11	233
	100	2,056

Source: IASC Annual Review, 1996. Copyright © International Accounting Standards Committee (IASC), 166 Fleet Street, London EC4A 2DY, United Kingdom.

5.5 OPERATION OF THE IASC

This section explains the procedures by which a proposal eventually becomes a standard. It then continues by exploring the challenges faced by the IASC which include the changing nature of membership of the Board; the potential lack of powers of enforcement; the impact of established national practices when a new standard is under development; political pressures on IASC; and the desire to survive as an organisation. A useful discussion of the operation of the IASC is provided by Cairns (1995).

5.5.1 Procedure for issuing a standard

First of all there has to be an idea. Ideas may come from board representatives, member bodies, members of the consultative group, other organisations and individuals and the IASC staff. Whatever the source, the first stage is a project proposal which is approved by the Board.

Following approval of a project proposal, the Board sets up a steering committee, chaired by a Board representative. There are usually representatives of the accountancy bodies in at least three other countries. The steering committee may also include experts in the subject. Where the topic forms part of IOSCO's list of core standards, an observer from IOSCO will be invited to join the steering committee.

The steering committee reviews all the accounting issues relating to the topic. It considers national and regional accounting requirements and practices and also has regard to the IASC's *Framework for the Preparation and Presentation of Financial Statements*. A statement of the key issues, called a Point Outline, is submitted to the Board.

The Board provides comments on the point outline, following which the steering committee prepares and publishes a draft statement of principles. The purpose of the draft statement is to set out the underlying accounting principles which will form the basis for the later preparation of an exposure draft (ED). It also describes alternative solutions considered by the steering committee and the reasons for rejection. The draft statement of principles is not reviewed by the Board at this stage and is thus not constrained by the Board's discussions. There is usually an exposure period of four months, during which comments are invited.

Once the comments have been received, the steering committee prepares a final statement of principles. This document is submitted to the Board for approval and then used for preparing an exposure draft of a proposed International Accounting Standard (IAS). Publication of the exposure draft includes an invitation to comment in an exposure period which may be as short as one month but is usually closer to six months.

After all the comments on the exposure draft have been received, the steering committee reviews the comments and prepares the IAS for review by the Board. There must be approval of at least three-quarters of the Board before publication is permitted.

This basic process may sometimes be augmented by issuing more than one exposure draft before developing an IAS. An example of the timing of a new project from start to completion is shown in Exhibit 5.7.

Exhibit 5.7 TARGET DATES FOR A NEW PROJECT: INTERIM FINANCIAL REPORTING

Commencement of project	November 1995
Issues Paper	May 1996
Comment deadline on Issues Paper	30 June 1996
Publish Draft Statement of Principles	31 August 1996
Comment deadline on Draft Statement of Principles (SOP)	30 November 1996
IASC Board approves final SOP	15 April 1997
IASC Board approves Exposure Draft (ED) based on SOP	30 June 1997
Comment deadline on ED	31 October 1997
IASC Board approves final Standard	31 March 1998

For many years, the publication of the IAS was the final stage of the process. In 1995 it was agreed that it would be desirable to have interpretations giving additional rulings on particular aspects of the standards. This would be an important aspect of ensuring the acceptance of IASs by the regulators of securities exchanges, particularly the US Securities and Exchange Commission (SEC). The work of preparing these interpretations will be in the hands of the Standing Interpretations Committee (SIC). The Committee will consider suggestions for agenda items from any source. The suggestion should be accompanied by a description of the problem and a brief proposal for a solution. When the Committee has agreed (maximum three out of 12 members dissenting) it will transmit the interpretation to the Board for final approval. The Board will not re-debate the issue but may veto publication if it sees a fundamental objection.

The first three SICs, issued in 1997, are listed in Exhibit 5.8.

Exhibit 5.8 LIST OF INTERPRETATIONS ISSUED BY STANDING INTERPRETATIONS COMMITTEE

SIC–D1	Consistency – Different Cost Formulas for Inventories
SIC–D2	Consistency – Capitalisation of Borrowing Costs
SIC–D3	Elimination of Unrealised Profits and Losses on Transactions with Associates

5.5.2 Membership

There has been an increasing tendency for representatives of national standard setters to take one of the seats allocated to the national board members. Membership is therefore changing from representatives of independent professional bodies to those holding the levers of power in national accounting standard setting. There has also been co-option to the Board in order to extend membership to producer and user groups. Observer status has been given to other regulators to reflect the wider business community.

Attention has been drawn to the apparent overrepresentation of the interests of developed nations on the Board of IASC. Questions have been raised as to whether the views and evidence of the developing countries, as a majority of the membership by number, are being heard and considered (Wallace, 1990). It was suggested in the same study that the most critical issue concerning the adoption of IASs was their relevance to developing countries.

5.5.3 Power of enforcement

The power of enforcement has diminished over time. When the IASC was founded its members agreed to use their best endeavours and persuasive influence to ensure compliance with the standards. It was intended that each professional accounting association within the IASC would ensure that the external auditors would satisfy themselves as to observance of the standards and would disclose cases of non-compliance; appropriate action was to be taken against any auditor who did not follow these recommendations. Later, revised wording of the agreement among members acknowledged that IASC pronouncements would not override the standards followed by individual countries. By 1982, the agreement no longer contained the requirement that the auditors should disclose the extent of non-compliance. The failure of the agreement to make any mention of obligations placed on auditors continues; the route to enforcement has now moved in the direction of applying the powers of national stock exchanges which subscribe to the IOSCO agreement on the acceptance of core standards.

5.5.4 Impact of national practices

Empirical research studies have from time to time been made on the effectiveness of IASC. A study of the application of accounting methods by major companies in a range of major accounting nations over the 1970s found that IASs had little impact on the accounting practices of the companies surveyed. Except for a few instances, companies which followed a particular accounting method prior to the promulgation of the standard continued to follow the same practice after the standard was issued (Evans and Taylor, 1982). Of the initial 16 standards issued, eight permitted alternative accounting treatments, and hence allowed flexibility (Choi and Bavishi, 1982). That flexibility was attributed to attempts to accommodate the variety of treatments that existed in reporting standards already adopted by developed countries.

By the mid-1980s researchers were observing that the IASs had not succeeded in changing existing national standards, or in establishing new standards. This was perceived as being due to lack of enforceability. The programme of IASs was seen as having value in so far as it succeeded in codifying generally accepted practice (McKinnon and Janell, 1984). By the end of the 1980s there was a high degree of flexibility within the standards. Studies showed that in eight of the 24 international standards issued up to 1984, alternative solutions were permitted (Most, 1984).

By 1989 research was observing that IASs were strongly influenced by the accounting practices of developed counties, and there appeared to be a potentially patronising assumption that the accounting standards of these countries should be adopted by others (Rivera, 1989). The author of the 1989 study identified problems as:

- lack of a structured theoretical accounting framework underlying the preparation of specific standards

- a multiplicity of permitted reporting options introduced in the current standards

- a tendency to address only those issues developed in or related to advanced economic environments where sophisticated markets and information prevail

- lack of enforceability of international standards at local and international level.

5.5.5 Political pressure

D.J. Hayes, US representative to the IASC, referred to the problem of 'intervention by international governmental bodies' such as the United Nations (Hayes, 1980).

A study comparing selected IASC standards to similar standards in the UK and USA concluded that those two countries exerted very significant levels of influence on IASC standards (Hove, 1990). The study suggested that this was because both countries had devoted a great deal of effort and resources to developing an extensive and well codified set of standards, and, therefore, would have the most to lose if an international standard were fundamentally different from their own. The study noted, however, that the influence of the UK and USA was unlikely to be in the interests of less developed countries

5.5.6 Survival as an organisation

The IASC faces the problems applying to any international organisation that seeks to survive on the basis of voluntary co-operation. In 1990, the IASC was described as an organisation with a will to survive which sustains itself by adapting to change and the demands of its internal and external environment (Wallace, 1990). Such an organisation would be risk averse, seeking to minimise the likelihood of not attaining its chosen objective. This in turn requires the organisation to ensure that any group likely to determine its continued survival as an organisation is not offended. For the IASC, this leads to standards which are acceptable to the majority of, although not necessarily to all, members.

That 1990 view of the IASC may be modified considerably in the light of the subsequent support from IOSCO which provides the potential for enforcement which IASC previously lacked. However, it is important to consider whether IOSCO is truly international in its influence or whether some members of IOSCO are more influential than others. If the IASC is now being directed down the route of serving the needs of capital markets of developed countries, there may remain a question of the balance of influence on IASC as between developed and developing economies.

5.6 CHANGING STYLES OF STANDARD SETTING BY IASC

Various phases have been identified in the standard setting process operated by the IASC (*see* Exhibit 5.9). This section discusses those phases and the factors which have influenced a change of direction.

Exhibit 5.9 PHASES IN THE DEVELOPMENT OF THE WORK OF THE IASC

Stage		
1	Issue of general standards	1973–9
2	Development of more detailed standards	1980–9
3	Reduction of flexibility – Comparability project	1990–5
4	IOSCO core standards project	1995–8

5.6.1 The early standards

The first standards from the IASC in the 1970s were basic, straightforward and largely non-controversial. They had a high level of generality and concentrated primarily on matters of presentation and disclosure rather than more controversial issues of measurement (Nair and Frank, 1981).

5.6.2 Increasing use of permitted alternatives

Standards issued during the 1980s dealt with more complex issues reflecting problematic subjects under active consideration in the leading accounting countries. That period of developing detailed standards led to increasingly frequent use of options within standards. These were deemed to be acceptable options within which the prevailing accounting practices of most of the major accounting nations could be accommodated. In this way the IASs did not pose a threat to national differences. It had been noted that most IASs had two acceptable alternative treatments because of the necessity of ensuring that the required 75% of the 14 voting members of the board voted in favour (see comments of Arthur R. Wyatt, IASC, in Fleming, 1991).

Purvis *et al.* (1991), analysing compliance with IASs as indicated in an IASC survey of 1988, found a high level of national conformity with those standards issued early in the life of the IASC but much lower levels of conformity for those issued closer to 1988. The authors observed that the results were not surprising since the nature of the earlier standards, addressing fundamental issues at a general level, meant that countries could comply with minimum need for change, especially in view of the permitted alternative treatments. Furthermore the passage of time permitted countries which initially had non-conforming standards to adopt new ones in line with IASs.

A reaction to the extent of choice in IASs began in 1989 with a project to reduce flexibility. A second phase began in 1995, intended to meet the demands of IOSCO for an acceptable set of core standards.

5.6.3 Comparability project

In 1989 the IASC launched a major initiative to bring greater comparability to financial statements.

5.6.3.1 Exposure draft E 32

The initiative was represented by an exposure draft, E 32, which contained proposals to reduce the number of alternative treatments allowed in the IASs issued to date. The exposure draft contained recommendations on matters of free choice that might have had a material effect on the definition, recognition, measurement and display of net income and assets and liabilities in the financial statements of an enterprise. E 32 was seen as the first stage in a continuing process of improvement; it acknowledged that free choice had been necessary in the past to gain acceptance of certain standards.

The IASC also decided to reformat all IASs in such a way as to highlight the significant points of principle in bold italic type. The document would also present, in normal type, explanations of each significant point of principle in the standard.

5.6.3.2 Need for change

The main impetus for these changes was the increase in cross-border financing. Wyatt (in Fleming, 1991) claimed that the American Institute of Certified Public Accountants (AICPA) along with other accounting bodies had agreed in writing to attempt to ensure that the standard setting bodies in their countries moved toward international standards. IOSCO encouraged the IASC in its project and, according to Wyatt, intended to encourage securities regulators in member countries to require use of IASs, providing that the IASC could produce results of adequate quality.

5.6.3.3 Statement of intent

The initial proposals contained in E 32 were modified and explained further in a Statement of Intent issued in 1990. The Statement of Intent explained that, where it was not possible to gain agreement on a single recommended approach, there would be a 'benchmark treatment' and an 'allowed alternative treatment'. The word 'benchmark' had gained greater acceptance than the word 'preferred' used in the exposure draft E 32. The benchmark treatment was to be regarded as a point of reference for the Board when making its choice between alternatives.

Following on from the comparability project, the trend was to make IASs more prescriptive. Some national accounting traditions appear to be at variance with the resulting standards and removal of previously permitted options to focus on one method only has inevitably been a process of robust negotiation. In that process, some observers have identified increasing dominance of the Anglo-Saxon model of reporting.

5.6.3.4 Potential for success

The potential for the comparability project to succeed depended on the level of conformity existing at the time of the project and the subsequent intentions of national standard setters with regard to the subsequent revision of IASs. Research has been undertaken assessing the extent to which the financial reporting practices of countries agreed with the accounting practices contained in the standards issued by the IASC following the comparability project. The results showed that there was substantial agreement (Salter *et al.*, 1996; Roberts *et al.*, 1996). Partners in major firms of accountants were asked to indicate the percentage of significant organisations in their country which already followed the recommended accounting treatments (benchmark or allowed alternative) contained in the IASs that were to take effect from January 1995. The average level of national agreement with the IASs was 68.4%, while the level of agreement for the countries included both in their study and in this book were: USA 75.96%, UK 74.78%, France 71.69%, Malaysia 70.80%, Australia 64.75%, The Netherlands 63.94%, Japan 63.86% and Germany 57.70%.

In no single country did corporate accounting practice exactly match the revised rules resulting from the comparability project. The countries with the least change required in bringing existing practice into line with the revised IASs tended to belong to the UK/US tradition. Countries with the greatest change required were typically 'code law' countries adopting a conservative approach to measurement of accounting income and assets.

5.6.3.5 Evaluation of the comparability project

Some of the more interesting debates resulting from the comparability project will be discussed in Chapter 6, in explaining the context of specific standards as they are operating in their revised form. The comparability project was a bold initiative to reduce options but there are views that it did not entirely succeed because of strong interest groups. It has been suggested that the standard setters of the member states of the EU did not give sufficient signs of unity on issues where the US influence was dominant (a detailed discussion has been provided by Gernon *et al.*, 1990). The comparability project did achieve some reduction of options compared with accounting practice in the UK and USA but left a number of allowed alternatives in areas where UK and US practice differed. There were also many controversial aspects of accounting which the comparability project did not address (Weetman *et al.*, 1993).

5.6.4 Acceptance of IASs by IOSCO: The core standards programme

5.6.4.1 Relations with IOSCO

In its present form IOSCO dates from the mid-1980s. Its objectives include

- the establishment of standards and effective surveillance of international securities transactions
- provision of mutual assistance to ensure the integrity of the markets by a rigorous application of standards and by effective enforcement against offenders.

A working party was established to cooperate with the IASC with a view to identifying accounting standards which security regulators might be ready to accept in the case of multinational offerings. At its annual conference in 1987 a resolution was passed to promote the use of common standards in accounting and auditing practice. In that same year IOSCO became a member of the IASC Consultative Group. IOSCO gave active support to the E 32 comparability project, and in 1996 IOSCO accepted observer status on the IASC board.

5.6.4.2 Core standards programme

In 1995 the IASC made a significant agreement with IOSCO. The agreement stated that the goal of both IASC and IOSCO was that financial statements prepared in accordance with IASs can be used in cross-border offerings and listings as an alternative to national accounting standards. The achievement of this goal was made conditional on completion of the IASC Work Programme, scheduled for 1999. The Work Programme concentrates on a core set of standards and has come to be referred to more commonly as 'the core standards programme'. By March 1996 the Board had revised the target date to March 1998, in response to requests from international companies and from members of IOSCO. The revised target saved 15 months on the original plan.

The core standards programme is a very significant agreement because hitherto companies which had a listing on stock exchanges outside their own country were sometimes required to prepare their financial statements using the generally accepted accounting principles of that country. That condition was applied in particular by the US SEC, and the detail of the additional disclosures was perceived as deterring many companies from seeking a listing in US stock markets. The initial acceptability of IASs and the various targets set for revision of core standards are shown in Exhibit 5.10.

5.6.4.3 Likelihood of success

During 1995, the European Commission moved towards putting the power of the EU behind the harmonisation process. It indicated that it would associate more closely with the work being undertaken by IASC and IOSCO towards harmonisation of accounting standards. The Commission took the view that only the IASC had the resources to produce harmonisation of accounting standards in a reasonable time scale.

The agreement with IOSCO regarding the establishment of core standards is consistent with the steps already being taken by many securities regulators in domestic markets. The London Stock Exchange accepts IASs where foreign issuers do not follow requirements of the UK, another member state of the EU, or the USA. Foreign companies using IASs are allowed to register on many stock exchanges in continental Europe and the Asia/Pacific region. The US SEC has agreed to accept cash flow statements which conform to IAS 7. It will also accept the treatment required by IASs on amortisation of goodwill, the definitions of acquisitions and pooling of interest, and the translation of financial statements of subsidiaries in hyperinflationary economies.

In effect, IASs were already acceptable for cross-border listings on most major stock exchanges before the core standards programme was put in place. The notable exceptions were the USA, Canada and Japan. Japan and Canada have indicated by various actions that they are favourably disposed to IASs and so the key factor for acceptability is the US SEC. In the view of one firm of international financial advisers, the widespread use of IASs, even before the IOSCO agreement, has lowered the analytical cost associated with global investing and increased investor interest in non-US stocks.[1]

---

[1] Merrill Lynch, *Accounting Bulletin*, 51 (1997), extract reproduced on IASC web pages

Exhibit 5.10 INITIAL ACCEPTABILITY OF IASs FOR THE PURPOSE OF IOSCO CORE STANDARDS

International Accounting Standards considered core and acceptable to IOSCO in their form as at 1995

IAS 2*	Inventories
IAS 7	Cash Flow Statements
IAS 8*	Net Profit or Loss for the Period, Fundamental Errors and Changes in Accounting Policies
IAS 11*	Construction Contracts
IAS 16*	Property, Plant and Equipment
IAS 18*	Revenue
IAS 20	Accounting for Government Grants and Disclosure of Government Assistance
IAS 21*	The Effects of Changes in Foreign Exchange Rates
IAS 22*	Business Combinations
IAS 23*	Borrowing Costs
IAS 24	Related Party Disclosure
IAS 27	Consolidated Financial Statements and Accounting for Investments in Subsidiaries
IAS 28	Accounting for Investments in Associates
IAS 29	Financial Reporting in Hyperinflationary Economies
IAS 31	Financial Reporting of Interests in Joint Ventures

International Accounting Standards considered core but are unacceptable to IOSCO in their form as at 1995

IAS 9*	Research and Development Costs
IAS 10	Contingencies and Events Occurring After the Balance Sheet Date
IAS 17*	Accounting for Leases

International Accounting Standards considered core by IOSCO but already subject to review by IASC as at 1995

IAS 1	Disclosure of Accounting Policies
IAS 5*	Information to be Disclosed in Financial Statements
IAS 13	Presentation of Current Assets and Current Liabilities
	(*all under review together for incorporation in a major revision of IAS 1*)
IAS 12	Accounting for Taxes on Income
IAS 14	Reporting Financial Information by Segments
IAS 19*	Retirement Benefit Costs
IAS 25*	Accounting for Investments

International Accounting Standards not considered core by IOSCO as at 1995

IAS 4	Depreciation Accounting
IAS 15	Information Reflecting the Effects of Changing Prices
IAS 26	Accounting and Reporting by Retirement Benefit Plans
IAS 30	Disclosure in the Financial Statements of Banks and Similar Financial Institutions
IAS 32	Financial Instruments: Disclosure and Presentation

Note: * Indicates that the IAS was listed for attention in the comparability project exposure draft E 32
Source: Cairns (1995), pp. 62–3, drawing on *IASC Insight*, September 1994. Reproduced with permission of David Cairns and Accountancy Books. *IASC Insight* material copyright © International Accounting Standards Committee (IASC), 166 Fleet Street, London EC4A 2DY, United Kingdom.

5.7 IASC FRAMEWORK

In 1989 the IASC issued a framework which may be regarded as a statement of key principles to be applied in accounting practices (IASC, 1989). The framework is not itself an accounting standard. The purpose of the framework document is to assist:

- the Board in development and review of International Accounting Standards
- the Board in promotion of harmonisation by providing a basis for reducing the number of alternative accounting treatments permitted by IASs
- national standard setting bodies in developing national standards
- preparers of financial statements in applying IASs and dealing with topics on which IASs do not yet exist
- auditors in forming an opinion as to whether financial statements conform to IASs
- users in interpreting financial statements prepared in conformity with IASs
- those interested in the formulation of IASs by providing information about the approach used by the IASC.

The framework deals with:

- the objectives of financial statements
- the qualitative characteristics that determine the usefulness of information in financial statements
- the definition, recognition and measurement of the elements from which financial statements are constructed
- concepts of capital and capital maintenance.

The framework document is concerned with general purpose financial statements which normally include a balance sheet, an income statement, a statement of change in financial position, and those notes and other statements and explanatory material that are an integral part of the financial statements. 'Financial statements' does not include reports by directors, statements by the chairman, or discussion and analysis by management that may be included in an entity's financial or annual report.

The users of financial statements are identified as present and potential investors, employees, lenders, suppliers and other trade creditors, customers, government and their agents and the public. Although all of the information needs of these users cannot be met by financial statements, it is reasonable to think that providing the information needs of investors will ensure that most of the needs of other users can be satisfied.

5.7.1 Objective of financial statements

The objective of financial statements is to provide information about the *financial position, performance* and *changes in financial position* of an enterprise that is useful to a wide range of users in *making economic decisions*. They do not provide all the information users need since they largely portray the financial effects of past events and do not necessarily provide non-financial information. Financial statements also show the results of the stewardship of management or the accountability of management for the resources entrusted to it. In particular:

1 *Economic decisions* taken by users require an evaluation of the ability of an enterprise to generate cash and the timing and certainty of their generation.

2 The *financial position* of an entity is affected by the economic resources it controls, its financial structure, its liquidity and solvency, and its capacity to adapt to changes in the environment in which it operates. Information about financial structure is useful in predicting future borrowing needs and how future profits and cash flows will be distributed amongst those with an interest in the enterprise and how further finance is likely to be raised.

3 Information about *performance* and the variability of performance of an enterprise is required to assess potential change in economic resources and is useful in predicting the capacity of the enterprise to generate cash flow and its efficiency in employing additional resources.

4 Information about *changes in financial position* is useful in order to assess an enterprise's investing, financing and operating activities.

In order to meet this objective financial statements are prepared on the underlying assumptions of an accruals based accounting system and that the enterprise is a going concern and will continue in operation for the foreseeable future.

5.7.2 Qualitative characteristics

In order that financial statements should be useful to the users, the following qualitative characteristics should be present and the constraints noted.

5.7.2.1 Understandability

Information should be readily understandable by users who have a reasonable knowledge of business and economic activities and accounting and a willingness to study the information with reasonable diligence.

5.7.2.2 Relevance

Information is relevant where it influences the economic decisions of users by helping them to evaluate past, present or future events or confirming, or correcting, their past evaluation. The relevance of information is affected by its materiality – i.e. whether its omission or misstatement could influence the economic decisions of users. Materiality provides a threshold or cut-off point for the provision of information.

5.7.2.3 Reliability

Reliability is expressed in terms of freedom from error and bias: information represents what it purports to represent. Within this concept of reliability are issues of faithful representation, substance over form, neutrality, prudence and completeness:

- *faithful representation*: a balance sheet and an income statement should represent faithfully the transactions and other events which meet the recognition criteria

- *substance over form*: information is presented in accordance with the substance and economic reality and not merely the legal form
- *neutrality*: information has not been selected or presented so as to encourage a predetermined result or outcome
- *prudence*: there is a degree of caution in the exercise of judgements such that assets or income are not overstated and liabilities or expenses are not understated, but not permitting the deliberate understatement or overstatement of items
- *completeness*: information must be complete within the bounds of materiality and cost.

5.7.2.4 Comparability

Financial statements of an entity should be capable of being compared through time. Financial statements of different entities should be comparable for the same period. Measurement and display of the financial effect of similar transactions and other events must be carried out in a consistent way throughout an enterprise and over time for that enterprise and in a consistent way for different enterprises.

5.7.2.5 Constraints on relevant and reliable information

The constraints are timeliness, balanced against benefits and costs. There are also constraints in selecting a balance of qualitative characteristics:

- *timeliness*: if there is undue delay in reporting information it may lose its relevance; management need to balance the relative merits of timely reporting and the provision of reliable information
- *balance between benefit and cost*: in imposing accounting standards on preparers accounting standard setting organisations should apply the constraint that benefits derived from information should exceed the costs of providing it
- *balance between qualitative characteristics*: there may be constraints in the balance between relevance and reliability – those seeking reliability may ask for more detail than would be considered necessary on grounds of relevance; those emphasising the relevance of information may have to recognise some sacrifice of reliability.

5.7.3 True and fair view or fair presentation

The IASC framework does not include a discussion of the concept of 'true and fair' but it asserts that the application of the principal qualitative characteristics and of appropriate accounting standards normally results in financial statements that convey what is generally understood as a true and fair view. The framework gives 'presenting fairly' as equivalent wording.

5.7.4 Definition, recognition and measurement

The broad classes of transactions portrayed in financial statements are called elements of financial statements. The elements relating to the measurement of financial position are assets, liabilities, and equity. Those relating to the measurement of performance are income and expenses. For an item to be reported in a balance sheet or income statement it must first of all meet the definition of an element and then satisfy the criteria for recognition. These elements are defined as follows:

- an *asset* is a resource controlled by the enterprise as a result of past events and from which future economic benefits are expected to flow to the enterprise
- a *liability* is a present obligation of the enterprise arising from past events, the settlement of which is expected to result in an outflow from the enterprise of resources embodying economic benefits
- *equity* is the residual interest in the assets of the enterprise after deducting all its liabilities
- *income* is increases in economic benefits during the accounting period in the form of inflows or enhancements of assets or decreases of liabilities that result in increases in equity, other than those relating to contributions from equity participants
- *expenses* are decreases in economic benefits during the accounting period in the form of outflows or depletions of assets or incurring of liabilities that result in decreases in equity, other than those relating to distributions to equity participants.

An item that meets the definition of an element should be recognised (i.e. incorporated in words and numerical amount in accounting statements) if (and only if):

(a) it is probable that any future economic benefits associated with the item will flow to or from the enterprise, and

(b) the item has a cost or value that can be measured with reliability.

Items that meet the definition of an element but fail to meet the criteria for recognition may warrant disclosure in the notes to the financial statements if knowledge of the item is considered to be relevant to the evaluation of the results of the enterprise.

5.7.4.1 Assets

An asset is recognised in the balance sheet when it is probable that the future economic benefit will flow to the enterprise and the asset has a cost or value that can be measured reliably. When expenditure has been incurred that meets the definition of an asset but fails the recognition test because it is considered improbable that economic benefit will flow to the enterprise beyond the current accounting period, the transaction should be recognised as an expense in the income statement.

5.7.4.2 Liabilities

A liability is recognised in the balance sheet when it is probable that an outflow of resources embodying economic benefits will result from the settlement of a present obligation and the amount at which the settlement will take place can be measured reliably.

5.7.4.3 Income

Income is recognised in the income statement when an increase in future economic benefits related to an increase in an asset or decrease of a liability has arisen that can be measured reliably.

5.7.4.4 Expenses

Expenses are recognised in income statements when a decrease in future economic benefits relating to a decrease in an asset or an increase of a liability has arisen that can be measured reliably.

5.7.5 Measurement: concepts of capital and capital maintenance

The IASC framework is least specific when discussing the measurement methods that should be used in recognising the elements of the financial statements. It merely lists the different measurement bases that are currently used, namely Historical cost; Current cost; Realisable value; and Present value. The framework declines to express a preference for any of these bases of measurement.

In the context of making no recommendation on measurement it is perhaps surprising that the framework ventures into capital maintenance. It offers the guidance that the selection of the appropriate concept of capital (i.e. invested money, invested purchasing power or physical output capacity) and hence concept of capital maintenance by an enterprise should be based on the needs of the users of its financial statements.

The concept of capital maintenance provides the link between the concepts of capital and profit and imposes some limitation on the measurement processes adopted.

The framework points out that selection from the available concepts of capital maintenance and measurement bases provides a wide range of accounting models that can be used in the preparation of financial statements. It is claimed that the framework is applicable to the range of accounting models and that at present there is no intention to prescribe one particular model for general adoption.

5.8 THE INTERNATIONAL ACCOUNTING STANDARDS

The IASs in issue at February 1998 are shown in Exhibit 5.11. In each case the title of the standard is followed by the date of first issue and the date of reformatting under the comparability project, or of subsequent re-issue through amendments brought about either by the comparability project or the achievement of the core standards programme. It will be seen from Exhibit 5.11 that all IASs have been revised or reissued in the 1990s, making them a comprehensively up-to-date collection.

Although it is useful to have the standards listed in numerical sequence, for purposes of considering the impact and relevance of the standards it is more convenient to rearrange them according to the accounting issues they address. This rearrangement is presented in Exhibit 5.12.

Chapter 6 contains summaries of the key aspects of each standard, explaining where there were controversial issues to settle in the comparability project. It gives an indication of the work required to move forward from the comparability project in meeting the IOSCO target of mid-1998.

Exhibit 5.11 IASs IN ISSUE, FEBRUARY 1998

IAS 1	Presentation of Financial Statements	Issued 1997, effective for accounting periods starting 1 July 1998, replaces IAS 1, 5 and 13
Former IASs remaining effective until 1 July 1998		
IAS 1	*Disclosure of Accounting Policies*	*Issued 1975, Reformatted 1995[1]*
IAS 5	*Information to be Disclosed in Financial Statements*	*Issued 1976, Reformatted 1995*
IAS 13	*Presentation of Current Assets and Current Liabilities*	*Issued 1979, Reformatted 1995*
IAS 2[2]	Inventories	Issued 1993,[3] superseding 1975 version
IAS 3	Consolidated Financial Statements	Superseded by IAS 27 and IAS 28
IAS 4	Depreciation Accounting	Issued 1976, Reformatted 1995
IAS 6	Accounting Responses to Changing Prices	Superseded by IAS 15
IAS 7[2]	Cash Flow Statements	Issued 1992, superseding 1977 version
IAS 8[2]	Net Profit or Loss for the Period, Fundamental Errors and Changes in Accounting Policies	Issued 1993,[3] superseding 1978 version
IAS 9	Research and Development Costs	Issued 1993,[3] superseding 1978 version
IAS 10	Contingencies and Events Occurring After the Balance Sheet Date	Issued 1978, Reformatted 1995
IAS 11[2]	Construction Contracts	Issued 1993,[3] superseding 1979 version
IAS 12	Income Taxes	Issued 1996, superseding 1979 version, Reformatted 1995
IAS 14	Reporting Financial Information by Segments	Issued 1997, superseding 1981 version, Reformatted 1995
IAS 15	Information Reflecting the Effects of Changing Prices	Issued 1981, Reformatted 1995
IAS 16[2]	Property, Plant and Equipment	Issued 1993,[3] superseding 1982 version
IAS 17	Leases	Issued 1997, superseding 1982[3] version Reformatted 1995
IAS 18[2]	Revenue	Issued 1993,[3] superseding 1982 version
IAS 19	Employee Benefits	Issued 1998, superseding 1993 and 1982[3] versions
IAS 20[2]	Accounting for Government Grants and Disclosure of Government Assistance	Issued 1983, Reformatted 1995
IAS 21[2]	The Effects of Changes in Foreign Exchange Rates	Issued 1993,[3] superseding 1983 version
IAS 22[2]	Business Combinations	Issued 1993,[3] superseding 1983 version
IAS 23[2]	Borrowing Costs	Issued 1993,[3] superseding 1984 version
IAS 24[2]	Related Party Disclosure	Issued 1984, Reformatted 1995
IAS 25	Accounting for Investments	Issued 1986,[3] Reformatted 1995
IAS 26	Accounting and Reporting by Retirement Benefit Plans	Issued 1987, Reformatted 1995
IAS 27[2]	Consolidated Financial Statements and Accounting for Investments in Subsidiaries	Issued 1989, Reformatted 1995
IAS 28[2]	Accounting for Investments in Associates	Issued 1989, Reformatted 1995
IAS 29[2]	Financial Reporting in Hyperinflationary Economies	Issued 1989, Reformatted 1995
IAS 30	Disclosure in the Financial Statements of Banks and Similar Financial Institutions	Issued 1990, Reformatted 1995
IAS 31[2]	Financial Reporting of Interests in Joint Ventures	Issued 1990, Reformatted 1995
IAS 32	Financial Instruments: Disclosure and Presentation	Issued 1995
IAS 33	Earnings per Share	Issued 1997
IAS 34	Interim Financial Reporting	1998
IAS xx[4]	Intangible Assets	1998
IAS xx	Discontinuing Operations	1998
IAS xx	Impairment of Assets	1998

[1] 'Reformatted 1995' indicates that the reformatted version applied from 1 January 1995
[2] Indicates that the IAS was acceptable to IOSCO as a core standard without further revision
[3] Indicates that the IAS was listed for attention in the Comparability Project exposure draft E 32
[4] xx Indicates that the IAS number has not been allocated at the time of writing

Exhibit 5.12 CLASSIFICATION OF IASs, BY ACCOUNTING ISSUE

Disclosure and presentation

General aspects consolidated in IAS 1
effective starting 1 July 1998

IAS 1   Presentation of Financial Statements
effective to 1 July 1998

IAS 1   Disclosure of Accounting Policies
IAS 5   Information to be Disclosed in Financial Statements
IAS 13   Presentation of Current Assets and Current Liabilities
Specific aspects
IAS 7   Cash Flow Statements
IAS 8   Net Profit or Loss for the Period, Fundamental Errors and Changes in Accounting Policies
IAS xx   Discontinuing Operations
IAS 14   Reporting Financial Information by Segments
IAS 24   Related Party Disclosure
IAS 33   Earnings per Share
IAS 34   Interim Financial Reporting

Asset recognition and measurement
IAS 2   Inventories
IAS 4   Depreciation Accounting
IAS 16   Property, Plant and Equipment
IAS xx   Impairment of Assets
IAS 23   Borrowing Costs
IAS 25   Accounting for Investments
IAS 9   Research and Development Costs
IAS xx   Intangible Assets

Liability recognition and measurement
IAS 10   Contingencies and Events Occurring After the Balance Sheet Date
IAS 12   Income Taxes
IAS 17   Leases
IAS 19   Employee Benefits
IAS 32   Financial Instruments: Disclosure and Presentation

Recognition of economic activity
IAS 11   Construction Contracts
IAS 18   Revenue
IAS 20   Accounting for Government Grants and Disclosure of Government Assistance

Measurement
IAS 15   Information Reflecting the Effects of Changing Prices
IAS 29   Financial Reporting in Hyperinflationary Economies

Group accounting
IAS 21   The Effects of Changes in Foreign Exchange Rates
IAS 22   Business Combinations
IAS 27   Consolidated Financial Statements and Accounting for Investments in Subsidiaries
IAS 28   Accounting for Investments in Associates
IAS 31   Financial Reporting of Interests in Joint Ventures

Specialist industries
IAS 26   Accounting and Reporting by Retirement Benefit Plans
IAS 30   Disclosure in the Financial Statements of Banks and Similar Financial Institutions

5.9 NATIONAL ACCOUNTING REQUIREMENTS

The agreement between IASC and IOSCO, if carried to a successful conclusion, may provide a very different emphasis on international accounting standards after the turn of the century. National standard setting bodies will be consulting their constituencies well ahead of the establishment of topics for the IASC agenda, so that national interests may be represented in the early stages of development.

We have already seen that during 1995 the European Commission decided that the establishment of a European accounting standards board was not on its agenda. The reasons for rejecting the idea were centred on fears that such a body would create an expensive and long-drawn-out process which would add another layer to EU national standards and might detract from the objective of global harmonisation.

Because the Commission is the custodian of European Law, derived from the Directives, there will be a need to ensure that, as the Work Programme of the IASC

Exhibit 5.13 EXAMPLES OF RECENT ACTIONS IN SPECIFIC COUNTRIES
(taken from IASC announcements)

- A spokesman for the German government has said that it proposes to accept consolidated financial statements prepared in accordance with International Accounting Standards [IASs] for domestic purposes in Germany.

- Malta put in place a new Companies Act with effect from 1 January 1996. This requires companies to use generally accepted accounting principles which are in turn defined by reference to International Accounting Standards

- The Institute of Chartered Accountants of Barbados will adopt all International Accounting Standards from January 1996 as the benchmark for generally accepted accounting principles in Barbados.

- China is about to issue a core set of accounting standards that are based on, and broadly comply with, International Accounting Standards.

- In Australia, the standard setting boards have agreed to start a project, with the support of the Australian Stock Exchange, with the aim of ensuring that compliance with Australian accounting standards results in compliance with International Accounting Standards.

- Zimbabwe has new Companies Act disclosure requirements from May 1996, based largely on requirements of International Accounting Standards

- From 1997 the UK's Chartered Association of Certified Accountants will allow its students – including over 70,000 based outside the UK – to sit examinations based on International Accounting Standards, as an alternative to UK standards or local variants.

- In May 1997, the Council of the IFAC admitted the Chinese Institute of Certified Public Accountants to membership of IFAC and IASC. As agreed by the IASC Board in June 1996, the People's Republic of China will now take up a seat as an observer at IASC Board meetings from July 1997.

Source: IASC Annual Review, 1995, 1996; IASC Insight, July 1996, June 1997. Copyright © International Accounting Standards Committee (IASC), 166 Fleet Street, London EC4A 2DY, United Kingdom.

moves forward, there is no conflict with the Fourth and Seventh Directives on company law. If differences are found there may be changes in the IASs. On the other hand it may be that international authoritative opinion is sufficiently strong to persuade the Commission that it should review the Directives.

More generally, it is clear that little will be gained from the agreement between IASC and IOSCO if multinational companies are required to present two sets of financial statements because national practice differs from the IASs. At present some countries use IASs as the basis for national standards, while others use them

| Exhibit 5.14 | CURRENT STATUS OF IASs IN 67 COUNTRIES |

● IASs used as national standards, with explanatory material added Croatia, Cyprus, Kuwait, Latvia, Malta, Oman, Pakistan, Trinidad and Tobago	8
● IASs used as national standards, plus national standards developed for topics not covered by IASs Malaysia, Papua New Guinea	2
● IASs used as national standards, with some cases of modification for local conditions or circumstances Albania, Bangladesh, Barbados, Colombia, Jamaica, Jordan, Kenya, Poland, Sudan, Swaziland, Thailand, Uruguay, Zambia, Zimbabwe	14
● National accounting standards separately developed but based on and similar to the relevant IAS, national standards generally provide additional explanatory material only China, Iran, Philippines, Slovenia, Tunisia	5
● National accounting standards separately developed but based on and similar to the relevant IAS in most cases; however, some standards may provide more or less choice than IASs; no reference is made to IASs in national standards Brazil, Czech Republic, France, India, Ireland, Lithuania, Mauritius, Mexico, Namibia, the Netherlands, Norway, Portugal, Singapore, the Slovak Republic, South Africa, Switzerland, Turkey	17
● As in previous case except that each standard includes a statement that compares the national standard with the relevant IAS Australia, Denmark, Hong Kong, Italy, New Zealand, Sweden, Yugoslavia	7
● National standards developed separately Austria, Belgium, Canada, Finland, Germany, Japan, Korea, Luxembourg, Spain, the UK, the USA	11
● National standards do not exist at the present time Romania	1
● No national standards, IASs not formally adopted but usually used Botswana, Lesotho	2

Source: *IASC Insight*, October 1997, p. 15. Copyright © International Accounting Standards Committee (IASC), 166 Fleet Street, London EC4A 2DY, United Kingdom.

as a benchmark against which to compare national practices. A few countries have practices which differ from IASs and there is strong national pressure for such differences to remain.

The standard setting bodies in many developing countries are using IASs as the basis for national requirements although there are some who question the desirability of wholesale adoption without regard for differing economic circumstances. Examples of recent national activities are set out in Exhibit 5.13.

The current status of IASs was surveyed and reported in *IASC Insight* in October 1997. The results of the survey are shown in Exhibit 5.14.

5.10 MULTINATIONAL COMPANIES

As indicated in subsection 3.4.1, it has become common for companies to express their accounting results by reference to an internationally accepted approach. This has been perceived as being more acceptable to the investing public and to stock exchange regulators. At present, companies have two internationally recognised approaches from which to choose – US GAAP and IASs.

There is an increasing number of companies now presenting financial statements that conform with IASs. Three approaches may be identified.

1 In some cases, national requirements conform with IASs. In such instances there may be no practical problem from the point of view of the company but it is important for the user of the financial statements to know that this is the case. There are examples of companies which provide an explicit statement of conformity with IASs as well as national standards.

   Groupe Saint Louis (France) (Exhibit 5.15) provides such an example. Schering (Germany) (Exhibit 5.16) presents its financial statements in accordance with IASs but explains that IASs and national law may not always agree in all respects. STORA (Sweden) (Exhibit 5.17) lists the ways in which accounting policies adopted differ from IAS. Fiat (Italy) (Exhibit 5.18) presents similar information.

Exhibit 5.15 GROUPE SAINT LOUIS: ACCOUNTING POLICIES

> Note 1 – ACCOUNTING POLICIES
>
> A – GENERAL
>
> The Saint Louis consolidated financial statements have been prepared in accordance with French accounting principles relating to consolidated accounts.
>
> The principles and methods used are also in conformity with the pronouncements of the International Accounting Standards Committee.

Source: Groupe Saint Louis SA (France), annual report, 1995, p. 45

Exhibit 5.16 SCHERING: ACCOUNTING POLICIES

NOTES ON THE CONSOLIDATED FINANCIAL STATEMENTS FOR 1996

(1) General principles

The Consolidated Financial Statements of Schering AG are prepared in accordance with the German Commercial Code (HGB). The Standards of the International Accounting Standards Committee which apply for 1996 are also observed where they do not conflict with the accounting and valuation principles of the German Commercial Code. Differences arise in particular from our application of the principles of recognition and prudence. However, they do not have a material effect on the 1996 Consolidated Financial Statements.

Source: Schering AG (Germany), annual report, 1996, p. 38

Exhibit 5.17 STORA: ACCOUNTING POLICIES

Accounting and valuation principles

GENERAL

In preparing the consolidated accounts, STORA has followed the recommendations of the Swedish Financial Accounting Standards Council. STORA also follows the recommendations issued by the International Accounting Standards Committee (IASC), with certain exceptions, as described below, under separate heading. No changes have been made in STORA's Accounting and Valuation Principles since the preceding year's consolidated financial accounts were published.

IMPORTANT DEVIATIONS FROM IASC RECOMMENDATIONS

Reporting of hydropower assets that were sold on a sale and leaseback basis
STORA holds an option to repurchase hydropower assets that were sold during 1986 and 1987. The option agreement gives STORA the right to repurchase these assets in any of the following years: 1998, 2003 and 2007. During the period up to the time the option may be exercised, STORA is responsible for the management of the assets and has pledged to purchase all produced power at a price that covers the owners' financing costs, among other expenses. The transaction has been reported as a sale of assets, which is not in accordance with the recommendations of the IASC.

Capitalization of interest expense in connection with major investments
The acquisition value of machinery and buildings does not include interest expense paid during the construction and assembly time. According to the IASC, such interest expense should be included in the acquisition value.

Revaluation of fixed assets
STORA has made a revaluation of its fixed assets in a manner that is not in accordance with the IASC recommendations.

Reporting of proposed dividend as a liability
In accordance with Swedish law, the proposed dividend is not reported as a liability.

Statement of changes in financial position
The way in which STORA presents its Statement of changes in financial position differs from the general form recommended by the IASC.

When translating the cash flow in foreign subsidiaries, STORA also deviates from the method prescribed by the IASC. As a result, the Statement of changes in financial position contains the exchange-rate differences that arise when translating the opening balance of the foreign subsidiaries.

Source: STORA (Sweden), annual report, 1996, pp. 51–2

Exhibit 5.18 FIAT: ACCOUNTING POLICIES

Notes to the Consolidated Financial Statements as of December 31, 1996 and 1995

PRINCIPLES OF CONSOLIDATION AND SIGNIFICANT ACCOUNTING POLICIES

The consolidated financial statements have been prepared from the statutory financial statements of the Group's single companies or consolidated Sectors approved by the Boards of Directors and adjusted, where necessary, by the directors of the companies to conform with Group accounting principles and to eliminate tax-driven adjustments. The Group's accounting policy respects the requirements of the effective Italian legislation and are consistent with International Accounting Standards, except for I.A.S. 9, which requires that development costs be recorded as an asset on the balance sheet. Consistent with prior years, the costs of developing new products and/or processes are included in the results of operations in the period in which such costs are incurred in line with the principle of conservatism and with international practice in the automobile sector, which is the Group's primary line of business.

Source: Fiat Group (Italy), annual report, 1996, p. 73

Exhibit 5.19 SAIPEM: ACCOUNTING POLICIES

Notes to the Consolidated Financial Statements

PREPARATION CRITERIA

The consolidated financial statements as of and for the year ended 31 December 1996 have been prepared in accordance with the criteria established by paragraph 3 of Decree Law No. 127 of 9 April 1991 and comply with accounting principles of the 'Consigli Nazionali dei Dottori Commercialisti e dei Ragionieri' and where silent, those of the International Accounting Standards Committee (I.A.S.C.)

The true and correct representation of the balance sheet and the income statement has not deviated from that laid out in Paragraph 4 of article 29 of the Decree.

The consolidated financial statements comprise the financial statements of Saipem S.p.A. and also the Italian and foreign subsidiaries over which Saipem S.p.A. exerts direct and indirect control by way of majority holdings of voting rights or of voting rights sufficiently large enough to exert a dominant influence at a general meeting. Those subsidiaries which are held as joint ventures are also stated using the proportionate method. Companies exclusively controlled within the scope of subsequent sale, those in liquidation and other minor shareholdings that are not relevant to the entity have been excluded from the consolidation.

The consolidation principles adopted are in line with those of the prior year.

Source: Saipem SpA (Italy), annual report, 1996, p. 34

Saipem (Exhibit 5.19) provides an instance of using International Accounting Standards where national accounting standards fail to cover a specific area.

2 Some companies include in the financial report a reconciliation showing the differences between national accounting practices and the requirements of IASs. Statoil (Norway) (Exhibit 5.20) provides such a reconciliation.

Exhibit 5.20 STATOIL: RECONCILIATION OF PROFIT TO IASs

19. Reconciliation of accounts between Norwegian Accounting Standards and International Accounting Standards

As stated in note 1, the NGAAP differ in some areas from the IAS. A reconciliation of profit before taxation and shareholder's equity from the IAS to the NGAAP is given below.

NOK million	1996	1995	1994
Profit before taxation – IAS	17 924	14 689	16 900
Net capitalised/expensed exploration costs	(368)	(277)	51
Net capitalised interest on building loans	(584)	(926)	(466)
Change in unrealised gains	228	(979)	(282)
Depreciation of capitalised exploration costs and building loan interest	659	573	536
Profit before taxation – NGAAP	17 859	13 080	16 739
Shareholder's equity – IAS	37 142	33 832	30 215
Capitalised exploration costs	(3 061)	(2 795)	(2 602)
Capitalised interest on building loans	(4 696)	(4 679)	(4 245)
Change in unrealised gains	(1 285)	(1 499)	(521)
Deferred taxation	6 133	6 264	5 323
Shareholder's equity – NGAAP	34 233	31 123	28 170

Source: Statoil Group (Norway), annual report, 1996, p. 54

3 Other companies present full financial statements in conformity with IASs, either as the main financial statements or in addition to the financial statements complying with national accounting practices.

Keramik Holdings AG Laufen (Switzerland) (Exhibit 5.21) presents full financial statements according to IASs. Statoil (Norway) (Exhibit 5.22) gives equal prominence to the IAS-based accounting statements and the national accounting statements. Nokia (Finland) (Exhibit 5.23) appears to give precedence to the financial statements prepared according to IASs. It provides a reconciliation between US GAAP and IAS results. The Nokia example provides insight into the competition between IASs and US GAAP. Time will tell which of these two becomes the dominant means by which non-US multinationals will choose to achieve the wider international acceptance of their annual reports.

In the *Annual Report* for 1995, the IASC reported that it was aware of more than 200 major companies using IASs in their financial statements. On the web pages in September 1997 IASC listed over 400 companies. At that date over 70 were companies in Switzerland (not a member of the EU and therefore not eligible for 'mutual' recognition). There were 41 companies registered in Kuwait, 36 in Canada, 32 in France, 21 in Sweden, 14 in Turkey, 12 in South Africa, 11 in Hong Kong, 11 in Finland, and smaller numbers in a wide spread of countries.

Germany is one country where companies have traditionally been reluctant to report using accounting principles other than those of Germany itself. Bayer became the first German conglomerate to announce that it would use IASs for its Group accounting financial statements of 1994 (*see* Exhibit 5.24). This followed a decision by Daimler–Benz to seek a full listing in the US securities market

Exhibit 5.21 KERAMIK HOLDINGS: STATEMENT OF POLICY ON CONSOLIDATION

> ## Consolidation and accounting principles
>
> The consolidated financial statements of the Laufen Group have been drawn up in accordance with the requirements of the International Accounting Standards Committee (IASC).

Source: Keramik Holdings AG Laufen (Switzerland), annual report, 1996, p. 32

Exhibit 5.22 STATOIL: INCOME STATEMENT

INCOME STATEMENT – STATOIL GROUP

Norwegian 1994	Accounting 1995	Standards 1996	NOK million	International 1996	Accounting 1995	Standards 1994
			Sales and other operating revenue			
98 535	101 080	**124 017**	Operating revenue	**124 017**	101 080	98 450
(14 820)	(15 705)	**(17 451)**	Sales tax, excise duties	**(17 451)**	(15 705)	(14 820)
448	1 149	**422**	Share of net profit in associated companies (12)	**415**	1 142	440
84 163	86 524	**106 988**	Net operating revenue (2, 3)	**106 981**	86 517	84 070
			Operating costs			
41 570	45 013	**54 883**	Cost of goods sold (3)	**54 883**	45 013	41 567
19 158	19 420	**23 100**	Operating and administration costs (4)	**23 100**	19 420	19 158
1 475	1 297	**1 644**	Exploration costs (6)	**1 277**	1 020	1 528
6 540	6 902	**8 828**	Depreciation (7)	**9 487**	7 474	7 076
68 743	72 632	**88 455**	Total operating costs	**88 747**	72 927	69 329
15 420	13 892	**18 533**	**Operating profit**	**18 234**	13 590	14 741
1 319	(812)	**(674)**	Financial items (8, 9)	**(310)**	1 099	2 159
16 739	13 080	**17 859**	**Profit before taxation (19)**	**17 924**	14 689	16 900
11 247	8 474	**12 752**	Taxation(10)	**12 627**	9 414	11 520
1	10	**16**	Minority shareholders' interest	**16**	10	1
5 491	4 596	**5 091**	**Net profit**	**5 281**	5 265	5 379

Source: Statoil Group (Norway), annual report, 1996, p. 39

Exhibit 5.23 NOKIA: RECONCILIATION OF US GAAP AND IAS RESULTS

U.S. GAAP

The principal differences between IAS and U.S. GAAP are presented below together with explanations of certain adjustments that affect consolidated net income and total shareholders' equity as of and for the years ended December 31:

	1996 MFIM	1995 MFIM
Reconciliation of net income		
Net income reported under IAS	3 263	2 232
U.S. GAAP adjustments:		
Deferred income taxes	−129	426
Pension expense	−19	133
Development costs	32	−844
Sale–leaseback transactions	4	4
Other adjustments	235	36
Deferred tax effect of U.S. GAAP adjustments	−84	176
Net income under U.S. GAAP	3 302	2 163
Presentation of net income under U.S. GAAP		
Income from continuing operations	2 954	3 884
Discontinued operations:		
Profit/loss from operations, net of income tax of FIM14 million in 1996 and FIM33 million in 1995	41	−249
Gain/loss on disposal, net of income tax of FIM124 million in 1996 and net of income tax benefit of FIM516 million in 1995	307	−1 472
Gain/loss from discontinued operations	348	−1 721
Net income	3 302	2 163
Reconciliation of shareholders' equity		
Total shareholders' equity reported under IAS	15 925	13 806
U.S. GAAP adjustments:		
Deferred income taxes	242	371
Pension expense	29	48
Development costs	−535	−567
Sale–leaseback transactions	−32	−36
Other adjustments	88	−256
Deferred tax effect of U.S. GAAP adjustments	123	207
Total shareholders' equity under U.S GAAP	15 840	13 573

Source: Nokia Corporation (Finland), annual report, 1996, p. 58

(*see* Chapter 3, Case study 3.1). Daimler–Benz consequently reported its 1993 financial statements under US GAAP as well as German accounting principles.

In December 1995 the German company Deutsche Bank announced that it would present financial statements in compliance with IASs. Others followed, and by September 1997 there were 10 German companies stating that they used IASs in their consolidated accounts.

| Exhibit 5.24 | ENCOURAGING GERMAN COMPANIES TO FOLLOW IASs |

> In relation to the decision by Bayer, Liesl Knorr, a partner in KPMG Cologne and the acting Secretary-General of IASC said:
>
> > Many large German companies would like to see Germany adopt the approach taken in France and Switzerland, where groups of companies use national requirements for the financial statements of individual enterprises, but are free to use International Accounting Standards in the group financial statements. Then we would see many more German groups presenting financial statements to international investors under internationally recognised principles without compromising the domestic investor and without the cost of producing consolidated financial statements under two or more sets of rules.

Source: *IASC Insight*, March 1995, p. 3. Copyright © International Accounting Standards Committee (IASC), 166 Fleet Street, London EC4A 2DY, United Kingdom.

5.11 SUMMARY AND CONCLUSIONS

This chapter has shown that there are many organisations working towards achievement of harmonisation and standardisation. Not all seek to be active at a global level, some being satisfied with regional action. The only international organisation which has sustained a programme of accounting standards is the IASC. The expertise and accumulated experience of the IASC has increasingly been recognised by other international bodies. Some bodies which are in a position to enforce use of accounting standards across national boundaries are now support-ing the work of the IASC in the context of developing and applying a set of core standards; however there remain some unanswered questions about the eventual acceptance which will be given by the most significant national standard setting bodies and the extent to which the IASC may have to lean towards such bodies in order to achieve acceptance. Chapter 6 continues this theme by explaining the key features of each standard and the progress made in each case towards reducing the options in international practice.

QUESTIONS

Objectives of the IASC (5.3)

1 To what extent do the stated objectives of the IASC duplicate work already done by other international organisations that have an interest in accounting matters?

2 To what extent do the stated objectives of the IASC provide something more than the work already done by other international organisations that have an interest in accounting matters?

Organisation of IASC (5.4)

1 What are the benefits and potential limitations of having an Advisory Council?

2 What are the benefits and potential limitations of having a Consultative Group?

3 What mechanisms exist to ensure the independence of the IASC as a standard setting body? Is there any potential risk that the financing arrangements for the IASC might jeopardise its independence? What other factors might influence independence?

Operation of the IASC (5.5)

1 Is the process for issuing a standard sufficient to ensure that all interested parties are consulted? What are the benefits and potential limitations of the process?

2 Is the IASC able to be effective in enforcing its standards? To what extent do established national practices in developed countries inhibit the work of the IASC?

3 Is there a long-term future for the IASC?

Changing styles of standard setting by the IASC (5.6)

1 How, and why, has the nature of the work of the IASC changed over time?

2 Was the 1989 comparability project a success?

3 What necessitated the implementation of the core standards project?

Framework (5.7)

1 Why did the IASC decide it was necessary to issue a framework document in 1989?

2 What possible explanations are there for the measurement section being the least well developed section of the framework document?

National accounting requirements (5.9)

1 To what extent will the work of the IASC in the core standards programme be acceptable to regulators in the EU?

Multinational companies (5.10)

1 What is the role of multinational companies in disseminating accounting practice which conforms to IASs?

REFERENCES

Cairns, D. (1995) *A Guide to Applying International Accounting Standards*. London: Accountancy Books/The Institute of Chartered Accountants in England and Wales.

Choi, F.D.S. and Bavishi, V.B. (1982) 'Financial Accounting Standards: A multinational synthesis and policy framework', *International Journal of Accounting*, Fall, 159–83.

Coopers and Lybrand International (1993) *International Accounting Summaries: A Guide for Interpretation and Comparison*. New York: John Wiley.

Evans, T.G. and Taylor, M.E. (1982) 'Bottom line compliance with the IASC: A comparative analysis', *International Journal of Accounting Education and Research*, Fall, 115–28.

Fleming, P.D. (1991) 'The growing importance of International Accounting Standards', *Journal of Accountancy*, September.

Gernon, H., Purvis, S.E.C. and Diamond, M.A. (1990) 'An analysis of the implications of the IASC's comparability project', School of Accounting, University of Southern California.

Hayes, D.J. (1980) 'The IASC – recent developments and current problems', *International Journal of Accounting*, Fall.

Hove, M.R. (1990) 'The Anglo-American influence on International Accounting Standards: The case of the disclosure standards of the IASC', *Research in Third World Accounting*, vol. 1. London: JAI Press.

IASC (1989) 'Framework for the Preparation and Presentation of Financial Statements', contained in *International Accounting Standards, 1997*. London: International Accounting Standards Committee.

McKinnon, S.M. and Janell, P. (1984) 'The International Accounting Standards Committee: A performance evaluation', *International Journal of Accounting Education and Research*, Spring, 19–34.

Most, K.S. (1984) *International Conflict of Accounting Standards, a Research Report*. Vancouver: The Canadian Certified General Accountants' Research Foundation.

Nair, R.D. and Frank, W.G. (1981) 'The harmonisation of International Accounting Standards, 1973–1979', *International Journal of Accounting, Education and Research*, Fall, 61–77.

Purvis, S.E.C., Gernon, H. and Diamond, M.A. (1991) 'The IASC and its comparability project', *Accounting Horizons*, 5(2), 25–44.

Radebaugh, L.H. and Gray, S.J. (1997) *International Accounting and Multinational Enterprises*, 4th edn. New York: John Wiley.

Rivera, J.M. (1989) 'The internationalisation of accounting standards: Past problems and current prospects', *International Journal of Accounting, Education and Research*, 24 (4), 320–41.

Roberts, C.B., Salter, S.B. and Kantor, J. (1996) 'The IASC comparability project and current financial reporting reality: An empirical study of reporting in Europe', *British Accounting Review*, 28, 1–22.

Salter, S.B., Roberts, C.B. and Kantor, J. (1996) 'The IASC comparability project: A cross-national comparison of financial reporting practices and IASC proposed rules', *Journal of International Accounting and Taxation*, 5(1), 89–111.

Wallace, R.S.O. (1990) 'Survival strategies of a global organisation: The case of the International Accounting Standards Committee', *Accounting Horizons*, 4(2), 1–22.

Weetman, P., Adams, C.A. and Gray, S. J. (1993) 'Issues in International Accounting Harmonisation: The Significance of UK/US Accounting Differences and Implications for the IASC's Comparability Project', *Research Report*, 33. London: Chartered Association of Certified Accountants.

This chapter also draws on material contained in IASC publications, particularly:

IASC Annual Review (various issues).

IASC Insight (published several times during a year).

IASC, International Accounting Standards, published annually.

Various Exposure Drafts and Statements, as indicated in the chapter.

The IASC web site.

Chapter 6

The international accounting standards

6.1 PURPOSE OF THE CHAPTER

The purpose of this chapter is to establish knowledge and understanding of the International Accounting Standards (IASs) produced by the IASC. The chapter also explains the progress towards reducing options which began with the comparability project of 1989 and culminated in the work programme establishing core standards to the satisfaction of the International Organization of Securities Commissions (IOSCO). The chapter will provide a background against which to evaluate the national accounting practices which are explained and discussed in later chapters.

Learning objectives

After reading this chapter you should be able to:

- Explain the key issues and main principles of each International Accounting Standard.

- Understand the aims and achievements of the comparability project and the subsequent work programme of the IASC in reducing options available under international standards.

- Relate the International Accounting Standards to the framework document in categories of assets, liabilities, recognition, measurement, group accounting and special needs of particular user groups.

- Compare the published accounting policies of any company listed on a national stock exchange with the relevant International Accounting Standards and form an opinion on the extent to which the company's policies are consistent with them

Exhibit 5.11 in Chapter 5 (p. 139) contains a table listing IASs in chronological order of date of first issue, Exhibit 5.12 (p. 140) then rearranges them according to the accounting issues they address. This rearrangement is repeated in Exhibit 6.1.

Exhibit 6.1 CLASSIFICATION OF IASs, BY ISSUE

Disclosure and presentation
General aspects consolidated in IAS 1
effective starting 1 July 1998
IAS 1   Presentation of Financial Statements
effective to 1 July1998
IAS 1   Disclosure of Accounting Policies
IAS 5   Information to be Disclosed in Financial Statements
IAS 13 Presentation of Current Assets and Current Liabilities
Specific aspects
IAS 7   Cash Flow Statements
IAS 8   Net Profit or Loss for the Period, Fundamental Errors and Changes in Accounting Policies
IAS xx Discontinuing Operations
IAS 14 Reporting Financial Information by Segments
IAS 24 Related Party Disclosure
IAS 33 Earnings per Share
IAS 34 Interim Financial Reporting

Asset recognition and measurement
IAS 2   Inventories
IAS 4   Depreciation Accounting
IAS 16 Property, Plant and Equipment
IAS xx Impairment of Assets
IAS 23 Borrowing Costs
IAS 25 Accounting for Investments
IAS 9   Research and Development Costs
IAS xx Intangible Assets

Liability recognition and measurement
IAS 10 Contingencies and Events Occurring After the Balance Sheet Date
IAS 12 Income Taxes
IAS 17 Leases
IAS 19 Employee Benefits
IAS 32 Financial Instruments: Disclosure and Presentation

Recognition of economic activity
IAS 11 Construction Contracts
IAS 18 Revenue
IAS 20 Accounting for Government Grants and Disclosure of Government Assistance

Measurement
IAS 15 Information Reflecting the Effects of Changing Prices
IAS 29 Financial Reporting in Hyperinflationary Economies

Group accounting
IAS 21 The Effects of Changes in Foreign Exchange Rates
IAS 22 Business Combinations
IAS 27 Consolidated Financial Statements and Accounting for Investments in Subsidiaries
IAS 28 Accounting for Investments in Associates
IAS 31 Financial Reporting of Interests in Joint Ventures

Specialist industries
IAS 26 Accounting and Reporting by Retirement Benefit Plans
IAS 30 Disclosure in the Financial Statements of Banks and Similar Financial Institutions

This chapter summarises the key issues and main content of each standard. It explains where there were controversial issues to settle in the comparability project of 1989 and indicates the further work required in order to meet the IOSCO target for completion of the core standards project.

When reading any IAS, it is important to note that, in the language of standard setting, 'should' is interpreted as 'must' and 'may' is interpreted as 'is permitted'.

6.2 DISCLOSURE AND PRESENTATION

Disclosure and presentation of information is fundamental to providing the users of financial statements with information which meets their particular needs. IASs have hitherto taken two routes to disclosure and presentation. One route dealt with general issues and the other with specific aspects. Standards of a general nature covered disclosure of accounting policies, types of information to be presented in financial statements and the presentation of current assets and current liabilities. Standards of a more specific nature focused on the reporting of cash flow; disclosure of fundamental errors; changes in accounting policy; segmental reporting; and the disclosure of related parties and their transactions with the enterprise. The common thread in all these standards is the tension between being open with those who have a legitimate right to information and preserving the commercial confidentiality which gives the enterprise its competitive advantage.

6.2.1 Presentation of financial statements

IAS 1, *Presentation of Financial Statements*, was issued in 1997, replacing three standards:

IAS 1   Disclosure of Accounting Policies (issued 1975)
IAS 5   Information to be Disclosed in Financial Statements (issued 1976)
IAS 13   Presentation of Current Assets and Current Liabilities (issued 1979)

All three IASs had been reformatted in 1995 without revision in principle. IAS 1 (revised) adopts the particular contents of those three standards but also contains new material and amends some aspects of presentation in other standards. IAS 1 (revised) takes effect for periods starting on or after 1 July 1998. The existing three standards continue to apply until that date.

6.2.1.1 Key issues

The objective of IAS 1 is to improve comparability of financial statements. This includes both comparability from one period of time to the next for a particular entity and comparability within the same period of time for more than one entity. IAS 1 brings up to date many of the ideas in the early standards which were forward-looking when issued but are now accepted as normal practice. It sets out concepts, guidelines and minimum requirements which reflect developments in thinking on presentation of financial statements.

6.2.1.2 Approach in IAS 1

Underlying concepts are listed as:

- fair presentation
- accounting policies
- going concern
- accrual basis of accounting
- consistency of presentation
- materiality and aggregation
- offsetting
- comparative information.

The most interesting of these is 'fair presentation' which was not an explicit criterion of the three IASs which are being replaced. It is defined in the standard as 'present fairly' without mentioning the phrase 'true and fair' which appeared in the framework document (para. 46) as an alternative phrase to 'present fairly' . The change in emphasis could be seen as indirect evidence of a stronger US influence. The US wording is 'fair presentation in accordance with generally accepted accounting principles'. The words 'true and fair view' may be seen on the one hand as allowing a higher degree of flexibility and judgement but on the other hand as permitting a looser approach to matters of detail.

The paragraphs on accounting policies emphasise the importance of selecting and applying accounting policies so as to achieve fair presentation. This is a different emphasis from that in the original IAS 1 which was to disclose accounting policies so as to permit comparisons. Disclosure of accounting policies has, over a period of years, become accepted as standard international practice and the change in emphasis in IAS 1 reflects that change of approach.

IAS 1 prescribes the minimum structure and content of basic financial statements as:

- balance sheet (current/non-current distinction not required)
- profit and loss account/income statement (operating/non-operating separation)
- cash flow statement
- statement showing changes in equity (various formats allowed).

It also deals with notes to the accounts; a summary of accounting policies; and disclosure of compliance with IASs. This must be genuine compliance with IASs and not merely a compliance with national standards which may have some similarities to, and some departures from, IASs. There is provision in IAS 1 of an 'override' to be used in very limited and rare circumstances to meet the requirement that financial statements should fairly present an enterprise's results and position. This means that a company may depart from an IAS for justifiable reason, but must give an explanation and disclose the effect of the departure. The circumstances are that a transaction is of a type that could not reasonably have been considered when the relevant standard was developed, and the use of the standard would be misleading. The existence of conflicting national requirements would not be sufficient to justify departures in financial statements prepared under IASs.

Illustrative structures of financial statement are appended to IAS 1. The appendix is not part of the proposed standard and is therefore not intended to be mandatory. The use of a suggested format for presentation, even in an appendix, is a new departure for IASs. The format has similarities with, although it is not identical to, formats of the type found in the Fourth and Seventh Directives of the EU.

The Statement showing changes in equity is a compromise which allows both the US format showing all changes in equity and the UK format showing total recognised gains and losses of the period. The UK approach must be accompanied by a note showing all changes in equity. The US-type format will include as a subtotal the total gains and losses of the period.

6.2.1.3 Reducing the options

IAS 1, IAS 5 and IAS 13 did not require attention in the comparability project of 1989. The exposure draft E 53, which led up to IAS 1, updated and brought into one document general aspects of disclosure and presentation.

E 53 sought to improve comparability and so effectively reduce options in disclosure. There is one topic where, in principle, an option remains. IAS 13 allowed a choice as to whether or not current assets and current liabilities should be presented as separate classifications in the balance sheet. That choice was preserved in E 53 and IAS 1. Such apparent freedom seems strange in a programme of reducing options. However it is of relatively minor importance because in practice few countries fail to make the distinction. Furthermore this is purely a disclosure issue. The classification of assets and liabilities does not affect the measurement of profit.

The exposure draft E 53 included a proposal for a 'statement of non-owner movements in equity' as a report which would highlight items, such as unrealised gains and movements due to foreign currency translation, moving through reserves rather than through the income statement. This did not receive support during the exposure period. Performance measurement is to be addressed in a separate project, addressing wider issues across a number of existing standards.

Comment on E 53 resulted in the inclusion in IAS 1 of the limited over-ride described earlier.

6.2.2 Cash flow statements

IAS 7, issued 1992, superseding funds flow statement of 1977.

6.2.2.1 Key issues

The purpose of IAS 7 is to provide information which is useful to users of financial statements in making economic decisions. It assumes that such economic decisions require an evaluation of the ability of an enterprise to generate cash and cash equivalents and also an assessment of the timing and certainty of the generation of cash. The standard requires an enterprise to present a cash flow statement as an integral part of its financial statements.

6.2.2.2 Approach in IAS 7

Cash flows should be classified according to whether they arise from operating, investing or financing activities.

There are two ways of reporting cash flows from operating activities. The *direct* method requires separate disclosure of each major class of gross cash receipt and gross cash payment. The *indirect* method permits adjustment to the net profit or loss identified in the profit and loss account to eliminate the effects of transactions of a non-cash nature. There is no **benchmark** guidance on these alternatives but enterprises are encouraged to report cash flows from operating activities using the direct method.

The total cash flows from operating, investing and financing activities will equal the change in *cash and cash equivalents*, defined as short-term, highly liquid investments (having a maturity of three months or less from the date of acquisition).

The standard also encourages enterprises to disclose, by way of a note to the accounts, additional information that may be relevant to users, including amounts of undrawn borrowing facilities; amounts in each major category of activity relating to joint ventures reported using proportional consolidation; and amounts in each major category of activity for each reported industry and geographical segment.

6.2.2.3 Reducing the options

IAS 7 was fundamentally revised in 1992. The previous version dealt with statements of changes in financial position, which concentrated on changes in the funding of the enterprise. The revision concentrates on changes in cash and cash equivalents. In making that change, the IASC was reflecting changing international thinking where it had been recognised that statements covering all changes in financial position were complex and did not help users' understanding so effectively as statements of changes in cash position. The revision did not reduce choice between the direct and indirect method of preparing the operating cash flow.

There are differences from one country to the next as to precisely what is included in 'cash and cash equivalents', but these should be seen in the context of a much more significant overall change in moving to a cash flow-based statement. IAS 7 is acceptable to IOSCO as a core standard.

6.2.3 Net profit or loss for the period, fundamental errors and changes in accounting policies

IAS 8, issued 1978, superseded 1993.

6.2.3.1 Key issues

Particular difficulties arise when unusual circumstances cause a change in the outcome of an event already reported. Difficulties for accounting practice are also encountered where a change in one accounting period invalidates comparability with earlier periods. An unusual item arising in one period may cause problems for comparability.

The general proposition underpinning the standard is that all items of income and expense recognised in a period should be included in the determination of the net profit or loss for the period. This proposition is applied in recommending treatment for four difficult areas: extraordinary items; discontinued operations; the effect of fundamental errors; and the cumulative effect of changes in accounting policy. The common aspect is that all give rise to problems of comparability from one accounting period to the next.

6.2.3.2 Approach in IAS 8

Extraordinary items arise from events or transactions that are clearly distinct from the ordinary activities of the enterprise and therefore are not expected to recur frequently or regularly. Ordinary activities of an enterprise are those activities undertaken as part of its business. Net income (net profit) should be divided into two components on the face of the profit and loss account: (a) profit or loss from ordinary activities; (b) extraordinary items.

The standard asserts that virtually all items of income and expenditure arise from ordinary activities and only on rare occasions does an event or transaction give rise to an extraordinary item. The two examples of events normally giving rise to extraordinary items are (a) expropriation of assets, (b) an earthquake or other natural disaster.

When items from ordinary activities are of such size, nature or incidence that they are relevant to explaining the performance of the enterprise, their nature and amount should be separately disclosed. Disclosure of such items is normally made in the notes to the financial statements.

The effect of a *discontinued operation*, while generally to be regarded as part of the ordinary activities of an enterprise, will demand separate and extended disclosure which should include (1) the gain or loss on discontinuance and the accounting policy used to measure that gain or loss and (2) the revenue and profit or loss from the ordinary activities of the operation for the current period and corresponding amounts for prior periods.

Fundamental errors are those which have such a significant effect on the financial statements of prior periods that those financial statements can no longer be considered to have been reliable. Adjustment of fundamental errors by restating the opening balance of retained earnings is the benchmark treatment. An allowed alternative is to correct the fundamental error in the current period without adjustment to comparative figures in the statutory accounts and to produce additional pro forma information adopting the prior year adjustment method.

Changes in accounting policy should only be made if required by statute or by accounting standard, or if the change results in a more appropriate presentation of events. The benchmark treatment is to adjust the opening balance of retained earnings. The allowed alternative treatment is similar to that allowed for adjusting for fundamental error, with disclosure of reasons for the change.

6.2.3.3 Reducing the options

The comparability project drew attention to the treatment of adjustments resulting from prior period items. E 32 proposed that the preferred treatment should be adjustment to opening retained earnings but that an allowed alternative should remain in passing the item through the income statement of the current year.

6.2.4 Discontinuing operations

E 58, issued August 1997. IAS expected 1998.

6.2.4.1 Key issues

Discontinuing operations cause the results of a period to be of limited usefulness for future forecasting by users of accounts. It would be desirable for companies to give separate disclosure of discontinuing operations but this raises questions of what should be disclosed, what should be measured, and what is meant by 'discontinuing'.

6.2.4.2 Approach in E 58

The exposure draft deals only with presentation and disclosure. Recognition and measurement principles of other IASs will apply, particularly those on impairments and provisions. A discontinuing operation should be an IAS 14 segment or part thereof, to be disposed of pursuant to a single plan. The initial disclosure will be by public announcement of a Board decision. In the financial statements there must be disclosed the carrying amounts of assets and liabilities, earnings and cash flows, and net selling prices of any assets for which there are binding sales agreements. Once there is a commitment to disposal, with no possibility of withdrawal, the discontinuing operation must be reported separately from the continuing operations.

6.2.4.3 Reducing the options

The revision of IAS 8 in 1992 also incorporated a requirement for certain disclosures about discontinuing operations. It resulted in variable practice and did not address the more difficult questions surrounding the recognition and measurement of the gain or loss on discontinuance. One difficult question is to decide on the precise date at which discontinuance should be recognised. A second difficult question is to decide precisely which costs are attributable to the discontinuing operation. The project on Discontinuing Operations was part of the package targeted for completion as a core standard. The title was chosen deliberately to reflect the Board's view that the discontinuance of an operation should be recognised in the financial statements before the process of discontinuing was completed. The Board also agreed, in giving approval for the project, that the operation would be treated as discontinuing once the enterprise was committed to discontinue the operation without any realistic possibilities of withdrawal. A draft Statement of Principles issued in November 1996 added further suggestions relating to disclosure, recognition and measurement. The recognition and measurement aspects were not taken forward in E 58.

6.2.5 Reporting financial information by segment

IAS 14, issued 1981, reformatted 1995, revised 1997.

6.2.5.1 Key issues

Expert users of financial statements will almost always say that the information about segments is by far the most interesting part of the total package. On the other hand, the competitive edge may be lost if business rivals and customers learn too much about the enterprise.

The key issues in segmental reporting are concerned with deciding how much detail is desirable and how to define segments so that the information provided is comparable across a range of enterprises and from one period to the next.

6.2.5.2 Approach in IAS 14

IAS 14 applies to enterprises whose securities are publicly traded and other economically significant entities. An enterprise should report financial information by segments – specifically, the different business segments and the different geographical areas in which it operates. It requires that an enterprise should look to its internal organisational structure and internal reporting systems for the purpose of identifying those segments. It is likely that most enterprises will identify their business and geographical segments as the organisational units for which information is reported to the Board of Directors and to the Chief Executive Officer.

Under IAS 14 one basis of segmentation is to be primary and the other secondary. For each primary segment the enterprise must disclose: revenue; operating result; the basis of intersegment pricing; carrying amount of segment assets and segment liabilities; cost of acquiring property, plant, equipment and intangibles; depreciation; non-cash expenses other than depreciation; and share of profit or loss of equity and joint venture investments. For secondary segments, disclosures are: revenue; assets; and costs of acquiring property.

The sum of the separate segments should equal the aggregate amounts in the financial statements. If that is not the case, a reconciliation statement should be disclosed explaining the difference. Other segmental disclosures are encouraged on a voluntary basis.

6.2.5.3 Reducing the options

Exposure draft E 51, *Reporting Financial Information by Segment,* was issued in June 1996. It reflected many of the reporting requirements of IAS 14 but added new disclosures and sought to change the way in which segments were identified. It looked to the company's organisational structure and internal reporting system for the purpose of identifying its reportable business and geographical segments. The IASC benefited from the extensive input from financial analysts to this project. The international organisations of analysts had confirmed to the IASC, in various comments prior to the issue of E 51, that segment information was essential to meet the needs of a range of users of financial statements.

The review of IAS 14 was undertaken in parallel with similar reviews of existing requirements in the USA and Canada. This was reflected in E 51 by the emphasis on the company's organisational structure and internal reporting system. However the IASC Board started with the objective of providing insight into how diversity affects the overall risks and returns. This in turn required enterprises to disclose information about segments based on industrial and geographical distinctions.

The standard setters in the USA and Canada seek to provide information about business activity. In consequence, they permit an enterprise to disclose segments based on the organisational structure of the enterprise, even where such segments cover a number of different industries or geographical areas.

The IASC Board approved IAS 14 in January 1997 but postponed publication until July 1997 to allow for harmonisation efforts by the US and Canadian standard setters. This resulted in particular in the idea of 'primary' and 'secondary' bases of segmentation. One other tightening of requirements is that the inter-segment transfers must be measured on the basis of the actual transfer pricing practice used in the enterprise (previously a different method could be used for segment disclosure purposes). The accounting policies used for segment reporting must be those of the main financial statements.

6.2.6 Related party disclosure

IAS 24, issued 1984, reformatted 1995.

6.2.6.1 Key issues

When close relationships exist between one enterprise and another, there may be concerns as to whether the relationship is beneficial or detrimental. Such relationships exist where one party has the ability to control the other party or exercise significant influence over its financial and operating decisions. In the absence of information the user of financial statements can not make an informed judgement about the relationship or about transactions resulting from the relationship.

The key issues in IAS 24 are the definition of related parties and the specification of what should be disclosed about relationships and the transactions resulting from those relationships.

6.2.6.2 Approach in IAS 24

Parties are considered to be related if one party has the ability to control the other party or exercise significant influence (participation in policy decisions) over the other party in making financial and operating decisions. 'Significant influence' is assumed when 20% or more of the voting power is held.

The following relationships are deemed *not* to be related parties;

- companies simply having a director in common without the ability to affect the policies of both companies in their mutual dealings
- providers of finance, trade unions, public utilities, government departments and agencies in their normal dealings with an enterprise
- business contacts such as a customer, supplier, franchisor, distributor or agent.

Related party relationships where control exists should be disclosed irrespective of whether there have been transactions between the parties. If there have been transactions between related parties, the reporting enterprise should disclose the nature of the related party relationship as well as the type of transaction. Aggregation of similar items can be made unless separate disclosure is necessary for an understanding of the effect on the financial statements.

No disclosure of transactions is required:

- in the consolidated financial statements in respect of transactions within a group
- in parent financial statements where these are published with the consolidated financial statements
- in financial statements of a subsidiary where its parent is incorporated within the same country and provides consolidated financial statements within that country
- in financial statements of state-controlled enterprises of transactions with other state-controlled enterprises.

6.2.6.3 Reducing the options

IOSCO indicated that IAS 24 was acceptable as a core standard and therefore no revision was planned before the 1998 target. However, in any future review of the standard it is likely that IASC will consider whether it is appropriate to continue allowing exclusions from disclosure of transactions in relation to subsidiary companies within a larger group. Future revisions may also consider disclosures such as remuneration of directors and key employees.

6.2.7 Earnings per share

IAS 33, issued 1997.

6.2.7.1 Key issues

The objective of IAS 33 is to set out principles for the disclosure and presentation of earnings per share which will improve performance comparison among different enterprises in the same period and among different accounting periods for the same enterprise. The standard pays particular attention to the number of shares issued, which forms the denominator of the formula for earnings per share.

6.2.7.2 Approach in IAS 33

The standard applies to enterprises whose ordinary shares are publicly traded. The enterprise should disclose basic earnings per share and diluted earnings per share with equal prominence on the face of the income statement. ('Basic earnings per share' indicates the earnings available to existing shareholders, while 'diluted earnings per share' indicates the earnings available if all potential conversions to ordinary shares took place.)

There should be disclosure of the amounts used in calculating the earnings per share. The method of calculation is also prescribed. In particular, a weighted average number of shares in issue should be calculated for use as the denominator. The IASC has worked closely with international organisations of financial analysts on this project.

6.2.7.3 Reducing the options

This is the first IAS dealing with earnings per share. Its main achievement is harmonisation with the US standard FAS 128, *Earnings per Share* (issued 1997) so far as the denominator (number of shares) is concerned. Initiatives by financial analysts to reach a worldwide consensus on the numerator (definition of earnings) have not yet led to agreement. IAS 33 was part of the agreed work programme of core standards.

6.2.8 Interim financial reporting

IAS 34, issued February 1998.

6.2.8.1 Key issues

National securities regulators have various rules as to which companies should publish interim financial reports and how frequent the interim reporting should be. The key accounting issues are:

1 Is the interim financial report intended to help predicting the current financial year's results, or is it intended to help with projections more generally?

2 Where the business activity is spread unevenly over the year, should it be reported as it occurs, or should there be smoothing of revenue and expenses over the year as a whole?

It is for national securities regulators and stock exchanges to decide which companies should be required to publish interim financial reports, and how frequently this should occur.

6.2.8.2 Approach in IAS 34

An interim report should include a condensed balance sheet, condensed income statement, condensed cash flow statement, condensed statement of changes in equity, and selected explanatory notes. Items should be reported in relation to the figures of the period (year-to-date basis) and not in relation to estimated annual data.

The accounting principles must be the same as those used in the company's annual financial statements. The same definitions of assets, liabilities, income and expenses must be used for interim reporting as for annual financial statements. The interim tax expenses must be measured using the expected effective annual income tax rate.

The standard applies if an enterprise is required, or elects, to publish an interim report. IASC will encourage at least half-yearly reporting for all public companies, within 60 days after the period end.

6.2.8.3 Reducing the options

A Point Outline paper, *Interim Financial Reporting*, issued early in 1996, was the first stage of a major initiative on this subject. The outline paper identified 27 basic issues of this type. The steering committee published a draft Statement of Principles in September 1996, and E 57 followed in August 1997. The standard was issued in February 1998.

6.3 ASSET RECOGNITION AND MEASUREMENT

Valuation of assets has an impact on reported net income: overstating assets leads to overstating net income. The application of prudence suggests that perceived risk arising from overstatement of assets is greater than perceived risk from understatement of the same magnitude. Standards dealing with asset valuation therefore show a common theme of prudence. Consistency is also an essential feature because users of financial statements need to understand the asset base from which income is generated. Disclosure of the nature of the asset is essential so that users can appreciate the relative risk, subjectivity of valuation and liquidity of the asset. Some or all of these factors are found in each of the IASs dealing with assets.

6.3.1 Inventories

IAS 2, issued 1975, revised 1993.

6.3.1.1 Key issues

The valuation of inventories is an important aspect of the determination of profit, or net income, of an enterprise. The standard is based firmly in historical cost accounting. It provides rules for valuation which ensure that profit is not anticipated until it is earned when the inventories are sold. It also ensures that inventories include all the costs of bringing them to their present condition and location.

6.3.1.2 Approach in IAS 2

The standard contains rules for valuation. Key aspects are:

- inventories should be measured at the lower of cost and net realisable value
- cost should comprise all costs of purchase, cost of conversion and other costs incurred in bringing the inventory to its present location and condition
- costs include a systematic allocation of fixed and variable production overheads based on the normal capacity of the production facilities; overhead costs are included to the extent that they are incurred in bringing the inventories to their present location and condition
- in limited circumstances borrowing costs are included in the cost of inventories (*see* IAS 23)
- standard cost or the retail method may be used to approximate to cost.

Where specific costs can not be attributed to identified items of inventory, the benchmark treatment is to use first-in-first-out (FIFO) or weighted average cost formulas. The allowed alternative is to use the last-in-first-out (LIFO) formula.
The standard also contains rules for disclosure.

6.3.1.3 Reducing the options

In implementation of the comparability project this standard was controversial. E 32 included LIFO as the allowed alternative but the Statement of Intent announced that LIFO and base stock would not be permitted. Subsequent strong opposition from countries using LIFO restored the LIFO approach as the allowed alternative but subject to disclosure of cost using the benchmarked FIFO or weighted average approaches. The standard is acceptable to IOSCO as a core standard.

6.3.2 Depreciation accounting

IAS 4, issued 1976, reformatted 1995

This was one of the early standards and is very general in nature. The most interesting aspects of depreciation are those relating to property, plant and equipment, which are dealt with in IAS 16 (see below). The review of core standards did not include IAS 4.

6.3.3 Property, plant and equipment

IAS 16 issued 1982, revised 1993.

6.3.3.1 Key issues

The principal issues in accounting for property, plant and equipment are the timing of recognition of the assets, the amount at which they are carried in the balance sheet, and the depreciation to be recorded. The standard also covers disclosure of information. The criteria for recognition should be those contained in the Framework. The benchmark treatment for measurement is to apply historical cost accounting. Revaluation is an allowed alternative.

6.3.3.2 Approach in IAS 16

An item of property, plant or equipment should initially be valued at cost, which includes all attributable costs of bringing the asset to working condition for its intended use. Further rules apply:

1 if an item is acquired in exchange or part exchange the cost is measured at the fair value of the asset given up adjusted by the amount of any cash transferred;

2 subsequent expenditure should be added to the carrying amount of the asset when that expenditure meets the framework document tests of definition and recognition of an asset;

3 subsequent to the initial recognition the benchmark treatment is that the asset should be carried at cost less accumulated depreciation; periodic review is required to assess whether the recoverable amount has declined below the carrying amount. If such a decline has taken place the amount of the reduction should be recognised as an expense;

4 if the circumstances and events that led to the write down cease to exist, the benchmark treatment is that the amount should be written back after adjusting for depreciation that would have been charged had the original write-down not occurred;

5 as an allowed alternative treatment the asset may be revalued, and it should then be carried in the balance sheet at its fair value at date of revaluation *less* accumulated depreciation; revaluation should be made with sufficient regularity

such that the carrying amount does not differ materially from its fair value at the balance sheet date;

6 when an item is revalued, the entire class of assets to which it belongs should be revalued;

7 revaluation that leads to an increase to the carrying amount should be credited directly to equity under the heading of revaluation surplus, unless it reverses a previous revaluation decrease that has been recognised as an expense; in that case, the revaluation should be treated as income;

8 revaluation that leads to a decrease to the carrying amount should be recognised as an expense unless it reverses a previous revaluation surplus in respect of that asset; in that case, it should be set off against the surplus.

Depreciation of an asset is a process of systematic allocation of the depreciable amount of an asset over its useful life. The depreciable amount is the cost minus the expected residual value. The allocation should reflect the pattern in which the asset's economic benefits are consumed by the enterprise. Rules of recognition and measurement are:

1 the depreciation charge for each period should be recognised as an expense unless it is included in the carrying amount of another asset held by the enterprise at the balance sheet date;

2 the enterprise should select the depreciation method appropriate for the particular asset and apply it consistently from period to period, unless there is a change in the expected pattern of economic benefit from that asset;

3 useful life and depreciation methods should be reviewed periodically; if changes are necessary, the depreciation charge for the current and future periods should be adjusted;

4 gains or losses arising from the disposal (or retirement) of an asset should be calculated as the difference between net disposal proceeds and the carrying amount of the asset and should be recognised as income or expense in the income statement.

Extensive disclosure requirements are set out for the primary financial statements and the notes to the accounts.

6.3.3.3 Reducing the options

In the comparability project, it was proposed in E 32 that the preferred treatment of gross carrying amount would be historical cost while the allowed alternative would be revaluation, using a prescribed approach. The wording of the resulting standard is different, referring to measurement *subsequent* to initial recognition, but the sentiment remained the same in regarding historical cost as the benchmark treatment and revaluation as the allowed alternative.

It is stated in IAS 16 that the carrying amount of an item of property, plant and equipment should not exceed its recoverable amount. In order to determine the recoverable amount of an asset it may be necessary to consider the extent of impairment. This is an issue which is relevant to any long-lived asset and the IASC has put in place a project to consider all forms of impairment (see below, p. 167). IAS 16 is acceptable to IOSCO for the core standards programme.

6.3.4 Impairment

E 55, issued May 1997. IAS expected 1998.

6.3.4.1 Key issues

It is an aspect of prudence in accounting that assets should not be overvalued in the balance sheet. There is a risk that this may arise under historical cost accounting where fixed assets are depreciated on the basis of historical cost but that depreciation may not take into account some change in circumstances which causes the value of the asset to decrease suddenly. Such an unexpected decrease would be an example of impairment of the asset, beyond normal depreciation, which would require recognition in the financial statements. The difficult issues are, first, to set conditions which recognise that impairment has occurred and, second, to specify a method or methods for measuring the impairment.

6.3.4.2 Approach in E 55

An asset is regarded as being impaired if its carrying amount exceeds its recoverable amount. Assets should be reviewed at each balance sheet date for indications of impairment. Where such indications are found, there must be a detailed calculation of recoverable amount, defined as the higher of an asset's net selling price and its value in use. 'Value in use' is the present value of the estimated future cash flows from continued use of the asset and disposal at the end of its useful life. 'Net selling price' is the amount obtainable from an arm's length sale between knowledgeable, willing buyers and sellers, *less* costs of disposal.

If the asset's carrying amount exceeds recoverable amount, an impairment loss is recognised. An impairment loss recognised in a prior period should be reversed, and income recognised, if there has been a favourable change in the estimates that were used when the last impairment loss was recognised.

Disclosure of impairment losses during the accounting period should be given for each class of asset. E 55 applies to all assets except for inventories, deferred taxes, financial assets, assets arising from construction contracts and employee benefits.

6.3.4.3 Reducing the options

Impairment became the subject of a project announced in June 1996. It is intended to make the impairment test identical for all intangible assets including goodwill (presently covered in IAS 22, *Business Combinations*). Impairment is also referred to in IAS 9, *Research and Development Costs*, IAS 16, *Property, Plant and Equipment* and IAS 25, *Accounting for Investments*. It is intended that the IAS on impairment should set the general principles to be applied to all assets. If additional reviews are required for particular assets, that will be dealt with in the specific standard (such as for intangible assets and goodwill).

6.3.5 Borrowing costs

IAS 23, issued 1984, revised 1993.

6.3.5.1 Key issues

In most instances, the interest charges on borrowed funds will be reported as an expense of the period in which they arise. There are occasions, however, when companies wish to argue that interest charges are an asset rather than an expense, because they create a benefit for the future. This argument might apply, for example, to interest charged on finance borrowed to pay for a development project.

6.3.5.2 Approach in IAS 23

The benchmark treatment is that borrowing costs should be recognised as an expense in the period in which they are incurred. The allowed alternative treatment is that borrowing costs may be capitalised as part of the cost of an asset where the borrowing costs are directly attributable to the acquisition, construction or production of an asset which necessarily takes a substantial period of time to get ready for its intended use or sale. Reporting the borrowing costs as an asset should cease when substantially all the activities necessary to prepare the asset for its use or sale are complete.

Disclosure is required of the amount of borrowing costs capitalised during the period and the capitalisation rate used.

6.3.5.3 Reducing the options

Prior to the comparability project, the standard allowed free choice of capitalising or not capitalising borrowing costs incurred on assets being made ready for their intended use. E 32 proposed a preferred treatment and an allowed alternative which were eventually reflected in the revised standard. However, initial reaction to E 32 resulted in a change of thinking by the IASC, indicated in the Statement of Intent, to require capitalisation of borrowing costs which met particular criteria. This revised thinking was presented in E 39, which evoked a range of comments. From that point IASC decided to revert, in revising IAS 23, to its proposals as set out in E 32.

IOSCO has indicated that IAS 23 is acceptable for the purpose of the core standards programme.

6.3.6 Accounting for investments

IAS 25, issued 1986, reformatted 1995.

6.3.6.1 Key issues

Enterprises hold investments for various reasons. IAS 25 distinguishes the accounting measurement and disclosure treatment of current and long-term investments. It sets out various options but describes the choices available rather than prescribing a benchmark in each case.

6.3.6.2 Approach in IAS 25

Investments classified as *current assets* should be carried in the balance sheet at market value or at the lower of cost and market value. The comparison of cost and market value can be performed either on an aggregate portfolio basis, in total or by category of investment, or on an individual investment basis. All adjustments to carrying value should be recognised in the income statement.

Investments classified as *long-term assets* should be valued in the balance sheet at cost or at revalued amount or, in the case of marketable equity securities, at the lower of cost and market value determined on a portfolio basis. If revalued amounts are used, a policy for the frequency of revaluation should be adopted and investments should be valued in entire categories. The resulting changes in carrying value can either be recognised through the income statement or adjusted on owners' equity as a revaluation surplus provided that the valuation is above cost. Any revaluation below cost is recognised as an expense in the income statement. The enterprise should recognise any decline in value below cost, other than on a temporary basis, on an item-by-item basis. This should be reported in the income statement.

Investment properties are investments in land or buildings that are not occupied by the investing enterprise or other enterprises in the same group. These can either be treated as any other property under IAS 16, in which case systematic depreciation will be calculated, or as long-term investments which may be carried either at cost or at fair value.

The standard also covers disclosure aspects in detail.

6.3.6.3 Reducing the options

For the comparability project, E 32 identified a preferred treatment of historical cost valuation for investments classified as long-term assets. Revaluation was offered as an allowed alternative, with disclosure of additional information. Revaluation would be applied to an entire class of long-term investments and reductions in value would be determined for each investment separately.

For investments classified as current assets the preferred treatment in E 32 was to carry at market value. The allowed alternative was to carry at the lower of cost and market value, with disclosure of additional information.

The realised gain on disposal of an investment would be reported in net income and any revaluation surplus from previous periods would be transferred to retained earnings and not to the income of the period.

These changes were not carried through in reformatting the standard because it was decided that in the move to set acceptable core standards there would be a larger project dealing with financial instruments more generally. The exposure draft E 48 (1994) deals with recognition and measurement of all financial instruments and will have an impact on IAS 25. That exposure draft contains controversial recommendations which may take some time to be agreed, but it is a part of the core standards programme. Until E 48 becomes a standard, IAS 25 has to be read in conjunctions with IAS 32 for disclosure and presentation requirements.

6.3.7 Research and development costs

IAS 9, issued 1993 superseding 1978 version; to be covered in new Intangible Assets standard.

6.3.7.1 Key issues

The key issue of IAS 9 is whether research and development expenditure should be reported as an expense or as an asset. The standard gives definitions:

- *research* is investigation undertaken with the prospect of gaining new scientific or technical knowledge and understanding
- *development* is application of research or knowledge for the production of new or substantially improved material, devices, products, processes, systems or services prior to the commencement of commercial production or use.

It is necessary to compare these definitions of research and development with the framework document definitions of an asset and an expense. Internationally there is little difficulty in accepting that research should be reported as an expense because of the uncertainty as to the expected future benefit. However opinion is divided on whether development expenditure may be reported as an asset.

6.3.7.2 Approach in IAS 9

The IAS states that:

1 *Research* costs should be recognised as an *expense* in the period in which they are incurred and should not be recognised as an asset in a subsequent period.

2 *Development* costs of a project should be recognised as an *expense* in the period in which they are incurred *unless certain criteria for asset recognition are all met*. In such a case that part of the recoverable cost of the project should be recognised as asset. The amount of development costs recognised as an asset should be amortised and recognised as an expense on a systematic basis so as to reflect the pattern in which the related economic benefits are recognised.

3 The *criteria for asset recognition* of development costs of a project are that the product or process: (i) is clearly defined and the costs can be separately identified and measured; (ii) is intended to be produced and marketed; (iii) is demonstrably marketable or useful within the enterprise; and (iv) is backed up by adequate resources so that it can be completed and marketed.

4 Financial statements should disclose the amount of research and development costs recognised as an *expense* in a period, *amortisation* method used and rates used; and a reconciliation of the opening and closing balances of unamortised development costs of the period.

6.3.7.3 Reducing the options

The original IAS 9, issued in 1978, permitted development cost to be reported as an asset and amortised, providing that such development cost met specified criteria. There was free choice for companies in this matter. In the comparability project, E 32 sought to have the **preferred treatment** as charging all research and development expenditure as an expense of the period, with the **allowed alternative** of recognising development expenditure as an asset under tightly controlled conditions. The Statement of Intent proposed a harder line, insisting that development cost must be reported as an asset if it met the specified conditions. The revised IAS 9 maintained this harder line.

Despite the firmer approach of the revised IAS 9, the standard was included in the list of core standards to be revised by 1998 for the agreement with IOSCO. This reflected concern in some countries that it would be preferable to account for research and development costs as one item, reporting all as an expense of the period. It was agreed in 1997 that the standard on Intangible Assets should also cover research and development activities for achievement of the core standards project.

6.3.8 Intangible assets

E 60, *Intangible Assets*, issued August 1997 with consequential changes in E 61, *Business Combinations*; E 50 issued 1995.

6.3.8.1 Key issues

E 60 and E 61 apply to purchased and internally developed intangible assets. An intangible asset may be recognised only if: the asset is identifiable; the asset is controlled by the enterprise; future economic benefits specifically attributable to the asset are probable; and cost is reliably measurable. A 20-year life would normally be the maximum for amortisation but the enterprise may justify a period longer than 20 years and disclose that justification. Review for impairment must be carried out at each reporting date. Detailed annual impairment calculations are required if the amortisation period is more than 20 years. Revaluation of an intangible asset (but not goodwill) is an allowed alternative only if there is an active market for the asset. In a purchase business combination, an intangible asset that cannot be recognised separately is included in goodwill, not written off immediately.[1]

6.3.8.2 Approach in IAS xx

The standard on Intangible Assets will cover research and development (previously IAS 9).

6.3.8.3 Reducing the options

The exposure draft E 50, *Intangible Assets*, had included controversial proposals that all intangible assets should be amortised over a useful life not exceeding 20 years; subsequent measurement should be made, under the allowed alternative treatment, by reference to an active secondary market; and there should be particular restrictions on initial recognition and measurement for intangible assets.

Having considered responses to the exposure draft, the Board announced in July 1996 that it would not impose a 20-year limit on the useful life but that there would be a rebuttable presumption that useful life does not exceed 20 years. Where asset lives were held to exceed 20 years an enterprise would be required to calculate recoverable amount every year in accordance with the Board's proposals on Impairment (see above, p. 167).

In July 1997 the Board approved E 60, to include research and development activities. In approving the exposure draft, the Board agreed to require an annual impairment test for internally generated intangible assets that are not yet available for use.

---

[1] IASC web page

6.4 LIABILITY RECOGNITION AND MEASUREMENT

Reporting of liabilities also has an impact on reported net income: understating liabilities leads to overstating net income. The application of prudence suggests that the risk of understatement of liabilities should be taken very seriously. Standards dealing with liabilities will therefore show a common theme of ensuring that all liabilities are acknowledged as fully as possible. Disclosure of the maturity date of the liability is very important. For longer-term liabilities the user of financial statements will be interested in the commitment of future cash flows to loan interest and capital repayments. There will also be an interest in the gearing (ratio of long-term loans to equity finance).

6.4.1 Contingencies and events occurring after the balance sheet date

IAS 10, issued 1978, reformatted 1995.

6.4.1.1 Key issues

There are many situations existing at the balance sheet date whose outcome will be determined by future events which may or may not occur. If the likelihood of occurrence is high, the liability will be accrued and reported in the balance sheet. If there is a lesser likelihood of occurrence, the liability may be declared *contingent* and reported in a note to the accounts.

6.4.1.2 Approach in IAS 10

The amount of a *contingent loss* should be recognised as an expense and a liability if (a) it is probable that future events will confirm that an asset has been impaired or a liability incurred at the balance sheet date; (b) a reasonable estimate of the amount of the resulting loss can be made. The existence of a contingent loss should be disclosed in notes to the financial statements if these conditions are not met. If the possibility of a loss is remote then no reporting is required.

A *contingent gain* should not be recognised as income or as an asset in financial statements. The existence of a contingent gain should be disclosed in a note to the accounts if it is probable that the gain will be realised.

Events which occur after the balance sheet date but before the date on which the financial statements are authorised for issue may indicate a need to make adjustments to assets and liabilities or may require disclosure. The essential test is whether the event provides additional evidence about conditions existing at the balance sheet date or provides information relating to the applicability of the going concern assumption. An example requiring adjustment is the loss on a trade receivable which is confirmed by the bankruptcy of the customer occurring after the balance sheet date.

Dividends of a period that are *proposed or declared* after the balance sheet date but before approval of the financial statements should be either adjusted for or disclosed in the financial statements.

6.4.1.3 Reducing the options

An essential element of the revision of core standards is the revision of IAS 10. IOSCO has called for review of the measurement requirements of IAS 10. Guidance is required to define more clearly the nature of contingencies. If this can be achieved the revised standard will provide a basis for distinguishing on-balance sheet and off-balance sheet items. There is also a particular concern with the use of provisions in financial statements which will also be addressed within the review of IAS 10.

A Discussion Paper, produced jointly by a working group of standard setting bodies in Australia, Canada, the UK, the USA and the IASC, served as a basis for developing the standard. The project continued as a joint project of the UK Accounting Standards Board (ASB) and the IASC. E 59, *Provisions, Contingent Liabilities and Contingent Assets*, was issued in August 1979, following from the draft Statement of Principles. The tentative conclusions brought forward in E 59 were that a provision should be recognised when the enterprise has no realistic alternative but to pay out resources. The provision should be measured at the discounted present value of the expected settlement amount. Provision should be made for restructuring when there was a detailed plan and a demonstrable commitment. There should be provision for future losses only in respect of onerous contracts.

6.4.2 Income taxes

IAS 12, issued 1979, reformatted 1995, revised 1996.

6.4.2.1 Key issues

Taxes on income are accrued as an expense of the period to which the income and operating expenses relate. To the extent that there are timing differences between an enterprise's accounting income and taxable income (as defined by the relevant tax authorities) the tax effect is included in the tax expense in the income statement and in the deferred tax balance in the balance sheet.

6.4.2.2 Approach in IAS 12

IAS 12 requires that a deferred tax liability should be recognised for all taxable temporary differences (apart from some specified exceptions). A deferred tax asset may be recognised (for the carry-forward of unused tax losses and unused tax credits) to the extent that it is probable that future taxable profit will be available against which the unused tax losses and unused tax credits can be utilised. The term 'temporary differences' is used because it covers temporary timing differences and also some differences between accounting treatment and tax treatment which are not due to timing.

Measurement of current tax liabilities and assets should be at the amount expected to be paid or recovered under law as enacted at the balance sheet date. Measurement of deferred tax liabilities and assets should be at the tax rates which are expected to apply when the liability is settled or the asset is realised.

The standard prohibits discounting of liabilities. It also sets out disclosure requirements for taxes.

6.4.2.3 Reducing the options

The previous version of IAS 12, *Accounting for Taxes on Income*, permitted either the deferral method or a liability method. The revised IAS 12 does not permit the deferral method. The revised IAS 12, *Income Taxes*, implements the proposal in exposure draft E 49 (October 1994) that partial application of deferred taxation accounting should not be permitted. In these and other more detailed matters the stricter attitude of the revised IAS 12 contrasts with the permissiveness of the original IAS 12 and the exposure draft E 33.

The approach adopted in the revised IAS 12 has similarities to that used by the FASB in FAS 109, *Accounting for Income Taxes*. The IASC Board consulted major accounting firms and over 100 multinational companies, in arriving at the conclusion that the new approach could be applied internationally.

6.4.3 Accounting for leases

IAS 17, issued 1982, reformatted 1995, project added to core standards agenda June 1996, revised 1997.

6.4.3.1 Key issues

The framework document states that transactions and other events ought to be accounted for and presented in accordance with their substance and financial reality and not merely with their legal form. A finance lease has the effect in substance of a loan-financed purchase, and should therefore be reported as such. The accounting standard covers the lessee and the lessor.

6.4.3.2 Approach in IAS 17

IAS 17 covers aspects of both lessee and lessor accounting.

1 *Lessee*

The standard requires a finance lease to be reported in the balance sheet as an asset and an obligation. The income statement should report depreciation of the asset and interest on the remaining balance of the liability.

An 'operating lease' is any lease other than a finance lease. The full rental payment under the lease should be charged to the income statement over the life of the lease, the allocation being made on a systematic basis that is representative of the time pattern of the user's benefit.

The commitment for minimum lease payments under finance leases and under non-cancellable operating leases with a term of more than one year should be disclosed in summary form, giving the amounts and periods in which the payments will become due.

2 *Lessor*

The problems lie in reporting income of the period and the nature of the asset. The income of the period should be calculated to achieve a constant rate of return on the lessor's net investment or net cash outstanding over the life of the asset. The asset should be recognised as an account receivable, at an amount equal to the net investment in the lease.

6.4.3.3 Reducing the options

In the comparability project, E 32 sought to reduce the flexibility available to lessors in reporting income and also sought to deal with leveraged leases (these are finance leases structured so as to distribute tax benefits advantageously). The Statement of Intent noted that further work would be required in this area. Consequently IAS 17 was reformatted but without significant change in principles. The options were not reduced as a result of the comparability project.

This meant that IAS 17 was among those standards not acceptable to IOSCO as a core standard. IOSCO asked for a review of IAS 17 in three areas considered essential: lessor accounting, leveraged leases and more specific disclosures. Within the work programme an exposure draft was planned to deal with these items in particular, and in the longer term a more fundamental review will be considered. A starting point was a joint Discussion Paper (July 1996) of a working group from the standard setting bodies of Australia, Canada, New Zealand, the UK and the USA, together with the IASC.

Exposure draft E 56 was issued in February 1997, proposing enhanced disclosure by lessees, enhanced disclosure by lessors, and that a lessor should use the net investment method to allocate final income (the net cash investment method would no longer be permitted). The enhanced disclosures were contained in the revised standard issued at the end of 1997. This requires enhanced disclosure by lessees, enhanced disclosure by lessors, and that a lessor should use the net investment method to allocate finance income (the net cash investment method is no longer permitted). The IASC also stated, when they issued the revised standard, that they planned to consider a more fundamental reform of the lease standard once they had finished their current work programme. This would involve the capitalisation of all leases with a term of more than one year.

6.4.4 Employee benefits

IAS 19, *Retirement Benefit Costs*, issued 1993; E 54, 1996; IAS 19 (revised) *Employee Benefits*, issued 1998.

6.4.4.1 Key issues

In many countries the provision of retirement benefits is a significant element of the remuneration package for an employee. The cost to the employer may fluctuate from one accounting period to the next, depending on whether the scheme is a defined contribution plan or a defined benefit plan. Employers also provide other benefits to employees such as paying salaries or wages during periods of absence from work, or bonuses in addition to normal rates of pay. The employer may pay for benefits which continue to be received after the employee has ceased to work for the employer in circumstances other than retirement. The common feature of all these benefits is that the payments made by the employer are not always spread evenly over time. The standard prescribes the amount of the cost that should be recognised and the information to be disclosed in the financial statements of the employing enterprise.

6.4.4.2 Approach in IAS 19

A *defined contribution plan* is a retirement benefit plan under which amounts to be paid as retirement benefits are determined by reference to the earnings of an investment fund which is created from the contributions made. An enterprise's contribution to the fund, in respect of service in a particular period, should be recognised as an expense in that period.

A *defined benefit plan* is an arrangement whereby an enterprise provides benefits for its employees such that the benefits are determined or estimated in advance of retirement from the provisions of a document or from the enterprise's practice. The reported expense in the current period must follow a series of rules which concentrate on the pension obligation as a liability and the assets relating to the plan, measured at fair value.

Extensive disclosures are required.

6.4.4.3 Reducing the options

The comparability project introduced a benchmark and an allowed alternative treatment for a defined benefit plan, in order to limit the free choice existing under the standard as originally issued.

Under either approach to a defined benefit plan, the important aspect was the measurement of the expense. Items were reported in the balance sheet in the categories of assets and liabilities. However these did not necessarily meet the framework document criteria for definition and recognition. The balance sheet entries were a result of the decision about the expense and therefore the standard contradicted the framework to some extent, in allowing the contents of the income statement to determine the nature of an asset or a liability.

Following on from the comparability project, it became clear that further work would be required for the core standards programme, particularly in considering those balance sheet items resulting from IAS 19 which do not meet the definition of an asset or a liability. There are two particular weaknesses. The nature of retirement benefit arrangements are not consistent in all countries. The standard also provides insufficient guidance on the balance sheet consequences of reporting retirement benefit costs in the income statement. The exposure draft E 54, *Employee Benefits* (1996), proposed a single actuarial method for measuring the expected liability for retirement benefits and also provided accounting procedures for other forms of employee benefits such as paid absences, bonuses and all forms of post-employment benefits. The revised IAS 19 was issued in January 1998.

6.4.5 Financial instruments: disclosure and presentation

IAS 32, issued 1995.

6.4.5.1 Key issues

International financial markets are changing rapidly, with widespread use of a variety of financial instruments. Some instruments, such as derivatives or interest rate swaps, may not previously have been reported in the financial statements. The standard prescribes requirements for presentation of some financial instruments on the balance sheet and for notes to be provided where financial instruments remain off the balance sheet.

6.4.5.2 Approach in IAS 32

Ideally a standard on this topic should address measurement issues as well as disclosure. It is explained below that the measurement issues are more difficult to resolve. Accordingly, IAS 32 is primarily a disclosure standard, information is also required on fair value.

The standard explains in detail matters of classification and presentation. In the balance sheet the reporting enterprise must classify the instrument according to the substance of the contractual arrangement on initial recognition. Where a financial instrument contains both a liability and an equity element, the enterprise should classify the component parts separately. Interest, dividends, losses and gains relating to a financial instrument must be reported in the income statement. Offsetting a financial asset and a financial liability is permitted only in specific circumstances.

In order to provide an understanding of risk, for each class of financial asset, liability and equity instrument disclosure is required of:

- terms, conditions and accounting policies
- interest rate risk
- credit risk
- fair value
- hedges.

6.4.5.3 Reducing the options

An exposure draft E 48 (January 1994) set out the results of a joint project with the Canadian Institute of Chartered Accountants. Comments from other standard setting bodies indicated that E 48 was too ambitious and could distance the IASC from those standard setting bodies which were reluctant to accept some of the proposals.

As a result of these views and of the comments from others on the exposure draft, the IASC decided to separate the disclosure and the measurement aspects into two separate projects. The disclosure aspects resulted in the issue of IAS 32. Recognition and measurement were set to follow as a priority. In March 1997 a Discussion Paper examined major recognition and measurement issues for financial instruments. An exposure draft was expected in October 1997 but somewhat surprisingly a press release from the IASC in September announced that the IASC staff would recommend to the Board that the IASC should adopt the US standards on financial instruments as an interim step, followed by joint work with international standard setters to agree a harmonised international standard. It was recognised by the IASC staff that it would be impossible to produce an international standard within the timescale for completion of the core standards programme. At its meeting in November 1997, the Board decided to develop both a comprehensive standard and an interim standard. The interim standard would be completed in 1998.

6.5 RECOGNITION OF ECONOMIC ACTIVITY

Recognition is dealt with in the framework document. Recognition becomes particularly significant where an economic activity of the enterprise extends over a period of time: the question arises as to when the economic activity may prudently be reported in the financial statements. Issues of recognition arise for construction contracts; revenue earned; and government grants received ahead of the activity earning those grants.

6.5.1 Construction contracts

IAS 11, issued 1979, revised 1993.

6.5.1.1 Key issues

Construction contracts may extend over more than one accounting period. The standard sets out recognition criteria for the allocation of revenue and costs to more than one period; recognition reflects the percentage of the contract completed in the period.

6.5.1.2 Approach in IAS 11

When the outcome of a construction contract can be estimated reliably, contract revenue and contract costs associated with the construction contact should be recognised as revenue and expenses, respectively, by reference to the stage of completion of the contract activity at the balance sheet date. When it is probable that total contract costs will exceed total contract revenue, the expected loss should be recognised as an expense immediately.

When the outcome of a contract cannot be estimated reliably, revenue should be recognised only to the extent of contract costs incurred that it is probable will be recoverable. Contract costs should be recognised as an expense in the period in which they are incurred.

For all contracts in progress at the balance sheet date, for which costs incurred *plus* recognised profit (*less* recognised losses) exceed progress billings, the net amount should be presented as an asset. Where progress billings exceed costs incurred *plus* recognised profits (*less* recognised losses) the net amount should be presented as a liability.

Disclosures are required to show how these rules have been applied in the period.

6.5.1.3 Reducing the options

Prior to the comparability project, IAS 11 allowed free choice in revenue recognition between the percentage of completion method and the completed contract method. Implementation of E 32 in the revised IAS 11 permitted only the percentage of completion method. IAS 11, as revised, is acceptable to IOSCO as a core standard.

6.5.2 Revenue

IAS 18, issued 1982, revised 1993.

6.5.2.1 Key issues

As a general principle, revenue is recognised when it is probable that future economic benefits will flow to the enterprise and these benefits can be measured reliably. The standard applies this principle to the sale of goods, the rendering of services and the use by others of enterprise assets yielding interest, royalties and dividends.

6.5.2.2 Approach in IAS 18

Revenue should be measured at the fair value of the consideration received or receivable.

Revenue from the *sale of goods* should be recognised when the enterprise has transferred to the buyer the significant risks and rewards of ownership of the goods. The enterprise should not retain a continuing management involvement of the type usually associated with ownership and should not retain effective control over the goods sold.

When the outcome of a transaction involving the *rendering of services* can be estimated reliably, revenue associated with the transaction should be recognised by reference to the stage of completion of the transaction at the balance sheet date. When the outcome of the transaction cannot be estimated reliably, revenue should be recognised only to the extent of the expenses recognised that are recoverable.

Interest should be recognised on a time proportion basis that takes into account the effective yield on the asset. *Royalties* should be recognised on an accrual basis in accordance with the substance of the relevant agreement. *Dividends* should be recognised when the shareholder's right to receive payment is established.

The enterprise should disclose the accounting policies adopted for the recognition of revenue, including the methods adopted to determine the stage of completion of transactions involving the rendering of services and the amount of each significant category of revenue recognised during the period, identifying the amount arising from barter exchange.

6.5.2.3 Reducing the options

In the original version of IAS 18 the recognition of revenue on service contracts allowed either the percentage of completion method or the completed contract method. Following the comparability project, the revised standard permitted only the percentage of completion method. The standard is acceptable to IOSCO as a core standard.

6.5.3 Accounting for government grants and disclosure of government assistance

IAS 20, issued 1983, reformatted 1995.

6.5.3.1 Key issues

Government grants may be received by the enterprise in advance of the performance of the activity which is financed by the grant. The activity may be the use of a fixed asset purchased with the grant, or the subsidisation of operating costs such as the training of the workforce. Government grants should not be recognised until there is reasonable assurance that:

- the enterprise will comply with the conditions attached to them
- the grant will be received.

6.5.3.2 Approach in IAS 20

Government grants should be recognised as income over the periods necessary to match them with the related costs which they are intended to compensate, on a systematic basis. They should not be credited directly to shareholders' interest.

A government grant that becomes receivable as compensation for expenses or losses already incurred or for the purpose of giving immediate financial support with no future related costs should be recognised as income of the period in which it becomes receivable.

Government grants relating to assets should be presented in the balance sheet either as deferred income or as a deduction in arriving at the carrying amount of the asset. The standard expresses no preference as to how the grants should be reported in the income statement.

Repayment of a grant relating to income should be first deducted from any deferred credit. The remaining amount of the repayment should be recognised immediately as an expense. Repayment of a grant related to an asset should be recorded by increasing the carrying amount of the asset or reducing the deferred income balance. Any appropriate additional depreciation to date should be recognised immediately as an expense.

Disclosures are also prescribed.

6.5.3.3 Reducing the options

IOSCO has accepted IAS 20 as a core standard. However there are indications[2] that some members of IOSCO would like to propose different treatments for particular types of grants which have come into existence since IAS 20 was issued. IASC would resist any attempt to create exceptions to the general principle of a standard and would expect new types of grant to be reported consistently with the principles stated.

6.6 MEASUREMENT IN GENERAL

The framework document says relatively little about measurement. In the separate standards there is a clear preference for historical cost accounting, although some specific alternatives are permitted (for example, in IAS 16). In addition there are two standards dealing particularly with changing prices (inflation). IAS 15 encourages enterprises to present a supplementary statement reflecting the effects of changing prices. IAS 29 insists on the use of the current unit of purchasing power in the primary financial statements where there is a hyperinflationary economy.

---

[2] Cairns (1995), p. 627

Measurement is not a significant theme of the agreement with IOSCO on core standards and has taken a relegated position in the accelerated work programme. That does not diminish the importance of the issue in economic terms, but does perhaps indicate the dominance of historical cost accounting.

6.6.1 Information reflecting the effects of changing prices

IAS 15, issued 1981, reformatted 1995.

6.6.1.1 Key issues

This standard applies, irrespective of the rate of inflation or the extent of specific price changes, to enterprises whose level of revenues, profit, assets or employment are significant in the economic environment in which they operate.

6.6.1.2 Approach in IAS 15

Enterprises should present information in the form of a supplementary statement using an accounting method reflecting the effect of changing prices. This information can be in terms of general purchasing power, current cost or a combination of the two approaches.

The enterprise should describe the method adopted to compute the information disclosed in the supplementary statement. The standard prescribes disclosures required in the supplementary statement.

6.6.1.3 Reducing the options

The Board stated in 1989 that international consensus had not reached the extent hoped for when IAS 15 was issued. Although the standard uses the word 'should' (which, in the terminology of standard setters indicates a firm requirement), the Board takes the view that compliance with IAS 15 is not necessary for conformity to IASs. Accordingly companies are 'encouraged' to present the information required by IAS 15. This state of affairs is consistent with the framework document which is relatively silent on aspects of measurement. IOSCO has not included IAS 15 as a core standard.

6.6.2 Financial reporting in hyperinflationary economies

IAS 29, issued 1989, reformatted 1995.

6.6.2.1 Key issues

Financial statements of an enterprise that reports in the currency of a hyperinflationary economy should be stated in terms of the measuring unit current at the balance sheet date.

6.6.2.2 Approach in IAS 29

The existence of hyperinflation is indicated by the following characteristics of a country's economic environment:

181

- the general population prefers to keep its wealth in non-monetary assets or a relatively stable foreign currency
- amounts of local currency held are immediately invested to maintain purchasing power
- prices may be quoted in a relatively stable foreign currency
- sales and purchase on credit take place at a price which compensates for the loss of purchasing power during the period of credit
- interest rates, wages and prices are linked to a price index
- the cumulative inflation rate over three years is approaching, or exceeds, 100%.

For accounting records maintained in *historical cost terms*, non-monetary balance sheet items are re-stated to current monetary units by applying a general price index. Monetary items need no re-statement as they are already expressed in monetary units current at the balance sheet date. Each item in the income statement needs to be re-stated by applying the change in the general price index from the date when that item was initially recorded.

For accounting records maintained in *current cost terms*, most balance sheet items will be expressed in monetary units of currency at the balance sheet date and will not need re-stating. Cost of sales and depreciation are recorded at current cost of the time they are consumed. Other expenses and all revenues are recorded at monetary amounts of the date they occur. All revenues and expenses must be re-stated into the measurement unit of the balance sheet date by applying an appropriate general price index.

The gain or loss on the net monetary position should be included in net income and separately disclosed.

6.6.2.3 Reducing the options

IAS 29 is acceptable to IOSCO as a core standard.

6.7 GROUP ACCOUNTING

Many countries which have firm preferences for domestic accounting practices in the financial statements of individual companies turn nevertheless to IASs for guidance on group accounting. Thus it is possible to encounter group accounts published under IAS accounting policies, accompanied by parent company accounts using domestic practices. In other countries there are established domestic standards for group accounting also. IASs deal with many of the problem areas of group accounting, such as foreign exchange rates (IAS 21); the nature of a business combination (IAS 22); consolidated financial statements and investments in subsidiaries (IAS 27); investments in associates (IAS 28); and interests in joint ventures (IAS 31).

All the standards relating to group accounting are acceptable to IOSCO for the core standards programme. Accounting for goodwill, dealt with in IAS 22, is probably the most controversial aspect of acquisition accounting.

6.7.1 The effects of changes in foreign exchange rates

IAS 21, issued 1983, revised 1993.

6.7.1.1 Key issues

The financial statements of an enterprise may be affected by foreign exchange rates in two ways. The enterprise may undertake transactions in foreign currencies; alternatively, it may operate part of its business in a foreign country which has a different currency. The standard sets out procedures for recording transactions undertaken in a foreign currency and translation of financial statements produced in a foreign currency. Each enterprise presents its financial statements in one currency, which is called the 'reporting currency'.

6.7.1.2 Approach in IAS 21

Foreign currency *transactions* should be recorded in the reporting currency of the enterprise by applying the exchange rate relevant at the date of the transaction. Exchange differences arising from settlement or reporting of monetary items should be recognised as income or expenses in the period in which they arise.

Translation of financial statements of foreign operations (controlled by the reporting enterprise) is a process which has some similarities to translation of a passage of text. The underlying meaning, as well as the technical terms, should be preserved as far as possible. The method of accounting to be used depends on whether the foreign operations are:

● integral to the operations of the reporting enterprise, where the foreign enterprise carries on its business as if it were an extension of the reporting enterprise's operations, or

● regarded as a foreign entity, where the foreign operation enjoys a significant degree of autonomy from the reporting enterprise.

The standard describes in some detail the methods to be used in each case. Although not defined as such, the descriptions correspond respectively to what some text books refer to as the 'temporal method' and the 'net investment method', respectively.

When there is a change in the classification of a significant foreign operation, details of the change should be provided, including the impact on shareholders' equity and net profit or loss of the current and previous years. The standard prescribes disclosures.

6.7.1.3 Reducing the options

The comparability project revised IAS 21 to clarify the required treatment of exchange differences on long-term foreign currency monetary items. It also provided some interim guidance on accounting for hedges, pending the production of an international accounting standard on financial instruments, and it transferred aspects of accounting in hyperinflationary economies to a specific standard on that topic. IAS 21 is acceptable to IOSCO as a core standard.

6.7.2 Business combinations

IAS 22, issued 1983, revised 1993.

6.7.2.1 Key issues

Most business combinations involve an acquisition of one enterprise by another. The result is a combined organisation where the location of control is clear, although the separate operations of each enterprise may continue to be identifiable. In relatively rare cases, two enterprises unite their interests in such a way that control continues to be located in the separate entities, but with mutual sharing of risks and benefits. These different kinds of combination are given different accounting treatments. The standard seeks to regulate the definition and accounting treatment of each type.

6.7.2.2 Approach in IAS 22

The standard classifies business combinations as either

- an *acquisition,* when one enterprise obtains control over the net assets and operations of another enterprise in exchange for the transfer of assets, incurring of a liability or issue of shares, or
- a *uniting of interests,* when the shareholders of the combining enterprise combine control over the whole of their net assets and operations to achieve a continuing mutual sharing in the risks and benefits attaching to the combined entity such that neither party can be identified as the acquirer.

The standard asserts that virtually all business combinations can be portrayed as acquisitions but in exceptional cases it is not possible to identify an acquirer. In such cases a uniting of interests is achieved.

A business combination which is an *acquisition* should be accounted for by use of the *purchase method* of consolidation accounting. In particular:

1 assets and liabilities should be taken into the consolidated accounts at their fair value by reference to their intended use by the acquirer; this does not permit the raising of a provision to cover future operating losses;

2 any excess of the cost of acquisition over the acquirer's interest in the fair value of the identifiable assets and liabilities acquired as at the date of the exchange transaction should be described as goodwill and recognised as an asset;

3 where the cost of acquisition is less than fair value, the difference is described as 'negative goodwill';

4 goodwill should be amortised by recognising it as an expense over its useful life: in amortising goodwill, the straight-line basis should be used unless another amortisation method is more appropriate in the circumstances; the amortisation period should not exceed five years unless a longer period, not exceeding twenty years from the date of acquisition, can be justified;

5 the unamortised balance of goodwill should be reviewed at each balance sheet date; any amount no longer recoverable should be recognised immediately as an expense.

For negative goodwill the benchmark treatment is that it should be eliminated by reducing proportionately the carrying values of non-monetary assets. Any balance that cannot be eliminated in this way should be treated as deferred income and recognised as income on a systematic basis over a period not exceeding five years, unless a longer period not exceeding 20 years is justified. The allowed alternative treatment for negative goodwill is for it to be treated in full as deferred income and amortised, normally over not more than five years.

For minority interests, at the date of acquisition, the benchmark treatment is to include the appropriate proportion of the pre-acquisition carrying amount of the net assets of the subsidiary. The allowed alternative is to include the appropriate proportion of the post-acquisition fair values of the net assets of the subsidiary.

A business combination that is a *uniting of interests* should be accounted for by use of the *pooling of interests method* of consolidation accounting, Under this method, the group accounts show the combined enterprises as though the separate businesses were continuing as before, though now jointly owned and managed. Minimum changes are made in aggregating the individual financial statements. The only relevant adjustments to asset and liability valuations are those needed to apply a uniform set of accounting policies. One important feature of this approach is that there is no calculation of goodwill.

Whatever the approach taken, extensive disclosures are prescribed.

6.7.2.3 Reducing the options

The comparability project tightened up the definition of a uniting of interests. In the case of acquisition accounting, the project discontinued the previous practice of permitting goodwill on acquisition to be set against shareholders' interests. Amortisation became the required treatment.

The preferred treatment for negative goodwill was proposed as allocation over the relevant assets. The allowed alternative was proposed as deferred income to be amortised over a period not normally exceeding five years.

The **preferred treatment** of minority interests was seen as according more closely with the historical cost basis of accounting. The **allowed alternative** reflects the opinion of those who regard the group as a consolidated economic entity.

IOSCO indicated that it would accept IAS 22 as a core standard but nevertheless the IASC decided in 1995 to revise those aspects of IAS 22 dealing with goodwill. The discussion of impairment tests for longer-lived assets and the production of a general standard covering intangible assets both had an impact on the goodwill aspects of IAS 22. In particular, the Board proposed eliminating the allowed alternative for negative goodwill.

6.7.3 Consolidated financial statements and accounting for investments in subsidiaries

IAS 27, issued 1989, reformatted 1995.

6.7.3.1 Key issues

A parent company (i.e. an enterprise that has one or more subsidiary companies that it controls) should normally present consolidated financial statements. There are two exceptions to this requirement:

- the parent enterprise is itself a wholly-owned subsidiary, or
- the parent owns virtually all (at least 90%) of the subsidiary and omission of consolidated accounts has the approval of owners of the minority interest.

IAS 27 applies the entity concept in regarding all the assets and liabilities of group enterprises as being controlled by the group as an entity. The strength of control requires all the assets and liabilities to be aggregated in the group balance sheet even where the parent company owns less than 100% of the equity of a subsidiary. The minority interest in net assets is presented as a separate line item.

6.7.3.2 Approach in IAS 27

'Control' in the context of this standard is the power to govern the financial and operating policies of an enterprise so as to obtain benefits from its activities.
A subsidiary should be excluded from consolidation when:

- control is intended to be temporary because it is acquired with a view to disposal in the near future, or
- it operates under severe long-term restrictions which significantly impair its ability to transfer funds to the parent.

Such excluded subsidiaries should be accounted for as investments under IAS 25 and the reason for non-consolidation disclosed.
The standard sets out in detail the procedures for consolidation and the disclosures required.

6.7.3.3 Reducing the options

The first standard on consolidated financial statements was issued in 1976 (IAS 3). This pre-dated the EU Seventh Directive and probably influenced the Directive as well as being available for member states in implementing it. IAS 27, in replacing IAS 3, brought the concept of control into IASs and removed some of the exemptions previously allowed in IAS 3. IAS 27 is acceptable to IOSCO as a core standard.

6.7.4 Accounting for investments in associates

IAS 28, issued 1989, reformatted 1995.

6.7.4.1 Key issues

Enterprise *A* may be regarded as an associate of enterprise *B* where *B* holds, directly or indirectly, more than 20% of the voting power of *A* or has significant influence in some other manner. An enterprise should include in its consolidated financial statements its share of the profits and losses of an associate.

6.7.4.2 Approach in IAS 28

An investment in an associate (i.e. an enterprise in which the investor has significant influence and which is neither a subsidiary nor a joint venture of the investor) should be accounted for in consolidated financial statements under the equity method. An exception to this is when the investment is acquired and held exclusively with a view to its disposal in the near future, in which case it should be accounted for under the cost method. 'Significant influence' is defined as the power to participate in the financial and operating policy decisions of the investee but not control over those policies. A holding of 20% is presumed to give significant influence unless it can be demonstrated that this is not the case.

Under the equity method the investment is initially recorded at cost and the carrying amount is increased or decreased to recognise the investor's share of the profits or losses and other changes in the equity of the investee after the date of acquisition. Associates accounted for using the equity method should be classified as long-term assets and disclosed separately in the balance sheet. The investor's share of profit or loss and of any extraordinary item should be separately disclosed in the income statement.

Disclosures are prescribed.

6.7.4.3 Reducing the options

IAS 28 replaced the aspects of IAS 3 dealing with associates. It was not revised in the comparability project and is acceptable to IOSCO as a core standard.

6.7.5 Financial reporting of interests in joint ventures

IAS 31, issued 1990, reformatted 1995.

6.7.5.1 Key issues

The standard identifies three broad types of joint venture structures. Each is characterised by the existence of a contractual arrangement entered into by two or more ventures that establishes joint control (i.e. the agreed sharing of the power to govern the financial and operating policies of an economic activity so as to obtain benefits from it).

An enterprise should include in its consolidated financial statements its proportionate share of assets, liabilities, income and expenses of a jointly controlled entity. The enterprise should also include in its separate financial statements (and hence in the consolidated financial statements) its share of assets and liabilities controlled jointly with other venturers. This requirement for proportional consolidation is in contrast to the normal practice of full consolidation as set out in IAS 27.

6.7.5.2 Approach in IAS 31

Definitions are provided to distinguish various types of joint activity:

- in *jointly controlled operations,* each venturer uses its own assets and incurs its own expenses and liabilities; the joint venture agreement provides a means by which the revenues from the sale of the joint product are shared amongst the venturers

- for *jointly controlled assets*, there is joint control and ownership of assets constructed or acquired and dedicated for the purpose of the joint venture – each venture takes a share of the output from the assets and each bears an agreed share of the expenses incurred; this does not involve the setting up of a new entity

- *jointly controlled entities* involve the creation of a new entity in which each venturer has an interest – this entity owns assets, incurs liabilities and expenses and earns income; each venturer is entitled to a share of the results of the jointly controlled entity, which will maintain its own accounting records and present financial statements.

The accounting treatment of jointly controlled operations and jointly controlled assets is relatively straightforward. For jointly controlled entities there are different approaches available. The benchmark treatment in such situations is that the consolidated financial statements of a venturer should report its interest in a jointly controlled entity using proportional consolidation. Within this benchmark treatment, there are choices of reporting formats.

The allowed alternative treatment is that a venturer should report its interest in a jointly controlled entity using the equity method as set out in IAS 28. Although equity accounting is an allowed treatment it is very much regarded as a second-best solution because proportional consolidation better reflects the substance and economic reality of a venturer's interest in a jointly controlled entity.

6.7.5.3 Reducing the options

IAS 31 did not feature in the comparability project of 1989 and is acceptable to IOSCO as a core standard.

6.8 SPECIALIST ORGANISATIONS AND INDUSTRIES

The World Bank has provided funding of approximately £350,000 for a project on agriculture. This is not part of the core standards programme under the agreement with IOSCO but is nevertheless important to member countries having agricultural economies. A Statement of Principles published in November 1997 proposed the use of fair values to measure biological assets as well as certain agricultural produce and agricultural land.

IASC has received requests for industry specific standards in areas such as insurance, mining and banking. It does not have the resources to do this while the accelerated standards programme is operating, but has indicated a willingness in principle. There are two existing specialist standards, one of which relates to retirement benefit plans and the other to banks and similar financial institutions. These are outlined in the following paragraphs.

6.8.1 IAS 26 Accounting and reporting by retirement benefit plans

This standard deals with the accounting practices required where a retirement benefit plan exists as a reporting entity separate from the enterprise which employs the persons concerned. There is a separate standard, IAS 19, which sets out the method by which the enterprise accounts for retirement benefit costs in its own financial statements.

6.8.2 IAS 30 Disclosure in the financial statements of banks and similar financial institutions

The standard recognises the special needs of banks in reporting matters of solvency, liquidity and relative risk attaching to different types of business. It covers aspects of accounting policies and disclosures which are particularly significant to those who use the financial statements of banks and financial institutions.

6.9 SUMMARY AND CONCLUSIONS

This chapter has set out the key issues and approach taken in each of the IASs. It has explained how options have been reduced in moving down the route of international harmonisation and has indicated the extent to which differences remain. In later chapters, the accounting practices of separate countries will be discussed in the context of adoption and implementation of the IASs.

QUESTIONS

Disclosure and presentation (6.2)

1 To what extent have the comparability project and the core standards project reduced options in relation to disclosure and presentation?

2 To what extent is reduction of options in disclosure and presentation necessary or desirable?

3 Which areas of disclosure and presentation have given the IASC particular problems in seeking to reduce options?

4 Which influences appear strongest where there is resistance to reducing options?

Asset recognition and measurement (6.3)

1 To what extent have the comparability project and the core standards project reduced options in relation to asset recognition and measurement?

2 To what extent is reduction of options in asset recognition and measurement necessary or desirable?

3 Which areas of asset recognition and measurement have given the IASC particular problems in seeking to reduce options?

4 Which influences appear strongest where there is resistance to reducing options?

Liability recognition and measurement (6.4)

1 To what extent have the comparability project and the core standards project reduced options in relation to liability recognition and measurement?

2 To what extent is reduction of options in liability recognition and measurement necessary or desirable?

3 Which areas of liability recognition and measurement have given the IASC particular problems in seeking to reduce options?

4 Which influences appear strongest where there is resistance to reducing options?

Recognition of economic activity (6.5)

1 To what extent have the comparability project and the core standards project reduced options in relation to recognition of economic activity?

2 To what extent is reduction of options in recognition of economic activity necessary or desirable?

3 Which areas of recognition of economic activity have given the IASC particular problems in seeking to reduce options?

4 Which influences appear strongest where there is resistance to reducing options?

Group accounting (6.6)

1 To what extent have the comparability project and the core standards project reduced options in relation to group accounting?

2 To what extent is reduction of options in group accounting necessary or desirable?

3 Which areas of group accounting have given the IASC particular problems in seeking to reduce options?

4 Which influences appear strongest where there is resistance to reducing options?

Questions linking Chapters 5 and 6

1 To what extent has the relatively short time scale for the core standards project allowed the full consultative process to take place? Discuss particular examples.

2 Of the standards originally identified for action under the core standards project (listed in Chapter 5), which types of standard have caused particular concern to IOSCO?

3 To what extent has the core standards project reduced options which were not resolved after the comparability project?

4 Are the circumstances of the core standards project sufficiently different from those of the comparability project to allow successful completion of the core standards?

5 Why is the position of the US regulators so significant in relation to the core standards project? Which areas attract the particular attention of the US regulators?

6 Which new themes have been added to the programme of standards since the comparability project was completed? What are the apparent reasons for adding these new themes?

REFERENCES

This chapter draws on material contained in IASC publications, particularly:

IASC Annual Review, various issues.

IASC Insight, published several times during a year.

IASC, International Accounting Standards, published annually.

Various Exposure Drafts and Statements, as indicated in the chapter.

The IASC web site.

Discussions based on recent material and covering the move towards the IOSCO targets are to be found in:

Cairns, D. (1995) *A Guide to Applying International Accounting Standards*. London: Accountancy Books/The Institute of Chartered Accountants in England and Wales.

Coopers and Lybrand (1996) *Understanding IAS: Analysis and Interpretation*. London: Coopers and Lybrand (UK).

Part 2

COUNTRY STUDIES

Introduction to Part 2

In Chapters 1–4 you have studied the factors influencing accounting rules and practice. These factors have been observed and recorded in academic studies. Some of those studies rely on descriptive classifications, others make use of quantitative methods of analysis to derive classifications and explanations of those classifications in terms of national characteristics.

Chapters 1–4 have explained not only the causes of difference in accounting rules and practice, but also the causes of similarities. They have shown how these similarities and differences may be traced through different types of classification systems.

Chapters 5 and 6 have explained in detail the most ambitious and far-reaching influence for harmonisation, represented by the work of the International Accounting Standards Committee (IASC). It has not worked in isolation, as Chapter 5 shows in describing the multitude of bodies and groups which have worked towards particular aspects of harmonisation across particular country groupings. However, the work of the IASC provides a comprehensive set of International Accounting Standards (IASs), described in Chapter 6. To some extent, that work lay in the background of national accounting standard setting for many years; it has now come to the fore in a very visible manner because of the desire to achieve a set of standards which will be acceptable to stock exchange regulators in markets around the world. Establishing confidence in such an approach will be tested over a number of years; but the direction is sufficiently well established to allow a text book to analyse the accounting practice of individual countries against the intended set of core standards.

Purpose of Part 2

The chapters of Part 2 have two major aims. The first is to explain how the national characteristics of a range of countries are likely to affect accounting principles and practice, using a framework derived from the studies explained in Part 1. The second is to indicate the extent to which national practice is already close to or in harmony with IASs and to indicate those areas of national practice which are particularly influenced by national characteristics, and therefore possibly more resistant to broader desires for harmonisation.

Structure of country chapters

Each chapter explains national institutions and characteristics under four headings:

- the country
- overview of accounting regulations
- institutions, broken down into:
  - political and economic system
  - legal system
  - taxation system
  - corporate financing system
  - the accounting profession
  - external influences
- societal culture and accounting subculture.

The influence of institutional factors has been explained in Chapter 1. The effect of cultural influences has been described in Chapter 2, and measurement of the differences arising from these influences in Chapter 3. The resulting classifications were summarised in Chapter 4, and each of the country chapters will refer the reader back to the relevant sections of those chapters. It is important to read those chapters again as each country is studied, so that the reader gains an increased understanding of the relative position of the country and avoids learning about one country in isolation.

The country chapters summarise the overall picture of accounting practice measured against the IASs and then identify key features of interest in national principles and practice measured against Gray's (1988) system of classification (described in Chapter 4). The classifications are:

- professionalism versus statutory control
- uniformity versus flexibility
- conservatism versus optimism
- secrecy versus transparency.

A final overview of the findings of empirical classification studies allows the chapter to draw conclusions about the relative position of the country within the four classification headings of Gray's system, using most recent accounting practices.

Choice of countries

Choosing which countries to include in detail was one of the most difficult aspects of writing this book. The total global diversity of accounting practice creates a classification range which makes international accounting a fascinating subject for study. Describing anything less than the total must necessarily leave the reader with an incomplete picture. However, constraints of time and space necessitate a choice which gives the reader the widest possible taste of the diversity and complexity, leaving an appetite to find out more by using the reference material cited in the chapters.

The choice was influenced by:

- relative size and importance of international capital markets
- residence of major multinational companies
- role in the International Accounting Standards Committee (IASC)
- origins of the accountancy profession
- distinctive national accounting principles and practice
- accounting classification systems which indicate an expectation of distinctive characteristics.

For the EU, Chapter 7 sets the scene for the Union as a whole. The choice of countries as France, Germany, The Netherlands and the UK takes four member states of the EU whose accounting practices have been identified as very different in many comparative studies. The USA has to be included in any international study because it is influential on any of the criteria used for choice here. By contrast another English-speaking country, Australia, is included as an indication that what is sometimes referred to as the 'Anglo' system has varieties in its influence.

In contrast to the present member states of the EU, with traditions of Western capital economies, there are now Eastern European countries emerging from command economies which seek membership of the EU and are arranging their accounting practices accordingly. Hungary will be among the first of these. There are emerging markets in the Far East which have derived their accounting practices from very different backgrounds. Japanese accounting practice has established an international reputation based on an international capital market. Countries such as China are developing internationally orientated accounting practices which will be consistent with their development as bases for international business activity. A number of countries are beginning to use IASs as the basis of their domestic regulations. Egypt is just one example of this.

Learning outcomes

In summary, the learning outcomes of each country chapter are, for each country:

- to know, in outline, the key characteristics of each country as summarised in published economic indicators
- to know the origins of accounting regulations and the historical development leading to the present state of practice
- to relate institutional factors for each country to the framework set out in Chapter 1 with particular reference to:
  - political and economic system
  - legal system
  - taxation system
  - corporate financing system
  - the accounting profession
  - external factors

- to be aware of the outcome of Hofstede's (1984) classification of societal culture of the country, described in Chapter 2, and its implications for approaches to accounting practice as classified by Gray's system, described in Chapter 4
- to know the position of national accounting practice in relation to the IASs described in Chapter 6
- to understand the characteristics of national accounting practice, as described in terms of specific practices, on scales of:
  - professionalism versus statutory control
  - uniformity versus flexibility
  - conservatism versus optimism
  - secrecy versus transparency
- to be able to relate specific practices to national characteristics and summarise the relative position of the country in the international spectrum of accounting practices.

Chapter 7

The European Union

PURPOSE OF THE CHAPTER

The purpose of this chapter is to set the scene for the first four countries considered in Part 2 of this book. These four countries are all member states in the EU. The reporting practices of these member states, and the regulatory framework of financial reporting, have all been influenced by membership of the Union. Each chapter will deal with particularly interesting characteristics of one country. This chapter sets the scene more generally by explaining the origins of the Union, the formation of community law and the common features which bind all member states in matters of accounting.

Learning objectives

After reading this chapter you should be able to:

● Explain the origins and nature of the EU.

● Explain how laws are made in the EU.

● Understand the main requirements of the EU Fourth and Seventh Directives.

● Relate the requirements of these Directives to the IASs.

It was shown in Chapter 4 that classification of accounting systems shows differing types of measurement practices in different clusters of companies. From the range of classifications in Chapter 4, Part 2 takes four EU countries for detailed consideration.

These countries are:

● France

● Germany

● The Netherlands

● the UK.

All are founder members of the IASC. France, Germany and the UK contain the major stock markets of the EU. The UK and The Netherlands have the longest established accountancy professional bodies of EU countries. The four countries also provide an interesting insight into the ways in which member states have preserved national characteristics in domestic legislation through use of options implementing directives on company law. In terms of the classification of accounting practice (Chapter 4, Exhibit 4.7) they occupy different strands of the hierarchy. Each is the home country of some major multinational companies.

7.2 ORIGINS AND NATURE OF THE EU

The present day EU emerged from the European Communities created in the 1950s by a series of treaties:

- European Coal and Steel Community (ECSC), 1950 (Treaty of Paris)
- European Economic Community (EEC), 1957 (Treaty of Rome)
- European Atomic Energy Community, 1957 (Euratom Treaty).

At that stage the emphasis was on industrial and trading partnerships between member states. The three communities became called collectively the 'European Communities' in 1965. Over the years the emphasis on political linkage, as well as trading co-operation, has become more apparent. The Single European Act of 1986 set the aim of removing all barriers, whether physical, technical or fiscal. The title 'European Union' was adopted in the Treaty on European Union signed at Maastricht in 1991. By the end of 1992, the Single Market was largely complete.

7.2.1 Purpose of the union[1]

The founders of the European Communities wanted to achieve a closer union among the peoples of Europe. This was stated in terms of achieving freedom of movement of persons, services and capital. The political ambitions varied, with some participants desiring to move eventually to a federation of European states and others more cautiously seeking only commercial benefits. Over the years there have been proposals for European integration and union on an increasingly ambitious scale, within the original aims of freedom of movement of persons, services and capital.

For those concerned with the practice of financial accounting and reporting, the most important of these aims is the freedom of movement of capital. Much of the work of the Council and Commission in the 1970s and 1980s related to bringing company law of member states into closer agreement. In the 1990s, more publicity has been given to the harmonisation of laws relating to the movement of persons and services, but the work on company law has continued to develop.

7.2.2 Main institutions[2]

Of the three treaties creating the European Communities, the most significant was the Treaty of Rome which led to the establishment of the European Parliament and the Court of Justice. In 1965 the Merger Treaty established a single Council of Ministers and a single Commission covering all three Communities.

---

[1] Kent (1996), pp. 3–7
[2] Kent (1996), pp. 10–24

The Council of Ministers is the legislative body, this means that it issues the laws. On receiving a proposal from the Commission (see below), the Council of Ministers will usually consult with the European Parliament before issuing legislation. The Council must act within the scope of the Treaties and must base its actions on the proposals of the Commission.

The Commission is the civil service of the EU, and Commissioners have considerable power. The Commission watches over the implementation of the treaties in each member state. It initiates policy and sets in place the procedures to implement policy, it helps Council meetings arrive at an agreed basis for action and has power to administer some of the rules.

The European Parliament is a body which is consulted on matters for legislation but it does not set legislation. Parliament may question the Commission and may, in theory, dismiss its members. There is also some scope for the exercise of a power of veto, preventing legislation from being issued.

The Court of Justice is the highest court for matters relating to community law. It examines the legality of Acts of the Council and of the Commission. It can also provide guidance to national courts in the interpretation of community law.

7.2.3 Member countries

Six countries signed the Treaty of Rome:

- Belgium
- West Germany
- France
- Italy
- Luxembourg
- The Netherlands.

In 1972 Denmark, the Republic of Ireland and the United Kingdom joined the European Communities.

The 1980s saw a Mediterranean enlargement, bringing into membership Greece (1981), Spain (1986) and Portugal (1986). Cyprus and Malta also wish to join at a future enlargement.

Unification of Germany brought the former German Democratic Republic ('East Germany') into membership in 1990. Closer links with countries in the European Free Trade Association (EFTA) brought Sweden, Austria and Finland into membership in 1995. At that point the total membership was 15 countries.

Many East European states signed 'Europe Agreements' following the Copenhagen Summit of 1993. These agreements encourage a relationship which will lead to convergence and regional co-operation and may eventually provide a route to full membership. In particular, Europe Agreements have been signed with Poland, Hungary, the Czech and Slovak Republics, Bulgaria, Romania and the Baltic States. In July 1997 the European Commission recommended that the EU should begin accession negotiations with five countries, one of which was Hungary (*see* Chapter 14).

7.3 ██ HOW LAWS ARE MADE[3]

There are two aspects to community law. Basic legislation, contained in treaties and protocols, sets out fundamental obligations of member states. When member states agree to accept the basic legislation, they give up some of their sovereign power over national affairs. This basic legislation passes directly into the law of the nation and there is no need for a member state to initiate its own laws. Secondary legislation creates obligations on the governments of member states which citizens of those states may refer to in courts of law. Consequently the member states are expected to incorporate secondary legislation in their national laws. The secondary legislation appears in more than one form:

1 a regulation has general application and is directly binding on all member states;

2 a directive explains a set of desirable outcomes, which must be achieved by member states – it indicates to member states a variety of options which they can use to achieve the required outcomes; member states select the option or options which best suit national circumstances;

3 a decision may be issued for a particular purpose such as an antitrust or a competition case, it is binding on the persons to whom it is addressed;

4 recommendations and opinions are also issued, but do not have binding force.

7.3.1 Company law directives[4]

Company law directives are published under the authority of the Treaty of Rome (Article 54(3)(g)). The Council and the Commission are required to co-ordinate 'safeguards' to protect the interests of member states and others, in such a way that these safeguards are equivalent across the Union. The safeguards must be consistent with freedom of movement of goods, persons, services and capital. The laws of member states must be brought sufficiently close to allow proper functioning of the common market.

The directives are the practical means of achieving these safeguards. The directives which have been issued in relation to company law are shown in Exhibit 7.1. The date given is that of adoption by the Council of Ministers. Incorporation in national law may take several years from the date of adoption. Where a directive is particularly controversial, such as the Fifth Directive, its adoption may be delayed for a long time.

7.3.2 The meaning of equivalence[5]

The purpose of harmonising company law across member states is to provide equivalent safeguards throughout the Union. The safeguards do not have to be identical. Equivalence allows a variety of options to be inserted in directives. Directives consist of a series of Articles, each containing a separate issue for attention. There are three types of Articles found in directives, namely:

---

[3] Kent (1996); Sealy (1996)
[4] Kent (1996), pp. 26–7; Sealy (1996), p. 9
[5] FEE (1993), pp. 15–22

Exhibit 7.1 EU COMPANY LAW DIRECTIVES

Directive	Date of adoption	Main purpose
First	1968	Powers of directors and powers of companies
Second	1976	Requirements for capital when forming a company; maintaining capital; distinction between private and public companies
Third	1978	Reconstructions within public companies
Fourth	1978	Disclosure of financial information and contents of annual accounts of individual companies
Fifth	–	[proposal] Company structure and employee participation
Sixth	1982	Merger and de-merger of public companies
Seventh	1983	Group accounts
Eighth	1984	Qualifications and independence of auditors
Ninth	–	[proposal] Relationships within a group structure
Tenth	–	[proposal] Mergers between plcs
Eleventh	1989	Disclosure in respect of branches of foreign companies located in the member state
Twelfth	1989	Single-member companies – memorandum and articles of association

● uniform rules to be implemented identically in all member states

● minimum rules which may be strengthened by the national government

● alternative rules giving member states options (choices).

7.3.3 Use of options in national law

Options are negotiated during the drafting of the directives as a result of lobbying or persuasion by the representatives of the various member states in the Council and the Commission. The options reflect areas where it was most difficult to obtain agreement at the negotiation stage.

In some cases the national government decides which options to adopt. As an example of options taken by governments, the Seventh Directive provided various options on the definition of 'control' for purposes of defining a subsidiary company. The UK government chose one set of options, while the German government chose another. In both cases, companies had to apply the law of their own country.

In other cases the national government preserves the options in its national law and allows the standard setters or the individual companies to decide which option to apply. It should be noted that the directives provide minimum standards for national law. It is open to national governments to be more exacting in the national legislation. As an example of options within the national law, the Fourth

Directive allowed more than one approach to valuation of assets in a balance sheet. The UK government allowed individual companies to choose either historical cost or an alternative valuation method (current cost). The French government did not allow individual companies the choice of departing from historical cost accounting.

7.3.4 The Fourth and Seventh Directives

This book will concentrate in particular on the contents and influence of the fourth and seventh directives. The Fourth Directive (1978) set the ground rules for the accounts of individual companies, giving standard formats for the balance sheet and profit and loss account.[6] The Seventh Directive (1983) established a common basis of presentation of accounts for groups of companies. Implementation in national law was faster in some countries than in others (Exhibit 7.2) but all member states now have both directives implemented. Together they have made a considerable impact on the presentation of companies' financial statements.

Exhibit 7.2 IMPLEMENTATION OF FOURTH AND SEVENTH DIRECTIVES IN NATIONAL LAW

Country	Fourth	Seventh
Denmark	1981	1990
UK	1981	1989
France	1983	1985
Netherlands	1983	1988
Luxembourg	1984	1988
Belgium	1985	1990
Germany	1985	1985
Ireland	1986	1992
Greece	1986	1987
Spain	1989	1989
Portugal	1989	1991
Italy	1991	1991
Sweden	1995	1995
Austria	1995	1995
Finland	1995	1995

7.3.5 Other measures

Other community measures which have had an impact on accounting practices include those on:

● admission to listing on a stock exchange

● mutual recognition of listing particulars (where a company resident in one country is allowed to have its shares listed on the stock exchange of another, without rewriting its financial statements)

---

[6] Watts (1979)

- disclosure of major shareholdings
- insider dealing
- information contained in a prospectus.

7.3.6 Mutual recognition[7]

Stock exchanges each have their own rules to ensure that companies obtaining a listing provide sufficient information to allow a fair market to operate. The rules are drawn up in terms of national accounting practices and consequently companies which have a listing on more than one international stock exchange may find themselves preparing more than one set of accounts. To avoid this problem, the stock exchanges in member states have agreed that they will recognise accounts prepared under the rules of any other member state. The agreement is 'mutual' because each stock exchange feels it has given something to the financial community by relaxing the rules, and has also gained something from the financial community, by encouraging international listing of shares.

Mutual recognition is based on the reassurance that member states now have minimum standards in common because they all apply the Fourth and Seventh Directives. Mutual recognition is less rigorous than the concept of equivalence (explained earlier).

7.4 THE FOURTH DIRECTIVE[8]

Drafting of the Fourth Directive began in 1965 when there were only six members of the European Communities but it was completed in 1978 when there were nine members. For Denmark, the UK and Ireland, who all joined the Community in 1978, some relatively late lobbying was required to reflect national concerns. In particular the UK argued forcefully for inclusion of the concept of 'a true and fair view'. The inclusion of the words 'true and fair' caused particular difficulty for translation into the languages of other member states. Not only were the words unfamiliar: the ideas behind the words were unfamiliar in continental Europe, and particular national approaches are dealt with in Chapters 8–11. (The influence of German chairmanship in the early stages of drafting the directive is seen in the detailed specification of the format of financial statements; such prescriptive formats were not known in the UK or Ireland prior to the Fourth Directive.)

7.4.1 Objective[9]

The directive applies to the accounts of an individual company and covers all aspects of the annual accounts. It aims to harmonise accounting principles, presentation, publication and audit by laying down minimum standards to be applied by member states. The intention in preparing the directive was that investors, lenders and suppliers should find it easier to obtain, understand and rely on the

---

[7] FEE (1993), pp. 15–22
[8] Watts (1979)
[9] Coleman (1984)

accounts of companies in other member states. The directive was also aimed at promoting fair competition among member state companies: managers of a business anywhere in the Union should be able to find out as much about a competitor company as the competitor can find out about their business. Furthermore, multinational corporations should not base decisions about location on differences in national accounting requirements.

7.4.2 'True and fair view'[10]

The Fourth Directive imposes an overriding requirement that the annual accounts (comprising the balance sheet, profit and loss account and notes to the accounts) present a true and fair view. In most cases it would be expected that complying with the requirement of the law would be sufficient. However, it may be necessary for companies to disclose more than the minimum specification in order to present a true and fair view. On relatively rare occasions, companies may have to depart from the requirements of the law in order to give a true and fair view. That is permissible but must be explained in the annual report.

The concept of a 'true and fair view' is essentially Anglo-Saxon in origin and was not readily accommodated within some national practices of Continental Europe, particularly where tax legislation had traditionally dominated accounting reporting. The first draft of the directive, issued in 1971, used words such as 'accuracy' and 'principles of regular and proper accounting'. Negotiations following the accession of the UK, the Republic of Ireland and Denmark resulted in the phrase 'true and fair' appearing. The company laws of each member state now include words approximating in translation to 'true and fair view', but the meaning of the words and application of the concept should be considered in the context of juridical tradition and cultural aspects.[11]

It has been suggested that there is a range of positions on the meaning of 'true and fair view'.[12] In the UK and Ireland, it may be used by standard setters to justify general rules and may be used by companies to justify overriding the specific requirements of law. In Germany, it is clear that the idea of a 'true and fair view' cannot be used to override the requirements of law. Between these two extremes lies a range of interpretations in various member states.

In the Netherlands 'true and fair' may be used by directors and auditors as a basic principle for interpretation of the law and guidelines. It is used in setting guidelines but is not used to override the requirements of the law. In France and Spain 'true and fair' has been used by law makers to allow some move towards substance rather than form. It may be used by companies as a justification for overriding the law, but only very exceptionally. It is used by directors and auditors as a basic principle for interpretation of the law. In Italy 'true and fair' may be used by directors and auditors as a basic principle for interpretation of the law but it is unlikely that it would be used to justify a departure from the law.

---

[10] Parker and Nobes (1994)
[11] Parker and Nobes (1994)
[12] Parker and Nobes (1994), p. 80

7.4.3 Framework of principles

There is no separate European framework of principles. However the Fourth Directive includes Article 31 setting out accounting principles for valuation:

- the company must be presumed to be a going concern unless evidence exists to the contrary

- methods of valuation must be applied consistently from one period to the next

- valuation must be made on a prudent basis and in particular:
  - only profits made may be included in the financial statements
  - all foreseeable liabilities and potential losses arising in the year should be taken into account, even where they become apparent between the balance sheet date and the date on which it is drawn up
  - account must be taken of depreciation, irrespective of whether there is a profit or a loss

- all income and charges must be brought into account (i.e. the accruals concept is applied)

- components of asset and liability items must be valued separately

- the opening balance sheet of a year must correspond to the closing balance sheet of the previous year.

7.4.4 Disclosure and presentation

The Fourth Directive includes Articles 9, 10 and 23–26, which list items for disclosure in the balance sheet and profit and loss account. The order of presentation may not be varied but there is some latitude allowed, such as the insertion of subtotals. National standard setting bodies may add further requirements. Companies have the discretion to provide more information than is prescribed by the Directives.

The layout of the annual accounts is prescribed in *formats*. There are descriptions of formats in the Articles of the Fourth Directive setting out the order of line items for one type of balance sheet and two types of profit and loss account, with a choice of horizontal and vertical presentation for both. Examples of some of the prescribed formats are set out in Appendix 7.1 (p. 215).

The first example in Appendix 7.1 is a full horizontal balance sheet as set out in Article 9. It shows, by using a variety of symbols, information required from all companies, information not required from small companies, and information not required from small companies or in published accounts of medium-sized companies. In that example, each line item carries a label. The major headings are labelled with capital letters A, B, C, and so on. The next level of headings is labelled with roman numerals I, II, III, and so on. The third level of headings is labelled with arabic numerals 1, 2, 3, and so on. Line items labelled with capital letters and roman numerals must appear on the face of the balance sheet. Those labelled with arabic numerals may appear in notes to the accounts. The example in the Appendix shows the fullest possible balance sheet where a company places all information on the face of the primary financial statement. Making use of notes to the accounts and the alternative classifications shown for some line items, plus concessions for company size, may reduce the density of information in particular cases.

A full vertical balance sheet is set out in Article 10. The second example in Appendix 7.1 shows the application of Article 10 where a company desires to produce a minimum balance sheet taking advantage of the concessions for small companies and making use of the facility for notes to the accounts.

There are four Articles dealing with formats of the profit and loss account because two quite different approaches are allowed, each in horizontal and vertical form. One approach permits the costs to be analysed by *type of expenditure* (e.g. purchase of goods, payment of wages and salaries) while the other gives categories based on the *function of the expenditure* (e.g. the function of selling goods is identified as cost of goods sold, while paying wages and salaries is reported as either administrative or distribution functions). This is also called the *operational basis*. These two approaches reflect different national practices in existence when the Directive was written. The resulting differences in presentation occur at the start of

Exhibit 7.3 COMPARISON OF ALTERNATIVE FORMS OF VERTICAL PROFIT AND LOSS ACCOUNT (based on Articles 23 and 25)

Type of expenditure	Functional basis (Operational basis)
1 Net turnover	1 Net turnover
2 Variations in stocks of finished goods and in progress	
3 Work performed by the undertaking for its own purposes and capitalised	2 Cost of sales (including value adjustments)
4 Other operating income	
5 (a) Raw materials and consumables (b) Other external charges	3 Gross profit or loss

6 Staff costs
  (a) Wages and salaries
  (b) Social security costs, with a separate indication of those relating to pensions	

	4 Distribution costs (including value adjustments)
7 (a) Value adjustments in respect of formation expenses and of tangible and intangible fixed assets (b) Value adjustments in respect of current assets, to the extent that they exceed the amount of value adjustments which are normal in the undertaking concerned	5 Administrative expenses (including value adjustments)
8 Other operating charges 9–21 Same as 7–19 for *functional basis*	6 Other operating income 7–19 Same as 9–21 for *type of expenditure*

each type of profit and loss account, and are set out for comparison in Exhibit 7.3. The *type of expenditure* basis is more detailed on the face of the profit and loss account, but has the disadvantage of not showing the gross profit or loss. Under the *functional basis* more detailed notes to the accounts are required, so the overall provision of information is the same under each.

7.4.5 Recognition and measurement

There are no criteria stated for recognition, but there is the general requirement that profits may only be reported when they are 'made'. The word 'made' is not defined, but has generally been equated with 'realised' (also not defined). The restriction to realisation of profit has an inevitable consequence on asset recognition in many instances. The Directive does not define 'made' and hence a great deal of discretion is left to national law and national standard setters. This area includes potentially controversial issues such as profits on long-term contracts, franchise income, fees received in advance of services rendered, and recognition of income for those who provide finance through leasing arrangements.

The general rule of measurement is that historical cost accounting must be applied, although there is an option in the Fourth Directive (Article 33) by which member states may permit or require companies or any classes of companies to:

- value tangible fixed assets with limited useful economic lives, and stocks, by the replacement value method
- value by other methods designed to take account of inflation the items shown in the annual accounts, including capital and reserves
- revalue tangible fixed assets and financial fixed assets.

Where national law provides for use of any these valuation methods, it must define their content and limits and the rules for their application (Article 33).

The Fourth Directive contains specific valuation rules for certain assets:

1 fixed assets with a limited useful economic life must be depreciated so as to write off their value systematically over the useful life (Article 35).

2 goodwill, research and development costs and formation expenses must in general be written off over five years. In exceptional circumstances, member states may permit a longer period (Article 37.1) (see later for the treatment of goodwill arising on consolidation);

3 current assets must be valued at purchase price or production cost. Value adjustments must be made where the market value is lower than purchase price or production cost (Article 39);

4 member states have options on the valuation of stocks of goods. They may permit the purchase price or production cost of stocks of goods of the same category, either on the basis of weighted average prices, or on the basis of first-in-first-out (FIFO) or on the basis of last-in-first-out (LIFO) (Article 40);

5 member states have the option to permit use of the equity method of valuing holdings in affiliated companies (the Fourth Directive left open the precise definition of 'affiliated' but the Seventh Directive gave guidance as a holding of 20% or more) (Article 59).

The recognition of liabilities is largely governed by the requirement for prudence, as explained earlier. There are fewer valuation rules than for assets, but particular items are:

1 under the heading 'accruals and deferred income', account must be taken of the income and charges of the year, irrespective of the date of receipt or payment (Article 31);

2 where the amount repayable under any debt is greater than the amount received (e.g. a discount on issue of a debenture loan) the difference may be shown as an asset and amortised, to be written off no later than the time of repayment of the debt (Article 41);

3 deferred taxation liabilities may be recognised, but there is no rule specified for valuation (Article 9/10, Article 43);

4 provisions for contingencies and charges must not be in excess of the amount necessary (Article 42).

7.4.6 Measurement approaches

As already explained, the Fourth Directive carries an initial presumption of historical cost accounting. Inflation accounting is considered in the Directive, where member states may permit or require companies or any classes of companies to:

● value tangible fixed assets with limited useful economic lives and stocks by the replacement value method

● value by other methods designed to take account of inflation the items shown in the annual accounts, including capital and reserves

● revalue tangible fixed assets and financial fixed assets.

Where national law provides for use of any these valuation methods, it must define their content and limits and the rules for their application (Article 33).

7.5 THE SEVENTH DIRECTIVE[13]

The Fourth Directive deals only with individual companies standing alone. The essential purpose of writing the Seventh Directive was to define a group. This was an extremely controversial matter because of the range of practices in existence across countries and because of the importance of the definition in relation to tax law in some countries. Many of the issues contained in the Fourth Directive, such as presentation, valuation rules and accounting principles, apply equally well to groups of companies. These matters are incorporated in the Seventh Directive by specific reference to the Fourth Directive.

7.5.1 Origins[14]

For some member states, consolidation is a development of recent years. An act of 1965 in Germany required a form of consolidation to be applied by public com-

---

[13] FEE (1993)
[14] Niessen (1993)

panies. Listed companies in France were required to apply consolidation from the early 1970s. The Seventh Directive was first published as a draft in 1976 and drew on the long-running experience which could be found in the UK, Ireland and the Netherlands. Consequently the Seventh Directive brought group accounting to some continental European countries which had not previously produced consolidated accounts as a widespread practice.

The Seventh Directive shows the influence of Anglo-Saxon practice, in contrast to the Fourth Directive which may be seen as having a clear base in continental European law. There are, however, some important indications of continental European influence in the definition of 'control'. Some countries regarded the group as being essentially an economic unit, defined by its economic activity, while others preferred to have strict definitions set out in law, defined by legal contracts. The considerable debate on the content of the Seventh Directive is reflected in the number of options it contains.

7.5.2 Extensive use of options

Options relate to aspects of consolidated accounting which were found to be too controversial to allow any agreement in a Directive. There are more than 50 options which represent political compromises rather than strong points of principle. The extent of the options available to member states means that variety of national practice is wide. The Directive has increased the number of companies that are required to produce consolidated accounts, but has not greatly increased harmonisation in the practices of consolidated accounting.

7.5.3 Approach to consolidation

Undertakings are required to draw up consolidated accounts which include subsidiaries irrespective of their location. 'Subsidiaries' are defined in terms of control by voting rights or dominant influence established by contract. Member states have the further option to require consolidation of companies managed on a unified basis and companies over which a dominant influence is exercised in the absence of a specific contract (Articles 1–4). Articles 5–15 begin the process of developing the options which are a particular feature of the Seventh Directive (Exhibit 7.4).

Exhibit 7.4   OPTIONS FOR CONSOLIDATION

> Member states may exempt financial holding companies that neither manage their subsidiaries nor take part in appointments to the board of directors (Article 5). They may also exempt small and medium-sized groups provided no listed company is involved (Article 6). A company is exempted from the requirement to consolidate its own subsidiaries if it is itself a subsidiary, but member states may insist on consolidation by listed companies, whether or not they are themselves subsidiaries. Other exemptions are available to member states under Articles 7–11. Member states may require horizontal consolidation where companies are managed by the same person (Article 12). Subsidiaries may be excluded from consolidation if they are immaterial, or if there would be disproportionate expense or delay (Articles 13–15).

Merger accounting is permitted where any cash payment represents less than 10% of the nominal value of shares issued (Article 20). Minority interests must be shown separately and all income of consolidated companies must be included (Articles 21–23). This means that proportional consolidation of income is not permissible for full subsidiaries.

Various practical rules for consolidation are set out in Articles 24–28. These are very detailed and reflect the lack of widespread experience of the process when the Directive was given approval.

Positive goodwill arising on consolidation must be amortised through the profit and loss account or else written off immediately against reserves. Negative goodwill should be taken to profit only if it is realised or is due to the expectation of future costs or losses (Articles 30, 31).

7.5.4 Similarities to Fourth Directive

The requirement for a true and fair view is contained in Article 16. Formats of the Fourth Directive are updated and expanded to take account of the additional line items of consolidation (Articles 16 and 17). Goodwill based on fair values should be calculated at the date of first consolidation or at the date of purchase (Article 18).

7.5.5 Valuation rules

The valuation rules of the Fourth Directive must be applied (Article 29). The Article specifies initially that the undertaking which draws up consolidated accounts must apply the same methods of valuation as are used in its individual accounts. However, the Article then provides the option that member states may require or permit the use of other valuation methods in the consolidated accounts, provided such methods are permitted by the Fourth Directive. Most member states give permission for use of other valuation rules, but none requires such an approach.

7.5.6 Associates and joint ventures

Member states may require or permit proportional consolidation for joint ventures (Article 32). Associated companies must be recorded as a single line item, using the equity method of valuation (Article 33). The remainder of the Directive deals extensively with disclosure requirements and transitional provisions.

7.6 THE ACCOUNTANCY PROFESSION IN EUROPE

The Fédération des Experts Comptables Européens (FEE) is the representative organisation for the accountancy profession in Europe. At the start of 1997 it encompassed 38 leading institutes in 26 countries, comprising the 15 member states of the EU, Cyprus, Iceland, Israel, Malta, Monaco, Norway, Switzerland, the Czech Republic, Hungary, Romania and Slovenia. Together this covers 375,000 accountants of whom about 40% work in public practice and 60% in industry, commerce, government and education. The major accountancy bodies in Europe are described briefly in Chapter 1, Exhibit 1.6, and particular bodies are described in more detail in the country-specific chapters.

FEE was created in 1986 to continue the work of previous organisations serving the European accountancy profession. Its principal objectives are:[15]

- to promote and advance the interests of the European accountancy profession
- to be the sole representative organisation of the European accountancy profession in relation to the institutions of the EU
- to represent the European accountancy profession at the international level
- to promote co-operation between the professional accountancy bodies in Europe in relation to issues of common interest
- to work towards the enhancement, harmonisation and liberalisation of the practice and regulation of accountancy in Europe, taking account of developments at a worldwide level and, where necessary, promoting and defending specific European interests.

FEE is one of the regional accountancy bodies consulted by the International Federation of Accountants (IFAC), which in turn works closely with the IASC.

This description might give the impression that FEE speaks for the accountancy bodies in Europe on international matters. However it is important to note from Chapter 5 that it is the EU Commission which has the observer status on the IASC and also that professional bodies of each country are directly members of the IASC. They may from time to time become Board members but that is in their capacity as national representatives. Furthermore the UK standard setters are working in the G4 group with the USA, Canada and Australia on a number of issues of international importance.

7.7 FUTURE DEVELOPMENTS OF ACCOUNTING IN THE EU

7.7.1 Extension to candidates for future entry

Other European countries beyond the member states of the EU are adopting the Fourth and Seventh Directive into their national laws. Harmonisation with European Law is a condition for new entrants to the Union. In particular the countries of Eastern Europe which seek closer links with the Union are adopting the Directives as the basis of national law; these are the countries which have signed 'Europe Agreements' following the Copenhagen Summit of 1993.

7.7.2 Relationship with IASs

It may be seen from Exhibit 7.4 that the options and areas of silence under the Directives mean that there is greater scope for harmonisation in the near future by following the IASs than there is by the process of European Law. The concern in Europe is that the balance of influence over the international standards gives a fair hearing to Europe and is not dominated by North America.

In November 1995, the Commission announced that it would look to the IASC to carry forward the work of harmonisation. This reversed earlier indications by the Commission that it would wish to develop a programme of European standards. The change of approach probably reflected acknowledgement of the

---

[15] *FEE Euronews*, Issue 1, March 1997, p. 4

continued diversity of measurement practices across EU countries, despite achievements of harmonisation in disclosure and presentation. By 1995 it was becoming apparent that only the IASC would be in a position to meet the needs for harmonisation within a relatively short timescale. It was reported in the IASC *Annual Review* of 1996 that a study had shown only two very minor conflicts between IASs and the rules contained in the European Directives.

To achieve harmonisation by use of IASs it will be important that member states take action to recognise IASs in their laws. By 1997, this process was under way in France and Germany. The directives will also have to be reviewed and kept in line with changing demands. The European Commission has indicated its awareness that amendments to the Fourth Directive may be required in order to permit some IAS practices, particularly that proposed for derivatives.[16]

7.7.3 Accounting for the Euro[17]

The aim of creating a single market leads inevitably to the aim of creating a single currency. A single unit of currency, called the Euro, has been proposed for introduction in member states by the year 2002. Not all member states wish to join the monetary union and until that discussion has been completed it is not clear whether the Euro will apply universally across all member states. A three-phase programme has been proposed. Phase A, the launch of monetary union, will start in 1998; Phase B, the practical development of monetary union and the introduction of the new currency unit, will run from the start of 1999 to the end of 2001; Phase C, the definitive changeover, will take place during 2002.

From 2002 onwards there should not be significant accounting problems if all member states use the same currency. If some remain outside monetary union there may be increased requirements for foreign currency translation and additional levels of detail required in bookkeeping systems. In the intervening years of transition there could be quite significant accounting problems, in reporting and in recording transactions, arising from dual operations. Two principles have been laid down as 'no compulsion' and 'no prohibition' during the transition period. This may cause a range of accounting issues to arise across and within member states until the completion of Phase C.

7.8 SUMMARY AND CONCLUSIONS

This chapter has explained the origins of the EU and the way in which it has expanded and continues to expand as more countries seek membership. It has explained the process by which laws are made, so that the development of national company law may be understood in its impact on national accounting practices. The most important aspects of the legal process of the EU, so far as accounting is concerned, are the Fourth and Seventh Directives. The chapter has explained these in some detail so that the practices of individual countries may be discussed in later chapters against this general background. Finally the chapter has indicated that the accounting practices of the EU may be starting to harmonise with IASs.

---

[16] *FT World Accounting Report*, May 1997, p. 3
[17] Directorate General XV (1997)

APPENDIX 7.1: FORMATS IN THE FOURTH DIRECTIVE

Horizontal balance sheet (Article 9)

Assets

A	Subscribed capital unpaid			θ
B	Formation expenses			θ
C	Fixed assets			θ
	I Intangible assets		⊗	
	1 Costs of research and development	φ		
	2 Concession, patents, licences, trade marks and similar rights and assets	φ		
	3 Goodwill	•		
	4 Payments on account	φ		
	II Tangible assets		⊗	
	1 Land and buildings	•		
	2 Plant and machinery	•		
	3 Other fixtures and fittings, tools and equipment	•		
	4 Payments on account and tangible assets in course of construction	•		
	III Financial assets		⊗	
	1 Shares in affiliated undertakings	•		
	2 Loans to affiliated undertakings	•		
	3 Participating interests	•		
	4 Loans to undertakings with which the company is linked by virtue of participating interests	•		
	5 Investments held as fixed assets	φ		
	6 Other loans	φ		
	7 Own shares	•		
D	Current assets			θ
	I Stocks		⊗	
	1 Raw materials and consumables	φ		
	2 Work in progress	φ		
	3 Finished goods and goods for resale	φ		
	4 Payments on account	φ		
	II Debtors		⊗	

(Amounts becoming due and payable after more than one year must be shown separately for each item)

	1 Trade debtors	φ		
	2 Amounts owed by affiliated undertakings	•		
	3 Amounts owed by undertakings with which the company is linked by virtue of participating interests	•		
	4 Other debtors	φ		
	5 Subscribed capital called but not paid (unless under A-Assets)	φ		
	6 Prepayments and accrued income (unless under E-Assets)	•		
	III Investments		⊗	
	1 Shares in affiliated undertakings	•		
	2 Own shares	•		
	3 Other investments	φ		
	IV Cash at bank and in hand		⊗	
E	Prepayments and accrued income (unless under D.II.6-Assets)			θ

θ

Liabilities

A Capital and reserves   θ
   I   Subscribed capital   ⊗
      (unless called-up capital shown under this item)
   II   Share premium account   ⊗
   III Revaluation reserve   ⊗
   IV Reserves   ⊗
      1   Legal reserve, in so far as required   φ
      2   Reserve for own shares, in so far as required   φ
      3   Reserves provided for by the articles of association   φ
      4   Other reserves   φ

   V   Profit or loss brought forward   ⊗
   VI Profit or loss for the financial year   ⊗
      (unless under F-Assets or E-Liabilities)

B   Provisions for liabilities and charges   θ
    1   Provisions for pensions and similar obligations   φ
    2   Provisions for taxation   φ
    3   Other provisions   φ

C   Creditors   θ
(Amounts becoming due and payable within one year and
after more than one year must be shown separately for each
item and in total)
    1   Debenture loans, showing convertible loans separately   •
    2   Amounts owed to credit institutions   •
    3   Payments received on account of orders in so far as they
       are not shown separately as deductions from stocks   φ
    4   Trade creditors   φ
    5   Bills of exchange payable   φ
    6   Amounts owed to affiliated undertakings   •
    7   Amounts owed to undertakings with which the company
       is linked by virtue of participating interests   •
    8   Other creditors including tax and social security   φ
    9   Accruals and deferred income (unless shown under
       D-Liabilities)   •

D Accruals and deferred income (unless shown under
    C.9-Liabilities)   θ
                                  θ

Key to symbols
θ   Required from all companies
⊗   Required from all companies
•   Not required for small companies
φ   Not required for small companies or published
    accounts of medium-sized companies

Minimum vertical balance sheet (Article 10)

C	FIXED ASSETS		θ
	I Intangible assets	⊗	
	II Tangible assets	⊗	
	III Financial assets	⊗	
D	CURRENT ASSETS		θ
	(showing separately for debtors amounts due in more than one year)		
	I Stocks	⊗	
	II Debtors	⊗	
	III Investments	⊗	
	IV Cash	⊗	
F	CREDITORS (due within one year)		(θ)
G	NET CURRENT ASSETS		θ
H	TOTAL ASSETS LESS CURRENT LIABILITIES		θ
I	CREDITORS (due in more than one year)		(θ)
J	PROVISIONS FOR LIABILITIES AND CHARGES		(θ)
L	CAPITAL AND RESERVES	⊗	
	I Called-up capital	⊗	
	II Share premium account	⊗	
	III Revaluation reserve	⊗	
	IV Reserves	⊗	
	V Profit or loss brought forward	⊗	
	VI Profit or loss for year	⊗	

Notes:

1 Items A, B, E and K are omitted here because national law can permit inclusion within other headings as shown in previous exhibit.

2 For larger companies the above layout assumes that national law requires or allows all items preceded by arabic numerals to be shown in the notes on the accounts.

3 The above layout also shows the form of balance sheet that would be published by small companies if all possible concessions relating to the balance sheet were granted to them (and making assumptions 1 and 2 above).

4 Net current assets will include amounts due from debtors after more than one year.

Key to symbols

⊗ Required from all companies

θ Required from all companies

217

Profit and loss account
Type of expenditure basis – vertical (Article 23)

1 Net turnover   φ
2 Variations in stocks of finished goods and work in progress   φ
3 Work performed by the undertaking for its own purposes and capitalised   φ
4 Other operating income   φ

5 (a) Raw materials and consumables   φ
   (b) Other external charges   φ

6 Staff costs
   (a) Wages and salaries   (•)
   (b) Social security costs, with a separate indication of those relating
       to pensions   (•)

7 (a) Value adjustments in respect of formation expenses and of
       tangible and intangible fixed assets   •
   (b) Value adjustments in respect of current assets, to the extent
       that they exceed the amount of value adjustments which are
       normal in the undertaking concerned   •

8 Other operating charges   (•)

9 Income from participating interests, with a separate indication of
   that derived from affiliated undertakings   •

10 Income from other investments and loans forming part of the fixed assets,
    with a separate indication of that derived from affiliated undertakings   •

11 Other interest receivable and similar income, with a separate indication
    of that derived from affiliated undertakings   •

12 Value adjustments in respect of financial assets and of investments
    held as current assets   (•)

13 Interest payable and similar charges, with a separate indication of
    those concerning affiliated undertakings   (•)

14 Tax on profit on ordinary activities   (•)

15 Profit or loss on ordinary activities after taxation   •

16 Extraordinary income   •

17 Extraordinary charges   (•)

18 Extraordinary profit or loss   •

19 Tax on extraordinary profit or loss   (•)

20 Other taxes not shown under the above items   •

21 Profit or loss for the financial year   •

Key to symbols
φ Small and medium-sized companies may be allowed to combine these items
    under one item called 'Gross profit or loss'. Small companies may be exempted
    from publishing, but not from preparing, a profit and loss account.
• Not required for small companies.

Profit and loss account
Functional (operational) basis – vertical (Article 25)

1	Net turnover	φ
2	Cost of sales (including value adjustments)	φ
3	Gross profit or loss	•
4	Distribution costs (including value adjustments)	(•)
5	Administrative expenses (including value adjustments)	(•)
6	Other operating income	
7	Income from participating interests, with a separate indication of that derived from affiliated undertakings	•
8	Income from other investments and loans forming part of the fixed assets, with a separate indication of that derived from affiliated undertakings	•
9	Other interest receivable and similar income, with a separate indication of that derived from affiliated undertakings	•
10	Value adjustments in respect of financial assets and of investments held as current assets	(•)
11	Interest payable and similar charges, with a separate indication of those concerning affiliated undertakings	(•)
12	Tax on profit or loss on ordinary activities	(•)
13	Profit or loss on ordinary activities after taxation	•
14	Extraordinary income	•
15	Extraordinary charges	(•)
16	Extraordinary profit or loss	•
17	Tax on extraordinary profit or loss	(•)
18	Other taxes not shown under the above items	(•)
19	Profit or loss for the financial year	•

Key to symbols

φ Small and medium-sized companies may be allowed to combine these items with item 3 under one item called 'Gross profit or loss'. Small companies may be exempted from publishing, but not from preparing, a profit and loss account.

• Not required for small companies.

219

APPENDIX 7.2: RELATING THE INTERNATIONAL ACCOUNTING STANDARDS TO THE FOURTH AND SEVENTH DIRECTIVES

	Fourth Directive	*Seventh Directive*	*Notes on contents EU Directives*
Framework for the preparation and presentation of financial statements	Art 3		Once a permitted format has been adopted it should be applied consistently
	Art 4	Art 16	Application of the concept of 'true and fair'
	Art 31		Sets out the general principles of valuation
	Art 32		Affirms the general application of historical cost valuation
	Art 33		Allows member states to permit or require the use of other methods of valuation
Disclosure and presentation			
IAS 1 Presentation of Financial Statements	Art 4	Art 16	Application of the concept of 'true and fair'
IAS 1 Presentation of Financial Statements	Art 43 1 (1)		Disclosure of methods of valuation and calculation of value adjustment
IAS 1 Presentation of Financial Statements	Arts 9, 10	Art 17	Layout of permitted balance sheet formats
	Arts 23–26	Art 17	Layout of permitted profit and loss account formats
	Art 4		Explains to what extent items can be combined on face of primary financial statements
	Arts 11, 27		Sets out criteria for and contents of abridged financial statements
IAS 1 Presentation of Financial Statements	Art 9, 10		Both permitted balance sheet formats require identification of current assets and current liabilities
IAS 7 Cash Flow Statements			
IAS 8 Net Profit or Loss for the Period, Fundamental Errors and Changes in Accounting Policies	Art 29		Amounts arising otherwise than in the course of 'ordinary activities' must be shown as 'extraordinary income and charges'
IAS xx Discontinuing Operations			
IAS 14 Reporting Financial Information by Segments	Art 43 1 (8)		Disclosure of segment turnover by activity and geographical markets
IAS 24 Related Party Disclosure			
IAS 33 Earnings per Share			
IAS 34 Interim Financial Reporting			
Asset recognition and measurement			
IAS 2 Inventories	Art 39 1		Current assets valued at the lower of cost or market value
	Art 39 2		Cost should include a reasonable proportion of production overheads
	Art 40		Cost defined as LIFO, FIFO, average cost or similar method
IAS 4 Depreciation Accounting	Art 35 1(b)		Fixed assets with limited useful life must be depreciated

	Fourth Directive	*Seventh Directive*	*Notes on contents EU Directives*
IAS 16 Property, Plant and Equipment	Art 35 1 (a), Art 35 3		Fixed assets valued at cost Cost of self-production includes a reasonable proportion of indirect production overheads
IAS xx Impairment of Assets			
IAS 23 Borrowing Costs	Arts 35 4, 39 2		Interest on borrowed funds to finance production of either current or fixed assets may be included in the total of production cost of the asset
IAS 25 Accounting for Investments	Art 36 Art 60		Investment companies may be allowed to charge depreciation directly against reserves Investment companies may be required or permitted to value investments at market value
IAS 9 Research and Development Costs	Art 37 1		If R&D treated as an asset it should be depreciated over a maximum of five years
IAS xx Intangible Assets	Art 35		Depreciation required for all fixed assets of finite life
Liability recognition and measurement			
IAS 10 Contingencies and Events Occurring After the Balance Sheet Date	Art 43 1 (7)		Disclosure of post-balance sheet financial commitments
IAS 12 Income Taxes	Art 43 1 (11)		Difference between tax charged and tax payable for the same years (deferred tax) should be disclosed as a note and may be separately identified on the balance sheet
IAS 17 Leases			
IAS 19 Employee Benefits			
IAS 32 Financial Instruments: Disclosure and Presentation			
Recognition of economic activity			
IAS 11 Construction Contracts			
IAS 18 Revenue			
IAS 20 Accounting for Government Grants and Disclosure of Government Assistance			
Measurement			
IAS 15 Information Reflecting the Effects of Changing Prices	Art 33		Allows member states to permit or require the use replacement cost or other methods of valuation that take account of inflation
IAS 29 Financial Reporting in Hyperinflationary Economies			
Group accounting			
IAS 21 The Effects of Changes in Foreign Exchange Rates			
IAS 22 Business Combinations	Arts 34, 37 2	Art. 30 1	Goodwill should be written off within five years but member states can permit companies to extend this period provided it does not exceed its useful economic life

	Fourth Directive	*Seventh Directive*	*Notes on contents EU Directives*
IAS 22 Business Combinations		Art 30 2	Member states may permit the immediate write-off of goodwill to reserves
		Art 31	Negative goodwill may be transferred to profit and loss account when the event to which it corresponds occurs
		Arts 18, 22	Consolidation of 100% of assets and liabilities and income and expenses of subsidiaries
		Art 19	Goodwill on consolidation calculated at date of acquisition; revaluation of assets and liabilities may be required or permitted
		Art 20	Merger accounting method may be required or permitted if conditions are met (90% plus shares held, cash part of consideration less than 10% of shares issued)
		Arts 21, 22	Minority interest should be shown separately in balance sheet and profit and loss account
		Art 25	Methods of consolidation should be applied consistently
IAS 27 Consolidated Financial Statements and Accounting for Investments in Subsidiaries		Arts 1, 2	Defines parent/subsidiary in terms of voting power and contractual control Member states may extend this to other non-contractual management relationships
		Art 5	Financial holding companies may be exempted from producing group accounts
		Art 6	Exemption on grounds of size from producing group accounts is permitted
		Art 7	Intermediate holding company is exempt from producing group accounts when 90% plus of its shares owned by parent
		Arts 13, 14	Non-consolidated subsidiaries can be justified on grounds of materiality; severe long-term restriction in control; disproportionate expense or undue delay; held as a current asset; or dissimilar activity
		Art 26	Elimination of intra-group trading and indebtedness
		Art 29	Member states may require or permit in the group accounts the use of methods of valuation not used in the parent's own accounts
IAS 28 Accounting for Investments in Associates		Art 33	Equity accounting method should be used when accounting for investments in associated undertakings
IAS 31 Financial Reporting of Interests in Joint Ventures		Art 32	Member states may permit or require jointly owned undertaking (joint ventures) to be consolidated using proportional consolidation method
Specialist industries			
IAS 26 Accounting and Reporting by Retirement Benefit Plans			
IAS 30 Disclosure in the Financial Statements of Banks and Similar Financial Institutions			

QUESTIONS

Origins and nature of the European Union (7.2)

1 To what extent is accounting practice in member states likely to be affected by the stated purpose of the union?

2 In which ways are each of the main institutions likely to have an influence or impact on accounting practice in member states?

How laws are made (7.3)

1 If a new company law directive were proposed today, what processes would be required? How long might it take for the directive to enter national law of each member state?

2 Is 'equivalence' the same as 'equality'?

3 Why is it necessary to have options in directives? What factors might cause options to be allowed in a new directive?

Fourth Directive (7.4)

1 What were the most significant features of the Fourth Directive?

2 Why may the words 'true and fair' have a different effect in different countries?

3 What are the similarities and differences between the 'type of expenditure' format and the 'functional basis' format of the profit and loss account?

4 To what extent do recognition and measurement feature in the Fourth and Seventh Directives?

Seventh Directive (7.5)

1 What were the most significant features of the Seventh Directive?

2 What are the problems in defining a group?

The accounting profession in Europe (7.6)

1 Is it necessary for FEE to carry out a co-ordinating role for the accountancy profession in Europe?

Future developments of accounting in the EU (7.7)

1 What are the key issues facing accounting practice in the EU?

2 Should the EU set its own European accounting standards independently of the IASC? What are the arguments for and against?

3 From the table in Appendix 7.2 (p. 220), which areas of the current IASC core standards project are closest to existing requirements in EU directives? Which areas are furthest from EU directives or not dealt with in them?

■ REFERENCES

Coleman, R. (1984) 'The aims of EEC company law harmonisation: Corporate accounting and disclosure issues', in Gray, S.J. and Coenenberg, A.G., *EEC and Accounting Harmonisation: Implementation and Impact of the Fourth Directive*. Amsterdam: North Holland.

Directorate General XV (1997) *Accounting for the Introduction of the Euro*. Brussels: European Commission.

FEE (1993) *Seventh Directive Options and their Implementation*. London: Fédération des Experts Comptables Européens/Routledge.

Flower, J. and Lefebvre, C. (eds) (1997) *Comparative Studies in Accounting Regulation in Europe*. Leuven: Acco.

Kent, P. (1996) *Law of the European Union*, 2nd edn. London: Pitman Publishing.

Niessen, H. (1993) 'The Seventh Directive on consolidated accounts and company law harmonization in the European Community', in Gray, S.J., Coenenberg, A.G. and Gordon, P. D. (eds), *International Group Accounting – Issues in European Harmonisation*. London: Routledge.

Parker, R.H. and Nobes, C.W. (1994) *An International View of True and Fair Accounting*. London: Routledge.

Sealy, L.S. (1996) *Cases and Materials in Company Law*, 6th edn. London: Butterworths.

Walton, P. (ed.) (1996) 'Country studies in international accounting – Europe', *The Library of International Accounting* series. Aldershot: Edward Elgar.

Watts, T.R. (ed.) (1979) *Handbook on the EEC Fourth Directive: The Impact on Company Accounts in the Nine Member States*. London: The Institute of Chartered Accountants in England and Wales.

Chapter 8

France

8.1 INTRODUCTION

French accounting practice is based in a tradition of a code set by law. The emphasis on a code of detail may be traced to Napoleonic times. Tax law has developed separately from accounting law, but has been highly influential on the choice of accounting practice within the accounting law. Being a founder member of the EU gave an opportunity for France to influence accounting practice in individual companies, through the Fourth Directive. France was in turn itself influenced, in the widespread adoption of consolidated accounting, by the Seventh Directive. The development of accounting practice in France has taken place largely within a political setting of a republic operating as a democracy. Swings in political power within that democracy may have slowed the pace of change in accounting practice compared with that of some other member states of the EU. On the other hand, the relative freedom of choice in preparation of group accounts has provided new opportunities for flexibility of practice and opened accounting thinking to new concepts and practices.

8.2 THE COUNTRY

8.2.1 Geography

France is the largest country, by area, in Western Europe. It is surrounded by three seas but also has common frontiers with Belgium, Luxembourg, Germany, Switzerland, Italy and Spain. Andorra and Monaco are independent territories on the French border having special relations with it. There is a varied landscape and a temperate climate.

The population is 57.7 million and almost 20% are under the age of 15. Life expectancy is high.

8.2.2 Economic indicators

Exhibit 8.1 FRANCE: COUNTRY PROFILE, TAKEN FROM EIU STATISTICS

Population	58.1 m.	
Land mass	543,965 sq.km	
GDP per head	US $24,973	
GDP per head in purchasing power parity	78	(USA=100)
Origins of GDP:	%	
Agriculture	2.6	
Industry	28.6	
Services	68.8	
	%	
Real GDP average annual growth 1985–95	2.2	
Inflation, average annual rate 1989–96	2.5	

Source: *The Economist Pocket World in Figures 1998 Edition*, The Economist (1997)

The economy has shown growth of 2.2% per annum over the period 1985 to 1995 (*see* Exhibit 8.1). More than two-thirds of gross domestic product (GDP) is created by services and less than one-third by manufacturing. Agriculture is a relatively small proportion (2.6%) of GDP. Manufacturing industry is directed in particular towards metal products (including cars) and machinery, with an identifiable concentration also in agriculture and food processing. There is diversification in 50% of manufacturing industry.

It should be noted that 50 years ago there was a very different mix of GDP with much stronger influence of agriculture and manufacturing.[1] That may seem like a long time ago, but it should be considered against the relatively slow pace of change in accounting regulation which will be explained later in the chapter.

Standards of living are high, indicated by a high life expectancy and relatively low population growth compared to the growth of GDP. Inflation has been low on the average during the period 1989–96 but there have been interludes of higher rates of inflation before that time which have periodically affected accounting practice.[2]

From EIU data it may be seen that a positive balance of trade on visible exports and imports is increased by a net inflow on invisibles such as tourism. Exports are diversified across a number of specialist manufactured products, the highest of which is capital equipment, perhaps not as well known to consumers in other countries as some of the cars and foodstuffs also exported. Export destinations are mainly other EU countries. Imports are similarly spread across a range of manufactured products and the source of imports is mainly other EU countries.

The trade links with other EU countries lead to an expectation that influences on accounting practice would lie predominantly in that area.

---

[1] Scheid and Walton (1992), pp. 12–13
[2] Scheid and Walton (1992), p. 19

8.3 OVERVIEW OF ACCOUNTING REGULATIONS

8.3.1 Early accounting law[3]

Accounting was introduced as a compulsory aspect of French business by the *Ordonnance* of Colbert in 1673, written in the form of an explanatory text by Jacques Savary. This law required traders to maintain daily records of transactions, to keep a record of correspondence and to make a list of assets once a year.

The Savary law was incorporated in the Commercial Code of 1807 as part of the reorganisation of French laws into codes during the period of rule by Napoleon. Company law was further reformed in 1867 covering matters which included the creation of the *Société Anonyme* as a form of business organisation. It also provided for a form of auditing for this type of corporation. The most significant subsequent development, so far as the present day is concerned, was the implementation of the Fourth Directive in the 1983 Accounting Law. Until that time, the *Plan Comptable Général* (published for the first time in 1947) was widely accepted as providing sufficient practical guidance despite the lack of clarity as to its legal status. Tax legislation referred to the *Plan Comptable Général* as an authoritative source. Major revisions to the *Plan Comptable Général* took place in 1957, 1982 and 1986. The dates of first issue and major revision of the *Plan Comptable Général* are linked to significant events in the country's history of economic development and law – emerging from the Second World War and implementation of the Fourth and Seventh Directives of the European Union. The revision of 1957, coinciding with the formation of the *Conseil National de la Comptabilité* (CNC, *see* subsection 8.3.3), did not disturb the basic approach of the 1947 version.

The development of accounting law is said to follow a tradition of French law which dates from Roman law and the influence of Napoleonic times. The Commercial Code remains the source of the general requirement to keep accounts and present annual accounts. The strong requirement is to record an action such as a commercial transaction; there has been relatively less attention given to the nature of the commercial organisation and its significance in economic terms. The separation of the management and ownership of companies has received less attention in French law than in some other countries. The emphasis on recording the transaction as it occurs has also placed historical limits on developing accounting practice to deal with representing the economic substance of a complex series of transactions such as capitalisation of a finance lease, revaluation of fixed assets and even the process of consolidation.

The law on auditing has developed separately from the law on accounting. Company audit was introduced in a law of 1867, strengthened in 1935 and further modified substantially in 1966. Auditors were given independence under the law and were seen as being part of the judicial system rather than technical advisers to company management. In particular, they are expected to defend the rights of minority shareholders.

---

[3] Scheid and Walton (1995), p. 68, (1992), pp. 26–30; Standish (1995), pp. 238–9; Fortin (1991)

8.3.2 Charts of accounts[4]

Early attempts had been made at creating a chart of accounts, particularly in 1942 (*see* also subsection 8.4.6). In 1946 the government of France established a commission on accounting standards leading to a code (*Plan Comptable Général*) in 1947 which contained some of the features of the 1942 code. One of the genuinely French features was to have no fixed relationship between management accounts and financial accounts (splitting the chart into two sets of related accounts). The code gradually became standard practice although it was not mandatory under law. It had a strong influence on the training of professional accountants and remained substantially unaltered until the implementation of the Fourth Directive in the 1982 *Plan Comptable Général*.

8.3.3 *Conseil National de la Comptabilité* (CNC)[5]

The National Accounting Council (*Conseil National de la Comptabilité*, CNC) came into existence in 1947, attached to the Ministry for Finance. It was the successor to various commissions and associations from 1918 onwards seeking to establish codes of accounting practice. The composition of the CNC acknowledged that accounting affected a wide range of economic and social interests. The mission of the CNC has been to function as a consultative organisation, to bring together information about the teaching and practice of accounting, and to give an opinion on accounting matters proposed by the state or its agents. The CNC has no powers to establish or enforce regulations. The large council meets relatively infrequently and works through subcommittees and working groups. Civil servants form a significant number of the council, and the Ministry of Finance provides secretariat support.

An important aspect of the work of the CNC is to comment on changes in the *Plan Comptable Général*. The existence of such a wide-ranging body of persons could be regarded as an interesting effort to produce a language of accounting which meets the needs of different users of financial reports, but the need for compromise and the consistent dominance of particular interest groups have placed practical limitations on the wider ideal. The dominance of government-based members has given a focus on macroeconomic issues of providing information for economic statistics and national economic planning. The needs of fiscal policy and tax administration have also had an influence.[6]

The work of the CNC was modified by the Ministry of Finance in 1996, reducing the number of members from 117 to 58. The CNC is still maintained in a study and advisory capacity but the active power in standard setting has been given to the CRC (*see* subsection 8.3.4).

In July 1977 the professional accountancy bodies, via the OEC and the CNCC (*see* subsection 8.4.5.1 and 8.4.5.2), sent a White Paper to the CNC outlining 50 recommendations for improved financial reporting. The focus of the recommendations was excessive latitude with regard to consolidated accounts and the

---

[4] Standish (1995), pp. 228–9
[5] Standish (1995), p. 235
[6] Standish (1995), p. 237

desirability for harmonisation with international practice as well as more disciplined approaches internally where variable practice existed.

8.3.4 *Comité de Réglementation Comptable* (CRC)[7]

Under a law passed in 1997, a *Comité de Réglementation Comptable* has been set up with 11 members. The chairman is the Minister of Finance and the vice-chairman is the Minister of Justice. Membership includes the presidents of the Bourse, the CNC, the CNCC and the OEC, plus three CNC members appointed by the Ministry of Finance. Some of these persons are likely to be professional accountants and so there will be accounting expertise included. The CRC is devoted to making mandatory, for all or some enterprises, the accounting standards which are prepared by the CNC or other institutions. For the first time in France, there will be a body with the power to impose accounting standards.

The CRC will approve all new accounting rules, subject to ratification by the appropriate government ministers. The CRC must act within the framework of the Accounting Law, but is empowered to prepare the necessary rules for applying the law. Provided the law allows certain companies to present accounts according to internationally recognised standards, the CRC will have to decide what is meant by 'internationally recognised standards'.[8]

8.3.5 Consolidated accounting[9]

Consolidated accounts have been a requirement of the Stock Exchange Council (*Commission des Opérations de Bourse*, COB) since 1971. Any group seeking COB permission for a new listing on the Bourse was required to include in its prospectus a set of consolidated accounts covering the most recent three years. Consolidated accounting had been adopted voluntarily by many other companies already having a listing. When it was announced in 1983 that consolidation was to become compulsory for listed companies, a survey by the COB showed that 75% of listed groups already carried out consolidation. Delays in implementation of the Seventh Directive eventually made consolidation compulsory for listed companies from 1986 and for unlisted companies from 1990. An audit report was required from 1984.

Prior to 1983 those companies which did apply consolidation had no clear guidance to follow. Practice varied from one group to the next, and comparisons could not readily be made.

In January 1998 the National Assembly approved a bill that would allow listed French companies to elect to follow IASs in their consolidated financial statements for domestic purposes. Until the year 2002 French companies would also be permitted, under the bill, to use US GAAP (generally accepted accounting principles) provided an official translation into French was published. The Senate had previously approved a bill endorsing the use of IASs in consolidated accounts by certain French companies. The two Bills were then sent for scrutiny so that differences could be reconciled with a view to preparing a new Law.

---

[7] *The Corporate Accountant*, November 1996, p. v
[8] *FT World Accounting Report*, May 1997, p. 6; January 1997, pp. 9–10
[9] Pham (1993), p. 60–1

8.4 INSTITUTIONS

8.4.1 Political and economic system

8.4.1.1 Nature of political system[10]

France is a republic led by a President elected by the people for a period of seven years. Legislative authority is held by two assemblies which together constitute the parliament, led by a Prime Minister. The Prime Minister, who is appointed by the President, is a person having majority support in the National Assembly. The President and the Prime Minister are not always members of the same political party. Elections to the National Assembly take place every five years and elections for President every seven years. The Assemblée Nationale is directly elected by the people and the Sénat is elected indirectly by local authority councillors. Since the inception of the Fifth Republic in 1958 a fundamental statute, called the Constitution, has organised the legislative, administrative and judicial functions in France.

The administration is organised into various ministries, such as the Ministry of Justice or the Ministry of Finance, regulating one particular aspect of administration across the whole of France. There are 22 administrative regions in France, and almost 100 Metropolitan Departments. Beyond that there are very many local authorities, called *communes*. Although there has been some decentralisation giving greater powers to the regions, departments and communes, there is a strong emphasis on uniform application of legal rights and responsibilities across the country as a whole.

France was a founder member of the European Economic Community (EEC), and the growth of its economy in the 1960s reflects that fact. In particular, the removal of trade barriers encouraged French businesses to modernise in order to compete.

8.4.1.2 Ministry of Finance and state control of business[11]

Within the Ministry of Finance there is a *Trésor* directorate which has a strong influence on business matters. While market-based solutions to problems form the official approach, there may be informal directions on how the solutions will be formed. Persuasion is used rather than legal powers. The *Trésor* will do its best to save companies which are in trouble and may persuade creditors or shareholders to delay action while a company is refinanced.

The Ministry of Finance also takes a role in relation to takeovers. There are few barriers in French law which prevent companies being taken over but the Ministry of Finance must give approval where the bidder is not in the EU and the acquisition involves more than 20% of the target. The Ministry may try to encourage a rival French bid.

---

[10] Scheid and Walton (1992), pp. 8–9
[11] Charkham (1994), pp. 121–2

8.4.1.3 Privatisation programme[12]

Some of the largest French companies are nationalised industries.[13] From 1945 onwards there was a move to reconstruct the economy by creating joint enterprise bodies owned by government and private enterprise. That began a tradition of state intervention mixed with private enterprise partnership. France has been subjected to waves of nationalisation and privatisation of industry, depending on the government in power. A wave of nationalisation in the early 1980s was followed by a programme of privatisation starting in 1993 and then in 1997 a further change of government which may slow down privatisation. As a result of these various changes, France has companies which may have been natural monopolies – such as electricity, gas and railways – and companies which have more autonomy and compete commercially.

8.4.1.4 Government services providing information[14]

The Ministry of Justice runs, through the *Tribunaux de Commerce*, the register of commerce. This is where all corporations of any kind must deposit for public access their articles of association. Limited liability corporations must also deposit their annual financial statements.

The *Centrale des Bilans*, run by the Bank of France, receives data voluntarily from 28,000 large companies. The companies receive in return reports about their own relative performance and balance sheets. A further analysis of the company's performance and financial health is available for a fee. The Bank of France also provides information on a company's indebtedness through the *Centrale des risques*. Ratings of companies for use by lenders are derived from the *Centrale des risques* and are available through the *Fichier bancaire des entreprises*.

8.4.2 Legal system

The French legal system is of the Romano-Germanic family but has taken on a European characteristic which is identifiably different from the German legal system. Other countries having a legal system similar to that of France include Belgium, Denmark, Italy, The Netherlands, Portugal and Spain.

8.4.2.1 Types of business organisation

Sociétés anonymes (SA) are the French equivalent of the public company in the UK or the AG in Germany. *Sociétés à responsibilité limité* (SARL) are private limited companies similar to the GmbH in Germany or the private limited company in the UK. They are not obliged to have a Board of Directors. A comparison of the membership of the SA and the SARL is provided in Exhibit 8.2.

---

[12] Scheid and Walton (1992), pp. 11–20
[13] Charkham (1994), p. 125
[14] Charkham (1994), p. 121

| Exhibit 8.2 | SA AND SARL: COMPARISON OF KEY FEATURES |

	SA	*SARL*
Number of members	Minimum of 7	Between 1 and 50
Minimum capital	Unquoted FFr250,000 Quoted FFr1.5m	FFr50,000
Shares	Generally registered but if quoted may be bearer shares	Shares may not be evidenced by any form of negotiable document
Transfer of shares	Quoted shares are recorded by a central registry, SICOVAM (see section 8.4.4.1) Almost all are bearer shares, transferred by delivery and held by an intermediary. Registered shares may be bought and sold but there are formalities regarding the debit or credit of the shareholders' stockholding account in the company's records	By written agreement being served on the company

8.4.2.2 Corporate governance[15]

In France, there is a choice of two distinct systems for *Sociétés anonymes*, one having a unitary board and the other a supervisory board. The traditional approach is the unitary board, appointed by the shareholders. A Président Directeur Générale (PDG) is the chairman and chief executive. The PDG is elected by the board, and as a matter of French law, the PDG has executive authority and the sole right to represent the company.

The PDG is in a strong position of control over the company and the system of corporate governance is largely dependent on the PDG's personality. Furthermore, the PDG gains support from loyal shareholders and particularly the shareholder representatives who take places on the board of directors. Undertakings not to sell shares may also be given by major shareholders.[16] A typical PDG may be a professional manager who has developed a career with the business, possibly as a founding owner. The PDG may also be a person brought in from outside because of his or her connections, particularly where relations with government are important.

The size of a unitary board varies with company size but no more than one-third may be executive; a high proportion of the board is thus non-executive. The

---

[15] Charkham (1994), pp. 130–7
[16] Charkham (1994), p. 152

board does not intervene in the day-to-day running of the business. Its role is to hire and fire the PDG, to authorise the raising of new finance and to authorise mergers or other links; meetings are relatively infrequent.

There is legislation dating from 1966 which allows the alternative of a supervisory board (*conseil de surveillance*) resembling that found in Germany. Management is in the hands of a *Directoire* (2–5 members) appointed by the supervisory board to run the company. This alternative system of corporate governance is relatively little used.

Companies over a specified size are required to have a *comité d'enterprise* on which the workforce is represented. This reflects the socialist politics of France in the early 1980s. The committee is not as strongly based as the German works council and the control of the company is very much in the hands of the PDG. One or two members of the *comité d'enterprise* attend meetings of the Board of Directors, but have no voting rights. The board does not deal with day-to-day activities and so it is possible for the PDG to take executive action without extensive consultation with the representatives of the *comité d'enterprise*.

8.4.3 Taxation system

8.4.3.1 Taxable income[17]

Taxes on income are levied by the state. For businesses the taxable income is calculated by starting with the accounting profit as determined by the *Plan Comptable Général*. Some further adjustments are made for the purposes of tax law. These adjustments involve the exclusion of expenses which relate to personal items associated with the owner of the business. Gifts to customers, expenses of entertaining and travel, and commissions paid to third parties are examples of transactions which are acceptable. The emphasis is on 'normal business practice', but it is essential that the expense item is included in the financial accounts.

The basis of the depreciation calculation is allocation of cost over the useful life of the asset but accelerated depreciation is allowed for specific assets provided it is used in the financial statements.

Provisions are widely used in French accounting practice. To be allowable for tax purposes the provision must meet specific criteria which ensure that the provision is probable, that it is specific and that it arises from an event which happened during the year (rather than an event after the balance sheet date).

8.4.3.2 Corporate income tax[18]

Companies pay corporation tax based on their accounting profits. The definition of 'profit' for corporate tax purposes is that used for commercial and industrial purposes. Corporate income taxes are paid by individual companies rather than by groups of companies. However, there are some specific rules for groups of companies.

Capital gains are determined in the same way as for unincorporated businesses, but a company pays a lower long-term rate of capital gains tax if the gain is transferred to

---

[17] Scheid and Walton (1992), pp. 45–6
[18] Scheid and Walton (1992), pp. 53–7; Coopers and Lybrand International Tax Network (1995), pp. F19–F37

special reserves. Short-term investments held by a company are valued at market price at the balance sheet date and a capital gain or loss calculated for tax purposes.

Dividend distributions are taxed under an imputation system. Where a company makes a distribution of dividend there is an extra payment of 50% of corporate tax but a tax credit of the same amount (*avoir fiscal*) is released for the shareholder. The effective rate of tax on the company increases but the overall tax rate on company and shareholder together is lower than in the absence of distribution.

8.4.4 Corporate financing system

8.4.4.1 Equity investors

Relatively few listed companies in France have widely dispersed shareholdings.[19] Most companies have major shareholders because of a history of flotation as a subsidiary, because of shareholdings by other companies, or because founders have retained their investment. Such shareholdings have in part been designed to discourage takeovers by creation of cross-shareholdings.

Historically, French companies have not generally used the stock market as a source of finance but in more recent years there has been an increase in new equity financing. Use of share options to reward management has caused greater interest in the stock market.[20] However there is a view that shareholders have a conservative view of expectations from dividends. Growth of the company, with corresponding increase in value of the shares, is the preference of many shareholders.[21]

From Chapter 1, Exhibit 1.3, it may be seen that the French stock exchange is relatively small in European terms, comparable in size to that of Germany, but the size of the companies listed, measured by market capitalisation, is large in comparison with GDP. Exhibit 1.4 shows that the French stock market's share of world market capitalisation is less than 5%, while Exhibit 1.5 shows that there is no dominant shareholder group and that shares are widely held.

Almost all shares in quoted companies are held in bearer form. That means the person in possession of the share certificate (the bearer) has ownership. Because this makes share certificates vulnerable to theft and fraud, they are generally held by custodian banks as intermediaries; there is no paper certificate. Ownership is recorded by a central registry, SICOVAM. Companies do not know who many of their shareholders are, and there is no mailing of information to shareholders, although the annual general meeting is advertised and shareholders have the choice of attending. Dividends are not sent to shareholders. They are paid by SICOVAM to intermediaries for onward distribution. Since 1987 there has been a new type of share, the identifiable bearer share (TPI), which will allow companies to find out more about their shareholders.

There has been some concern that small shareholders may not be paid sufficient attention, and many companies now make efforts to contact their shareholders. Because companies do not know who owns them, communication relies on press

---

[19] Charkham (1994), pp. 126–7
[20] Charkham (1994), pp. 126–7
[21] Charkham (1994), p. 142

announcements and on information given in briefings to analysts meetings. It is interesting to note that the World Wide Web pages of Rhône-Poulenc carry the text of questions and answers from the briefing meeting with analysts.

In France, there is no equivalent to the pension funds of the UK or the USA as equity investors. The major insurance companies are significant investors, tending to concentrate their investments, and often having a representative on the company's board of directors.[22]

There is a tradition of family business in France and some of these family businesses prefer borrowing rather than issuing further shares to raise finance. This, combined with state ownership of some large companies, means that companies issue bonds to raise new capital, rather than equity.

8.4.4.2 Top companies[23]

From the Financial Times annual survey *FT 500* there are 19 French companies in the top 500 world companies, measured by market capitalisation. No group based in France featured in the top 20 European companies ranked by market capitalisation, reflecting to some extent the slow pace of industrial restructuring in France. The top ten listed French companies in 1997 are shown in Exhibit 8.3.

Exhibit 8.3 TOP 10 FRENCH LISTED COMPANIES

Name	*Market cap $m*	*Rank in Europe*	*Sector*
1 Elf Aquitaine	35,997	21	Oil, internationals
2 Total	27,540	36	Oil, internationals
3 L'Oréal	26,734	38	Cosmetics
4 Carrefour	23,676	45	Retail grocery chain
5 Axa-UAP	21,878	49	Insurance – Property and accident
6 Alcatel Alsthom	21,276	53	Communications equipment
7 LVMH	18,391	64	Beverages, distillers
8 Générale des Eaux	15,578	78	Utilities
9 Suez Lyonnaise des Eaux	13,861	84	Utilities
10 Société Générale	13,663	87	Commercial banks and other banks

Source: Survey *FT 500*, *Financial Times*, 22 January 1998, p. 15

8.4.4.3 Bank lending

Historically, deposit-taking banks did not participate in the financing of their industrial and commercial customers;[24] merchant banks were the source of lending to business. The two types of banks are, since 1984, similar in status under banking law, all being called *établissements de crédit*. The provision of bank lending

---

[22] Charkham (1994), p. 147
[23] *Financial Times*, *FT 500 Survey*, 22 January 1998
[24] Charkham (1994), p. 144–5

is concentrated in a small number of large banks. This factor, in combination with the relative lack of spread of equity shareholding mentioned earlier, means that a few banks are relatively influential in matters of raising corporate finance. Banks also take equity shareholdings in companies. This may be encouraged by the company which sees a source of cheaper capital and a protection against takeover. For the banks, the strategy of increasing their involvement in corporate finance has resulted from comparative evaluation of the systems in Germany and in the UK, with the conclusion favouring the German approach. This gives a long-term orientation to bank financing by loans and by equity investment.[25]

8.4.4.4 *Commission des Opérations de Bourse* (COB)[26]

The French stock market, which comprises the Paris Bourse, provincial stock exchanges and the second market, ranks third in Europe (*see* Chapter 1, Exhibit 1.4). Although there is a significant number of companies listed, many have a relatively low proportion of their capital available through the market. Family shareholdings control a high proportion of shares, even in the top companies.[27] The COB is a state-appointed body which acts as the regulatory authority for the French stock market. It is modelled on the US SEC and works with the Ministry of Finance, the Banque de France and the Conseil des bourses de valeurs. It regards itself as a key player within IOSCO.[28]

The COB has a staff concerned with matters of accounting practice and the head of that unit could be regarded as comparable to the Chief Accountant of the US SEC. This group of staff scrutinises prospectuses and other documents issued by companies seeking to raise finance. It also investigates irregularities in the functioning of the financial markets, covering issues such as insider dealing and the provision of false or misleading information. The COB has powers to investigate auditors of listed companies and, since 1987, a special committee of the CNCC has undertaken a regular review of audits of listed companies on behalf of the COB.

In addition to setting rules for obtaining and maintaining listings, the COB operates rules governing takeover bids such as the rule requiring a general offer once a specified shareholding is reached. The 1996 *Annual Report* of the COB confirmed a continuing commitment to an increase in transparency in company information and to good practices in corporate governance.

8.4.4.5 Mergers and acquisitions[29]

Major French companies have acquired shareholdings in companies outside France in order to consolidate their international position. The interlocking shareholdings and the complex networks of interactions, where key investors have significant holdings in many leading companies, may give cause for concern about conflict of interest where mergers between two French companies are contemplated. Fear of takeover could be a factor influencing the behaviour of company management, but in practice many PDGs expect solid support from existing shareholders.

---

[25] Charkham (1994), p. 146
[26] Standish (1995), p. 237; Scheid and Walton (1992), p. 71
[27] Charkham (1994), p. 147
[28] *FT World Accounting Report*, July 1996, p. 7
[29] Charkham (1994), pp. 150–1

Demergers are also a feature. In the late 1980s and early 1990s management buyouts by employees were also increasing at a rapid rate.

8.4.5 The accounting profession

The reform of company law in 1967 established the profession of auditor (*Commissaire aux Comptes*). Historically, the profession of auditor had been separate, in the eyes of the law, from that of accountant. However in practice most auditors also belong to the accountancy profession. A range of professional bodies existed in the later part of the nineteenth and early twentieth century. These were rationalised by government action in formation of the *Ordre des experts comptables et des comptables agréés* (OEC) in 1945.[30] This was formed as a two-tier body of the *expert comptable* who was authorised to prepare annual accounts and the *comptable agréé* who operated the bookkeeping system.

8.4.5.1 *Ordre des experts comptables* (OEC)[31]

Only members of the OEC are permitted to call themselves *expert comptable*. They have a monopoly position, protected by law, in the public supply of certain accounting services. Only partners or employees of an accountancy practice may use the title *expert comptable*; those who move to work in industry lose their membership of the professional body. This means there is no professional accountancy body representing accountants working in industry and commerce.

Those seeking membership of the OEC must undergo a period of training and pass professional examinations, including the writing of a dissertation.

In 1996 the OEC published a draft conceptual framework, rejecting the Anglo-Saxon/US/IASC approach of starting with the balance sheet and emphasising the importance of the profit and loss account as the essential statement of wealth creation.[32]

8.4.5.2 *Compagnie nationale des commissaires aux comptes* (CNCC)

The CNCC was formed in 1969 as part of a continuing reform of auditing under government jurisdiction. Although the statutory position of the auditor was established by the law of 1867, there was no professional organisation at that time and it was only after a reform of the law in 1935 that the duties of the auditor were extended and professional organisations began to appear.

Formation of the CNCC was related to changes in the law which widened the responsibilities of auditors and fixed their fees in relation to the size of the client. They were required to certify the *regularité* (conforming with legal requirements) and the *sincerité* (application of accepted valuation methods in good faith) of the accounts. Most *commissaires aux comptes* are also *experts comptables*, as members of the OEC.

---

[30] Scheid and Walton (1995), p. 169
[31] Scheid and Walton (1995), p. 169; Standish (1995), pp. 239–40
[32] *FT World Accounting Report*, July 1996, p. 2

8.4.6 External influences

There is a history of independent development of accounting practice in France. Early tendencies towards charts of accounts may be traced to a commission formed in 1918 which included in its remit the idea of standardisation. No specific chart appeared in France at that time but in the 1920s Schmalenbach proposed a model chart of accounts in Germany. The German occupation of France in 1940 brought ideas of German economic organisation to industry and administration in France; this drew attention to potential deficiencies in French accounting practice and a code was prepared in 1942 as a detailed manual.

As a founder member of the EU France has influenced the content of the directives affecting company law in the community. It has in turn been influenced by other members joining the EU, particularly the UK request that the Fourth Directive should include the requirement for a 'true and fair view' (*see* Chapter 11).

Colonisation of Africa in the late nineteenth century left a legacy of French accounting tradition in many African countries which are now independent. In particular, that legacy reflects the notion that accounting regulations should apply to all business entities, whether or not incorporated, and that there should be a uniform chart of accounts. It has been suggested that the French approach has made it easier to regulate unincorporated businesses and provide bookkeeping training, provided there is adequate literacy among small traders.[33]

8.5 SOCIETAL CULTURE AND ACCOUNTING SUBCULTURE

It has been suggested[34] that French people think deeply about the origins and developments of their institutions in an analytical, political and historical way. The strong authority of the president of a company is comparable to that given to a state president. Politics does not draw a clear boundary between government and industry. The state has a presence.

8.5.1 Hofstede's cultural dimensions

Exhibit 8.4 reproduces part of the table set out in Chapter 2, Exhibit 2.4, showing the scores and rankings for France from Hofstede's (1984) research on cultural dimensions.

8.5.2 Culture and accounting

Exhibit 8.5 links Gray's (1988) accounting values for France to the cultural dimensions measured by Hofstede. Section 8.7 of this chapter expands on practical applications, illustrating the relevance of Gray's general analysis.

The cultural values identified by Hofstede are such that in the final column the quality of high individualism acts in the opposite direction to strong uncertainty avoidance and high power distance. Gray's classification of France in the 'more developed Latin' grouping brings out the impact of these conflicting quali-

---

[33] Walton, P., 'Special rules for a special case', *Financial Times*, 18 September 1997, p. 11
[34] Charkham (1994), p. 119

238

Exhibit 8.4 FRANCE: SCORES AND RANKINGS FOR INDIVIDUAL COUNTRIES FROM HOFSTEDE'S (1984) CULTURAL DIMENSIONS RESEARCH

Individualism versus collectivism		*Large power distance versus small power difference*		*Strong uncertainty avoidance versus weak uncertainty avoidance*		*Low nurture versus high nurture*	
Score	*Rank*	*Score*	*Rank*	*Score*	*Rank*	*Score*	*Rank*
71	10/11	68	15/16	86	10/15	43	35/36

Exhibit 8.5 LINKING GRAY'S (1988) ACCOUNTING VALUES TO HOFSTEDE'S (1984) CULTURAL DIMENSIONS, IN THE MANNER PROPOSED BY GRAY

Gray's accounting values – classification	*Cultural dimensions affecting the country's accounting values*	*Interpretation of Hofstede's scores of cultural values for France (based on scores in Exhibit 8.4)*
Professionalism (marginal)	Professionalism tends to be associated with: ● Individualism ● Weak uncertainty avoidance ● Small power distance	High individualism Strong uncertainty avoidance High power distance
Uniformity (strong)	Uniformity tends to be associated with: ● Strong uncertainty avoidance ● Large power distance ● Collectivism	Strong uncertainty avoidance High power distance High individualism
Conservatism (strong)	Conservatism tends to be associated with: ● Strong uncertainty avoidance ● Collectivism ● High nurture	Strong uncertainty avoidance High individualism Tendency to high nurture
Secrecy (marginal)	Secrecy tends to be associated with: ● Strong uncertainty avoidance ● Large power distance ● Collectivism ● High nurture	Strong uncertainty avoidance High power distance High individualism Tendency to high nurture

ties. Professionalism is marginal because of strong uncertainty avoidance modifying high individualism. Uniformity and conservatism are strong for the same reason. Secrecy is marginal because high individualism and a tendency to high nurture outweigh the strength of uncertainty avoidance and power distance.

Gray indicated, in making his classification, the traditional position in France where the professional accountant's role has been concerned primarily with the implementation of relatively prescriptive and detailed legal requirements.

8.6 ACCOUNTING REGULATIONS AND THE IASC

Salter *et al.* (1996) showed that, following the IASC comparability project, France was above the average score for percentage agreement between the IASs and the national accounting practice (*see* Chapter 5, subsection 5.6.3.4). That may well reflect the fact that in consolidated accounts French companies have relative freedom of accounting choice and some major companies choose to apply IASs. An example of a company which has selected accounting methods conforming to IASs is IMS International Metal Services. This company uses IASs in its group accounts while applying the PCG in the accounts of the holding company (*see* Exhibit 8.6).

The extent to which French accounting practice is broadly in agreement with IASs is shown in Exhibit 8.7.

Exhibit 8.6 IMS GROUP AND IMS PARENT COMPANY: NOTES ON ACCOUNTING POLICY

NOTES TO THE CONSOLIDATED FINANCIAL STATEMENTS

PRINCIPLES AND METHODS OF CONSOLIDATION

The consolidated financial statements of the IMS Group have been prepared according to the accounting principles generally accepted at international level, recommended by the International Accounting Standards Committee and in conformity with the French law dated 3rd January 1985 and its implementing decree dated 17th February 1986. They have not been changed over recent financial years.

APPENDIX TO THE BALANCE SHEET AND INCOME STATEMENT FOR THE 1995 FINANCIAL YEAR

1 – ACCOUNTING RULES AND METHODS

The company's statements have been drawn up according to the regulations, principles and methods in the General Accounting Plan (Plan Comptable Général : PCG) 1982 (approved by order dated 27th April 1982), the requirements of Law N°83.353 dated 30th April 1983 and decree 83–1020 dated 29th November 1983.

Nevertheless, by a departure from the classification in the PCG, the item 'Banking and similar services' has been reclassified under the heading 'Financial costs'.

The rules for evaluating and determining the result have undergone no changes in relation to previous financial years.

The basic method for evaluating the elements recorded in the accounts is the historic cost method.

The notes and tables presented as a supplement to the balance sheet and income statement form the appendix and are, in this respect, an integral part of the annual accounts.

Source: IMS International Metal Service, annual report, 1995, pp. 26, 39

Exhibit 8.7 COMPARISON OF ACCOUNTING PRACTICES IN FRANCE WITH
REQUIREMENTS OF IASs: KEY SIMILARITIES AND DIFFERENCES

IAS	Subject of IAS	Practice in France	Ref
Disclosure and presentation			
	General aspects consolidated in IAS 1 (revised)		
IAS 1	Fair Presentation	'True and fair' requirement	7.2.5 7.5.1
	Disclosure of Accounting Policies (former IAS 1)	Group accounts generally in agreement	
	Information to be Disclosed in Financial Statements (former IAS 5)	Group accounts generally in agreement	
	Presentation of Current Assets and Current Liabilities (former IAS 13)	Group accounts generally in agreement	
	Specific aspects		
IAS 7	Cash Flow Statements	Not required by regulation but some form of funds flow or cash flow provided by most companies in group accounts	7.2.4
IAS 8	Net Profit or Loss for the Period, Fundamental Errors and Changes in Accounting Policies	Practice is different in several respects	7.2.4
IAS xx	Discontinuing Operations	Not required by regulation	
IAS 14	Reporting Financial Information by Segments	Disclosure requirement is significantly less than IAS 14	7.5.2
IAS 24	Related Party Disclosure	No general requirement, some specific items	
IAS 33	Earnings per Share	No specific requirement	
IAS 34	Interim Financial Reporting		
Asset recognition and measurement			
IAS 2	Inventories	Generally in agreement	7.4.2
IAS 4	Depreciation Accounting	Generally in agreement	
IAS 16	Property, Plant and Equipment	Generally in agreement	7.4.3 7.4.4
IAS xx	Impairment of Assets	Not required by regulation	
IAS 23	Borrowing Costs	Generally in agreement	
IAS 25	Accounting for Investments	More conservative than IAS 25	
IAS 9	Research and Development costs	Generally in agreement	7.4.5
IAS xx	Intangible Assets	Generally in agreement	7.4.5
Liability recognition and measurement			
IAS 10	Contingencies and Events Occurring After the Balance Sheet Date	More conservative on recognising contingencies as liabilities	7.4.6
IAS 12	Income Taxes	Deferred tax in group accounts only – generally in agreement	
IAS 17	Accounting for Leases	Group accounts may follow IAS 17	7.4.3
IAS 19	Employee Benefits	No requirement in regulations	
IAS 32	Financial Instruments: Disclosure and Presentation	Not in legislation	
Recognition of economic activity			
IAS 11	Construction Contracts	Completed contract more common but percentage of completion used	7.4.1
IAS 18	Revenue	Generally in agreement	
IAS 20	Accounting for Government Grants and Disclosure of Government Assistance	Generally in agreement but unexpired balance shown as equity	

►

Exhibit 8.7	continued

IAS	Subject of IAS	Practice in France	Ref
Measurement			
IAS 15	Information Reflecting the Effects of Changing Prices	Permitted in group accounts but rarely used	
IAS 29	Financial Reporting in Hyperinflationary Economies	Not relevant to French economy	
Group accounting			
IAS 21	The Effects of Changes in Foreign Exchange Rates	No regulation – flexibility of practice	7.3.3
IAS 22	Business Combinations	Purchase method generally used; goodwill amortised over 2–40 years	7.4.5
IAS 27	Consolidated Financial Statements and Accounting for Investments in Subsidiaries	Generally in agreement	7.3.5
IAS 28	Accounting for Investments in Associates	Equity method used in group accounting, but not in accounts of individual companies	
IAS 31	Financial Reporting of Interests in Joint Ventures	Proportional consolidation available; equity accounting also used; flexible interpretation of rules	7.3.4

Note: This exhibit deals primarily with group accounts; much of the content of individual company accounts is determined by the Chart of Accounts which is less closely aligned to IASs.

It was explained in section 8.3.4 that establishment of the CRC has strengthened arrangements for setting accounting standards in France and will allow recognition of standards which are acceptable for use. It seems likely that IASs will be accepted for use in the preparation of consolidated accounts by companies which have stock market listings outside France.[35] A survey of the top 100 French companies has shown slow progress which indicates that many companies are waiting for the outcome of the debate in Parliament.[36] The survey found 19 companies which had adopted IASs and 10 which had adopted US GAAP.

The IASC web pages list 32 companies which refer to the use of IASs in their financial statements (*see* Exhibit 8.8)

8.7 THE ACCOUNTING SYSTEM

8.7.1 Outline of current regulation[37]

As explained earlier, the Commercial Code contains the basic requirement of law regarding the keeping of accounts and the presentation of annual accounts. Implementation of that general requirement has been carried out historically through the *Plan Comptable Général*, the most recent version being that of 1982, modified in 1986.

[35] IASC, *Annual Review 1996* and IASC *Insight*, March 1998
[36] *The Corporate Accountant*, January 1997, p. v
[37] Scheid and Walton (1992), pp. 26–8; Standish (1995), pp. 239–40

Exhibit 8.8	FRENCH COMPANIES REFERRING TO THE USE OF IASs IN THEIR FINANCIAL STATEMENTS, WITH RANK IN EUROPE

	Rank in Europe		*Rank in Europe*
Aerospatiale	–	Lectra Systèmes	–
Air France	–	LVMH	64
Banque Indosuez	–	Moulinex	–
Bongrain	–	Office Commercial Pharmaceutique	–
Canal +	223	Peugeot	183
Cap Gemini Sogeti	303	Primagaz Group	–
Carnaud Metalbox	–	Rémy Cointreau	–
Compagnie de Suez	–	Renault	170
DMC	–	Saint-Gobain	89
ECIA	–	Saint Louis	–
Eridania Beghin-Say	295	Schneider	131
Essilor	398	Sligos	–
Eurocopter	–	Technip	468
Hermès International	375	Thomson-CSF	308
IMS	–	Usinor Sacilor	251
Lafarge	173	Valeo	267

Source: extracted from IASC web pages; *Financial Times, FT 500*, January 1998

Present practice depends on the 1983 accounting law (the 1983 Accounting Act), which implemented the Fourth Directive, and the 1985 Act which contains the requirements of the Seventh Directive. Each Act was implemented by a Decree, issued in 1983 and 1986 respectively. It is a requirement of the 1983 Accounting Act that annual accounts are consistent, honest and give a true and fair view of the wealth of the enterprise, its financial position and its results. Where the application of an accounting requirement is insufficient to give a true and fair view, further information may be provided in notes to the accounts. In exceptional circumstances, a departure from an accounting requirement may be necessary for the presentation of a true and fair view. The 1983 Accounting Act requires the enterprise to establish an accounting manual which contains a record and explanation of the organisation of the accounting system, the data processing procedures and the accounting principles used in preparation of the financial statements.

The annual accounts of companies must be filed with the Register of Commerce in the *Tribunal de Commerce* and there is public access to these records. There is no significant penalty for companies which file accounts late, and there is more than one Tribunal where accounts may be filed. Efficient interrogation of all files requires the use of a commercial electronic facility.

The law on auditing is separate from the accounting law.

8.7.2 Professionalism versus statutory control

Gray (1988) placed French accounting in the position of being marginally professional, less so than Germany, for example. This may reflect the strong influence of tax law on statutory accounts, limiting the scope for exercise of professional judgement. The influence of the French accounting profession on direct development of accounting practices has been relatively limited historically but, with the changes in the CNC, could be improving.

8.7.2.1 Relation between tax law and statutory accounts[38]

French fiscal law has paid close attention to the balance sheet and particularly the end-of-period accruals. The general rule, that expenses are tax-deductible only if they are reported in the annual accounts, has ensured that tax law has a strong influence on accounting practice. However the flexibility of some aspects of tax law has left scope for professionalism, particularly in the choice of depreciation calculation. The potential scope for exercise of professionalism has also been seen in case law decisions.

The adoption of the Fourth Directive in French law through the 1983 Accounting Act gave accounting a higher profile than it had previously held. As a result, there was some harmonisation of work sheets between the fiscal authorities and the legislators. However the fiscal authority subsequently established new rules within a principle of autonomy of fiscal law. Special provisions continue to be stipulated in the fiscal law and additional conditions have been inserted to deal with the apparent freedom created by new accounting practices.

8.7.2.2 *Conseil national de la comptabilité*[39]

The work of the CNC is organised through Sections, Commissions and Working Groups. Part of its work is to consider matters of continuing or long-term significance for standardisation. Other work is more short-term in nature. There are Commissions dealing with management accounting, consolidated accounts, financial instruments and small and medium-sized enterprises (SMEs). There is a permanent secretariat of persons qualified in accountancy and law. The nature of this work is heavily influenced by, and dependent on, the public sector, although the recent reforms of the CNC should increase the professional accountancy influence.

8.7.2.3 Recommendations of professional bodies[40]

The professional recommendations of the OEC are contained in the Members' Handbook. Volume II in particular contains accounting principles, recommendations on specific tasks such as stock control procedures, and professional conduct. The recommendations of the OEC are not binding on members and do not form part of the legal requirements for financial disclosure. There are relatively few recommendations compared with the major standard setting activities in the UK or the USA. The OEC also has an input to the recommendations of the CNC.

Other activities of the OEC which spread information on good practice are the technical publications and guides to practice. Annual congresses are also held, discussing issues concerned with the organisation and conduct of professional

---

[38] Standish (1995), p. 241; Frydlender and Pham (1996)
[39] Standish (1995), p. 235
[40] Standish (1995), pp. 244–5

practice. The activities of the accounting and auditing professions are significant but much less influential than those of the UK or the USA.

The CNCC issues the main auditing recommendations. There is a Handbook on Audit Standards and Ethics and a Handbook on Audit Controls and Procedures.

8.7.2.4 Financial statements formats[41]

Obligatory formats follow the Fourth Directive. For individual accounts the balance sheet must be in horizontal format but for group accounts it may be in vertical or horizontal format. The profit and loss account may be in horizontal or vertical format. For individual companies the expenses must be presented by nature, but for group accounts they may be presented by function.

In the balance sheet of the individual company the assets are on the left (*actif*) and liabilities and equity on the right (*passif*). Liabilities are categorised by their nature but not by date of maturity. The separation of current and non-current liabilities is given in notes to the accounts. The categories gross cost, accumulated depreciation (or provision for depreciation) and net book value are used for all assets, whether current or fixed. Some consolidated accounts will contain financial statements in a format very similar to that required of the parent company, with all the required detail on the face of the balance sheet (*see* Exhibit 8.9).

The 1986 Act allowed consolidated balance sheets and profit and loss accounts to be presented in a more simple format. Many of the details included in the primary financial statements for individual companies may be included in the notes to the accounts. Aerospatiale (see Exhibit 8.10), in its group accounts, shows the depreciation column applying to all assets. Many other companies, in their group accounts, prefer to present the depreciation information in notes to the accounts, as in Exhibit 8.11.

A typical full profit and loss account is presented by some companies (*see* Exhibit 8.12), while a simplified presentation on the face of the profit and loss account is presented by other companies (*see* Exhibit 8.13), using notes to the accounts to provide the detail.

For individual companies the expenses are presented by nature as a tradition dating from the *Plan Comptable Général* 1947. The Fourth Directive imposes a requirement that there is a split between ordinary activities and extraordinary activities. So each expense classified by nature might have an ordinary and an extraordinary component. *The Plan Comptable Général* 1982 overcomes this problem by specifying the types of expense by nature which might have an extraordinary expense included. However considerable flexibility remains. The OEC issued a recommendation on ordinary and extraordinary items which effectively implemented IAS 8. Most major companies follow this recommendation.

8.7.2.5 'True and fair view'

The wording used in French legislation is 'une image fidèle', translated as 'a faithful picture'. The use of the word 'faithful' had historical precedents and left sufficient ambiguity to satisfy national legislators. Parker and Nobes (1994, p. 80)

---

[41] Scheid and Walton (1992), Chapter 8

Exhibit 8.9   ASSYSTEM: BALANCE SHEET

Consolidated financial statements

Consolidated Balance Sheet as at December 31, 1996 (in FRF)

Assets		31.12.96		31.12.95
	Gross	Depreciation & Provisions	Net	Net
Shares subscribed but not called (0)				
INTANGIBLE FIXED ASSETS				
Preliminary expenses	325,226	166,788	158,438	230,080
Research and development costs				
Franchises, patents, licenses	16,474,344	13,682,775	2,791,569	1,462,436
Goodwill other than acquisition goodwill	19,318,819	14,913,543	4,405,276	3,981,703
Downpayments and prepayments				
Other intangible assets	77,740	10,431	67,309	249,164
Acquisition goodwill	157,415,150	48,870,431	108,544,719	38,986,228
TANGIBLE FIXED ASSETS				
Land	1,706,711	172,056	1,534,655	1,554,544
Leases of land				
Buildings	47,686,020	18,156,659	29,529,361	31,147,678
Leased buildings				
Plant, machinery & equipment	8,246,079	4,681,097	3,564,982	2,244,427
Leased plant, machinery and equipment				
Other tangible fixed assets	108,949,630	69,534,851	39,414,779	35,644,122
Other leased fixed assets				
Tangible fixed assets-in-progress	59,400		59,400	471,651
Prepayments	331,318		331,318	
INVESTMENTS				
Other long-term equity investments	8,147,285	3,230,085	4,917,200	6,764,895
Receivables from corporate investments	411,845	84,323	327,522	
Other long-term investments	5,867,828	487,961	5,379,867	4,576,941
Loans	3,041,233		3,041,233	265,088
Other	7,585,675	65,425	7,520,250	5,318,564
Securities in companies consolidated using the equity method	5,640,158		5,640,158	2,895,935
TOTAL I	**391,284,461**	**174,056,425**	**217,228,036**	**135,793,456**
INVENTORIES AND WORK-IN-PROGRESS				
Raw materials & other supplies	1,745,935	74,948	1,670,987	1,715,086
Work-in-progress/goods				1,372,663
Work-in-progress/services	54,649,001	511,000	54,138,001	43,709,224
Semi-finished and finished products				
Goods held for resale	595,896		595,896	540,406
Payments on account to suppliers	1,717,244		1,717,244	1,791,444
OPERATING RECEIVABLES				
Trade notes and other trade receivables	677,940,200	6,330,938	671,609,262	514,807,852
Other	110,903,677	13,258,328	97,645,349	123,253,997
Sundry receivables	2,270,852	450,000	1,820,852	
Capital subscribed, called and unpaid				
Investments: own shares				
Investments : other securities	167,057,887		167,057,887	134,360,801
Cash and other liquid assets	77,838,401		77,838,401	147,860,989
Prepaid expenses	5,294,640		5,294,640	3,305,905
TOTAL II	**1,100,013,733**	**20,625,214**	**1,079,388,519**	**972,718,367**
Expenditure to be charged over several periods III	1,912,468		1,912,468	
Deferred taxation IV	9,555,694		9,555,694	2,328,173
Premiums on redemption of bonds V				
Foreign exchange differences VI	12,391		12,391	600,830
Contras/eliminations VII				
TOTAL (0 TO VII)	**1,502,778,747**	**194,681,639**	**1,308,097,108**	**1,111,440,826**

Exhibit 8.9 continued

Consolidated financial statements

Liabilities	31.12.96	31.12.95
SHAREHOLDERS' FUNDS		
Capital stock	51,148,630	50,368,000
Share premiums and other paid-in capital	70,826,278	34,555,605
Revaluation reserve		
Legal reserve	5,036,800	4,936,800
Other reserves	69,074,794	64,666,347
Holdings by the company of its own shares		
Retained earnings	57,561,685	308
Specially-regulated provisions		
Investment grants		
Group share of consolidated reserves	140,724,378	99,650,530
Exchange differences		
Group share of earnings for year	86,226,188	143,938,600
TOTAL I	**480,598,753**	**398,116,190**
Minority interests' share of reserves	8,749,419	12,286,404
Minority interests' share of exchange differences		
Minority interests' share of net earnings for year	6,535,448	3,628,252
TOTAL II	**15,284,867**	**15,914,656**
OTHER SHAREHOLDERS' FUNDS III	**1,050,000**	**350,000**
Provisions for contingencies	23,612,749	18,407,103
Provisions for expenses	29,920,313	24,964,254
Provisions for deferred taxation	1,992,486	
Provisions resulting from acquisition goodwill (-)		
TOTAL IV	**55,525,548**	**43,371,357**
FINANCIAL LIABILITIES		
Convertible bonds		
Other bonds		
Bank borrowings and short-term debts from financial institutions	165,175,489	84,730,927
Leasing finance		
Sundry borrowings and financial liabilities	20,199,183	24,527,004
Payments on account from clients	3,060,577	31,393,036
OPERATING LIABILITIES		
Trade notes and other accounts payable	141,846,425	151,403,145
Taxes and dividends payable, and payments to and in respect of employees	388,077,224	342,152,293
Other	1,343,810	735,163
OTHER LIABILITIES		
Liabilities re fixed assets and related accounts	439,727	3,521,236
Tax liabilities (corporate taxes)		
Other	16,419,516	10,318,294
Prepaid income	19,072,884	4,906,128
TOTAL V	**755,634,835**	**653,687,226**
Foreign exchange differences VI	3,105	1,397
Contras/eliminations VII		
TOTAL (I TO VII)	**1,308,097,108**	**1,111,440,826**

Source: Assystem Group, annual report, 1996, pp. 38–9

Exhibit 8.10 AEROSPATIALE: EXTRACT FROM BALANCE SHEET

CONSOLIDATED BALANCE SHEET

ASSETS

(FF millions)

		Dec. 31, 1996			Dec. 31, 1995	Dec. 31, 1994
		Gross	Depreciation, amortization and provisions	Net	Net	Net
FIXED ASSETS						
Intangible assets	*(Note 1)*	1,907	1,499	408	405	610
Tangible assets	*(Note 2)*	25,191	17,032	8,159	8,817	9,215
Companies accounted for by the equity method	*(Note 3)*	1,046		1,046	940	691
Financial assets	*(Note 4)*	1,923	288	1,635	1,550	1,921
Total		**30,067**	**18,819**	**11,248**	**11,712**	**12,437**
CURRENT ASSETS						
Inventories and work-in-process	*(Note 5)*	24,166	2,867	21,299	20,120	23,600
Advances and payments on account on orders		3,632		3,632	3,884	3 300
Accounts receivable		17,425	1,317	16,108	17,681	17,716
Sundry receivables		4,181	1	4,180	3,780	4,130
Marketable securities	*(Note 9)*	6,416		6,416	5,457	6,693
Cash and equivalents	*(Note 9)*	1,715		1,715	4,042	3,250
Prepaid expenses	*(Note 6)*	1,102		1,102	760	1,694
Total current assets		**58,637**	**4,185**	**54,452**	**55,724**	**60,383**
Expenses to amortize over several years		50		50	69	139
Bond redemption payments		7		7	13	16
TOTAL ASSETS		**88,761**	**23,004**	**65,757**	**67,518**	**72,975**

Source: Aerospatiale Group, annual report, 1996, p. 16

classify the French approach as allowing the arrival of the true and fair view to permit some change towards substance rather than form. It became available to directors and auditors to be used as a basis for interpretation or for guidance where no rules existed (*see* Chapter 6).

Exhibit 8.11 CARBONE LORRAINE: EXTRACT FROM BALANCE SHEET

CARBONE LORRAINE GROUP

ASSETS

At December 31, (FF in millions)	1996	1995	1994
FIXED ASSETS			
Intangible assets			
– Goodwill	127.3	125.5	89.1
– Other intangible assets	35.2	36.0	36.2
Tangible assets			
– Land	29.5	28.4	24.9
– Buildings	178.9	180.0	169.0
– Plant, equipment and other tangible assets	445.5	440.7	353.3
– Capital expenditure in progress	69.2	74.8	37.7
Financial assets			
– Investments	106.4	90.0	76.8
– Other financial assets	19.2	20.2	28.2
TOTAL FIXED ASSETS	**1,011.2**	**995.6**	**815.2**
CURRENT ASSETS			
– Inventories	568.9	626.6	487.0
– Trade accounts receivable and related receivables	671.3	638.7	477.8
– Other receivables	90.3	88.6	63.3
– Short-term advances	1.0	0.3	0.3
– Marketable securities	0.1	—	8.1
– Cash at bank and in hand	67.8	109.6	52.0
TOTAL CURRENT ASSETS	**1,399.4**	**1,463.8**	**1,088.5**
TOTAL ASSETS	**2,410.6**	**2,459.4**	**1,903.7**

The accompanying notes are an integral part of these financial statements.

Source: Carbone Lorraine Group, annual report, 1996, p. 10

8.7.3 Uniformity versus flexibility

Gray (1988) placed France at the highly uniform end of the scale. That may have reflected the historical dominance at that time of the accounting practices of individual companies which were highly regulated. The later 1980s saw increasing production of consolidated accounts where French companies took advantage of the flexibility available under the less stringent regulatory framework. The practical extent of that flexibility is seen in annual surveys.[42] The *Plan Comptable Général* is probably the most significant factor in determining the level of uniformity.

---

[42] 11th annual survey of annual reports of industrial and commercial companies, referred to in *FT World Accounting Report*, January 1997, p. 10

Exhibit 8.12 ASSYSTEM: PROFIT AND LOSS ACCOUNT

INCOME STATEMENT	1996	1995
OPERATING REVENUE		
Sales of goods held for resale	731,382	1,281,546
Sales of manufactured goods and services	1,623,540,857	1,411,832,700
Net turnover	**1,624,272,239**	**1,413,114,246**
Increase/decrease in inventory of work-in-progress	1,840,686	31,222,272
Fixed assets produced for own use	411,673	814,021
Operating subsidies	408,756	971,790
Recovery from provisions and depreciation and expense transfers	17,370,636	35,014,655
Other income	8,127,474	6,510,161
TOTAL I	**1,652,431,464**	**1,487,647,145**
OPERATING EXPENSES		
Purchases of goods for resale	538,846	1,213,396
Change in inventory	19,520	- 38,483
Purchases of raw materials and other supplies	5,054,122	5,750,865
Change in inventory	- 114,342	- 1,516,996
Other external purchases	454,578,865	437,133,941
Taxation and other dues	47,964,497	32,424,918
Wages and salaries	647,633,426	505,968,562
Social charges	245,493,996	190,296,040
Depreciation and amortization of fixed assets	23,889,497	20,285,087
Provisions in respect of fixed assets		10,020
Provisions in respect of current assets	2,371,968	2,020,809
Contingency and expense provisions	16,143,320	10,925,286
Other expenses	2,765,302	3,276,372
TOTAL II	**1,446,339,017**	**1,207,749,817**
NET OPERATING INCOME (I-II)	**206,092,447**	**279,897,328**
Profit transferred (III)		
Loss transferred (IV)		
FINANCIAL INCOME		
– from corporate investments	1,760,209	537,217
– from other securities and capitalized receivables	268,662	269,866
– other interest and similar income	1,222,286	2,452,339
– recovery from provisions and expense transfers	4,568,200	429,483
– foreign exchange gains	43,125	28,506
– net proceeds of disposal of short-term investments	4,502,000	4,500,581
TOTAL V	**12,364,482**	**8,217,992**

▶

Exhibit 8.12 continued

INCOME STATEMENT	1996	1995
INTEREST AND OTHER FINANCIAL CHARGES		
Allowance for amortization, depreciation and provisions	13,220,860	7,831,721
Interest and similar expenses	12,985,249	6,190,604
Foreign exchange losses	170,827	268,671
Losses on disposals of short-term investments		
TOTAL VI	26,376,936	14,290,996
NET FINANCIAL INCOME (V-VI)	- 14,012,454	- 6,073,004
INCOME BEFORE TAX AND EXCEPTIONAL ITEMS	**192,079,993**	**273,824,324**
EXCEPTIONAL GAINS		
From operations	2,512,774	238,179
From capital transactions	2,937,939	2,044,481
Recovery from provisions and expense transfers	1,440,090	2,055,592
TOTAL VII	6,890,803	4,338,252
EXCEPTIONAL LOSSES (VII-VIII)		
In respect of operations	2,665,658	2,342,006
In respect of capital transactions	3,489,571	1,358,631
In respect of amortization, depreciation and provisions	935,279	594,507
TOTAL VIII	7,090,508	4,295,144
NET EXCEPTIONAL INCOME (VII-VIII)	- 199,705	43,108
Employee profit-sharing (IX)	19,779,625	20,193,115
Income tax expense (X)	68,492,368	95,186,079
Deferred taxes (XI)	- 5,157,711	3,787,994
EARNINGS OF FULLY CONSOLIDATED COMPANIES (before amortization of acquisition goodwill)	108,766,006	154,700,244
SHARE OF EARNINGS OF COMPANIES CONSOLIDATED USING THE EQUITY METHOD (before amortization of acquisition goodwill)	79,544	1,413,758
CONSOLIDATED EARNINGS (before amortization of acquisition goodwill)	**108,845,550**	**156,114,002**
Minority interests (before amortization of goodwill)	6,535,448	3,628,252
Parent company interest (before amortization of goodwill)	**102,310,102**	**152,485,750**
Net allowance for amortization of goodwill on acquisition of fully consolidated companies	15,527,298	8,363,768
Net allowance for amortization of goodwill on acquisition of equity-method companies	556,616	183,382
CONSOLIDATED NET EARNINGS	**92,761,636**	**147,566,852**
Share of minority interests	6,535,448	3,628,252
Share of parent company	**86,226,188**	**143,938,600**

Source: Assystem Group, annual report, 1996, pp. 40–1

Exhibit 8.13 RENAULT: SIMPLIFIED PROFIT AND LOSS ACCOUNT

Consolidated Statements of Income

(In millions of French Francs)	1996	1995	1994
Sales of goods and services	176,023	175,596	169,659
Revenues from financial services (Note 4)	8,055	8,469	8,878
Revenues (Note 3)	184,078	184,065	178,537
Cost of goods and services sold (a)	(147,036)	(144,959)	(138,712)
Cost of sales financing (Note 4)	(4,716)	(5,000)	(5,739)
Research and development expenses (a)	(9,125)	(9,220)	(9,074)
Selling, general and administrative expenses	(25,002)	(23,406)	(22,164)
Other operating income and expenses, net (Note 5)	(4,186)	(221)	(531)
Total costs and operating expenses	(190,065)	(182,806)	(176,220)
Operating income	(5,987)	1,259	2,317
Interest income (expense), net	65	526	2
Other financial income and expense, net	259	128	686
Financial income (Note 7)	324	654	688
Net income (loss) from companies accounted for under the equity method (Note 11)	18	63	480
Group pretax income	(5,645)	1,976	3,485
Current and deferred tax (Note 8)	379	305	219
Income before minority interest (Group)	(5,266)	2,281	3,704
Minority interest	(18)	142	68
Net income (Renault)	(5,248)	2,139	3,636
Earnings per share in French Francs (Note 1-J)	(22.07)	9.03	15.65
Average number of shares (in thousands)	237,750	236,887	232,391

(a) The figures for fiscal years 1995 and 1994 are presented pro-forma (cf. note 1-E)

Source: Renault Group, annual report, 1996, p. 92

8.7.3.1 The *Plan Comptable Général*[43]

The national accounting code (*Plan Comptable Général*) is at the heart of financial reporting and accounting. It is issued under the authority of the French national accounting council (CNC). The Code is revised at relatively infrequent intervals, with amendments and additions occurring more frequently. There are two central objectives of the *Plan Comptable Général*:

- standardising the organisation of the accounting system of the enterprise
- standardising the presentation of financial results and position.

---

[43] Standish (1995), pp. 224–8; Scheid and Walton (1992), pp. 117–27

Taken together, these ensure that the accounting records are maintained in a form which permits production of the required form of financial statements.

The *Plan Comptable Général* is very detailed, using a decimal numbering system to specify major headings and greater levels of detail. The highest level of heading is shown in Exhibit 8.14.

The detailed accounts under each heading are also specified using further digits. Two-digit examples are given in Exhibit 8.15.

Exhibit 8.14 ACCOUNT CODES FOR FINANCIAL ACCOUNTS

1	Capital (share capital, reserves, loans)
2	Fixed assets
3	Stocks (inventory) and work-in-progress
4	Debtors and creditors
5	Financial assets and liabilities
6	Expenses
7	Revenues
8	Special accounts
9	Management accounts

Exhibit 8.15 EXAMPLES OF TWO-DIGIT CODES IN THE *PLAN COMPTABLE GÉNÉRAL*

21	Tangible assets (part of fixed assets)
40	Trade creditors (part of debtors and creditors)
x9	Any two-digit account ending in 9 indicates a provision against an asset

Three-digit codes are also used for detailed recording. They can be aggregated to the two-digit level in order to present information for financial reporting.

As well as containing specification of account codes, the *Plan Comptable Général* also contains the following:

- terminology
- valuation and measurement rules
- rules linking the chart of accounts to the financial statements
- regulations for special situations
- methodology for consolidated accounts
- guidance on management accounting.

Effectively it is a very detailed manual for the preparation of accounts. It does not have the status of a law, but application of the classification is compulsory. Furthermore there are industry-specific versions. However the *Plan Comptable Général* requires interpretation of some of the rules and it is not a full source of information on all matters. It does, however, contain extensive guidelines for explanation of the principles.

The general principles of the *Plan Comptable Général* are intended to produce a true and fair view (*image fidèle*) by application of prudence, consistency (*régularité*) and faithful reckoning (*sincérité*). There are no statements of accounting standards in France.

8.7.3.2 Relationship between company law and tax law[44]

Accounting law in France has been shaped by fiscal policy as enacted in tax law. Tax law has concentrated on the construction of the balance sheet to ensure that the recording of transactions is carried out without the exercise of discretion over matters such as end-of-period adjustments. There is a general rule that expenses are tax-deductible only if treated as expenses in the annual accounts.

Tax law has sometimes had an influence for greater flexibility than the accounting codes, particularly so in permitting accelerated depreciation which would not be justified by economic circumstances. In times of high inflation tax law has permitted specific revaluations of fixed assets. The court of appeal in tax matters is the *Conseil d'État*, which has indicated a willingness to apply general accounting principles to tax matters. The relationship between tax law and accounting law is therefore complex, and it is not always the case that tax law dictates the outcome.

8.7.3.3 Foreign currency translation[45]

The PGC 1982 allows both historic rate and closing rate to be used for foreign currency transactions in the accounts of individual companies. Where there is translation of a long-term monetary item denominated in a foreign currency, any exchange difference may be reported at the foot of the assets section or the liabilities section of the balance sheet. There are no prescribed rules for translation of the accounts of foreign subsidiaries, and there is thus considerable choice of practice.

8.7.3.4 Accounting for joint ventures[46]

Legislation requires that jointly controlled entities should be accounted for using proportional consolidation, in line with the benchmark treatment contained in IAS 31. From surveys of published accounts it would appear that the proportional consolidation method is used only by a minority of companies. The law sets out general principles which are not elaborated elsewhere, so in practice it may be difficult to decide where proportional consolidation should be used. Equity accounting produces a single line in the balance sheet and conceals the extent of gearing when compared to the proportional consolidation method. Thus the flexibility taken under the law limits comparability. An example of joint venture accounting using proportional consolidation is provided by Colas Group (see Exhibit 8.16), a company primarily in the business of road construction and maintenance. It should be noted also that Colas uses the permitted flexibility of non-consolidation in respect of partnerships in areas of dissimilar activity, namely manufacturing asphalt concrete.

---

[44] Standish (1995), pp. 241–2; Scheid and Walton (1992), pp. 85–7
[45] Scheid and Walton (1992), pp. 247–8
[46] Scheid and Walton (1992), pp. 251–3

Exhibit 8.16 COLAS GROUP: PROPORTIONAL ACCOUNTING FOR JOINT VENTURE

PRINCIPLES OF CONSOLIDATION

Subsidiary companies controlled by more than 50% are fully consolidated.

As in previous years, investments in Moroccan subsidiaries have been fully consolidated even though the company's interest is slightly less than 50%.

Joint-venture construction partnerships have been consolidated by including the company's proportional share in the venture's assets, liabilities, revenues and expenses, in all cases where the said share exceeds 20%.

On the other hand, companies or partnerships formed for the manufacturing of asphalt concrete and other similar products, which are jointly owned with other construction companies, are not consolidated.

Uncontrolled companies subject to significant activity are consolidated using the equity method.

Companies in the process of liquidation, with non significant activity or which are located in countries with restrictions on currency transfers, are not included in the consolidated financial statements.

SCOPE OF CONSOLIDATION

Number of companies consolidated by consolidation method

	1996	1995
Full consolidation	316	255
Proportional consolidation	41	43
Accounted for on the equity method	5	4
Total	362	302

Source: Colas Group, annual report, 1996, pp. 19, 18

8.7.3.5 Influence of EU on French accounting

The Fourth Directive reflects the French practice as contained in the *Plan Comptable Général* and reflects in particular the preference for financial statement formats. Implementation of the Fourth Directive required a major revision of the *Plan Comptable Général* in 1982 but this had the effect of confirming the uniformity of presentation in the financial statements of individual companies. A late addition to the Fourth Directive was the requirement for a true and fair view, translated into French as *image fidèle*. This was dealt with in a manner similar to that of Germany in declaring that the true and fair view is established by reading the balance sheet, profit and loss account and notes taken together. Uniformity in the financial statements was thus preserved in the context of potential flexibility in the notes to the accounts.

Implementation of the Seventh Directive in France made consolidation a more familiar process than it had previously been. The lack of established codification gave French companies considerable latitude in preparation of consolidated accounts and this latitude is a feature of the many options available under the Directive. Examination of consolidated accounts may thus give an impression of flexibility. It has been suggested that the open-minded approach to consolidation owes much to the lobbying by French multinational companies during implementation of the Seventh Directive.[47] Comparability has consequently been relatively limited.

8.7.4 Conservatism versus optimism

Gray (1988) placed French accounting practice at the highly conservative end of the spectrum, clustered with other more developed Latin countries and Japan. The extent of conservatism is illustrated here in relation to long-term contracts, inventories, asset valuation and provisions. It will be seen that the potential for conservatism could be modified by the flexibility available, but in practice the dominance of tax law tends to encourage conservative practices.

8.7.4.1 Long-term contracts[48]

In France, the percentage of completion method is not mandatory but is commonly used. If the percentage of completion method is applied then conditions as to certainty of overall outcome are specified in the Commercial Code. The work-in-progress must be valued, the customer must have accepted the work done, costs to completion must have been estimated and it must be possible to estimate the final profit with a reasonable degree of certainty. There are also requirements of the PGC 1982. For contracts involving public works, there are further conditions in the law which reflect the greater certainty attached to such contracts. Use of a mixture of percentage of completion and completed contract methods is illustrated in Exhibit 8.17.

In general terms, the conditions applied in France are those of IAS 11. In particular the payments on account by the customer must be kept in a separate liability account until the project is completed. However in conformity with the Fourth Directive the profit recognised on the contract is reported as an amount receivable from the customer rather than as an element of work-in-progress. Overall, the French practice shows the optimism on long-term contracts which is found in IAS 11 and other continental European countries, but it is flavoured with conservatism in respect of the conditions imposed by law and the lack of compulsion under the law.

8.7.4.2 Inventories[49]

All the provisions of IAS 2 are applied in France. The 'lower of cost and net realisable value' rule is applied. The presentation of the information in the balance sheet requires the disclosure of the full amount of historical cost followed by a sep-

---

[47] Pham (1993), p. 93
[48] Scheid and Walton (1992), pp. 186–8
[49] Scheid and Walton (1992), p. 196

Exhibit 8.17 GROUP EIFFAGE: NOTE TO THE ACCOUNTS REGARDING LONG-TERM CONTRACTS

NOTES TO THE CONSOLIDATED ACCOUNTS FOR THE FINANCIAL YEAR 1995

II. VALUATION METHODS

Long-term contracts

Earnings from long-term contracts are included at the completion of work. However, the percentage-of-completion method is applied in the following cases:
– construction projects of short duration or low unit value, notably roadworks and earthworks,
– certain types of contract due to their special characteristics, method of payment ('cost plus' etc.) or special contractual or regulatory factors, particularly in certain foreign countries,
– after completion of major constructions forming part of exceptionally long-term projects.

Provisions for contingent liabilities or loss of value of work in progress are included to cover foreseeable losses at completion, these being assessed on the basis of an analysis of the economic and financial forecasts for each contract, account possibly being taken of sums likely to be obtained in respect of claims filed.

Source: Group Eiffage, annual report, 1995, pp. 12, 13

arate provision to arrive at realisable value. Where prices of inventories are changing, the FIFO method is permitted for both individual accounts and group accounts but the LIFO method is available only for group accounts. In practice, most French companies use the average cost method; there is no appearance of greater conservatism in French accounting than elsewhere in this respect.

8.7.4.3 Valuation of assets[50]

Historical cost valuation of tangible assets is prescribed in the 1983 Accounting Act, in terms of purchase price for goods purchased by the company, market value for goods acquired free of charge and production cost for goods manufactured by the company. Further detail is provided in the 1983 Accounting Decree defining such terms as 'purchase price', 'market price' and 'cost of production'.

Purchase price and production cost

Some evidence of conservatism may be seen in relation to purchase price where items such as any interest content of the price, or any subsequent variation in price due to currency fluctuations, would not be included. Items such as fees and commissions paid to acquire a fixed asset may be capitalised and amortised for accounting purposes but must be treated as an expense for tax purposes. Most companies follow the tax rule.

'Production cost' includes all direct costs and an allocation of indirect costs based on full absorption costing and a 'normal' level of production. Where there is

---

[50] Scheid and Walton (1992), pp. 194–8

a shortfall in production and a consequent under-recovery of overheads, the PGC requires the shortfall to be taken directly to profit and loss account. In this regard, the French practice is conservative in not allowing the additional cost to be taken to stock values but no more conservative than UK practice.

Leasing

Where a business uses an asset which it does not own, the law allows the asset to appear on the balance sheet of the enterprise provided there is an agreement at the outset to transfer title at a point in the future. This includes the grant of a trading right such as a concession to provide public transport. However, where assets are held under finance lease there is no capitalisation in the balance sheet of the individual companies. This is consistent with the emphasis on using accounting practice which is consistent with the tax law. Capitalisation of finance leases is optional in group accounting; there are no regulations and so groups tend to follow IAS 17.

8.7.4.4 Revaluation[51]

The 1983 Accounting Act permits voluntary revaluation of the whole of the tangible fixed assets and investments. The revaluation surplus must be taken to a non-distributable reserve; this reflects the previous practice of making revaluations from time to time under government order, usually in times of high inflation. Until 1959, the government made orders for revaluation for tax purposes and companies usually incorporated these in the published accounts. Since 1960, the government has changed to the use of accelerated depreciation rather than asset revaluation in dealing with economic factors. During the 1960s and early 1970s there was uncertainty about the tax implications of asset revaluation and so it did not occur. A government-authorised revaluation was made by companies at the end of December 1976 under clear conditions of establishing a revaluation reserve which was not subject to tax. However, in general, the tax authorities will continue to regard revaluations as taxable.

Revaluation in the accounts of individual companies is thus not found and revaluations in the group accounts are rare despite the relative freedom for group accounting. The conservatism of accounting practice appears to be based in the traditional impact of tax law.

8.7.4.5 Intangible assets[52]

Purchased goodwill has traditionally been thought of as the value of the customer base of an organisation (*fonds de commerce*) and is valued according to established professional practice. It is not amortised where it is seen as having an enduring value. At the point of consolidation the *fonds de commerce* goodwill is regarded as an identifiable intangible asset, similar to a patent or a trade mark. Other purchased intangible assets may be subject to systematic depreciation if their value is associated with a specific period of legal protection (such as a patent). When the value of a category of intangible asset is based on economic advantage which has no limit of time, then amortisation is not required (trade names and brands, for example).

---

[51] Scheid and Walton (1992), pp. 207–10
[52] Scheid and Walton (1992), Chapter 13

The more specific type of goodwill is that arising on acquisition by one company of another and is dealt with in the 1986 Decree. It is calculated as the difference between the acquisition cost and the accounting value of the equity acquired. This difference must be allocated first to the different elements in the balance sheet, although the law does not specify the basis. Any remaining amount is 'true goodwill' (*survaleur*) and is amortised through the profit and loss account. Some aspects of accounting for goodwill are not clear in the 1986 Decree or in the PGC 1982. The value of the assets acquired may be the fair value at the date of acquisition, the fair value at the date of first consolidation or the book value at the date of acquisition. Immediate write-off against reserves is permitted by the 1986 Decree, but with imprecise conditions.

Amortisation of goodwill is the most common practice but other variants are found because of the flexibility allowed by the law. The law shows no particular leanings towards conservatism, but in practice companies choose the conservative approach. In practice, the time period for systematic allocation of amortisation varies from 2 to 40 years.

It is possible for companies to think creatively about the range of identifiable intangible assets against which goodwill on acquisition may be allocated. IMS (Exhibit 8.18) provides an illustration of this process, where the assignment of goodwill is extended to intangible assets. The result is intangible assets of long life on which there is no depreciation in the reporting period.

Brand valuation without depreciation is seen in the financial statements of Danone (*see* Exhibit 8.19). The company does depreciate the purchased goodwill, regarded as the *fonds de commerce*, and other intangibles.

Exhibit 8.18   IMS: NOTE ON INTANGIBLE ASSETS

■ BALANCE SHEET ACCOUNTS

2.1 Intangible assets

The development of the Group through external growth is resulting in IMS acquiring market shares, customers and trading networks which are not generally stated in the balance sheet of acquired companies. The assignment of goodwill arising on acquisition has therefore been extended to intangible assets. These intangible assets are then valued with reference to the gross margin and the operating profit which are the two most representative criteria.

In the years subsequent to the acquisition, the value of intangible assets created is systematically audited and, if necessary, a provision for depreciation may be allocated to reflect the loss in value of these assets.

At the end of 1996, the intangible assets created in respect of assigning goodwill on acquisition amounted to 113 million French francs. A depreciation reserve of FRF 6 million was entered in 1996 for Scert.

Source: IMS International Metal Service, annual report, 1996, p. 39

Exhibit 8.19 DANONE: NOTE ON BRANDS AND OTHER INTANGIBLE ASSETS

Brands and other intangible assets
The brands which have been separately identified are only premium brands, with a value that is substantial and considered to be of a long-term nature, sustained by advertising expenses.
The valuation of these brands is determined with the assistance of specialized consultants, taking into account various factors including brand recognition and earnings contribution. These brands, which are legally protected, are not amortized. In the event that the recorded value of a brand becomes permanently impaired, an allowance would be charged to income.
Purchased goodwill ('fonds de commerce'), licenses, patents and leasehold rights are recorded at cost. They are amortized on a straight-line basis over their estimated useful lives, not exceeding forty years.

Source: Danone Group, annual report, 1996, p. 46

A particularly full description of accounting policies applied to intangible assets is provided by Pinault-Printemps-Redoute (*see* Exhibit 8.20). The note also makes a distinction between purchased goodwill and the goodwill arising on consolidation.

Research and development expenditure may be treated as an asset under French accounting. Pure research is never reported as an asset but applied research may be treated comparably with development expenditure. If there is capitalisation then amortisation is usually over a maximum of five years. This is more flexible than IAS 9 with regard to optional capitalisation of development expenditure and is more conservative than IAS 9 in the period allowed for amortisation.

8.7.4.6 Provisions and contingencies[63]

There is a relatively high incidence in French accounting of provisions for risks and charges. They can cover matters such as:

- guarantees given to customers
- amounts in respect of ongoing litigation
- restructuring and reorganisation
- taxation
- pensions
- redundancy of employees
- future discounts to employees
- services due to clients
- losses in subsidiaries which are guaranteed by the parent.

Many of these items would, in UK accounts, be reported in notes on contingencies rather than as provisions on the face of the balance sheet. This has led researchers in the past to suggest that French accounting is relatively conservative. That conservatism appears to have survived the introduction of the Fourth and

---

[53] Scheid and Walton (1992), p. 190; Alexander *et al.* (1996)

Exhibit 8.20 PINAULT-PRINTEMPS-REDOUTE: ACCOUNTING POLICIES ON INTANGIBLE ASSETS

NOTES TO THE CONSOLIDATED FINANCIAL STATEMENTS

1 – ACCOUNTING POLICIES

The consolidated financial statements are presented in accordance with the provisions of the law of January 3, 1985 and the application decree of February 17, 1986, and with the rules and principles set out in the French Accounting Plan (Plan Comptable Général). The financial statements of consolidated companies prepared in accordance with local accounting standards in their country of operation, are restated to reflect the accounting policies applied by the Group.

1-1 Consolidation [extract]
Significant undertakings over which the Pinault-Printemps-Redoute Group exercises exclusive control are fully consolidated. Exclusive control is presumed to exist where the Group holds more than 40% of the voting rights and has enjoyed, for two consecutive years, the right to appoint the majority of the members of the Board of Directors, executive management, or the Supervisory Board of the undertaking in question. Undertakings in which the Pinault-Printemps-Redoute Group exercises significant influence over management or financial policy are accounted for under the equity method. Significant influence is presumed to exist where 20% of the voting rights are held. Undertakings involved in financial services or insurance activities over which the Group has majority control are accounted for under the equity method, due to the distinct nature of their business activities and the different form in which their financial statements are presented.

1-5 Goodwill
When the Group acquires an interest in a consolidated subsidiary, all identifiable assets and liabilities of the company acquired are restated according to Group accounting policies and revalued at their value in use to the Group. A period of one year from the date of the acquisition is allowed to finalize the valuation. Minority interests are also valued on the basis of the fair value of the identifiable net assets of the subsidiary. The difference between the cost to the Group of acquiring the interest (including incidental costs) and the share of the restated and revalued net assets acquired is recorded as 'goodwill' in the consolidated balance sheet (see Note 9). Goodwill is amortized on a straight line basis over a maximum period of 40 years, unless circumstances dictate a shorter period.

1-6 Other intangible assets
Because of the nature of the Group's operations, intangible assets such as brands, trade names, market shares, lease hold interest, and purchased goodwill often account for a significant proportion of differences arising on the acquisition of controlling interests in consolidated companies.
Only those intangible assets which have established worth and are separately indentifiable, and in respect of which changes in value can be measured, are capitalized by the Group. They are valued by independent experts, using appropriate criteria for the business concerned, making direct reference to sales and profitability (see Note 10). The Group takes appropriate action to ensure that the value of these intangible assets is maintained. A provision is charged against income when there is a permanent diminution in the current use value of such an asset. The valuation of these assets is reviewed on a regular basis using consistent methods.
The Group also confirms that these intangible assets are properly valued by ensuring that the net book value of the entity to which they relate, as shown in the consolidated financial statements, is less than the current use value to the Group. This value is determined using established methods: theoretical market capitalization, discounted future cash flow, and revalued net assets (excluding intangibles).

Source: Pinault-Printemps-Redoute Group, annual report, 1996, pp. 82–3

Seventh Directives and, as we have seen, may be attributed to the influence of tax law on accounting practice. Furthermore it has been noted that many French companies are not dependent on the capital market for a source of finance and so are not concerned about the impact of reported earnings on share price.

The notion of a 'contingent liability' is not used in France, and items which in the UK would be reported as contingencies will be analysed differently. If the outcome is predictable, there will be a provision for risks and charges. If predictability is relatively low, then there will be a note on a commitment. Although there is a phrase in French accounting corresponding to contingent liabilities, such items do not appear in practice. The treatment is dependent on likelihood of occurrence.

The different practice in France, as compared with that of the UK, may be regarded as an interesting example of a situation where both countries have a similar concept – that of 'probability of occurrence' – but the situations in each country result in very different interpretations of the concept.

8.7.5 Secrecy versus transparency

Gray (1988) classified French accounting as relatively low on the secrecy scale compared with Germany or the less developed Latin countries. This is consistent with the extensive use of notes to the accounts and various types of additional disclosure such as segmental reporting, the management report and the social balance sheet.

8.7.5.1 Notes to the accounts[54]

The balance sheet, profit and loss account and notes to the accounts must be read as a whole. It is specifically stated in the PGC 1982 that the three documents form *un tout*, and it is also stated in the Commercial Code in the phrase *un tout indissociable*.

The notes are regarded as complementing and commenting on the information in the balance sheet and profit and loss account. They may also supply additional information where the rules are not sufficient to give a true and fair view. Their role also covers describing and justifying changes in accounting policies or presentation of information. It is clear from the Commercial Code that the notes should be used to provide the additional information necessary for a true and fair view. Giving additional information in the balance sheet and profit and loss account is not acceptable.

Two sets of notes are required – one for the parent company and one for the group. It should be noted that in English-language versions of group accounts the parent company accounts and notes are often omitted.

8.7.5.2 Segmental reporting[55]

French legislation reflects the Seventh Directive in its segmental requirements, which are consequently limited in scope. The disclosures are analysis of turnover by type of activity and by geographical market. Disclosure is not required where it would significantly damage the interests of the company. In practice, many listed companies exceed the requirements of law in their consolidated accounts, reflecting IAS 14 or even the US standard.

Examples of the range of segmental disclosure in published accounts may be seen in Exhibit 8.21 (GTM–Entrepose) and Exhibit 8.22 (PSA Peugeot Citroën). GTM–Entrepose is a multinational company undertaking trading in many parts of the world. It presents information in the financial statements identifying sales

---

[54] Parker (1996)
[55] Scheid and Walton (1992), pp. 250–1

Exhibit 8.21 GTM–ENTREPOSE: SEGMENTAL DISCLOSURE

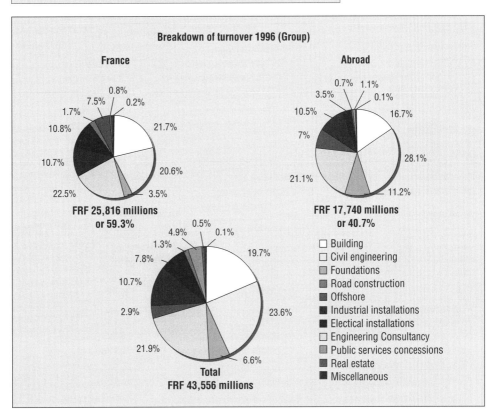

NOTES RELATING TO THE INCOME STATEMENT

1. Sales

	1996 (1)	1995 PRO FORMA (2)	1995 (3)
Sales inside France	24,171	22,855	23,379
Sales outside France	15,620	16,783	14,666
TOTAL	**39,791**	**39,638**	**38,045**

(1) With full consolidation of the DUMEZ-GTM group, with the exception of WIEMER UND TRACHTE, accounted for by the equity method, with FRIEDLANDER being excluded from the scope of consolidation.
(2) With full consolidation of the DUMEZ-GTM group for the whole year, except for WIEMER UND TRACHTE and FRIEDLANDER, accounted for by the equity method.
(3) With consolidation on a proportional basis (50%) of the DUMEZ-GTM group for the first half-year, full consolidation of this group for the second half-year and full consolidation of FRIEDLANDER over the whole year.

Breakdown of turnover 1996 (Group)

France

0.8%, 7.5%, 0.2%, 1.7%, 21.7%, 10.8%, 10.7%, 20.6%, 22.5%, 3.5%

FRF 25,816 millions or 59.3%

Abroad

0.7%, 1.1%, 3.5%, 0.1%, 10.5%, 16.7%, 7%, 28.1%, 21.1%, 11.2%

FRF 17,740 millions or 40.7%

0.5%, 0.1%, 4.9%, 1.3%, 19.7%, 7.8%, 10.7%, 2.9%, 23.6%, 21.9%, 6.6%

Total FRF 43,556 millions

☐ Building
☐ Civil engineering
▨ Foundations
▨ Road construction
■ Offshore
■ Industrial installations
■ Electical installations
☐ Engineering Consultancy
▨ Public services concessions
■ Real estate
■ Miscellaneous

Source: GTM–Entrepose Group, annual report, 1996, pp. 65, 7

Exhibit 8.22   PSA PEUGEOT CITROËN: SEGMENTAL DISCLOSURE

■ NOTE 2 – Segment information

a – Industry segments

Year ended December 31, 1996

| *(in millions of French francs)* | Peugeot S.A. | Automotive | | | | | Mechanical and services activities | Finance companies | Eliminations | Consolidated |
		Automobiles Peugeot	Automobiles Citroën	Common activities (1)	Total automotive				
Net sales:										
– to third parties	4	97,165	66,169	168	163,506	9,162	–	–	172,668
– intra-group, inter-segment	514	9,887	10,689	3,968	25,058	9,840	–	(34,898)	–
Total	518	107,052	76,858	4,136	188,564	19,002	–	(34,898)	172,668
Working capital provided from operations	750	6,171	2,375	(24)	9,272	1,349	539	–	11,160
Net income/(loss) before income taxes	662	830	(2,693)	(31)	(1,232)	1,016	1,270	–	1,054
Total assets	14,790	65,773	48,501	304	129,368	9,104	6,735	–	145,207
Capital expenditure	–	4,963	4,588	–	9,551	722	–	–	10,273
Depreciation and amortization of property, plant and equipment and special tools	17	5,242	4,739	–	9,998	601	–	–	10,599

(1) Common activities include centralized purchasing and research and development units.

b – Geographic areas

Year ended December 31, 1996

The information below is presented by geographic location of the subsidiary and not by destination of the products sold:

(in millions of French francs)	France	Spain	United Kingdom	Other European countries	Other countries	Eliminations	Consolidated
Net sales:							
– within the geographic area (third parties)	95,784	15,965	21,186	39,489	244	–	172,668
– transfers between geographic areas (group)	59,748	12,582	1,795	694	–	(74,819)	–
Total	155,532	28,547	22,981	40,183	244	(74,819)	172,668
Working capital provided from operations	9,611	994	414	142	(1)	–	11,160
Net income before income taxes	322	499	290	(53)	(4)	–	1,054
Total assets	118,592	8,931	7,348	10,186	150	–	145,207
Capital expenditure	8,184	1,486	347	256	–	–	10,273
Depreciation and amortization of property, plant and equipment and special tools	9,597	590	243	166	3	–	10,599

Transfers between geographic areas concern primarily vehicles, accessories and replacement parts sold to group subsidiaries.

Source: PSA Peugeot Citroën, annual report, 1996, pp. 65–6

within and beyond France. Further segmental information is given in a piecemeal fashion in the unaudited sections of the annual report. This extends only to identifying the level of sales in each of the ten business specialities. In contrast, PSA Peugeot Citroën presents a more detailed note on segmental information within its financial statements section.

8.7.5.3 Management report[56]

The 1985 Act incorporates the provision of the Seventh Directive for a review of the development of the business and discussion of important post-balance sheet events, likely future developments and research and development. This may be seen as comparable to the Directors' Report in UK companies' annual reports.

8.7.5.4 The social balance sheet[57]

French undertakings which have a significant number of employees (more than 300) are required to present to the staff committee a *bilan social*, or employment report. The *bilan social* is not part of the notes to the accounts but is sometimes published in the annual report. It may be regarded as a type of social balance sheet although it is presented as a narrative report. The requirements are contained in a 1977 law relating to company law reform in non-accounting matters. The information provided covers employment, wages and related costs, health and safety conditions, other working conditions, staff training, industrial relations and living conditions where these are the responsibility of the employer.

8.8 EMPIRICAL STUDIES

8.8.1 Classification studies

In Chapter 4 (subsection 4.4.1) it was shown that Mueller (1967) classified France as a uniform system where accounting was seen as a means of governmental control. Nobes (1984) classified French accounting as tax based and macro-uniform, grouped with Italy, Belgium and Spain (Exhibit 4.7). Nair and Frank (1980) classified France with the main body of European countries on the basis of measurement (Exhibit 4.10) but with Belgium, Italy and Spain as European countries, on the basis of disclosure (Exhibit 4.11). Using more recent survey data Doupnik and Salter (1993) (Exhibit 4.8) classified France as part of a core macro-uniform group from which other macro-uniform countries had been distinguished by legal system, attitude to uncertainty, market capitalisation of the stock market, level of economic development, relative inflation and relative nurture.

8.8.2 Comparability measures

Approaches to measuring comparability were explained in Chapter 3. French companies have not, as a common matter, restated their accounts under the policies of

---

[56] Scheid and Walton (1992), p. 168
[57] Parker (1996), p. 335; Scheid and Walton (1992), p. 164

other countries and so there has in the past been little data for comparability studies. One exception is France Telecom, which made a US filing in 1997 in order for shares to be traded in New York. Delays to privatisation delayed the actual listing but the information published in the USA showed a loss of FFr33.9 billion in 1996 under US GAAP compared with a profit of FFr2.1 billion under French rules.[58] The difference lay in a special payment to the state in return for the transfer of pension liabilities which was recorded in the profit and loss account under US rules but not under French rules. (It should be noted this was a very special case particular to this company.) Other companies which make full filings with the US SEC are shown in Exhibit 8.23.

Exhibit 8.23 COMPANIES HAVING A FULL LISTING ON THE NEW YORK STOCK EXCHANGE

> Alcatel Alsthom Compagnie Générale d'Électricité
> AXA
> Bouygues Offshore SA
> Compagnie Générale de Géophysique
> Elf Aquitaine
> Groupe AB SA
> Pechiney
> Rhône–Poulenc SA
> SCOR
> SGS–Thomson Microelectronics NV
> Total

Source: http://www.nyse.com at September 1997

In the hypothetical study by Simmonds and Azières (1989), it was shown that French accounting practice gave a most likely profit, as well as maximum and minimum measures, in the middle of the range across EU countries surveyed. Profits could be minimised by increasing the goodwill charge and valuing stocks on a LIFO basis. Profits could be maximised by reducing the goodwill charge. Net asset values were also in the middle of the range across the EU countries surveyed.

A simulation comparing French and UK accounting was undertaken by Walton (1992) and is described in Case study 3.2, appended to Chapter 3. He showed that on separate line items, UK respondents to a case study were often more conservative than their French counterparts. Moreover there was considerable variety within each country as well as between them. The overall conservatism of French accounting is probably based in the use of provisions rather than the treatment of each item of the accounts.

8.8.3 Harmonisation studies

Harmonisation studies were explained in Chapter 4. Archer *et al.* (1995) included France in their eight-country sample which showed a low level of harmony on

---

[58] *Financial Times*, 1 July 1997

deferred tax both between countries and within countries. No increase was seen in relation to consolidated goodwill over the period studied.

Hermann and Thomas (1995) found that, of the countries classed as legalistic (Belgium, France, Germany and Portugal), France had the highest bicountry I index when compared to the fairness orientated countries (Denmark, Ireland, the UK and the Netherlands). This was explained by Hermann and Thomas as reflecting French use of Anglo-Saxon methods of consolidation and the influence of IASs on French group accounting practices.

The flexibility of measurement practices in large French companies, compared with those of German and UK companies, was confirmed by Emenyonu and Gray (1992) in respect of stock valuation and depreciation methods.

8.9 SUMMARY AND CONCLUSIONS

In this chapter you have seen how characteristics of accounting principles and practice in France are related to the predictions made by Gray and others based upon analysis of cultural factors. Using the scores developed by Hofstede (1984), Gray's (1988) method of analysis may be used to predict that the accounting system in France will be characterised by marginal professionalism, strong uniformity, strong conservatism and marginal secrecy. You have seen that the political and legal institutions provide a basis of statutory control for accounting within the individual company. However, there is more flexibility available for group accounting. Uniformity is influenced by the Fourth and Seventh Directives, but is particularly strong in relation to the application of the chart of accounts. Conservatism is seen in the accounting treatment of provisions and contingencies and is influenced by the interaction of accounting and tax law. Secrecy is less prevalent in accounting practice in France compared with some other countries of the EU, and there are extensive disclosures required by regulation.

French accounting has influenced practice in many former French colonies, so that there is an international sphere of influence for French accounting practices. Until relatively recent times there has been no specific attention given in the law to the IASs, but there is now a desire to allow consolidated accounts of major multinational companies to adopt IASs within the bounds of French law.

QUESTIONS

Business environment (8.2)

1 To what extent does the business environment of France provide clues as to possible influences on accounting practices?

Early developments in accounting (8.3)

1 To what extent do early developments in accounting practice indicate the likely directions of: professionalism/statutory control; uniformity/flexibility; conservatism/optimism; and secrecy/transparency in current practice?

Institutions (8.4)

1 How does the political and economic system of France fit into the classifications described in Chapter 1?

2 How does the legal system of France fit into the classifications described in Chapter 1?

3 How does the taxation system of France compare to the descriptions given in Chapter 1?

4 How does the corporate financing system of France compare to the descriptions given in Chapter 1?

5 How does the accounting profession in France compare to the descriptions given in Chapter 1?

6 How do the external influences on accounting practice in France compare to those described in Chapter 1?

7 Which institutional factors are most likely to influence French accounting practice?

Societal culture and accounting subculture (8.5)

1 What is the position of France relative to the UK, Germany and the Netherlands, according to Hofstede's (1984) analysis (Chapter 2)?

2 What are the features of French societal culture identified by Hofstede which led Gray to his conclusions regarding the likely system of accounting in France?

3 What is the position of France relative to the USA, Japan and Australia according to Hofstede's analysis (Chapter 2)?

IASs (8.6)

1 In which areas does accounting practice in France depart from that set out in IASs?
   For each of the areas of departure which you have identified, describe the treatment required or applied in France, and identify the likely impact on net income and shareholders' equity of moving from French accounting practice to the relevant IAS.

2 What explanations may be offered for these departures from IASs, in terms of the institutional factors described in the chapter?

3 What are the most difficult problems facing accounting in France if it seeks harmonisation with the IASC core standards programme?

EU membership (8.7)

1 What have been the most significant changes in accounting practice in France arising from the Fourth and Seventh Directives?

2 Which factors make it relatively easy or relatively difficult for French accounting practices to harmonise with those of other European countries?

Professionalism/statutory control (8.7.2)

1 Identify the key features supporting a conclusion that marginal professionalism is a characteristic of French accounting.

2 Explain which institutional influences cause marginal professionalism to be a characteristic of French accounting.

3 Discuss whether a classification of marginal professionalism is appropriate for the 1990s.

Uniformity/flexibility (8.7.3)

1 Identify the key features supporting a conclusion that uniformity, rather than flexibility, is a dominant characteristic of French accounting.

2 Explain which institutional influences cause uniformity, rather than flexibility, to be a dominant characteristic of French accounting.

3 Discuss whether a classification of strong uniformity is appropriate for the 1990s.

Conservatism/optimism (8.7.4)

1 Identify the key features supporting a conclusion that conservatism, rather than optimism, is a dominant characteristic of French accounting.

2 Explain which institutional influences cause conservatism, rather than optimism, to be a dominant characteristic of French accounting.

3 Discuss whether a classification of strong conservatism is appropriate for the 1990s.

Secrecy/transparency (8.7.5)

1 Identify the key features supporting a conclusion that marginal secrecy is a characteristic of French accounting.

2 Explain which institutional influences cause marginal secrecy to be a characteristic of French accounting.

3 Discuss whether a classification of marginal secrecy is appropriate for the 1990s.

Empirical studies (8.8)

1 What is the relative position of France as indicated by research studies into classification, comparability and harmonisation?

REFERENCES

Alexander, D. and Archer, S. (1996) 'Goodwill and the difference arising on first consolidation', *European Accounting Review*, 5(2), 243–70.

Alexander, D., Archer, S., Delvaille, P. and Taupin, V. (1996) 'Provisions and contingencies: An Anglo-French investigation', *European Accounting Review*, 5(2), 271–98.

Archer, S., Delvaille, P. and McLeay, S. (1995) 'The measurement of harmonisation and the comparability of financial statement items: Within-country and between-country effects', *Accounting and Business Research*, 25 (98), 67–80.

Burlaud, A., Messina, M. and Walton, P. (1996) 'Depreciation: Concepts and practices in France and the UK', *European Accounting Review*, 5(2), 299–316.

Charkham, J.P. (1994) *Keeping Good Company: A Study of Corporate Governance in Five Countries*. Oxford: Clarendon Press.

Collins, L. (1984) 'The Fourth Directive and France', in Gray, S.J. and Coenenberg, A.G. *EEC and Accounting Harmonisation: Implementation and Impact of the Fourth Directive*. Amsterdam: North-Holland.

Coopers and Lybrand Tax Network (1995) *1995 International Tax Summaries: A Guide for Planning and Decisions*. New York: John Wiley.

Di Pietra, R. (1997) 'Accounting regulation models in Italy, France and Spain', Chapter 9 in Flower, J. and Lefebvre, C. (eds), *Comparative Studies in Accounting Regulation in Europe*. Leuven: Acco.

Emenyonu, E.N. and Gray, S.J. (1992) 'EC accounting harmonisation: An empirical study of measurement practices in France, Germany and the UK', *Accounting and Business Research*, Winter, 49–58.

Flower, J. (1997) 'The national systems for the regulation of financial reporting: A synthesis', Chapter 13 in Flower, J. and Lefebvre, C. (eds), *Comparative Studies in Accounting Regulation in Europe*. Leuven: Acco.

Fortin, A. (1991) 'The 1947 French accounting plan: Origins and influences on subsequent practice', *Accounting Historians Journal*, 19(2), December, 1–25.

Frydlender, A. and Pham, D. (1996) 'Relationships between accounting and taxation in France', *European Accounting Review*, 5, supplement, 845–57.

Hermann, D. and Thomas, W. (1995) 'Harmonisation of accounting measurement practices in the European Community', *Accounting and Business Research*, 25(100), 253–65.

Parker, R.H. (1996) 'Harmonising the notes in the UK and France: A case study in *de jure* harmonisation', *European Accounting Review*, 5(2), 317–38.

Parker, R.H. and Nobes, C.W. (1994) *An International View of True and Fair Accounting*. London: Routledge.

Pham, D. (1993) 'Group accounting in France', in Gray, S.J., Coenenberg, A.G. and Gordon, P.D. (1993) *International Group Accounting – Issues in European Harmonisation*. London: Routledge.

Salter, S.B., Roberts, C.B. and Kantor, J. (1996) 'The IASC comparability project: A cross-national comparison of financial reporting practices and IASC proposed rules', *Journal of International Accounting and Taxation*, 5(1), 89–111.

Scheid, J.-C. and Walton, P. (1992) *European Financial Reporting – France*. London: Routledge.

Scheid, J.-C. and Walton, P. (1995) 'France' in Alexander, D. and Archer, S. (eds), *European Accounting Guide*. New York: Harcourt Brace Professional Publishing.

Simmonds, A. and Azières, O. (1989) *Accounting for Europe – Success by 2000 AD?*. London: Touche Ross.

Standish, P. (1995) 'Financial reporting in France', in Nobes, C. and Parker, R. *Comparative International Accounting*, 4th edn. Englewood Cliffs, NJ: Prentice-Hall.

Walton, P. (1992) 'Harmonization of accounting in France and Britain: Some evidence', *Abacus*, 28(2), 186–99.

Newspapers and journals

FT World Accounting Report, published monthly by *Financial Times* Publications.

The Corporate Accountant, Insert in *The Accountant*, UK monthly. London: Lafferty Publications.

Financial Times, UK.

Chapter 9

Germany

9.1 INTRODUCTION

Germany has a comparatively short history as a unified country.[1] From a relatively loose confederation of states, unification of Germany was completed only in 1871 under the Prussian monarchy (1871–1918). Following the end of the First World War, the Weimar Republic, as a federation with a constitution, operated from 1918 to 1933. The National Socialists seized power in 1933, operating in the name of a republic but in practice as a dictatorship, from 1933 to 1945. Following the end of the Second World War there was a period of occupation by the Allied powers of France, the USSR, the USA and the UK (1945–9). In 1949, Germany was divided by the occupying powers. The German Federal Republic, also known as 'West Germany' was established as a federal state. It has been described as a 'social democratic federal state',[2] but care should be taken in using this description so as not to confuse the general type of classification with any particular political party. Alongside, the German Democratic Republic, also known as 'East Germany', was established as a 'socialist constitution'. Reunification took place in 1990, bringing the social democratic federal state to the whole of Germany.

Chapter 9 focuses on the accounting practices of the former West Germany in relation to the development of accounting in the EU. East Germany operated accounting systems appropriate to a command economy (socialist state) which are not discussed here.

9.2 THE COUNTRY

It may be seen from Exhibit 9.1 that general standards of living are high and the economy has shown consistent growth.

Gross national product (GNP) is created two-thirds by services and one-third by manufacturing. Agriculture makes a negligible contribution to GNP. In manufacturing industry there is a strong presence of machinery and transport, but there is also diversification into other areas. Inflation has been controlled over a period of years, and a feature of that control is an independent central bank.

---

[1] Ordelheide and Pfaff (1994), p.6
[2] Ordelheide and Pfaff (1994), p.6

| Exhibit 9.1 | GERMANY: COUNTRY PROFILE, TAKEN FROM EIU STATISTICS |

Population	81.6 m.	
Land mass	357,868 sq.km	
GDP per head	US $27,604	
GDP per head in purchasing power parity	74	(USA=100)
Origins of GDP:	%	
Agriculture	1.1	
Industry	33.4	
Services	65.5	
	%	
Real GDP average annual growth 1985–95	2.8	
Inflation, average annual rate 1989–96	2.9	

Source: The Economist Pocket World in Figures 1998 Edition, The Economist (1997)

These overall figures conceal differences between the parts of Germany formerly distinguished as West and East Germany.[3] The prosperity of the economy has developed largely in West Germany. The population of East Germany is relatively younger on average. Population density is relatively high and has been augmented in West Germany by an influx of foreign workers. There have also been movements from villages to cities and conurbations. There is an elaborate social security system, reflecting the social aspect of the market economy.

Germany has a consistent pattern of a positive balance of trade, comparing exports with imports, although this is reduced when invisible items are added.[4] The main destination for exports is France. Overall the countries of the EU are an important export market, but Germany is forging links with Eastern European countries which will extend exports potential. Imports are also closely dependent on EU member countries for supply.

The Deutschmark is generally a strong currency on foreign exchanges, reflecting the priority given in Germany to price stability. Inflation over the period 1989–96 was 2.9% per annum.

9.3   OVERVIEW OF ACCOUNTING REGULATIONS[5]

9.3.1   Early accounting law

From the earliest codification of commercial law in 1794 (the Prussian General Act, 1794), the development of accounting law has been linked to the formation of the national state. The *Allgemeines Deutsches Handelsgesetzbuch* (General German Commercial Code, 1861) required an inventory and a balance sheet. In this con-

---

[3] Ordelheide and Pfaff (1994), pp. 3–4
[4] Ordelheide and Pfaff (1994), Chapter 2, p. 14
[5] Ordelheide and Pfaff (1994), Chapter 6

text, an 'inventory' means a list of all assets and liabilities. Assets and liabilities were to be valued at 'attributed value', which could be interpreted as current value.

The profit and loss account emerged later as a separate financial statement as a basis for declaring dividends during the lifetime of a business. There was concern at the risks of distributing dividends based on uncertain profits, and so it became seen as important to determine profits on a prudent basis.

However, the law continued to concentrate on the balance sheet in its approach to valuation. The Stock Corporation Act 1884 required historical cost to be the upper limit of valuation of fixed assets as reported by stock corporations. At that time, the valuation rules required of a stock corporation were not binding upon other forms of business that were regulated by the General German Commercial Code. A new Commercial Code in 1897 used more general wording in requiring assets to be valued according to the *Grundsätze ordnungsmäßiger Buchführung* (*GoB*) or Principles of Regular Accounting; this phrase remains in use at the present time. Accounting law became more flexible after the 1987 Commercial Code but there was a legal requirement to follow the GoB in accounts. Until the amendment of the Commercial Code in 1985 it was not clear whether historical cost accounting was really required for forms other than stock corporations, although it was a majority belief.[6]

Strict historical cost accounting and prudence in the treatment of provisions date from regulations of 1931 and 1937; there was considerable scope for the creation of 'secret reserves'. The potential over-enthusiasm for prudence was cut back in the *AktG* of 1965 in the case of corporations (see below).

9.3.2 Consolidated accounting[7]

The first regulations dealing with consolidated accounts appeared after the Second World War, under the Allied occupation authorities. Consequently an American model was adopted in particular industries (coal, iron and steel) and provided a model for other industries to follow. The German government had taken the authority to issue regulations on group accounts in 1931, but had not acted on that authority. Codification of the rules on group accounting took place in the Joint Stock Corporations Act (*AktG*) of 1965. It required only the consolidation of German-owned subsidiaries and hence foreign-resident subsidiaries were not required by law to be included. However large groups were including foreign-resident subsidiaries voluntarily.[8] The Disclosure Act of 1969 regulated holding companies existing in a legal form other than that of a stock corporation. It required group accounts to be prepared by such holding companies above a specified size.

Group accounting as it is now practised in Germany applies the Seventh Directive as enacted in the Accounting Directives Act (*Bilanzrichtlinien-Gesetz*) 1985. A draft law on the simplification of raising capital, passed in mid-1998 will, if enacted, allow German companies operating in foreign capital markets to present consolidated financial statements which are accepted by those markets instead of in accordance

---

[6] Ballwieser (1995)
[7] Ordelheide and Pfaff (1994), Chapter 8
[8] We are obliged to Prof Dr Wolfgang Ballwieser for this observation

with German statutory requirements (the *Kapitalaufnahmeerleichterungsgesetz*, abbreviated as *KapAEG*). The new law will require that consolidated financial statements must comply with the Seventh Directive, be approximately equal to those stipulated under German statutory requirements, explain they are not German financial statements and comply with special audit and disclosure requirements.[9]

9.4 INSTITUTIONS

There is a general introduction in Chapter 1 to the impact of institutions on accounting practice. This section expands on that work in relation to Germany.

9.4.1 Political and economic system

The German political system has been described as one of social democracy in a federated state. However there is more than one political grouping and the general term 'social democracy' should not be equated with a particular political party.

9.4.1.1 Federal structure

Since reunification in 1990, the German Federal Republic (GFR) comprises 16 states, collectively called *Länder*. Each *Land* (singular) has its own legislature, executive and judiciary under its own written constitution. There is a complex division of responsibilities between federal and state regulation in constitutional, political and legal matters. Very often this puts the onus on the levels of government to achieve a high degree of co-operation. This interdependence is clearly illustrated in the the structure of the federal legislature which is composed of the *Bundestag* and the *Bundesrat*. The Bundestag comprises politicians elected for four years by the German people. It has overriding authority at the federal level and may be compared to what is termed the 'lower chamber' in other countries. The *Bundesrat* comprises members of the *Länder* (states). It may be regarded as comparable to the 'upper chamber' of other countries and is the means through which the states have an input into the legislative process, to the extent that the interests of the states are affected.

The federal system is generally responsible for law-making while the states are generally responsible for administering the law. Accounting practitioners and people of business who wish to influence the formation of law must consequently work with the Federal Ministry of Justice.

9.4.1.2 Social market economy

The economic system[10] of Germany is that of the 'social market economy', a tradition of the Federal Republic of Germany prior to reunification. There is a tradition of co-operation as a basic social and cultural value. This is a strong modifying force on the concept of unrestricted competition. The economic environment of business consequently reflects a need for a mixture of competition and co-operation between companies.

---

[9] *FT World Accounting Report*, January 1997, p. 7; IASC *Insight*, March 1998
[10] Ordelheide and Pfaff (1994), p. 11

9.4.1.3 State regulation of the economic system

The state is given an important role in regulating the economic system. The law sets the framework within which the economic system operates. This involves such matters as preventing concentration of companies which would dominate the market. It limits the free market where this conflicts with social concerns such as working conditions and the provision of social security. Economic policy has been based on the 1967 Economic Stability and Growth Act. The federal and state authorities must co-ordinate economic and financial measures for maintaining the value of the domestic currency. Higher rates of unemployment in the 1990s have put the social aspect of economic policy under some strain.

9.4.1.4 Social values in the economic system

Whereas a fully competitive economic system might be seen as being based on self-interest, in Germany the pursuit of self-interest both by individuals and by organisations is constrained by a sense of obligation to the community.[11] This has been seen traditionally in the attitude of companies to education and training in the workplace. Companies will often be found to be training individuals in excess of the immediate requirements of the business but with a conscious aim of contributing to the skills of the national workforce.

There is a consensus of views in Germany about the purpose of companies. Immediate shareholder value is not seen as the overriding yardstick of corporate success, shareholders being seen as one set of stakeholders amongst several. It has been suggested that German management thinks of its customers and employees first.

From the German point of view, accounting is a very important part of business economics.[12]

9.4.2 Legal system

The German legal system is of the Romano-Germanic family, with the German approach as a unique branch of the European grouping. Consequently German accounting practice, which is strongly contained in law, might be expected to show unique characteristics.

9.4.2.1 Types of business organisation[13]

German law recognises various types of organisations. Although business might operate in a manner which includes sole proprietorship, partnership, or co-operatives, the vast bulk of German industry is undertaken through one of two main types of corporations (*Kapitalgesellschaft*). One is the *AG (Aktiengesellschaft)* (joint stock company) and the other is the *GmbH (Gesellschaft mit beschränkter Haftung)* (limited liability company). The joint stock company resembles the UK public limited company and the GmbH resembles the UK private company. These have some features in common, such as a separate legal personality and the power to act independently of shareholders. Owners of the company are liable for the

---

[11] Charkham (1994), pp. 6–7
[12] Busse von Colbe (1996)
[13] Charkham (1994), Chapter 2, p. 15

debts only to the limit of their capital contributed. The GmbH is not permitted to have a stock exchange listing. While the AG is permitted to have a listing, only about 700 out of a total of 3,000 seek a listing on a stock exchange.

The supervisory board (*Aufsichtsrat*) is an essential feature of the AG and large GmbHs. It is not generally compulsory for a smaller GmbH to have a supervisory board, unless it is required by the articles of association.

A group of companies linked by share ownership (*Konzerne*) is not a separate legal person in German law. Formal contractual relationships are often entered into within a group by means of control contracts and profit-sharing contracts. There is in Germany a Group Governance Law (*Konzernverfassungsrecht*) which sets out rules for the relations between companies within groups.[14] However groups are regulated in Germany by a variety of laws, especially the Commercial Code, the Stock Corporation Act and the Disclosure Act. In particular, obligations are imposed on the management of holding company and subsidiaries to protect the position of minority shareholders and creditors of subsidiary companies. In this area of company law the German legal system has made major contributions to the development of law reform in Europe and forms the basis of the EU's proposed Ninth Directive on the Conduct of Groups.

9.4.2.2 Corporate governance

The German system of corporate governance for companies of a substantial size (all AGs and GmbHs of more than 500 employees) is based on a 'two-tier principle. This means there are two layers of management control – the shareholders and the employees are stakeholders and share in the appointment of the supervisory board; the supervisory board appoints an executive board. In the case of an AG, this is called a *Vorstand*, in the case of a GmbH, it is called a *Geschäfts-führung*.

There are strict rules on the composition of the supervisory board. For the largest companies, the membership of the supervisory board is split equally between persons appointed by the shareholders and persons appointed by the employees. Where there are less than 2,000 employees two-thirds of the members are appointed by the shareholders. The chairman of the board is always drawn from the shareholder representatives, and has the casting vote in a situation of deadlock.

The area of activity of the supervisory board is prescribed by law and covers:

- the company's accounts for a specified period
- major capital expenditure and strategic acquisitions or closures
- appointments to the executive board
- approval of the dividend.

The main function is to ensure the competence of general management, but a second role is the approval of the annual profit and loss account and balance sheet. Both are audited (where the corporation is at least of medium size) and the supervisory board may question the external auditors. The employees' representatives also function effectively because they draw on material provided by the

---

[14] Ordelheide and Pfaff (1994), p. 30

Works Councils which allows them to play an effective part in the work of the supervisory board.

Banks also take a seat on the supervisory board of a company. They do this as part of the shareholder representation. The banks are pre-eminent as suppliers of capital and they also provide a range of other services. There are therefore strong personal links with the company beyond the formal links of the supervisory board. The banks themselves have advisory boards of which industrialists are members, and there are therefore some intricately interwoven links between banks and companies. It has been suggested that the combination of direct ownership, deposited share voting rights, length of lending period and breadth of services, provides the following benefits:

- deep relationships between companies and banks whereby the bank becomes a counsel and guide to the company on a long-term basis
- a considerable flow of information into the banks
- deep knowledge by the banks about sectors of industry which can be used to the advantage of customers
- development of well trained staff in the banks
- banks having the knowledge, motivation and authority to exert influence on company management.[15]

A new law on aspects of corporate governance, *Gesetz zur Kontrolle und Transparenz im Unhternehmensbereich (KonTraG)*, came before parliament in 1997. It seeks to match the corporate governance standards of other countries and has been influenced significantly by the report of the Cadbury Committee in the UK.[16] The legislation was a response to problem cases arising in well known companies in the mid-1990s.

9.4.2.3 Executive board

The executive board of directors is a decision-making body which acts collectively and therefore the idea of a powerful chief executive has historically been unusual in Germany. The chair of the board has been held by members of the board in rotation.

Members of the executive board are appointed by the supervisory board, and a two-thirds majority is usually required for this decision. Where such a majority cannot be achieved then a simple majority will suffice, with the chairman having the casting vote. In practice, therefore, shareholders have more potential than employees to influence the composition of the board of directors.

German industrial relations have developed under the principle of co-determination, that is the right of employees' representatives to participate in decisions that affect them. Central to this is the provision of detailed information, including internal accounting information, at the level of plant, company and group. Co-determination is practised through the institutions of works councils, legally defined trade union bargaining rights and employee board representation. Traditionally, German trades unions have been organised on a industry-by-industry

---

[15] Charkham (1994), Chapter 2, p. 43
[16] *The Corporate Accountant*, April 1997, p. 1

rather than on a craft basis, which tends to encourage industrial harmony. Works councils have existed in Germany since the early 1970s.

9.4.3 Taxation system[17]

In Germany, there is a close link between the annual accounts and the tax accounts. Small businesses in particular prefer to produce one set of accounts which satisfy the tax law as well as the accounting rules. Where the tax burden may be reduced or postponed, businesses will be influenced by that factor in their accounting practice. Tax on companies is levied on each company separately, rather than on a group of companies.

9.4.3.1 Taxable income

Taxable income is determined by comparing the net assets of a company at the start and end of the accounting year. For this purpose, special tax balance sheets are used. It is important for tax purposes that the information has also been reported in the accounting balance sheet. The difference in net assets is then adjusted for dividend distributions, addition or withdrawal of capital, and particular items specified in the tax law. There are special rules for deductions and there are some expenses which are not deductible.

The approach used, in equation form, is:

	Net assets at the end of the accounting year
minus	Net assets at the start of the accounting year
plus	Distributions of profit and return of capital
minus	Contributions of capital
equals	Profits subject to corporation tax

This balance sheet approach means that asset valuation is very important for tax purposes, and that in turn affects accounting practice.

9.4.3.2 Corporate income tax

Resident corporations are subject to corporate income tax. Where the profits of a corporation are distributed, the tax rate on the distributed profits is reduced. Resident shareholders may claim a tax credit in respect of the tax paid by the company on the distributed profits. This means that the individual is not taxed twice on the same source of income (in contrast to those countries where the individual shareholder suffers tax on the company profits and then a further tax on the dividend distributed).

9.4.3.3 Trade tax

There was a trade tax regulated by federal law and collected by municipalities (local government units); the tax was based on business profit and business capital (measured as net assets). The basic rate was set by federal authorities but the municipalities multiplied the basic rate by municipal factors. The trade tax was an

---

[17] Coopers and Lybrand International Tax Network (1995)

allowable deduction in arriving at taxable profits for purposes of corporate income tax; however the tax has been abolished as from 1998 and the German constitution amended accordingly.

9.4.4 Corporate financing system[18]

Shares in AG companies are mainly bearer shares, which means that possession is evidence of ownership. Consequently they need to be taken care of, and the usual place for safe custody is a bank. Because they are bearer shares, not carrying the owner's name, it is difficult to gain information on the pattern of share ownership.

9.4.4.1 Equity investors

It may be seen from Chapter 1, Exhibit 1.3 that the German stock market is of comparable size to that of France but smaller than that of the UK. The domestic companies listed have a market capitalisation which is a relatively low percentage of GDP, indicating that equity funding is not as significant as in the Netherlands or the UK. Exhibit 1.4 indicates that the market capitalisation of the German stock market is less than 5% of the world market, which is dominated by the US and Japanese markets. From Exhibit 1.5 it is clear that pension funds and insurance companies are relatively insignificant investors. The most significant shareholder group is non-financial corporations, a situation where companies hold shares in each other. Such systems of cross-holdings make companies very secure against takeover bids, but also foster secrecy.

Institutional investors are thus not in general a strong force in the financing and governance of companies. Because shares are in bearer form and held by banks, there is strong power in the hands of the banks when voting at general meetings is required. The banks hold proxy votes authorised by the owners of the shares; banks are obliged to consult the owners of the shares and have dealt with this obligation by asking for a 15-month proxy covering all the shareholdings of the investor. It would not be unusual for the banks collectively to control more than half of the votes cast at an annual general meeting of a major German company. A survey by the Deutsche Bundesbank indicated that 19.4% of shares were held by individuals, 39.3% by miscellaneous companies, 2.7% by insurance companies, 11.4% by banks, 7.1% by the state and 20% by foreign investors.[19]

Companies seeking a listing must present a prospectus. Listed companies are also required to disclose an interim report. The content of this report is regulated by the Stock Exchange Act (*Börsengesetz*) and the Ordinance regulating Stock Exchange Listing (*Börsenzulassungsverordnung*).[20] There has been expansion of foreign listings on the German stock exchanges since the early 1990s. Listings of domestic companies between 1992 and 1996 increased by 2.4% (from 665 in 1992 to 681 in 1996) but listings of foreign companies over the same period increased by 117% (from 594 in 1992 to 1,290 in 1996).

---

[18] Charkham (1994), p. 27
[19] Rathbone (1997), p. 184
[20] Ballwieser (1995), pp. 1529–31

9.4.4.2 Top companies[21]

From the *Financial Times* annual FT 500 survey there are 21 German companies in the top 500 world companies, measured by market capitalisation. Five German companies featured in the top 20 European companies. The top ten listed German companies are shown in Exhibit 9.2.

Exhibit 9.2 TOP 10 LISTED GERMAN COMPANIES

Name	Market cap $m	Rank in Europe	Sector
1 Allianz	56,013	9	Insurance – multiline
2 Deutsche Telekom	52,515	12	Telephone companies
3 Daimler-Benz	42,710	15	Automobiles
4 Siemens	37,358	18	Electrical equipment
5 Deutsche Bank	36,991	20	Commercial and other banks
6 Bayer	28,756	31	Chemicals (diversified)
7 Veba	28,498	32	Diversified holding companies
8 Münchener Rückversicherung	28,004	34	Insurance – multiline
9 Hoechst	25,798	42	Chemicals (diversified)
10 Dresdner Bank	24,825	44	Commercial and other banks

Source: Survey *FT 500, Financial Times*, 22 January 1998, p. 12

9.4.4.3 Bank lending

Management of German companies are generally unenthusiastic for the stock market. Total market capitalisation of German listed companies is relatively low. However, there are high volumes of transactions in the relatively small number of major listed companies. In the main, companies finance themselves by internally generated finance and by borrowing. It is commonly asserted in text books that the debt:equity ratios of German companies are higher than those of the USA or the UK but this is not borne out by national income statistics (OECD, 1996) and is challenged by research (Rajan and Zingales, 1995).

Banks approach lending as a long-term arrangement. This creates what is called 'relationship' banking rather than 'transaction' banking. Bankers have to understand their customers and the industries in which they are located. The major banks have developed a range of services so that a company may receive all types of banking service, including lending, from one source – referred to as *Universalbanken*.

Banks are also shareholders in companies, to a significant extent. This has to some extent happened by accident, because banks will accept equity as repayment of debt when a company falls into difficulties. A Banking Directive of the EU in 1989 limited the shareholdings of banks in relation to their overall capital.

---

[21] *Financial Times, Financial Times FT 500 Survey*, 22 January 1998

9.4.4.4 Mergers

Contested takeover bids are unlikely to be observed. Friendly mergers may arise for normal commercial reasons, such as the need to find a successor to operate a business. The banks play a leading part where companies are encouraged to merge because of financial difficulties in one of the companies.

9.4.5 The accounting profession[22]

Audit is required for large corporations and large enterprises. According to the law, only *Wirtschaftsprüfer* and firms of *Wirtschaftsprüfer* may act as auditors. For medium-sized limited liability companies there is a second category, the sworn-in auditors (*vereidigter Buchprüfer*) and their firms. Those seeking to become *Wirtschaftsprüfer* normally require a university degree and to have at least four years of practical auditing experience.[23] There is a demanding final examination. As in most other countries, a high degree of independence is demanded of the Wirtschaftsprüfer. Links with the company under audit are forbidden, both for the auditor and for the audit firm.

There is legislation setting out the legal position of the *Wirtschaftsprüfer* and the sworn-in auditor. The legislation allows the profession to be self-governing. All *Wirtschaftsprüfer* and sworn-in auditors are required to be members of the chamber of *Wirtschaftsprüfer* (*Wirtschaftsprüferkammer*) which is a public law body under the official supervision of the Federal Minister of Economics. With around 8,000 persons entitled to describe themselves as *Wirtschaftsprüfer*, they may be regarded as an elite body.

At a conference in 1995 a senior official at the Federal Ministry of Justice invited German accountants to enter detailed discussions about professional standards. The Institute of German Public Accountants and the *Wirtschaftsprüferkammer* entered into detailed negotiations with the ministry. The fruits of the discussions were incorporated in proposed legislation in 1997, *Gesetz zur Kontrolle und Transparenz im Unternehmensbereich (KonTraG)*.[24] Among other aspects of corporate governance, the proposed law requires German accountants to comment on the company's year-end business report as well as the accounts. They are also required to scrutinise the company's risk management system and mention any risks which might threaten the company as a going concern. This creates a new volume of work and adds new complexity to the statutory audit. Most significant however is the change from regarding auditing as an examination of past business alone. The *KonTraG* requires auditors to express a view about ongoing business.

Some proposals from the Federal Ministry were not incorporated in the new law. A clause requiring rotation of auditors was removed and the Ministry was persuaded against its initial intention of increasing statutory liability. The *KonTraG* stipulates automatic liability of DM2 million for statutory audits (previously established at DM500,000 in 1965) and four times that figure for consultancy. In practice lawsuits are rare.

---

[22] Ordelheide and Pfaff (1994), Chapter 10
[23] *Wirtschaftsprüferordnung*, section 9, para.1
[24] *The Accountant*, May 1997, p. 13

9.4.6 External influences

Historically, accounting practice in Germany has developed independently with distinctive national characteristics.[25] As a founder member of the EU, Germany has had a significant influence on the directives affecting company law. Because of historical political links and continuing commercial links, German accounting has an influence on practices in countries such as Austria and Hungary. During periods of occupation of other countries during wartime, the German influence affected some accounting practices in countries such as France, there is also evidence of a German influence on Japanese accounting. Germany itself was occupied briefly after the Second World War, and there has been a resulting impact on consolidated accounting in some sectors.

As other countries have joined the EU, Germany has found its own approach modified from time to time. This is particularly significant in the case of the 'true and fair view' being imported under UK influence and being seen as an infringement of the tax-driven approach to accounting.

Multinational companies are a vehicle of change in accounting practice. It is reported that Daimler–Benz, the first German company to obtain a full listing on a US stock exchange (*see also* Case study 3.1),[26] has stated that it is now using US GAAP figures both internally and externally as a result of the change of culture caused by taking a full listing. In its 1996 annual report, it presents its financial statements in accordance with GAAP while at the same time complying with German and EU requirements.[27]

9.5 SOCIETAL CULTURE AND ACCOUNTING SUBCULTURE

There is a tradition of co-operation as a basic social and cultural value.[28]

9.5.1 Hofstede's cultural dimensions

Exhibit 9.3 reproduces part of the table set out in Chapter 2, section 2.4, showing the scores and rankings for Germany from Hofstede's (1984) research on cultural dimensions.

Exhibit 9.3 GERMANY: SCORES AND RANKINGS FOR INDIVIDUAL COUNTRIES FROM HOFSTEDE'S (1984) CULTURAL DIMENSION RESEARCH

Individualism versus collectivism		*Large power distance versus small power difference*		*Strong uncertainty avoidance versus weak uncertainty avoidance*		*Low nurture versus high nurture*	
Score	*Rank*	*Score*	*Rank*	*Score*	*Rank*	*Score*	*Rank*
67	15	35	42/44	65	29	66	9/10

[25] Schneider (1995)
[26] Radebaugh *et al.* (1995)
[27] *FT World Accounting Report*, June 1997, p. 3
[28] Charkham (1994)

9.5.2 Culture and accounting

Exhibit 9.4 links Gray's (1988) accounting values for Germany to the cultural dimensions measured by Hofstede (1984). Section 9.7 of this chapter expands on practical applications illustrating the relevance of Gray's general analysis.

Gray's classification of German practice as reflecting professionalism and uniformity may be seen to match closely the cultural values identified by Hofstede. In classifying German practice as also embodying conservatism and secrecy, Gray draws on the work of other researchers for conservatism and on anecdotal evidence, such as the use of hidden reserves, for secrecy. Taking only the cultural values measured by Hofstede, the picture is less clear unless relative weightings are attached to the various cultural values.

Exhibit 9.4 LINKING GRAY'S (1988) ACCOUNTING VALUES TO HOFSTEDE'S (1984) CULTURAL DIMENSIONS, IN THE MANNER PROPOSED BY GRAY

Gray's accounting values – classification	Cultural dimensions affecting the country's accounting values	Interpretation of Hofstede's scores of cultural value (as in Exhibit 9.3)
Professionalism (moderate)	Professionalism tends to be associated with: ● Individualism ● Weak uncertainty avoidance ● Small power distance	 Tendency to individualism Tendency to uncertainty avoidance Clearly small power distance
Uniformity (marginal)	Uniformity tends to be associated with: ● Strong uncertainty avoidance ● Large power distance ● Collectivism	 Tendency to uncertainty avoidance Clearly small power distance Tendency to individualism
Conservatism (marginal)	Conservatism tends to be associated with: ● Strong uncertainty avoidance ● Collectivism ● High nurture	 Tendency to uncertainty avoidance Tendency to individualism Tendency to low nurture
Secrecy (strong)	Secrecy tends to be associated with: ● Strong uncertainty avoidance ● Large power distance ● Collectivism ● High nurture	 Tendency to uncertainty avoidance Clearly small power distance Tendency to individualism Tendency to low nurture

9.6 ACCOUNTING REGULATIONS AND THE IASC

Research by Salter *et al.* (1996) showed that, on completion of the IASC comparability project, accounting practice in the UK ranked lowest of the countries studied, in compliance with IASs (*see* Chapter 5, subsection 5.6.3.4).

Exhibit 9.5 shows the current position of compliance with IASs.

Exhibit 9.5 COMPARISON OF ACCOUNTING PRACTICES IN GERMANY WITH REQUIREMENTS OF IASs: KEY SIMILARITIES AND DIFFERENCES

IAS	Subject of IAS	Practice in Germany	Ref
Disclosure and presentation			
	General aspects consolidated in IAS 1 (revised)		
IAS 1	Fair Presentation	'True and fair' requirement	7.2.5 7.2.4
	Disclosure of Accounting Policies (former IAS 1)	Generally in agreement	
	Information to be Disclosed in Financial Statements (former IAS 5)	Generally in agreement	
	Presentation of Current Assets and Current Liabilities (former IAS 13)	Generally in agreement	7.2.3
	Specific aspects		
IAS 7	Cash Flow Statements	Not required by regulation, but provided voluntarily by large companies	7.2.3
IAS 8	Net Profit or Loss for the Period, Fundamental Errors and Changes in Accounting Policies	Prior-period adjustments must pass through reported profit	7.2.3
IAS xx	Discontinuing Operations	Not required by regulation	
IAS 14	Reporting Financial Information by Segments	Disclosure requirement is significantly less than IAS 14	7.5.2
IAS 24	Related Party Disclosure	No general requirement, some specific items	
IAS 33	Earnings per Share	DVFA calculation used on a voluntary basis	7.5.5
IAS 34	Interim Financial Reporting	Required by Stock Exchange; relatively liberal rules on estimation	
Asset recognition and measurement			
IAS 2	Inventories	Write-downs permitted in excess of IAS 2	7.4.4
IAS 4	Depreciation Accounting	Generally in agreement	7.4.4
IAS 16	Property, Plant and Equipment	Revaluation not permitted	7.4.4
IAS xx	Impairment of Assets	Not in regulation	
IAS 23	Borrowing Costs	Generally in agreement	
IAS 25	Accounting for Investments	More conservative than IAS 25	
IAS 9	Research and Development Costs	Normally all R&D is reported as an expense of the period	7.4.4
IAS xx	Intangible Assets	Generally in agreement	7.4.4
Liability recognition and measurement			
IAS 10	Contingencies and Events Occurring After the Balance Sheet Date	More conservative than IAS 10	7.4.5
IAS 12	Income Taxes	Generally in agreement for consolidated accounts	7.3.3
IAS 17	Leases	No capitalisation of finance leases	

Exhibit 9.5   continued

IAS	Subject of IAS	Practice in Germany	Ref
IAS 19	Employee Benefits	Provision made for commitment to direct support; contributions to outside funds reported as incurred.	
IAS 32	Financial Instruments: Disclosure and Presentation	Not in legislation	
Recognition of economic activity			
IAS 11	Construction Contracts	Completed contract method normally	7.4.4
IAS 18	Revenue	Generally in agreement	
IAS 20	Accounting for Government Grants and Disclosure of Government Assistance	Professional guidance in agreement with IAS 20 – not followed by all	
Measurement			
IAS 15	Information Reflecting the Effects of Changing Prices	No comparable requirement	
IAS 29	Financial Reporting in Hyperinflationary Economies	Not relevant to German economy	
Group accounting			
IAS 21	The Effects of Changes in Foreign Exchange Rates	No regulation – flexibility of practice	7.4.7
IAS 22	Business Combinations	Differences in treatment and calculation of goodwill	7.3.4 and 7.4.4
IAS 27	Consolidated Financial Statements and Accounting for Investments in Subsidiaries	Differences in: definition of control; scope of consolidation; and some detailed aspects of practice	7.3.5
IAS 28	Accounting for Investments in Associates	Allows different method of valuing equity interest	
IAS 31	Financial Reporting of Interests in Joint Ventures	Proportional consolidation or equity accounting may be used	

In 1998 the IASC published, in German, a first official translation of IASs. German companies are permitted to follow the IASs to the extent that these conform to German law. An example of a company which has selected accounting methods conforming to IASs is provided by the Bayer Group. Exhibit 9.6 sets out the statement of accounting policies and the audit report which refers to International Auditing Standards and IASs.

The contrast with the more commonly produced statement disclosing compliance with domestic accounting standards and the wording of the domestic auditor's opinion is provided by Bosch Group (Exhibit 9.7).

The accounting policy note produced by Hoechst (Exhibit 9.8) explains how the methods of valuation used in the group accounts differ from those used in the holding company.

Exhibit 9.6   BAYER GROUP: STATEMENT OF ACCOUNTING POLICIES AND THE AUDIT REPORT

Notes to the Consolidated Financial Statements of the Bayer Group

Accounting policies
The consolidated financial statements of the Bayer Group are prepared according to German law. As in previous years, they also comply with the rules issued by the International Accounting Standards Committee (IASC), London, in the versions in effect at the closing date.

The financial statements of the consolidated companies are prepared according to uniform recognition and valuation principles. Valuation adjustments made for tax reasons are not reflected in the Group statements. The individual companies' statements are prepared as of the closing date for the Group statements.

Certain income statement and balance sheet items are combined for the sake of clarity, as explained in the Notes.

The 21 business groups were reallocated to five (previously six) business segments effective January 1, 1997. Our reporting for 1996 is already based on these new segments; the 1995 figures are restated accordingly

Independent Auditors' Report

We have audited the consolidated balance sheet of the Bayer Group as of December 31, 1996 and the related consolidated statements of income and cash flows for the year then ended. These financial statements are the responsibility of the Group's management. Our responsibility is to express an opinion on these financial statements, based on our audit, and about their compliance with the International Accounting Standards.

We conducted our audit in accordance with the International Standards on Auditing issued by the International Federation of Accountants (IFAC). Those standards require that we plan and perform the audit to obtain reasonable assurance about whether the financial statements are free of material misstatement. An audit includes examining, on a test basis, evidence supporting the amounts and disclosures in the financial statements. It also includes assessing the accounting principles used and significant estimates made by the management, as well as evaluating the overall financial statement presentation. We believe that our audit provides a reasonable basis for our opinion.

In our opinion, the aforementioned financial statements (pages 58–85) give a true and fair view of the financial position of the Bayer Group as of December 31, 1996, and of the results of its operations and its cash flows for the year then ended in accordance with the International Accounting Standards issued by the International Accounting Standards Committee (IASC).

The financial statements of the Bayer Group also comply with the German Commercial Code. We therefore issue the following unqualified opinion:

The financial statements of the Bayer Group, which we have audited in accordance with professional standards, comply with the German statutory provisions. Prepared in accordance with generally accepted accounting principles, they give a true and fair view of the net worth, financial position and earnings of the Group. The management report of the Bayer Group, which is combined with the management report of Bayer Aktiengesellschaft, is consistent with the financial statements of the Bayer Group.

Essen, February 28, 1997

C&L Deutsche Revision
Aktiengesellschaft
Wirtschaftsprüfungsgesellschaft

C.-F. Leuschner   *J. Schilling*
Wirtschaftsprüfer   *Wirtschaftsprüfer*
(Certified Public Accountant)   *(Certified Public Accountant)*

Source: Bayer Group, annual report, 1997, pp. 61, 57

Exhibit 9.7 BOSCH GROUP: GENERAL REMARKS AND AUDITOR'S OPINION

Financial Statements of Bosch Group Worldwide
Appendix 1996

(1) General remarks

The consolidated statements of the Bosch Group Worldwide conform to the Regulations of the Commercial Code.

In order to ensure better understanding of these financial statements, we combined a number of individual balance-sheet items and profit and loss statement items into key groupings. These items are stated separately in the Appendix. Required comments for individual items are also contained in the Appendix. The consolidated profit and loss statement follows the format of the total cost method.

Auditor's opinion

The accounting and the consolidated financial statements of Robert Bosch GmbH as of December 31, 1996, which we have audited in accordance with professional standards, comply with legal provisions. With due regard to generally accepted accounting principles the consolidated financial statements give a true and fair view of the company's assets, liabilities, financial position and profit and loss. The management report to the consolidated financial statements is consistent with the contents thereof.

Stuttgart, March 12, 1997

Schitag Ernst & Young
Deutsche Allgemeine Treuhand AG
Wirtschaftsprüfungsgesellschaft

Dörner   Dr. Pfitzer
Wirtschaftsprüfer   Wirtschaftsprüfer

Source: Bosch Group, annual report, 1996, pp. 35, 41

The IASC web pages list ten German companies which refer to the use of IASs in their financial statements (Exhibit 9.9)

As the IASC moved forward in achieving its target of issuing the core standards by 1998, the European Commission gave its support to the IASs. That did not of itself produce harmonisation with national laws, because of the options. Germany appears likely to follow the example set by France in establishing a new law which would provide a system for recognising nationally a system of international standards. Interest in international accounting harmonisation in Germany was stimulated strongly when Deutsche Bank in 1996 published its annual results in accordance with IASs. By April 1998 legislation to allow the use of IASs in Germany was making good progress.[29]

---

[29] IASC, *Annual Review*, 1996; IASC *Insight*, March 1998

Exhibit 9.8   HOECHST: ACCOUNTING POLICY NOTE

Notes to the consolidated financial statements

(figures in the tables are in DM million)

(1) Accounting principles

The 1996 consolidated financial statements are based on the International Accounting Standards (IAS) of the International Accounting Standards Committee (IASC) in the version valid on the balance sheet date. IAS 12 "Income Taxes" (revised 1996), which is compulsory as of 1998, was adopted effective January 1, 1996. In order to comply with the provisions of the German Commercial Code, appropriate use is made of the existing options under the German Commercial Code and IAS, thereby permitting conformity with both sets of accounting standards. Insofar as classification rules are stipulated by the German Commercial Code for the consolidated financial statements, this is taken into consideration in the balance sheet or in the form of additional information and explanations in the notes. Classification is based on the principles of clarity, understandability and materiality.

Certain prior year balances have been reclassified to conform with 1996 presentation.

Source: Hoechst AG, annual report, 1996, p. 69

Required disclosure for stand-alone Hoechst AG financial statements

Hoechst AG is required to prepare stand-alone financial statements pursuant to the German Commercial Code. In preparing these stand-alone financial statements, certain accounting principles and methods have been used that deviate from those used in preparing the consolidated financial statements. These differences arise because IAS has not been fully adopted for purposes of preparing the stand-alone financial statements. The differences are required to be disclosed in the consolidated financial statements, as follows:

Patents and licenses are amortized over a period of maximally five years.

Movable fixed assets and factory buildings are amortized by the declining-balance method.

The write-downs of inventories to the lower realizable value and provisions for losses arising from sales contracts include all costs incurred up to the sale. In the case of inventories, a profit margin is additionally deducted.

Short-term liabilities and receivables stated in a foreign currency are only recorded in the balance sheet at closing rates as long as the unrealized exchange difference is a loss. Gains are only recognized when the transaction is settled.

Original values are only reinstated so long as taxable gains are not generated.

Valuation adjustments made solely in accordance with German tax regulations are taken into consideration.

Provisions are set up for maintenance expenses not incurred in the year under review but postponed until the first three months of the following year.

Deferred tax assets are not recorded.

Source: Hoechst AG, annual report, 1996, p. 71

---

(7) Explanatory remarks on the use of IAS

In comparison with the previous accounting and valuation methods, the application of IAS in the 1995 Group financial statements had the following effects on the profit before taxes on income (rounded off, in DM m):

Valuation of inventories and loss contracts at lower realizable values	250
Use of straight-line depreciation with respect to tangible fixed assets acquired in 1995 as well as write-downs of intangible fixed assets	200
Uniform statement of foreign currency receivables and liabilities at the closing rate	80
Elimination of provisions for maintenance	40
Valuation of pension provisions abroad in accordance with IAS 19	– 320
Gains in the year under review	**250**

Source: Hoechst AG, annual report, 1995, p. 59

Exhibit 9.9 GERMAN COMPANIES REFERRING TO THE USE OF IASs IN THEIR FINANCIAL STATEMENTS, WITH RANK IN EUROPE BY MARKET CAPITALISATION

	Rank in Europe
Adidas AG	212
Alsen-Breitenburg Zement	–
Bayer	31
Deutsche Bank	20
Dyckerhoff AG	–
Heidelberger Zement	334
Hoechst	42
Merck KgaA	185
Puma AG	–
Schering	167

Source: extracted from IASC web pages and *Financial Times, FT 500*, January 1998

9.7 THE ACCOUNTING SYSTEM

9.7.1 Outline of current regulation[30]

All enterprises must comply with the *Handelsgesetzbuch (HGB)* or Commercial

Exhibit 9.10 MAIN HEADINGS OF *HANDELSGESETZBUCH (HGB)*

- Bookkeeping and inventory (making a list of all assets and liabilities)
- Obligation to prepare accounts, principles of preparation
- Recognition of assets and liabilities
- Valuation rules
- Retention and production of evidence.

Code. The main headings are indicated in Exhibit 9.10.
There are further specific rules applying to corporations. These are found in:

- specific sections of the HGB relating to corporations
- *Aktiengesetz (AktG)* or Joint Stock Corporation Act
- *Gesetz betreffend die Gesellschaften mit beschränkter Haftung (GmbHG)* or Act Concerning Limited Liability Companies.

---

[30] Ordelheide and Pfaff (1994), pp. 86–7

The major distinction is that the *AktG* applies to public companies, including those having a listing on the stock exchange, while the *GmbHG* applies to private companies. The distinctions between the *AG* and *GmbH* are set out in the earlier section describing the types of business organisation.

9.7.2 Professionalism versus statutory control

Gray (1988) classified German accounting as lying towards the professionalism end of this scale rather than being heavily influenced by statutory control. That may seem on first impression to be counter to the considerable amount of legislative framework in place, but this section will show that professional interpretation has a strong influence on the implementation of the requirements of legislation.

The extent of professionalism modifying the statutory control means that a combination of the Commercial Code, Tax law and professional recommendations presents a multitude of options for the company. This has implications for uniformity/flexibility and conservatism/optimism, and is discussed further below.

9.7.2.1 Accounting rules as part of the legal system[31]

In Germany, the accounting rules are regarded as part of the legal system which enacts policy decisions having a broad social basis. There is consequently a political dimension to the enactment of accounting policy in legal rules which may explain the absence of a body of accounting experts to establish accounting rules.

The traditional regard for the role of the legal system has been consistent with the approach of the Directives which have permitted national options. Consequently the determination of the profit of individual enterprises has continued to follow rules enacted in law. Laws are written in the form of general principles, but require to be supplemented by detailed explanation. In Germany, there are three sources of such detailed explanations: interpretations provided by judges in the courts of law; opinions provided by professional associations or organisations; and a commercial market for interpretations.

Legal interpretations are established by judges as part of case law. Judges give interpretations of the law which are regarded as precedent to be followed in subsequent practice. The tax courts are the most significant in terms of the importance of the judgments they pass. This is because many small and medium-sized companies (SMEs) prepare only one set of accounts for taxation and financial reporting purposes. The taxation courts also interpret the Principles of Regular Accounting (*GoB* of the *HGB*).

Other interpretations are developed by a committee of the Institut der Wirtschaftsprüfer. Such opinions are not legally binding on members, but are a strong indication of good practice.

The third source of interpretations of the law emerges from the experts who participate in a substantial market for information on interpretations. In particular, the major accountancy firms write or edit commentaries on the interpretation of accounting law.

---

[31] Ordelheide and Pfaff (1994), pp. 82–3, 85–6, 92

9.7.2.2 Tax law and impact on statutory accounts[32]

It has been explained already that the German tax authorities are more concerned with the balance sheet than with the profit and loss account. The principles of recognition and valuation applied in the commercial accounts must in general be incorporated into the tax balance sheet. On some occasions, tax law requires specific accounting principles which differ from accounting regulations; this is usually to allow a degree of objectivity. The close relationship between accounting and tax principles is referred to as the authoritativeness principle (the *Maßgeblichkeitsprinzip*) (*see also* subsection 9.7.3.3). (It is also translated in texts as the principle of 'congruency' or 'bindingness'.)

Because of this close relationship there may be conflict between the desire to report high profit as a measure of success and the desire to minimise tax liabilities. Undervaluation of assets for tax reasons leads to a more pessimistic presentation of the financial position and economic situation of a company than does the principle of prudence acting as an accounting constraint.

9.7.2.3 Financial statement formats[33]

Balance sheet

The basic format for the balance sheet (*Bilanz*) is set out in the *HGB*. There are main captions within a prescribed format, as shown in Exhibit 9.11.

Where it is permitted to disclose further detail by way of notes, companies will produce notes rather than further detail on the face of the balance sheet, in order

Exhibit 9.11 MAIN CAPTIONS FOR BALANCE SHEET (*HGB*)

Assets	*Equity and liabilities*

A Fixed assets
  I Intangible assets
  II Tangible assets
  III Financial assets
	A Equity
	  I Subscribed capital
	  II Capital reserves
	  III Revenue reserves
	  IV Retained profits/accumulated
	    losses brought forward

B Current assets
  I Inventories
  II Receivables and other current assets
  III Securities
  IV Liquid funds
	V Result for the year
	
	B Accruals

C Pre-paid expenses	C Liabilities D Deferred income

---

[32] Haller (1992), p. 266
[33] Seckler (1995)

to avoid overloading the balance sheet. In particular the detailed categorisation of liabilities will be found in notes.

For listed companies, the *AktG* increases the disclosures required but does not alter the basic structure of the balance sheet. In particular, it requires the subheadings to be broken down further into prescribed items.

Profit and loss account

In English-language translations the terms 'profit and loss account' and 'income statement' are both used. The German title is *Gewinn- und Verlustrechung*. The format of the profit and loss account is prescribed in basic form in the *HGB*. It must be in a vertical format but may take either the 'type of expenditure' or the 'functional' format. The analysis by type of expenditure is the traditional form in Germany, and is orientated towards production. The view of the company is that it produces goods for sale and goods for inclusion in the inventory of finished goods at the end of the accounting period. An example of this format is provided by the VIAG Group (*see* Exhibit 9.12).

Exhibit 9.12 VIAG GROUP: PROFIT AND LOSS ACCOUNT FORMAT SHOWING TYPE OF EXPENDITURE

Statement of Income for the period January 1, 1996 to December 31, 1996

	Notes	1996 DM thousand	1995 DM million
Sales	(18)	**42,452,285**	41,932
Increase or decrease in inventories and other own work capitalized	(19)	**94,236**	362
Total operating performance		**42,546,521**	42,294
Other operating income	(20)	**1,715,731**	1,919
Cost of materials	(21)	**28,473,723**	28,763
Personnel expenses	(22)	**6,188,212**	6,457
Depreciation	(23)	**2,232,814**	2,340
Other operating expenses	(24)	**4,961,059**	4,870
Net loss (1995: income) from participations	(25)	**– 85,248**	+ 33
Financial result	(26)	**– 60,989**	– 150
Results from ordinary activities		**2,260,207**	1,666
Extraordinary result	(27)	**89,928**	575
Taxes on income	(28)	**1,290,147**	921
Consolidated net income for the year	(29)	**1,059,988**	1,320

Source: VIAG Group, annual report, 1996, p. 55

The functional format has been a more recent feature of German accounting, following its inclusion in the Commercial Code as a result of the Fourth Directive. An example is provided by the Bayer Group (Exhibit 9.13).

Extraordinary revenues and expenses are transactions outside the ordinary course of business which are of an unusual character, not regularly recurring and material. Prior-year items are not normally treated as extraordinary items.[34] This is at variance with IAS 8, which would require an additional proforma in such circumstances. There is no common understanding or interpretation of precisely what should be reported as an extraordinary item.[35] Professional judgement has a significant role in this regard.

As with the balance sheet, the notes to the accounts are particularly important in disclosing detail to supplement the information presented in the format.

Exhibit 9.13   BAYER GROUP: PROFIT AND LOSS ACCOUNT IN FUNCTIONAL FORMAT

Bayer Group Consolidated Statements of Income

(DM million)	*Note*	*1996*	*1995*
Net sales	[1]	**48,608**	**44,580**
Cost of goods sold		(28,050)	(25,613)
Gross profit etc		**20,558**	**18,967**
Selling expenses		(10,531)	(9,734)
Research and development expenses	[2]	(3,608)	(3,259)
General administration expenses		(1,635)	(1,562)
Other operating income	[3]	789	779
Other operating expenses	[4]	(1,063)	(1,080)
Operating result	[5]	**4,510**	**4,111**
Expense from investments in affiliated companies – net	[6]	(15)	(2)
Interest income (expense) – net	[7]	(87)	11
Other non-operating income – net	[8]	56	65
Non-operating result		**(46)**	**74**
Income before income taxes		4,464	4,185
Income taxes	[9]	(1,717)	(1,764)
Income after taxes		**2,747**	**2,421**
Minority interests in consolidated subsidiaries	[11]	(22)	(27)
Net income		**2,725**	**2,394**

Source: Bayer Group, annual report, 1996, p. 58

---

[34] Ordelheide and Pfaff (1994), pp. 118–19
[35] Seckler (1995), p. 239

Cash flow statements

Cash flow statements are not a mandatory requirement of legislation. Nevertheless they are commonly produced in the annual reports of multinational companies. Formats vary from one company to the next. In some cases, the cash flow statement is a primary financial statement and in others a note to the accounts or a table in the management report. However a new recommendation from the accounting profession is likely to reduce this variation. The professional recommendation is very similar to IAS 7.[36]

Examples of cash flow statements are taken from Fried. Krupp AG Hoesch–Krupp (Exhibit 9.14), which shows a table in the management report, and Hoechst (Exhibit 9.15), which produces a primary statement in accordance with IAS 7.

9.7.2.4 Importance of Notes to the accounts[37]

Notes on the accounts are a mandatory part of the financial statements. The German view is that the balance sheet, profit and loss account and notes must, taken together, produce a true and fair view. The 'true and fair' test is not applied to each element separately. Particularly important use of Notes to the accounts are:

- disclosure of methods of accounting and valuation
- effects of accounting methods applied solely for tax reasons
- information on receivables and liabilities
- information on changes in equity as shown in the statement of appropriation of profit
- information on employees
- remuneration and benefits of board members
- information on shareholdings.

Before 1987, notes had to be prepared and disclosed only by public companies and certain large private companies. The extension of notes to financial statements of all companies is therefore regarded as an important change resulting from the Fourth Directive.

9.7.2.5 'True and fair view'

The wording in the law which enacts the fourth directive is '*(unter Beachtung der Grundsätze ordnungsmässiger Buchführung) ein den tatsächlichen Verhältnissen entsprechendes Bild*'. It is translated as '(in compliance with accepted accounting principles) a picture in accordance with the facts'. The German legislators found it difficult to bring the concept of 'true and fair' into German law, and their wording differs from that of the official German-language version of the directive. Parker and Nobes (1994) classify the German approach to 'true and fair' as one which cannot be used to justify a departure from the law (*see* Chapter 6).

---

[36] We are obliged to Professor Dr Wolfgang Ballwieser for this observation
[37] Ordelheide and Pfaff (1994), p. 161

Exhibit 9.14 FRIED. KRUPP AG HOESCH–KRUPP: NOTE ON CASH FLOW IN MANAGEMENT REPORT

The financial situation of the Krupp Group in 1996 was marked by a further reduction in financial borrowings.

The statement of changes in financial position printed here shows that cash flow decreased against the previous year by DM471 million to DM1,228 million. This fall is mainly due to the lower net income for the year.

Most of the cash flow stems from current business activity. Only around a third (DM356 million) comes from retirement of fixed assets and disposals.

As the DM945 million decrease in liabilities from current business was financed fully by funds released from current assets, almost all the inflow of funds from current business activity (DM1,156 million) was available for investment and reducing financial borrowings.

In addition to the influx of funds from current business activity, further inflows of DM445 million from the retirement of fixed assets and disposals were available for Group financing.

The DM2,025 million investment in fixed assets also includes the acquisition of shares in Uhde GmbH.

The other changes in Group assets mainly stem from the initial consolidation of the Uhde group and the deconsolidation of Krupp MaK Maschinenbau GmbH and its subsidiaries.

Altogether DM692 million was available for financing. Almost all of this amount (DM662 million) was used for the further redemption of financial borrowings.

After deduction of liquid assets, net financial borrowings at DM2,844 million now amount to only 81% of the Group's equity funds.

(DM in millions)	1996	1995
Net income for the year	**208**	**505**
Amortisation, depreciation and write-downs	1026	957
Decrease/increase in accruals for pensions and other long-term accruals	− 275	63
Decrease/increase in special items	− 14	60
Other expenditures and earnings not entailing payments	283	114
DVFA/SG cash flow	**1228**	**1699**
Income from retirement of fixed assets and disposals	− 356	− 69
Decrease/increase in inventories and payments received on account, receivables and other assets	1209	− 317
Increase in short-term accruals	20	269
Decrease/increase in trade payables and other liabilities	− 945	437
Inflow of funds from current business activity	**1156**	**2019**
Inflows from the retirement of fixed assets and disposals	445	412
Investment in fixed assets	− 2025	− 1513
Other changes in Group assets due to changes in the consolidated Group	1066	− 474
Outflow of funds from investment activity	**− 514**	**− 1575**
Decrease in financial borrowings	− 662	− 985
Capital increase at Fried. Krupp AG Hoesch-Krupp	92	25
Dividend payments to minority shareholders	− 231	− 26
Decrease/increase in securities classified as current assets	172	− 55
Decrease/increase in equity from changes to the consolidated Group and translation differences	− 63	405
Outflow from financing activity	**− 692**	**− 636**
Decrease in liquid assets	**− 50**	**− 192**

Source: Krupp Group, annual report, 1996, p. 19

9.7.3 Uniformity versus flexibility

Gray (1988) classified German accounting practice as a mixture of uniformity and flexibility.

Exhibit 9.15   HOECHST: CASH FLOW STATEMENT IN ACCORDANCE WITH IAS 7

Consolidated cash flow statement

	See Notes	1996 DM million	1995 DM million
Profit after taxes		2774	2245
Depreciation of non-current assets	(19) (20) (21)	3632	3381
Gain on disposals of non-current assets		− 1234	− 787
Undistributed earnings from equity method investments		− 134	− 129
Net interest expense		742	600
Changes in inventories		160	− 777
Changes in receivables, other assets and deferred income		− 160	−260
Changes in provisions		− 808	1433
Changes in liabilities (excluding corporate debt)		799	166
Other		− 149	− 80
Cash flows from operating activities		**5622**	**5792**
Capital expenditure on property, plant and equipment and investments in intangible assets	(19) (20)	− 4021	− 3757
Acquisitions of businesses and purchases of investments	(21)	− 2145	− 10589
Proceeds from disposals of affiliates, operations and shareholdings	(8)	2409	1092
Proceeds from the sale of property, plant and equipment and intangible assets		720	463
Proceeds from the sale of investments		311	514
Proceeds from the sale of marketable securities		277	1209
Interest received		337	356
Cash flows used for investing activities		**− 2112**	**− 10712**
Capital increases		175	203
Retirement/Increase in long-term corporate debt	(31)	− 586	4284
Change in short-term corporate debt	(31)	− 1163	1491
Dividends paid	(27)	− 984	− 767
Interest paid		− 1105	− 838
Cash flows used for financing activities		**− 3663**	**4373**
Cash flows from operating, investing and financing activities		**− 153**	**− 547**
Effect of exchange rate changes on cash		10	− 59
Effect of consolidation changes on cash		− 89	− 41
Change in cash and cash equivalents		**− 232**	**− 647**
Liquid assets excluding marketable securities:			
at beginning of year		614	1261
at end of year		382	614

Source: Hoechst AG, annual report, 1996, p. 68

9.7.3.1 Charts of accounts and the work of Schmalenbach[38]

There are two meanings of the phrase 'chart of accounts' in Germany. One is an accounts framework (*Kontenrahmen*), setting an outline chart for companies in a particular sector. The other is a detailed accounts plan (*Kontenplan*) developed by a business for its own use. Both use a decimal system of classification. Ten classes of accounts, numbered 0–9, are each divided into ten account groups. Each account group has ten account types and each account type has ten subaccounts; further subdivision is permitted. The numbers so created form the account number.

Charts of accounts have a long history in Germany, first appearing around 1900. A comprehensive system was developed by Schär in 1911, but the leading authority was the work of Schmalenbach published in 1927, called *The Kontenrahmen*. Since 1945 it is not mandatory to use a particular *Kontenrahmen* for a sector. Industry frameworks have continued to be issued by the Association of German Industry and have been adapted to take account of the Fourth Directive.

Although the German charts of accounts are not compulsory, they have an interesting history and a strong influence on the *Plan Comptable* in France (*see* Chapter 8).

9.7.3.2 The stakeholder perspective[39]

In relation to the function of the annual accounts, there is a perspective of stakeholders extending beyond the owners of a business. One purpose of the annual accounts is to report the amount of profit available to be distributed to the owners, but thereafter the purpose is to provide information about the economic position of the enterprise to the management, the creditors and the employees as well as to the shareholders.

It has been stated that, in Germany, so far as the purpose of the annual accounts is concerned, disclosure for investment purposes takes second place to the determination of distributable profit. The annual report is not the sole source of information to stakeholders because they have access to inside information through formal mechanisms such as the supervisory board and the workers' council.

The uniformity of the annual accounts is thus a means of ensuring comparable treatment of stakeholders, but in practice it is modified by the flexibility of access to additional relevant information.

9.7.3.3 Relationship between company reporting and tax law[40]

It is essential to be aware that commercial accounts in Germany are linked directly to tax accounts. The German Income Tax Law incorporates an authoritative principle (the *Maßgeblichkeitsprinzip*) which states that commercial *Grundsätze ordnungsmäßiger Buchführung* (Principles of Regular Accounting, or *GoB*) form an authoritative basis for tax accounts unless there are other explicit tax rules. Tax accounts are thus derived from commercial accounts.

However the tax legislation is also very detailed in relation to accounting treatment and tax incentives. The availability of tax incentives usually requires the

---

[38] Ordelheide and Pfaff (1994), pp. 94–100
[39] Ordelheide and Pfaff (1994), p. 79
[40] Seckler (1995), p. 228; Ordelheide and Pfaff (1994), pp. 79–83

values of tax accounting to be used also in commercial accounting. This has been called 'the reverse authoritativeness principle'.[41] So, in reality, tax practices influence the starting point for preparation of the commercial accounts. In particular there is pressure on German companies to value assets at the lowest amount possible and liabilities at the highest amount possible.[42]

These interactive influences between tax law and company reporting are relevant only to the annual accounts of individual companies; the authoritativeness principle does not have the same effect on group accounts. Consolidated accounts must apply the principle of prudence, but do not necessarily have to adopt the valuations contained in the individual accounts. Nevertheless it may be that consolidated accounts are driven by tax influences, either because it is expensive to prepare two different sets of accounts or because stakeholders persuade management to use an approach in the consolidated accounts which is consistent with that of the individual accounts, so that the messages conveyed by both are comparable.

The common view that the influence of tax law in German accounting leads to uniformity of practice is therefore an oversimplification. For individual companies, there is flexibility of practice within the authoritativeness principle and there may be a range of options even where the reverse authoritativeness principle applies. For group accounting there is no statutory requirement to apply the authoritativeness principle but there may be commercial pressures to do so.

9.7.3.4 Calculation of goodwill[43]

The unusual aspect of German practice is the variability allowed in valuing the net assets of the subsidiary on acquisition. Under one method, the book values of the subsidiary's assets and liabilities are compared with the cost of the investment. If the cost of the investment is greater, there is an implication that the price paid has covered hidden reserves as well as recorded net assets. A portion of the excess is consequently allocated to balance sheet headings for assets and liabilities; any amount remaining is recorded as goodwill. The consequence is that asset values in the group accounts may vary from one enterprise to the next. If the cost of the investment is less than the book value of net assets, negative goodwill or 'badwill' may result as the consolidation difference.

Under the alternative current value method, the hidden reserves are eliminated by replacing book values by market values. The upper limit is that the proportional net equity of the subsidiary must not exceed the cost of the investment. Negative goodwill cannot then arise.

9.7.3.5 Influence of the EU on German accounting

The Fourth Directive reflects German practice, which is heavily orientated towards historical cost accounting and the use of financial statements formats.[44] Implementation of the Fourth Directive was therefore not problematic in Germany except perhaps for the requirement to show a true and fair view which was a late

---

[41] Pfaff and Schröer (1996)
[42] Ballwieser (1995), pp. 1430–1
[43] Seckler (1995), p. 248
[44] Wysocki (1984), p. 59

addition to the Fourth Directive as a result of the Anglo-Saxon influence. The requirement is contained in the *HGB* as an addition to the principles of regular accounting. The approach of a 'true and fair view' could be seen as opening a door to flexibility but German legislation chose to emphasise that the true and fair view is established by reading the balance sheet, profit and loss account and notes taken together. The principle of reverse authoritativeness, with regard to tax law, also modified the approach to 'true and fair' taken in the German law. Uniformity in the primary financial statements was thus preserved, with flexibility directed towards the notes to the accounts.

Implementation of the Seventh Directive in Germany made use of the options which preserved traditional national practice. At the time of implementation of the Seventh Directive in German law, one observer stated that consolidated accounts prepared under EU influence would be less easy to compare with each other than was the case under previous German law.[45] It was seen as a trend of moving away from regimentation of accounting practice. It may thus be concluded indirectly that the concept of a true and fair view has had some influence on the relative position of German accounting practice on the scale of uniformity versus flexibility.

9.7.4 Conservatism versus optimism

Gray's (1988) system classified German accounting as moderately conservative.

9.7.4.1 Long-term view[46]

German shareholders are said to take a long-term view, favouring slow steady increases in real earnings and heavy reinvestment rather than a high level of distribution. This would support placing German accounting in a category of relatively high conservatism.

9.7.4.2 Pre-eminence of the calculation of distributable profit[47]

The profits calculated according to the law are the basis on which distributable profits are shared by the owners of the enterprise. It is an important feature of the law that the distribution limits to a reasonable level the risk that creditors will not receive their entitlement to interest and repayment of capital. Historical experience of corporate collapse and the importance of long-term credit as a source of finance has ensured that protection of creditors is a primary feature of commercial law as it affects accounting.

In particular, the corporation is required to build up a legal reserve in the balance sheet through appropriation of profit each year. In addition, the articles of association or the powers of management may allow further appropriations to reserves. Thereafter the decision on distribution rests with the shareholders. They may resolve to make transfers to reserves, or they may decide to take all distributable profit as dividends.

---

[45] Wysocki (1993), p. 99
[46] Charkham (1994), p. 52
[47] Ordelheide and Pfaff (1994), pp. 72–5

The importance of the calculation of distributable profit and the potential adverse consequences of overdistribution provide a ready explanation of the need for caution and conservatism in reporting profit of individual companies.

9.7.4.3 Emphasis on creditor protection[48]

As well as protecting existing creditors, it is a function of the annual accounts that they will aid the decisions of potential creditors in granting or withholding credit. The banking legislation requires credit institutions to take a close interest in the annual accounts of those to whom money is loaned; the banking regulators may also ask to see accounts in some circumstances. Analysis of accounts pays particular attention to the ability of the borrower to service debt.

There is therefore a close connection between the granting of credit and the annual accounts. This explains a potentially high degree of conservatism which is in practice modified by the availability of other sources of information to be used by creditors. In particular, lenders may exercise influence and gain information through representation on the supervisory board.

9.7.4.4 Valuation

The valuation of *tangible fixed assets*[49] must not exceed acquisition cost. Revaluation upwards is not permitted. No specific method of depreciation[50] is prescribed by law, the most common methods being the straight-line and the reducing-balance methods. Commercial law requires the useful economic life to be estimated conservatively.[51] Estimated useful lives are generally dependent on tax tables relevant to the industry, which avoids the need to prepare two sets of accounts.

Intangible fixed assets[52] which are purchased must be capitalised and amortised. Internally generated intangibles, including internally generated development expenditure, may not be recognised – in respect of development expenditure, this is in conflict with IAS 9.[53] Goodwill arising on consolidation can either be written off against reserves or amortised through profit and loss account. The law mentions a period of four years for depreciation, but in practice a much wider range of asset life is used, which is also in accordance with the law.

Inventories[54] must be stated at the lower of historical cost and market value. The determination of market value is complex. For raw materials and supplies, the market value is the replacement cost in the purchase market. For finished goods, the market value is the net realisable value in the sales market. For work-in-progress, either market may apply. This leads to a situation where the inventory value may be reduced to replacement cost despite the net realisable value being above historical cost. This 'lower of cost and market' rule is therefore more conservative than the 'lower of cost and net realisable value' rule of some other EU countries which is also used in IAS 2. Where net realisable value is used, the enter-

---

[48] Ordelheide and Pfaff (1994), p. 78
[49] Ordelheide and Pfaff (1994), p. 134
[50] Seckler (1995), p. 257
[51] Ordelheide and Pfaff (1994), p. 140
[52] Seckler (1995), pp. 248, 259
[53] Ordelheide and Pfaff (1994), p. 250
[54] Seckler (1995), p. 263

prise may deduct from sales price a mark-down to reflect an adequate profit for the entrepreneur. This is a tax rule which allows further conservative practice. It is also possible to anticipate expected future price reductions by use of inventory reserves.

In the commercial accounts, it is compulsory to include in inventory valuation the costs of direct material, direct labour and special production costs. This variable cost approach is not accepted for tax law, which requires in addition an element of overhead costs of materials and labour plus overheads of depreciation, general administration and costs of pension or other social benefits. To avoid duplication of effort, many companies follow the tax rules.

Where prices are changing, LIFO is acceptable for tax purposes and may be used in the commercial accounts.[55] This is an allowed alternative under IAS 2. However, the average cost and FIFO remain the common methods.[56]

Profits on long-term contracts[57] may be reported on completion of the project rather than on the basis of the percentage of work completed. Reporting on completion is accepted for tax purposes. However, the percentage of completion is permitted where there is adequate evidence of that portion of the work being finished. The percentage of completion method is accepted in German accounting practice, although there is no evidence of a direct link with IAS 11.

9.7.4.5 Provisions[58]

There are requirements in the law for, and conditions set upon, making provisions for uncertain liabilities. There has to be a liability to a third party outside the business. (The German view of the entity regards provisions for expenses as an obligation of the enterprise to itself.) There is a second condition that, at the balance sheet date, the business event giving rise to the uncertain liability should have occurred. The third condition relates to measurement. There must be uncertainty concerning the existence or amount of the liability but also sufficient likelihood that the business has a commitment, and the amount must be measured according to sound business judgement.

These conditions appear, in principle, comparable to those applying in other EU countries. Nevertheless German accounting has a reputation for making provisions in excess of those found elsewhere in similar circumstances. The meaning of 'sound business judgement' may be influenced by cautious business practice and the principle of authoritativeness.

One particular explanation lies in the requirement for provisions for losses on incomplete transactions, which could be regarded elsewhere as anticipating future losses. These provisions are allowed for tax purposes and consequently are used wherever permissible. They form a significant part of an enterprise's financing, effectively providing state finance through lower tax charges. Legislation on social and environmental protection is strict and contributes to the need for such provisions. There are also specific requirements to provide for items such as repairs and maintenance. One exception is that German companies are not obliged to create a

---

[55] Ordelheide and Pfaff (1994), p. 147
[56] Seckler (1995), p. 262
[57] Seckler (1995), p. 265; Ordelheide and Pfaff (1994), p. 150
[58] Ordelheide and Pfaff (1994), p. 130; Macharzina and Langer (1995), p. 277

separate trust for employees' pensions. Many carry the liability on the balance sheet although some take out an insurance scheme.

Taken together, these requirements of law and their application lead to relatively high levels of provisions in the accounts of German companies. A large part of these provisions is due to pension liabilities because of direct commitments to employees. A significant portion of the other provisions would be regarded under IAS 10 as contingent liabilities, disclosed in notes to the accounts rather than reported in the balance sheet.

9.7.4.6 Legal concepts of hidden reserves[59]

Hidden reserves, by their nature, become apparent only in a crisis. These are reserves of shareholder wealth which are not shown specifically on the face of the balance sheet. They arise through undervaluation of assets and overvaluation of liabilities, and they come to light when a company is in crisis or is liquidated and the values of assets and liabilities are placed under scrutiny. Historical cost accounting will tend to undervalue assets compared with their current value. There is a legal prohibition on the capitalisation of internally generated intangible fixed assets. Tax-permitted write-down of assets beyond economic depreciation will also lead to undervaluation. Exhibit 9.16 shows the impact on profit of additional depreciation taken in accordance with tax legislation.

Corporations are permitted to create discretionary reserves. Together with the scope for interpretation in the creation of mandatory reserves, this provides possibilities for hidden reserves of value.

To some extent Germany's reputation is historical and not out of line with practice of that time elsewhere. The rules in the 1937 *AktG*, for example, were interpreted as prohibiting overvaluation but placing no lower limit on undervaluation. The reform of the *AktG* in 1965 imposed the test of reasonable business practice in such a way as to oppose certain kinds of valuation practices where there was a feeling that those practices were in conflict with the interests of shareholders. A limitation on excessive conservatism was extended to GmbHs by the Accounting Directives Act of 1985. Overall, however, the continuing scope for hidden reserves, within a framework of limiting historical excesses, leads to continuing conclusions that German accounting practices are conservative.

9.7.4.7 Foreign currency translation[60]

Legislation requires only that the method of translation is disclosed. There is therefore total flexibility in practice but it may be seen that the flexibility tends towards conservative practices. Two instances are explained in this section, the first relating to current assets and liabilities and the second to the overall process of translation.

The prevalent practice of translation is to apply the rate of exchange at the closing date (balance sheet date). An exception is that in the current assets section of the balance sheet the amounts receivable which are denominated in foreign currencies may be translated at the lower of the closing date rate and the

---

[59] Ordelheide and Pfaff (1994), pp. 157–61
[60] Seckler (1995), p. 265; Ordelheide and Pfaff (1994), p. 179; Macharzina and Langer (1995), p. 281

Exhibit 9.16 KARSTADT: IMPACT ON PROFIT OF ADDITIONAL DEPRECIATION TAKEN IN ACCORDANCE WITH TAX LEGISLATION

Notes to the consolidated financial statements and financial statements of Karstadt AG at December 31, 1996

(4) Principles of accounting and valuation, and translation of foreign currencies (Extract)

Tangible assets are shown at purchase or production cost, *less* scheduled depreciation. Depreciation on buildings is charged in accordance with Art. 7 of the Income Tax Act and, in the case of movable assets, for the most part using initially the declining balance and later the straight-line methods. Minor value assets are fully expensed in the year of acquisition; in the fixed assets move-ments schedule, however, the related cost and accumulated depreciation are maintained for a period of five years, before being eliminated in the sixth year. Where accelerated depreciation has been applied to certain assets, we have calculated the scheduled depreciation rates in subsequent years straight-line from the starting value for a maximum of five years, in accordance with the Development Areas Act, while in all other cases they are based on the residual values and estimated remaining useful lives.

Movable assets acquired in the first half of the year are generally charged with a full year's depreciation, half a year's depreciation being applied to those assets acquired in the second half of the year.

As in previous years, additional depreciation has been taken, and untaxed special reserves set up or released, in accordance with the tax regulations, during the financial year. We refer in respect of 1996 to Notes 18, 25, and 29.

The Karstadt Group's 1996 profit has been reduced by some 67%, and that of Karstadt AG has been increased by about 23%, as a result of these measures; this will result in higher tax charges in future years, which will however be spread over up to 48 years, and will therefore not have a material effect on any individual future year (disclosure in accordance with Art. 314 (1) No. 5 and 285 No. 5 HGB).

Source: Karstadt AG, annual report, 1996, pp. 56, 58–9

historical rate. In the current liabilities section the amounts payable in foreign currencies are translated at the higher of the closing rate and the historical rate. This practice is conservative because it considers translation losses but not trans-lation gains. It results in unequal treatment of assets and liabilities, even where the asset and liability are matching, and this unequal treatment is demonstrated in the following illustration.

Exchange rate at date of transaction (historical rate) : DM2 = \$1

Exchange rate at balance sheet date
(1) DM5 = \$1 (Closing rate is lower – German currency is weaker)
(2) DM1 = \$1 (Closing rate is higher – German currency is stronger)

Amount receivable German company will receive \$100	*Amount payable* German company will pay \$100
(1) Amount receivable falls from DM50 to DM20. The translation loss is recorded (2) Amount receivable increases from DM50 to DM100. The translation gain is not recorded	(1) Amount payable falls from DM50 to DM20. The translation gain is not recorded (2) Amount payable increases from DM50 to DM100. The translation loss is recorded

When translating the full accounts of a subsidiary, German companies may apply the closing rate method or the temporal method. If the temporal method is applied then gains and losses arising on translation are generally reported through reserves. This could be regarded as more conservative than the recommendation of IAS 21, which is for such gains and losses to be reported through the profit and loss account.

9.7.5 Secrecy versus transparency

Gray (1988) classified German accounting as highly secretive by reputation. However, the extent of information provided is quite extensive and the reputation for secrecy may have been created by concentrating on a few items such as hidden reserves.

9.7.5.1 Notes to the accounts

As indicated in previous sections, the notes to the accounts are extensive. The note on fixed assets is particularly detailed in its analysis of movement on fixed assets.[61] Accounts receivable and accounts payable are analysed extensively according to the due date and nature,[62] but the detail in the notes is in contrast to the limited detail required on the face of the balance sheet. Extraordinary items[63] of revenues and expenses must be disclosed with a comment in the notes regarding their amount and nature. However, enterprises define the nature of the requirements in a restrictive manner and in practice disclose relatively little. This tendency towards secrecy is aided by interpretations in the legal commentaries on the *HGB*. There are therefore indications that the pressures for secrecy remain evident in the interpretations which effectively reverse some of the intentions of the Directives.

---

[61] Seckler (1995), p. 261
[62] Ordelheide and Pfaff (1994), p. 164
[63] Ordelheide and Pfaff (1994), pp. 118–19

9.7.5.2 Segmental reporting[64]

Segmental information was relatively unknown prior to 1985. Revision of the *HGB* to meet the requirements of the EU Directives set out regulations for segmental reporting which corresponded to the requirements of the Fourth and Seventh Directives but did not exceed them. A corporation is obliged to disclose segmented sales only if there are different forms of sales organisation in different product or regional markets. Neither the nature of the products nor the production process is relevant for the requirements of segmental disclosure. It has been found that, because of the weak interpretation of the *HGB*'s segmental reporting requirements in commentaries on the *HGB*, the practical implementation of segmental reporting has been slow. That may be taken as an indication of the continuation of a tradition of secrecy in the accounting philosophy. However, the competing pressure lies in international capital markets where multinational companies find they must adopt internationally accepted practices such as those recommended by the IASC. BMW is one of a number of German multinationals that go further than the requirements of IAS 14 in the range of segmental information disclosed, but it will often be necessary to look further than the note to the accounts to find the relevant information.

9.7.5.3 The management report[65]

The management report is a statutory requirement for corporations of at least medium size. In many ways, it is comparable to the Management Discussion and Analysis required of US companies. It provides a commentary by management on the performance of the enterprise and information on its business situation and development. Management, in making the report, may take a view of aspects of the business of the enterprise in terms of technical, legal, social and economic aspects. The report must provide current information and must deal with some future orientated matters such as post-balance sheet events, immediate prospects and research and development. However a tendency towards secrecy may be seen in the nature of the comments on research and development, which are often restricted to a general statement of the number of persons employed in that activity.

The management report must be audited. Groups of companies must produce a group management report in addition to reports on the separate companies. A combined management report on the parent and the group is permissible, and is commonly found.

9.7.5.4 Supervisory board

The report of the supervisory board is made to shareholders by way of the annual report. It is a formal document, covering one or two pages, confirming that the supervisory board has carried out its duties, noting the audit report and approving the financial statements.

Informal communication is achieved by the flow of information to the works council and to the bankers on the supervisory board. Bankers in turn draw on

---

[64] Haller and Park (1994), p. 563
[65] Ordelheide and Pfaff (1994), p. 203

other flows of information from their own contacts with the company, from colleagues, and from the bank's research department. These supplementary flows make the supervisory board meetings important.[66]

9.7.5.5 Voluntary disclosure[67]

It may be argued that voluntary disclosure of information is a means of overcoming conservatism in measurement. Voluntary disclosure is evidenced in:

- value added statements
- information for shareholders regarding share price, type of shareholder and size of shareholdings
- environmental reporting
- management analysis of performance.

Value added statements are relatively common in annual reports, sometimes being shown in the management report and at other times appearing in the notes to the accounts. In the management report the value added statement is often given equal prominence with commentaries on the profit and loss account; this reflects the stakeholder perspective of German accounting. The variety of value added statements is illustrated by examples taken from the Karstadt Group (Exhibit 9.17), the VIAG Group (Exhibit 9.18) and the Bayer Group (Exhibit 9.19).

The practice of voluntary disclosure is strongest in multinational companies. It is also seen in the presentation of results according to the German Association for Financial Analysts and Investment Consultants (*DVFA*) and the Schmalenbach Society/German Association for Business Economics (*SG*).[68] This presentation starts with the published consolidated profit or loss and makes adjustments which allow the corporation to show trends over time, present a reliable basis for the forecasting of future results and permit comparisons between enterprises. This is all in the context of the conservatism of German accounting principles but has the benefit of disclosing information not made available elsewhere.

Companies often make reference to the DVFA/SG analysis in their management report and include information in highlight statements. Examples are provided by Hoechst (Exhibit 9.20) and Karstadt (Exhibit 9.21).

9.8 EMPIRICAL STUDIES

This chapter has shown that the principles of German accounting are strongly codified in law but that practice is subject to interpretations which allow characteristics of conservatism and secrecy to persist in some matters. The existence of these interpretations creates scope for flexibility, but this is in practice curtailed by the influence of tax law.

---

[66] Charkham (1994), Chapter 2, p. 44
[67] Meek, Roberts and Gray (1995), pp. 555–72
[68] Ordelheide and Pfaff (1994), pp. 206–9

Exhibit 9.17   KARSTADT GROUP: VALUE ADDED STATEMENT

KARSTADT GROUP:
VALUE ADDED

	1996 Mio DM	1995 Mio DM
Source		
Total group output	**28 367**	28 448
Less: intermediate input	**22 100**	22 156
Added value	**6 267**	6 292
taken out of the group	**51**	1
Distribution	**6 318**	6 293
Employees	**5 127**	5 112
Government	**806**	796
Providers of funds	**229**	228
Shareholders	**156**	156
Outside shareholders	**–**	1

Total group output includes turnover
and, with minor deviations, other
income, including VAT.

Intermediate input mainly includes
cost of sales, non-personnel expenditure,
and depreciation of tangible fixed
assets. The VAT relating to the intermediate input has been added. The portion of the added value distributed to
the employees includes wages and salaries, social security levies and the cost
of pension plans and related benefits.
The net amount of VAT payable to the
government is shown together with
the normal tax charges, the corporation
tax credit on the dividends is included
in the part shown as distributed to the
shareholders.

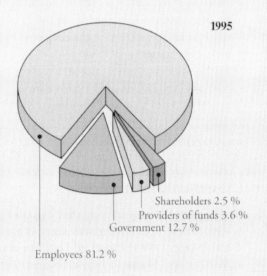

1996

Shareholders 2.5 %
Providers of funds 3.6 %
Government 12.8 %

Employees 81.1 %

1995

Shareholders 2.5 %
Providers of funds 3.6 %
Government 12.7 %

Employees 81.2 %

Source: Karstadt Group, annual report, 1996, p. 67

| Exhibit 9.18 | VIAG GROUP: VALUE ADDED STATEMENT |

VIAG Group Statement of value added

	1996		1995	
	DM million	%	DM million	%
Creation of value added				
Total operating performance	**42,546**	**95**	42,295	94
Other income	**2,271**	**5**	2,514	6
Total operating performance	**44,817**	**100**	44,809	100
less: Purchased goods and services	**33,210**	**74**	32,951	74
Gross valued added	**11,607**	**26**	11,858	26
less: Depreciation on tangible and intangible assets	**2,233**	**5**	2,340	5
Net value added	**9,374**	**21**	9,518	21
Distribution of value added				
Employees (Personnel expenses)	**6,188**	**66**	6,457	68
Public authorities (Taxes)	**1,429**	**15**	1,066	11
Creditors (Interest)	**697**	**8**	675	7
Company/Stockholders	**1,060**	**11**	1,320	14
Net value added	**9,374**	**100**	9,518	100

Statement of value added

The statement of value added reveals the value contributed to the wealth generated in an economy by the products manufactured, and services provided, by a company. In addition, it shows the extent to which this value is accounted for by the individual groups involved in the company directly and indirectly.

At DM9.4 billion, the net value added of the VIAG Group is around the same level as in 1995 (DM9.5 billion). Compared with 1995, however, there have been appreciable shifts in the value added distribution statement. The employee share of value added fell from 68% to 66%. As a consequence of the drop in consolidated net income, the share attributable to shareholders and the company itself fell by 3%. In contrast, the share taken by the public sector increased to 15% (1995: 11%) due to the return of the tax expense to normal levels in 1996.

Source: VIAG Group, annual report, 1996, p. 18

9.8.1 Classification studies

In Chapter 4 it was shown that Mueller (1967) classified Germany as a uniform system where accounting was seen as a means of government control (subsection 4.4.1). Nobes (1984) classified German accounting alongside that of Japan (Exhibit 4.7). Nair and Frank (1980) classified Germany with the main body of European

Exhibit 9.19 BAYER GROUP: VALUE ADDED STATEMENT

Bayer Group: Value Added
(DM million)

Source		Distribution	
Net sales	48,608	Stockholders and minority	
Other income	1,405	interests	1,253
Total operating performance	**50,013**	Employees	15,096
Cost of materials	(16,608)	Governments	2,049
Depreciation	(2,594)	Lenders	611
Other expenses	(10,308)	Earnings retention	1,494
Net inputs	**(29,510)**		
Value added	**20,503**	**Value added**	**20,503**

Total operating performance and value added

The value added of the Group rose DM 0.8 billion or 4.2 percent to DM 20.5 billion. Of this, DM 15.1 billion, or 74 percent, went to our employees. Governments received Dm 2 billion. Interest expense rose 5 percent to DM 611 million, accounting for 3 percent of value added. Stockholders and minority interests received DM 1.3 billion. The remaining DM 1.5 billion will be retained as stockholders' equity.

Source: Bayer Group, annual report, 1996, p. 13

Exhibit 9.20 HOECHST: EXTRACT FROM HIGHLIGHTS STATEMENT

Financial highlights

Figures per Hoechst share

Amounts in DM	1996	1995
Hoechst AG dividend per DM 5 share	1.40[1]	1.30
Tax credit	0.60	0.56
Net income	3.60	2.91
DVFA/SG result	2.75	2.40
Book value	24.67	21.16
Number of Hoechst shares on Dec. 31 in millions	588	588
Total market value at the end of 1996 (DM bn)	41.92	22.93

[1] Proposed dividend

Source: Hoechst, annual report, 1996, inside front cover

Exhibit 9.21 KARSTADT: EXTRACT FROM MANAGEMENT REPORT

Key figures per DM 50 Karstadt shares

	1996	1995
Dividend	10.00	13.00
Tax credit	4.29	5.57
Profit for the year	6.95	12.85
DVFA/SG result	– 20.92	– 21.42
Cash flow per DVFA/SG	75.06	91.67
Capital and reserves	277.32	291.46
Stock market price (31.12.)	512.00	590.00
Highest stock market price	624.00	679.00
Lowest stock market price	491.00	524.00
Number of shares (in millions)	8.4	8.4
Stock market value (31.12. in million DM)	4301	4956

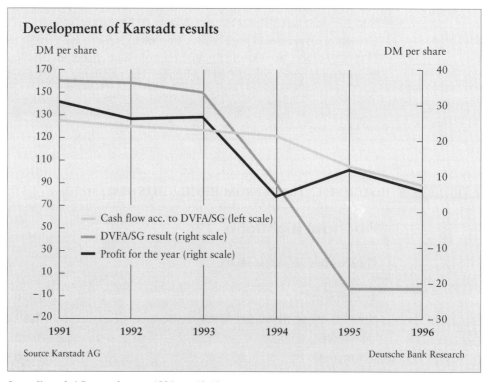

Source: Karstadt AG   Deutsche Bank Research

Source: Karstadt AG, annual report, 1996, pp. 18–19

countries on the basis of measurement (Exhibit 4.10) but with Japan and the USA on the basis of disclosure (Exhibit 4.11). Using more recent survey data, Doupnik and Salter (1993) (Exhibit 4.8) classified Germany as identifiably different within a group of macro-uniform countries. However while their analysis confirmed that German accounting practice was very distinct, they were not able to identify conclusively the factors which were causing Germany to be different.

9.8.2 Comparability measures

Chapter 3 explained the methods used to measure comparability. There is little opportunity to carry out analysis of quantified differences in reported profit because few German companies re-state their accounts under the policies of other countries or the IASC. One exception was Daimler–Benz, taking a listing on the New York stock exchange, as discussed in Chapter 1 (*see also* Case study 3.1). In the first year of listing (1993) it reported a loss under US GAAP compared with a profit under German GAAP, causing some surprise in the context of accepted views that German accounting is relatively conservative. The differences in profits of Daimler–Benz between German and US GAAP in 1993 were due in very large part to extraordinary profits in the German presentation which were subtracted for the US presentation. More recent examples of the reconciliations provided by Daimler–Benz can be seen in Exhibit 9.22.

In the hypothetical exercise undertaken by Simmonds and Azières (1989), it was shown that German accounting practice allowed achievement of a lower minimum reported profit than any other EU member country in 1989. Similarly, the most likely and the maximum values were each the lowest in their respective ranges. Profits could be minimised by use of LIFO stock valuation, the ability to exclude certain overheads from stock valuation, and the ability to increase the charge for amortisation of goodwill. Simmonds and Azières (1989) also showed that the German accounting practices gave the lowest fixed asset figure of any EU country.

9.8.3 Harmonisation studies

Harmonisation studies are described in Chapter 3. Archer *et al* (1995) found that within-country comparability decreased, due mainly to a number of German companies changing their methods of amortisation of goodwill over the period of study. Increasing disclosures by German companies on deferred tax were observed over the period of study (Chapter 3, subsection 3.5.4).

Hermann and Thomas (1995), using accounting reports of 1992/3, found that across the range of European companies studied, Germany was the only country where all companies sampled used strict historical cost. Depreciation policy in the German sample, based on declining balance in the early years and then straight line in later life, was significantly different from the straight-line approach used by most other companies. This was attributed by Hermann and Thomas to the influence of tax law on accounting practice in Germany. In respect of accounting for goodwill they detected a change in practice in the accounts examined for 1992/3 year ends, with 20 out of 30 companies capitalising and amortising goodwill. Emenyonu and Gray (1992), using 1989 data, found that write-off to reserves predominated. Policy on research and development expenditure was not disclosed in 27 out of 30 companies. LIFO inventory valuation was used by 15 out of 30 and 11 gave no disclosure. In foreign currency translation, where the majority of companies across EU countries used the current rate method for all assets and liabilities, 11 out of the 30 German companies used a mixture of current and historical rates. In bicountry I indices, Germany was second lowest to Portugal in harmonisation with other EU countries in this range of accounting matters.

Exhibit 9.22 DAIMLER–BENZ: RECONCILIATION OF PROFIT REPORTED UNDER GERMAN AND US GAAP

Additional Information in Accordance with the U.S. Generally Accepted Accounting Principles (U.S. GAAP)

With the listing of Daimler–Benz stock on the New York Stock Exchange, we are obligated to file an annual report on Form 20-F with the Securities and Exchange Commission (SEC). Much of the information contained in this report is taken from our annual report; however, additional data and financial information are provided that were determined on the basis of U.S. accounting principles. Since there are substantial differences, especially in net income and stockholders' equity, the reconciliations (see page 49) are required to convert certain financial data from the German consolidated financial statements to the values calculated using the U.S. GAAP. An explanation of the most important items is provided on page 80.

Reconciliation of Consolidated Net Income/Loss and Stockholders' Equity to U.S. GAAP

– in millions of DM –	1995	1994
Consolidated net (loss) income in accordance with German HGB (Commercial Code)	(5,734)	895
+/- Changes in appropriated retained earnings:		
provisions, reserves and valuation differences	(640)	409
	(6,374)	1,304
Additional adjustments		
+/- Long-term contracts	(9)	53
Goodwill and business acquisitions	(2,241)	(350)
Deconsolidation of MBL Fahrzeug-Leasing GmbH & Co. KG	369	(652)
Pensions and other postretirement benefits	(219)	(432)
Foreign currency translation	52	(22)
Financial instruments	49	633
Securities	238	(388)
Other valuation differences	(215)	232
Deferred taxes	2,621	496
Consolidated net (loss) income in accordance with U.S. GAAP before cumulative effect of a change in accounting principle	(5,729)	874
Cumulative effect of change in accounting for certain investments in debt and equity securities as of January 1, 1994, net of tax of DM 235 million	–	178
Consolidated net (loss) income in accordance with U.S. GAAP	(5,729)	1,052
Net (loss) income per share in accordance with U.S. GAAP	DM (111.67)	DM 21.53
Net (loss) income per American Depositary Share[1] in accordance with U.S. GAAP	DM (11.17)	DM 2.15
Stockholders' equity in accordance with German HGB	13,842	20,251
+ Appropriated retained earnings:		
provisions, reserves and valuation differences	5,604	6,205
	19,446	26,456
Additional adjustments		
+/- Long-term contracts	253	262
Goodwill and business acquisitions	(559)	1,978
Deconsolidation of MBL Fahrzeug-Leasing GmbH & Co. KG	(283)	(652)
Pensions and other postretirement benefits	(2,469)	(2,250)
Foreign currency translation	115	63
Financial instruments	1,058	1,013
Securities	525	27
Other valuation differences	(1,073)	(336)
Deferred taxes	5,847	2,874
Stockholders' equity in accordance with U.S. GAAP	22,860	29,435

[1] Corresponds to one tenth of a share of stock of DM 50 par value.

Exhibit 9.22 continued

Notes to the Reconciliation of Consolidated Net Income/Loss and Stockholders' Equity to U.S. GAAP

Appropriated Retained Earnings: Provisions, Reserves and Valuation Differences

U.S. accounting principles by far do not allow provisions and reserves to the same extent as the German Commercial Code. Non-recognized provisions and reserves have to be eliminated, which has an effect on net income as well as stockholders' equity. According to U.S. GAAP, the stockholders' equity increased for that reason alone by DM 5.3 billion in 1995. The changes not only affected provisions but also property, plant and equipment, net inventories and receivables. We use the term 'appropriated retained earnings' to disclose to the American investors that such retained earnings are not available for distribution as dividends. This term also establishes a bridge between the two different accounting cultures.

Long-Term Contracts

Customer revenues and cost of sales are recorded under German law in accordance with the completed contract method, whereas U.S. principles generally require that the percentage of completion method be used. The majority of contracts within the group require partial prepayment as well as partial recognition of profits based upon payments received. Contracts of this nature are also customary in the U.S.A., and are recognized under its accounting regulations. The resulting differences are therefore not material.

Goodwill and Business Acquisitions

Under German accounting regulations, goodwill can be offset against stockholders' equity, or capitalized and amortized generally over the expected useful life, which in Germany ranges up to 20 years. Under U.S. GAAP, goodwill must be capitalized and amortized over a period not exceeding 40 years. The expenses of 1995 are based on additional amortization of such goodwill that must be taken in accordance with U.S. GAAP.

Deconsolidation

Under German accounting principles, a company can be deconsolidated once the majority of the shares have been sold. According to U.S. GAAP, however, a leasing company of which a majority interest has been sold to nongroup entities must remain consolidated until the economic risks and rewards have been fully transferred.

Pensions and Other Postretirement Benefits

According to U.S. accounting principles, the determination of provisions for pensions is based, among other things, on anticipated increases in wages and salaries. The calculation is not based on a discount rate of 6%, which is applicable under German Tax Law, but instead, on the interest rate of the countries involved. Another difference relates to the requirement that health care costs for retirees be actuarially calculated and accrued for in the U.S.A.

Foreign Currency Translation and Financial Instruments

Unrealized profits and losses related to the valuation of amounts denominated in foreign currencies and to financial instruments are treated differently in the two accounting systems. Under German law, according to the imparity principle, only unrealized losses are to be recorded, whereas under U.S. GAAP, as well unrealized profits must be recognized.

Securities

Under German accounting principles, securities are valued at the lower of cost or market. In contrast, U.S. GAAP requires that securities be marked to higher market value. The changes in the market value are recorded either directly in the statements of income or in the stockholders' equity.

Other Valuation Differences

Additional differences between German and American accounting methods may occur with respect to inventories, minority interests and leasing activities.

Deferred Taxes

In the German consolidated financial statements, deferred tax assets result primarily from elimination entries affecting net income. According to U.S. GAAP, future advantages from (temporary) differences between tax and book values and from tax losses carried forward are also taken into consideration.

Source: Daimler–Benz, annual report, 1995, pp. 48, 49, 80

Emenyonu and Gray (1992) using earlier data from 1989, obtained similar results to those of Hermann and Thomas with respect to Germany, except for the change in practice with regard to capitalisation of goodwill mentioned in the previous paragraph.

9.9 SUMMARY AND CONCLUSIONS

In this chapter you have seen how characteristics of accounting principles and practice in Germany are related to the predictions made by Gray and others based upon analysis of cultural factors. Using the scores developed by Hofstede (1984), Gray's (1988) method of analysis may be used to predict that the accounting system in Germany will be characterised by moderate professionalism, marginal uniformity, marginal conservatism and strong secrecy. You have seen that the political and legal institutions provide a strong basis of statutory control which then requires a body of professional interpretation in application of the law. Uniformity is influenced by the Fourth and Seventh Directives, but their influence is augmented by the importance of tax law as an influence on accounting practice. The principle of 'reverse authoritativeness', in particular, is a unique feature of German accounting in its interaction with tax law. Conservatism is the underlying factor in the emphasis on protection of creditors and in the pre-eminence of the calculation of distributable profit. In accounting practice, this is seen particularly in the absolute prohibition on asset revaluation, the use of provisions and the legal concept of hidden reserves. The reputation for secrecy may be due in part to the factor of hidden reserves, because in some respects German accounting is informative; there is a management report required by law, and there is evidence of voluntary disclosure in group accounts by larger German companies. However, segmental reporting is less developed than in some other countries and the notes to the accounts may be used to give a true and fair view where the balance sheet alone is not sufficient. In some respects the notes to the accounts are provided in considerable detail but in other respects there are indications of a tendency to secrecy.

German accounting is unique in many respects and tends to create a category of its own in any classification system. It has been influential on accounting in other countries, particularly its close neighbours and trading partners in Europe, but also as far afield as Japan. There is a desire to allow companies to use IASs within the bounds of the legal system controlling accounting practice, and steps are being taken in that direction.

QUESTIONS

Business environment (9.2)

1 To what extent does the business environment of Germany provide clues as to possible influences on accounting practices?

Early developments in accounting (9.3)

1 To what extent do early developments in accounting practice indicate the likely directions of professionalism/statutory control; uniformity/flexibility; conservatism/optimism; and secrecy/transparency in current practice?

Institutions (9.4)

1 How does the political and economic system of Germany fit into the classifications described in Chapter 1?

2 How does the legal system of Germany fit into the classifications described in Chapter 1?

3 How does the taxation system of Germany compare to the descriptions given in Chapter 1?

4 How does the corporate financing system of Germany compare to the descriptions given in Chapter 1?

5 How does the accounting profession in Germany compare to the descriptions given in Chapter 1?

6 How do the external influences on accounting practice in Germany compare to those described in Chapter 1?

7 Which institutional factors are most likely to influence German accounting practice?

Societal culture and accounting subculture (9.5)

1 What is the position of Germany relative to the UK, France and the Netherlands, according to Hofstede's (1984) analysis (Chapter 2)?

2 What are the features of German societal culture identified by Hofstede which led Gray (1988) to his conclusions regarding the likely system of accounting in Germany?

3 What is the position of Germany relative to the USA and Japan according to Hofstede's analysis (Chapter 2)?

IASs (9.6)

1 In which areas does accounting practice in Germany depart from that set out in IASs?

2 For each of the areas of departure which you have identified, describe the treatment prescribed in German accounting, and identify the likely impact on income and shareholders' equity of moving from German practice to the relevant IASs.

3 What explanations may be offered for these departures from IASs, in terms of the institutional factors described in the chapter?

4 What are the most difficult problems facing accounting in Germany if it seeks harmonisation with the IASC core standards programme?

EU membership (9.7.3.5)

1 What have been the most significant changes in accounting practice in Germany arising from the Fourth and Seventh Directives?

2 Which factors make it relatively easy or relatively difficult for German accounting practices to harmonise with those of other European countries?

Professionalism/statutory control (9.7.2)

1 Identify the key features supporting a conclusion that moderate professionalism, rather than statutory control, is a characteristic of German accounting.

2 Explain which institutional influences cause moderate professionalism, rather than statutory control, to be a characteristic of German accounting.

3 Discuss whether a classification of moderate professionalism is appropriate for the 1990s.

Uniformity/flexibility (9.7.3)

1 Identify the key features supporting a conclusion that marginal uniformity is a characteristic of German accounting.

2 Explain which institutional influences cause marginal uniformity to be a characteristic of German accounting.

3 Discuss whether a classification of marginal uniformity is appropriate for the 1990s.

Conservatism/optimism (9.7.4)

1 Identify the key features supporting a conclusion that marginal conservatism is a characteristic of German accounting.

2 Explain which institutional influences cause marginal conservatism to be a characteristic of German accounting.

3 Discuss whether a classification of marginal conservatism is appropriate for the 1990s.

Secrecy/transparency (9.7.5)

1 Identify the key features supporting a conclusion that secrecy, rather than transparency, is a dominant characteristic of German accounting.

2 Explain which institutional influences cause secrecy, rather than transparency, to be a dominant characteristic of German accounting.

3 Discuss whether a classification of strong secrecy is appropriate for the 1990s.

Empirical studies (9.8)

1 What is the relative position of Germany, as indicated by research studies into classification, comparability and harmonisation?

REFERENCES

Archer, S., Delvaille, P. and McLeay, S. (1995) 'The measurement of harmonisation and the comparability of financial statement items: Within-country and between-country effects', *Accounting and Business Research*, 25(98), 67–80.

Ballwieser, W. (1995) 'Germany – Individual accounts', in Ordelheide, D. and KPMG (eds), *Transnational Accounting*, I, 1395–1546.

Busse von Colbe, W. (1996) 'Accounting and the business economics tradition in Germany', *European Accounting Review*, 5(3), 413–34.

Charkham, J.P. (1994) *Keeping Good Company: A Study of Corporate Governance in Five Countries*. Oxford: Clarendon Press.

Coopers and Lybrand Tax Network (1995) *1995 International Tax Summaries: A Guide for Planning and Decisions*. New York: John Wiley.

Emenyonu, E.N. and Gray, S.J. (1992) 'EC accounting harmonisation: An empirical study of measurement practices in France, Germany and the UK', *Accounting and Business Research*, Winter, 49–58.

Haller, A. (1992) 'The relationship of financial and tax accounting in Germany: A major reason for accounting disharmony in Europe', *International Journal of Accounting*, 27(4) 310–23.

Haller, A. and Park, P. (1994) 'Regulation and practice of segmental reporting in Germany', *European Accounting Review*, 3(3) 563–80.

Hermann, D. and Thomas, W. (1995) 'Harmonisation of accounting measurement practices in the European Community', *Accounting and Business Research*, 25(100), 253–65.

Macharzina, K. and Langer, K. (1995) 'Financial Reporting in Germany', in Nobes, C. and Parker, R., *Comparative International Accounting*, 4th Edn. Englewood Cliffs, NJ: Prentice-Hall.

Meek, G.K., Roberts, C.B. and Gray, S.J. (1995) 'Factors influencing voluntary annual report disclosures by US, UK and continental European multinational corporations', *Journal of International Business Studies*, third quarter, 555–72.

OECD (1996) *Financial Statements of Non-Financial Enterprises*. Paris: Organization for Economic Co-operation and Development.

Ordelheide, D. (1995) 'Germany – Group accounts', in Ordelheide, D. and KPMG (eds), *Transnational Accounting*, I, 1547–1658.

Ordelheide, D. and Pfaff, D. (1994) *European Financial Reporting – Germany*. London: Routledge.

Parker, R.H. and Nobes, C.W. (1994) *An International View of True and Fair Accounting*. London: Routledge

Pfaff, D. and Schröer, T. (1996) 'The relationship between financial and tax accounting in Germany – The authoritativeness and reverse authoritativeness principle', *European Accounting Review*, 5, Supplement, 963–79.

Radebaugh, L.H., Gebhardt, G. and Gray, S.J. (1995) 'Foreign stock exchange listings: A case study of Daimler–Benz', *Journal of International Financial Management and Accounting*, 6(2), 158–92.

Rajan, R.G., and Zingales, L. (1995) 'What do we know about capital structure?', *Journal of Finance*, 50(5), 1421–60.

Rathbone, D. (ed.) (1997) *The LGT Guide to Word Equity Markets 1997*. London: Euromoney Publications plc.

Salter, S.B., Roberts, C.B. and Kantor, J. (1996) 'The IASC comparability project: A cross-national comparison of financial reporting practices and IASC proposed rules', *Journal of International Accounting and Taxation*, 5(1), 89–111.

Schneider, D. (1995) 'The history of financial reporting in Germany', in Walton, P., *European Financial Reporting: A History*. New York: Academic Press.

Seckler, G. (1995) 'Germany', in Alexander, D. and Archer, S. (eds), *European Accounting Guide*. New York: Harcourt Brace Professional Publishing.

Simmonds, A. and Azières, O. (1989) *Accounting for Europe – Success by 2000 AD?*. London: Touche Ross.

Wysocki, K.V. (1984) 'The Fourth Directive and Germany' in Gray, S.J. and Coenenberg, A.G. (1984) *EEC and Accounting Harmonisation: Implementation and Impact of the Fourth Directive*. Amsterdam: North-Holland.

Wysocki, K.V. (1993) 'Group Accounting in Germany' in Gray, S.J., Coenenberg, A.G. and Gordon, P.D. (1993) *International Group Accounting – Issues in European Harmonisation*. London: Routledge.

Newspapers and journals

FT World Accounting Report, published monthly by *Financial Times* Publications.

The Corporate Accountant, Insert in *The Accountant*, UK monthly. London: Lafferty Publications.

Chapter 10

The Netherlands

10.1 INTRODUCTION[1]

The Netherlands is part of a region which has at times in history been called the Low Countries. The national language is Netherlandish, referred to in the English language as Dutch. There has been a long history of active involvement in commerce and sea trade. There is a treatise on double entry bookkeeping, written in Dutch, published in 1543, and double entry bookkeeping was used by merchants in the Low Countries at an early date in relation to the rest of northern Europe. The Reformation split the Low Countries in terms of religious affiliation, with protestantism dominating in the north and Roman Catholicism in the south. The United Provinces, containing the provinces of the present Netherlands, gained independence in the seventeenth century. Two of those provinces have the name 'Holland' (North Holland and South Holland) and the name is sometimes used incorrectly in English to refer to The Netherlands as a country. The Kingdom of The Netherlands was formed in 1831. The Netherlands was subject to German occupation from 1940 to 1945, the kingdom being restored thereafter.

10.2 THE COUNTRY[2]

The Netherlands has a relatively high population density and occupies low-lying land, much below sea level, which has been progressively reclaimed from the sea.

It may be seen from Exhibit 10.1 that the economy has shown growth of 2.6% per annum over the period 1985–95. Gross domestic product (GDP) is created two-thirds by services, almost one-third by industry, and less than 5% by agriculture. Although apparently quite low, agricultural activity in The Netherlands is higher in percentage terms than in France, Germany or the UK. There has been a sustained period of low inflation and the guilder has remained a strong currency. In manufacturing industry there is no heavy dependency on any one industry. Agriculture has become highly intensive and specialised, producing mostly milk, meat, vegetables and flowers. The insurance and banking sector is particularly significant in the Dutch economy.

The country does not have many natural resources and so the discovery of natural gas in the 1960s in the Dutch sector of the North Sea was very

---

[1] Dijksma and Hoogendoorn (1993), pp. 5–6
[2] Dijksma and Hoogendoorn (1993)

Exhibit 10.1 THE NETHERLANDS: COUNTRY PROFILE, TAKEN FROM EIU STATISTICS

Population	15.5 m.	
Land mass	41,526 sq. km	
GDP per head	US $23,966	
GDP per head in purchasing power parity	74	(USA=100)
Origins of GDP:	%	
Agriculture	3.4	
Industry	29.7	
Services	66.9	
	%	
Real GDP average annual growth 1985–95	2.6	
Inflation, average annual rate 1989–96	2.6	

Source: *The Economist Pocket World in Figures 1998 Edition*, The Economist (1997)

important. Salt is also found in quantities in the north-west. Raw materials are largely imported. The country also serves as a base for transit trade by road and by water (using the River Rhine).

The Netherlands has a positive balance of payments, both on visible and invisible trade. Exports are chiefly of manufactured goods, the largest single category being machinery and transport equipment. Food, drink and tobacco are also a significant export category. The main export destinations are in the EU. Imports are of manufactured goods and raw materials, again mainly from EU countries. Germany is the chief trading partner.

10.3 OVERVIEW OF ACCOUNTING REGULATIONS

10.3.1 Early accounting law[3]

As mentioned in the Introduction, the merchants of the Low Countries were the first in northern Europe to use double entry bookkeeping, described in a Dutch text of 1543 by Jan Ympyn Christoffels. The first statutory accounting rule was published in the 1837 Commercial Code, requiring merchants to keep a daily journal. Company law was revised further in 1928 and 1929, with the next major revision occurring in 1970.

The first statutory accounting law, in 1928, contained rules dealing with the assets side of the balance sheet but saying little about the liabilities or the profit and loss account. For a period of 40 years thereafter, much discussion ensued and working papers were written by consultative groups from time to time, but there was no substantial change in the law. Managers of large companies would adopt

---

[3] Bouma and Feenstra (1997), pp. 177–8; Hoogendoorn (1995), p. 577; Zeff (1993); Camfferman (1995)

good practices indicated in non-mandatory recommendations but in the main companies enjoyed considerable flexibility.

The emphasis changed with the Act of 1970 on Annual Financial Statements. This started a stronger emphasis on the influence of law on accounting practice. The Act had been ten years in development, having been prepared by a committee of the Ministry of Justice. Parliamentary debate and related processes had taken five of those years. (As a technical matter, the 1970 Act was incorporated in the Civil Code in 1976.) Dutch law introduced the Fourth and Seventh Directives by Acts of 1983 and 1988, causing further amendment to the Civil Code.

The apparent lack of urgency to develop statutory regulation of accounting before 1970 may be attributed to the strong influence of the business economics approach. The term 'business economics' (*bedrijfseconomie*) is commonly encountered in discussions of Dutch accounting theory and practice. Historically accounting has been considered to be part of business economics, although the links may have diminished in recent years. Business economics is an educational programme designed by Theodore Limperg (1879–1961) as a set of different disciplines comprising theories of:

- value (as replacement value), capital and income measurement
- product costing
- finance
- industrial organisation
- organisation and management
- auditing.

The subject of business economics has had academic status since around 1920, and accounting theory developed out of business economics. In particular, Limperg wrote a theory of current values (replacement cost accounting) which had considerable influence on accounting thought in The Netherlands and which was taken up by some companies, in whole or in part, as will be explained later.

10.3.2 The introduction of consolidated accounting[4]

Since 1971 almost all public companies and most smaller companies have prepared consolidated financial statements. Consequently many aspects of the Seventh Directive were in place before its formal implementation in the 1988 Act. The 1988 Act defines a group as an economic unit in which legal entities are linked through organisational ties. The Dutch legislators, in implementing the relevant Articles of the Seventh Directive, mainly applied the options which were close to the rules already in existence for the definition of a group. However the definition of a subsidiary moved towards a majority of the voting rights rather than the previous approach based on participation in the share capital. Joint ventures are accounted for either by proportional consolidation or by equity accounting.

---

[4] Klaassen (1993), Chapter 13; Hoogendoorn (1995), p. 574

INSTITUTIONS

10.4.1 Political and economic system[5]

The Netherlands has a constitutional monarchy. The constitution divides the government into three branches: the legislative, represented by the States General (Parliament); the executive, represented by the Crown; and the judiciary. The States General has an Upper Chamber (First Chamber) of 75 members and a Lower Chamber (Second Chamber) of 150 members. The Upper Chamber is elected indirectly by the members of the provincial governing bodies. General elections to the Lower Chamber must be held at least every four years. Legislation originates in the Lower Chamber and is passed subject to the approval of the Upper Chamber. The Crown is formed by the sovereign (Queen) and the cabinet of Ministers. The sovereign has a symbolic function, without direct influence on political issues. The prime minister presides over a cabinet in government. The cabinet members are not members of Parliament but are responsible to Parliament. There is a Council of State which, as a non-political advisory body, advises on all legislation.

Legislation was enacted in 1950 to provide councils of persons appointed from various sectors of the economy. These councils were intended to help the government cope with the complexities of modern life and provide, on a regular basis, expert advice to the government. They also have defined legislative powers. The Social Economic Council is the most important.

The Netherlands is a highly industrialised nation.[6] It has a history of being a centre for commerce and banking, and today there is a particularly strong insurance industry. The economy is characterised by an open market and an international orientation, and there is a mixture of public and private ownership of companies. The business sector is dominated by a relatively small number of multinational companies. Strong economic growth in 1990 and 1991 was followed by a period of stabilisation.

The Social Economic Council supervises production associations and commodity boards. It implements various Acts, including the Act on Structure Companies. Among other activities, it also oversees the work of the Council for Annual Reporting. The role of the Council for Annual Reporting is consequently strengthened.

10.4.2 Legal system[7]

The Dutch legal system is based on laws, jurisprudence (verdicts), treaties and custom. The laws are passed by Parliament. The courts will recognise international treaties and will use long-established customs as an aid to the interpretation of statutes. The system of law in The Netherlands is within the Romano-Germanic family and of the European tradition, alongside France but distinguished from Germany. This common basis of underlying legal systems might lead to an expectation of some similarities with accounting in continental European countries.

---

[5] CCH (1997)
[6] Dijksma and Hoogendoorn (1993), pp. 6, 25–6
[7] CCH (1997)

10.4.2.1 Sources of corporate law[8]

Corporate law in The Netherlands is contained in Book 2 of the Civil Code. The Civil Code is a major item of legislation covering all aspects of corporate law as it affects business entities. In particular, the Fourth and Seventh Directives have been incorporated in the Code. The Act on Annual Accounts of 1971 was incorporated in the Civil Code in 1976. Amending rules, bringing into effect the Fourth Directive, were applied in 1983. The law was further amended for the Seventh Directive in 1988. Simplifications and improvements relating to small and medium-sized companies (SMEs) were added in 1990.

10.4.2.2 Types of business organisation[9]

The legal forms of business entity are regulated by the Civil Code. Public limited companies (*Naamloze vennootschap*) have the letters 'NV' before or after their name. Private limited companies (*Besloten vennootschap*) use the letters 'BV'. Both types of company are incorporated with limited liability. The chief distinction is that private limited companies may not be listed or traded on a stock exchange, while listed companies must be public companies. The shares of the private limited company must be registered with the company but the shares of a public limited company may be either bearer shares or registered shares (*see* Exhibit 10.2). In practice, the BV form is almost always chosen for wholly-owned subsidiaries and for joint venture situations with a limited number of shareholders.

Exhibit 10.2 NV AND BV: COMPARISON OF KEY FEATURES

	NV	*BV*
Shares	May have either registered or bearer shares, share certificates may be issued for either type	Only registered shares, share certificates may not be issued
Minimum capital	Hfl100,000	Hfl40,000
Transferability	No restrictions on transferability	Articles of association must contain certain restrictions on the transferability of shares
Restriction on acquisition and holding of own shares	May hold up to 10% of issued share capital	May hold up to 50% of issued share capital
Loans for purchase of own shares	Not allowed	Allowed in certain circumstances

---

[8] CCH (1997); Schoonderbeek (1994), p. 134
[9] Dijksma and Hoogendoorn (1993), pp. 19–21

Larger companies in both categories have a special description of 'structure-NV' or 'structure-BV'. Special rules exist for these companies. The size criteria are based on the equity of the company, number of employees (at least 100) and the presence of a works council.

10.4.2.3 Enterprise Chamber[10]

The Enterprise Chamber is a special chamber of the Courts of Justice which gives rulings on allegations of failure to comply with the legal requirements of financial accounting. The verdicts are specific to the cases considered, but may also have a wider influence. The Chamber may state that the financial accounts are incorrect and may give an order to the company containing precise requirements as to the preparation of financial statements, now or in the future. It may also give instructions of a more general nature which may cause a particular accounting policy to become unacceptable. The verdict may include comment on the auditor, which may in turn lead to professional disciplinary action being taken by the professional body.

10.4.2.4 Council for Annual Reporting

The Council for Annual Reporting (*Raad voor de Jaarverslaggeving, or RJ*) is a third stage in the process of setting accounting standards (the first being the Civil Code and the second the Enterprise Chamber). It is not part of the formal legal system but is an essential element in the implementation of the law. It operates under the oversight of the Social Economic Council (*see* subsection 10.4.1). The first two steps are the establishment of statute law (*see* subsection 10.4.2.1) and the work of the Enterprise Chamber (*see* subsection 10.4.2.3). The Council for Annual Reporting was established in 1982, replacing an earlier body set up in 1971 at the request of the government. The Council acts on behalf of the Foundation for Annual Reporting and comprises representatives of three interest groups – users, preparers and auditors. The users are represented by the two main trade unions and a representative from the Dutch Financial Analysts' Society, the preparers by the principal industrial confederation and the auditors by their professional body, NIVRA. It is interesting to note the emphasis placed on employees as users.

The Council reviews the accounting principles which are applied in practice and gives its opinion on the acceptability of those principles within the framework of the law. Opinions are published as Guidelines for Annual Reporting.

10.4.2.5 Corporate governance[11]

A Dutch corporation is managed by a *board of management* comprising one or more members. They are all called 'managing directors' but the closest Anglo-Saxon equivalent would be executive director. These directors are appointed and dismissed by the general meeting. The managing board as a whole is responsible for the proper management of the corporation. For a structure corporation, the supervisory board appoints and dismisses the managing director.

---

[10] Bouma and Feenstra (1997), p. 182; Schoonderbeek (1994), pp. 134–5; Klaassen (1980)
[11] Dijksma and Hoogendoorn (1993), pp. 21–6; CCH (1997)

For structure corporations (large companies) a *supervisory board* is a requirement. Other companies may have a supervisory board if they wish to do so. The functions and responsibilities of the supervisory board are laid down in the Civil Code and include the following powers:

- to appoint and dismiss members of the managing board
- to determine the financial statements
- to approve certain decisions of the managing board.

In particular, the supervisory board adopts the annual accounts. It has unrestricted access to the corporate premises and the right to inspect the books and records. Each member of the supervisory board must sign the annual accounts, and members of the supervisory board may be personally liable for the consequences of issuing misleading accounts. Members of the supervisory board of a structure corporation are appointed by co-option (existing members invite new members to join them). The general meeting, the works council and the managing board have the right to recommend for co-option. The general meeting and the works council have the right to object to a recommended co-option.

The *works council* is compulsory for larger companies. Its purpose is to allow the workforce to debate with the executive board twice a year on important issues. The works council must receive the annual accounts and a report on the company's social policy. It must be allowed to give advice when significant plans are being made and it must be consulted on matters regarding conditions of employment.

Audit committees are found in some companies in The Netherlands, as a relatively recent introduction. An important function of the audit committee is to formalise contact between the supervisory board and the internal and external auditors. It appears that the idea originated around 1978 in the supervisory board of Royal Dutch/Shell, drawing on the company's experience in Canada and the USA. Its use appears limited to larger listed companies, particularly those in the financial sector. The audit committee will typically comprise a mixture of members of the supervisory board, representatives of the financial management and representatives of the internal audit department. Effectively, the audit committee is a subcommittee of the supervisory board. The audit committee will typically meet prior to the annual audit to discuss the audit plan and shortly after completion of the audit to discuss the results of the audit and the annual financial statements.

Internal audit developed particularly strongly in Philips NV in the 1950s and 1960s, giving an opinion on the financial statements in a form comparable to that given by the external auditor. However, as the use of internal audit spread across other companies the operational functions increased and the financial audit aspect decreased in relative terms. International influences from the 1970s onwards caused the major Dutch companies to look to the examples of the USA and the UK in the use of the internal audit function.

The *external auditor* is appointed by the general meeting, the supervisory board or the management board (in that order) and may be dismissed by the appointing group or by the general meeting.

10.4.3 Taxation system

10.4.3.1 Tax law[12]

In The Netherlands accounting and taxation are formally independent, both for individual accounts and group accounts. Both sets of regulations leave scope for flexibility. Tax law relating to incorporated businesses is contained in the Law on Corporation Tax.

10.4.3.2 Taxable profit

Taxable profit is based on the annual profit of the company, calculated according to tax rules. The calculation requires comparison of the shareholders' equity at the start and end of the year, excluding contributions and distributions. The difference is taxable profit. Profit should be determined using 'sound business practice'. There is flexibility in that the accounting policy used for the calculation of taxable profit may differ from that used for accounting profit. The net income for tax purposes is normally lower than that reported for accounting purposes because of this flexibility.

Tax rules place some limits on flexibility. Only historical cost depreciation is allowed and, although depreciation rates are not explicitly specified, there are acceptable ranges for each type of asset. Inventory may be valued using FIFO, LIFO, average cost or base stock methods. Income from participating interests (subsidiaries and associates) is not taxable, to avoid double taxation of the same profit.

In calculating annual profit for tax purposes, transfers to tax-free reserves are permitted. These are the asset replacement reserve, the reserve for equalisation of expenses and the self-insurance reserve.

10.4.3.3 Tax on distributions

There is a dividend withholding tax based on dividend income. Withholding tax on dividends is seen as an advance personal income tax. The tax is withheld by companies resident in The Netherlands. Shareholders receive a tax credit in respect of the withholding tax and the dividends are partly exempt.

10.4.4 Corporate financing system[13]

10.4.4.1 Equity investors

There is an established stock market in Amsterdam and other related markets including the European Options Exchange, the Amsterdam Futures Market, the Rotterdam Energy Futures Exchange, the over-the-counter (OTC) market and a market for private arrangements.

The Amsterdam Stock Exchange (Chapter 1, Exhibit 1.3) is relatively significant in relation to the GDP of the country. However, the frequent turnover is dominated by a relatively small number of companies and the Amsterdam exchange is not a

---

[12] Dijksma and Hoogendoorn (1993), Chapter 4; Coopers and Lybrand (1992)
[13] Dijksma and Hoogendoorn (1993), Chapter 3

significant source of new capital. The companies listed are relatively large in market capitalisation. Exhibit 1.4 shows that the stock market in The Netherlands is very small in international terms.

10.4.4.2 Top companies[14]

From the *Financial Times FT 500* annual survey there are ten Dutch companies in the top 500 world companies, measured by market capitalisation. In addition there are three companies jointly located in The Netherlands and the UK and one jointly located in The Netherlands and Belgium. Two of the joint Dutch/UK companies, Royal Dutch Petroleum (the UK company is Shell) and Unilever, feature in the top 20 European companies, as does one wholly Dutch Company, ING Group. The top ten listed companies in The Netherlands are shown in Exhibit 10.3.

Exhibit 10.3 TOP TEN LISTED COMPANIES IN THE NETHERLANDS, BY MARKET CAPITALISATION

Name	Market cap $m	Rank in Europe	Sector
1 Royal Dutch Petroleum[1]	118,725	1	Oil international
2 ING Group	37,346	19	Insurance – multiline
3 Unilever NV[1]	33,790	8	Food processors
4 Philips	29,016	29	Electronical equipment
5 ABN Amro Holdings	27,864	35	Commercial banks
6 Aegon	22,874	46	Insurance, multiline
7 KPN	18,292	65	Telephone companies
8 Fortis AG[2]	16,095	75	Insurance, multiline
9 Ahold	13,808	85	Retail – grocery chain
10 Akzo-Nobel	12,038	98	Chemicals (diversified)

[1] Joint with UK
[2] Joint with Belgium, joint company having higher ranking in total
Source: Survey *FT 500*, extracted from *Financial Times*, 22 January 1998, p. 19

10.4.4.3 Banking

There is an active banking sector. Credit banks grant loans to businesses, and specialist financial institutions offer finance for special purposes such as business start-ups and export finance.

10.4.5 The accounting profession[15]

The origins of the accounting profession may be traced to the last decades of the nineteenth century when the role of accountants developed from bookkeeping to auditing as limited companies grew in importance. The separation of management

---

[14] *Financial Times*, FT 500 Survey, 22 January 1998
[15] Bouma and Feenstra (1997), pp. 192–3; Hoogendoorn (1995), pp. 555–7

and ownership of companies created a demand for auditors having independent and professional judgement. Other duties such as internal auditing, governmental auditing and management advisory work also developed.

The Netherlands Institute of Accountants was established in 1895 with the purpose of creating statutory rules for the accounting profession, although the rules did not materialise. No further significant legislative action arose until the Chartered Accountants Act of 1962, which reserved the auditing of financial statements for *registeraccountants* (*RA*). The same law created the *Nederlands Instituut van Registeraccountants*, *NIVRA*, as the Dutch institute of chartered accountants. Another body, the *Accountants-Administratieconsulenten* (*AA*) came into existence in 1974, providing accounting services directed more at SMEs. Implementation of the Eighth Directive in Dutch Law in 1993 gave the right of auditing to both *NIVRA* and *AA*, but in practice large companies choose *NIVRA* members as their auditors.

The education and examination of *RA*s is considerably more onerous than that required by the Eighth Directive. It lasts from 8 to 12 years, embracing undergraduate and postgraduate study as well as professional training.

NIVRA issues auditing guidelines but does not issue accounting standards or guidelines. It does, however, participate in accounting guidelines through membership of the Council for Annual Reporting. However, departures from the Guidelines for Annual Reporting are not referred to in the report of the independent auditor.

10.4.6 External influences

The accounting system of The Netherlands is very clearly individualistic and has developed under internal national influences. It could be said that the Napoleonic influence may be seen in the legacy of a Commercial Code, although the French model was soon replaced by a domestic Code.

As a founder member of the EU, The Netherlands influenced the formation of directives. The Netherlands was also a founder member of the IASC. Former colonies of The Netherlands, mainly the Dutch East Indies (now Indonesia), have accounting practices reflecting the Dutch influence. It has been suggested that the Dutch influence made it relatively easy for Indonesia to create national rules closely aligned with IASs.[16]

The large multinational companies which have their base in The Netherlands have created their own mixture of harmonised accounting practices to meet their specific needs and have in some matters influenced domestic practices of competitors.

It has been suggested that a willingness to consider foreign ideas has been a continuing characteristic of Dutch accounting, but uncritical reception has been rare.[17] Until the 1970s unique features of Dutch accounting were a source of pride. Perceptions of the value of harmonisation are seen as a feature of more recent years.

---

[16] *FT World Accounting Report*. August/September 1996, pp. iii–v
[17] Camfferman (1995)

10.5 SOCIETAL CULTURE AND ACCOUNTING SUBCULTURE

10.5.1 Hofstede's cultural dimensions

Exhibit 10.4 reproduces part of the table set out in Chapter 2, section 2.4, showing the scores and rankings for The Netherlands from Hofstede's (1984) work on cultural dimensions.

Exhibit 10.4 THE NETHERLANDS: SCORES AND RANKINGS FOR INDIVIDUAL COUNTRIES FROM HOFSTEDE'S (1984) CULTURAL DIMENSION RESEARCH

Individualism versus collectivism		*Large power distance versus small power difference*		*Strong uncertainty avoidance versus weak uncertainty avoidance*		*Low nurture versus high nurture*	
Score	*Rank*	*Score*	*Rank*	*Score*	*Rank*	*Score*	*Rank*
80	4/5	38	40	53	35	14	51

10.5.2 Culture and accounting

It was shown in Chapter 2 that Hofstede grouped The Netherlands in the cultural area he described as Nordic, a group which also contained Denmark, Finland, Norway and Sweden. Gray (1988) maintained this single Nordic grouping in his analysis relating Hofstede's cultural dimensions to accounting values of a country (*see* Chapter 4, Exhibit 4.5). That grouping is somewhat general for the purposes of this chapter, particularly since other studies of clusters of accounting characteristics have identified The Netherlands as having very distinctive accounting values. Exhibit 10.5 sets out an interpretation of Hofstede's scores of cultural values, for use in later sections of this chapter, and indicates Gray's classification for the Nordic group as a whole. Each of the subsections 10.7.1–10.7.4 will provide an evaluation consistent with Gray's general approach but specific to The Netherlands. Those sections indicate that Gray's analysis points in the right direction in each case, but may understate the strength of the accounting values in being averaged over a larger group. It is worth noting at this stage that while all Hofstede's scores would contribute to an expectation of strong professionalism and flexibility in accounting values (rather than Gray's classifications as 'moderate' or 'marginal'), the accounting values of optimism and transparency are linked to conflicting pressures where strong individualism acts in the opposite direction to other cultural values.

Exhibit 10.5 LINKING GRAY'S (1988) ACCOUNTING VALUES TO HOFSTEDE'S (1984) CULTURAL DIMENSIONS, IN THE MANNER PROPOSED BY GRAY

Gray's accounting values – classification	Cultural dimensions affecting the country's accounting values	Interpretation of Hofstede's scores of cultural values for The Netherlands (based on scores in Exhibit 10.4)
Professionalism (moderate)	Professionalism tends to be associated with: • Individualism • Weak uncertainty avoidance • Small power distance	Strong individualism Tendency to uncertainty avoidance Clearly small power distance
Flexibility (marginal)	Uniformity tends to be associated with: • Strong uncertainty avoidance • Large power distance • Collectivism	Tendency to uncertainty avoidance Clearly small power distance Strong individualism
Optimism (moderate)	Conservatism tends to be associated with: • Strong uncertainty avoidance • Collectivism • High nurture	Tendency to uncertainty avoidance Strong individualism High nurture
Transparency (moderate)	Secrecy tends to be associated with: • Strong uncertainty avoidance • Large power distance • Collectivism • High nurture	Tendency to uncertainty avoidance Clearly small power distance Strong individualism High nurture

10.6 ACCOUNTING REGULATIONS AND THE IASC[18]

Salter *et al.* (1996) showed that, following the IASC comparability project, The Netherlands was below the average score for percentage agreement between the IASs and the national accounting practice (*see* Chapter 5, subsection 5.6.3.4). Exhibit 10.6 shows the current position.

---

[18] Bouma and Feenstra (1997), p. 193; Hoogendoorn (1995), pp. 567, 573, 616

Exhibit 10.6 COMPARISON OF ACCOUNTING PRACTICES IN THE NETHERLANDS WITH REQUIREMENTS OF IASs: KEY SIMILARITIES AND DIFFERENCES

IAS	Subject of IAS	Practice in The Netherlands	Ref
Disclosure and presentation			
	General aspects consolidated in IAS 1 (revised)		
IAS 1	Fair Presentation	'True and fair' requirement	7.2.3 7.5.1
	Disclosure of Accounting Policies (former IAS 1)	Generally in agreement	
	Information to be Disclosed in Financial Statements (former IAS 5)	Generally in agreement	
	Presentation of Current Assets and Current Liabilities (former IAS 13)	Generally in agreement	
	Specific aspects		
IAS 7	Cash Flow Statements	Not required by regulation except for new Stock Exchange listings, but provided by most listed companies	7.2.2
IAS 8	Net Profit or Loss for the Period, Fundamental Errors and Changes in Accounting Policies	Certain unusual items may be taken directly to reserves; interpretation varies	7.3.2 7.5.1
IAS xx	Discontinuing Operations		
IAS 14	Reporting Financial Information by Segments	Disclosure requirement is less than IAS 14	7.5.2
IAS 24	Related Party Disclosure	Generally in agreement	
IAS 33	Earnings per Share		
IAS 34	Interim Financial Reporting		
Asset recognition and measurement			
IAS 2	Inventories	Generally in agreement	7.4.3
IAS 4	Depreciation Accounting	Generally in agreement	7.4.2
IAS 16	Property, Plant and Equipment	Generally in agreement, current value permitted	7.4.2
IAS xx	Impairment of Assets		
IAS 23	Borrowing Costs	Generally in agreement	
IAS 25	Accounting for Investments	More conservative than IAS 25	
IAS 9	Research and Development Costs	Capitalisation permitted, but not required	7.4.6
IAS xx	Intangible Assets	Generally in agreement	7.4.6
Liability recognition and measurement			
IAS 10	Contingencies and Events Occurring After the Balance Sheet Date	Generally in agreement	7.4.5
IAS 12	Income Taxes	Full liability method but permits discounting; other detailed differences	7.3.1
IAS 17	Leases	No specific requirement	7.5.3
IAS 19	Employee Benefits	Differs in detail on back service costs – The Netherlands requires immediate recognition	7.4.5
IAS 32	Financial Instruments: Disclosure and Presentation	Not in legislation	
Recognition of economic activity			
IAS 11	Construction Contracts	No specific requirement	7.4.3
IAS 18	Revenue	Generally in agreement	
IAS 20	Accounting for Government Grants and Disclosure of Government Assistance	Generally in agreement	

▶

331

Exhibit 10.6 continued

IAS	Subject of IAS	Practice in The Netherlands	Ref
Measurement			
IAS 15	Information Reflecting the Effects of Changing Prices	Generally in agreement	7.4.1
IAS 29	Financial Reporting in Hyperinflationary Economies	Not relevant to Dutch economy	
Group accounting			
IAS 21	The Effects of Changes in Foreign Exchange Rates	More flexible than IAS 21	7.3.3
IAS 22	Business Combinations	Generally in agreement	
IAS 27	Consolidated Financial Statements and Accounting for Investments in Subsidiaries	More flexible on exclusion from consolidation	7.5.3
IAS 28	Accounting for Investments in Associates	Generally in agreement, except that entity's own accounts must record investment using equity method, while IAS 28 permits use of cost	
IAS 31	Financial Reporting of Interests in Joint Ventures	Allows both proportionate consolidation and equity accounting	3.2 7.5.3

The IASC web pages give only two companies which have selected accounting methods conforming to IASs; these are Group 4 and Intrum Justitia. Neither is in the *FT 500* for Europe.

The Council for Annual Reporting (*RJ*) has issued opinions which, among other matters, effectively introduce IASs to The Netherlands. It is not compulsory to follow the *RJ*'s guidelines but it is helpful.

The general accounting principles of going concern, consistency, accrual, prudence, substance over form and materiality are contained in the Civil Code (derived from the Fourth Directive). The *RJ* in 1996 published a Dutch translation of the IASC's *Framework for the Preparation and Presentation of Financial Statements*. The Council compares new guidelines with this framework document, indicating that there is a growing influence of the IASC on the work of the Council.

Generally there are strong similarities between Dutch accounting practices and IASs. There is a tendency towards convergence, the use of IAS 7 as a base for cash flow accounting being a specific example. However differences are found where the independent development of highly specific Dutch practices may have preceded the IAS, causing a reluctance to abandon national approaches.

Dutch accounting will probably continue to be influenced by pressures for international harmonisation because there are calls within The Netherlands for less flexibility and for the adoption of IASs as much as possible. Some multinational Dutch companies have indicated a desire for harmonisation by using FASB standards. It may be that when the core IASs are accepted by IOSCO the Dutch companies will prefer these to US standards.

10.7 THE ACCOUNTING SYSTEM

10.7.1 Current regulation[19]

The Civil Code deals with financial statements and related matters in Title 9 of Book 2, *Annual Accounts and Directors' Report*. The 15 sections are shown in Exhibit 10.7.

Exhibit 10.7 SECTIONS OF THE CIVIL CODE

1, 2	General provisions
3	Regulations concerning the balance sheet and the notes
4	Regulations concerning the profit and loss account and the notes
5	Special regulations concerning the notes
6	Regulations concerning valuation principles and the principles underlying the determination of financial results
7	Executive directors' report
8	Other data
9	Audit requirements
10	Publication
11	Exemptions based on the size of the company
12	Specific industries
13	Consolidated financial statements
14	Provisions for banks
15	Provisions for insurance companies

As explained earlier, there are three sources for companies which intend to follow generally acceptable accounting principles in The Netherlands. The word 'acceptable' is used here rather than 'accepted'[20] because there is no specific book of accounting standards such as that found in the USA or the UK. The first source is to follow the Civil Code as statute law. The second is to take note of the verdicts of the Enterprise Chamber and the third is to apply the recommendations of the Council for Annual Reporting (*RJ*). This combination is essential as the key rule for accounting in The Netherlands (comparable to achieving a 'true and fair view' in the UK).

The Enterprise Chamber can only react to complaints – it cannot initiate action. The person making a complaint must prove a direct interest in the financial statements of the company and must state the perceived deficiency. The court hears the complainant, the company's view and the auditor's explanation. Because the Chamber is part of a formal legal process, the number of judgments is relatively small. The formation of the Chamber was seen as being an alternative to creating a supervisory body like the US SEC.

As explained earlier (*see* subsection 10.4.2.4), the recommendations of the Council for Annual Reporting (*RJ*), published in the form of guidelines, are not a

---

[19] Dijksma and Hoogendoorn (1993), p. 57
[20] Parker (1995), p. 208

statutory requirement. They are, however, regarded as authoritative pronouncements and an important frame of reference for the auditor in forming an opinion on financial statements. Departures from the guidelines of the *RJ* are possible and are not referred to in the auditor's report.

10.7.2 Professionalism versus statutory control

The strength of the business economics background in The Netherlands has resulted in strong professionalism in many respects. In that context Gray's (1988) classification as moderate professionalism is perhaps surprising. However the regulatory framework does circumscribe the exercise of professional judgement in that the recommendations of the *RJ* should be noted as interpretations of law and statements of best practice. Formats of consolidated accounts normally reflect those of the parent company. Although there is a lack of direct governmental involvement in the standard setting process there is an elaborate network established under statute and regulation which provides an indirect constraint.

10.7.2.1 Council for Annual Reporting[21]

The composition of the Council for Annual Reporting (*RJ*) reflects the fundamental legal requirement of financial accounts that the bases underlying the valuation of assets and liabilities and the determination of the financial results comply with standards acceptable in the business environment.

The Council reviews accounting principles used in practice and gives opinions on the acceptability of the principles within the framework of law. It does not in itself have statutory powers or duties and there is no government representative on the Council. The Council's opinions have no statutory backing, although they do provide an important frame of reference for the auditor and for the courts in arriving at views on the application of accounting policies. The Council contains a range of interest groups working together to achieve a consensus. It cannot strictly be proposed as an example of professionalism because the influence of *NIVRA* is only one of the voices on the Council, but it indicates the potential for interesting social interaction where statutory control is not imposed.

10.7.2.2 Formats of financial statements[22]

The financial statements comprise the balance sheet, the profit and loss account, the notes and other prescribed information. The formats of the Fourth Directive have been adopted. Both horizontal and vertical balance sheet forms are in use by companies. The profit and loss account is usually in vertical format but both functional formats and type of expenditure formats are used (*see* Chapter 7 on the EU).

Group accounts follow formats similar to those of individual companies. Accounting policies of groups are normally the same as those used in the legal entity's own financial statements; different principles may be used only for valid reasons which are to be disclosed in the notes. Group account financial statements

---

[21] Schoonderbeek (1994), pp. 135–6; Hoogendoorn (1995), p. 561
[22] Hoogendoorn (1995), pp. 565–82

are illustrated by Akzo-Nobel (*see* Exhibit 10.8) where the profit and loss account is in 'type of expenditure' format. The balance sheet is a list of assets, subdivided as non-current and current, but does not highlight a net current assets position.

A cash flow statement is not obligatory except that the Stock Exchange requires it for new companies seeking a listing. The guidelines of the *RJ* recommended in 1996 that large companies should include a cash flow statement based on IAS 7.

Exhibit 10.8 AKZO-NOBEL: CONSOLIDATED BALANCE SHEET AND CONSOLIDATED INCOME STATEMENT

Consolidated statement of income

Millions of guilders	NOTE	1996	1995
Net sales	1	22,438	21,488
Cost of sales		(13,684)	(13,159)
Gross margin		8,754	8,329
Selling expenses		(4,591)	(4,247)
Research and development expenses		(1,137)	(1,112)
General and administrative expenses		(1,083)	(1,086)
Miscellaneous revenue from operations		88	89
		(6,723)	(6,356)
Operating income		2,031	1,973
Financing charges	2	(263)	(260)
Operating income less financing charges		1,768	1,713
Taxes	3	(507)	(495)
Earnings of consolidated companies from normal operations, after taxes		1,261	1,218
Earnings from nonconsolidated companies	4	91	137
Earnings from normal operations, after taxes		1,352	1,355
Extraordinary items after taxes	5		2
Earnings before minority interest		1,352	1,357
Minority interest		(34)	(43)
Net income		1,318	1,314

See notes on pages 61 and 62.

| Exhibit 10.8 | continued |

Consolidated balance sheet

AFTER ALLOCATION OF PROFIT

Millions of guilders, December 31	NOTE	1996		1995	
Assets					
Noncurrent assets					
Intangible assets	7		**167**		146
Property, plant and equipment	8		**9,486**		8,479
Financial noncurrent assets:	9				
– nonconsolidated companies		**1,236**		1,157	
– other financial noncurrent assets		**383**		268	
			1,619		1,425
			11,272		10,050
Current assets					
Inventories	10	**3,878**		3,632	
Receivables	11	**4,366**		4,202	
Cash and cash equivalents	12	**891**		699	
			9,135		8,533
Total			**20,407**		18,583
Equity and liabilities					
Equity	13				
Akzo Nobel N.V. stockholders' equity		**7,703**		6,605	
Minority interest		**238**		193	
			7,941		6,798
Provisions	14		**3,531**		3,387
Long-term debt	15		**2,148**		2,718
Short-term debt					
Short-term borrowings	16	**2,485**		1,619	
Current liabilities	17	**4,302**		4,061	
			6,787		5,680
Total			**20,407**		18,583

Source: Akzo-Nobel NV, annual report, 1996, pp. 58–9

10.7.2.3 'True and fair view'

The wording of the Dutch law, incorporating the Fourth Directive, uses the phrase *'een getrouw beeld'*, which may be translated as 'a faithful picture'. Nobes's (1984) classification of The Netherlands in respect to 'true and fair view' is that it is used by directors and auditors as the basic principle in interpreting the law and guidelines. The 1970 law had used wording which could be translated as 'presents faithfully, clearly and consistently over time' and also 'presents an insight such that a well-founded opinion can be formed'.[23] Thus in The Netherlands, as in the UK and Ireland, the notion of a true and fair view predated the Fourth Directive.

10.7.3 Uniformity versus flexibility

Gray's (1988) classification was of marginal flexibility. There is high flexibility in the separation of tax law from accounting law and relative freedom in reporting extraordinary items. Foreign currency translation allows considerable flexibility. In the light of these examples, Gray's classification seems somewhat strange. However, there are matters which lead to conservatism (see below) where the regulatory influence is stronger, such as the requirement for making legal reserves, which in practice limit the amount of distributable profit so that the flexibility of accounting practice on separate line items is modified by a cautious attitude to the overall result.

10.7.3.1 Relationship between tax law and accounting law[24]

The differences between profit for tax purposes and profit for accounting purposes may be grouped as temporary differences and permanent differences. Temporary differences arise from:

- choosing different accounting policies for each profit calculation
- the use of tax-free reserves
- early recognition of costs for accounting purposes which is not accepted by tax rules
- tax loss carryforward
- use of current cost accounting.

Permanent differences arise from:

- gains or losses recognised as changes in shareholders' equity (such as cumulative effects of changes in accounting policy)
- accounting costs which are not allowed for tax purposes (such as business gifts)
- gains reported for accounting purposes such as income from subsidiaries and associated companies.

It is possible for the taxable income and the accounting income to be the same, especially in small companies. For most larger companies the taxable income will be lower than the accounting income, and so there will be a provision for doubtful

---

[23] Zeff (1990)
[24] Hoogendoorn (1996), pp. 875–7; Hoogendoorn (1995)

debts included with the debtors. The accounting rules allow the provision for deferred tax to be carried in the balance sheet at book value or at discounted present value, but in practice the discounted present value is rarely used. The accounting law on deferred tax is generally consistent with the revised IAS 12, except that the IAS does not permit discounting.

10.7.3.2 Extraordinary items[25]

The Civil Code requires extraordinary items to be reported separately in the profit and loss account. Frequency of occurrence is an important factor in identifying extraordinary items. The definition is not dissimilar to that of IAS 8 but the interpretation is very different. Examples of items which would be treated as extraordinary in The Netherlands but not under IAS 8 are:

- gains or losses on the disposal of participating interests
- changes arising from reorganisation or related to discontinuity
- special provisions, such as those for litigation
- insurance recoveries, to the extent that they differ from the book value of the assets lost.

10.7.3.3 Foreign currency translation[26]

Foreign currency translation appeared as a problem in Dutch accounting when currencies first floated in the 1970s. Neither accounting theory nor business economics provided a solution, and there was no guidance in the 1970 Act. Some Dutch corporations turned to FASB or the AICPA guidance provided in the USA, others did not disclose their policy, and there was considerable lack of uniformity. From the 1980s the existence of IAS 21, together with the UK SSAP 20 (*Foreign Currency Translation*) and the USA SFAS 52 (*Foreign Currency Translation*) have created greater comparability as multinationals switched to the closing rate method of translation of foreign subsidiaries. This is an area in which there has been considerable flexibility and where multinational companies have led the development of a national practice. The motivation for companies to prefer the closing rate method was to avoid having swings in exchange rates reflected in the profit and loss account.

In relation to translation of the financial statements of subsidiary companies, IAS 21 requires a distinction to be made between those foreign operations that are integral to the operations of the reporting enterprise and those foreign entities that are more independent of the reporting enterprise. The *RJ* allows all foreign-based operations to be grouped in one of these categories for practical reasons, depending on the nature of the major subsidiaries.

10.7.3.4 Joint Dutch/UK companies

The top ten listed companies in The Netherlands include two joint Dutch/UK companies. These are Royal Dutch/Shell and Unilever. Reed Elsevier is also a major

---

[25] Hoogendoorn (1995), p. 613
[26] Bouma and Feenstra (1997), pp. 189–90; Hoogendoorn (1995), p. 620

Dutch/UK company, ranked 62nd in Europe. They create their own flexibility, each in a different way, and none refers specifically to compliance with IASs.

Royal Dutch/Shell (Exhibit 10.9) produces accounts conforming to GAAP of The Netherlands and US GAAP. The flexibility of approach in The Netherlands allows the company to choose accounting methods which are acceptable in the more restrictive US regime. The company claims its approach is substantially similar to UK accounting practice other than in the provision for deferred taxation.

Exhibit 10.9 ROYAL DUTCH/SHELL: NOTES ON ACCOUNTING POLICIES

NOTES TO FINANCIAL STATEMENTS

1 The Royal Dutch/Shell Group of Companies

The Parent Companies, Royal Dutch Petroleum Company (Royal Dutch) and The "Shell" Transport and Trading Company, p.l.c. (Shell Transport) are holding companies which together own, directly or indirectly, investments in numerous companies known collectively as the Royal Dutch/Shell Group. Group companies are engaged in all principal aspects of the oil and natural gas business throughout the world. They also have substantial chemical and coal interests. These activities are conducted in more than 120 countries and are subject to changing economic, regulatory and political conditions.

Arrangements between Royal Dutch and Shell Transport provide *inter alia*, that notwithstanding variations in shareholdings, Royal Dutch and Shell Transport shall share in the aggregate net assets and in the aggregate dividends and interest received from Group companies in the proportion 60:40. It is further arranged that the burden of all taxes in the nature of or corresponding to an income tax leviable in respect of such dividends and interest shall fall in the same proportion.

The 60:40 arrangements referred to above have been supplemented by further arrangements, beginning with Group dividends payable to the Parent Companies in respect of 1977, whereby each Parent Company is to bring into account towards its share in the 60:40 division of dividends from Group companies, tax credits and other tax benefits which are related to the liability to tax of a Group company and which arise to the Parent Company or which would arise to the holders of its ordinary shares if there were to be an immediate full onward distribution to them of Group dividends (for which purpose all shareholders are assumed to be individuals resident and subject to tax in the country of residence of the Parent Company in question).

2 Accounting policies

Nature of the financial statements

The accounts of the Parent Companies are not included in the financial statements, the objective of which is to demonstrate the financial position, results of operations and cash flows of a group of undertakings in which each Parent Company has an interest in common whilst maintaining its separate identity. The financial statements reflect an aggregation in sterling of the accounts of companies in which Royal Dutch and Shell Transport together, either directly or indirectly, have control either through a majority of the voting rights or the right to exercise a controlling influence. Investments in companies over which Group companies have significant influence but not control are classified as associated companies and are accounted for on the equity basis. Certain joint ventures are taken up in the financial statements in proportion to the relevant Group interest.

The financial statements have been prepared under the historical cost convention. They have been prepared in all material respects in accordance with generally accepted accounting principles in the Netherlands and the United States. Group accounting policies are also substantially consistent with accounting principles generally accepted in the United Kingdom, with the notable exception of the provision for deferred taxation.

The preparation of financial statements in conformity with generally accepted accounting principles requires management to make estimates and assumptions that affect the amounts reported in the financial statements and notes thereto. Actual results could differ from those estimates.

REPORT OF THE AUDITORS

To Royal Dutch Petroleum Company and The "Shell" Transport and Trading Company, p.l.c.

In our opinion, the financial statements referred to above present fairly, in all material respects, the financial position of the Royal Dutch/Shell Group of Companies at December 31, 1996 and 1995 and the results of its operations and its cash flows for each of the three years in the period ended December 31, 1996 in accordance with generally accepted accounting principles in the Netherlands and the United States.

KPMG Accountants N.V., The Hague

Ernst & Young, London

Price Waterhouse LLP, New York

March 13, 1997

Source: Royal Dutch/Shell Group, annual report, 1996, pp. 39, 33

Unilever (Exhibit 10.10) makes no mention in the English-language version of the accounting policy as regards the system of GAAP being followed. However, the auditor's report confirms that the practices used give a true and fair view in accordance with the Civil Code and the UK Companies Act.

Reed Elsevier (Exhibit 10.11) refers to UK GAAP and Dutch GAAP.

Exhibit 10.10 UNILEVER: ACCOUNTING POLICY NOTE AND EXTRACT FROM REPORT OF THE AUDITORS

Unilever Group

Accounting policies

Group companies

Group companies are those companies in whose share capital NV or PLC holds an interest directly or indirectly, and whose consolidation is required for the accounts to give a true and fair view.

In order that the consolidated accounts should present a true and fair view, it is necessary to differ from the presentational requirements of the United Kingdom Companies Act 1985 by including amounts attributable to both NV and PLC shareholders in the capital and reserves shown in the balance sheet. The Companies Act would require presentation of the capital and reserves attributable to PLC and NV shareholders as minority interests in the respective consolidated accounts of NV and PLC. This presentation would not give a true and fair view of the effect of the Equalisation Agreement, under which the position of all shareholders is as nearly as possible the same as if they held shares in a single company.

Net profit and profit of the year retained are presented on a combined basis on page 8, with the net profit attributable to NV and PLC shareholders shown separately. Movements in profit retained are analysed between those attributable to NV and PLC shareholders in note 19 on page 19.

Report of the auditors

Report of the auditors to the shareholders of Unilever N.V. and Unilever PLC

Opinion

In our opinion the accounts give a true and fair view of the state of affairs of the Unilever Group, Unilever N.V. and Unilever PLC at 31 December 1996 and of the profit, total recognised gains and cash flows of the Group for the year then ended. In our opinion the accounts of the Unilever Group, and of Unilever N.V. and Unilever PLC respectively, have been properly prepared in accordance with Book 2 of the Civil Code in the Netherlands and the United Kingdom Companies Act 1985.

Coopers & Lybrand N.V.
Registeraccountants
Rotterdam
As auditors of Unilever N.V.

Coopers & Lybrand
Chartered Accountants and Registered Auditors
London
As auditors of Unilever PLC

10 March 1997

Source: Unilever Group, annual report, 1996, pp. 6 and 5

Exhibit 10.11 REED ELSEVIER: ACCOUNTING POLICIES AND ADDITIONAL INFORMATION FOR US INVESTORS

Accounting Policies

These financial statements adopt accounting policies that are in compliance with both UK and Dutch Generally Accepted Accounting Principles ('GAAP') and are presented under the historical cost convention as modified by the revaluation of land and buildings.

BASIS OF COMBINATION

The equalisation agreement between Reed International P.L.C. and Elsevier NV has the effect that their shareholders can be regarded as having the interests of a single economic group. The principal financial statements are, therefore, the combined Reed Elsevier accounts ("the combined financial statements").

The combined financial statements encompass the businesses of Reed Elsevier plc and Elsevier Reed Finance BV and their respective subsidiaries and associates, together with the parent companies, Reed International P.L.C. and Elsevier NV ("the combined businesses").

These financial statements are not for a legal entity and do not, therefore, include all the information required to be disclosed by a company in its accounts under the UK Companies Act or Dutch Civil Code. Full statutory information is given in the Reed Elsevier plc financial statements and in the accounts of the parent companies, Reed International P.L.C. and Elsevier NV, each of which are available from their registered addresses. A list of principal businesses is set out on pages 70 and 71.

Additional Information for US Investors

APPROXIMATE EFFECTS ON NET INCOME OF DIFFERENCES BETWEEN UK AND DUTCH GAAP AND US GAAP

£ million	1996	1995
Net income under UK and Dutch GAAP	604	554
US GAAP adjustments:		
Amortisation of goodwill and other intangibles	(107)	(120)
Deferred taxation	(27)	(31)
Acquisition accounting	(9)	(14)
Sale and lease back	14	1
Pension and other	18	2
Sale of businesses	–	301
Net income under US GAAP	493	693
Analysed:		
Continuing operations	488	304
Discontinued operations – Income from operations	5	36
– Gain on sales net of provisions	–	353
	493	693

The adjustment in relation to the disposal of businesses in 1995 reflects the substantially lower goodwill and intangible asset values attributed to the businesses concerned under US GAAP due to amortisation in prior periods.

Discontinued operations shown in 1996 represent the consumer book publishing operations where it remains the intention to sell the business in due course.

Source: Reed Elsevier, annual report, 1996, pp. 46, 65

10.7.4 Conservatism versus optimism

Gray (1988) classified accounting practice in The Netherlands as having moderate optimism. The availability of current value accounting is perhaps the best known feature of Dutch accounting practice. The flexibility of Dutch accounting allows current value to be reported, but the rules are set to discourage excessive optimism. The law states that the principles of valuation should be applied 'with prudence'.

Where flexibility has allowed an apparently less conservative approach (such as capitalisation of research expenditure) this is countered by a requirement to establish a legal reserve, restricting distributions to shareholders. Provisions also show a tendency to conservatism. Widespread use of direct write-off for goodwill on acquisition leads to lower balance sheet values but higher reported profit.

10.7.4.1 Principles of valuation[27]

General principles are stated in the Civil Code and are consistent with IASs. The general rule is that financial statements should give a true and fair view of capital and income. Specifically, two bases of valuation are allowed: historical cost accounting and current value. Current value accounting is limited to financial and tangible fixed assets and inventories. Regular adjustment for the effect of changing prices (current purchasing power accounting) is not permitted under the Civil Code, contrasting with IAS 15. The Asset Valuation Decree contains rules on the application of current value which may be the replacement value, the recoverable amount or the net realisable value. The choice between the historical cost and current value principles is a free choice, but once the choice has been made the balance sheet and profit and loss account must be consistent within that choice. Furthermore, once current values are used, the revaluations must be regular. Changes in current value are reported in a revaluation reserve.

The use of full current value accounting is relatively rare. One example is Heineken (*see* Exhibit 10.12) which gives a detailed description of the system. There is no mention in the audit report that current cost accounting has been used.

An example of the partial approach is provided by CSM (*see* Exhibit 10.13) which has in past years charged supplementary depreciation on tangible fixed assets. The fixed assets are not revalued. The supplementary depreciation has been charged to a supplementary reserve. However, the company changed its policy to charge historical cost depreciation with effect from 1995/6.

10.7.4.2 Tangible fixed assets[28]

The *RJ* suggests that, where companies choose to adopt current value accounting for some categories of assets, they should do so for all tangible fixed assets or all inventories. However in practice companies will apply current value accounting to subgroups of fixed assets, leaving others at historical cost. However, those reported at current value are revalued regularly and systematically. At the start of the 1990s a survey showed that very few companies used full current value accounting but almost half of listed companies revalued some subset of tangible fixed assets.

---

[27] Hoogendoorn (1995), p. 597
[28] Hoogendoorn (1995), pp. 597–600; Dijksma and Hoogendoorn (1993), p. 123

Exhibit 10.12 HEINEKEN: NOTES DESCRIBING FULL REPLACEMENT COST ACCOUNTING

Accounting policies for the valuation of assets and liabilities

Fixed assets Tangible fixed assets have been valued on the basis of replacement cost and, with the exception of sites, after deduction of cumulative depreciation. The replacement cost is based on valuations by internal and external experts, taking technical and economic developments into account. They are supported by the experience gained in the construction of establishments all over the world. Projects under construction are stated at cost of acquisition. The non-consolidated participations in which a significant influence is exercised over management policy are stated at the Heineken share in the net asset value. This net asset value is determined as far as possible on the basis of the Heineken accounting policies. The other non-consolidated participations are valued at the cost of acquisition, after deduction of provisions considered necessary. Loans to non-consolidated participations and other financial fixed assets are shown at par value, less a provision for bad debts.

Current assets Stocks obtained from third parties have been valued on the basis of replacement cost. The replacement cost is based on the prices of current purchase contracts and on market prices applicable on the balance sheet date. Finished products and products in process are valued at manufacturing cost, based on replacement cost and taking into account the stage of processing. Stocks and spare parts are depreciated on a straight-line basis in view of the reduction of the possibility of use. Provisions on stocks are made up to the recoverable amount or net realizable value, respectively, if this is lower than the replacement value. Prepayments on stocks are stated at par value. Accounts receivable are shown at par value, after deduction of a provision for bad debts and less the amount of deposits due on account of the obligation to take back own packaging materials.

Securities have been valued at the cost of acquisition, unless the market price or the estimated market value of unlisted securities is lower. Cash at bank and in hand is stated at par value.

Revaluations Differences in valuation resulting from revaluation are credited or debited to the Group funds, if applicable after deduction of an amount for deferred tax liabilities.

Auditors' Report

We have audited the 1996 financial statements of Heineken N.V., Amsterdam, as included on pages 45 to 68 of this report. These financial statements are the responsibility of the company's management. Our responsibility is to express an opinion on these financial statements based on our audit.

We conducted our audit in accordance with auditing standards generally accepted in the Netherlands. Those standards require that we plan and perform the audit to obtain reasonable assurance about whether the financial statements are free of material misstatement. An audit includes examining, on a test basis, evidence supporting the amounts and disclosures in the financial statements. An audit also includes assessing the accounting principles used and significant estimates made by management, as well as evaluating the overall financial statement presentation. We believe that our audit provides a reasonable basis for our opinion.

In our opinion, the financial statements give a true and fair view of the financial position of the company as of 31 December 1996 and of the result for the year then ended in accordance with accounting principles generally accepted in the Netherlands and comply with the financial reporting requirements included in Part 9, Book 2, of the Netherlands Civil Code.

Amsterdam, March 13, 1997
KPMG Accountants N.V.

Source: Heineken NV, annual report, 1996, pp. 51, 69

Exhibit 10.13 CSM: NOTES DESCRIBING FORMER USE OF SUPPLEMENTARY DEPRECIATION BASED ON REPLACEMENT VALUE

ACCOUNTING PRINCIPLES

CHANGE IN DEPRECIATION SYSTEM

Up to and including the financial year 1994/95 the depreciation on tangible fixed assets charged in the profit and loss account was based on the replacement value of those assets. Starting with the financial year 1995/96 the depreciation charged in the profit and loss account has been calculated on the basis of purchase price/production cost (historical cost). The comparative figures for 1994/95 in the accounts and in the 'Principal data' on page 1 and the figures for prior financial years in the table 'Ten years in figures' on pages 62 and 63 have been adjusted accordingly.

The table below shows the effect of the change in the depreciation system on the relevant principal data for the year under review and the comparative figures:

	System applied from 1995/96 (historical cost)		System applied up to and including 1994/95 (replacement value)	
	1995/96	1994/95	**1995/96**	1994/95
In millions of guilders				
Depreciation	**93.9**	92.0	**104.5**	102.1
Operating profit	**293.0**	269.7	**282.4**	259.6
Net profit	**201.6**	186.5	**191.0**	176.4
Per share in guilders				
Net profit	**5.17**	4.89	**4.90**	4.62
Cash flow	**7.58**	7.30	**7.58**	7.30

The balance sheet values of the tangible fixed assets are not affected by the change in the depreciation system since they were already valued on the basis of purchase price/production cost.
With effect from 30 September 1995 the supplementary depreciation reserve, amounting to NLG 133.3 million, has been added to the reserves.

Source: CSM, annual report, 1995/6, p. 43

The depreciation method used for accounting purposes may differ from that used for taxation purposes. It is common to find straight-line depreciation used in the accounting profit and loss account. Under the Civil Code there are other reductions in the value of an asset which may have to be recognised. Permanent reductions in value must be charged to profit and loss account. The charge must be reversed if the reduction in value subsequently reverses. Special write-downs allowed for tax purposes may not be reported in the commercial financial statements if they are in excess of what would be justifiable commercially.

10.7.4.3 Stocks and work-in-progress[29]

In general, the Civil Code is similar to IAS 2 in dealing with valuation of stocks. There is a choice between historical cost and current value. FIFO, LIFO, weighted average and base stock are all permitted methods of dealing with changes in the cost of inventories. Accounting for work-in-progress may follow either the percentage of completion or the completed contract method, as permitted under IAS 11. However the Civil Code is more prudent with regard to situations where no reliable estimate can be made of the outcome of the contract. IAS 11 requires revenue in such situations to be reported as equal to costs incurred that are recoverable, so that costs and revenues are reported to give a zero profit measure. This is not permitted in The Netherlands, where the completed contract method is required in these circumstances. Although the outcome in terms of reported profit is zero in both situations, the Dutch approach is more conservative with regard to reported turnover.

10.7.4.4 Legally required reserves[30]

The Civil Code specifies headings for shareholders' equity within the accounts of individual companies. The list of reserves includes the revaluation reserve, other legally required reserves and statutory reserves. The general principle underlying all legally required reserves is protection of creditors from excessive distribution to shareholders.

The revaluation reserve is regarded as a non-distributable reserve, but it may be converted into share capital. Downward valuation reduces the revaluation reserve, but the law requires preservation of a minimum amount represented by values of assets held at the balance sheet date.

Other legal reserves include:

- a reserve for capitalised incorporation expenses and share issue expenses and capitalised research and development costs
- a reserve for undistributed profits of subsidiaries and associated companies accounted for under the equity method, unless the profits can be distributed on the authority of the company and received without limitations.

The reserves may be created by a charge against the profit appropriation account or by a transfer from free reserves, including reserves of accumulated past profit.

10.7.4.5 Provisions and liabilities[31]

Accounting practice in The Netherlands follows that of other continental European countries in being conservative in the creation of provisions. The Civil Code requires the balance sheet to show provisions against liabilities and losses, risks existing at the balance sheet date and costs that will lead to an expense in a subsequent financial year, the final item of these essentially being an income-smoothing device. The criteria for recognising provisions under the first two categories are comparable to the conditions under IAS 10 for the reporting of contingent losses.

---

[29] Hoogendoorn (1995), pp. 605–6
[30] Hoogendoorn (1995), pp. 590–2
[31] Hoogendoorn (1995), pp. 593–7

The Civil Code requires disclosure of provisions in some detail, and specifically requires separate disclosure of the provision for deferred taxation and the provision for pension commitments. The *RJ* also defines categories of provisions which might be expected.

Liabilities which do not appear on the balance sheet are contingent liabilities and *pro memoria* liabilities. (A *pro memoria* liability is the liability arising out of a contract under which both performance and consideration are due to take place after the balance sheet date.) Financial commitments for a number of years ahead are disclosed in notes. These *pro memoria* liabilities usually relate to investments, rent and leasing agreements.

One area where Dutch practice does not follow international practice is in relation to retirement benefit costs. These must be accounted for as they arise in The Netherlands, while IAS 19 allows the cost to be allocated over the remaining working lives of the participants.

10.7.4.6 Intangible fixed assets[32]

Intangible fixed assets are dealt with in the Civil Code by stating rules on capitalisation of some categories of cost which allow them to be reported in the balance sheet where specific conditions are met. This is generally consistent with IASs, but differs in respect of goodwill and research and development costs.

Dutch companies are not allowed to capitalise internally created goodwill. The argument against is that of reliability of measurement, indicating that some aspects of theory may have affected practice. The accounting regulation leaves several options for the treatment of goodwill. Treatment as an asset is permitted, with systematic amortisation within the useful economic life. Extension beyond five years requires explanation. Immediate write-off against reserves is also permitted, and it appears that more than 90% of Dutch listed companies use this option. This gives a conservative view of assets in the balance sheet, but is less conservative in the profit and loss account. Immediate write-off against income is a third possibility, but is applied only rarely.

Research and development costs are both subject to conditions where they may be reported as an asset if conditions of relative certainty are met. Although this is a prudent approach in the context of Dutch law, it is less conservative than IAS 9, which prohibits the capitalisation of any research expenditure, and also more flexible than IAS 9 in being permissive rather than mandatory on capitalisation of development expenditure which meets specific criteria.

Major publishing companies report issuing rights bought from third parties, although the law does not list this category as an intangible fixed asset.

10.7.5 Secrecy versus transparency

Gray (1988) classified accounting in The Netherlands as moderately transparent. This section shows that The Netherlands takes a firm approach to notes to the accounts, requiring these to supplement the financial statements rather than con-

---

[32] Bouma and Feenstra (1997), pp. 190–2; Hoogendoorn (1995), pp. 602–3, 619

tribute to a true and fair view. On the other hand there is little regulation and considerable variety in practice on segmental reporting. A report by the managing board is compulsory, but social reporting on a voluntary basis is not widespread.

10.7.5.1 Notes to the accounts[33]

Much of the information provided in the notes is specified in the Civil Code. However, it is important that the balance sheet and the profit and loss account should comply with the statutory requirement to show a true and fair view, even before the notes are considered. The notes should not be used to rectify a deficient or incorrect picture in the balance sheet and profit and loss account. This means that the main function of the notes (as indicated by the *RJ*) is to be explanatory and informative in support of the primary statements.

Because reserve accounting is allowed in The Netherlands, the notes on movements on reserves are especially important. In particular the notes will show direct movements on reserves due to:

- revaluation of assets under current cost accounting
- goodwill elimination against reserves
- adjustments to the provision for deferred taxation, related to the revaluation of assets
- some consequences of financial reorganisation
- losses resulting from uninsured destruction of assets in a disaster
- losses resulting from forms of nationalisation or expropriation
- the cumulative effect of changes in accounting policies.

The foregoing list shows items which will change the total of shareholders' equity but will not pass through the profit and loss account. It is a departure from the 'all-inclusive' approach generally used in reported profit and is less strict than IAS 8, which indicates that such items would be expected to flow through the profit and loss account.

10.7.5.2 Segmental reporting[34]

The basic requirement for segmental reporting is set out in the Civil Code but further guidance is provided by the *RJ*. Net sales (turnover) should be reported according to business activities and to geographic regions. The requirements of the Civil Code are less demanding than those of IAS 14. When the Fourth Directive was implemented the debate in Parliament indicated more concern with the damage which might be caused to loss of international competitive position than with the benefits of segmental disclosure. Companies are therefore left with considerable discretion in segmental reporting. The *RJ* guidance recommends disclosure of segmental operating results by type of activity and by geographical area. Surveys have shown that most companies give some form of geographical data, but the level of detail is very variable. A company may apply for exemptions

---

[33] Dijksma and Hoogendoorn (1993), pp. 99–100; Hoogendoorn (1995), p. 593
[34] Dijksma and Hoogendoorn (1993), pp. 162–5

from disclosures that are deemed to be competitively harmful; permission for this exemption is given by the Minister of Economic Affairs.

An interesting example of the matrix approach to segmental reporting is provided by Koninklijke BolsWessanen (*see* Exhibit 10.14).

It is less usual to see segmental information over a long time series, and so the practice of Akzo-Nobel (Exhibit 10.15) is interesting in this respect.

Exhibit 10.14 KONINKLIJKE BOLSWESSANEN: SEGMENTAL REPORTING OF SALES IN MATRIX FORM

Notes to the consolidated financial statements 1996

amounts in thousands of Dutch guilders unless otherwise indicated

The accounting principles applied are set forth on pages 27 through 30.

Consolidated income statement

Net sales

Analysis of net sales to country of consumption and product groups:

(x NLG 1 million)		The Netherlands	Other Europe	USA and Canada	Other countries	Total
Dairy	1996	59	639	1,552	–	2,250
	1995	60	664	1,353	–	2,077
Convenience Food and Cereals	1996	180	521	3	4	708
	1995	203	514	63	16	796
Natural and Specialty Foods	1996	–	–	1,028	–	1,028
	1995	–	–	857	–	857
Spirits and Wines	1996	247	344	35	83	709
	1995	246	411	28	210	895
Total	1996	486	1,504	2,618	87	4,695
	1995	509	1,589	2,301	226	4,625

Source: Koninklijke BolsWessanen NV, annual report, 1996, p. 36

Exhibit 10.15 AKZO-NOBEL: SEGMENTAL INFORMATION PRESENTED FOR 10 YEAR
HISTORICAL SUMMARY

| Business segment statistics | | | | pro forma | | | | | | | |
Millions of guilders	1996	1995	1994	1993	1993	1992	1991	1990	1989	1988	1987
Pharma											
Net sales	3,952	3,774	3,669	3,421	3,421	3,246	3,064	2,775	2,647	2,412	2,218
Operating income	795	750	655	590	590	532	514	429	383	335	330
Invested capital*	2,392	1,973	1,803	1,780	1,780	1,616	1,484	1,338	1,330	1,390	1,152
Operating income, as percentage of net sales	20.1	19.9	17.9	17.2	17.2	16.4	16.8	15.5	14.5	13.9	14.9
Operating income, as percentage of invested capital	36.4	39.7	36.6	34.7	34.7	34.3	36.4	32.2	28.2	26.4	29.7
Gross cash flow	971	900	796	711	711	641	616	525	472	408	396
Expenditures for PP&E	236	273	238	226	226	195	178	147	149	159	152
Average number of employees	15,100	14,300	14,100	14,000	14,000	13,600	13,200	12,800	12,500	12,300	11,800
Coatings											
Net sales	7,436	6,840	6,887	6,503	4,024	4,062	3,851	3,929	3,659	2,794	2,415
Operating income	592	474	521	398	199	203	221	251	281	210	164
Invested capital*	3,120	2,972	2,798	2,970	1,873	1,903	1,879	1,683	1,708	1,291	1,089
Operating income, as percentage of net sales	8.0	6.9	7.6	6.1	4.9	5.0	5.7	6.4	7.7	7.5	6.8
Operating income, as percentage of invested capital	19.4	16.4	18.1	13.4	10.5	10.7	12.4	14.8	18.7	17.6	15.2
Gross cash flow	811	675	729	601	321	325	334	355	373	286	232
Expenditures for PP&E	254	254	233	270	172	143	169	170	170	158	140
Average number of employees	21,800	21,500	21,900	22,600	14,200	15,000	14,500	15,300	14,000	12,100	10,800
Chemicals											
Net sales	7,695	7,342	7,902	7,525	5,816	5,671	5,737	5,760	6,420	6,020	4,651
Operating income	576	608	712	478	351	359	328	379	703	700	470
Invested capital*	5,705	5,111	5,180	5,220	3,476	3,406	3,476	3,461	3,607	3,455	2,765
Operating income, as percentage of net sales	7.5	8.3	9.0	6.4	6.0	6.3	5.7	6.6	11.0	11.6	10.1
Operating income, as percentage of invested capital	10.7	11.8	13.7	9.3	10.2	10.4	9.5	10.7	19.9	22.5	18.2
Gross cash flow	1,081	1,055	1,212	998	712	719	685	725	1,043	1,016	736
Expenditures for PP&E	932	753	733	545	423	309	341	450	516	423	355
Average number of employees	14,900	15,300	16,000	16,900	12,900	13,400	14,400	14,700	14,500	13,800	12,000
Fibers											
Net sales	3,393	3,584	3,626	3,239	3,239	3,762	4,262	4,852	5,210	4,678	4,291
Operating income	82	158	80	(21)	(21)	127	102	218	268	195	129
Invested capital*	2,546	2,554	2,117	2,653	2,653	2,193	2,372	2,735	2,750	2,464	2,329
Operating income, as percentage of net sales	2.4	4.4	2.2	(0.6)	(0.6)	3.4	2.4	4.5	5.1	4.2	3.0
Operating income, as percentage of invested capital	3.2	6.8	3.4	(0.9)	(0.9)	5.6	4.0	7.9	10.3	8.1	5.8
Gross cash flow	305	383	314	225	225	380	384	516	552	438	336
Expenditures for PP&E	318	309	321	311	311	250	261	294	368	470	358
Average number of employees	14,500	15,200	16,700	18,500	18,500	20,100	23,500	26,200	26,900	26,400	26,300

* At December 31

Source: Akzo-Nobel, annual report, 1996, p. 76; similar information presented for geographical segments

10.7.5.3 Off-balance sheet finance[35]

There are possibilities for companies to have sources of finance for their activities which are not recorded on the face of the balance sheet. The reader has to look for clues in the notes to the accounts. Such possibilities exist in:

- contingent liabilities and *pro memoria* liabilities
- lease obligations not reported in the balance sheet
- non-consolidation of highly geared subsidiary companies
- financial instruments such as swaps and futures contracts.

Non-consolidation is relatively flexible in its use. The Civil Code stipulates that where consolidation would conflict with the true and fair view, due to a major difference in activities, the financial statements of the excluded subsidiary must be disclosed separately in the notes. IAS 27 does not allow exclusion from consolidation of group companies with dissimilar activities. In any event, among the major listed Dutch groups this reason is rarely used. For joint ventures, proportionate consolidation and equity accounting are similar options. The law gives no preference to either method.

Heineken (Exhibit 10.16) explains the basis of consolidation and indicates a selective approach to proportional consolidation.

Exhibit 10.16 HEINEKEN: BASIS OF CONSOLIDATION

Basis of consolidation

In the consolidated balance sheet and statement of income Heineken N.V. and its subsidiaries, with which Heineken N.V. constitutes a group, are shown as fully consolidated. The minority interests in the Group funds and in the Group profit are indicated separately. Proportional consolidation takes place in the case of participations in which the Heineken Group has a direct interest and, in co-operation with other shareholders, exercises control with regard to management policy if the activities of the participations concerned are closely linked with those of the Heineken Group. Under the heading "Changes in the consolidation" the following statements of the movements of various assets and liabilities show the movements which relate to the increase in or reduction of our interests in consolidated participations.

Source: Heineken NV, annual report, 1996, p. 50

---

[35] Dijksma and Hoogendoorn (1993), pp. 106–11, 172–3

DSM (Exhibit 10.17) explained in its 1995 accounts that there would be a change in accounting policies from 1996 to introduce proportional consolidation, but only in respect of 'core activities'.

Exhibit 10.17 DSM: PROPOSED CHANGES IN CONSOLIDATION POLICIES

Notes to the consolidated financial statements

Changes in consolidation policies with effect from 1996

A number of DSM's core activities have been organized into joint ventures in which policy decisions are made jointly by DSM N.V and third parties. The proportion of DSM activities organized into such partnerships is expected to increase.

To provide a better insight into the significance for DSM of the activities of these joint ventures, we have decided – as announced in the 1995 Annual Report – to include the financial data of 50% participations which are important to DSM in the consolidated financial statements according to the proportional-consolidation method, from the financial year 1996 onwards. A '50% participation which is important to DSM' is a participation in a company which is directly involved in DSM's core activities and which is of sufficient size.

As from 1 January 1996 the following 50% participations are proportionally consolidated: Holland Sweetener Company VoF, DSM Idemitsu Company Ltd., Chemferm VoF and Chemferm SA. The 50/50 DEX-Plastomers joint venture is included in the consolidated financial statements as from 1 January 1996 and is also proportionally consolidated.

The change in our consolidation policies will have no consequences for the net result and the shareholders' equity, but it will affect the composition of the result and the equity. If in 1996 we had still applied the previous consolidation policies, net sales would have been more than NLG 200 million lower. The influence on the operating result and the result of non-consolidated participations is very limited. In the statements of changes the effects of the change in consolidation policies on the major balance-sheet items are shown under 'Introduction of proportional consolidation'.

(1) INTANGIBLE FIXED ASSETS

	total	concessions and permits	licenses and patents	pre-operating and start-up expenses
balance at January 1, 1996				
cost	108	3	26	79
amortization	54	1	19	34
book value	54	2	7	45
changes in book value:				
– introduction of proportional consolidation	21	–	14	7
– capital expenditure	26	–	5	21
– acquisitions	6	–	6	–
– amortization	-18	–	-9	-9
– other changes	7	–	18	-11
	42	–	34	8
balance at December 31, 1996				
cost	166	3	71	92
amortization	70	1	30	39
book value	96	2	41	53

Source: DSM NV, annual report, 1996, p. 47

10.7.5.4 Report by the managing board of directors[36]

The report by the managing board of directors is prescribed in the Civil Code. The report should contain a general review, information on the dividends and financial results, a balance sheet profile and an indication of prospects. In this way, past present and future issues are discussed. It reports also on issues of employment and research and development activities. The indication of prospects relates to capital investments, finance, employees' development, circumstances related to net sales development and profitability analysis. The requirement to show a true and fair view applies to this report.

There are therefore similarities with the operating and financial review provided by UK companies, the management report provided by German companies and the management discussion and analysis required in the USA.

10.7.5.5 Social accounting[37]

Laws dealing with the restructuring of enterprises, the establishment of workers' councils, and the supervisory board were all passed in the late 1960s and early 1970s, as part of the social developments of the 1950s and 1960s. In parallel, social accounting reports developed as employee orientated documents. The economic difficulties of the 1980s meant that the focus on social accounting diminished, and there is thus no strong concept of wider social reporting in Dutch accounting practice. There is, however, a requirement that the management board has to discuss the financial report with the works council.

10.8 EMPIRICAL STUDIES

This chapter has shown that accounting practice in The Netherlands is unique in its mixture of a high level of flexibility and some elements of quite strong conservatism. Tax law is not an influential factor and statutory regulation of accounting practice is relatively recent in the context of the strong historical influence of business economics.

10.8.1 Classification studies

In Chapter 4 it was shown that Mueller (1967) classified The Netherlands as having a microeconomic system where accounting is seen as a branch of business economics and primarily as aiding the objectives of the individual business (subsection 4.4.1). No other country shared this classification. Nobes (1984) classified accounting in The Netherlands as an isolated type, being micro-based (serving the needs of stakeholders) and in the family of business economics (Exhibit 4.7). Nair and Frank (1980) classified The Netherlands with the UK and the 'British Commonwealth' group on the basis of measurement (Exhibit 4.10) and with the North American group as well as the UK group on the basis of disclosure (Exhibit 4.11). It should be noted that the work of Nair and Frank dates from the early 1970s when regulation

---

[36] Hoogendoorn (1995), p. 579
[37] Bouma and Feenstra (1997), pp. 188–9

of accounting by statute was still a relatively new phenomenon in The Netherlands. In that respect, they were looking for a match in other countries where professional judgement was stronger than detailed regulation. At the time, that was also true of the UK and the USA. The work of Nobes was published in the early 1980s, and therefore probably gives a more representative picture. Using more recent survey data Doupnik and Salter (1993) (Exhibit 4.8) classified The Netherlands as micro-based and in a group dominated by characteristics of a well developed capital market, the attitude to uncertainty and the legal system.

10.8.2 Comparability measures

Studies on measures of comparability were explained in Chapter 3. A small group of Dutch companies re-state their accounts under US GAAP for the purposes of SEC registration. Weetman and Gray (1991) examined the reconciliations produced by six Dutch companies in 1988. The results showed a mixture of reported profit under Dutch practice both above and below the US GAAP figure. The only company which reported higher Dutch profit in the three years to 1988 was Philips, using current cost accounting. The current cost profit was higher than historical cost, possibly because of the benefits of gearing flowing to the profit and loss account. Income smoothing was a feature of other companies, with adjustments bypassing the Dutch profit and loss account but flowing through under US GAAP. The income-smoothing approach may be related to the 'business economics' approach, seeking to iron out unpredictable distortions in recurring profit. Systematic conservatism was not observed.

A more recent study is that of Vergoossen (1996), published in Dutch, which showed that the reported net income of 11 Dutch companies under Dutch GAAP was consistently higher than under US GAAP, with differences ranging from 2% to 41% of Dutch net income. The reported equity of the same companies under Dutch GAAP was consistently lower than under US GAAP, with differences ranging from 1% to 96% of Dutch equity.

In the hypothetical exercise undertaken by Simmonds and Azières (1989), it was shown that accounting practice in The Netherlands gave a 'most likely' figure for reported profit which was relatively low compared with the UK and Ireland. The minimum achievable was the second lowest of the European countries studied (only Germany being lower). The maximum achievable was less than that of the UK, Ireland, France or Belgium. Relative conservatism in profit measurement was indicated. In particular, profits could be minimised by valuing stocks on a LIFO valuation and by increasing the goodwill charge. Profits could be maximised by reducing the goodwill charge.

The study by Simmonds and Azières also showed that accounting practices in The Netherlands gave a tangible fixed assets figure higher than that of Ireland or Germany but comparable to Spain and France and marginally lower than Belgium or the UK. The position of The Netherlands reflects the requirement that when there is a desire to revalue fixed assets an entire class must be revalued. Capitalisation of finance leases is a requirement in The Netherlands as well as in Belgium and the UK.

10.8.3 Harmonisation studies

Harmonisation studies were explained in Chapter 3. Archer *et al.* (1995) (Chapter 3, subsection 3.5.4) found that within-country comparability in relation to deferred taxation continued to be influenced by the clustering of policy choices within countries. A majority of disclosing companies in The Netherlands used the full provision method. Between-country comparability increased over the period 1986/7 to 1990/1 but The Netherlands was constant over the period because full provision was recommended by the *RJ* throughout the period and the liability method was required by the *RJ* (although the deferral method was permitted until 1992).

On goodwill, Archer *et al.* found that a small number of Dutch companies, which had followed generally accepted Dutch practice in 1986/7, decided in 1990/1 to switch to another method accepted in several countries other than The Netherlands, or not to specify the method used. This led to an overall decrease in within-country comparability.

Hermann and Thomas (1995) found that the bicountry I index was relatively high for pairings within the fairness orientated grouping (Denmark, Ireland, The Netherlands and the UK). In the sample examined by Hermann and Thomas, the use of modified historical cost valuation of fixed assets was relatively rare, writing-off goodwill against reserves was common and the costing used in inventory valuation was not disclosed in many cases, so that only one actual case of LIFO usage was detected in 30 examined.

10.9 SUMMARY AND CONCLUSIONS

In this chapter you have seen how characteristics of accounting principles and practice in The Netherlands are related to the predictions made by Gray (1988) and others based upon analysis of cultural factors. Using the scores developed by Hofstede (1984), Gray's method of analysis may be used to predict that the accounting system in The Netherlands will be characterised by moderate professionalism, marginal flexibility, moderate optimism and moderate transparency. You have seen that the regulation of accounting is within a unique system reliant on social co-operation. There are three layers of accounting regulation – the Civil Code law; the Enterprise Chamber and the Council for Annual Reporting (*RJ*). These allow professionalism to influence the application of the law, while retaining a basis of statutory control. Flexibility exists in the separation of accounting and tax law. Flexibility is also influenced by major multinational companies which are seeking to meet the needs of practice in the UK and the USA as well as The Netherlands. Flexibility underlies the permissive nature of valuation, including the revaluation of fixed assets. Transparency is indicated in the extent of notes to the accounts and there is considerable discretion over segmental reporting.

Dutch accounting tends to create a category of its own in any classification system. It has been influential on accounting in other countries, particularly its former colonies. Accounting practices show substantial areas of agreement with IASs.

■ QUESTIONS

Business environment (10.2)

1 To what extent does the business environment of The Netherlands provide clues as to possible influences on accounting practices?

Early developments in accounting (10.3)

1 To what extent do early developments in accounting practice indicate the likely directions of professionalism/statutory control; uniformity/flexibility; conservatism/optimism; and secrecy/transparency in current practice?

Institutions (10.4)

1 How does the political and economic system of The Netherlands fit into the classifications described in Chapter 1?

2 How does the legal system of The Netherlands fit into the classifications described in Chapter 1?

3 How does the taxation system of The Netherlands compare to the descriptions given in Chapter 1?

4 How does the corporate financing system of The Netherlands compare to the descriptions given in Chapter 1?

5 How does the accounting profession in The Netherlands compare to the descriptions given in Chapter 1?

6 How do the external influences on accounting practice in The Netherlands compare to those described in Chapter 1?

7 Which institutional factors are most likely to influence Dutch accounting practice?

Societal culture and accounting sub-culture (10.5)

1 What is the position of The Netherlands relative to the UK, Germany and France, according to Hofstede's (1984) analysis (Chapter 2) and Gray's (1988) analysis (Chapter 4)?

2 What are the features of Dutch societal culture identified by Hofstede which led Gray to his conclusions?

3 What is the position of The Netherlands relative to the USA, Japan and Australia according to Hofstede's analysis (Chapter 2) and Gray's analysis (Chapter 4)?

IASs (10.6)

1 In which areas does accounting practice in The Netherlands depart from that set out in IASs?

2 For each of the areas of departure which you have identified, describe the treatment required under the Dutch accounting system and identify the likely impact on the income and shareholders' equity of moving from Dutch GAAP to the relevant IAS standards.

3 What explanations may be offered for these departures from IASs, in terms of the institutional factors described in the chapter?

4 What are the most difficult problems facing accounting in The Netherlands if it seeks harmonisation with the IASC core standards programme?

EU membership (10.7)

1 What have been the most significant changes in accounting practice in The Netherlands arising from the Fourth and Seventh Directives?

2 Which factors make it relatively easy or relatively difficult for Dutch accounting practices to harmonise with those of other European countries?

Professionalism/statutory control (10.7.2)

1 Identify the key features supporting a conclusion that moderate professionalism is a characteristic of Dutch accounting.

2 Explain which institutional influences cause moderate professionalism to be a characteristic of Dutch accounting.

3 Discuss whether a classification of moderate professionalism is appropriate for the 1990s.

Uniformity/flexibility (10.7.3)

1 Identify the key features supporting a conclusion that marginal flexibility is a characteristic of Dutch accounting.

2 Explain which institutional influences cause marginal flexibility to be a characteristic of Dutch accounting.

3 Discuss whether a classification of marginal flexibility is appropriate for the 1990s.

Conservatism/optimism (10.7.4)

1 Identify the key features supporting a conclusion that moderate optimism is a characteristic of Dutch accounting.

2 Explain which institutional influences cause moderate optimism to be a characteristic of Dutch accounting.

3 Discuss whether a classification of moderate optimism is appropriate for the 1990s.

Secrecy/transparency (10.7.5)

1 Identify the key features supporting a conclusion that moderate transparency is a characteristic of Dutch accounting.

2 Explain which institutional influences cause moderate transparency to be a characteristic of Dutch accounting.

3 Discuss whether a classification of moderate transparency is appropriate for the 1990s.

Empirical studies (10.8)

1 What is the relative position of The Netherlands, as indicated by research studies into classification, comparability and harmonisation?

REFERENCES

Archer, S., Delvaille, P. and McLeay, S. (1995) 'The measurement of harmonisation and the comparability of financial statement items: Within-country and between-country effects', *Accounting and Business Research*, 25(98), 67–80.

Bollen, L.H.H. and Nuffel, L.L.-V. (1997) 'Financial reporting regulation in Belgium and The Netherlands', Chapter 2 in Flower, J. and Lefebvre, C. (eds), *Comparative Studies in Accounting Regulation in Europe*. Leuven: Acco.

Bouma, J.L. and Feenstra, D.W. (1997) 'Accounting and business economics tradition in The Netherlands', *European Accounting Review*, 6(2), 175–97.

Camfferman, K. (1995) 'The history of financial reporting in The Netherlands', in Walton, P., *European Financial Reporting: A History*. New York: Academic Press.

CCH (1997) *Doing Business in Europe: The Authoritative Guide to European Legal Systems*. London: CCH Publications.

Coopers and Lybrand Tax Network (1995) *1995 International Tax Summaries: A Guide for Planning and Decisions*. New York: John Wiley.

Dijksma, J. and Hoogendoorn, M.N. (1993) *European Financial Reporting – The Netherlands*. London: Routledge

Hermann, D. and Thomas, W. (1995) 'Harmonisation of accounting measurement practices in the European Community', *Accounting and Business Research*, 25(100), 253–65.

Hoogendoorn, M.N. (1995) 'The Netherlands', in Alexander, D. and Archer, S. (eds), *European Accounting Guide*. New York: Harcourt Brace Professional Publishing.

Hoogendoorn, M.N. (1996) 'Accounting and taxation in The Netherlands', *European Accounting Review*, 5, Supplement, 871–82.

Klaassen, J. (1980) 'An accounting court: The impact of the Enterprise Chamber on financial reporting in The Netherlands', *The Accounting Review*, 15(2), 327–41

Klaassen, J. (1993) 'Group accounting in The Netherlands', in Gray, S.J., Coenenberg, A.G. and Gordon, P.D. (1993) *International Group Accounting – Issues in European Harmonisation*. London: Routledge.

Parker, R. (1995) 'Financial reporting in The Netherlands', in Nobes, C. and Parker, R., *Comparative International Accounting*, 4th edn. Englewood Cliffs, NJ: Prentice-Hall.

Salter, S.B., Roberts, C.B. and Kantor, J. (1996) 'The IASC comparability project: A cross-national comparison of financial reporting practices and IASC proposed rules', *Journal of International Accounting and Taxation*, 5(1), 89–111.

Schoonderbeek, J.W. (1994) 'Setting accounting standards in The Netherlands', *European Accounting Review*, 1, 132–42.

Simmonds, A. and Azières, O. (1989) *Accounting for Europe – Success by 2000 AD?* London: Touche Ross.

Van Hoepen, M.A. (1984) 'The Fourth Directive and The Netherlands', in Gray, S.J. and Coenenberg, A.G., *EEC and Accounting Harmonisation: Implementation and Impact of the Fourth Directive*. Amsterdam: North Holland.

Vergoossen, R.G.A. (1996) 'Invloed beursnotering in Verenigde Staten op Stelselkeuze en additionele informatieverschaffing' [trans. 'Impact of US Stock Exchange listing an accounting choice and additional disclosure'], *Maandblad voor Accountancy en Bedrijfseconomie*, 11, November, 597–608.

Weetman, P. and Gray, S.J. (1991) 'A comparative international analysis of the impact of accounting principles on profits: The USA versus the UK, Sweden and The Netherlands', *Accounting and Business Research*, 21(84), 363–79.

Zeff, S. (1990) 'The English language equivalent of '*Geeft ein getrouw beeld*', *De Accountant*, 2, October.

Zeff, S.A. (1993) 'The regulation of financial reporting: Historical development and policy recommendations', *De Accountant*, 3, November.

Newspapers and professional journals or magazines

De Accountant (publishes some articles in English).

The *Financial Times* (UK).

Chapter 11

The UK

11.1 INTRODUCTION

Accounting practice in the UK has a strong tradition of professionalism. Statute law and accounting standards set general bounds on requirements but the professional accountant determines the detail of practice. The accounting profession is well established and there is a relatively wide requirement for audit of company accounts.

Tax law has developed separately from accounting law and there is no requirement that accounting profit must be calculated under fiscal rules to be an acceptable base for taxable profit. Membership of the EU, and the adoption of the Fourth and Seventh Directives, brought more specific requirements in the shape of accounting formats not hitherto known. Group accounting, and in particular consolidated accounting, was well established from 1948 onwards.

Company law concentrates primarily on protection of shareholders and creditors. Other sources of authority indicate a concern with wider stakeholders. From time to time there have been concerns to ensure that the needs of employees are addressed and that the public interest is taken into account; this depends to some extent on the political views of the government of the day.

The current approach to standard setting places particularly strong emphasis on the needs of users, although there is no clear statement of their needs.

11.2 THE COUNTRY

11.2.1 Geography

The UK comprises England, Wales, Scotland and Northern Ireland. The Channel Islands and the Isle of Man have their own Treasuries and separate systems of direct taxation. The term 'Great Britain' denotes the main land mass of the British Isles. Great Britain includes England, Scotland and Wales, it is a geographical description rather than a political unit. The term 'British Isles' is also a geographical description, covering England, Wales, Scotland, all of Ireland and the various islands around the coastline of these countries. Completion of the Channel Tunnel was a significant factor in allowing commercial freight traffic more ready access to continental Europe.

359

The population is 58 million and has a relatively low rate of growth. Population density is greatest in the south-east of England.

11.2.2 Economic indicators

The economy has shown growth of 2.2% per annum over the period 1985–95 (*see* Exhibit 11.1). Gross domestic product is created 70% by services and almost 30% by manufacturing industry. Agriculture is a relatively small proportion (2%) of gross domestic product. Manufacturing industry is directed 30% towards machinery and transport, 15% towards agriculture and 50% towards a diversified range of activity.

Standards of living are relatively high in terms of life expectancy and a rate of population growth which is lower than the rate of growth of gross domestic product (GDP). The rate of inflation, at 4.6% per annum over the period 1989–96, reflects a period of activity in the economy where government spending was underpinned by the proceeds of privatisation.

Visible imports have exceeded exports but there has been a net inflow on invisibles. Exports comprise mainly manufactured and semi-manufactured products, with the USA remaining an important export destination but the EU as a whole taking a larger portion of UK exports. In 1996 the largest single export market lay in Germany, whereas in 1995 it was the USA. Imports also came from the EU but a significant amount of trade exists with the USA and Japan. Trade with former Commonwealth countries has fallen significantly since the UK joined the EU.

Exhibit 11.1 THE UK: COUNTRY PROFILE, TAKEN FROM EIU STATISTICS

Population	58.1 m.	
Land mass	242,534 sq.km	
GDP per head	US $18,849	
GDP per head in purchasing power parity	71	(USA=100)
Origins of GDP:	%	
Agriculture	2.0	
Industry	27.1	
Services	70.9	
	%	
Real GDP average annual growth 1985–95	2.2	
Inflation, average annual rate 1989–96	4.6	

Source: The Economist Pocket World in Figures 1998 Edition, The Economist (1997)

11.3 OVERVIEW OF ACCOUNTING REGULATIONS[1]

11.3.1 Early company law[2]

The first Companies Act was passed in 1844, allowing limited liability companies to form by incorporation as joint stock companies; prior to that time a separate Act of Parliament was required for each company formed. The Companies Act set out basic rules for accounting and auditing, but these were not effective until 1900. The company was seen as a private arrangement involving shareholders and directors, and secrecy in business matters was regarded as a virtue.

From 1907, there was a requirement to produce an audited balance sheet, but no stipulation as to format or content. A major change in public opinion about accounting disclosure resulted from the *Royal Mail Steam Shipping* case (1932) (R v Lord Kylsant (1932) I KB 442, [1931] 1 All ER Rep 179), where a company produced a false prospectus by drawing on 'secret reserves' to give the appearance of profitability. That change in opinion led to the Companies Act 1948 specifying minimum levels of disclosure in annual accounts; an audited profit and loss account and balance sheet; group accounts; and enhancement of the rights and duties of auditors. The 1948 Act concentrated on disclosure and the protection of shareholders and creditors.

Matters of valuation, formats of financial statements and the method of recording transactions were all left to directors. There persisted a strong philosophy of minimal intervention by government and a defence of the rights of directors and shareholders to take decisions on corporate matters. Some minor changes extending disclosure were made in 1967, but these concentrated primarily on the report of the directors and additional notes to the balance sheet. The principles of 1948 remained.

The most significant change in approach was taken in 1981 when the Fourth Directive was implemented in UK company law. This brought formats and valuation rules to company law for the first time. Concepts such as prudence, consistency, accruals and going concern were introduced to law, as was the requirement to report only realised profit in the profit and loss account. The 1981 Act was additional to the 1948 and subsequent Acts. All were consolidated in 1985. Implementation of the Seventh Directive was by way of the 1989 Act amending the principal Act of 1985.

11.3.2 Consolidated accounts[3]

Evidence of consolidation by particular companies may be traced to the early years of the twentieth century but it was not until the aftermath of the *Royal Mail Steam Shipping* case (1932) that the doubts of accountants were overcome. One aspect of that case had been reporting the results of subsidiaries only on receipt of dividends. Group accounting was made compulsory under the Companies Act 1948,

---

[1] Napier (1995)
[2] Gordon and Gray (1994), Chapter 2
[3] Ma, Parker and Whittred (1991)

based on definitions of a subsidiary which held until the incorporation of the Seventh Directive in the 1989 Act. The Companies Act 1948 gave no guidance on the method of group accounting, not even consolidation was compulsory. It was left to the professional accountant to determine the method of group accounting, and it would have satisfied the requirements of law to staple together all the accounts of parent and subsidiary. In this context, the influence of leading text book writers was important.

The initial reaction to the Seventh Directive was that UK accounting already satisfied its requirements and the options on definition allowed the approach of the 1948 Act to continue. However the experiences of the late 1980s, when companies began to avoid consolidation by working round the 1948 definitions, led to adoption of the more widely embracing options in the Seventh Directive which emphasised effective control rather than relying solely on percentage of ownership. The Companies Act 1989 extended the UK definition of a subsidiary and included recommendations on consolidation not previously found in UK law.

11.3.3 Accounting standards[4]

Prior to 1970 there was no system of written accounting standards in the UK. Professional bodies issued guidance to their members. The Institute of Chartered Accountants in England and Wales (ICAEW) in particular had a detailed Handbook of Recommendations on accounting and auditing matters; these were advisory in nature. Following some well publicised company failures in the 1960s the major accountancy bodies established the Accounting Standards Committee (ASC), jointly owned by themselves. They each retained the power of veto over any standard and all proposals for new standards had to be approved by the Council of each member body.

Accounting standards have from time to time tried to meet economic needs of the day. High inflation in the early 1970s stimulated debate and practice in a variety of approaches to the problem. Initial inclinations towards general price levels in current purchasing power accounting then switched to specific price levels in current cost accounting, as advocated by the authors Edwards and Bell.

A major review of the standard setting process (the Dearing review) recommended that accounting standards should remain, as far as possible, the responsibility of preparers, users and auditors, rather than becoming a matter of regulation by law. An independent standard setting body was seen to be necessary, with adequate financial support to carry out its work. Dearing also made recommendations about the organisation of the standard setting process.

Most of Dearing's recommendations were adopted in 1990, when the government announced the establishment of the Financial Reporting Council (FRC) to cover, at a high level, a wide range of interests. The chairman is appointed by the Secretary of State for Trade and Industry and the Governor of the Bank of England. The FRC guides the standard setting body on matters of policy, ensures it is adequately financed, and acts as an influence on good practice. The Accounting Standards Board (ASB) as one arm of the FRC, is a panel of experts having a full-time chairman and technical director. There are seven other members, all part-time, drawn from the

---

[4] Gordon and Gray (1994), Chapter 5

accountancy profession and from business. A two-thirds majority of the Board is required for approval of an accounting standard. A second arm of the FRC is the Financial Reporting Review Panel (FRRP) which enquires into annual accounts where it appears that the requirements of the Companies Act might have been breached. The ASB is helped by an Urgent Issues Task Force (UITF) in dealing with matters of detail arising out of existing legislation or standards where clarification or a change of practice is required.

11.4 INSTITUTIONS

11.4.1 Political and economic system[5]

The UK is a constitutional monarchy, having a parliamentary system of government. There are two Houses of Parliament at Westminster, in London. The House of Commons has over 600 elected members. Called Members of Parliament (MPs), they are elected by the adult population of the UK on a 'first-past-the-post' system. This system of election normally results in one of two political parties taking a clear majority as the basis of government for a term of office lasting up to five years. The House of Lords comprises hereditary peers of the realm and also life peers appointed in recognition of public service. Legislation originates in the House of Commons and after approval there is passed to the House of Lords. In the House of Lords there may be detailed amendments to the proposed legislation, but only rarely is it defeated completely. The House of Commons has the power to restore legislation opposed by the House of Lords: the House of Lords may consequently modify or delay legislation, but cannot prevent its passage.

The House of Commons is led by the Prime Minister who is usually also the leader of the parliamentary party holding the parliamentary majority. The monarch is head of state, but must act on the advice of the government of the day.

The dominant position of the House of Commons and the lack of conflict between the leader of the government and the majority party in Parliament means that business legislation desired by the government is likely to become law. From 1979 to 1996 the UK had a conservative government. A marked change of electoral mood led to the election of a left-of-centre Labour government in 1997.

The economic system is generally based on a free market approach. Government regulation is applied to particular aspects of economic activity such as the control of monopolies and mergers, or the prevention of price-fixing arrangements. In 1996 the Bank of England was given independent power to determine interest rates, taking this power from previous control by the government. The purpose of this change was to allow interest rates to move more closely with market forces in the economy.

The period of conservative government from 1979 saw a policy of privatisation of companies which had been in government control, nationalisation having dated from the late 1940s. Privatisation was seen as a political ideal but also placed large capital funds at the disposal of the government of the day and reduced the

---

[5] Gordon and Gray (1994), Chapter 1

borrowing requirements of the public sector. The privatisation policy was largely completed before the Labour government came to power, and despite earlier threats to reverse the policy, on achieving power the new Labour government showed no apparent desire to carry out such reversal. However, regulation of the privatised companies is extensive, particularly for the utilities, covering pricing of products and provides another means of government control.

Rates of exchange between the pound sterling and other currencies are determined by market forces. The Bank of England has regard to the rate of exchange when setting interest rates. Although the UK is a member of the EU, there is reluctance to join the European Monetary System (EMS) and take up the Euro as a common currency.

11.4.2 Legal system[6]

Statute law is established by Parliament and sits alongside common law which has been established by tradition through the courts of law. There is a national system of law for the UK as a whole but there is also a separate legal system in Scotland, derived from the historical position of Scotland as an independent country prior to the Act of Union in 1707. Business law is usually applicable on a UK-wide basis. There are some separate laws established by the UK Parliament to be applied in Northern Ireland and Wales, recognising their separate historical origins.

In the seventeenth and eighteenth centuries, trading and commercial companies could be formed only by royal charter or by private Act of Parliament. Company law, allowing relatively straightforward incorporation of business companies, came into existence in the middle of the nineteenth century. The law at that stage was not excessively intrusive, taking the view that the regulation of a company was essentially a matter for the shareholders and the directors. A series of business scandals in the early years of the twentieth century led to the view that more intervention was required through business legislation. This led, in the Companies Act 1948, to much more detailed prescription on disclosure of information and general conduct of the business. That legislation survived, with some modification in 1967, until the UK joined the EU and was required to adopt the Fourth and Seventh Directives. Initially, legislation in 1980 and 1981 modified the earlier law but major consolidation of company law resulted in the comprehensive Companies Act 1985. Further legislation in 1989 modified the Companies Act 1985 in respect of the Eighth Directive and made some amendments to the definition of a subsidiary company.

Statute law also covers matters such as insolvency, financial services, and insider trading on the stock market. There is a strong tradition of judge-made law, passed down through decisions in courts of law which are taken as binding precedent for future cases of a similar type.

Although parliamentary process is required for primary legislation, such as the approval of the Companies Act 1985, some amendments to legislation may thereafter be implemented without debate in Parliament. Thus the Companies Act is amended from time to time by Statutory Instrument. This method is used to

---

[6] Gordon and Gray (1994), Chapter 2

change disclosure exemption limits, or to delete minor unwanted items of disclosure, or to add new items of detail within an overall existing heading.

The UK legal system may be classified as from the common law family, and of British type. Within the UK, Scots law is based on Roman law. Laws affecting business are set by the UK Parliament but may have an additional section relating to Scots law.

11.4.2.1 Types of business organisation

Unincorporated businesses operate as sole traders or partnerships. Both carry the disadvantage that the owner has unlimited liability for the obligations of the business. The need to grow and seek a larger capital base may eventually force the expanding business to seek incorporation as a limited liability company. There are two types of limited liability company: the public limited company (plc) and the private limited company (Ltd). Exhibit 11.2 sets out the key differences.

11.4.2.2 Corporate governance[7]

The day-to-day management of companies is in the hands of the Board of Directors. The single-tier board comprises both executive and non-executive directors. It is led by a chairman who is usually a non-executive director. A report issued in 1992 (the Cadbury Report, see below) stated that it was desirable in public companies for the chairman and the chief executive to be separate persons. The Board of Directors is expected to act as a single group of persons, all taking collective responsibility for the decisions of the board. In practice, everyday activity is delegated by the board to a senior executive director who leads the other executives in running the company.

Exhibit 11.2 DIFFERENCES BETWEEN PRIVATE AND PUBLIC COMPANIES

Public limited company (plc)	Private company (Ltd)
Minimum 2 directors	Minimum 1 director
Minimum share capital £50,000	No minimum share capital
Shares and debentures may be offered to the public by advertisement	Prohibition on offer to the public
Restrictions on making loans to directors	Fewer restrictions on dealing with directors
General prohibition on assisting others to purchase the company's own shares	Giving assistance to purchase own shares is allowed, subject to safeguards for creditors and minority shareholders
Company may purchase its own shares provided fixed capital is not reduced	Own shares may be purchased out of fixed capital

---

[7] Charkham (1994), Chapter 6

Directors are elected, and may be removed, by the shareholders in annual general meeting. Directors are required to act as agents of the shareholders, as a body, and in that context have duties defined by law. The directors must act in good faith in the best interests of the company.

In 1992 there was a major report into corporate governance in the UK. It was chaired by Sir Adrian Cadbury, so that the report is known as the 'Cadbury Report'. It recommended, among other things:

- a Code of Best Practice to be followed by company directors
- appointment of non-executive directors to all company boards
- formation of an audit committee, comprising non-executive directors, to review accounts and audit
- formation of a remuneration committee, comprising non-executive directors
- limitations on length of directors' service contracts
- disclosure of directors' remuneration and benefits in kind
- clear statements in the annual report setting out the respective responsibilities of directors and auditors
- confirmation by the directors that the company is a going concern
- confirmation by the directors concerning the adequacy of internal controls.[8]

The recommendations for disclosure of directors' emoluments were taken forward by Sir Richard Greenbury, resulting in the Greenbury Report (1995). It made more specific the items to be disclosed and the separate disclosures required for each director. In particular, the benefits expected from pension funds should be quantified and policy on remuneration should also be disclosed.

A promised review of the report of the Cadbury Committee, planned for 1995, eventually took place in 1997. It was chaired by Sir Ronald Hampel and took a broader view of the conditions required for good corporate governance. The Hampel Report took the view that entrepreneurship should not be stifled by excessive regulation.

11.4.3 Taxation system[9]

Companies pay corporation tax while owners of unincorporated businesses pay income tax. The two types of tax operate under different rules and may have different rates of tax applied. However, for the determination of taxable business profits the rules are similar. The starting point is the reported accounting profit, modified by specific aspects of tax law.

11.4.3.1 Taxable income

A distinction is drawn between income arising from revenue transactions and that arising from capital receipts. Income is subdivided according to its source and different rules are applied to each source. The aggregate amount is subject to corporation tax. For companies the main sources are:

---

[8] Chambers (1996)
[9] Gordon and Gray (1994), Chapter 4; Coopers and Lybrand International Tax Network (1995)

- trading profit
- non-trading income
- chargeable gains

Trading profit is based on reported accounting profit with adjustments specified in tax law. The most significant adjustment is that tax law does not allow accounting depreciation as an expense but substitutes instead a system of capital allowances at prescribed rates. Trading stock may not be valued on a LIFO basis. Profits and losses on the disposal of fixed assets are not included in taxable profits. Provisions are not allowed unless they can be shown to be specific to a defined item of expected loss. Some expenses, such as business entertaining, are not allowed for tax purposes.

Non-trading income includes investment income, rental income, interest and royalties. These are generally taxed on the basis of cash received rather than on an accruals basis.

Chargeable gains are the profits calculated on disposal of fixed assets. Indexation allowances, calculated to eliminate the inflationary element of the gain, were available until 1998.

11.4.3.2 Tax treatment of dividends

Dividends are paid to UK shareholders net of a withholding tax. The individual shareholder may set the amount of the withholding tax against the personal tax bill but large institutional shareholders such as pension funds, which are exempt from tax, may not reclaim the amount withheld. This selective imputation system reflects a change in political power in 1997, ending almost 25 years of a widely applied imputation system. Companies which receive dividend income from other companies may not claim any deduction for the tax withheld and they must pay corporation tax on the dividend income. Relief is available within groups of companies.

11.4.4 Corporate financing system[10]

11.4.4.1 Equity investors

Periodic surveys of company share registers indicate that individuals hold no more than 20% by value of the equity of listed companies. More than 60% is held by insurance companies, pension funds and a range of financial institutions including unit trusts. Chapter 1, Exhibit 1.5 shows that the relative strength of investment by financial institutions is an unusual characteristic by comparison with other countries.

Institutional investors tend not to become involved in the management of the company, but where strong concerns arise the institutional investors will use their powers in general meeting.

11.4.4.2 London Stock Exchange[11]

The London Stock Exchange dates from the seventeenth century. For a period of time there were regional trading floors but these closed in the mid-1960s and business focused on London. A major change in the nature of trading operations in the

---

[10] Gordon and Gray (1994), Chapter 3
[11] London Stock Exchange, *Fact File*, 1997

1980s meant that a dealing floor was no longer maintained, and trading now takes place by use of telephones and computer screens. The main market is the London Stock Exchange, on which companies have a full listing. For new, smaller companies there is the Alternative Investment Market (AIM). It is regulated by the London Stock Exchange but has rules which are are less onerous. The AIM may provide a step towards full membership.

Movement on share prices is measured by a number of indices, the most frequently mentioned being the FTSE-100 index. This index is operated jointly by the *Financial Times* and the Stock Exchange, based on the 100 largest companies measured by market capitalisation.

The Stock Exchange is a Self-Regulatory Organisation (SRO) under the Financial Services Act and so may issue rules, under the general umbrella of official approval.

The relative importance of the UK stock exchange in Europe can be seen in Chapter 1, Exhibit 1.3, although Exhibit 1.4 shows that it remains less significant than US and Japanese markets in terms of the market capitalisation of listed companies.

11.4.4.3 Top ten companies

From the *Financial Times* annual survey,[12] the top 500 world companies at January 1998 included 51 UK companies and also three companies registered in both the UK and the Netherlands. The top ten UK listed companies are shown in Exhibit 11.3.

11.4.4.4 Bank lending

London is one of the major banking centres of the world. The Bank of England is the central bank, exercising regulatory control over lending by commercial and

Exhibit 11.3 TOP TEN UK LISTED COMPANIES

	Market cap $m	Rank in Europe	Sector
1 HSBC Holdings	56,987	3	Commercial banks
2 British Petroleum	53,596	4	Oil international
3 Glaxo Wellcome	49,735	6	Drugs, pharmaceuticals
4 Shell Transport & Trading	45,094	1*	Oil international
5 Lloyds TSB Group	44,980	7	Commercial banks
6 SmithKline Beecham	33,256	11	Drugs, pharmaceuticals
7 BT	26,215	16	Telephone company
8 Barclays	25,353	17	Commercial banks
9 Zeneca	19,176	24	Drugs, pharmaceuticals
10 Halifax	18,323	27	Commercial banks, other banks

Note: *Jointly as Royal Dutch/Shell
Source: Survey FT 500, *Financial Times*, 22 January 1998, p. 23

---

[12] *Financial Times*, FT 500 Survey, 22 January 1998

merchant banks. Commercial banks are reluctant to become involved in ownership of companies and therefore concentrate on very short-term lending to companies. The medium-term and longer-term lending originates with merchant banks or venture capitalists.

Commercial banks also seek to offer services beyond pure lending, particularly for small and medium-sized enterprises (SMEs). They do not play a significant part in corporate governance but may find themselves linked to a customer on a more long-term basis where short-term loans are repeatedly rolled over.

Merchant banks are interested in the larger companies or those medium-sized companies which intend to grow. The merchant banks offer all types of corporate finance services including dealing in foreign exchange markets; swaps; financial futures; forward rate agreements; interest rate and currency options; money market loans and deposits. Strengths of individual banks depend on their chosen specialisms but most will offer advice on takeovers and mergers; corporate reorganisation and reconstruction; management buyouts; stock exchange flotations; and bond issues on foreign currency markets.

11.4.4.5 Mergers and acquisitions[13]

Activity in takeovers and mergers varies with economic cycles. Accounting practice distinguishes a true merger from an acquisition, but in practice nearly all business combinations in the UK involve one party acquiring another. Takeover activity is regulated by the Takeover Panel, a self-regulating mechanism which has existed since 1968. It sets a Code of practice for takeovers and can impose penalties ranging from a private reprimand to removal of the shares from stock exchange listing. The underlying themes of the Code are openness, timeliness and even-handedness.

Government policy to discourage creation of monopolies is administered by the Monopolies and Mergers Commission. The Commission will investigate a proposed acquisition and is required to state whether the proposal is, or is not, against the public interest.

Accounting information often plays an important part in takeovers, especially where these are contested. The Stock Exchange sets out rules for disclosure in circulars issued in connection with a takeover proposal. The Takeover Code dictates who shall receive such information; often companies will voluntarily exceed the minimum requirement and more may be learned about the parties involved than would ordinarily appear in the annual report.

11.4.5 The accounting profession[14]

The UK has a long history of professional accountancy bodies. Over time specialist groupings have emerged. The major professional bodies are:

- The Institute of Chartered Accountants in England and Wales (ICAEW)
- The Institute of Chartered Accountants of Scotland (ICAS)
- The Institute of Chartered Accountants in Ireland (ICAI)

---

[13] Sudarsanam (1995), pp. 79–94
[14] Gordon and Gray (1994), Chapter 5

- The Association of Chartered Certified Accountants (ACCA)
- The Chartered Institute of Management Accountants (CIMA)
- The Chartered Institute of Public Finance and Accountancy (CIPFA).

All set examinations as a precondition of membership. Those persons wishing to become company auditors must obtain the status of Registered Auditor which normally means membership of the ICAEW, ICAS, ICAI or ACCA, together with relevant practical experience.

Before 1990 these professional bodies worked together, through the Accounting Standards Committee (ASC), in setting accounting standards. The process was found to be too slow and accused of being controlled too closely by the profession. In 1990 the ASB was established as an independent authority and the professional bodies lost their power of veto over the issue of a standard. They continue to make representations to the ASB and to contribute indirectly through the work of members.

Auditing standards continue to be set by the professional bodies through the Auditing Practices Board (APB), owned and financed by them collectively. Concerns at excessive professional control are addressed by including lay members on the APB.

11.4.6 External influences

Historically, UK accounting has developed as an approach which has been exported to other parts of the world, particularly the countries which were once colonies but today form part of the Commonwealth.[15] Those countries, on gaining independence, looked to wider global practices and adapted their UK-based accounting systems to include practices found in major trading partner countries. It has been suggested that accounting in the USA is an adaptation, rather than wholesale adoption, of the UK accounting system, carried to that country by pioneering accountants emigrating to the USA.[16]

The most significant inward influence on UK accounting has been membership of the EU.[17] This has required significant changes in company law to adopt the various directives. In particular, the concept of having formats and valuation rules contained in company law was a major change resulting from the Fourth Directive. However, the UK also had an influence on accounting in the EU. At the date of UK membership, the Fourth Directive was still in draft form and did not give any scope for the 'true and fair' approach which was the UK tradition. The 'true and fair' amendment to the Fourth Directive was a very significant concession to UK requests.

Multinational companies are an agent for the import and export of international practices. Where these companies have found themselves producing different sets of financial statements for different jurisdictions, they have tended to choose options which were common to more than one country. Such companies have from time to time referred to their own attempts to find common approaches to specific issues, or frustration at the lack of common approaches.

---

[15] Parker (1995)
[16] Parker (1989)
[17] Nobes and Parker (1984); Nobes (1993)

11.5 SOCIETAL CULTURE AND ACCOUNTING SUBCULTURE

11.5.1 Hofstede's cultural dimensions

Exhibit 11.4 reproduces part of the table set out in Chapter 2, section 2.4, showing the scores and rankings for the UK from Hofstede's (1984) research on cultural dimensions.

11.5.2 Culture and accounting

Hofstede grouped the UK in what he called the 'Anglo' cultural area, which included the USA as well as Australia, Canada, Ireland and New Zealand, all countries more recently under UK accounting influence. Exhibit 11.5 sets out an interpretation of Hofstede's scores of cultural values and indicates Gray's (1988) classification for the Anglo group as a whole. More detailed analysis is given in section 11.7.

11.6 ACCOUNTING REGULATIONS AND THE IASC

UK accounting standards always indicate, in an appendix, whether or not they are consistent with IASs. Companies which apply UK standards are therefore to a considerable extent applying IASs implicitly but seldom acknowledge that fact in their annual reports. Research by Salter *et al.* (1996) showed that, on completion of the IASC comparability project, accounting practice in the UK ranked relatively high in compliance with IASs (*see* Chapter 5, subsection 5.6.3.4).

The ASB has identified three different strategies for reacting to the mounting pressure for harmonisation:

- adopt international standards for domestic purposes
- develop domestic requirements without regard to international standards, or
- harmonise national requirements with international standards where possible.

Analysis of benefits and limitations led the ASB to support the third strategy.[18] The Board has taken the view that it will depart from international consensus only when:

Exhibit 11.4 THE UK: SCORES AND RANKINGS FOR INDIVIDUAL COUNTRIES FROM HOFSTEDE'S (1984) CULTURAL DIMENSIONS RESEARCH

Individualism versus collectivism		*Large power distance versus small power difference*		*Strong uncertainty avoidance versus weak uncertainty avoidance*		*Low nurture versus high nurture*	
Score	*Rank*	*Score*	*Rank*	*Score*	*Rank*	*Score*	*Rank*
89	3	35	42/44	35	47/48	66	9/10

---

[18] Financial Reporting Council, *Annual Review 1996*, p. 45

Exhibit 11.5 **LINKING GRAY'S (1988) ACCOUNTING VALUES TO HOFSTEDE'S (1984) CULTURAL DIMENSIONS, IN THE MANNER PROPOSED BY GRAY**

Gray's accounting values – classification	*Cultural dimensions affecting the country's accounting values*	*Interpretation of Hofstede's scores of cultural values for the UK*
Professionalism (strong)	Professionalism tends to be associated with: ● Individualism ● Weak uncertainty avoidance ● Small power distance	 High individualism Weak uncertainty avoidance Small power distance
Flexibility (strong)	Uniformity tends to be associated with: ● Strong uncertainty avoidance ● Large power distance ● Collectivism	 Weak uncertainty avoidance Small power distance High individualism
Optimism (strong)	Conservatism tends to be associated with: ● Strong uncertainty avoidance ● Collectivism ● High nurture	 Weak uncertainty avoidance High individualism Low nurture
Transparency (strong)	Secrecy tends to be associated with: ● Strong uncertainty avoidance ● Large power distance ● Collectivism ● High nurture	 Weak uncertainty avoidance Small power distance High individualism Low nurture

● there are particular legal or fiscal problems which dictate such a course, or

● the Board genuinely believes that the international approach is wrong and that an independent UK standard might point the way to an eventual improvement in international practice.

Exhibit 11.6 shows the extent to which UK standards are broadly in agreement with IASs and the key areas of difference.

11.7 THE ACCOUNTING SYSTEM[19]

11.7.1 Current regulation

Accounting standards are defined in the Companies Act 1985 as a result of an amendment introduced in 1989. The Act requires directors of companies, other than SMEs, to disclose whether accounts have been prepared in accordance with applicable accounting standards and to explain any departure from those

---

[19] Davies *et al.* (1997)

Exhibit 11.6 COMPARISON OF ACCOUNTING PRACTICES IN THE UK WITH
REQUIREMENTS OF IASs: KEY SIMILARITIES AND DIFFERENCES

IAS	Subject of IAS	Practice in UK	Ref
Disclosure and presentation			
	General aspects consolidated in IAS 1 (revised)		
IAS 1	Fair Presentation	'True and fair' requirement	7.2.2
	Disclosure of Accounting Policies (former IAS 1)	Generally in agreement	
	Information to be Disclosed in Financial Statements (former IAS 5)	Generally in agreement	
	Presentation of Current Assets and Current Liabilities (former IAS 13)	Generally in agreement	
	Specific aspects		
IAS 7	Cash Flow Statements	Generally in agreement. Difference in categories	7.3.1
IAS 8	Net Profit or Loss for the Period, Fundamental Errors and Changes in Accounting Policies	Generally in agreement	
IAS xx	Discontinuing Operations	FRS 3 similar	7.3.1
IAS 14	Reporting Financial Information by Segments	Generally in agreement	7.5.2
IAS 24	Related Party Disclosure	Generally in agreement	
IAS 33	Earnings per Share	New FRED* aligns with IAS 33 on measurement; differences on disclosure	
IAS 34	Interim Financial Reporting	New FRED aligns with IAS	7.5.4
Asset recognition and measurement			
IAS 2	Inventories	Generally in agreement	7.4.1
IAS 4	Depreciation Accounting	Generally in agreement	7.4.1
IAS 16	Property, Plant and Equipment	Generally in agreement; investment properties must be revalued	7.4.1
IAS xx	Impairment of Assets	New FRED aligns with IAS	7.4.2
IAS 23	Borrowing Costs	No specific requirement	
IAS 25	Accounting for Investments	No specific requirement – market value of current asset investments used by some companies	7.4.1
IAS 9	Research and Development Costs	Capitalisation permitted, but not required	7.4.5
IAS xx	Intangible Assets	FRS 10 generally in agreement	7.4.5
Liability recognition and measurement			
IAS 10	Contingencies and Events Occurring After the Balance Sheet Date	Generally in agreement	
IAS 12	Income Taxes	Partial provision method used	7.3.4
IAS 17	Leases	Generally in agreement	
IAS 19	Employee Benefits	Differences exist	
IAS 32	Financial Instruments: Disclosure and Presentation	Under discussion	

▶

Exhibit 11.6 continued

IAS	Subject of IAS	Practice in UK	Ref
Recognition of economic activity			
IAS 11	Construction Contracts	Generally in agreement	
IAS 18	Revenue	Generally in agreement	
IAS 20	Accounting for Government Grants and Disclosure of Government Assistance	Generally in agreement	
Measurement			
IAS 15	Information Reflecting the Effects of Changing Prices	No specific requirement – companies may use current value as alternative valuation	
IAS 29	Financial Reporting in Hyperinflationary Economies	Not relevant to UK economy	
Group accounting			
IAS 21	The Effects of Changes in Foreign Exchange Rates	Generally in agreement; more flexible on translation of profit and loss account items	
IAS 22	Business Combinations	Generally in agreement	7.3.5
IAS 27	Consolidated Financial Statements and Accounting for Investments in Subsidiaries	Generally in agreement	7.3.5 7.4.3
IAS 28	Accounting for Investments in Associates	Generally in agreement	
IAS 31	Financial Reporting of Interests in Joint Ventures	Proportionate consolidation not permitted for incorporated businesses	

Note: *Financial Reporting Exposure Draft (FRED)

standards. Where the accounts of a company do not comply with the requirements of the Act, the legislation gives power to the Courts to order preparation of a revised set of accounts, at the cost of the directors who approved the defective accounts.

From 1970 to 1990 Statements of Standard Accounting Practice (SSAPs) were issued by the ASC. The ASB has adopted all the SSAPs issued by the ASC and remaining in force at 1990. New standards issued for the first time by the ASB are called Financial Reporting Standards (FRSs).

The process of consultation prior to the issue of an FRS includes the issue of a Financial Reporting Exposure Draft (FRED) which in turn may be preceded by a Discussion Paper seeking views on major points of principle. Letters of comment to the ASB will be placed on the public record, unless confidentiality is requested. Other forms of consultation and discussion take place in private. The ASB seeks to operate the maximum possible consultation.

From time to time urgent matters are drawn to the attention of the ASB and these will be dealt with by the UITF. The matters addressed by the UITF are often detailed aspects of an existing standard or of company law.

Bodies which represent industry sectors may develop Statements of Recommended Practice (SORPs). The ASB does not specifically endorse the SORP, but will give an assurance that the SORP does not appear to conflict with existing standards.

11.7.2 Professionalism versus statutory control

The history of accounting practice in the UK is strongly dependent on professional expertise developing practices to satisfy the general requirements of the law. This is consistent with the development of other professions such as law and medicine.

When the law was required to adopt a more prescriptive approach in relation to incorporating the Fourth and Seventh Directives in national law, those drafting the law made extensive use of options in order to preserve the capacity for professional judgement. The preservation of the concept of a 'true and fair view' was a particularly important aspect of the strength of professionalism in the UK, because it allowed continuation of the practice of evolving generally accepted accounting principles.

11.7.2.1 Generally accepted accounting principles

For all limited liability companies the Companies Act 1985 imposes on directors the requirement to present a true and fair view of the financial position and performance of the period. After stipulating that very onerous requirement the legislation leaves many important decisions to professional judgement. Under the influence of the Fourth and Seventh Directives the statute law prescribes formats, but it imposes very little hard practice on valuation.

The Companies Act 1985 uses wording which indicates the existence in the UK of a concept of generally accepted principles or practices. In relation to merger accounting the words 'accords with generally accepted accounting principles or practice' are used and in relation to realised profits there is the wording 'in accordance with principles generally accepted, at the time when the accounts are prepared'. Legislation does not define the wording further. Guidance is contained in Technical Release TR 481, issued by the Consultative Committee of Accounting Bodies (CCAB) in 1982.

Popularisation of the abbreviation 'UK GAAP' may be attributed to the book of that title first published by the accountancy firm of Ernst and Young in the late 1980s, now in its 5th edition (September 1997). The abbreviation may however be found earlier than that in the documents lodged with the SEC by companies having a full listing on a major US stock exchange, where the companies were creating terminology which would appear familiar to US readers.

The use of the phrase in the UK must be seen in the context of the statutory requirement for financial statements to present a 'true and fair view' which is widely regarded in UK accounting practice as having a broader range than the US phrase 'fairly present'.

11.7.2.2 'True and fair view'[20]

There is no definition of the phrase 'a true and fair view' although much has been written about it. The ASB has sought the advice of legal counsel on the matter and that advice is presented as an appendix to the *Foreword to Accounting Standards*. The emphasis is very much on the dynamic nature of the concept. 'What is required to show a true and fair view is subject to continuous rebirth' (Appendix, para. 14). The legal opinion is that the courts will hold that compliance with accounting

---

[20] Parker and Nobes (1994)

standards is necessary to meet the true and fair requirement. The courts would probably give special weight to the view of the ASB as a standard setting body.

It thus seems inescapable that accounting standards are a necessary component of a true and fair view, although they may not in themselves be sufficient in all situations. Professional judgement remains an essential additional element.

11.7.3 Uniformity versus flexibility

Gray (1988) classified UK accounting as exhibiting strong flexibility. When prescribed formats first appeared, as a result of the influence of the Fourth Directive, there were concerns in the accountancy profession that this would curtail professional freedom. However the formats allow flexibility and the standard setting body has taken presentation of primary financial statements well ahead of the legal minimum prescription. The formal separation of tax law and accounting law permits flexibility although in practice it may be constrained by interactions of the two approaches to profit. It was found in the late 1980s that too much flexibility, in relation to defining a group of companies, can lead to problems and the definition was tightened.

11.7.3.1 Financial statement formats

The formats set out in the Fourth Directive have been incorporated in the Companies Act 1985 (consolidating earlier legislation). The Act sets out two formats of balance sheet and four formats of profit and loss account, thus permitting both vertical and horizontal arrangements. In practice, most companies choose the vertical form of balance sheet, and the vertical form of profit and loss account in the functional version. This allows the matching of cost of goods sold against turnover to report gross profit. A smaller number of companies use the version of the profit and loss account which shows type of expenditure. The vertical form of balance sheet is shown for Rentokil Initial plc (1996) (Exhibit 11.7). The profit and loss account in functional version is presented for Dixons (1997) (Exhibit 11.8). There is a requirement in the UK to disclose exceptional items separately, but within the expenditure category where possible. Some companies, such as Dixons, show the exceptional items in an extra column. Others, such as United Biscuits (1996) (Exhibit 11.9) have a line item within the vertical presentation. United Biscuits also gives an example of the disclosure of the results of discontinued operations, reported in a separate note to the profit and loss account.

A cash flow statement is prescribed by FRS 1, first issued in 1991 and amended in 1996 following a review of experience of its use. The revised format contains eight headings, considerably more detailed than IAS 7. The first version was unpopular with preparers of accounts because it reported the movement in 'cash and cash equivalents'. There was some concern that the definition of 'cash equivalents' did not match commercial thinking. The revised version takes a simpler view of cash and appears to have dealt with the objections.

A relatively novel primary financial statement is the Statement of Total Recognised Gains and Losses (STRGL), required by FRS 3, *Reporting Financial Performance* (*see* subsection 11.7.3.2). Additionally there is a requirement in FRS 3

Exhibit 11.7 RENTOKIL INITIAL PLC: BALANCE SHEET IN VERTICAL FORMAT

Balance Sheets

At 31st December	Notes	Consolidated 1996 £m	Consolidated 1995 £m	Parent 1996 £m	Parent 1995 £m
Fixed assets					
Tangible assets	8	725.0	157.1	18.0	17.4
Investments	9	16.4	3.3	734.9	177.3
		741.4	160.4	752.9	194.7
Current assets					
Stocks	10	61.0	30.6	-	-
Debtors	11	481.9	190.6	130.7	175.1
Taxation recoverable	12	13.0	6.7	12.8	6.7
Short term deposits and cash		189.8	173.8	1.3	90.0
		745.7	401.7	144.8	271.8
Current liabilities due within one year					
Creditors	13	(622.9)	(228.2)	(220.4)	(108.4)
Bank and other borrowings	14	(166.0)	(75.1)	(96.1)	(78.4)
		(788.9)	(303.3)	(316.5)	(186.8)
Net current (liabilities)/assets		(43.2)	98.4	(171.7)	85.0
Total assets less current liabilities		698.2	258.8	581.2	279.7
Deferred liabilities due after one year					
Creditors	15	(77.9)	(6.5)	-	-
Bank and other borrowings	16	(533.7)	(1.7)	(396.8)	-
Provisions for liabilities and charges	17	(214.5)	(19.7)	-	(0.9)
Net (liabilities)/assets	1	(127.9)	230.9	184.4	278.8
Equity capital and reserves					
Called up share capital	18	28.5	19.7	28.5	19.7
Share premium account	19	21.3	16.7	21.3	16.7
Merger reserve	20	1,644.4	-	-	-
Revaluation reserve	21	4.0	4.6	1.4	1.4
Other reserves	22	7.2	10.6	-	-
Profit and loss account	23	623.5	495.2	133.2	241.0
Goodwill reserve	24	(2,459.2)	(317.1)	-	-
Equity shareholders' funds		(130.3)	229.7	184.4	278.8
Equity minority interests		2.4	1.2	-	-
Capital employed		(127.9)	230.9	184.4	278.8

Source: Rentokil Initial plc, annual report, 1996, p.43

Exhibit 11.8 DIXONS GROUP: PROFIT AND LOSS ACCOUNT IN VERTICAL FORMAT, FUNCTIONAL PRESENTATION

Consolidated Profit and Loss Account

	Note	Before exceptional items £million	Exceptional items £million	53 weeks ended 3 May 1997 Total £million	52 weeks ended 27 April 1996 Total £million
Turnover					
Continuing operations		2,421.6	–	2,421.6	1,919.7
Acquisitions		20.9	–	20.9	–
	2	2,442.5	–	2,442.5	1,919.7
Operating profit					
Continuing operations		177.9	(9.0)	168.9	128.1
Acquisitions		0.5	–	0.5	–
	3	178.4	(9.0)	169.4	128.1
Exceptional profit on partial disposal	4	–	19.0	19.0	–
Exceptional amount written off investment		–	–	–	(33.7)
Profit on ordinary activities before interest		178.4	10.0	188.4	94.4
Net interest	5	11.8	–	11.8	7.1
Profit on ordinary activities before taxation		190.2	10.0	200.2	101.5
Taxation on profit on ordinary activities	10	(50.3)	2.8	(47.5)	(30.9)
Profit for the period		139.9	12.8	152.7	70.6
Dividends – Preference	11			(9.3)	(9.3)
– Ordinary	11			(44.4)	(35.2)
Retained profit for the period	27			99.0	26.1
Earnings per Ordinary share (pence)					
Basic	12			34.3p	15.3p
Adjusted basic	12			31.2p	23.7p
Fully diluted	12			32.1p	15.7p
Adjusted fully diluted	12			29.4p	22.7p

Source: Dixons Group, annual report, 1997, p. 40

for a note reconciling the changes in shareholders' funds and movements on reserves. Where there is a difference between pure historical cost profit and the profit reported, there must be a note reconciling the two figures.

11.7.3.2 Statement of total recognised gains and losses

In 1993, the ASB proposed a new primary financial statement which would report the total of all gains and losses of the reporting entity that are recognised in a period and are attributable to shareholders. The first line of this statement is taken from the profit and loss account which reports the net profit realised for

Exhibit 11.9   UNITED BISCUITS: PROFIT AND LOSS ACCOUNT AND NOTE ON DISCONTINUED OPERATIONS

Consolidated profit and loss account

for the 52 weeks ended 28 December 1996

	Notes	1996 £m	1995 £m
Turnover			
Continuing operations		1,887.2	1,824.3
Discontinued operations		99.5	1,176.8
		1,986.7	3,001.1
Cost of sales		(1,271.5)	(1,755.2)
Gross profit		715.2	1,245.9
Distribution, selling and marketing costs		(434.6)	(983.5)
Administrative expenses		(147.9)	(166.3)
Other income		5.3	2.5
Employee profit sharing		(1.0)	–
Operational reorganisations	2	–	(27.4)
Operating profit			
Continuing operations before exceptionals		129.2	123.8
Discontinued operations		7.8	(25.2)
		137.0	98.6
Operating exceptional items		–	(27.4)
Total operating profit		137.0	71.2
Amounts written off investments	2	(3.2)	(4.3)
Loss on disposal of businesses	2 & 21	(82.9)	(102.3)
Profit/(loss) on disposal of fixed assets	2	1.4	(16.3)
Profit/(loss) before interest	2	52.3	(51.7)
Interest	3	(27.9)	(48.9)
Profit/(loss) on ordinary activities before tax			
Continuing operations before exceptionals		101.3	74.9
Discontinued operations before exceptionals		7.8	(25.2)
Total operations before exceptionals		109.1	49.7
Total exceptional items		(84.7)	(150.3)
Profit/(loss) on ordinary activities before tax		24.4	(100.6)
Taxation			
Tax charge on profit before exceptionals	5	(29.7)	(23.0)
Tax credit/(charge) on exceptionals	5	23.6	(1.2)
Taxation		(6.1)	(24.2)
Profit/(loss) on ordinary activities after tax		18.3	(124.8)
Minority interests		(1.3)	(1.4)
Profit/(loss) attributable to shareholders		17.0	(126.2)
Dividends – payable	6	(18.5)	(18.5)
– proposed	6	(34.5)	(32.8)
Reduction in reserve	19	(36.0)	(177.5)

▶

Exhibit 11.9 continued

Notes to the accounts

continued

2 Profit before interest (continued)

Full analysis of turnover down to profit before interest is set out below:

	Continuing operations £m	Discontinued operations £m	1996 Total £m	Continuing operations £m	Discontinued operations £m	1995 Total £m
Turnover	1,887.2	99.5	1,986.7	1,824.3	1,176.8	3,001.1
Cost of sales	(1,212.4)	(59.1)	(1,271.5)	(1,193.7)	(561.5)	(1,755.2)
Gross profit	674.8	40.4	715.2	630.6	615.3	1,245.9
Distribution, selling and marketing costs	(412.7)	(21.9)	(434.6)	(389.4)	(594.1)	(983.5)
Administrative expenses	(137.7)	(10.2)	(147.9)	(120.2)	(46.1)	(166.3)
Other income	5.8	(0.5)	5.3	2.8	(0.3)	2.5
Employee profit sharing	(1.0)	–	(1.0)	–	–	–
Operational reorganisations	–	–	–	(27.4)	–	(27.4)
Operating profit/(loss) before exceptional items	129.2	7.8	137.0	96.4	(25.2)	71.2
Amounts written off investments	(3.2)	–	(3.2)	(4.3)	–	(4.3)
Non-operating exceptional items	(8.4)	(73.1)	(81.5)	(13.6)	(105.0)	(118.6)
Profit/(loss) before interest	117.6	(65.3)	52.3	78.5	(130.2)	(51.7)

Source: United Biscuits, annual report, 1996, pp. 38, 46

shareholders, but it continues by adding in unrealised items, particularly increases in value of fixed assets and foreign currency translation effects. The information contained in the STRGL could be found in the note of movements on reserves, but these are not easy to find or to understand. The ASB felt that creating a new primary statement, to be presented in close proximity to the profit and loss account, would draw attention to the unrealised gains and losses.

Respondents to the earlier exposure draft had asked that the STRGL should be extended to provide a complete reconciliation of movements in shareholders' funds. The ASB decided the reconciliation would be useful but preferred a separate note which would not divert attention from the components of performance in the STRGL. The appearance of the full page of information is shown for Rentokil Initial plc (1996) (Exhibit 11.10).

Exhibit 11.10 RENTOKIL INITIAL PLC: STATEMENT OF TOTAL RECOGNISED GAINS AND LOSSES, NOTE OF HISTORICAL COST PROFITS AND LOSSES AND RECONCILIATION OF MOVEMENTS IN SHAREHOLDERS' FUNDS

Statement of Total Recognised Gains and Losses

For the year ended 31st December	Consolidated		Parent	
	1996	1995	**1996**	1995
	£m	£m	**£m**	£m
Profit attributable to shareholders	**219.2**	139.3	**(29.8)**	92.0
Exchange adjustments	**(22.7)**	5.8	**(5.8)**	3.2
Total recognised gains/(losses) for the year	**196.5**	145.1	**(35.6)**	95.2

Note of Historic Cost Profits and Losses

No historic cost statement for the group or the parent company has been presented as the difference between the reported profit and the historic cost profit is immaterial.

Reconciliation of Movements in Shareholders' Funds

For the year ended 31st December	Consolidated		Parent	
	1996	1995	**1996**	1995
	£m	£m	**£m**	£m
Profit attributable to shareholders	**219.2**	139.3	**(29.8)**	92.0
Dividends	**(72.2)**	(41.4)	**(72.2)**	(41.4)
New share capital issued	**1,657.8**	8.3	**1,657.8**	8.3
Utilisation of merger reserve	**-**	-	**(1,644.4)**	-
Goodwill written-off (note 24)	**(2,142.1)**	(56.8)	**-**	-
Exchange adjustments	**(22.7)**	5.8	**(5.8)**	3.2
Net change in shareholders' funds	**(360.0)**	55.2	**(94.4)**	62.1
Opening shareholders' funds	**229.7**	174.5	**278.8**	216.7
Closing shareholders' funds	**(130.3)**	229.7	**184.4**	278.8

Source: Rentokil Initial plc, annual report, 1996, p. 42

11.7.3.3 Relationship between company law and tax law[21]

Accounting profit for tax purposes is reported separately from accounting profit for accounting purposes; separate laws govern each measure of profit. There is therefore formal independence of the two approaches to measurement of profit, and this permits financial reporting to be flexible without fiscal impact. However, despite formal independence there have developed effective interdependencies, primarily because the judgment of the courts in relation to taxable profit is that it should be based on the profits reported under generally accepted accounting principles. Where flexibility exists under accounting practice, there have therefore been instances of choosing the approach likely to lead to the most favourable taxation outcome, and on occasions this flexibility has been challenged in the courts by the tax authorities. The results of such court decisions have had some influence on subsequent accounting practice in regard to this particular issue.

11.7.3.4 Accounting for deferred taxation

It has been explained that the rules for calculating taxable profit may lead to a different figure from that reported for accounting purposes. This may lead to postponement (deferral) of some part of the liability which might be expected from the accounting profit. The liability will eventually become payable, and so provision should be made.

The standard SSAP 15 requires provision for deferred taxation to the extent that it is probable that a liability or asset will crystallise. This standard replaced an earlier version, SSAP 11, which required full provision for the expected liability. Under that approach, companies found that the provision was accumulating in the balance sheet year after year and did not appear to diminish by reversal. Because of the memory of that experience, companies have been unenthusiastic for the ASB to bow to the strong international pressure to revert to full provision. Furthermore UK companies have enjoyed flexibility in applying the partial provision method. Surveys have shown that the word 'partial' appears to cover any proportion of the full amount, from almost zero up to 99%. The amount of the full provision must be shown by way of note.

11.7.3.5 Nature of the group[22]

In 1989 the amendment to the Companies Act 1985 took on the maximum flexibility permitted by the Seventh Directive, in defining the group for the purposes of consolidation. This use of flexibility was somewhat surprising because earlier the Department of Trade and Industry had argued for not departing from the well tried majority voting rule of the Companies Act 1948. The change in thinking was caused by concern that the 1948 rules were allowing companies to remain off the consolidated balance sheet despite behaviour which made them indistinguishable from subsidiaries included in the consolidation.

The new wording in 1989 tightened up the definition of a subsidiary but a further net was provided by the accounting standard FRS 5, *Reporting the Substance of*

---

[21] Lamb (1996); McMahon and Weetman (1997)
[22] Nobes (1993)

Transactions, in defining a quasi-subsidiary as any entity which, although not ful-filling the definition of a subsidiary, is directly or indirectly controlled by the reporting entity and gives rise to benefits which are in substance no different from those that would arise from a subsidiary.

11.7.4 Conservatism versus optimism

Gray (1988) classified UK accounting practice as demonstrating strong optimism, rather than conservatism. Companies are permitted to revalue upwards from his-torical cost and at present the rules on matching this with revaluation downwards are under review for tighter procedures. Provisions have in the past been given very varied and flexible treatment but that also is under review, paradoxically because companies have sometimes used provisions to be very conservative in one accounting period and leaving a very optimistic scene for the next accounting period. Intangible assets have also been an area for potential optimism which are now under review by the standard setters. The mood of the standard setters is to allow optimism only under carefully controlled conditions.

11.7.4.1 Valuation

The Companies Act 1985 permits either historical cost accounting or the use of an alternative basis of valuation. The alternative basis must be current value. After many years of debate on the application of alternative valuations within an overall histori-cal cost system, an exposure draft FRED 17 was issued in October 1997.[23] The exposure draft codifies as a proposed standard the existing best practice. There was a long process of consultation leading to FRED 17. The former ASC issued the exposure draft ED 51[24] which included some of the ideas emerging in FRED 17. In a Discussion Paper[25] on valuation in financial reporting the ASB acknowledged general anxieties about moving away from historical cost accounting to full current value accounting and indicated its inclination to concentrate on making pronouncements where there is already a requirement in law to provide supplementary information on current values and where the assets are already traded on a ready market.

Consistent with IAS 16, FRED 17 proposes that where an entity adopts a policy of revaluation, all assets of the same class should be revalued and the revaluations kept up to date. Previously companies were not required to revalue regularly and they could choose which assets to revalue. An example of the *ad hoc* nature of valuation may be seen in ASDA Group plc (1996) (Exhibit 11.11) which produces a full fixed assets note.

The ASB's interpretation of 'current value' is largely replacement cost, based on the 'deprival value' ideas from models in accounting theory. The justification for this approach is set out in the Statement of Principles.[26] The ASB is also consider-ing the use of discounting for the valuation of some long-term liabilities and impaired fixed assets. Those ideas are at a relatively early stage.[27]

---

[23] ASB (1997a)
[24] ASC (1990)
[25] ASB (1993a)
[26] ASB (1995)
[27] ASB (1997b)

Exhibit 11.11 ASDA: NOTES TO THE ACCOUNTS ON FIXED ASSETS, SHOWING REVALUATION

Group Accounting Policies

Accounting basis

The accounts are prepared under the historical cost convention modified to include the revaluation of certain fixed assets.

The accounts are prepared in accordance with applicable accounting standards.

Notes to the Accounts

7. TANGIBLE FIXED ASSETS	Freehold properties £m	Leasehold properties £m	Plant fixtures & fitting £m	Total £m
Cost or valuation				
At beginning of year	986.7	792.3	545.9	2,324.9
Reclassification	11.1	(15.3)	4.2	–
Acquisitions	351.9	11.5	0.5	363.9
Additions	142.7	41.8	91.0	275.5
Disposals	(7.5)	(19.3)	(40.1)	(66.9)
At end of year	1,484.9	811.0	601.5	2,897.4
Cost or valuation at end of year is represented by:				
Valuation at 2 May, 1992	544.1	410.3	–	954.4
Cost	940.8	400.7	601.5	1,943.0
	1,484.9	811.0	601.5	2,897.4
Depreciation				
At beginning of year	86.1	127.4	301.2	514.7
Reclassification	0.2	(0.9)	0.7	–
Acquisitions	–	–	0.3	0.3
Charge for the year	14.7	16.8	65.0	96.5
Disposals	–	(0.8)	(31.8)	(32.6)
At end of year	101.0	142.5	335.4	578.9
Net book amounts at end of year	1,383.9	668.5	266.1	2,318.5
Assets under construction (1995: £117.5 million)				184.1
Net book amounts at end of year				2,502.6
Net book amounts at beginning of year				1,927.7

Exhibit 11.11 continued

Food retailing properties were revalued at 2 May, 1992 by the group's own surveyors. This was carried out on the basis of open market valuation for existing use, with the exception of certain properties which, in the opinion of the directors, had a limited future life in existing use. In respect of these properties, a directors' valuation was undertaken on the basis of their lower, alternative use value. This valuation was further reviewed at 30 April, 1994 when additional properties were written down to their alternative use value.

The cumulative amount of capitalised interest included in the net book value of fixed assets is £10.4 million (1995: £10.2 million). Details of interest capitalised during the year are given in note 3 on page 43.

The historical cost of food retailing properties included at valuation is as follows:

	1996 £m	1995 £m
Freehold properties	693.8	694.8
Leasehold properties	474.6	474.6
	1,168.4	1,169.4

The net book amount of plant, fixtures and fittings for the group includes £13.9 million (1995: £10.5 million) in respect of leased assets after charging depreciation of £5.1 million (1995: £9.3 million).

The net book amount of leased property includes:	Group	
	1996 £m	1995 £m
Leases with 50 years or more unexpired	481.7	507.4
Leases with less than 50 years unexpired	186.8	157.5
	668.5	664.9

Source: ASDA plc, annual report, 1996, pp. 36, 45, 46

11.7.4.2 Impairment

The ASB has issued an exposure draft FRED 15, which generally adopts the approach taken by the IASC in E 55 Impairment of Assets. The accounting standard setters in Australia, Canada, the UK, the USA and New Zealand (referred to as 'the G4+1'), working with the IASC, are also preparing a paper on impairment which contrasts the approach followed in the FRED and the IASC exposure draft with that of the US standard.

The approach taken by the FRED is that impairment should be measured by comparing the carrying amount of a fixed asset or income-generating unit with the higher of its net realisable value and its value in use. Value in use is to be calculated by discounting the expected future cash flows at an estimate of the rate that the market would expect on an equally risky investment. There are some matters of technical detail where FRED 15 differs from E 55, but the principles are comparable.

11.7.4.3 Goodwill

When the Fourth Directive was introduced into UK law in 1981 it included a requirement that all fixed assets of finite life should be depreciated. At that time, companies and groups which had acquired goodwill had traditionally left the asset in the balance sheet, without amortisation, on the grounds that it was a long-term benefit to the company or group which was constantly being replenished. In the light of the Fourth Directive, this no longer appeared acceptable under law.

It was the view in the UK at the time that amortisation of the asset would be unpalatable and so it was decided that the favoured UK treatment would be immediate write-off against reserves. This preserved the profit and loss account from reporting any expense of amortisation. However, over a period of years during the 1980s, groups of companies making regular acquisitions found that in their balance sheets the equity base was being eroded by repeated write-offs. This reached the point that some companies such as advertising agencies, where goodwill is a high proportion of the acquisition, had negative equity. In some cases, the gearing ratios, comparing debt to equity, rose to what appeared to be unacceptable levels. Companies disliked reporting the goodwill write-off against reserves of accumulated past profit; some created a 'goodwill write-off reserve', starting with a nil balance and gradually becoming more negative. An example is Rentokil Initial plc (1996) (Exhibits 11.12 and 11.13). Looking back to the balance sheet of this company (Exhibit 11.7) you will see that continually writing-off goodwill has led to a position of negative equity.

The ASC made unsuccessful attempts, from time to time, to persuade preparers of accounts to consider reporting goodwill as an asset, with amortisation through the profit and loss account. Its final attempt was the exposure draft ED 57. During the 1990s the ASB continued the debate, persisting against considerable opposition and using a variety of methods of consultation. FRS 10, Goodwill and Intangible Assets, was issued in December 1997.

FRS 10 requires amortisation of the asset and on a systematic basis with the assumption that the asset life will not be longer than 20 years. Where the reporting entity wishes to argue for an asset life beyond 20 years it will have to apply impairment tests to show that the asset has maintained its value. The impairment tests are consistent with impairment tests proposed by the ASB in FRED 15 for a wider range of both tangible and intangible asset.

11.7.4.4 Provisions

Provisions, and movements on provisions, are often significant in the measurement of financial position and performance, but there has until recently been little published guidance on their measurement and disclosure. The exposure draft FRED 14 established three basic principles:

1 a provision should be recognised only where the entity has an obligation to transfer economic benefits as a result of past events;

2 the amount recognised as a provision should be a realistic and prudent estimate of the expenditure required to settle the obligation that existed at the balance sheet date;

3 specific disclosures, for each class of provision, should be given about the year-end position and about movements during the year; the exposure draft also deals with provisions for environmental liabilities.

Exhibit 11.12 RENTOKIL INITIAL PLC: ACCOUNTING POLICY AND NOTE TO THE
ACCOUNTS SHOWING GOODWILL RESERVE AND FAIR VALUE ADJUSTMENTS
ON ACQUISITION

Accounting Policies

Consolidation

The consolidated accounts comprise those of the parent company and its subsidiary undertakings ("subsidiaries" or "subsidiary companies") together with the group's share of the pre-tax profits, tax and net tangible assets of the associated undertakings ("associates" or "associated companies").

The results of newly acquired companies and businesses are consolidated from the date of acquisition.

For acquisitions involving deferred consideration, estimated deferred payments are accrued in the balance sheet. Interest due to vendors on deferred payments is charged to the profit and loss account as it accrues.

Goodwill represents the difference between the costs of acquisition and the fair value of the net tangible assets acquired. Goodwill is transferred to a separate reserve in the year of acquisition. Fair value adjustments are reviewed in the accounts for the year following the year of acquisition.

Notes on the Accounts

		Consolidated	
		1996	1995
		£m	£m
24 **Goodwill** **reserve**	At 1st January	**317.1**	260.3
	Additions in year	**2,142.1**	56.8
	At 31st December	**2,459.2**	317.1

29
Acquisitions

The group purchased 15 companies and businesses during the year as set out on page 63 for a total consideration of £2,230.3m of which £2,221.7m was in respect of the acquisition on 29th April 1996 of BET Public Limited Company. The total adjustments required to the balance sheet figures of companies and businesses acquired in order to present the net assets of those companies and businesses at fair values in accordance with group accounting principles were £260.8m, of which £259.7m related to BET, details of which are set out on pages 58 and 59 together with the matching adjustment to goodwill. All of these businesses have been accounted for as acquisitions.

Source: Rentokil Initial plc, annual report, pp. 45, 55, 57

Exhibit 11.13 FAIR VALUE ADJUSTMENTS

29 **Acquisitions** (continued)	From the dates of acquisition to 31st December 1996 the acquisitions contributed £1,334.6m to turnover (BET £1,331.7m), £116.9m to profit before interest (BET £116.1m) and £85.2m to profit after interest (BET £84.6m). BET contributed £138.6m to the group's net operating cash flows, paid £31.5m in respect of interest, £15.5m in respect of taxation and utilised £114.2m for capital expenditure. In its last financial year to 30th March 1996, BET made a profit after tax and minority interests of £101.8m. For the period since that date to the date of acquisition, BET's management accounts show:

	£m
Turnover	169.7
Operating profit	7.2
Profit before taxation	5.3
Taxation and minority interests	(2.3)
Profit attributable to shareholders	3.0
Exchange adjustments	(0.5)
Total recognised gains for the period	2.5

BET acquisition

	Book value	Revaluations	Consistency of accounting policy	Other	Fair value
	£m	£m	£m	£m	£m
Tangible fixed assets	609.2	(24.1)	(22.9)	-	562.2
Investments	33.0	(3.4)	(18.3)	(1.0)	10.3
Stock	35.0	(3.3)	-	-	31.7
Debtors	372.5	12.4	(0.6)	-	384.3
Creditors	(472.1)	(61.4)	(6.0)	-	(539.5)
Provisions					
- Vacant property	(20.7)	-	-	(47.5)	(68.2)
- Environmental	(4.4)	-	-	(49.9)	(54.3)
- Subsidiary	-	-	-	(33.0)	(33.0)
- Pre-acquisition					
restructuring	(1.8)	-	-	(5.0)	(6.8)
Taxation	(108.2)	3.5	-	-	(104.7)
Net debt	(130.5)	-	-	-	(130.5)
	312.0	(76.3)	(47.8)	(136.4)	51.5
Minority interests	(1.7)	0.8	-	-	(0.9)
Net assets acquired	310.3	(75.5)	(47.8)	(136.4)	50.6

Special dividend to BET shareholders	38.2
Adjusted assets	88.8
Goodwill	2,132.9
Consideration	2,221.7
Satisfied by	
Shares issued	1,653.2
Cash (including special dividend paid of £38.2m and deducting	
cash received from exercise of share options of £18.0m)	568.5
	2,221.7

Source: Rentokil Initial plc, annual report, 1996, p. 58

These principles are intended to prevent companies from making provision in anticipation of future events or commitments. Where this has occurred in past practice, it has been criticised by commentators as being over conservative. In developing FRED 14, the ASB worked closely with the IASC in a joint project. The proposals in FRED 14 are largely consistent with those of the IASC document.

11.7.4.5 Intangible assets

During the 1980s, some groups of companies found their equity diminishing through writing-off goodwill. They found a remedy in intangible assets other than goodwill, particularly brand names purchased or developed by the company. Where brand names had been acquired by corporate takeover, that element was taken out of the goodwill calculation and reported as a separate asset of the group. It was argued that brands have a long life and therefore amortisation was not required. Other companies took the further step of reporting as an asset the brand names developed internally, using a valuation supplied by expert advisers. The ASC and then the ASB sought, in various exposure drafts and discussion papers, to prohibit the reporting of internally generated intangible assets and to discourage the separate identification of brand names acquired in a takeover or merger.

After taking account of the arguments presented, the ASB decided to allow purchased intangible fixed assets to be distinguished from goodwill, provided they met specific recognition criteria. To achieve comparability of accounting treatment, the ASB will include intangible assets with goodwill in the new standard where the rules for amortisation of intangible assets are the same as those for goodwill (section 11.7.4.3).

Research and development expenditure remains in a separate standard, SSAP 13, which requires all research expenditure to be reported as an expense of the period in which it is incurred. Development expenditure which meets the criteria for recognition as an asset may be reported as such, but there is no compulsion. This is different from the IAS 9 insistence on reporting as an asset certain types of development expenditure. Software development companies have expressed concern that international acceptance of IAS 9 would lead to their global competitors showing higher profits under the 'capitalise and amortise' approach than is presently shown under the 'total write-off' approach where the UK companies match the conservative approach of their US competitors.[28]

11.7.5 Secrecy versus transparency

Gray (1988) classified UK accounting as strongly transparent. Notes to the accounts and additional voluntary disclosures are evidence of such transparency. Segmental reporting, the operating and financial review, interim reporting and disclosures regarding directors' remuneration are examples of transparency in UK reporting practice. It has been observed that non-financial disclosures in annual reports of major companies are greater in the UK than in the USA or in continental European countries.[29]

---

[28] *Accountancy Age*, 11 September 1997, p. 3
[29] Meek, Robert and Gray (1995)

11.7.5.1 Notes to the accounts

Notes to the accounts are required by company law and, for listed companies, by stock exchange regulations. Where the primary financial statements fail to show a true and fair view, this cannot be rectified by providing information in the notes to the accounts. The notes provide additional explanation to support what is contained in the financial statements.

There is considerable evidence that leading UK companies make voluntary disclosures well ahead of the minimum requirement of the law. This is particularly so where the companies have multinational activities. The annual reports of such companies are more informative than the basic prescription of law might lead the reader to expect.[30] Such companies are using the annual report to project their image on international stock exchanges.

11.7.5.2 Segmental reporting

The accounting standard SSAP 25 was the final standard issued by the ASC, and was broadly in line with IAS 14 at the time of issue, with some exceptions. SSAP 25 did not require the basis of intersegment pricing to be disclosed. SSAP 25 required 'segment net assets', while IAS 14 referred to 'assets employed'. Perhaps most significant was the exemption provided in SSAP 25, which stated that an entity need not disclose segmental information if disclosure would be seriously prejudicial to its interests.

The ASB returned to segmental reporting in 1996 in a Discussion Paper seeking views on the proposals in the USA and Canada as well as those of the IASC. It is likely that further UK proposals will follow on from the revised IAS and the changes made in the US and Canada.

11.7.5.3 Operating and financial review[31]

The Operating and financial review (OFR) is a form of disclosure recommended by the ASB in a non-mandatory Statement of best practice. The OFR is a framework for the directors to discuss and analyse the performance of the business and the factors underlying its results and financial position, in order to assist users to assess for themselves the future potential of the business.

There is no standard format for the OFR because directors are encouraged to design the OFR in the manner best suited to the needs of the business and its users. The ASB was keen to avoid the stereotyped image of some of the Management Discussion and Analysis documents (MD&A) issued in the United States. Essential features of the OFR are a top-down structure; a balanced and objective account, reference to matter discussed previously which have not turned out as expected; analytical discussion; explanations of ratios calculated; and analysis of trends. In discussing trends it should indicate trends and factors which have affected the results but are not expected to continue in the future, and also known events, trends and uncertainties which are expected to have an impact on the business in the future.

---

[30] Gray and Roberts (1993)
[31] ASB (1993b)

11.7.5.4 Interim reporting

Listed companies are required to provide interim reports on a half-yearly basis. Some provide quarterly reports voluntarily. The regulations on disclosure are largely those set by the Stock Exchange, increased at the recommendation of the Cadbury Report. The ASB has issued a non-mandatory Statement of best practice which is consistent with the IAS standard on the subject.[32] It sets out the recommended timing, contents and measurement basis of interim reports. On timing it encourages publication within 60 days of the interim period-end. The 'discrete' method is recommended, where the interim period is regarded as a distinct accounting period. Seasonal businesses may consequently report markedly different results in each half or quarter of the year.

11.7.5.5 Preliminary announcements

Under Stock Exchange rules a listed company is required to make an announcement of its results for the year in such a way that the information reaches all stock market participants at the same time. This is done through an organised announcements service; however, the amount of information announced varies from one company to the next. Some give little more than the annual profit and a summary balance sheet; others provide detail almost as great as that of the annual report which follows later. The ASB has issued an exposure draft of a Statement on preliminary announcements which will improve the timeliness, quality, relevance and consistency of preliminary announcements. The recommendations have similarities to the statement on interim reports.

11.7.5.6 Directors' remuneration[33]

As explained earlier, concerns about corporate governance in the UK led in particular to recommendations of increased disclosure of directors' emoluments and other benefits. The general recommendations of the Cadbury Committee were made specific by the Greenbury Committee and implemented by the Stock Exchange as requirements for listed companies. In 1997, the requirements were extended by Statutory Instrument to all limited companies, although with less demanding rules for unlisted companies. The essence of the changes is that:

- new disclosures are required for long-term incentive schemes, share options and pension benefits
- more information is required about the highest paid director
- differential levels of disclosure are applied to listed companies, compared with unlisted companies.

The Stock Exchange adds to the requirements for listed companies.

---

[32] ASB (1997c)
[33] Chandler (1996)

11.8 EMPIRICAL STUDIES

11.8.1 Classification studies

In Chapter 4 it was shown that Mueller (1967) classified the UK as an independent discipline system where accounting is seen as a service function derived from business practices and is characterised by the use of professional judgment (subsection 4.4.1). Nobes (1984) classified UK accounting as micro-based, in the family of business practice, being pragmatic and of British origin and setting the basis for a UK influence (Exhibit 4.7). Nair and Frank (1980) classified the UK with new and old Commonwealth countries (other than Canada) on the basis of measurement (Exhibit 4.10) and of disclosure (Exhibit 4.11). However it should be noted that the classification by Nair and Frank pre-dates the adoption of the Fourth and Seventh Directives. Using more recent survey data, Doupnik and Salter (1993) (Exhibit 4.8) classified the United Kingdom as micro-based and in a group dominated by characteristics of a well developed capital market, the attitude to uncertainty and the legal system.

11.8.2 Comparability measures

Research methods for studying comparability were explained in Chapter 3. Studies based on the restatement of UK accounts under US GAAP (Weetman and Gray, 1990, 1991) have shown that UK reported profits are higher than those under US GAAP. The principal cause of difference has been non-amortisation of goodwill, but there have been other factors, such as partial provision for deferred tax, which have caused profits under UK GAAP to be systematically less conservative than US GAAP. In the balance sheet, the reported UK equity has been lower due to writing off goodwill but higher due to revaluation of fixed assets and to the use of partial rather than full provision for deferred taxation. An example of the re-statement presented to the US SEC is given in the annual report of Tomkins plc (1997) (Exhibit 11.14), where the US reported profit is lower than that reported in the UK, due mainly to amortisation of goodwill in the USA. The US shareholders' funds are much greater than the UK figure, the difference again being dominated by goodwill.

In the hypothetical study by Simmonds and Azières (1989), it was shown that UK accounting practice gave the highest measure of 'most likely' profit by a considerable margin. The maximum achievable and the minimum achievable were also the highest in their respective ranges, across the EU countries studied. The lack of a goodwill charge was the key item.

11.8.3 Harmonisation studies

Harmonisation studies were described in general terms in Chapter 3. Archer *et al.* (1995) included the UK in their eight-country sample which showed a low level of harmony on deferred tax both between countries and within countries. However the changes in practice during the period of their study were more prevalent in the other countries than in the UK.

Hermann and Thomas (1995) grouped the UK with Denmark, Ireland and the Netherlands as a fairness orientated country. They found relatively high use of

Exhibit 11.14 TOMKINS PLC: RECONCILIATION TO US ACCOUNTING PRINCIPLES

Results under US accounting principles

Reconciliation to US Accounting Principles

The following is a summary of the estimated adjustments to profit and shareholders' funds which would be required if US GAAP had been applied instead of UK GAAP.

	1997 £ million	1996 £ million	1997 $ million	1996 $ million
PROFIT ATTRIBUTABLE TO SHAREHOLDERS				
Profit attributable to shareholders as reported in the consolidated profit & loss account	282.6	223.9	457.3	362.3
Estimated adjustments:				
Goodwill amortisation	(41.2)	(31.4)	(66.7)	(50.8)
Write back of impaired goodwill previously amortised	3.5	–	5.7	–
Pension costs	(1.2)	–	(1.9)	–
Deferred income tax	(1.9)	–	(3.1)	–
Estimated profit attributable to all shareholders (net income) as adjusted to accord with US GAAP	241.8	192.5	391.3	311.5
Preference share dividends	(26.4)	–	(42.7)	–
Estimated profit attributable to ordinary shareholders (net income) as adjusted to accord with US GAAP	215.4	192.5	348.6	311.5

	Per share	Per share	Per ADR	Per ADR
EARNINGS				
APB OPINION NO 15				
Primary	17.97p	16.14p	$1.16	$1.04
Fully diluted	17.67p	16.11p	$1.14	$1.04
SFAS NO 128				
Basic	18.08p	16.23p	$1.17	$1.05
Diluted	17.67p	16.11p	$1.14	$1.04

	1997 £ million	1996 £ million	1997 $ million	1996 $ million
SHAREHOLDERS' FUNDS				
Shareholders' funds as reported in the consolidated balance sheet	1,437.3	1,096.8	2,325.8	1,774.8
Estimated adjustments:				
Dividends	100.4	86.2	162.5	139.5
Pension liabilities	(12.6)	–	(20.4)	–
Deferred income tax	82.8	–	134.0	–
Redeemable convertible cumulative preference shares	(391.4)	–	(633.4)	–
Goodwill	1,708.8	1,272.3	2,765.2	2,058.8
Cumulative amortisation of goodwill	(225.8)	(155.2)	(365.4)	(251.1)
Estimated shareholders' funds (shareholders' equity) as adjusted to accord with US GAAP	2,699.5	2,300.1	4,368.3	3,722.0

The exchange rate used to translate the above figures (including comparatives) is that ruling at the 1997 balance sheet date (£1 = $1.6182).

Source: Tomkins plc, annual report, 1997, p. 72

modified historical cost in fixed asset valuation, uniform use of straight-line depreci-ation, predominant write-off for goodwill, expensing of research and development, poor disclosure of the details of the costing approach used in stock valuation and similar policies in all companies on matters of foreign currency translation. Overall the UK was found to be the most harmonised country in the EU countries surveyed.

Emenyonu and Gray (1992) found statistically significant differences between the measurement practices of large French, German and UK companies.

11.9 SUMMARY AND CONCLUSIONS

In this chapter you have seen how characteristics of accounting principles and practice in the UK are related to the predictions made by Gray and others based upon analysis of cultural factors. Using the scores developed by Hofstede (1984), Gray's (1988) method of analysis may be used to predict that the accounting system in the UK will be characterised by strong professionalism, strong flexibility, strong optimism and strong transparency. The profession has a long history of development in the UK and has traditionally operated in a framework where statu-tory control is limited to prescribing minimum standards only, leaving the profession to determine best practice. Flexibility has been consistent with this pro-fessional approach, uniformity in matters such as presentation of formats being a relatively new feature caused by implementation of directives. Optimism, rather than conservatism, is seen in the use of alternative valuation rules to historical cost accounting. Transparency is seen in the extensive disclosures required of com-panies by way of notes to the accounts.

UK accounting has developed in its own mould but has also been exported to former UK colonies and trading partners. IASs are acknowledged indirectly in notes to domestic accounting standards, which indicate compliance, or lack of compli-ance. The UK standard setting body is an active participant in the core standards programme of the IASC.

QUESTIONS

Business environment (11.2)

1 To what extent does the business environment of the UK provide clues as to possible influences on accounting practices?

Early developments in accounting (11.3)

1 To what extent do early developments in accounting practice indicate the likely directions of professionalism/statutory control; uniformity/flexibility; conser-vatism/optimism; and secrecy/transparency in current practice?

Institutions (11.4)

1 How does the political and economic system of the UK fit into the classifica-tions described in Chapter 1?

2 How does the legal system of the UK fit into the classifications described in Chapter 1?

3 How does the taxation system of the UK compare to the descriptions given in Chapter 1?

4 How does the corporate financing system of the UK compare to the descriptions given in Chapter 1?

5 How does the accounting profession in the UK compare to the descriptions given in Chapter 1?

6 How do the external influences on accounting practice in the UK compare to those described in Chapter 1?

7 Which institutional factors are most likely to influence UK accounting practice?

Societal culture and accounting subculture (11.5)

1 What is the position of the UK relative to Germany, France and the Netherlands, according to Hofstede's (1984) analysis (Chapter 2)?

2 What are the features of UK societal culture identified by Hofstede which led Gray to his (1988) conclusions regarding the likely system of accounting in the UK?

3 What is the position of the UK relative to Germany, Australia and Japan, according to Hofstede's analysis (Chapter 2)?

IASs (11.6)

1 In which areas does accounting practice in the UK depart from that set out in IASs?

2 For each of the areas of departure which you have identified, describe the treatment prescribed or applied in UK accounting, and identify the likely impact on the income and shareholders' equity of moving from US GAAP to the relevant IASs.

3 What explanations may be offered for these departures from IASs, in terms of the institutional factors described in the chapter?

4 What are the most difficult problems facing accounting in the UK if it seeks harmonisation with the IASC core standards programme?

EU membership (11.3.1, 11.3.2, 11.4.6 and 11.7.3.1)

1 What have been the most significant changes in accounting practice in the UK arising from the Fourth and Seventh Directives?

2 Which factors make it relatively easy or relatively difficult for UK accounting practices to harmonise with those of other European countries?

Professionalism/statutory control (11.7.2)

1 Identify the key features supporting a conclusion that professionalism, rather than statutory control, is a dominant characteristic of UK accounting.

2 Explain which institutional influences cause professionalism, rather than statutory control, to be a dominant characteristic of UK accounting.

3 Discuss whether a classification of strong professionalism is appropriate for the 1990s.

Uniformity/flexibility (11.7.3)

1 Identify the key features supporting a conclusion that flexibility, rather than uniformity, is a dominant characteristic of UK accounting.

2 Explain which institutional influences cause flexibility, rather than uniformity, to be a dominant characteristic of UK accounting.

3 Discuss whether a classification of strong flexibility is appropriate for the 1990s.

Conservatism/optimism (11.7.4)

1 Identify the key features supporting a conclusion that optimism, rather than conservatism, is a dominant characteristic of UK accounting.

2 Explain which institutional influences cause optimism, rather than conservatism, to be a dominant characteristic of UK accounting.

3 Discuss whether a classification of strong optimism is appropriate for the 1990s

Secrecy/transparency (11.7.5)

1 Identify the key features supporting a conclusion that transparency, rather than secrecy, is a dominant characteristic of UK accounting.

2 Explain which institutional influences cause transparency, rather than secrecy, to be a dominant characteristic of UK accounting.

3 Discuss whether a classification of strong transparency is appropriate for the 1990s.

Empirical studies (11.8)

1 What is the relative position of the UK, as indicated by research studies into classification, comparability and harmonisation?

QUESTIONS TO BE ANSWERED ON COMPLETION OF THE EUROPEAN SECTION OF PART 2

Institutional factors (8.4, 9.4, 10.4 and 11.4)

1 Compare the political and economic systems of France, Germany, the Netherlands and the UK, in terms of the classifications described in Chapter 1. Explain how the similarities or differences may relate to relative accounting practices in these countries.

2 Compare the legal systems of France, Germany, the Netherlands and the UK, in terms of the classifications described in Chapter 1. Explain how the similarities or differences may relate to relative accounting practices in these countries.

3 Compare the taxation systems of France, Germany, the Netherlands and the UK, in terms of the classifications described in Chapter 1. Explain how the similarities or differences may relate to relative accounting practices in these countries.

4 Compare the corporate financing systems of France, Germany, the Netherlands and the UK, in terms of the classifications described in Chapter 1. Explain how the similarities or differences may relate to relative accounting practices in these countries.

5 Compare the accounting professions of France, Germany, the Netherlands and the UK, in terms of the classifications described in Chapter 1. Explain how the similarities or differences may relate to relative accounting practices in these countries.

6 Compare the external influences on accounting in France, Germany, the Netherlands and the UK, in terms of the classifications described in Chapter 1. Explain how the similarities or differences may relate to relative accounting practices in these countries.

Comparison with IASs (8.6, 9.6, 10.6 and 11.6)

1 Rank the UK, Germany, France and the Netherlands, in order of decreasing comparability with IASs, giving reasons for your approach.

2 Discuss the rankings you have obtained in 1 in the light of institutional factors in each country.

3 Evaluate the relative impact on accounting practice in each country of the completion of the IASC core standards programme.

EU membership (*see* Chapter 7 and EU sections in Chapters 8 to 11)

1 Explain how EU membership has affected the accounting practices of each of the UK, Germany, France and the Netherlands, compared with practices in operation before the Fourth and Seventh Directives were incorporated in law.

2 Relate your answer to 1 to the relative strength of institutional factors in each country.

Professionalism/statutory control (8.7.2, 9.7.2, 10.7.2 and 11.7.2)

1 Compare the characteristics of professionalism and statutory control in accounting practice across Germany, France, the Netherlands and the UK.

2 Explain how the relative professionalism or statutory control in this group of countries is related to institutional influences in each.

Uniformity/flexibility (8.7.3, 9.7.3, 10.7.3 and 11.7.3)

1 Compare the characteristics of uniformity and flexibility in accounting practice across Germany, France, the Netherlands and the UK.

2 Explain how the relative uniformity or flexibility in this group of countries is related to institutional influences in each.

Conservatism/optimism (8.7.4, 9.7.4, 10.7.4 and 11.7.4)

1 Compare the characteristics of conservatism and optimism in accounting practice across Germany, France, the Netherlands and the UK.

2 Explain how the relative conservatism or optimism in this group of countries is related to institutional influences in each.

Secrecy/transparency (8.7.5, 9.7.5, 10.7.5 and 11.7.5)

1 Compare the characteristics of secrecy and transparency in accounting practice across Germany, France, the Netherlands and the UK.

2 Explain how the relative secrecy or transparency in this group of countries is related to institutional influences in each.

REFERENCES

Archer, S., Delvaille, P. and McLeay, S. (1995) 'The measurement of harmonisation and the comparability of financial statement items: within-country and between-country effects', *Accounting and Business Research*, 25(98), 67–80.

ASB (1993a) 'The role of valuation in financial reporting', *Discussion Paper*, Accounting Standards Board.

ASB (1993b) *Operating and Financial Review*, Statement issued by the Accounting Standards Board.

ASB (1995) Draft *Statement of Principles*, Chapter 5, Accounting Standards Board.

ASB (1997a) *Measurement of Tangible Fixed Assets*, FRED 17, Acounting Standards Board.

ASB (1997b) 'Discounting in financial reporting', *Working Paper*, Accounting Standards Board.

ASB (1997c) *Interim Reports*, Statement by the Accounting Standards Board.

ASC (1990) *Accounting for Fixed Assets and Revaluations*, Exposure Draft ED 51, Accounting Standards Committee.

Chambers, A. (1996) 'Directors' reports on internal financial control', in Skerratt, L.C.L. and Tonkin, D.J. (eds), *Financial Reporting 1995–96: A Survey of UK Reporting Practice*. London: Accountancy Books, 105–29.

Chandler, R. (1996) 'Directors' remuneration', in Skerratt, L.C.L. and Tonkin, D.J. (eds), *Financial Reporting 1995–96: A Survey of UK Reporting Practice*. London: Accountancy Books, 131–57

Charkham, J.P. (1994) *Keeping Good Company: A Study of Corporate Governance in Five Countries*. Oxford: Clarendon Press.

Coopers and Lybrand Tax Network (1995) *1995 International Tax Summaries: A Guide for Planning and Decisions*. New York: John Wiley.

Davies, M., Paterson, R. and Wilson, A. (1997) *UK GAAP*, 5th edn. London: Macmillan.

Edwards, E. and Bell, P. (1961) *The Theory and Measurement of Business Income*, Berkley, CA: University of California Press.

Emenyonu, E.N. and Gray, S.J. (1992) 'EC accounting harmonisation: An empirical study of measurement practices in France, Germany and the UK', *Accounting and Business Research*, Winter, 49–58

Gordon, P.D. and Gray, S.J. (1994) *European Financial Reporting – United Kingdom*. London: Routledge.

Gray, S. and Roberts, C. (1993) 'Voluntary information disclosure: The attitude of UK multi-nationals', in Gray, S.J., Coenenberg, A.G. and Gordon, P.D. (eds), *International Group Accounting – Issues in European Harmonisation*. London: Routledge.

Hermann, D. and Thomas, W. (1995) 'Harmonisation of accounting measurement practices in the European Community', *Accounting and Business Research*, 25(100), 253–65.

Lamb, M. (1996) 'The relationship between accounting and taxation: The United Kingdom', *The European Accounting Review*, 5: Supplement, 933–49.

Ma, R., Parker, R.H. and Whittred, G. (1991) *Consolidation Accounting*. London: Longman Cheshire.

McMahon, F. and Weetman, P. (1997) 'Commercial accounting principles: Questions of fact and questions of tax law', *British Tax Review*, 1, 6–18.

Meek, G.K., Roberts, C.B. and Gray, S.J. (1995) 'Factors influencing voluntary annual report disclosures by US, UK and continental European multinational corporations', *Journal of International Business Studies*, Third Quarter, 555–72.

Napier, C. (1995) 'The history of financial reporting in the United Kingdom', in Walton, P. (ed.), *European Financial Reporting: A History*. New York: Academic Press

Nobes, C. (1993) 'Group Accounting in the United Kingdom', in Gray, S.J., Coenenberg, A.G. and Gordon, P.D. (eds), *International Group Accounting – Issues in European Harmonisation*. London: Routledge.

Nobes, C.W. and Parker, R.H. (1984) 'The Fourth Directive and the United Kingdom', in Gray, S.J. and Coenenberg, A.G. (eds), *EEC and Accounting Harmonisation: Implementation and Impact of the Fourth Directive*. Amsterdam: North Holland.

Parker, R. (1995) 'Financial reporting in the United Kingdom and Australia', in Nobes, C.W. and Parker, R. (eds), *Comparative International Accounting*, 4th edn. Englewood Cliffs, NJ: Prentice-Hall.

Parker, R. (1989) 'Importing and exporting accounting: The British experience', in Hopwood, A.G. (ed.), *International Pressures for Accounting Change*. London: Prentice Hall/ICAEW, 7–29.

Parker, R.H. and Nobes, C.W. (1994) *An International View of True and Fair Accounting*. London: Routledge.

Salter, S.B., Roberts, C.B. and Kantor, J. (1996) 'The IASC comparability project: A cross-national comparison of financial reporting practices and IASC proposed rules', *Journal of International Accounting and Taxation*, 5(1), 89–111.

Simmonds, A. and Azières, O. (1989) *Accounting for Europe – Success by 2000 AD?*. London: Touche Ross.

Sudarsanam, P.S. (1995) *The Essence of Mergers and Acquisitions*. Englewood Cliffs, NJ: Prentice-Hall.

Weetman, P. and Gray, S.J. (1990) 'International financial analysis and comparative corporate performance: The impact of UK versus US accounting principles on earnings', *Journal of International Financial Management and Accounting*, 2(2/3), 111–29.

Weetman, P. and Gray, S.J. (1991) 'A comparative international analysis of the impact of accounting principles on profits: The USA versus the UK, Sweden and the Netherlands', *Accounting and Business Research*, 21(84), 363–79.

Newspapers and professional journals/magazines

FT World Accounting Report, published monthly by *Financial Times Publications*.

The Corporate Accountant, Insert in *The Accountant*, UK monthly. London: Lafferty Publications.

The Accountant (UK).

OECD, *Economic Surveys*. Paris: Organization for Economic Co-operation and Development.

Financial Times (UK).

Sources of regularly updated information on accounting standards and related matters

Accounting Standards (annual publication). London: Accountancy Books.

The London Stock Exchange Fact File (annual publication). London: London Stock Exchange.

Financial Reporting: A Survey of UK Reporting Practice. London: Accountancy Books.

Chapter 12

Australia

INTRODUCTION

Accounting practice in Australia has a strong tradition of professionalism. Statute law has been mostly concerned about the protection of shareholders and has been almost exclusively concentrated upon disclosure rules. Tax laws have developed separately from accounting rules and there is no requirement that accounting profits must be calculated using fiscal rules. Tax law has therefore had relatively little influence on financial reporting practices.

There is a very large and highly developed profession that is self-regulating. The profession was initially responsible for setting accounting standards that were primarily concerned with reducing the choice of measurement methods. Now, an independent public sector body, the Australian Accounting Standards Board (AASB) issues standards that companies have to follow by virtue of the Corporations Law.

Australia was one of the founder members of the IASC. The AASB has clearly stated its support for international harmonisation. It has begun a process of actively reconsidering those standards that conflict with IASs in an attempt to ensure that 'compliance with Australian accounting standards results in compliance with IASs'.[1]

THE COUNTRY

Indigenous Aboriginal races have inhabited Australia for hundreds of thousands of years while European settlers began to arrive towards the end of the eighteenth century. The earliest settlers were Anglo-Irish and this was the largest group of immigrants until the Second World War, since then, Australia experienced a significant influx of European migrants. More recently significant immigration from South East Asia has played an important role in developing Australia into a multicultural society.

The earliest settlers formed largely self-contained colonies. The modern-day Commonwealth of Australia finally came into being in 1901,[2] and Australia is now a federal system consisting of six states and two territories.

As can be seen from Exhibit 12.1, Australia is an immensely large country with a small population. However, it is highly urbanised and most of the population live on the coast, mainly in the south-east of the continent. It is

---

[1] AASB, *Policy Statement*, 6 (1996)
[2] Miller (1994)

relatively wealthy and economically successful. Its *per capita* GDP, approximately US$19,000 placed it 21st in the world in 1995.[3]

Exhibit 12.1 AUSTRALIA: COUNTRY PROFILE, TAKEN FROM EIU STATISTICS

Population	17.9 m.	
Land mass	7,682,300 sq.km	
GDP per head	US $18,914	
GDP per head in purchasing-power parity	70	(USA=100)
Origins of GDP:	%	
Agriculture	8.0	
Industry	23.4	
Services	68.6	
	%	
Real GDP average annual growth 1985–95	2.9	
Inflation, average annual rate 1989–96	3.7	

Source: *The Economist Pocket World in Figures 1998 Edition,* The Economist (1997)

Despite the size of the continent, agriculture is now relatively unimportant, accounting for only 8.0% of GDP. However, natural resources provide much of the country's foreign reserves, with the most important exports being ores and minerals and coal and oil. While the UK was originally the country's largest trade partner, regional trade has become increasingly important with the major export markets now being Japan (21.6%), ASEAN countries (15.4%) and the EU (11.1%). Imports come primarily from the USA (25.0%), the EU (22.6%) and Japan (13.9%).[4]

12.3 DEVELOPMENT OF ACCOUNTING REGULATIONS

There are four bodies involved in the setting or enforcement of accounting regulations:

● Australian Securities Commission (ASC)

● Australian Accounting Standards Board (AASB) (or, for public sector bodies, the Public Sector Accounting Standards Board (PSASB)

● Australian Accounting Research Foundation (AARF)

● Australian Stock Exchange (ASX).

The ASC was set up by the Australian Securities Commission Act 1989. It is responsible for administering all corporate legislation in the Commonwealth of Australia. Corporation Law ss 292 and 293 require directors to present shareholders with true and fair accounts. S 298 requires directors to ensure that the company's financial statements are made out in accordance with applicable accounting standards. The

---

[3] *The Economist* (1997), p. 24
[4] *The Economist* (1997), p. 99

Corporation Law includes a number of specific disclosure requirements, but most accounting regulations are contained in accounting standards.

The AASB has a number of functions, including the development of accounting standards, as described in Exhibit 12.2.

FUNCTIONS OF THE AASB

> 1 To develop a conceptual framework, not having the force of an accounting standard, for the purpose of evaluating proposed accounting standards
>
> 2 To review proposed accounting standards
>
> 3 To sponsor or undertake the development of possible accounting standards
>
> 4 To engage in such public consultation as may be necessary to decide whether or not it should make a proposed accounting standard
>
> 5 To make such changes in the form and content of a proposed accounting standard as it considers necessary.

Source: S 226, Australian Securities Commission Act 1989, quoted in Deegan (1996), p. 5

In carrying out its responsibilities the AASB is helped by the Australian Accounting Research Foundation. The AARF was set up by the accounting profession, it provides resources and expertise to the AASB as well as having a number of its own committees.

All nationally listed companies also have to comply with the disclosure requirements of the Australian Stock Exchange (ASX) (the Main Board rules). The ASX disclosure requirements are primarily concerned with the timely release of price-sensitive information to the market. Each state has its own responsibility for the listing requirements for companies that are listed only at state level, and these requirements may vary from state to state.

12.3.1 Company law

Historically, each state was responsible for setting its own Companies Acts. These were originally modelled upon several of the pre-1967 UK Companies Acts.[5] This led to increasing problems especially with regard to the multijurisdictional control and regulation of companies that increasingly operated in more than one state. After several attempts at reducing differences in the legislation of the various states, all states adopted the 1989 Corporation Law and Australian Securities Commission Law.[6] The latter led to the formation of the Australian Securities Commission (ASC), which was given the responsibility to administer and enforce the Corporation Law, including the examination of annual reports to ensure compliance. The ASC is an independent statutory commission accountable to the Attorney-General and through him to the Commonwealth Parliament.

---

[5] Parker (1989)
[6] McKinnon (1993)

12.3.2 Consolidated accounting[7]

Exhibit 12.3 illustrates the history of consolidated accounting in Australia. From this it can be seen that while federal statutory or legal regulations significantly lagged behind the UK and the USA, the stock markets began to require some group information at a relatively early date.

The first legislative requirement was contained in the 1938 Victorian Companies Act, which preceded UK legislation by a decade. This Act was the first in either Australia or the UK to require a detailed income statement, and also the first to require either separate statements for each subsidiary or consolidated statements of parent and subsidiaries. While some other states introduced similar requirements in the following years, consolidated statements were not required in all of the country until the Uniform Companies Act 1961.

These legislative requirements came after Stock Exchange listing requirements. The earliest of these was the Sydney and Melbourne Listing Requirements 1925, which required companies to disclose subsidiary balance sheet and income statements. Various other requirements were set by the stock markets over the period until 1941, when consolidated accounts were first required. (Prior to this, the requirements were for aggregated statements which did not involve the elimination of intra-group transactions.) However, until 1954, stock exchange listing requirements applied only to companies seeking a listing. They did not apply to companies that already had a listing. Therefore, before 1954 the majority of companies did not produce consolidated accounts.

Exhibit 12.3 NEW SOUTH WALES: HISTORY OF CONSOLIDATED ACCOUNTING, 1925–62

	1925	1927	1931	1936	1941	1946	1956	1962
Sydney Stock Exchange	Separate subsid accounts	Separate subsid accounts or aggregation parent and subsid	First consolid accounts	Separate subsid accounts or aggregation of subsid	Separate subsid accounts or consolidation			
NSW Statutes				Disclose investment in subsids				Uniform Companies Act
Professional requirements: ICAA						Disclose Holding co.		
ASA								Notes on preparation of cons accounts

Source: Whittred (1986), p. 107. Copyright © Accounting Foundation. Reproduced by kind permission of Blackwell Publishers

---

[7] Whittred (1986)

12.3.3 Accounting standards

Originally the accounting bodies saw themselves very much as employee organisations or professional associations. Their roles were to determine entrance into the profession and to ensure the continuing professional conduct of members. As such, they were not primarily concerned with accounting regulations as applied to companies. This began to change in the 1940s and 1950s. The Institute of Chartered Accountants in Australia (ICAA) first began to issue accounting recommendations in 1945,[8] followed in 1951 by auditing recommendations. The Australian Society of Accountants (ASA) began its Statement of Accounting Practices series in 1955 and in the following year launched its series of Technical Bulletins (see Appendix 12.1). Until the 1970s these were recommendations that were mainly concerned with presentation issues. This began to change with the formation jointly by the ICAA and the ASA of the Australian Accountancy Research Foundation (AARF) in 1965. Following the realisation that the two professional accounting bodies were developing separate standards on the same issues, they agreed in 1971 to issue Australian Accounting Standards (AAS), endorsed by both bodies.

Members of the institutes were required to ensure that companies complied with the AASs, but they were not legally binding. Instead, professional accountants were expected 'to support the Statements of Accounting Standards approved by the profession'.[9] The only penalty for non-compliance was disciplinary action by the accounting bodies and the level of compliance with these standards was often relatively low.

This changed with the formation of the public sector-based Accounting Standards Review Board (ASRB) in 1985. This body was given the legal authority to approve standards from the profession or other sources. Most, but not all, AASs were approved by the ASRB. Companies had to follow these standards under the Companies Code. Directors were subject to a legal penalty for non-compliance and auditors were similarly subject to legal penalties for non-reporting of any such cases. (As discussed later, non-compliance could originally have been justified by the need to report a 'true and fair view', but this is now no longer the case.)

The ASRB was itself succeeded by the Australian Accounting Standards Board (AASB) in 1991. The AASB approved all extant ASRB standards and also began to issue its own. Now, the profession no longer issues its own AASs and has only an indirect role in standard setting via AARF. As discussed above, the AARF provides research and administrative support to the AASB. It also co-ordinates the work of the AASB and a similar Public Sector Accounting Standards Board (PSASB) and administers three bodies itself: the Auditing Standards Board, the Legislative Review Board and the Urgent Issues Group (UIG).

---

[8] Gibson (1979)

[9] Australian Professional Statement 1 *Conformity with accounting standards*, quoted in Miller (1995)

12.4 INSTITUTIONS

12.4.1 Political and economic system

Australia is a developed democratic country with its political and economic systems both being similar to other western countries. Australia has a federal system of government – each state parliament has the power to legislate in all areas not specifically entrusted to the federal government. It is a parliamentary system, with state and federal parliaments organised in a manner similar to that of the UK, with no separation of executive and legislative powers. At the federal level, the Prime Minister, and at the state level the Premiers, come from the majority party in the lower house and policy making is very largely carried out by Cabinets appointed by the Prime Minister/Premiers.

While Australia is a capitalist country that supports the growth of private companies, there is a significant public sector. The government not only runs a variety of public services (for example, education, including tertiary education, and the health service) but it has owned many utilities (electricity, gas and water) and transport (railways, airline). However, as is happening in other countries, the government has been privatising many of these industries, with complete or partial sell-off to the private sector (or, failing this, it has increasingly imposed private sector-style policies).[10]

The history of corporate legislation largely mirrors the economic development of the country. The earliest corporate legislation was concerned with the regulation and reporting of banks and mining companies (*see* Appendix 12.1). Even now, there are some different laws relating to mining companies (*see* section 12.4.2.2).

12.4.2 Legal System

12.4.2.1 Accounting regulations

The legal system is a common law-based system. Law comprises both statute law, developed at the federal and state levels, and common law, developed through the courts. Australia has a strong and independent judiciary with the authority to rule on the legal status of all legislation.[11]

As with the UK and other common law countries, corporate regulations have developed in a piecemeal fashion over the years. Accounting and reporting requirements have often been imposed following crises such as the collapse of companies or other perceived problems. The main impetus for these regulations has been the desire to protect shareholders and, through this, to encourage the growth of limited liability stock companies. Because the regulations have been largely designed to increase investor protection, rather than other objectives such as providing information for government planning or for tax calculations, the emphasis has been on disclosure. Most of the legislative requirements relate to the disclosure of information, and relatively little emphasis has been placed on measurement issues.

---

[10] Miller (1994)
[11] Miller (1994)

Companies must disclose a full set of audited financial statements – parent and group income statement (or, as it is more commonly known in Australia, a profit and loss account), balance sheet, notes, audit report and directors' report. (A statement of cash flows is required as an accounting standard rather than as part of the Corporation Law requirements.)

12.4.2.2 Types of business organisations[12]

Unincorporated business can operate as either a sole proprietor or a partnership. Partnerships can be set up without any formal written contract or agreement. Partnerships, while easy to set up, usually have the major disadvantage that the partners have unlimited liability and are personally responsible for any debts of the business. Thus, most businesses of any size form a company which acts as a separate legal entity from its owners able to enter into contracts in its own name. Companies may be limited by shares or by guarantee, or even be no-liability companies. A company limited by guarantee is one where the owners agree in advance the maximum amount to which they will be personally liable in the event of the company winding up. Mining companies can be formed as no-liability companies, where the owners will have no obligations to pay for any calls on their shares in the event of a winding-up. However, most companies are limited by shares; nearly 98% of these are proprietary companies while the rest are public companies. The main difference relates to the freedom given to owners or shareholders to buy and sell their shares in the company. Exhibit 12.4 lists the major differences between a proprietary company and a public company.

The accounting and disclosure requirements of large proprietary and public companies are virtually identical, the only difference is that public companies have to disclose directors' remuneration. However, there are also small and exempt proprietary companies. The latter are companies where none of the shares is held by a public company. In this case, the financial statements need contain substantially fewer notes to the accounts and, if all members agree, no auditor need be

Exhibit 12.4 MAIN DIFFERENCES BETWEEN TYPES OF AUSTRALIAN COMPANIES

	Proprietary company	*Public company*
Minimum number members	At least 2	At least 5 (300 for listing)
Maximum number members	50	No upper limit
Number directors	At least 2	At least 3
Financing	No public issue of equity or debt	Can issue debt and equity to the general public
Owners' rights	Restricted in who can sell investment to	Free to sell investment on open market

[12] Miller (1994)

appointed. A non-exempt small company (defined as one with assets of less than A$10 million or revenues of less than $20 million) need not disclose some information in the notes (economic dependency, asset revaluations, superannuation commitments, interests in business undertakings and corporations).

12.4.3 Taxation system

The tax system plays no direct role in the regulation of accounting. Financial reports and accounts are produced to inform and protect shareholders and accounting regulations are set with this in mind. If the taxation authorities require any information, this is provided in special-purpose reports and not the annual report and accounts. The tax authorities have many of their own rules for calculating taxable income based upon the Income Tax Assessment Act and case law. There is not always an obvious link between taxable income and reported or accounting income; however, the accounting records form the basis from which companies compile their tax returns. In cases of disputes with the tax authorities, the use of AASB standards is taken as indicating that the figures produced are appropriate. Where there is more than 15% difference between the tax actually payable and the amount that apparently should be payable based upon reported income, companies must provide a note to the accounts that gives a reconciliation of the two figures. The main reasons for differences between the two figures are listed in Exhibit 12.5.[13]

| Exhibit 12.5 | REASONS FOR DIFFERENCES BETWEEN TAXABLE AND ACCOUNTING INCOME |

Permanent differences

- Tax loss carry-forward
- Investment allowances
- Non-deductible expenses
- Exempt or non-assessable income (i.e. gold mining income)
- Non-allowable depreciation
- R&D allowances
- Overseas tax differentials

Temporary differences

- Gross profit on instalment sales
- R&D costs
- Rent received in advance
- Provisions for guarantees, warranties and long service leave
- Accelerated depreciation allowances

---

[13] Crasswell (1995)

Shareholders have to pay tax on the dividends received and on any capital gains made through trading in shares. Since the mid 1980s capital gains have been taxed at the same rate as earned income. Taxes have to be paid on dividends only to the extent that the company has not already paid taxes. The shareholder is therefore liable only to the extent that their personal marginal taxation rate is higher than the corporation tax rate. Prior to these changes, investors tended to prefer capital appreciation rather than dividends. Following these changes, dividend income has become more attractive and companies are therefore tending to re-invest less and instead to raise capital through new issues on the stock market or through dividend reinvestment plans.

12.4.4 Corporate financing system

Australia has a well organised and active stock market alongside a number of countrywide commercial banks and other financial institutions including merchant and investment banks. Until changes in the tax laws in the late 1980s (*see* section 12.4.3), companies were largely financed by internal funds which historically provided approximately half of all finance. The next most popular source of finance was generally debt, with equity financing being relatively unimportant, However, recent years have seen a swing towards increasing equity financing.[14]

12.4.4.1 Stock Exchange[15]

Australia has a relatively long history of stock market activity. The first stock exchange opened in Sydney in 1837 and this was shortly followed by further exchanges in the other states. Until 1962 there were different listing requirements in each of the six stock markets, then the Australian Associated Stock Exchanges issued uniform listing requirements. In 1987, the stock exchanges were all amalgamated to form the Australian Stock Exchange (ASX). The ASX is a private non-profit making organisation. It is a member of IOSCO as well as the Paris-based Fédération International des Bourses de Valeurs and the East Asian and Oceanic Stock Exchange Federation (EAOSEF).

As discussed in section 12.3, the stock exchange does not play a role in the legislative and standard setting processes. However, it does issue listing requirements that all companies with a listing must adhere to. These listing requirements add further disclosure requirements to those of the Corporations Law and accounting standards. In particular, they require the immediate disclosure of price-sensitive information so that companies have a responsibility to disclose certain types of information to the market as soon as possible, rather than waiting until the annual or interim reports are published. They also mandate the maximum period taken to produce the accounts. Thus, interim or half-yearly reports and preliminary final statements must both be made public within 75 days and the final annual report must be given to shareholders within four months of the year-end (the only exception being mining exploration companies).

---

[14] Miller (1994)
[15] Australian Stock Exchange (1997)

The ASX has nearly 1,200 listed companies. As we saw in Chapter 1 (Exhibit 1.3) it was the tenth largest stock market in the world at the end of 1996, as measured by the market capitalisation of its domestic companies, with a stock market capitalisation of GB£185 billion.

In their latest survey (March 1995) the ASX found that the share ownership structure was as shown in Exhibit 12.6.

Exhibit 12.6 SHARE OWNERSHIP STRUCTURE, 1995

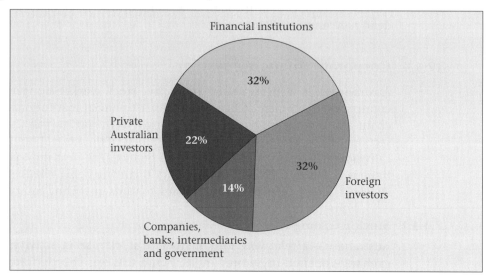

What is most striking about these figures is the importance of foreign investors. Foreign investors hold nearly one-third of the market and account for more than one-fifth of all market trading. This makes it one of the most international stock markets in the world, although there are very few foreign companies listed (only 55 at the end of 1996, *see* Exhibit 1.3). Also relatively important are institutional investors. While they are far less important than are institutional investors in the UK (62% of the UK market is held by institutional investors, as was shown in Exhibit 1.5), they are a significant source of funds. Institutional investors are certainly far more important in Australia than they are in many other countries.

12.4.4.2 Top ten companies

The top ten listed Australian companies are shown in Exhibit 12.7, with their rank in the Asia–Pacific group in the *Financial Times FT 500* annual survey. Of these, eight also featured in the FT 500, which lists the top 500 world companies, measured by market capitalisation.

12.4.5 The accounting profession

The first accountancy body formed in Australia was the Adelaide Society of Accountants formed in 1885.[16] This was followed by a number of other societies so

---

[16] Morris and Barbera (1990)

Exhibit 12.7 TOP TEN LISTED AUSTRALIAN COMPANIES, 1998

	Name	*Market cap, US $m*	*Rank in world (Asia–Pacific)*	*Sector*
1	Broken Hill Proprietary	23,491	147 (8)	Iron and steel
2	National Australia Bank	21,755	162 (9)	Commercial and other banks
3	ANZ Bank	12,314	325 (15)	Commercial and other banks
4	Commonwealth Bank of Australia	11,470	350 (19)	Commercial and other banks
5	Westpac Banking Corp	11,206	361 (21)	Commercial and other banks
6	News Corporation	9,992	408 (24)	Publishing – newspapers
7	Rio Tinto	9,647	121* (27)	Non-ferrous metals
8	Coca-Cola Amatil	9,018	452 (31)	Beverages – soft drinks
9	Woodside Petroleum	6,355	– (46)	Petroleum products including refineries
10	Lend Lease Corp	5,921	– (51)	Real estate

Note: * Rio Tinto is ranked 121st on the basis of the combined value of its UK and Australian listings.
Source: *Financial Times*, *FT 500 Survey*, 22 January 1998

that by 1904 all states had at least one accountancy body.[17] Following a series of mergers, there are now only two. The newer and larger is the Australian Society of Certified Practising Accountants (ASCPA) formed in 1958 and originally called the Australian Society of Accountants (ASA). The ASCPA has approximately 62,000 members while the second body, the Institute of Chartered Accountants of Australia (ICAA), which was formed in 1928, has about 27,000 members.[18] There is relatively little overlap in the membership of these two bodies, so that Australia has more accountants per head of population than almost any other country in the world (*see* Exhibit 1.6).

Both institutes are self-regulating. They determine their own entrance requirements, run examinations and are responsible for disciplinary matters. While the profession carries out supervisory activities, anyone acting as an auditor must be a registered company accountant, as required by the corporations legislation. There have been several unsuccessful attempts to merge the two institutes, however, this issue is far from dead and various calls for a merger can still be heard from bodies such as the Group of 100 (a group of finance executives of major companies).[19]

As described in section 12.3.3, each accounting society initially issued its own standards. Following a series of changes in the standard setting process the profession now plays only an indirect role in standard setting via the AARF. The AARF is also responsible, *inter alia*, for the Urgent Issues Group (UIG). This was set up in October 1994 to provide guidance on urgent reporting issues 'to avoid the development of divergent or unsatisfactory financial reporting practices in areas not dealt

---

[17] Parker (1989)
[18] Miller (1994): *FT World Accounting Report* (March 1996), p. 5
[19] *FT World Accounting Report* (December 1996), p. 7

with, or not dealt with specifically, in Accounting Standards'.[20] The UIG offers interpretations of existing accounting standards as well as considering issues not covered by any standard. It will not look at issues that are specific to the circumstances of a particular company, or issues that are under consideration by the AASB or the PSASB, nor may its interpretations change or conflict with existing standards or accounting concepts.

The UIG has 16 members, at least 11 of whom must vote for the view and no more than two against. These then become UIG Abstracts which while not legally enforceable are binding on ASCPA and ICAA members. However, while the UIG is situated inside the AARF, the AASB has the power to veto any pronouncement it disagrees with. Issues the UIG has considered include the reporting of directors' remuneration, accounting for the acquisition of gold mining companies, de-recognition of internally generated identifiable intangible assets and accounting for certain uninsured losses.[21]

Exhibit 12.8 lists the composition of the UIG while Exhibit 12.9 lists the abstracts issued as at November 1996.

Exhibit 12.8 COMPOSITION OF THE UIG, 1997

- Senior partner from each major accounting firm (currently six)

- Senior partner from a medium-sized or small accounting firm

- Four members from industry and commerce, of which at least two will be preparers – appointed with assistance from groups such as:
  - Business Council of Australia
  - Group of 100
  - Australian Institute of Company Directors
  - Australian Investment Managers' Association
  - Securities Institute of Australia
  - Australian Shareholders Association

- Two members from the public sector (one local government and one governmental department)

- An Auditor-General (or a senior staff member from an Auditor-General's office)

- One member from the Commonwealth Department of Finance or a state or territory Treasury or Department of Finance or equivalent

- A member of the AASB or PSASB appointed by the AASB and the PSASB

- One observer, being the Australian Securities Commission's Executive Director Accounting Practice or equivalent.

Source: AASB, *Accounting Handbook 1997*, vol. 1, p. 749

---

[20] UIG Charter, para. 1, quoted in Miller (1995)
[21] *FT World Accounting Report* (various issues)

Exhibit 12.9 **UIG ABSTRACTS, 1997**

1 Lessee accounting for surplus leased space under a non-cancellable operating lease

2 Accounting for non-vesting sick leave

3 Lessee accounting for lease incentives under a non-cancellable operating lease

4 Disclosure of accounting policies for restoration obligations in the extractive industry

5 Methods of amortisation of goodwill (withdrawn)

6 Accounting for acquisitions – deferred settlement of cash consideration

7 Accounting for non-current assets – de-recognition of intangible assets and a change in the basis of measurement of a class of assets

8 Accounting for acquisitions – recognition of restructuring provisions

9 Accounting for acquisitions – recognition of acquired tax losses

Source: AASB, *Accounting Handbook 1997*, vol. 1. p. 745

It is also proposed to create a Financial Reporting Review Board. This Board would tighten the surveillance of corporate reporting by ruling on whether companies have fully complied with all laws and standards as well as providing interpretations of extant standards.[22]

12.4.6 External influences

As we saw above, modern Australia started life as a colony of the UK, it therefore naturally turned to the UK when setting up many of its institutions and its laws. This included importing the UK model of professional accountancy bodies and all the early societies were based to varying extents upon the English and Scottish institutes.[23]

The UK influence can also be seen in the legal and parliamentary systems, in the taxation system and its relationship to financial reporting, and in the early accounting rules and regulations. This includes the use of 'true and fair'. This concept was imported from the UK and, until 1991, was interpreted in the same way as it is understood in the UK. The removal of the 'true and fair' override and its replacement with additional disclosure requirements reflects a move away from UK-inspired accounting regulations.

Australia has increasingly looked less and less towards the UK as either a trade partner or as a source of accounting regulations, instead, the USA and South East Asian countries have increasingly dominated trade. UK accounting regulations have also perhaps become less relevant to Australia as the UK has become more influenced by the EU. Australia has harmonised its accounting standards with New Zealand, all standards now include a comparison of Australian and New Zealand rules, while the AASB has set out to both attempt to narrow existing areas

[22] *FT World Accounting Report* (December 1996), p. 6
[23] Parker (1989)

of differences and to encourage the 'concurrent development of accounting standards wherever possible'.[24] Indeed, the requirement to consult with New Zealand is laid down in the Securities Commission Act 1989. Australia is also a member of the 'G4+1' group, which is made up of representatives of the standard setting bodies in Australia, Canada, the UK and the USA plus the IASC.

Australia's policy of looking at standards from, and consulting with, the standard setters in a number of other Anglo-American countries is best described in the words of the AASB itself in the foreword to its 'Financial Reporting Pronouncements' (Exhibit 12.10).

Exhibit 12.10 AASB FINANCIAL REPORTING PRONOUNCEMENTS: INTERNATIONAL FOCUS

> The AASB monitors closely the work of the . . . IASC and national standard setting bodies, particularly those of the [USA], Canada, New Zealand, the United Kingdom and South Africa. The AASB uses the work of these standard-setting bodies in the development of Australian pronouncements and endeavours to ensure that, where possible, the pronouncements are consistent with those of its international counterparts . . .
>
> The AASB and the AARF are also involved in meetings of standard setters from the USA, the UK, Canada, New Zealand and South Africa. These meetings occur several times each year.
>
> Through these close working relationships the AASB is able both to contribute directly to the international development of financial reporting and to work towards the harmonisation of Australian and international financial reporting requirements.

Source: AASB (1995)

12.5 SOCIETAL CULTURE AND ACCOUNTING SUBCULTURE

12.5.1 Hofstede's cultural dimensions

Exhibit 12.11 reproduces part of the table set out in Chapter 2, section 2.4, showing the scores and rankings for Australia from Hofstede's research on cultural dimensions.

What is most obvious from Exhibit 12.11 is how similar Australia is to both the UK and the USA. However, Australia can increasingly be described as a multicultural country and it remains to be seen whether or not it will continue to be quite so culturally similar to the UK and USA. (Remember that Hofstede's work dates from the early 1980s, and while culture does not change rapidly, neither is it immutable.)

From Hofstede's data, Australia can be described as being extremely individualistic, with low power distance, weak to moderate uncertainty avoidance and weak to moderate nurturing. Using these characteristics, Hofstede grouped Australia along-

---

[24] AASB (1994)

Exhibit 12.11 AUSTRALIA: SCORES AND RANKINGS FROM HOFSTEDE'S (1984) CULTURAL DIMENSION RESEARCH

	Individualism versus collectivism		Large power distance versus small power difference		Strong uncertainty avoidance versus weak uncertainty avoidance		Low nurture versus high nurturing	
	Score	Rank	Score	Rank	Score	Rank	Score	Rank
Australia	90	2	36	41	51	34	61	16
UK	89	3	35	42/44	38	47/48	66	9/10
USA	91	1	40	38	46	43	62	15

side a group of other western, developed Anglo-American countries and described the 'typical' organisation using the analogy of a village market.

12.5.2 Culture and accounting

Exhibit 12.12 links Gray's (1988) accounting values to Hofstede's cultural dimensions and uses this to describe the expected characteristics of the Australian accounting system.

This shows that we should be able to describe the Australian financial accounting system as one that exhibits strong professionalism, is flexible rather than uniform, is relatively optimistic and is open or transparent.

12.6 ACCOUNTING REGULATIONS AND THE IASC

Australian accounting standards are generally in conformity with IASs. Australia's largest industrial company, the mining company BHP, for example, stated that it materially complied with IASs, as shown in Exhibit 12.13.

It is likely that there will be even more conformity with IASs in the future. The Australian Stock Exchange has funded an A$1 million review of Australian standards aimed at ensuring that they comply with IASs. The importance for the IASC of this move towards increased harmonisation can be seen in the description accorded to the move by the Chair and Secretary General of the IASC reproduced in Exhibit 12.14.

The AASB and the ASX have agreed that, by December 1998, companies preparing accounts under Australian standards will be able to state that they also comply with IASs. This will involve the introduction of many new or amended standards.[25] Exhibit 12.15 lists the ten exposure drafts and four standards re-issued in the first eight months of 1997. These cover a wide variety of areas such as the depreciation of non-current assets; cash flows; inventories; long-term contracts; and leases. Exhibit 12.15 also describes the rest of the AASB work programme up until the end of 1998. This programme is designed to harmonise Australian standards and IASs.

---

[25] *FT World Accounting Report* (various issues)

Exhibit 12.12 LINKING GRAY'S (1988) ACCOUNTING VALUES TO HOFSTEDE'S (1984) CULTURAL DIMENSIONS, IN THE MANNER PROPOSED BY GRAY

Gray's accounting values – classification	Cultural dimensions affecting the country's accounting values	Interpretation of Hofstede's scores of cultural values for Australia
Professionalism (strong)	Professionalism tends to be associated with: ● Individualism ● Weak uncertainty avoidance ● Small power distance	High individualism Weak uncertainty avoidance Small power distance
Flexibility (strong)	Uniformity tends to be associated with: ● Strong uncertainty avoidance ● Large power distance ● Collectivism	Weak uncertainty avoidance Small power distance High individualism
Optimisim (strong)	Conservatism tends to be associated with: ● Strong uncertainty avoidance ● Collectivism ● Strong nurturing	Weak uncertainty avoidance High individualism Weak nurturing
Transparancy (strong)	Secrecy tends to be associated with: ● Strong uncertainty avoidance ● Large power distance ● Collectivism ● Strong nurturing	Weak uncertainty avoidance Small power distance High individualism Weak nurturing

Exhibit 12.13 BROKEN HILL PROPRIETARY CO. LTD STATEMENT OF ACCOUNTING POLICIES, 31 MAY 1995

The financial statements comply with the requirements of the Corporations Law and with all applicable Australian accounting standards.

The accounts are consistent, in all material respects, with International Accounting Standards except that the effect of accounting for investments in associated companies by the equity method is disclosed by note and not in the consolidated results.

Source: Broken Hill Proprietary Co. Ltd, annual report, 1995

Exhibit 12.14 STATEMENT OF IASC CHAIR AND SECRETARY GENERAL ON THE
AUSTRALIAN COMPATIBILITY PROJECT, 1997

> A landmark development in Australia may point the way for future relationships
> between the IASC and national standard setters. A project has been started to
> review Australian standards with the objective that compliance with Australian
> standards should secure compliance with international standards also. This would
> mean that Australian standards might have more requirements than international
> standards but they would not have fewer and they would not have requirements
> which conflicted with those of international standards. IASC has undertaken to
> work with the Australian bodies and will consider any suggestions that come out of
> the Australian project for improving international standards.

Source: IASC Annual Review 1996 (1997)

Exhibit 12.15 SCHEDULE OF IASC HARMONISATION PROGRAMME PROJECTS, JUNE 1997
UPDATE

Date	Action	Topic
Jan. 1997	Issued ED 74	Depreciation
Mar. 1997	Issued: ED75 ED76 ED77 ED78	 Borrowing costs After balance sheet events Cash flow statements Construction contracts
Jun. 1997	Issued: ED79 ED80 Reissued AASB1016	 Joint ventures Inventories and Cost of Goods Sold (CoGS) disclosure Equity accounting
Jul. 1997 (now 9/97)	Issued: ED85 ED82 ED81	 Earnings per share Leases Revenue
Aug. 1997 (now 9/97)	Reissued: AASB 1021 AASB 1002 AASB 1026	 Depreciation After balance sheet date Cash flow statements Construction contracts
Sept. 1997	Issue EDs	Revaluations Segment reporting Foreign currency translation Employee entitlements Tax Consolidations

Exhibit 12.15 continued

Date	Action	Topic
Dec. 1997	Issue EDs	Acquisitions of assets and goodwill Intangibles Research and development Related party disclosures Set-off and extinguishment debt Borrowing costs
	Issue Standard	Revenue Inventories and CoGS disclosures
	Reissue Standards	Earnings per share Leases Joint ventures
Mar. 1998	Issue EDs	Accounting policies Disclosures/presentations Profit and loss statement
Jun. 1998	Reissue Standards	Revaluations Segment reporting Foreign currency translation Research and development
Sept. 1998	Reissue Standards	Set-off and estinguishment debt Related party disclosures
Dec. 1998	Reissue Standards	Accounting policies Disclosure/presentation Profit and loss statements Acquisition assets and goodwill Consolidations Tax Intangibles Employee benefits

Source: ICAA (1997)

Exhibit 12.16 describes the extent to which Australian regulations are currently in harmony with IAS standards.

12.7 THE ACCOUNTING SYSTEM

12.7.1 Outline of current regulations

All company financial statements must comply with the requirements of the Corporations Law which sets out requirements to publish financial statements. The Law mandates the disclosure of information both in the accounts and in the notes to the accounts. These are mainly disclosure requirements. The financial statements must also be drawn up in accordance with applicable accounting standards as laid down by the AASB. The AASB is an independent body consisting of the chair and

Exhibit 12.16 COMPARISON OF ACCOUNTING PRACTICES IN AUSTRALIA WITH
REQUIREMENTS OF IASs: KEY SIMILARITIES AND DIFFERENCES

IAS	Subject of IAS	Practice in Australia	Ref
Disclosure and presentation			
	General aspects consolidated in IAS 1 (revised)		
IAS 1	Fair Presentation	'True and fair' requirement	7.2.2
	Disclosure of Accounting Policies	Generally in agreement	7.3.1
	Information to be Disclosed in Financial Statements	Generally in agreement	7.3.2
	Presentation of Current Assets and Current Liabilities	Generally in agreement	
	Specific aspects		
IAS 7	Cash Flow Statements	Generally in agreement	
IAS 8	Net Profit or Loss for the Period, Fundamental Errors and Changes in Accounting Policies	Generally in agreement	
IAS xx	Discountinuing Operations		
IAS 14	Reporting Financial Information by Segments	Generally in agreement	
IAS 24	Related Party Disclosure	More information required	7.5.1
IAS 33	Earnings per Share	Generally in agreement	
IAS 34	Interim Financial Reporting	Generally in agreement	
Asset recognition and measurement			
IAS 2	Inventories	LIFO not allowed	
IAS 4	Depreciation Accounting	New exposure draft fully in agreement	7.4.2
IAS 9	Research and Development Costs	Generally in agreement	7.2.5
IAS 16	Property, Plant and Equipment	Allowed alternative treatment common	7.4.2
IAS xx	Impairment of Assets		
IAS 23	Borrowing Costs	Generally in agreement	
IAS 25	Accounting for Investments	Generally in agreement	
IAS xx	Intangible Assets		
Liability recognition and measurement			
IAS 10	Contingencies and Events Occurring After the Balance Sheet Date	Generally in agreement	
IAS 12	Income Taxes	Generally in agreement	
IAS 17	Leases	Generally in agreement	
IAS 19	Employee Benefits	More information required	7.5.2
IAS 32	Financial Instruments: Disclosure and Presentation	Generally in agreement	
Recognition of economic activity			
IAS 11	Construction Contracts	Generally in agreement	
IAS 18	Revenue	Generally in agreement	
IAS 20	Accounting for Government Grants and Disclosure of Government Assistance	Generally in agreement	
Measurement			
IAS 15	Information Reflecting the Effects of Changing Prices	Recommended, seldom found	7.4.1
IAS 29	Financial Reporting in Hyperinflationary Economies	Not relevant to Australia	

Exhibit 12.16 continued

IAS	Subject of IAS	Practice in Australia	Ref
Group accounting			
IAS 21	The Effects of Changes in Foreign Exchange Rates	Generally in agreement	
IAS 22	Business Combinations	Generally in agreement	
IAS 27	Consolidated Financial Statements and Accounting for Investments in Subsidiaries	Generally in agreement	7.3.3
IAS 28	Accounting for Investments in Associates	Generally in agreement	
IAS 31	Financial Reporting of Interests in Joint Ventures	Generally in agreement	7.3.3

ten members appointed by the Commonwealth Attorney-General. Its members are part-time and drawn from the profession and business community. Thus, it is very similar to the US FASB. The main differences are that its members are part-time; its meetings were not open to the public (this changed in mid-1997); it does not publish dissenting opinions; and, there is no Emerging Issues Task Force. However, as with the FASB, it goes through an extensive series of consultations, including exposure drafts, before standards are issued. The AASB also set up a consultative group which first met in January 1995. This has 25 members representing various preparers, users and regulators. It is consulted about the following matters:

● Major technical issues

● Work programme

● Project priorities

● Due process

● Controversial matters of relevance to the Board.

Exhibit 12.17 lists the membership of the Consultative Group.

The AASB has also issued a series of policy statements, statements of accounting concepts and accounting guidance releases (*see* Appendix 12.2).

12.7.2 Professionalism versus statutory control

12.7.2.1 Co-regulation

Until 1989, the Australian system could be characterised in terms of very high professionalism. Statute, in the form of Companies Acts, was mainly concerned with regulating the disclosures of general purpose financial statements and the profession was responsible for setting accounting standards. Now, the system is often described as a 'co-regulation system', with the ASC and the AASB operating in the public sector and the ASX and the AARF both being private sector bodies. However, it would be too simplistic to assume that the public sector has taken over. For example, it is argued[26] that the AASB still has to be concerned about the

---

[26] Miller (1996)

Exhibit 12.17 CONSULTATIVE GROUP MEMBERSHIP (NOVEMBER 1996)

- Accounting Association of Australia and New Zealand
- Association of Superannuation Funds of Australia
- Australian Bankers Association
- Australian Chamber of Commerce and Industry
- Australian Financial Institutions Commission
- Australian Institute of Company Directors
- Australian Institute of Valuers and Land Economists
- Australian Investment Managers' Group
- Australian Securities Commission
- Australian Shareholders Association
- Australian Society of Certified Practising Accountants
- Australian Society of Corporate Treasurers
- Australian Stock Exchange
- Business Council of Australia
- Council of Small Business Organisations of Australia
- Group of 100
- Insurance Council of Australia
- International Banks and Securities Association of Australia
- Investment Funds Association of Australia
- Law Council of Australia
- Life Insurance Federation of Australia
- Institute of Actuaries of Australia
- Institute of Chartered Accountants in Australia
- Securities Institute of Australia

acceptability of its standards even though they have legal backing. The AASB has to maintain the support of the business community, government and the profession if it wishes to continue to issue standards.

12.7.2.2 True and fair

Until 1991, the most important requirement was that companies provided a 'true and fair' view. This took precedence over any specific legal requirements or accounting standards. Following growing concerns regarding the disclosures made by a number of companies, the requirement to comply with all laws and standards takes precedence. If this fails to result in the disclosure of a true and fair view of a company's position and performance, the company must provide further information and explanations. Thus, 'true and fair' may no longer be used as a reason to depart from regulations.[27] Standards have full legal backing and must always be followed.

---

[27] Parker and Nobes (1994)

The profession in Auditing Standard 702 'The audit report on a general purpose financial report' requires auditors to states whether, in their opinion, the statements 'present fairly in accordance with applicable accounting standards and other mandatory professional reporting requirements'. The Corporations Law requires the audit report to state whether or not the accounts provide a 'true and fair' view. Exhibit 12.18, the audit report of Foster's Brewing Company, illustrates the use of both sets of wording.

Exhibit 12.18 FOSTER'S BREWING GROUP LTD: AUDIT REPORT, 1997

**Independent Audit Report
to the Members of
Foster's Brewing Group Limited**

Scope

We have audited the financial statements of Foster's Brewing Group Limited (the Company) for the financial year ended 30 June 1997 as set out on pages 48 to 93. The financial statements consist of the accounts of the Company and the consolidated accounts of the economic entity comprising the Company and the entities it controlled at the end of, or during, the financial year. The Company's directors are responsible for the preparation and presentation of the financial statements and the information they contain. We have conducted an independent audit of these financial statements in order to express an opinion on them to the members of the Company.

Our audit has been conducted in accordance with Australian Auditing Standards to provide reasonable assurance as to whether the financial statements are free of material misstatement. Our procedures included examination, on a test basis, of evidence supporting the amounts and other disclosures in the financial statements, and the evaluation of accounting policies and significant accounting estimates.

These procedures have been undertaken to form an opinion as to whether, in all material respects, the financial statements are presented fairly in accordance with Accounting Standards, other mandatory professional reporting requirements, being Urgent Issues Group Consensus Views, and the Corporations Law so as to present a view which is consistent with our understanding of the Company's and the economic entity's state of affairs, the results of their operations and their cash flows.

We have not acted as auditors of the controlled entities as identified in note 33 to the financial statements. We have, however, received sufficient information and explanations concerning these controlled entities to enable us to form an opinion on the consolidated accounts.

The audit opinion expressed in this report has been formed on the above basis.

Audit Opinion

In our opinion, the financial statements of the Company are properly drawn up:

(a) so as to give a true and fair view of:
　(i) the state of affairs at 30 June 1997 and the results and cash flows for the financial year ended on that date of the Company and the economic entity; and
　(ii) the other matters required by Divisions 4, 4A and 4B of Part 3.6 of the Corporations Law to be dealt with in the financial statements;

(b) in accordance with the provisions of the Corporations Law; and

(c) in accordance with applicable accounting standards and other mandatory professional reporting requirements.

Price Waterhouse

Price Waterhouse
Chartered Accountants

Paul V Brasher
Partner

Melbourne, 25 August 1997

Source: Fosters Brewing Group Ltd, annual report, 1997

12.7.2.3 Statements of Accounting Concepts

The profession plays an important role in determining accounting practices via the conceptual framework project. This started with ASRB 100 and ASRB 101 in 1985 followed by SAC1, SAC2 and SAC3 in 1990. Exhibit 12.19 lists the benefits that the profession felt would flow from this conceptual framework project.

Exhibit 12.19 BENEFITS OF A CONCEPTUAL FRAMEWORK

- Accounting standards should be more consistent and logical, because they are developed from an orderly set of concepts
- Increased international compatibility of Accounting Standards should occur, because they are based on a conceptual framework that is similar to the explicit conceptual frameworks used by International Accounting Standards Committee and other overseas standard setters
- The Boards should be more accountable for their decisions, because the thinking behind specific requirements should be more explicit, as should any departures from the concepts which may be included in particular Accounting Standards
- The process of communication between the Boards and their constituents should be enhanced, because the conceptual underpinnings of proposed Accounting Standards should be more apparent when the Boards seek public comment on them
- The development of Accounting Standards should be more economical because the concepts developed by the Boards will guide the Boards in their decision making.

Source: AASB, Policy Statement, 5, *The Nature and Purpose of Statements of Accounting Concepts*, March 1995

The first three SACs covered the three areas of definition of reporting entity; objectives of general purpose financial statements; qualitative characteristics of financial information. These were essentially the same as those of the IASC and the UK and USA,[28] and were relatively non-controversial. SAC4, 'The definition and measurement of the elements of financial statements', was first issued in May 1992. It was very similar to equivalent overseas concepts, however, if it were to be implemented, it would have had significant implications for many areas of accounting such as various types of operating leases, R&D, financial instruments and off-balance sheet financing. Following public disagreements over the proposals, SAC4 was re-issued in March 1995 and the statements no longer have general legislative backing. However, not all areas of accounting are codified, and members of the profession are expected to use these concepts to guide them in those areas where there are no standards.

12.7.2.4 Substance over form

This is an increasingly important concept in accounting, in that it plays a major role in determining how many assets and liabilities are to be accounted for.

---

[28] Corsi and Staunton (1994)

Australia, in common with the IASC, has come down quite firmly in favour of reporting assets and liabilities in terms of their economic substance rather than in terms of their legal form. SAC4 thus defines assets and liabilities in terms of control rather than ownership. Assets are defined as 'service potential or future economic benefits *controlled* by the entity as a result of past transactions or *other* past events' (italics added). Once an asset has been identified, the next step is to decide whether or not it should be reported. SAC4 states that it should be recognised if it is probable that the service potential or future economic benefits will eventuate; and it possesses a cost or other value that can be reliably measured. It is interesting to note that SAC4 actually attempts to define what is meant by 'probable'. It defines it in probability terms as 'more likely rather than less likely'.

A liability is defined to cover legal obligations and equitable or constructive obligations (that is, obligations that arise from social or moral pressures or which may be inferred from the particular circumstances or actions of the company).[29] A liability is thus defined as 'future sacrifice of service potential or future economic benefits that the entity is presently obliged to make to other entities as a result of past transactions or other past events'.

These definitions are essentially the same as those contained in the IASC framework document. Their influence can be seen in many standards – for example, leases (ASRB 1008) are treated in the same way as required by IAS 17 with finance leases being capitalised. AASB 1033, 'Presentation and disclosure of financial instruments' and the revised AASB 1014, 'Set-off and extinguishment of debt', both came into force at the end of 1997. They are based upon IAS 32, although they go further both in terms of disclosure and coverage of certain types of commodity contracts.

12.7.2.5 R&D costs

Some other standards conflict with the SAC definitions of the elements of the financial statements. For example, AASB 1011 requires R&D to be charged to the income statement as incurred unless it is expected beyond reasonable doubt, to be recoverable; then it must be capitalised. This is a far more strict definition of an asset than that described in SAC4, which instead uses the term 'probable'. However, a similar strict definition of an asset is also used by the IASC in IAS 9. AASB 1011 also differs from SAC4 with respect to the write-back of R&D expenses. Under AASB 1011, if a company charges R&D costs to the profit and loss account it cannot at a future date change the policy and write-back the costs and treat the R&D as an asset. SAC4 allows companies to capitalise costs if events or circumstances change even if they had originally been treated as a period expense.[30]

12.7.3 Uniformity versus flexibility

12.7.3.1 Accounting policies

The accounting system is generally fairly flexible, as can be seen by reference to many of the accounting rules. Companies have to disclose the major accounting

---

[29] Crasswell (1995), p. 99
[30] Deegan (1996), p. 97

policies employed. AASB 1011 exempts companies from having to disclose certain basic principles such as accruals and going concern. However, they are explicitly required to disclose others, including whether or not the historical cost basis has been used, as it cannot be assumed that all companies use the same cost basis (*see* Appendix 12.3 for an example of such a disclosure).

12.7.3.2 Format of statements

In some areas, the Australian system is fairly uniform. One of these is the format of the financial statements. AASB 1034, 'Information to be disclosed in the financial statements', incorporates some of the disclosure requirements of Schedule 5 of the Corporations Act as well as other disclosure requirements. While it allows preparers to determine the format of the financial statements, it lays down principles for determination of appropriate classifications and presentations, and prescribes specific disclosures with respect to certain assets and liabilities, equity reserves and expenses.

The balance sheet appears dissimilar to that found in the UK or most other European countries though it would be more familiar to the US reader (*see* Appendix 12.3 for an example). Assets are listed in reverse order from that found in the UK – from most liquid (cash) to least liquid (intangible non-current assets). Current liabilities and non-current liabilities are then deducted from total assets to give shareholders' equity. Net current assets are thus not calculated – while this may simply be considered a cosmetic difference, as it is only a matter of presentation, it can confuse less knowledgeable users. There are also those who would argue that what is reported is what managers will be most concerned with controlling. The form of presentation of the statements may thus affect managers' behaviour.

12.7.3.3 Consolidated accounts

According to ASRB 1013, positive purchased goodwill must be amortised over a period not exceeding 20 years. Negative goodwill must be used to write down the fair values of the non-monetary assets acquired. If, after this, some negative goodwill still remains it must then be recognised in the income statement as a gain. Accounting for goodwill was tightened up further, in that sum-of-years amortisation is no longer allowed and only straight-line amortisation is now permitted.

Merger accounting or pooling of interests is not allowed. Proportional consolidation is required for joint ventures and companies must consolidate all subsidiaries including those carrying on dissimilar activities.

One important area of difference between Australia and the IASC and other countries such as the USA used to be with respect to the use of equity accounting for associates. Until 1997, equity accounting was not allowed in the financial statements and companies could only report the effects of equity accounting in a note to the accounts.

12.7.4 Conservatism versus optimism

Conservatism or prudence is not generally considered to be an important concept in Australia. While AASB 1001 lists prudence as one of the factors that should be considered in choosing accounting policies (alongside relevance, materiality, consistency and substance over form), it is usually seen as one of the criteria that has to be followed to ensure that the information produced is reliable rather than being a separate and desirable characteristic in its own right.[31]

12.7.4.1 Valuation of non-current tangible assets

The revaluation of non-current (or fixed) assets is widespread. This is covered by AASB 1010 which is far from prescriptive in terms of revaluing assets, although it is more prescriptive with regard to write-downs. Companies have to write down assets if their value is less than the amount they are shown at, but companies do not have to write up the value of assets if they are worth more than the amount they are shown at. However, if land and buildings are not shown at their current value, Corporation Law, Schedule 5 requires most companies to disclose their current value in a note to the accounts.

Given that companies have to revalue assets if they are to meet this note disclosure requirement, it is not at all surprising to find that approximately three-quarters of the largest 100 companies also revalue land and buildings in their financial statements.[32] The Corporation Law requires assets to be valued at least every three years; for this purpose, 'current value' is taken to mean the recoverable amount, and is defined as the total expected cash inflows *less* associated cash outflows from the assets continued use or sale (*see* Exhibit 12.20). This requirement is fairly controversial because it does not require the use the discounted cash flows: companies can discount the future expected cash flows, but they do not have to.[33]

The requirements are fairly strict in that if assets are revalued in the accounts, all assets of the same class must be revalued using the same basis – partial revaluations are not permitted (although there has recently been some relaxation of this rule in that companies can now systematically revalue assets over a three-year period). If the carrying amount of an asset exceeds its recoverable amount, the company must write it down to the lower amount. Any write-down in the value of an asset must be charged to the income statement, unless it is simply a reversal of a previous write-up – in which case it, like the initial write-up, is taken direct to the revaluation reserve. This method of revaluing assets is fully consistent with IAS 16, although the benchmark treatment of the IAS is not to revalue assets but to carry them at cost.

The treatment of depreciation (AASB 1021) is also generally consistent with the IAS requirements. However, a new Exposure Draft was issued in January 1997, to bring it fully in line with IAS 16. This standard excludes investment properties, which need not be written down unless the carrying amount is greater than the recoverable amount.

12.7.4.2 Intangible assets

As discussed above, purchased goodwill has to be written off to the income statement over time. This has an adverse impact upon reported earnings, and many companies have therefore sought to minimise the impact. One way that this can be done is through the valuation of other intangible assets. AASB 1021 permits all intangible assets except self-generated goodwill to be treated in the same way as

---

[31] Crasswell (1995), p. 99
[32] Crasswell (1995), p. 99
[33] Whittred *et al.* (1996)

Exhibit 12.20 VALUATION OF PROPERTY, PLANT AND EQUIPMENT 1997

Property, Plant and Equipment

Depreciable property, plant and equipment are shown in the accounts at cost or valuation less accumulated depreciation.

Land, land improvements and buildings are revalued from time to time and differences arising from revaluations are not included in profit for the year. During 1996/97 the Economic Entity revalued land, land improvements and buildings and the new independent valuations adopted are shown in Note 11.

In addition to valuations undertaken, the carrying amounts of all property, plant and equipment are reviewed annually. If the carrying amount of a property, plant and equipment exceeds its recoverable amount, the asset is written down to the lesser amount. In assessing recoverable amounts, the relevant cash flows are not discounted to their present value.

	Consolidated		Amcor Limited	
	1997 **$ million**	**1996** **$ million**	**1997** **$ million**	**1996** **$ million**
NOTE 11. PROPERTY, PLANT AND EQUIPMENT				
Land:				
• At cost	–	47.7	–	–
• At independent valuation 1994	–	247.3	–	52.4
• At independent valuation 1997 (1)	381.7	–	67.7	–
	381.7	295.0	67.7	52.4
Land improvements:				
• At cost	–	14.3	–	2.2
• At independent valuation 1994	–	40.3	–	17.3
• At independent valuation 1997 (1)	51.6	–	16.6	–
Accumulated depreciation	–	(3.1)	–	(1.1)
	51.6	51.5	16.6	18.4
Buildings:				
• At cost	–	281.0	–	6.5
• At independent valuation 1994	–	422.6	–	139.3
• At independent valuation 1997 (1)	644.0	–	186.6	–
Accumulated depreciation	–	(63.2)	–	(8.5)
	644.0	640.4	186.6	137.3
Plant and equipment:				
• At cost	4,449.8	4070.2	1,480.6	1,304.4
Accumulated depreciation	(1,970.4)	(1,750.5)	(564.5)	(531.6)
	2,479.4	2,319.7	916.1	772.8
Leased assets:				
• Finance leases	74.5	84.0	117.1	117.6
Accumulated amortisation	(23.1)	(23.3)	(74.7)	(70.0)
	51.4	60.7	42.4	47.6
Standing timber at cost (2)				
Plantation costs – refer Note 1(4)	105.0	97.0	–	–
Capitalised interest – refer Note 1(7)	83.3	79.3	–	–
	188.3	176.3	–	–
Total property, plant and equipment	3,796.4	3,543.6	1,229.4	1,028.5

(1) An independent valuation, as at June 1997, of the Economic Entity's land, land improvements and buildings was carried out by Mr G R Longden A.V.L.E (Val) of Jones Lang Wootton, licensed agents and approved valuers, on the basis of existing use. Directors adopted the independent valuation of land, land improvements and buildings which were written up in aggregate by $70.0 million – refer note 21.

(2) The Economic Entity's plantations in Victoria are insured against fire and certain other specified risks. Younger trees are insured for their current replacement costs whilst more mature trees are insured for a value equal to estimated wood volume multiplied by the Department of Conservation and Natural Resources royalty. The cost value shown is lower than both the recoverable amount and the insured value of standing timber.

Source: Amcor, annual report, 1997, pp. 49 and 51

tangible assets – that is, they may be carried in the balance sheet at cost or value and amortised over their economic life. While this requirement is subject to the general principle of materiality and intangible assets must meet the definition of an asset in terms of future benefits, there is no annual impairment test requirement. Many companies therefore capitalise acquired intangible assets, and as Exhibit 12.21 (The News Corporation) illustrates, these assets are not always amortised as it is argued that they have an indefinite life.

12.7.5 Secrecy versus transparency

12.7.5.1 Objectives of general purpose financial statements

Until the mid-1980s Australia lagged behind the UK in terms of the amount of information disclosed. 1986 and 1987 both saw significant increases in the disclo-

---

Exhibit 12.21 THE NEWS CORP. LTD: VALUATION OF INTANGIBLE ASSETS, 1997

Publishing rights, titles and television licences
These assets are stated at cost or valuation. No amortisation is provided on publishing rights and titles since, in the opinion of the Directors, they do not have a finite useful economic life. Although television licences in the United States are renewable every five years, the Directors have no reason to believe that they will not be renewed and, accordingly, no amortisation has been provided.

15 PUBLISHING RIGHTS, TITLES AND TELEVISION LICENCES

At cost	8,362	3,294
At valuation June 1990		
Original cost	6,198	5,938
Revaluation increment	3,753	3,436
	9,951	9,374
	18,313	12,668

During the 1996 year, in accordance with AASB 1010 Revaluation of Non-Current Assets, the Directors considered a revaluation of the group's publishing rights, titles and television licences, with the exception of those rights, titles and licences acquired during the year. The primary valuation technique used was a methodology based on the maintainable earnings of the publishing rights, titles and television licences. This incorporates multiples which take account of the market factors particular to the rights, titles and licences and which reflect the composition of the revenues and profitability, the loyalty of readership, the risk attaching to the advertising revenue and the potential for future growth. The Directors resolved not to reflect in the financial statements the increase in the value of the group's publishing rights, titles and television licences at that time. Where the value of the publishing right, title or television licence had declined, the full decrement was recognised. A decrement of $306 million was taken to the asset revaluation reserve in the 1996 year.

Source: The News Corp. Ltd, annual report, 1997, pp. 20 and 36

sure requirements, and Australia can now best be described as having a relatively transparent or open system with extensive disclosure requirements in a number of areas. Miller (1994, p. 342) argues that the Statements of Accounting Practice all provide conceptual support for a non-secretive system. The objectives of reporting in general purpose financial reports are laid down in SAC2. The main objective is described as being to 'provide information useful to users for making and evaluating decisions about the allocation of scarce resources'. SAC3 then goes on to require them to 'include all financial information which satisfies the concepts of relevance and reliability'. Several recent standards have similarly demanded fairly extensive disclosures. Some of the more interesting of these are described below.

12.7.5.2 Related parties

AASB 1017 calls for extensive related party information. This standard was re-issued in February 1997 to ensure that it was consistent with the Corporations Regulations. The major change was with respect to the basis used to calculate directors' remuneration. This standard is compatible with IAS 24 in that it also defines a 'related party' in terms of control or significant influence. However, far more information is required – in particular, the nature of the terms and conditions of each different type of transaction, aggregate amounts for each combination of type of transaction and nature of terms and conditions. It has been suggested that these regulations arose because of a number of financial scandals not only in Australia but also in other countries such as the UK, the USA and Canada.[34]

Director-related transactions are deemed to be material (and therefore reportable) regardless of the amounts involved. Other related-party transactions are material and so reportable if non-disclosure has the potential to affect either the decisions of users or the discharge of accountability by the directors. Exhibit 12.22 reproduces just some of the related-party information provided by BHP (in all, five pages of information are provided).

12.7.5.3 Pensions

AASB 1028, 'Accounting for employee entitlement', is compatible with IAS 19, although it requires far more disclosures. The Corporation Law, Schedule 5, requires companies to disclose details of pension plans, latest actuarial valuations and company commitments to the plans. AASB 1028 extends these requirements to include the disclosure of aggregate expenses and liabilities, the basis of measurement of liabilities for each type of employee entitlement (including average inflation and discount rates applied), and the effects of material changes in pensions plans. Exhibit 12.23 reproduces some of the information provided in the notes to the accounts by Qantas.

12.7.5.4 Directors

Extensive information about directors must be disclosed. This includes the related-party information as described in section 12.7.5.1 that must be included in the notes. The directors' report must also disclose information on qualifications,

---

[34] Deegan (1996)

Exhibit 12.22 BHP: NOTES TO THE ACCOUNTS, RELATED-PARTY TRANSACTIONS (EXTRACTS)

	Notes	BHP Group 1997	1997	1996	BHP Entity 1997	1996
		$ million	US$ million	$ million	$ million	$ million
46 RELATED PARTY DISCLOSURES (continued)						
Related party transactions and balances included throughout the accounts (in the notes as referenced) are as follows:						
Interest received or due and receivable from related parties						
Wholly owned controlled entities					990.765	849.670
Associated companies (a)		6.009	4.585	0.076	–	–
Directors						
– of the BHP Entity		–	–	0.001	–	0.001
– of controlled entities		0.002	0.002	0.010	0.002	0.010
	3	6.011	4.587	0.087	990.767	849.681
Dividends received or due and receivable from related parties						
Wholly owned controlled entities					738.521	1 394.844
Associated companies (a)		109.986	83.919	134.046	–	–
	3	109.986	83.919	134.046	738.521	1 394.844
Interest paid or due and payable to related parties						
Wholly owned controlled entities					668.472	640.738
Associated companies (a)		0.218	0.166	0.131	0.003	0.005
	5	0.218	0.166	0.131	668.475	640.743
Current trade receivables due from related parties						
Wholly owned controlled entities					145.620	106.566
Other controlled entities					0.717	1.155
Associated companies (a)		26.780	20.433	12.256	0.505	1.529
	12	26.780	20.433	12.256	146.842	109.250
Current sundry receivables due from related parties						
Wholly owned controlled entities					14 415.164	13 205.627
Other controlled entities					0.016	0.717
Associated companies (a)		19.419	14.817	7.469	0.201	–
Other related parties		–	–	1.190	–	–
Directors						
– of the BHP Entity (b)		0.004	0.003	0.001	0.004	0.001
– of controlled entities (b)		1.196	0.887	1.232	1.021	1.217
	12	20.619	15.707	9.892	14 416.406	13 207.562
Non-current sundry receivables due from related parties						
Wholly owned controlled entities					3 068.703	3 282.764
Other controlled entities					62.750	92.750
Directors						
– of controlled entities (b)		8.354	6.374	8.857	8.089	8.522
	16	8.354	6.374	8.857	3 139.542	3 384.036
Current trade creditors due to related parties						
Wholly owned controlled entities					110.192	144.163
Other controlled entities					0.082	0.050
Associated companies (a)		0.517	0.394	13.351	0.009	0.017
	22	0.517	0.394	13.351	110.283	144.230
Current sundry creditors due to related parties						
Wholly owned controlled entities					12 819.900	12 028.630
Associated companies (a)		1.739	1.327	20.797	0.199	–
	22	1.739	1.327	20.797	12 820.099	12 028.630
Other non-current borrowings owing to related parties						
Wholly owned controlled entities	24				5 624.161	5 539.289

Exhibit 12.22 continued

Notes on financial statements   *The Broken Hill Proprietary Company Limited*

	Notes		BHP Group			BHP Entity	
		1997	1997	1996	1997	1996
		$ million	US$ million	$ million	$ million	$ million

46 RELATED PARTY DISCLOSURES *(continued)*

Related party transactions and balances included throughout the accounts (in the notes as referenced) are as follows: *(continued)*

Related party contingent liabilities at balance date, not otherwise provided for in these accounts, are categorised as arising from:

Controlled entities (c)

	Notes	1997 $ million	1997 US$ million	1996 $ million	1997 $ million	1996 $ million
Unsecured...					14 445.604	14 819.182
Amounts uncalled on shares					51.292	51.324
Associated companies (a) (d)						
Unsecured...		50.659	38.653	2.132	1.694	2.132
	35	50.659	38.653	2.132	14 498.590	14 872.638

(a) For details of major associated companies refer note 31.

(b) Current and non-current sundry receivables due from Directors represent the appropriate portion of loans to Directors engaged in full-time employment within the BHP Group, mainly for acquisition of shares in the BHP Entity.

(c) The BHP Entity amount includes guarantees, mainly in relation to funding arrangements and financial instruments, given in regard to certain controlled entities which are eliminated on consolidation.
The BHP Entity has given written assurances to certain controlled entities which may lead to it becoming liable to those controlled entities in respect of debts incurred by them.

(d) This category includes mainly lease and loan guarantees.

Investments in controlled entities are shown in note 17.
Directors' remuneration is shown in note 39.
Major interests in unincorporated joint ventures are shown in note 43.
Details of controlled entities are shown in note 45.

Other Director transactions with Group entities

Where the Director was a shareholder in the BHP Entity, transactions included the receipt of dividends, and participation in the Dividend Investment Plan and Bonus Share Plan (refer note 26). These transactions were conducted on a commercial basis on conditions no more beneficial than those available to other shareholders.

Some eligible Directors, who were Directors of the BHP Entity and/or BHP's controlled entities, were issued with ordinary shares paid to one cent, priced at market value (refer note 27 for details of the Executive Share Scheme). These transactions were conducted on conditions no more beneficial than those available to other eligible senior executives.

Where the Director was an employee of the BHP Group, transactions include:

– reimbursement of transfer expenses
– minor purchases of products and stores
– participation in the Employee Share Plan (refer note 27)
– insurance with Group insurance companies.

All these transactions (which were trivial in amount) were conducted on conditions no more beneficial than those available to other employees.

A number of Directors of the BHP Entity hold positions in other companies, where it may be said they control or significantly influence the financial or operating policies of these entities. Accordingly, the following entities are considered to be director-related entities for the purpose of the disclosure requirements of Australian Accounting Standard AASB 1017: Related Party Disclosures:

Director of the BHP Entity	Director-related entity	Position held in director-related entity
D A Crawford	KPMG (Southern Region of Australia)	Partner and Chairman
J C Conde	Broadcast Investments Pty Ltd (and related entities)	Chairman and Managing Director
M A Chaney	Wesfarmers (Group)	Managing Director
D R Argus	National Australia Bank (Group)	Managing Director and Chief Executive Officer

Exhibit 12.22 continued

Notes on financial statements   The Broken Hill Proprietary Company Limited

46 RELATED PARTY DISCLOSURES *(continued)*

Transactions between the BHP Group and these director-related entities are detailed below:

– The chartered accounting firm KPMG (worldwide) received $1.681 million (1996 – $0.248 million) in fees for services provided to the BHP Group.

– The Wesfarmers Group received $0.669 million (1996 – $0.470 million) for products and services provided to the BHP Group. The Wesfarmers Group paid $17.968 million (1996 – $14.038 million) to the BHP Group for various products.

– Transactions with the National Australia Bank Group since 30 November 1996 are as follows:

  – *Foreign exchange cash management* – foreign exchange cash management transactions were made on a regular basis to convert foreign currency receipts into Australian dollars. These resulted in a loss of $0.443 million to the BHP Group during the year ended 31 May 1997.

  – *Foreign exchange hedging* – the BHP Group entered into forward foreign exchange contracts and options to hedge revenues denominated in foreign currencies. These resulted in a gain of $4.310 million to the BHP Group during the year ended 31 May 1997.

  – *Short term money market* – borrowings were made for periods of up to six months, but typically overnight. The National Australia Bank Group was paid $0.081 million in interest payments on such borrowings. In addition, overnight deposits and purchases of securities such as bank bills, negotiable certificates of deposit and promissory notes were typically made for periods of between 30 and 180 days. The BHP Group received $0.500 million in interest on these transactions.

  – *Long term funding* – at 31 May 1997, the BHP Group had outstanding borrowings from the National Australia Bank Group of $280 million. The BHP Group paid the National Australia Bank Group $7.073 million in interest during the year ended 31 May 1997 in relation to these borrowings. In addition, a separate $100 million standby facility exists, but was not drawn during the year. The BHP Group paid $0.025 million in fees for this facility.

  – *Bank accounts* – the BHP Group has various accounts with the National Australia Bank Group. These accounts operate under normal commercial terms and conditions. Fees paid to the National Australia Bank Group totalled $0.277 million in 1997.

  – *Housing loans* – the BHP Group has paid interest amounting to $0.535 million on subsidised loans for employees' housing.

These transactions occurred under normal commercial terms and conditions.

Some Directors of the BHP Entity are also Directors of other public companies which have transactions with the BHP Group. Except as disclosed above the relevant Directors do not believe they have the capacity to control or significantly influence the financial or operating policies of those companies. The companies are therefore not considered to be director-related entities for the purpose of the disclosure requirements of Australian Accounting Standard AASB 1017: Related Party Disclosures.

There were no transactions between Directors and director-related entities and the BHP Group other than those already disclosed.

Transactions with associated companies
The following material transactions with related parties of the BHP Group occurred:

– sales of manganese ore to Elkem Mangan KS amounting to $41.669 million (1996 – $39.538 million). These sales were conducted under normal commercial terms and conditions.

– sales of steel products to Tubemakers of Australia Ltd prior to acquisition amounting to $494.635 million in 1996. These sales were conducted under normal commercial terms and conditions. The BHP Group completed the acquisition of Tubemakers of Australia Ltd in April 1996 which resulted in the BHP Group's shareholding increasing from 47.6% to 100%.

Source: BHP, annual report, 1997, pp. 128–30.

experience, social responsibilities, the number of meetings held during the year and the number attended (*see* Exhibit 12.24, WMC Ltd). At least two of the directors are required to state that the financial statements give a true and fair view; there are reasonable grounds to believe that the company will be able to pay its debts when they become due; and that the accounts have been drawn up in accordance with the relevant statutes (*see* Exhibit 12.24).

Exhibit 12.23 QANTAS AIRWAYS LTD: PENSION AND EMPLOYEE ENTITLEMENTS
INFORMATION, 1997

NOTE 26: SUPERANNUATION COMMITMENTS

The Economic Entity maintains five superannuation plans covering Australian based staff. The Economic
Entity also maintains a number of superannuation and retirement plans for local staff in overseas countries.
Plan trustees are indemnified by the Economic Entity against actions, claims and demands arising from their
lawful administration.

The superannuation plan for the Chief Entity's Australian based employees (including employees of certain
controlled entities) provides either accumulation benefits (with a guaranteed minimum benefit for members
of Division 1 of the Qantas Airways Limited Staff Superannuation Plan (QALSSP)) or a combination of
accumulation and defined benefits payable as a lump sum. The Chief Entity is committed to making
contributions to the plan, the commitment being legally enforceable on the basis of actuarial advice of
amounts required to fully fund the superannuation benefits provided for in the rules of the plan, after
allowing for employee contributions. In addition, the Economic Entity is required to provide a minimum
level of contributions under the Australian Superannuation Guarantee legislation.

The various plans were last actuarially assessed as detailed in the following table. The actuarial valuations
confirmed that the value of the assets of the plans were sufficient to meet all anticipated liabilities, including
vested benefits of the plans in the event of termination of the plans and voluntary or compulsory termination
of employment of each employee at balance date.

The actuarial valuation of QALSSP determined that the Chief Entity's contribution to fund the defined
benefit portion of the plan was in surplus.

The Regional Airlines Superannuation Plan comprises several categories of membership according to the
employers, being Eastern Australia Airlines Pty Limited, Southern Australia Airlines Pty Limited or
Sunstate Airlines (Qld) Pty Limited.

The last actuarial reviews of the funds were as follows:

FUND	TYPE OF FUND	NAME AND QUALIFICATION OF ACTUARY*	DATE
Qantas Airways Limited Staff Superannuation Plan	Defined Benefit Accumulation	K.N. Lockery FIA, FIAA Not applicable	30 June 1996
TAA Pilots' Superannuation Scheme (1977)	Defined Benefit	C.B. Twomey FIA, FIAA	30 June 1994
Australian Airlines Pilots' Accumulation Fund (1989)	Accumulation	Not applicable	
Australian Airlines Flight Engineers' Superannuation Plan	Defined Benefit	C.B. Twomey FIA, FIAA	30 June 1994
Regional Airlines Superannuation Plan	Accumulation	Not applicable	

* Actuarial valuations performed by actuaries employed by Towers, Perrin, Forster & Crosby, Inc.

Certain controlled entities have a legally enforceable obligation under various awards to contribute to
industry plans on behalf of some employees. These plans operate on an accumulation basis and provide
lump sum benefits for members on resignation, retirement or death.

▶

Exhibit 12.23 continued

The following defined benefit superannuation plans are sponsored by the Economic Entity:

FUND	Present value of accrued benefits*	Net market value of fund assets^	Excess/ (deficit)	Employer contributions to fund^	Vested benefits^	Present value of accrued benefits*	Net market value of fund assets^	Excess/ (deficit)	Employer contributions to fund^	Vested benefits^
	1997 CONSOLIDATED $ m					**1997 CHIEF ENTITY $ m**				
Qantas Airways Limited Staff Superannuation Plan	**2,078.6**	**2,332.9**	**254.3**	**156.8**	**1,986.0**	**1,866.4**	**2,094.7**	**228.3**	**140.8**	**1,783.2**
TAA Pilots' Superannuation Scheme (1977)	**9.4**	**17.5**	**8.1**	**0.2**	**10.5**	–	–	–	–	–
Australian Airlines Flight Engineers' Superannuation Plan	**11.9**	**19.2**	**7.3**	**0.1**	**13.3**	–	–	–	–	–
Total	**2,099.9**	**2,369.6**	**269.7**	**157.1**	**2,009.8**	**1,866.4**	**2,094.7**	**228.3**	**140.8**	**1,783.2**
	1996 CONSOLIDATED $ m					1996 CHIEF ENTITY $ m				
Qantas Airways Limited Staff Superannuation Plan	1,499.4	2,007.1	507.7	94.0	1,920.9	1,346.4	1,803.7	457.3	84.5	1,726.2
TAA Pilots' Superannuation Scheme (1977)	9.4	16.2	6.8	0.2	9.7	–	–	–	–	–
Australian Airlines Flight Engineers' Superannuation Plan	11.9	18.4	6.5	–	12.6	–	–	–	–	–
Total	1,520.7	2,041.7	521.0	94.2	1,943.2	1,346.4	1,803.7	457.3	84.5	1,726.2

* *As at date of last actuarial review.*
^ *As at the last set of audited financial statements prepared by the plans.*

Source: Qantas Airways Ltd and Controlled Entities, annual report, 1997, p. 55

12.7.5.5 Shareholders

Companies have to disclose a significant amount of information about their shareholders. As in most countries, they must disclose the interests of directors and changes in directors' shareholdings. They must also disclose information about their major shareholders. For each type of share (ordinary and each class of preference) they must disclose number of shareholders; distribution of shareholdings by size; largest 20 shareholders; and proportion of shares held by each significant shareholder (*see* Exhibit 12.25).

12.8 EMPIRICAL STUDIES

12.8.1 Classification studies

Virtually without exception, classification studies have placed Australia alongside the UK in a British Commonwealth group. As we saw in Chapter 4, Nobes (1984) placed Australia in a micro-based, pragmatic group of UK-influenced countries. Doupnik and Salter (1993) likewise grouped Australia alongside the UK in a micro-group and while they also described the USA as a micro-system, they placed it in a different subgroup. Using empirical data of actual practices, Frank

Exhibit 12.24 WMC LTD: STATEMENT OF DIRECTORS AND EXTRACTS FROM DIRECTORS' REPORT, 1997

WMC Limited and Controlled Entities

Statement by Directors

In the opinion of the Directors:

a The financial statements set out on pages 52 to 93 are drawn up in accordance with Divisions 4, 4A and 4B of Part 3.6 of the Corporations Law and so as to give a true and fair view of:

- the state of affairs as at 30 June 1997, and the profit and cash flows for the financial year ended on that date of the Company and the economic entity; and
- the other matters with which they deal;

b at the date of this statement there are reasonable grounds to believe that the Company will be able to pay its debts as and when they fall due; and

c at the date of this statement there are reasonable grounds to believe that the Company and the subsidiaries identified in Note 34 will as an economic entity be able to meet any obligations or liabilities to which they are, or may become, subject by virtue of the deed of cross guarantee described in Note 34. The deed of cross guarantee has been entered into by the parties identified in Note 34 to take advantage of relief from accounting requirements available through Class Order 97/1018 issued by the Australian Securities Commission. At the date of this statement the Company and the subsidiaries identified in Note 34 are within the classes of companies affected by that Class Order.

The financial statements are drawn up in accordance with applicable Accounting Standards and other mandatory professional reporting requirements (Urgent Issues Group Consensus Views).

This statement is made in accordance with a resolution of the Directors.

AH Parbo
Melbourne, 13 August 1997

HM Morgan

Exhibit 12.24 continued

The Directors

Sir Arvi Parbo AC (Chairman) BE Hons FTSE FAusIMM Hon MIMM Hon FIE Aust Hon FAIM Hon DEng (Monash) Hon DSc (Deakin) Hon DSc (Curtin) Hon DUni (Flinders) (Age 71)

Non-Executive Chairman since his retirement in December 1990. Sir Arvi joined WMC in 1956, became Managing Director in 1971 and Chairman and Managing Director in 1974. He was Chairman of Alcoa of Australia Limited from 1978 to June 1996 and became a director of the Aluminum Company of America in 1980. He was a director of the Broken Hill Proprietary Company Limited from 1987 to 1992 and Chairman from 1989 to 1992. He is Chairman of Zurich Australian Insurance Group and Munich Reinsurance Company of Australia Limited, a director of Hoechst Australia Limited and Sara Lee Corporation, a member of Chase International Advisory Committee and the China International Trust and Investment Corporation (CITIC) International Advisory Council. He was President of the Australasian Institute of Mining and Metallurgy in 1990 and is the current President of the Australian Academy of Technological Sciences and Engineering. Sir Arvi lives in Melbourne.

Hugh M Morgan AO (Managing Director) LLB BCom FCPA FTSE FAusIMM FAIM Comp IEAust (Age 56)

A director since 1976 and Chief Executive Officer since December 1990. Mr Morgan has been a director of Alcoa of Australia Limited since 1977. He is a member of the Board of the Reserve Bank of Australia; a member and past President of the Minerals Council of Australia, a member of the Business Council of Australia, Vice-President of the Australia Japan Business Co-operation Committee and Vice-Chairman of the International Council on Metals and the Environment. He is President of the Australian German Association, a Trustee of The Asia Society New York and the Chairman of the Asia Society AustralAsia Centre. Mr Morgan lives in Melbourne.

Donald M Morley (Director of Finance) BSc MBA FAusIMM (Age 57)

Mr Morley joined WMC in 1970 and was appointed a director in 1983. He is Chairman of the World Gold Council, a director of Alcoa of Australia Limited and a director of The Centre for Independent Studies. Mr Morley lives in Melbourne.

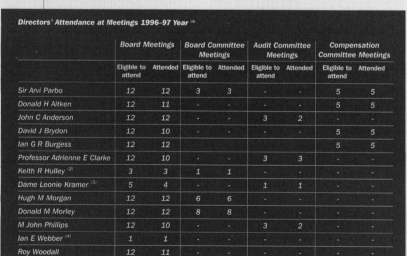

Directors' Attendance at Meetings 1996–97 Year [1]

	Board Meetings		Board Committee Meetings		Audit Committee Meetings		Compensation Committee Meetings	
	Eligible to attend	Attended	Eligible to attend	Attended	Eligible to attend	Attended	Eligible to attend	Attended
Sir Arvi Parbo	12	12	3	3	-	-	5	5
Donald H Aitken	12	11	-	-	-	-	5	5
John C Anderson	12	12	-	-	3	2	-	-
David J Brydon	12	10	-	-	-	-	5	5
Ian G R Burgess	12	12					5	5
Professor Adrienne E Clarke	12	10	-	-	3	3	-	-
Keith R Hulley [2]	3	3	1	1	-	-	-	-
Dame Leonie Kramer [3]	5	4	-	-	1	1	-	-
Hugh M Morgan	12	12	6	6	-	-	-	-
Donald M Morley	12	12	8	8	-	-	-	-
M John Phillips	12	10	-	-	3	2	-	-
Ian E Webber [4]	1	1	-	-	-	-	-	-
Roy Woodall	12	11	-	-	-	-	-	-

(1) Mr PJ Knight was appointed a director of the Company on 13 August 1997 after the end of the financial year
(2) Resigned as a director on 30 September 1996
(3) Retired as a director on 15 November 1996
(4) Appointed a director on 10 June 1997

Source: WMC Ltd, annual report, 1997, pp. 94 and 40

Exhibit 12.25 THE NEWS CORP. LTD: SHAREHOLDER INFORMATION, 1997

Shareholder Information

At 20 August, 1997

Corporate Ownership

Number of ordinary shareholders	33,833
Voting rights - ordinary shares	
On show of hands - one vote for each member.	
On poll - one vote for each share held.	
Distribution of shareholding	
1 - 1,000	17,177
1,001 - 5,000	12,574
5,001 - 10,000	1,955
10,001 - 100,000	1,765
100,001 and over	362
Holding less than a marketable parcel	1,384

Top twenty ordinary shareholders as at 20 August, 1997

Cruden Investments Pty. Limited and controlled entities	601,630,928
Citicorp Nominees Pty. Limited	181,927,636
Westpac Custodian Nominees Limited	159,304,282
A.N.Z. Nominees Limited	151,671,012
National Nominees Limited	107,542,979
Chase Manhattan Nominees Limited	101,669,276
Pendal Nominees Pty, Ltd.	47,676,044
Australian Mutual Provident Society	44,711,737
SAS Trustee Corporation	35,403,915
Queensland Investment Corporation	31,792,026
Permanent Trustee Co. Limited	27,130,435
HKBA Nominees Limited	18,639,617
Perpetual Trustees Nominees Limited	17,736,958
News Nominees Pty. Limited	17,501,882
Commonwealth Custodial Services Limited	15,910,797
MLC Limited	15,780,718
The National Mutual Life Association of Australasia Limited	14,447,003
Perpetual Trustee Co. Limited	13,180,906
Prudential Corporation Australia Limited	11,914,131
Commonwealth Superannuation Board of Trustees	9,655,856
	1,625,228,138

Percentage of issued ordinary shares held by twenty largest holders	83.33%
Substantial Shareholders	
Cruden Investments Pty. Limited and controlled entities	601,630,928

Source: The News Corp. Ltd, annual report, 1997, p. 75

and Nair (1980) likewise placed Australia in a British Commonwealth group for both disclosures and measurement practices. The USA and Australia were again placed in different groups.

It appears clear that the classification studies all support the assertion that Australia has been heavily influenced by the UK. We have argued above that Australia is increasingly following the lead of other countries and is turning not just to the UK but also to the USA and the IASC when developing its own standards. It remains to be seen whether this will result in future classification studies instead categorising Australia alongside the USA rather than in a British Commonwealth group alongside the UK.

12.8.2 Comparability measures

While a number of studies have examined the differences between IASs and Australian regulations, none has quantified the differences between reported profits under Australian standards and IASs. However, if this were done, it would be expected that the differences between IAS-based and Australian GAAP-based figures would generally not be significant.

There have been a few studies that have compared the figures produced under US and Australian GAAP. For example, Norton (1995) looked at the form '20-F' (*see* section 13.4.2.3) of 13 Australian companies that were listed in the USA for the period 1985–93. She found that there were no significant differences in the profit figures and in no year was the average US GAAP reported profit less than the Australian GAAP figure (contrary to what had been expected). There was much stronger support for the hypothesis that US GAAP-based equity is significantly less than Australian GAAP-based equity. However, it is not clear if significant differences still exist today. The main causes of the differences in the reported figures were goodwill (Australia has since then prohibited the immediate write-off of goodwill to reserves); use of equity accounting (since 1997 permitted in Australia); elements of cost recognition (the USA being stricter in disallowing deferrals of costs); and taxation adjustments.

12.8.3 Harmonisation studies

As we have seen, Australia is attempting to move further towards the IASC. However, there will still be differences between the IASs and Australian standards, with Australian standards often being more prescriptive or covering areas not covered by IASs. The two will thus be harmonised, but will not be identical.

Virtually all empirical studies comparing the reported figures of companies from various countries have looked at various European countries or the USA. This literature has very largely ignored Australia, although Rahman *et al.* (1996) compared requirements in Australia and New Zealand, and found that there is considerable scope for further harmonisation of the accounting standards. The Stock Exchange requirements in the two countries were found to be virtually identical while, in contrast, considerable differences still existed in the accounting standard requirements. Lack of comparability was particularly great with respect to disclosure of reserves and liabilities and the measurement of investment properties, pensions and earnings per share.

12.9 SUMMARY AND CONCLUSIONS

In this chapter you have seen how the accounting principles and practices of Australia are related to the predictions made by Gray (1988) based upon analysis of cultural factors. Using the scores developed by Hofstede (1984), Gray's work can be used to predict that the Australian accounting system will be one that can be described as exhibiting strong professionalism, is flexible rather than uniform, is relatively optimistic and is open or transparent. These predictions have been generally supported by the analysis of the practices in Australia. Australia has a strong independent accounting profession. The legal system is a common law one and Corporation Law is relatively silent with respect to the regulation of financial reporting. Many of the regulations that exist are flexible, as is perhaps most obviously seen in the choices that companies have with respect to the use of historical costing, current costing or historical costing modified by the revaluation of certain non-current assets. However, the Corporations Law and accounting standards together result in the disclosure of a considerable amount of information and the financial statements are relatively open or transparent. The taxation system is independent of the accounting regulations and has no direct impact upon accounting practices, although it does have an indirect impact.

Australia developed many of its institutions using the model of the UK. Many of the early accounting laws were imported from the UK and the Australian financial reporting system has typically been categorised alongside the UK system in a group of British Commonwealth countries. More recently, Australia has looked further afield, the USA has been increasingly influential and international pronouncements have had an impact in many of the newest standards. This is likely to continue, with the IASC becoming more important. Australia is currently in the middle of a project aimed at ensuring that Australian companies will be able to comply with all IASC standards – while Australian and IASC standards are likely to continue to be somewhat different, a company that meets all the Australian requirements will also meet international requirements.

APPENDIX 12.1: CHRONOLOGY OF DEVELOPMENTS IN CORPORATE FINANCIAL REPORTING IN AUSTRALIA (1817–1988) (excerpts from Morris and Barbera, 1990)

1817 First Australian company formed – Bank of New South Wales (Westpac)

1840 NSW banks required to publish standard format quarterly average balance sheets – based on British colonial banking Model Regulations (1840)

1855 First mining company legislation – Victorian Mining Companies Act based on cost book system developed in South-West England
Requires two-monthly balance sheet and reports
Extended 1858 to require audit if more than 20 shareholders

1858 Western Australia Co. Act – based on UK Companies Act 1856
Followed by similar acts in the other states

1885 Adelaide Society of Accountants formed

1896 Victorian Companies Act based on UK Davey Co Law Committee (1895)
Standard format audited balance sheet sent to all shareholders (precedes UK law of 1907)

1901 Commonwealth of Australia formed

1908 Australasian Corporation of Public Accountants formed

1910 Amend Victorian Companies Act – also require annual audited income statement

1928 Institute of Chartered Accountants of Australia (ICAA) formed

1931 First consolidated accounts published – Hoyts Theatres Ltd

1938 Victorian Companies Act – detailed profit and loss and balance sheet, separate subsidiary accounts or consolidated accounts; disclose movement reserves, unusual items

1946 ICAA issue first six Recommendations on Accounting Principles – most based on ICAEW recommendations

1951 ICAA Auditing recommendations issued

1952 Australian Society of Accountants (ASA) formed by merger of various bodies

1955 ASA begin series of Statements of Accounting Practice

1956 ASA begin series of Technical Bulletins

1958 Victorian Companies Act based upon UK Companies Act 1948

1961 Uniform Companies Act – countrywide company law based on 1958 Victorian Act

1965 Australian Accounting Research Foundation (AARF) formed

1971 Amend 1961 Act – considerable increase disclosure, alternatives for group accounts, auditors report breach Act to state Corporate Affairs Commission

1972 ICAA and ASA begin to issue joint exposure drafts

1974 Authority to issue exposure drafts moves to AARF

1977 NSW Government set up Accounting Standards Review Committee

1978 Co-operative scheme for regulating companies – Ministerial Council of state Attorney-Generals, national companies and Securities Commission (NCSC) and state and territory Corporate Affairs Commissions

1982 Auditing Standards Board use International Guidelines as basis for standards

1984 Establishment Australian Standards Review Board (ASRB) – determine priorities, sponsor development standards, review and approve them

1984 Accounting standards given legislative backing

1988 ICAA establishes Accounting Practices Taskforce – monitor reporting and identify controversial practices

1988 Merger ASRB and Accounting Standards Board of AARF – one set of standards only

APPENDIX 12.2: STANDARDS, CONCEPTS, POLICY STATEMENTS, GUIDANCE RELEASES AND UIGS (1986–97)

ASRB/AASB Statements and Standards

ASRB 100	Nature of approved accounting standards (AASs) and SACs and criteria for evaluation of proposed AASs	August 1990
AASB 1001	Accounting policies	October 1995
ASRB 1002	Events occurring after balance date	July 1986
ASRB 1004	Disclosure of operating revenue	March 1986
ASRB 1005	Financial reporting by segments	April 1986
ASRB 1006	Accounting for interests in joint ventures	April 1986
ASRB 1008	Accounting for leases	November 1987
ASRB 1009	Accounting for construction contracts	November 1986
AASB 1010	Accounting for the revaluation of non-current assets	June 1996
ASRB 1011	Accounting for research and development costs	May 1987
ASRB 1012	Foreign currency translation	July 1988
AASB 1013	Accounting for goodwill	June 1996
AASB 1014	Set-off and extinguishment of debt	December 1996
ASRB 1015	Accounting for the acquisition of assets	September 1988
AASB 1016	Accounting for investments in associates	June 1997
AASB 1017	Related party disclosures	February 1997
AASB 1018	Profit and loss accounts	October 1995
ASRB 1019	Measurement and presentation of inventories in historical cost system	October 1989
ASRB 1020	Accounting for income tax	October 1989
AASB 1021	Depreciation	August 1997
ASRB 1022	Accounting for extractive industries	October 1989
AASB 1023	Financial reporting of general insurance activities	November 1996
AASB 1024	Consolidated accounts	May 1992
AASB 1025	Application of reporting entity concept and other amendments	July 1991
AASB 1026	Statement of cash flows	December 1991
AASB 1027	Earnings per share	November 1992
AASB 1028	Accounting for employee entitlements	March 1994
AASB 1029	Half-year accounts and consolidated accounts	December 1994
AASB 1030	Application of accounting standards to disclosing entities other than companies	December 1994
AASB 1031	Materiality	October 1995
AASB 1032	Specific disclosures by financial institutions	December 1996

AASB 1033	Presentation and disclosure of financial instruments	December 1996
AASB 1034	Information to be disclosed in financial reports	December 1996
AASB 1035	Amendments to AASB 1034	June 1997

Accounting Guidance Releases

AAG1	Purpose and scope of AGRs and procedures for issuance	June 1990
AAG2	Accounting for change in rate of company income tax	December 1985
AAG3	Classification of leases by lessees and lessors	December 1985
AAG8	Accounting for capital gains tax	July 1986
AAG10	Measurement of monetary assets and liabilities	April 1988
AAG11	Debtors accounting for debt restructuring	June 1990
AAG13	Determination of discount rates for measuring certain liabilities at present value	July 1993
AAG14	Recognition of contributions to local governments	September 1993

Recent UIG Summaries

97-1	Depreciation of owner-occupied hotel properties	
97-2	Accounting for costs of modifying computer software for year 2000	
97-3	Directors remuneration	
97-4	Accounting for share buy-backs	
97-5	Early termination of foreign currency hedges	
97-6	Developer and customer contributions	

Accounting Policy Statements

1	Development of statements of accounting concepts and standards	July 1993
2	Operation of consultative group to AASB and PSAB	July 1994
3	Operation of project advisory panels	April 1994
4	Australia–New Zealand harmonisation policy	July 1994
5	Nature and purpose of statements of accounting concepts	April 1994
6	International harmonisation policy	April 1996

Statements of Accounting Concepts

SAC1	Definition of reporting entity	August 1990
SAC2	Objective of general purpose financial reporting	August 1990
SAC3	Qualitative characteristics of financial information	August 1990
SAC4	Definition and recognition of elements of financial statements	March 1995

APPENDIX 12.3: QANTAS AIRWAYS LTD, FINANCIAL STATEMENTS AND NOTES TO THE ACCOUNTS, 1997

PROFIT AND LOSS ACCOUNTS

FOR THE YEAR ENDED 30 JUNE 1997

	NOTES	CONSOLIDATED		CHIEF ENTITY	
		1997 **$ m**	1996 $ m	**1997** **$ m**	1996 $ m
Operating profit before interest and tax		**517.2**	504.4	**441.9**	284.7
Net interest expense	2	**(96.3)**	(103.0)	**(67.9)**	(92.1)
PROFIT FROM OPERATIONS		**420.9**	401.4	**374.0**	192.6
Abnormal items before tax	3	**(17.2)**	–	**(102.0)**	–
OPERATING PROFIT	2	**403.7**	401.4	**272.0**	192.6
Income tax expense attributable to operating profit	4	**(151.0)**	(154.7)	**(59.1)**	(59.3)
OPERATING PROFIT AFTER INCOME TAX		**252.7**	246.7	**212.9**	133.3
Outside equity interests in operating profit		**–**	(0.5)	**–**	–
OPERATING PROFIT AFTER INCOME TAX ATTRIBUTABLE TO MEMBERS OF THE CHIEF ENTITY		**252.7**	246.2	**212.9**	133.3
Retained profits at the beginning of the financial year		**824.9**	712.4	**486.6**	486.8
Adoption of Accounting Standard AASB 1021: "Depreciation of Non-Current Assets"	1k	**(2.2)**	–	**(1.3)**	–
TOTAL AVAILABLE FOR APPROPRIATION		**1,075.4**	958.6	**698.2**	620.1
Dividends provided for or paid	32	**(128.0)**	(133.7)	**(128.0)**	(133.5)
RETAINED PROFITS AT THE END OF THE FINANCIAL YEAR		**947.4**	824.9	**570.2**	486.6

The profit and loss accounts above are to be read in conjunction with the notes to and forming part of the financial statements set out on pages 35 to 65.

BALANCE SHEETS

AS AT 30 JUNE 1997

	NOTES	CONSOLIDATED		CHIEF ENTITY	
		1997	1996	**1997**	1996
		$ m	$ m	**$ m**	$ m
CURRENT ASSETS					
Cash	8	**53.5**	79.4	**39.5**	74.9
Receivables	9	**1,648.2**	1,327.2	**1,950.3**	1,634.9
Net receivables under hedge/swap contracts		**182.9**	52.9	**181.9**	52.9
Inventories	10	**149.5**	136.4	**102.7**	90.3
Other	12	**34.1**	57.7	**21.5**	41.1
TOTAL CURRENT ASSETS		**2,068.2**	1,653.6	**2,295.9**	1,894.1
NON-CURRENT ASSETS					
Receivables	9	**665.8**	663.2	**1,018.1**	1,000.1
Net receivables under hedge/swap contracts		**1,240.2**	1,026.7	**1,203.4**	997.8
Investments	11	**16.6**	235.1	**342.9**	342.4
Property, plant and equipment	13	**5,807.2**	5,586.8	**4,256.5**	4,021.9
Intangibles	14	**30.3**	8.3	**–**	–
Other	12	**83.7**	47.9	**11.7**	13.9
TOTAL NON-CURRENT ASSETS		**7,843.8**	7,568.0	**6,832.6**	6,376.1
TOTAL ASSETS		**9,912.0**	9.221.6	**9,128.5**	8,270.2
CURRENT LIABILITIES					
Accounts payable	15	**1,154.4**	1,032.7	**1,058.3**	911.1
Borrowings	16	**541.9**	147.7	**798.7**	373.5
Net payables under hedge/swap contracts		**177.1**	175.5	**168.5**	167.8
Provisions	17	**550.3**	364.5	**437.4**	293.6
Revenue received in advance		**647.7**	600.2	**610.0**	572.1
Deferred lease benefits/income		**46.4**	47.5	**43.8**	45.6
TOTAL CURRENT LIABILITIES		**3,117.8**	2,368.1	**3,116.7**	2,363.7
NON-CURRENT LIABILITIES					
Accounts payable	15	**–**	0.4	**–**	–
Borrowings	16	**2,649.4**	2,966.0	**2,490.1**	2,579.4
Net payables under hedge/swap contracts		**246.2**	323.7	**246.2**	323.7
Provisions	17	**760.4**	702.5	**513.3**	489.1
Deferred lease benefits/income		**440.7**	400.2	**415.8**	376.2
Other	18	**26.5**	24.1	**26.5**	24.1
TOTAL NON-CURRENT LIABILITIES		**4,123.2**	4,416.9	**3,691.9**	3,792.5
TOTAL LIABILITIES		**7,241.0**	6,785.0	**6,808.6**	6,156.2
NET ASSETS		**2,671.0**	2,436.6	**2,319.9**	2,114.0
SHAREHOLDERS' EQUITY					
Share capital	19	**1,111.7**	1,035.5	**1,111.7**	1,035.5
Reserves	20	**609.9**	574.4	**638.0**	591.9
Retained profits		**947.4**	824.9	**570.2**	486.6
Shareholders' equity attributable to members of the Chief Entity		**2,669.0**	2,434.8	**2,319.9**	2,114.0
Outside equity interests in controlled entities	21	**2.0**	1.8	**–**	–
TOTAL SHAREHOLDERS' EQUITY		**2,671.0**	2,436.6	**2,319.9**	2,114.0

The balance sheets above are to be read in conjunction with the notes to and forming part of the financial statements set out on pages 35 to 65.

STATEMENTS OF CASH FLOWS

FOR THE YEAR ENDED 30 JUNE 1997

	CONSOLIDATED		CHIEF ENTITY	
	1997	1996	**1997**	1996
	$ m	$ m	**$ m**	$ m
CASH FLOWS FROM OPERATING ACTIVITIES				
Receipts from customers	**7,851.4**	7,549.2	**6,795.0**	6,691.6
Payments to suppliers and employees	**(6,668.5)**	(6,511.4)	**(5,943.9)**	(5,973.1)
Interest received	**99.4**	93.2	**102.6**	98.4
Interest paid	**(202.8)**	(211.3)	**(179.1)**	(203.9)
Dividends received	**32.3**	22.0	**111.4**	17.4
Income taxes paid	**(1.0)**	(5.3)	**(0.5)**	(1.3)
Net cash provided by operating activities (refer note 36)	**1,110.8**	936.4	**885.5**	629.1
CASH FLOWS FROM INVESTING ACTIVITIES				
Payments for property, plant and equipment	**(610.6)**	(503.5)	**(569.4)**	(421.9)
Payments for aircraft security deposits	**(14.2)**	(87.1)	**(13.4)**	(78.6)
Total payments for purchases of property, plant, equipment and aircraft security deposits	**(624.8)**	(590.6)	**(582.8)**	(500.5)
Proceeds from sale of equity investments	**371.5**	–	–	–
Proceeds from sale of property, plant and equipment	**2.2**	52.3	**5.7**	41.9
Proceeds from sale and leaseback of non-current assets	**215.3**	396.0	**215.3**	396.0
Payments for investments net of cash acquired	**(44.3)**	(10.1)	**–**	–
Loans repaid by other entities	**9.0**	–	**4.6**	–
Net funding to related parties	**–**	–	**421.1**	130.3
Net cash provided by/(used in) investing activities	**(71.1)**	(152.4)	**63.9**	67.7
CASH FLOWS FROM FINANCING ACTIVITIES				
Repayments of borrowings	**(151.6)**	(148.2)	**(105.7)**	(104.6)
Net repayments of swaps	**(418.2)**	(141.5)	**(410.5)**	(134.0)
Debt prepayments	**(251.7)**	(396.0)	**(251.7)**	(396.0)
Total debt repayments	**(821.5)**	(685.7)	**(767.9)**	(634.6)
Proceeds from borrowings/swaps	**77.2**	11.4	**74.5**	6.1
Proceeds from issue of shares	**40.1**	–	**40.1**	–
Dividends paid	**(40.1)**	(46.7)	**(40.1)**	(46.3)
Net cash used in financing activities	**(744.3)**	(721.0)	**(693.4)**	(674.8)
RECONCILIATION OF CASH PROVIDED BY/ (USED IN):				
Operating activities	**1,110.8**	936.4	**885.5**	629.1
Investing activities	**(71.1)**	(152.4)	**63.9**	67.7
Financing activities	**(744.3)**	(721.0)	**(693.4)**	(674.8)
Net increase in cash held	**295.4**	63.0	**256.0**	22.0
Cash at the beginning of the financial year	**457.2**	394.2	**187.2**	165.2
Cash at the end of the financial year (refer note 36)	**752.6**	457.2	**443.2**	187.2

The statements of cash flows above are to be read in conjunction with the notes to and forming part of the financial statements set out on pages 35 to 65.

NOTES TO AND FORMING PART OF THE FINANCIAL STATEMENTS
FOR THE YEAR ENDED 30 JUNE 1997

NOTE 1: STATEMENT OF SIGNIFICANT ACCOUNTING POLICIES

In order to assist in an understanding of the figures presented, the following summarises the significant policies which have been adopted in the preparation of these financial statements.

a. Basis of Preparation

The financial statements are a general purpose financial report which have been drawn up in accordance with Accounting Standards, Urgent Issues Group Consensus Views and the Corporations Law. They have been prepared on the basis of historical costs and do not take into account changing money values or, except where stated, current valuations of non-current assets. Unless otherwise noted, the accounting policies have been consistently applied with those of the previous year.

b. Principles of Consolidation

The consolidated accounts of the Economic Entity comprise the accounts of Qantas Airways Limited, being the Chief Entity, and its controlled entities as at 30 June 1997, and the results for the year then ended. Results of controlled entities which were acquired or disposed of during the year are included from the date control commenced or to the date control ceased. The consolidation process eliminates inter-entity balances and transactions. Outside equity interests in the results and equity of controlled entities are shown separately in the consolidated profit and loss account and balance sheet respectively.

c. Foreign Currency Transactions
Foreign currency transactions

Foreign currency transactions, except those subject to specific hedging arrangements, are translated to Australian currency at the rate of exchange ruling at the date of each transaction. At balance date, amounts receivable and payable in foreign currencies are translated at rates of exchange ruling at that date. Resulting exchange differences are brought to account as exchange gains or losses in the profit and loss account in the financial year in which the exchange rate changes.

Translation of controlled foreign entities

All controlled entities incorporated overseas are self-sustaining foreign operations and as such, their assets and liabilities are translated at the rates of exchange ruling at the balance date. The profit and loss accounts are translated at the average rate for the year. Exchange differences arising on translation are taken directly to the foreign currency translation reserve.

Hedging of foreign currency commitments

Gains and losses on derivatives used to hedge the purchase or sale of capital equipment and goods and services are deferred in the balance sheet and included in the related purchase or sale. Net deferred losses associated with hedges of foreign currency revenues relating to future transportation services are included in the balance sheet as receivables. As at 30 June 1997, the net amount deferred was $219.4 million (1996: $122.4 million). These losses will be included in the measurement of the relevant future foreign currency revenues at the time the transportation services are provided.

Revenues and expenses from currency swap transactions and amounts owing to/from swap counterparties are set-off and disclosed on a net basis where the requirements of Accounting Standard AASB 1014: "Set-off and Extinguishment of Debt" are satisfied.

d. Derivative Financial Instruments

The Economic Entity is subject to foreign currency, interest rate and aviation fuel price risks. Derivative financial instruments are used to hedge these risks. Economic Entity policy is not to enter, issue or hold derivative financial instruments for trading purposes.

Gains and losses on derivatives used as hedges are accounted for on the same basis as the underlying exposures to which they relate. Accordingly, hedge gains and losses are included in the profit and loss account when the gains and losses arising on the related hedged positions are recognised in the profit and loss account. Further details are outlined in note 30.

e. Passenger and Freight Sales Revenues

Passenger and freight sales revenues are included in the profit and loss account net of sales discounts. Passenger and freight sales commissions are treated as a cost of sales.

f. Revenue Received in Advance

Passenger and freight sales are credited to revenue received in advance and subsequently transferred to revenue when tickets are utilised or freight uplifted. The liability relating to sales of other airlines' tickets is included in trade creditors.

g. Taxation

The Economic Entity adopts the liability method of tax effect accounting.

Income tax expense is calculated on operating profit adjusted for permanent differences between taxable and accounting income. The tax effect of timing differences which arise from items being brought to account in different years for income tax and accounting purposes is carried forward in the balance sheet as a future income tax benefit or a deferred tax liability.

Future income tax benefits relating to timing differences are not brought to account as an asset unless realisation is assured beyond reasonable doubt. Future income tax benefits relating to tax losses are only brought to account as an asset when their realisation is considered to be virtually certain.

NOTES TO AND FORMING PART OF THE FINANCIAL STATEMENTS

FOR THE YEAR ENDED 30 JUNE 1997

NOTE 1: STATEMENT OF SIGNIFICANT ACCOUNTING POLICIES cont.

g. Taxation cont.

Capital gains tax is provided in the financial statements in the years in which an asset is sold. Capital gains tax is not provided for when an asset is revalued.

The Economic Entity is taxed as a public company and provides for income tax in overseas countries where a liability exists. Generally, these taxes are assessed on a formula or percentage of sales basis.

h. Inventories and Work in Progress

Engineering expendables, consumable stores and work in progress which are held for consumption are valued at weighted average cost, less any applicable allowance for obsolescence. Assets held for disposal are valued at the lower of cost and net realisable value.

i. Non-Current Assets

The carrying amounts of non-current assets are reviewed at least annually to determine whether or not they are stated in excess of their recoverable amounts. Assets which primarily generate cash flows, such as aircraft, are assessed on an individual basis whereas infrastructure assets are examined on a class by class basis, and compared to net surplus cash inflows. Expected net cash flows used in determining recoverable amounts have been discounted to their net present value, using a rate reflecting the cost of funds.

Appropriate provisions are made where the carrying amount exceeds recoverable amount. To the extent that a revaluation decrement reverses a revaluation increment previously credited to, and still included in the balance of, the asset revaluation reserve for the same class of assets, the decrement is debited directly to the reserve. Otherwise, the decrement is recognised as an expense in the profit and loss account.

j. Investments

All investments are recorded at the lower of cost and recoverable amount.

Controlled entities

Dividend income from controlled entities is included in revenue of the Chief Entity when proposed.

Associated companies

An associated company is one in which the Economic Entity exercises significant influence, but not control. Dividend income from associated companies is included in revenue when received.

Other entities

Dividends from investments in corporations which are not controlled entities or associated companies are included in revenue when received.

k. Property, Plant and Equipment

Cost and valuation

Freehold land and buildings and leasehold improvements are independently valued at least every three years. Major modifications to aircraft and the costs associated with placing the aircraft into service are capitalised as part of the cost of the asset to which they relate. All aircraft maintenance costs are expensed as incurred.

Depreciation and amortisation

Depreciation and amortisation are provided on a straight line basis on all property, plant and equipment, other than freehold and leasehold land, at rates calculated to allocate the cost or valuation less estimated residual value at the end of the useful lives of the assets, over their estimated useful lives. The cost of improvements to or on leasehold properties is amortised over the unexpired period of the lease or the estimated useful life of the improvement, whichever is the shorter. The principal asset depreciation periods are:

	Years	Residuals %
Buildings and leasehold improvements	10-50	0
Plant and equipment	3-10	0
Jet aircraft and spare engines	20	0-25
Non-jet aircraft and spare engines	10-30	0-20
Aircraft spare parts	15-20	0-25

Depreciation rates are reviewed annually and reassessed having regard to commercial and technological developments.

AASB 1021: Depreciation of Non-Current Assets

Depreciation of non-current assets has been calculated in accordance with Accounting Standard AASB 1021: "Depreciation of Non-Current Assets". The financial effect of the adoption of this Accounting Standard has been to decrease retained profits at the beginning of the financial year by $2.2 million (Chief Entity: $1.3 million).

Leased and hire purchased assets

Leased assets under which the Economic Entity assumes substantially all the risks and benefits of ownership are classified as finance leases and capitalised.

At the inception of the lease, a lease asset and liability equal to the present value of the minimum lease payments are created. Any gains and losses under sale and leaseback arrangements are included as part of the cost of the leased asset. Capitalised leased assets are amortised on a straight line basis over the period in which benefits are expected to arise from the use of those assets. Lease payments are allocated between the reduction in the principal component of the lease liability and interest expense.

NOTES TO AND FORMING PART OF THE FINANCIAL STATEMENTS

FOR THE YEAR ENDED 30 JUNE 1997

NOTE 1: STATEMENT OF SIGNIFICANT ACCOUNTING POLICIES cont.
k. Property, Plant and Equipment cont.

In respect of a number of finance leases, debt funding has been provided to the lessor. This debt funding has been offset against the lease liability and the balance sheet reflects the net position (refer note 22). Interest received on the debt funding is also offset against interest paid (refer note 2).

Hire purchased assets are accounted for in the same way as finance leases.

Operating lease payments are charged to the profit and loss account in the years in which they are incurred.

In respect of any premises rented under long-term operating leases which are subject to sub-tenancy agreements, provision is made for any shortfall between primary payments to the head lessor less any recoveries from sub-tenants. These provisions are determined on a discounted cash flow basis, using a rate reflecting the cost of funds.

Non-cancellable operating leases

Non-cancellable operating leases are generally for a term of 12 years extendable at the option of the Chief Entity to 15 years. The leases are non-cancellable on the basis that there are likely to be financial penalties associated with a termination prior to year twelve.

l. Intangible Assets
Goodwill

Goodwill, representing the excess of the purchase consideration over the fair values of identifiable net assets acquired, is amortised on a straight line basis over the period in which future benefits are expected to arise, or 20 years, whichever is the shorter.

Other intangible assets

Trademarks, tradenames and licences are amortised on a straight line basis over the period in which future benefits are expected to arise, or 20 years, whichever is the shorter.

m. Frequent Flyer liability

The obligation to provide travel rewards to members of the Frequent Flyer program is progressively accrued as a current liability as points are accumulated. This accrual is based on the incremental cost of ultimately providing the travel rewards.

As members redeem awards or their entitlements expire, the accrual is reduced accordingly to reflect the acquittal of the outstanding obligation.

n. Employee Entitlements
Wages and salaries, annual leave, sick leave and statutory entitlements

Liabilities for wages and salaries, annual leave (including leave loading), sick leave vesting to employees and statutory overseas termination entitlements are recognised and measured as the amount unpaid at balance date at current wage and salary rates, including all related on-costs in respect of the employees' services provided up to that date.

Long service leave

The liability for long service leave represents the present value of the estimated future cash outflows to be made by the employer resulting from employees' services provided up to the balance date. Liabilities for employee entitlements which are not expected to be settled within 12 months are discounted using rates attached to national government securities at balance date which most closely match the timing of maturity of the related liability. In determining the liability for employee entitlements, consideration has been given to future increases in wage and salary rates and experience with staff turnover. The liability includes all related on-costs.

Superannuation

The Economic Entity contributes to employee superannuation funds. Contributions to these funds are recognised in the profit and loss account as they are made. Further details are disclosed in note 26.

Qantas Staff Share Plan II

Eligible Employees of the Chief Entity and its wholly-owned controlled entities are participants in the Qantas Staff Share Plan II. Further details are disclosed in note 31. Other than the costs incurred in administering the plan, which are expensed as incurred, the plan does not result in any expense to the Economic Entity.

o. Workers' Compensation

The Chief Entity is a licensed self-insurer under the New South Wales Workers Compensation Act and the Accident Compensation Act 1985 (Victoria), and has made provision for all assessed workers' compensation liabilities based on an independent actuarial assessment. Workers' compensation liabilities for non-New South Wales and Victorian employees are insured commercially.

Australian Airlines Limited, a controlled entity, has made provision for outstanding self-insured pre 1 July 1989 workers' compensation claims including an estimate for incurred but non-reported claims, both based on an independent actuarial assessment. Post 1 July 1989, all workers' compensation liabilities have been insured commercially.

NOTES TO AND FORMING PART OF THE FINANCIAL STATEMENTS
FOR THE YEAR ENDED 30 JUNE 1997

NOTE 1: STATEMENT OF SIGNIFICANT ACCOUNTING POLICIES cont.

p. Deferred Lease Benefits/Income
Gains/losses on instantaneous sale and operating leaseback of aircraft, benefits derived from cross-border leasing arrangements and variations between actual lease payments and minimum lease payments are treated as deferred lease benefits/income. These are brought to account as income/expenses over the period of the respective lease or on a basis which is representative of the pattern of benefits derived from the leasing transactions.

q. Segment Information
Segment information is provided in note 33.

Industry segments
The Economic Entity operates predominantly in one industry segment, being the transportation of passengers and freight on services within and to or from Australia.

Geographical segments
Passenger, freight and contract services revenue from domestic services within Australia is attributed to the Australian area. Passenger, freight and contract services revenue from inbound and outbound services between Australia and overseas is allocated to the area where the sale was made. Other revenue is not allocated to a geographic area as it is impractical to do so.

Segmental analysis of net assets and profit contribution
For the year ended 30 June 1997, the principal assets of the Economic Entity comprised the aircraft fleet, all except one of which, were registered and domiciled in Australia. These assets are used flexibly across the Economic Entity's worldwide route network. Accordingly, there is no suitable basis of allocating such assets and the related liabilities between geographic areas.

Operating profit resulting from turnover generated in each geographic area according to origin of sale is not disclosed as it is neither practical nor meaningful to allocate operating expenditure on that basis.

Disclosure is made of a more appropriate measure of profit contributions in accordance with the Economic Entity's internal reporting system, between the earnings before interest and tax contributions from international and domestic operations and controlled entity operations (refer note 33).

r. Earnings per Share
Earnings per share is determined by dividing the Economic Entity's operating profit after income tax attributable to members of the Chief Entity by the weighted average number of ordinary shares on issue during the financial year (refer note 34).

s. Statements of Cash Flows
For the purposes of the statements of cash flows (refer note 36), cash includes cash on hand, at bank and money market investments readily convertible to cash, net of outstanding bank overdrafts and short-term cash borrowings. Bank loans obtained through the use of commercial paper funding facilities and funding provided to related parties have been disclosed on a net basis due to the rapid turnover and the high volume of transactions.

t. Comparative Figures
Where applicable, comparatives have been adjusted to reflect disclosure on a comparable basis with current year figures.

Source: Qantas Airways Ltd and Controlled Entities, annual report, 1997, pp. 32–8

◼ QUESTIONS

Business environment (12.2–12.5)

1 To what extent does the business environment of Australia provide clues as to possible influences on accounting practices?

Early developments in accounting (12.3)

1 To what extent do early developments in accounting practice indicate the likely directions of: professionalism/statutory control; uniformity/flexibility; conservatism/optimism; secrecy/transparency in current practice?

Institutions (12.4)

1 How does the political and economic system of Australia fit into the classifications described in Chapter 1?

2 How does the legal system of Australia fit into the classifications described in Chapter 1?

3 How does the taxation system of Australia compare to the descriptions given in Chapter 1?

4 How does the corporate financing system of Australia compare to the descriptions given in Chapter 1?

5 How does the accounting profession in Australia compare to the descriptions given in Chapter 1?

6 How do the external influences on accounting practice in Australia compare to those described in Chapter 1?

7 Which institutional factors are most likely to influence Australian accounting practice?

Societal culture and accounting sub-culture (12.5)

1 What is the position of Australia relative to the UK and continental European countries, according to Hofstede's (1984) analysis (Chapter 2)?

2 What are the features of Australian societal culture identified by Hofstede which led Gray to his (1988) conclusions regarding the likely system of accounting in Australia?

3 What is the position of Australia relative to USA and Japan according to Hofstede's (1984) analysis (Chapter 2).

IASs (12.6)

1 In which areas does accounting practice in Australia depart from that set out in International Accounting Standards (IASs)?

2 What explanations may be offered for these departures from IASs, in terms of the institutional factors described in the chapter?

Professionalism/statutory control (12.7.2)

1 Identify the key features supporting a conclusion that professionalism, rather than statutory control, is a dominant characteristic of Australian accounting.

2 Explain which institutional influences cause professionalism, rather than statutory control, to be a dominant characteristic of Australian accounting.

3 Discuss whether a classification of strong professionalism is appropriate for the 1990s.

Uniformity/flexibility (12.7.3)

1 Identify the key features supporting a conclusion that flexibility, rather than uniformity, is a dominant characteristic of Australian accounting.

2 Explain which institutional influences cause flexibility, rather than uniformity, to be a dominant characteristic of Australian accounting.

3 Discuss whether a classification of strong flexibility is appropriate for the 1990s.

Conservatism/optimism (12.7.4)

1 Identify the key features supporting a conclusion that optimism, rather than conservatism, is a dominant characteristic of Australian accounting.

2 Explain which institutional influences cause optimism, rather than conservatism, to be a dominant characteristic of Australian accounting.

3 Discuss whether a classification of strong optimism is appropriate for the 1990s.

Secrecy/transparency (12.7.5)

1 Identify the key features supporting a conclusion that transparency, rather than secrecy, is a dominant characteristic of Australian accounting.

2 Explain which institutional influences cause transparency, rather than secrecy, to be a dominant characteristic of Australian accounting.

3 Discuss whether a classification of strong transparency is appropriate for the 1990s.

Empirical studies (12.8)

1 What is the relative position of Australia as indicated by research studies into classification, comparability and harmonisation?

REFERENCES

Australian Accounting Standards Board (1994) *Policy Statement 4, Australian–New Zealand harmonisation policy*. Sydney: AASB.

Australian Accounting Standards Board (1995) *Financial Reporting Pronouncements 1995*. Sydney: ASSB, xi–xiii.

Australian Accounting Standards Board (1996) *Policy Statement 6, International Harmonisation Policy*. Sydney: AASB.

Australian Society of CPAs, Institute of Chartered Accountants in Australia (1996) *Accounting Handbook 1997*. Sydney: Prentice-Hall.

Australian Society of CPAs, Institute of Chartered Accountants in Australia (1996) *Auditing Handbook 1997*. Sydney: Prentice-Hall

Australian Stock Exchange (1997) *Web page*, http://www.asx.com.au (October).

Corsi, R.A. and Staunton J.J. (1994) 'Australian accounting standard setting and the conceptual framework project', *Advances in International Accounting*, 6, 15–41.

Crasswell, A. (1995) 'Australia', in Ordeldeide, D. and KPMG (eds), *Transnational Accounting*. London: Macmillan.

Deegan, C. (1996) *Australian Financial Accounting: A practical conceptual and theoretical analysis*. Sydney: Irwin.

Doupnik, T.S. and Salter, S.B. (1993) 'An empirical test of a judgmental international classification of financial reporting practices', *Journal of International Business Studies*, 24(1), 41–60.

The Economist (1997) *Pocket World in Figures 1998 Edition*. London: Profile Books.

Gibson, R.E. (1979) 'Developments in corporate accounting in Australia', *The Accounting Historians' Journal*, Fall, 23–38.

Gray, S.J. (1988) 'Towards a theory of cultural influence on the development of accounting systems internationally', *Abacus*, 24(1), 1–15.

Hofstede, G. (1984) *Culture's Consequences: International Differences in Work-related Values*. Beverly Hills, CA: Sage Publications.

Institute of Chartered Accountants in Australia (1997) *Major Changes and New Directions in Accounting and Auditing*. London: ICAA (November).

McKinnon, J. (1993) 'Corporate disclosure regulation in Australia', *Journal of International Accounting, Auditing and Taxation*, 2(1), 1–21.

Miller, M.C. (1994) 'Australia', in Cooke, T.E. and Parker, R.H. (eds), *Financial Reporting in the West Pacific Rim*. London: Routledge, 333–82.

Miller, M.C. (1995) 'The credibility of Australian financial reporting: Are the co-regulation arrangements working?', *Australian Accounting Review*, 5(2), 3–16.

Miller, M.C. (1996) 'Accounting regulation and the roles assumed by the government and the accounting profession: The case of Australia', *Working Paper Series*, University of New South Wales, School of Accounting.

Morris, R.D. and Barbera, M.R. (1990) 'A chronology of the development of corporate financial reporting in Australia: 1817 to 1988', in Parker, R.D. (ed.), *Accounting in Australia*. New York: Garland Publishing.

Nair, R.D. and Frank, W.G. (1980) 'The impact of disclosure and measurement practices on international accounting classifications', *Accounting Review*, July, 426–50.

Nobes, C.W. (1984) *International Classification of Financial Reporting*. London: Croom Helm.

Norton, J. (1995) 'The impact of financial accounting practices on the measurement of profit and equity: Australia versus the United States', *Abacus*, 31(2), 178–200.

Parker, R.H. (1989) 'Importing and exporting accounting: The British experience', in Hopwood, A.G. (ed.), *International Pressures for Accounting Change*. London: Prentice Hall/ ICAEW.

Parker, R.H. and Nobes C.W. (1994) *An International View of True and Fair Accounting*. London: Routledge.

Rahman, A., Perera, H. and Ganeshanandam, S. (1996) 'Measurement of formal harmonisation in accounting: An exploratory study', *Accounting and Business Research*, 26(4), 325–40.

Whittred, G. (1986) 'The evolution of consolidated financial reporting in Australia', *Abacus*, 22(1), 103–20.

Whittred, G., Zimmer, I. and Taylor, S. (1996) *Financial Accounting: Incentive Effects and Economic Consequences*, 4th edn. Sydney: Harcourt Brace.

Chapter 13

The USA

INTRODUCTION

The accounting principles and practices of the United States of America (USA) are influential beyond the country's national boundary and have, of themselves, provided a means of harmonisation for those other countries and business enterprises choosing to follow the US lead. They act also as a block to harmonisation where the US regulators will not accept any practices other than those conforming to US standards without a statement of reconciliation of the differences. The source of the widespread influence of US accounting lies in its worldwide political and economic dominance and in the importance of its capital market. The market is closely regulated by an agency of the federal government, the Securities and Exchange Commission (SEC). Those companies which seek a listing for their shares must comply with SEC regulations.

Within this framework of close regulation, there is considerable scope for application of professional judgement in accounting matters. Accounting standards are greater in volume and more detailed than those of almost any other country of the world, but they are set by an independent standard setting body rather than by statute law. The standard setting body has been well supported financially, and has therefore researched issues to an extent not feasible in other countries.

The entirety of US accounting principles and practices is referred to as 'US GAAP', short for 'US generally accepted accounting principles'. The concept of such a set of written principles originates in the USA, although the abbreviation is used in reference to other countries also. Accounting disclosure is characterised by openness and accounting measurement by general conservatism and historical cost. Such conservatism originated in the stock market crash of 1929, modified by business pragmatism and flexibility in response to events of more recent years.

13.2 THE COUNTRY

13.2.1 Geography

The USA is a land mass stretching from the Atlantic to the Pacific ocean and including Alaska and Hawaii as states. There are five major units of physical geography. The coastal plain of the east extends down the entire Atlantic coast. Behind the coastal plain rise the Appalachian mountains in

453

a succession of plateaux and ridges. Moving west, a fertile interior basin is drained by the Mississippi river. Further west again the Rocky mountains extend from Canada to Colorado and finally the Pacific mountain system contains the Central Valley of California, a rich agricultural area. Mineral resources include iron ore and coal. Agricultural specialisation varies according to location and climate. The population is 267 million and has a relatively low growth rate.

13.2.2 Economic indicators

The economy showed growth of 2.5% per annum over the period 1985–95 and general standards of living are high (*see* Exhibit 13.1).

Gross domestic product (GDP) is created almost three-quarters by services. Manufacturing industry provides less than one-quarter of GDP. In manufacturing industry, the highest single contribution is provided by machinery and transport but half of manufacturing industry is diversified into a range of activities. Manufacturing is largely concentrated in a belt reaching from New England to the Midwest. This area contains much of the steel industry, the automotive industry, specialised and electrical engineering and the textile and clothing trades.

The main export product is capital goods, excluding vehicles. The main export destination is Canada. Japan is the most significant trading partner after Canada. The European Union (EU) features relatively little in the export destinations of US products, with the UK and Germany being the only countries listed.

The main import product is also capital goods, excluding vehicles. The origins of imports are primarily Canada and Japan. Again the EU is not significant as a source of imports, with mention being made only of Germany and the UK.

Imports exceed exports, giving a negative balance of trade. Inflows of invisibles exceed outflows, reducing the overall negative balance.

Exhibit 13.1   THE USA: COUNTRY PROFILE, TAKEN FROM EIU STATISTICS

Population	267.1 m
Land mass	9,372,610 sq.km
GDP per head	US $26,580
GDP per head in purchasing-power-parity	100
Origins of GDP:	%
Agriculture	1.9
Industry	23.4
Services	74.9
	%
Real GDP average annual growth 1985–95	2.5
Inflation, average annual rate 1989–96	3.6

Source: The Economist Pocket World in Figures 1998 Edition, The Economist (1997)

13.3 OVERVIEW OF ACCOUNTING REGULATIONS[1]

Accounting practices were to some extent imported from the UK by early pioneers establishing business practices in the USA. Some of the best known accounting firms have founding fathers of UK origin.[2]

13.3.1 Early regulation of accounting

The American Association of Public Accountants, formed in 1886, and the Institute of Bookkeepers and Accountants, encouraged a New York State law establishing the profession of Certified Public Accountant in 1896, and similar laws followed in other states. The Association established the *Journal of Accountancy* as a means of professional communication and published a terminology of accounting in 1915. The American Institute of Certified Public Accountants (AICPA) emerged in 1957 from various changes of name and mergers. In the early years, maintaining good standards of accountancy practice was very much in the hands of individual practitioners; companies generally did not disclose their accounting practices.

The stock market crash of 1929 caused fundamental changes in many aspects of US business practice. From 1930, the AICPA began working with the New York Stock Exchange (NYSE) to develop accounting principles to be followed by all companies listed on the exchange. The initial approach was to continue allowing companies relative freedom of choice but to emphasise disclosure. The Securities and Exchange Commission (SEC) was formed by Congress in 1933, establishing its rules in 1934 under which it received for filing a copy of the accounts of each listed company. The SEC took a harder line that where listed companies filed accounts which did not have substantial authoritative support, those accounts would not be accepted – effectively, the SEC was deciding on accounting practice.

During the late 1940s and the 1950s the AICPA worked to produce Accounting Research Bulletins (ARBs). Where the SEC felt there was an insufficiently strict approach in the ARBs, it would indicate that filing of accounts might be refused even though the ARBs had been applied. This caused the AICPA to form the Accounting Principles Board (APB) in 1959. However the ARBs survived in the form of ARB 43, which was a restatement and revision of the first 40 ARBs. Many parts of ARB 43 remain authoritative today.

The APB produced Accounting Research Studies and a series of APB Opinions; these did not dispel the controversies of the earlier periods and there were situations where the SEC indicated dissatisfaction with particular APB Opinions. More generally, it was felt that drafts of APB Opinions were not sufficiently exposed for comment and that resolution of some problems took too long a time. A major enquiry established by the AICPA (called the Wheat Committee) recommended in 1972 the formation of a Financial Accounting Standards Board (FASB). In particular, the Wheat Committee noted that the members of the APB were all accountants, creating a potential conflict of interest; it recommended the broader base of membership seen in the FASB today. A further enquiry, undertaken for the AICPA, by the

[1] Wolk and Tearney (1997), Chapter 3
[2] Nobes (1995), p. 145

Trueblood Study Group (AICPA, 1973), identified major objectives of financial statements which were subsequently taken by the FASB as guidance for its approach to standard setting. The present process is discussed further in section 13.7.

The FASB was guided in its work by a series of Statements of Financial Accounting Concepts (SFACs) in the late 1970s and early 1980s. These statements emphasise a balance sheet approach of defining and recognising assets and liabilities. Owners' equity is the residual item in the equation. Changes in assets and liabilities must be reported through the income statement. This tends to lead to fluctuations in reported profit when compared to the alternative approach of matching income and expenses so as to smooth reported profit from one period to the next. The FASB is sometimes accused of failing to adhere strictly to the balance sheet approach and returning instead to the approach of income smoothing.

13.3.2 Consolidated accounting[3]

Consolidated financial statements have been published in the USA since the end of the nineteenth century. They are produced so commonly that single company statements are generally published only by entities having no subsidiaries. There is no law in the USA that mandates their publication; the requirement to publish has emerged within US GAAP, the most important requirments being ARB 51, dating from 1959, and the more recent SFAS 94. Other standards address particular aspects of consolidation and the totality sets the consolidation policy to be followed under US GAAP.

Business combinations are normally accounted for using the purchase (acquisition) method of accounting. On relatively rare occasions, where there is a uniting of interests by exchange of equity shares, the pooling of interests (merger) method is required by APB 16. The criteria for applying 'uniting of interests' under IAS 22 are based on a general principle of sharing risks and benefits in the combined entity. These include an ownership condition, a size condition and a condition of shared management.

The conditions for pooling of interests contained in APB 16 are much more detailed than those of IAS 22 and yet are less restrictive because there is no condition of comparable fair value. What the US rules seek is to restrict the pooling of interest method to a straightforward exchange of shares between two parties which preserves the relative rights of each group of shareholders in the total entity. Pooling of interests has been discouraged as much as possible because it allowed profits to be combined without calculation and amortisation of goodwill.

Joint venture accounting has not been addressed specifically although it is included in the FASB's long-term project on consolidation. The present treatment is that joint ventures are accounted for using equity accounting. Proportionate consolidation is generally not used because the SEC objects; however, the SEC has made an exception for extractive industries such as oil and gas.

---

[3] Kubin (1993)

13.4 INSTITUTIONS

13.4.1 Political and economic system

The USA is a federal republic of separate states. Each state has its own constitution, but the separate states unite under a federal government operating under a federal constitution. The federal government has the power to impose taxes, the responsibility for national defence and foreign relations, the power to create a national currency and the authority to set countrywide laws regulating commercial and business practice. States also have power to regulate business practice.

The federal constitution divides the federal government into the executive, the legislative and the judicial branches. The President of the USA leads the executive branch, while the legislative branch consists of the Congress, the House of Representatives and the Senate. The judicial branch is led by the Supreme Court and, below it, a system of federal courts. Each of the three branches of the constitution is independent but there are checks and balances. The President has a power of veto over legislation, but the veto may be overcome by a two-thirds majority of both the House of Representatives and the Senate. The judiciary may declare acts of the executive unconstitutional.

The President is elected every four years, and only permitted two terms in total. The members of the House of Representatives and Senate are also elected. One-third of Senate members are elected by rotation every two years, House of Representatives members are elected every two years. Depending on swings in political mood, it is possible for the majority in Senate and the House of Representatives to be of a different political party from the President.

The economic system is that of the open market. Historically, the nature of the economic system has developed and changed as the political climate has changed and as technological change has allowed exploitation of new opportunities. The USA has always attracted high wealth in terms of human capital, more than once because persecution elsewhere drove individuals to seek freedom there. Development of the railways opened up the country to industrial production, that has now declined in relation to service industry, but remains a strong minority element of the economy.

The economic boom of the 1960s allowed political activity to strengthen. There was a heavy cost to the USA in its involvement in war in Vietnam, and in the 1970s inflation and economic depression were dominant problems. President Reagan in 1980 promised economic reform and a strong America overseas, and by 1997 it was claimed that there had been ten years of long-term growth potential. Indicative factors were cited as: increasing globalisation of US business; considerable increase in trade as a proportion of GDP; weakening of the power of trade unions; and competitive pressures among US companies. The alternative interpretation is that the improvement has resulted from a coincidence of short-term factors.[4]

---

[4] 'Miracle or myth? – that is the question', *Financial Times* (19 September 1997), Survey, *World Economy and Finance*, Part 1, 3

13.4.2 Legal system

The political doctrine of separation of powers in the federal constitution means that business may be affected by each of the executive, the legislative and the judicial arms. Independent regulatory agencies are also in existence as a fourth arm to the processes of the legal system. However the chairman and chief accountant of the SEC are appointed by the executive (President). (Regulatory agencies are under the rule of the executive, and so there is not a fourth arm to the constitution; however, the regulatory agencies are approved by Congress.)

Legislation is introduced through committees of each House of Congress. If compromise is required to meet the requirements of each separate House, it will be negotiated in committee before being submitted to the full House of Representatives and Senate. Implementation of the law through the courts begins in federal districts, each having a federal court called a District Court which applies federal law. Appeal from the District Court is made to the Courts of Appeal, and the Supreme Court reviews decisions of the lower federal courts.

The federal government has general regulatory powers, but much regulation of business enterprises is by state law. One general theme of the federal legislative approach is 'truth in securities', leading to regulation of those who issue shares to the public. Another is free and open competition, leading to what is called 'antitrust legislation'. This makes illegal any restraint of trade created by unfair business combinations, including those established on the basis of what some might regard as mutual trust but others would see as conspiracy.

The legal system of the USA is that of the common law family but has developed uniquely American characteristics, it is therefore not surprising to find similarly unique aspects to the development of accounting law in the USA.

13.4.2.1 Federal and state law[5]

Federal law deals with matters such as the registration of securities, taxation and antitrust law. Powers not specifically delegated to the USA by the constitution are reserved to the states. State laws apply to matters such as enforcement of contract, agency, conveyancing, bills of exchange, and debtor–creditor relationships; they also overlap with federal law on issues such as securities, taxation and antitrust law.

There is some element of competition between federal and state law. This leads also to interesting competition between states in attracting businesses. Many leading companies are registered in Delaware. This is because, in 1913, the state legislature of New Jersey introduced a restrictive approach to corporations. The corporations transferred their registration to Delaware, having a flexible incorporation law. Delaware has subsequently developed expertise in matters of business law. The restriction in New Jersey was short-lived but the corporations stayed in Delaware.

One important feature of US law is its Freedom of Information Acts, which give access to government papers that might in other countries be locked away. The openness of practices of governmental administration leads to openness in non-governmental organisations (NGOs) also. Information lodged with the government later becomes available as a government paper.

---

[5] Charkham (1994), pp. 174–5

13.4.2.2 Types of business organisation[6]

Businesses may operate as sole traders, partnerships or corporations. Corporations are established and governed by the law of the state in which they are incorporated. A foreign company may incorporate in any state, regardless of where the production facilities and management are located. Incorporation is achieved by filing articles of incorporation and bylaws with the relevant state official. State laws will cover matters such as the initial capital required; classes and powers of voting stock; corporate powers; the number of directors and their duties; payment of dividends; requirements for accounting records; and the cessation of the company. A corporation may acquire and hold its own shares.

All corporations have a board of directors elected by the shareholders and responsible to them for the running of the company. Directors and officers have duties of loyalty and care to the corporation. Any shareholder has the right to sue on behalf of the corporation where there has been a perceived breach of duty. The corporation is a taxable entity. The USA has many more unlisted than listed companies. The focus of this chapter is on listed companies which are the group regulated by the SEC. In particular, the SEC prescribes the reporting requirements for published accounting information.

The Chief Executive Officer (CEO) is always a member of the board of the company. The CEO is the focus of attention as the person driving the company; there is relatively little press interest in the directors. Typically a CEO will serve for six to eight years. The directors elect the chairman of the board, although in many cases the CEO is the chairman. Active management is delegated by the directors to paid officials. Directors focus on policy issues.

13.4.2.3 SEC

The Securities Act 1933 has the intention to create 'truth in securities', aiming to provide information for investors and prohibit misrepresentation. Any company planning to offer its securities for sale must register with the SEC, which imposes regulations based on registration forms requiring extensive disclosure. Domestic US companies must prepare an annual registration form referred to as '10-K'. Foreign companies seeking to offer securities for sale in the US must present an annual registration form called a '20-F' and must restate their financial statements using US GAAP. The essential power of the SEC lies in its authority to reject the filing of accounts: without that filing a company cannot continue to have a stock exchange listing. This gives the SEC effective control over accounting practice without being directly a standard setting body.

The SEC is a federal agency, and has a strong tradition of being activist in its work.[7] There are detailed rules on what information should be provided, where it should be lodged and where it should be sent. The SEC largely controls information issued by companies. It interacts with state law on some matters of specific disclosure but is prevented by the Supreme Court from encroaching too much on state law. The most important disclosure regulations are Regulation S-X, covering financial statements, and Regulation S-K, covering non-financial disclosure about the operations of the business.

---

[6] Charkham (1994), p. 183
[7] Charkham (1994), pp. 174–5

There are some 5,000 new registrations every year. The SEC regulates over 10,000 securities brokers and dealers and monitors all trading on the stock exchanges. It has an electronic filing system called EDGAR (Electronic Data Gathering Analysis and Retrieval) whereby companies may lodge information electronically. Access to the EDGAR filings is starting to become available through the World Wide Web.

13.4.2.4 Corporate governance[8]

Corporate governance, as a means of promoting trust, loyalty and commitment among the various parties, has grown in the USA over many years but its precise nature has depended on the concerns of the time regarding the behaviour of corporate entities. The most recent concerns have been related to seeing corporations slim down by shedding employees while at the same time giving progressively greater rewards to senior executives. This could appear to indicate a lack of social responsibility and too much emphasis on creating wealth for shareholders; on the other hand, it may indicate the economic efficiency which maintains the competitive position of US business in world markets. Either interpretation leads to emphasis on 'stakeholders' as a wider constituency than the shareholders and creditors who are seen by the legal process as having the primary need to know about the operation of a corporation.

The emphasis on stakeholders encourages corporations to be accountable and report to a wider group. In practice, the market for stocks and shares remains the primary mechanism for corporate governance. In particular, it is noticeable that major institutional shareholders will use their voting power at company meetings to express their views on corporate governance and are aware that they are expected to show an element of social responsibility as well as safeguarding their position as investors.

Structure of the board of directors

Members of the board of directors may be drawn from the entire USA, and the company's operations may be widely dispersed. Directors receive information quite frequently because of the obligation on listed companies to report quarterly to shareholders. The board of directors meets relatively infrequently, delegating detailed matters to committees of the board. These might cover remuneration packages, finance, public policy, planning, human resources and similar matters. The most important are the audit committee, the compensation committee, the nominating committee and the executive committee.

It is a condition of stock exchange listing that a corporation has an audit committee to review all aspects of external and internal auditing. The audit committee must comprise independent (non-executive) directors. Compensation committees also comprise the independent directors and decide the remuneration packages of senior executives including the CEO. Nominating committees screen policy proposals put forward by the CEO and offer advice on the composition and membership of the board of directors. Executive committees deal with urgent business between meetings of the main board. For corporations progressing at a steady

---

[8] Charkham (1994), Chapter 5; OECD (1996), pp. 118–21

rate, the committee structure is the effective form of governance and the board of directors takes an oversight role, becoming more active in intervention only where a crisis is looming.

Remuneration of CEOs

There are often references to the package of remuneration available to the CEO which, in the USA is referred to as 'compensation'. It means the basic salary paid in cash plus all the other benefits received such as membership of a health care scheme; use of a company car; contributions to a retirement benefit package; bonus payments related to corporate performance and profits; and options (rights) to purchase ordinary shares at an agreed price over a stated period of time. The long-term performance-related aspects are a much greater proportion of the total package than in other countries. (An OECD report[9] indicates long-term benefits as 32% of the total package of CEOs' compensation in the USA compared with 11% in France and the UK and nil in Japan.)

This compensation package provides the potential for the CEO to be self-seeking where the profits of the company are threatened or the CEO's position in the business is at risk. Restricting the compensation package might reduce the CEO's entrepreneurial spirit, and so the present emphasis in corporate governance is on disclosure to shareholders of the full compensation package and the use of a compensation committee comprising the non-executive members of the board of directors.

13.4.3 Taxation system

The US congress passes the laws that govern income taxes. The legislation is contained in the Internal Revenue Code and administered by the Internal Revenue Service (IRS). Generally, taxes are imposed on each company separately, but an affiliated group of domestic corporations may file a consolidated return and be taxed as one corporation. It is relatively unusual to find a country allowing tax to be based on the group as a whole.

13.4.3.1 Corporate income tax

Taxable income is determined as the excess of taxable revenue over deductible expenses. The general rule is that all revenue is taxable and expenses are deductible provided they are ordinary and necessary. The resulting taxable profit may differ from the accounting profit because the tax code is intended to generate revenue for the government in a manner consistent with specific social and economic goals, while financial accounting information is intended to be useful to investors and lenders. US corporations are taxable on their worldwide income.

Accrual accounting is used for tax purposes in the USA. However, some expenses such as losses on sales of assets (e.g. buildings) must be realised in cash before they are allowed to be deductible. The tax rules also cover revenue recognition, tax rates and tax credits. Some revenue and expenses are not taxable – a fine imposed for an illegal activity, for example, would not be allowable as an expense. Timing

---

[9] OECD (1996), p. 129

differences occur where the expense is recognised differently under tax rules compared with accounting practice, due to accelerated depreciation, delayed revenue recognition and delayed recognition of expenses.[10]

Accelerated depreciation is used for tax purposes but not necessarily for accounting profit. Under the Modified Accelerated Cost Recovery System, assets are placed in one of six groups defining asset life; a depreciation schedule is available for each class. The effect of the acceleration is to write off substantially more than 50% of the cost in the first half of the asset's life: the percentage written off in the early years is greatest for the shortest life group.

An example of delayed revenue is where the business uses the percentage of completion method to report contract profits for accounting purposes but uses the completed contract method for taxation purposes. An example of delayed expenses is a provision for repairs under warranty where the tax rules require the actual repair cost to be incurred.

Companies pay federal taxes and local state taxes, the local taxes being deductible in determining income for federal tax purposes. The federal government may give tax credits, which are direct reductions of the income tax itself, in contrast to tax deductions which reduce the level of taxable income.

13.4.3.2 Tax on distributions

Dividends paid by domestic corporations to US citizens and residents are taxable to such individuals. Dividend income paid to a non-resident alien is generally subject to a withholding tax. Stock dividends are not taxable.

13.4.4 Corporate financing system

13.4.4.1 Equity investors[11]

The US stock exchanges provide an important primary market for raising new capital. They attract listings by foreign registrants which seek to raise capital in the US market. The stock exchanges are also a secondary market for the purchase and sale of shares already in issue. There are some 7,000 listed companies. Institutional shareholders hold an average of 51% of the ordinary shares of the top 1,000 Group of companies.[12]

Chapter 1, Exhibit 1.3, indicates the relative size of US stock market in relation to those of Europe. However it is interesting to note the relatively low proportion of foreign companies listed on US markets compared with the higher proportion in the UK. This may be related to the strict reporting requirements in the USA, explained later. Chapter 1, Exhibit 1.4 shows that the US and Japanese markets together dominate world stock markets by size. Exhibit 1.5 indicates quite a different pattern of shareholding from that of the UK, with a household proportion which is higher than in Japan or the UK.

The two major national stock exchanges are the New York Stock Exchange (NYSE) and the American Stock Exchange (AMEX), and there are five regional

---

[10] Horngren *et al.* (1996), p. 639
[11] Charkham (1994), pp. 214–15; Fabozzi and Modigliani (1996), Chapter 13
[12] Charkham (1994), Chapter 5, Appendix 5A

stock exchanges. There is an over-the-counter market (OTC) for unlisted stocks. Dealers in the OTC are regulated by the National Association of Securities Dealers which uses an electronic Automatic Quotation system (NASDAQ). A stock may be listed on an exchange and traded in the OTC market. Trading such stocks in the OTC is called the 'third market'. Transactions may occur directly between buyers and sellers in what is called the 'fourth market'.

The stock exchanges are approved and regulated by the SEC in order to ensure the market's fairness, competitiveness and efficiency. There was concern in the past that investors were not necessarily receiving the best price, and trading rules are now in place to ensure fairness.

13.4.4.2 Top companies

From the *Financial Times* annual *FT 500* survey there are 222 US companies in the top 500 world companies, measured by market capitalisation. The top ten listed US companies are shown in Exhibit 13.2.

13.4.4.3 Bank lending[13]

Commercial banks are prevented from owning controlling blocks of shares in non-banking companies. They may not underwrite issues of shares or link with investment banks which do so. The basis of these restrictions is historical: the banks were blamed significantly for the stock market crash of 1929. Banks do act as trustees, holding shares on behalf of clients, but the banks prefer the clients to exercise their voting rights directly. The main financial link between banks and corporations is therefore that of lender and borrower. However the concept of 'relationship banking', where the bank provides services beyond the loan facility, is

Exhibit 13.2 TOP TEN LISTED US COMPANIES

Name	Market cap $m.	Rank in world	FT Sector
1 General Electric Company	222,748	1	Electrical equipment
2 Microsoft Corp	159,660	3	Computer software & services
3 Exxon Corp	157,970	4	Oil international
4 Coca-Cola	151,288	5	Beverages, soft drinks
5 Intel Corp	150,838	6	Electronics
6 Merck	120,757	8	Drugs, pharmaceuticals
7 IBM Corporation	104,120	11	Computers
8 Philip Morris	100,666	12	Tobacco manufacturers
9 Procter & Gamble	93,292	13	Soaps
10 Wal-Mart Stores	82,533	18	Retail – general merchandise

Source: *Financial Times FT 500 Survey*, 22 January 1998

[13] Charkham (1994), pp. 196–8

relatively unfamiliar; the bank may not always have the closer knowledge of the business which might be found in some continental European companies.

13.4.4.4 Mergers and acquisitions[14]

The ability of corporations to merge is restricted by antitrust legislation which seeks to prevent monopoly positions arising. Where a merger or acquisition is not prevented by antitrust law, the process of acquisition is regulated by state law and federal law. There is no equivalent of the voluntary self-regulation applied by the Take-over Panel in the UK. The SEC requires that acquisitions of 5% or more of voting shares are to be disclosed within ten days; changes of more than 1% thereafter must be notified. Tender offers are regulated by the SEC under the Williams Act 1968. Under a tender offer, the prospective purchaser offers a price for a specified quantity of shares. The company issues the tendered shares at the best price offered.

Contested takeover bids have led to defensive practices which may not be in the best interests of all shareholders – 'Poison pills' allow management, at short notice, to place blocks of shares with friendly persons in order to block a bid; 'Crown jewels' provisions place a desirable asset with a friendly corporation elsewhere; 'Greenmail' means paying a price above the market price for shares held by an investor who is threatening to start a takeover bid; 'Supermajority' means requiring a 75% majority vote to remove directors. All these tactics would be forbidden under the UK Takeover Code; they are contested from time to time under State law, but survive or emerge in a modified form.

13.4.5 The accounting profession

The historical development of the accounting profession has been described in an earlier section. It no longer has a direct role in setting accounting standards, but remains the professional organisation to which many of those involved in standard setting belong. The AICPA retains exclusive authority in the private sector for promulgating auditing rules. The Auditing Standards Board (ASB) of the AICPA issues Statements on Auditing Standards, and members of the AICPA must adhere to all applicable Statements on Auditing Standards in conducting audits. Audit is required by the SEC in the case of listed companies. For other companies, it is voluntary or else carried out at the request of a third party such as a bank lender.[15]

The AICPA has sought to curb what is sometimes called 'opinion shopping', which refers to the practice where listed companies offer the audit to the firm which gives the most sympathetic interpretation of GAAP. As well as strengthening professional standards of conduct, the AICPA has sponsored a major enquiry into the needs of users of financial reporting. The result of this enquiry, referred to as the Jenkins Report, was published in 1994 and is explained in section 13.7.5.6.

On a wider spectrum than the AICPA, specialisation has developed in aspects of the accountancy profession.[16] Specialist professional examinations in the US now recognise Certified Public Accountants; Certified Internal Auditors; Certified Management Accountants; and Chartered Financial Analysts. The AICPA itself has

---

[14] Sudarsanam (1995), p. 95
[15] Wolk and Tearney (1997), p. 79
[16] Choi and Mueller (1992), p. 9

Exhibit 13.3 MEMBERSHIP OF THE AICPA, 1996

Public practice	133,000
Industry	136,000
Local, state and federal government	15,000
Academia	8,000
Not active	3,600
Retirees	18,000
Students	13,000

Source: AICPA, cited in *The Accountant*, March 1996, p. 10

membership divisions reflecting various activities, being divided almost equally between public practice (accountancy firms) and industry, as shown in Exhibit 13.3.

There have been six leading accounting firms in the USA, often referred to as the 'big 6', which have undertaken the audits of some 97% of companies listed on the NYSE. These are Andersen Worldwide, Ernst & Young, Deloitte & Touche, KPMG Peat Marwick, Coopers & Lybrand and Price Waterhouse. However, current activities in merger discussions mean that the 'big 6' may become the 'big 4' or perhaps the 'big 3'.

13.4.6 External influences

The USA has developed by importing know-how and expertise. That includes accounting, which travelled to the USA with early pioneers from the UK. Accounting practice in the USA has subsequently been imbued with increasingly national characteristic. (Chapter 1, section 1.8 provides more details on this process of import and export.) In more recent years, the USA has exported its brand of accounting to countries under its economic influence, particularly Canada, central and south America, and countries in South East Asia (*see* also Chapter 1, Case Study 1). USA influence on Japanese accounting is discussed in Chapter 15 and a brief period of influence on German accounting is discussed in Chapter 9. One particularly significant export has been the idea of setting standards through a professional route rather than by government regulation, culminating in an independent standard-setting body.

As a founder member of IASC, the USA has had a significant influence on global accounting practices. Opinions are divided as to whether the USA influence has been excessive or not.[17]

13.5 SOCIETAL CULTURE AND ACCOUNTING SUBCULTURE

13.5.1 Hofstede's (1984) cultural dimensions

Exhibit 13.4 (overleaf) reproduces part of the table set out in Chapter 2, section 2.4, showing the scores and rankings for the USA from Hofstede's (1984) work on cultural dimensions.

---

[17] Flower (1997); Cairns (1997)

Exhibit 13.4 USA: SCORES AND RANKINGS FOR INDIVIDUAL COUNTRIES FROM HOFSTEDE'S (1984) CULTURAL DIMENSION RESEARCH

Individualism versus collectivism		*Large power distance versus small power difference*		*Strong uncertainty avoidance versus weak uncertainty avoidance*		*Low nurture versus high nurture*	
Score	*Rank*	*Score*	*Rank*	*Score*	*Rank*	*Score*	*Rank*
91	1	40	38	46	43	62	15

13.5.2 Culture and accounting

Hofstede grouped the USA in what he called the 'Anglo' cultural area, which included Australia, Canada, Ireland, New Zealand and the UK. Exhibit 13.5 sets out an interpretation of Hofstede's scores of cultural values, for use in later sections of this chapter, and indicates Gray's (1988) classification for the Anglo group as a whole. It may be misleading to group the USA with the other countries which have retained a link with UK accounting for much longer than the USA, and so Gray's analysis will be approached with caution. Each of the sections 13.7.2 to 13.7.5 will provide an evaluation consistent with Gray's general approach, but specific to the USA.

13.6 ACCOUNTING REGULATIONS AND THE IASC

As explained earlier, the regulation of accounting practice lies jointly in the hands of the FASB and the SEC. They have different sets of regulations but the SEC, in accepting filing of financial statements, effectively endorses the authority of the independent FASB. As explained in Chapter 5, the SEC is a member of the International Organization of Securities Commissions (IOSCO), which is moving towards acceptance of a core set of IASs as common usage for international companies seeking international listings.

Many similarities may be seen when comparing existing IASs and the corresponding SFASs. However, the SFASs contain more detail, and so differences emerge. Despite these differences the research by Salter *et al.* (1996) (*see* Chapter 5, section 5.6.3.4) showed that on completion of the IASC comparability project, the USA was high in the rankings of agreement between national standards and IASs.

Towards the end of 1996, the FASB published a book (FASB, 1996b) claiming more than 255 differences between FASB standards and IASs. The IASC has denied that this is evidence of any failure to meet the level of quality for US purposes, and has identified three categories of difference. Some arise because the US has industry standards which are not on the work programme agreed with IOSCO. Others arise where an IAS has already been accepted by IOSCO as satisfactory without amendment. That suggests concordance on principles, with perhaps minor differences in detail. The third category lies in projects still under development at the time of the FASB survey. The IASC took the view that the US analysis would be helpful to the IASC work programme although that did not mean agreement on every point of detail.[18]

---

[18] IASC, *Annual Review* (1996)

Exhibit 13.5	LINKING GRAY'S (1988) ACCOUNTING VALUES TO HOFSTEDE'S (1984) CULTURAL DIMENSIONS, IN THE MANNER PROPOSED BY GRAY

Gray's accounting values – classification	*Cultural dimensions affecting the country's accounting values*	*Interpretation of Hofstede's scores of cultural values*
Professionalism (strong)	Professionalism tends to be associated with: • Individualism • Weak uncertainty avoidance • Small power distance	 Strong individualism Weak uncertainty avoidance Small power distance
Flexibility (strong)	Uniformity tends to be associated with: • Strong uncertainty avoidance • Large power distance • Collectivism	 Weak uncertainty avoidance Small power distance Strong individualism
Optimism (strong)	Conservatism tends to be associated with: • Strong uncertainty avoidance • Collectivism • High nurture	 Weak uncertainty avoidance Strong individualism Moderate low nurture
Transparency (strong)	Secrecy tends to be associated with: • Strong uncertainty avoidance • Large power distance • Collectivism • High nurture	 Weak uncertainty avoidance Small power distance Strong individualism Moderate low nurture

US interest in international accounting was demonstrated by an act of Congress, signed by the President in October 1996, confirming the importance of IASs in attracting foreign corporations to gain access to listing in the US markets. To that end, Congress urged the SEC to support vigorously the development of high-quality IASs.

The IASC Framework for the Preparation and Presentation of Financial Statements (1989) owes much of its development and direction to the prior work of FASB published earlier in the 1980s as a series of Statements of Financial Accounting Concepts (SFACs). Exhibit 13.6 shows the extent to which US standards are broadly in agreement with IASs, and the key areas of difference.

US companies do not specifically acknowledge that their accounting practices are related to the IASs; this may be taken to confirm the relatively low profile of IASs in the scheme of what comprises 'generally accepted accounting principles' (*see* section 13.7.2.1).

Exhibit 13.6 COMPARISON OF ACCOUNTING PRACTICES IN THE US WITH
REQUIREMENTS OF IASs: KEY SIMILARITIES AND DIFFERENCES

IAS	Subject of IAS	Practice in USA	Ref
Disclosure and presentation			
	General aspects consolidated in IAS 1 (revised)		
IAS 1	Fair Presentation	'Fair presentation' requirement	7.2.2
	Disclosure of Accounting Policies (former IAS 1)	Generally in agreement[1]	
	Information to be Disclosed in Financial Statements (former IAS 5)	Generally in agreement	7.2.3
	Presentation of Current Assets and Current Liabilities (former IAS 13)	Generally in agreement	
	Specific aspects		
IAS 7	Cash Flow Statements	Generally in agreement	7.2.3
IAS 8	Net Profit or Loss for the Period, Fundamental Errors and Changes in Accounting Policies	Generally in agreement	7.2.3
IAS 14	Reporting Financial Information by Segments	Generally in agreement	7.5.3
IAS 24	Related Party Disclosure	Generally in agreement	
IAS 33	Earnings per Share	Generally in agreement	7.2.5
IAS 34	Interim Financial Reporting	Differences in approach to measurement	7.5.4
Asset recognition and measurement			
IAS 2	Inventories	Generally in agreement	7.4.5
IAS 4	Depreciation Accounting	Generally in agreement	7.3.2
IAS 16	Property, Plant and Equipment	Generally in agreement; revaluation not permitted	7.3.2 7.4.1
IAS xx	Impairment of Assets	Differences in approach	7.4.2
IAS 23	Borrowing costs	Generally in agreement, allowed alternative applied	7.3.3
IAS 25	Accounting for Investments	Current asset investments more conservative than IAS 25; notes show fair value	7.4.4
IAS 9	Research and Development costs	Development expenditure may not be capitalised	7.4.3
IAS xx	Intangible Assets	Generally in agreement	7.4.3
Liability recognition and measurement			
IAS 10	Contingencies and Events Occurring After the Balance Sheet Date	Generally in agreement	
IAS 12	Income Taxes	Generally in agreement	7.4.6
IAS 17	Leases	Generally in agreement	
IAS 19	Employee Benefits	Generally in agreement	
IAS 32	Financial Instruments: Disclosure and Presentation	Generally in agreement	7.3.4
Recognition of economic activity			
IAS 11	Construction Contracts	Generally in agreement	7.4.5
IAS 18	Revenue	Generally in agreement	

Exhibit 13.6 continued

IAS	Subject of IAS	Practice in USA	Ref
IAS 20	Accounting for Government Grants and Disclosure of Government Assistance	Generally in agreement	
Measurement			
IAS 15	Information Reflecting the Effects of Changing Prices	FAS 33 withdrawn – supplementary information not normally shown	
IAS 29	Financial Reporting in Hyperinflationary Economies	Not relevant to US economy	
Group accounting			
IAS 21	The Effects of Changes in Foreign Exchange Rates	Generally in agreement	
IAS 22	Business Combinations	Generally in agreement	7.5.5
IAS 27	Consolidated Financial Statements and Accounting for Investments in Subsidiaries	Generally in agreement; criteria for pooling of interest are more permissive on size criteria	3.2
IAS 28	Accounting for Investments in Associates	Generally in agreement	
IAS 31	Financial Reporting of Interests in Joint Ventures	Normally does not permit proportional consolidation	3.2

Note: [1]In this exhibit, 'generally in agreement' indicates broad comparability in principle. US accounting standards are very much more detailed in aspects of practical application.

13.7 THE ACCOUNTING SYSTEM

13.7.1 Current regulations

Since 1973, standards have been set by the FASB. This is an independent, private sector organisation, financed by a spread of contributions from accountancy firms, industry, organisations representing investors and creditors, and other related organisations. The FASB comprises seven members who must maintain total independence of other business activity during their term of office. The seven members of the FASB have diverse business backgrounds, and so could be said to be 'professional' in general terms; they are not all recruited from professional accountancy firms.

There is a substantial secretariat supporting the FASB, and an extensive consultative process, called 'due process', has been put in place. The FASB sponsors systematic and thorough research prior to developing a standard. The principle of openness is an essential element of the work of the FASB, extending to holding public hearings to discuss exposure drafts of standards, their deliberations are open to public attendance.

The 'due process' of consultation on developing standards involves:

● appointing a task force of experts to advise on the project

● sponsoring research studies and reviewing existing literature on the subject

● publishing a discussion of issues and potential solutions

- holding a public hearing
- issuing an exposure draft for public comment.

The result of the process is a Statement of Financial Accounting Standards (SFAS), and enforcement is effectively through the audit process. Implicitly there is a position of power for the SEC because it may refuse to accept a filing by a corporation where the auditor is not satisfied. The AICPA expects its members to apply FASB pronouncements. The report of the auditors to a public company does not refer directly to SFASs but uses the wording 'fairly present . . . in accordance with generally accepted accounting principles'.

The FASB is complemented by an Emerging Issues Task Force (EITF), which considers new issues requiring rapid guidance. Its views are published and are influential, without carrying the compulsion of an SFAS.

13.7.2 Professionalism versus statutory control

Gray's (1988) analysis, based on Hofstede's (1984) framework, indicates an expectation of strong professionalism. This means a preference for the exercise of individual professional judgement and professional self-regulation. The practical reality is complex, because the standard setting process is self-regulatory and makes considerable use of professional expertise. However standard setting is subject to indirect statutory control through the SEC which may, if it chooses, exercise a strong influence on particular accounting practices. The accountancy profession is independent and self-regulating so that the institutional arrangements do support the classification of strong professionalism. Professional judgement is exercised in the format of presentation and the use of notes to the accounts, on the other hand, professionalism is limited by industry standards and by some of the factors listed in later sections as indicative of other aspects of Gray's classification.

A litigious society ready to take action against professional accountants and auditors causes them to seek refuge in the protection of statute and regulation. However, it is hoped that the Private Securities Litigation Reform Bill (1995) will put a stop to disgruntled investors bringing frivolous lawsuits against companies and their professional advisers.[19]

13.7.2.1 Generally accepted accounting principles

A hierarchy of US GAAP is set out in the US Auditing Standard SAS 69 (1992) as follows:

- FASB Statements and Interpretations, APB Opinions and AICPA Accounting Research Bulletins [This is a set of documents for which the UK equivalent would be FRSs and SSAPs], Rules and interpretative releases of the SEC [The UK equivalent would be the Stock Exchange Listing Rules, or 'Yellow Book']
- FASB Technical Bulletins, AICPA Industry Audit and Accounting Guides and AICPA Statements of Position
- AICPA AcSEC Practice Bulletins and consensuses of the FASB Emerging Issues Task Force (EITF)

---

[19] *The Accountant* (March 1996), p. 10

- AICPA accounting interpretations, implementation guides (Qs&As) published by FASB staff and practices that are widely recognised and prevalent either generally or in the industry.

SAS 69 also indicates that other accounting literature may be considered, extending through various professional guidance to textbooks, handbooks and articles. IASs are contained in this miscellaneous grouping.

Acceptance of this list by the FASB was indicated by its inclusion in SFAS 111, 'Rescission of FASB statement no 32 and technical corrections', whereby the wording of SAS 69 was incorporated as a technical correction to APB 20, 'Accounting changes'.

The origins of the phrase 'generally accepted accounting principles' in the USA lie in the APB Opinion no 4 (issued by the AICPA in 1970), which refers to these principles being rooted in 'experience, reason, custom, usage, and . . . practical necessity'. The principles are said there to 'encompass the conventions, rules and procedures necessary to define accepted accounting practice at a particular time'.

The emphasis on GAAP in the USA necessitates having comprehensive and authoritative statements. This in turn has led the FASB to develop a significant volume of Statements of Financial Accounting Standards (SFASs) and an even greater volume of interpretations. The SFASs and the interpretations are quite lengthy in their detail and make a sharp contrast with the IASs which are primarily statements of broad standards.

13.7.2.2 Fair presentation

The US equivalent of the phrase 'true and fair view' found in European accounting is the somewhat different wording 'fairly presented in conformity with generally accepted accounting principles'. It is different because of the specific emphasis placed on GAAP. The European interpretation of 'true and fair' is not uniform, but the UK view is that 'true and fair' stands above any specific set of rules. Some commentators have drawn the distinction by describing the US approach as highly legalistic when compared with a much more judgmental approach in the UK.[20]

13.7.2.3 Financial statement formats

In the annual report of US companies there are four primary financial statements:

- Balance sheet
- Income statement (statement of earnings, profit and loss account)
- Cash flow statement
- Statement of shareholders' equity (stockholders' equity).

These four financial statements, augmented by footnotes and supplementary data, are interrelated. Collectively, they are intended to provide relevant, reliable and timely information essential to making investment, credit, and similar decisions, thus meeting the objectives of financial reporting.[21] (From 1998, companies will also be required to report comprehensive income under SFAS 130.)

---

[20] Davies *et al.* (1997), p. 10
[21] White *et al.* (1994), p. 6

Balance sheet

There is no universal form of balance sheet. The objectives are clarity and adequate disclosure of all pertinent and material facts. Some use the account form (a two-sided balance sheet corresponding to debit and credit); others use a report form (where the debit and credit sections of the account form are placed one above the other); and others again use a financial position form which corresponds to the vertical form used in the UK. Within the account form the assets are shown on the left-hand side, starting with cash and proceeding to the least liquid assets. The liabilities are on the right-hand side, starting with current liabilities and proceeding to long-term liabilities and equity. In all cases, there is classification of the main categories of assets and liabilities.

As an example, Philip Morris Companies Inc uses the account form (Exhibit 13.7) while Sears, Roebuck and Co uses the report form (Exhibit 13.8).

Income statement

There are essentially two forms of income statement (profit and loss account). One is the multiple-step and the other the single-step approach. The multiple-step approach sets out various intermediate balances, including gross profit, as in Philip Morris (Exhibit 13.9). The single-step approach presents one grouping of all revenue items, another grouping of expenses, and a resulting net income figure. General Motors uses the single-step approach (Exhibit 13.10). Those who favour the single-step approach argue that it is more neutral in its presentation while the multiple-step approach makes assumptions about priority of cost recovery. Combinations of both methods may be used; there is no rigid format or chart of accounts. The title 'statement of income' is most widely used, but not universal. Some use 'statement of earnings' and some use 'operations statement'. Both the single-step and the multi-step income statements have separate sections for discontinued items, extraordinary items and the effect of a change in accounting principle.

The flexibility of presentation of the income statement is illustrated in the case of Ford Motor Company, where the pre-tax profit on Automotive activities is reported separately from that of financial services. Both are then combined in the statement of income to give a figure of overall net income (Exhibit 13.11).

A particular feature of the income statement is the separate disclosure of the results of discontinued operations. Although this is consistent with the revised IAS 8, the US practice was established considerably earlier (under APB Opinion no 30 in 1973) and probably influenced the revision of IAS 8. There may be discussion to accompany the financial statement disclosure, as in AT&T (1996) (*see* Exhibit 13.12)

Cash flow statement

The FASB has prescribed the nature of the cash flow statement in SFAS 95. The reconciliation of operating profit and cash flow from operating activities is generally included as part of the statement rather than as a note. The categories within the cash flow statement and the level of disclosure are very similar to those of IAS 7.

Exhibit 13.7 PHILIP MORRIS COMPANIES, INC: ACCOUNT FORM OF BALANCE SHEET, 1996

Consolidated Balance Sheets (in millions of dollars, except per share data)

at December 31,	1996	1995
Assets		
Consumer products		
Cash and cash equivalents	$ 240	$ 1,138
Receivables, net	4,466	4,508
Inventories:		
Leaf tobacco	4,143	3,332
Other raw materials	1,854	1,721
Finished product	3,005	2,809
	9,002	7,862
Other current assets	1,482	1,371
Total current assets	15,190	14,879
Property, plant and equipment, at cost:		
Land and land improvements	664	726
Buildings and building equipment	5,168	4,976
Machinery and equipment	12,481	11,542
Construction in progress	1,659	1,357
	19,972	18,601
Less accumulated depreciation	8,221	7,485
	11,751	11,116
Goodwill and other intangible assets		
(less accumulated amortization of $4,391 and $3,873)	18,998	19,319
Other assets	3,015	2,866
Total consumer products assets	48,954	48,180
Financial services and real estate		
Finance assets, net	5,345	4,991
Real estate held for development and sale	314	339
Other assets	258	301
Total financial services and real estate assets	5,917	5,631
Total Assets	**$54,871**	$53,811

Exhibit 13.7 **continued**

	1996	1995
Liabilities		
Consumer products		
Short-term borrowings	$ 260	$ 122
Current portion of long-term debt	1,846	1,926
Accounts payable	3,409	3,364
Accrued liabilities:		
Marketing	2,106	2,114
Taxes, except income taxes	1,331	1,075
Employment costs	942	995
Other	2,726	2,706
Income taxes	1,269	1,137
Dividends payable	978	834
Total current liabilities	14,867	14,273
Long-term debt	11,827	12,324
Deferred income taxes	731	356
Accrued postretirement health care costs	2,372	2,273
Other liabilities	5,773	5,643
Total consumer products liabilities	35,570	34,869
Financial services and real estate		
Short-term borrowings	173	671
Long-term debt	1,134	783
Deferred income taxes	3,636	3,382
Other liabilities	140	121
Total financial services and real estate liabilities	5,083	4,957
Total liabilities	40,653	39,826
Contingencies (Note 13)		
Stockholders' Equity		
Common stock, par value $1.00 per share (935,320,439 shares issued)	935	935
Earnings reinvested in the business	22,478	19,779
Currency translation adjustments	192	467
	23,605	21,181
Less cost of repurchased stock (124,871,681 and 104,150,433 shares)	9,387	7,196
Total stockholders' equity	14,218	13,985
Total Liabilities and Stockholders' Equity	$54,871	$53,811

Source: Philip Morris Companies, Inc., annual report, 1996, pp. 32–3

Exhibit 13.8 | SEARS, ROEBUCK AND CO.: REPORT FORM OF BALANCE SHEET, 1996

Consolidated *Balance Sheets*

millions	1996	1995
ASSETS		
Current Assets		
Cash and invested cash	$ 660	$ 606
Credit card receivables	22,371	20,932
Less: Allowance for uncollectible accounts	808	826
	21,563	20,106
Other receivables	335	444
Merchandise inventories	4,646	4,033
Prepaid expenses and deferred charges	348	360
Deferred income taxes	895	892
Total current assets	28,447	26,441
Property and equipment		
Land	445	387
Buildings and improvements	5,080	4,382
Furniture, fixtures and equipment	4,279	3,775
Capitalized leases	433	313
	10,237	8,857
Less accumulated depreciation	4,359	3,780
Total property and equipment, net	5,878	5,077
Deferred income taxes	905	879
Other assets	937	733
TOTAL ASSETS	**$36,167**	**$33,130**
LIABILITIES		
Current Liabilities		
Short-term borrowings	$ 3,533	$ 5,349
Current portion of long-term debt and capitalized lease obligations	2,737	1,730
Accounts payable and other liabilities	7,225	6,133
Unearned revenues	840	887
Other taxes	615	508
Total current liabilities	14,950	14,607
Long-term debt and capitalized lease obligations	12,170	10,044
Postretirement benefits	2,748	2,825
Minority interest and other liabilities	1,354	1,269
TOTAL LIABILITIES	**31,222**	**28,745**
SHAREHOLDERS' EQUITY		
Preferred shares ($1 par value, 50 shares authorized)		
8.88% Preferred Shares, First Series (3.25 shares issued and outstanding as of Dec. 30, 1995)	—	325
Common shares ($.75 par value, 1,000 shares authorized, 391.4 and 390.5 shares outstanding)	323	322
Capital in excess of par value	3,618	3,634
Retained income	3,330	2,444
Treasury stock—at cost	(1,655)	(1,634)
Minimum pension liability	(277)	(285)
Deferred ESOP expense	(230)	(253)
Cumulative translation adjustments	(164)	(168)
TOTAL SHAREHOLDERS' EQUITY	**4,945**	**4,385**
TOTAL LIABILITIES AND SHAREHOLDERS' EQUITY	**$36,167**	**$33,130**

See accompanying notes.

Source: Sears, Roebuck and Co., annual report, 1996, p. 26

Exhibit 13.9 PHILIP MORRIS: MULTIPLE-STEP APPROACH IN INCOME STATEMENT, 1996

Consolidated Statements of Earnings (in millions of dollars, except per share data)

for the years ended December 31,	1996	1995	1994
Operating revenues	**$69,204**	$66,071	$65,125
Cost of sales	**26,560**	26,685	28,351
Excise taxes on products	**14,651**	12,932	11,349
Gross profit	**27,993**	26,454	25,425
Marketing, administration and research costs	**15,630**	15,337	15,372
Amortization of goodwill	**594**	591	604
Operating income	**11,769**	10,526	9,449
Interest and other debt expense, net	**1,086**	1,179	1,233
Earnings before income taxes and cumulative effect of accounting changes	**10,683**	9,347	8,216
Provision for income taxes	**4,380**	3,869	3,491
Earnings before cumulative effect of accounting changes	**6,303**	5,478	4,725
Cumulative effect of changes in method of accounting		(28)	
Net earnings	**$ 6,303**	$ 5,450	$ 4,725

Source: Philip Morris Companies, Inc., annual report, 1996, p. 34

Exhibit 13.10 GENERAL MOTORS: SINGLE-STEP APPROACH IN INCOME STATEMENT, 1996

Consolidated Statements of Income

(Dollars in Millions Except Per Share Amounts) Years Ended December 31,	1996	1995	1994
Net sales and revenues (Note 1)			
Manufactured products	$145,341	$143,666	$134,760
Financial services	12,674	11,664	9,419
Other income (Note 3)	6,054	4,942	4,320
Total net sales and revenues	164,069	160,272	148,499
Costs and expenses			
Cost of sales and other operating charges, exclusive of items listed below	123,922	121,300	113,585
Selling, general and administrative expenses	14,580	12,550	11,319
Depreciation and amortization expenses (Note 1)	11,840	11,213	9,645
Interest expense (Note 11)	5,695	5,182	5,392
Plant closings reserve adjustments (Note 17)	(727)	—	—
Other deductions (Note 3)	2,083	1,678	1,460
Total costs and expenses	157,393	151,923	141,401
Income from continuing operations before income taxes	6,676	8,349	7,098
Income taxes (Note 7)	1,723	2,316	2,232
Income from continuing operations before cumulative effect of accounting changes	4,953	6,033	4,866
Income from discontinued operations (Note 2)	10	900	793
Cumulative effect of accounting changes (Note 1)	—	(52)	(758)
Net income	4,963	6,881	4,901
Preference shares tender offer premium (Note 19)	—	153	—
Dividends on preference stocks (Note 19)	81	211	321
Earnings on common stocks	$4,882	$6,517	$4,580
Earnings attributable to common stocks (Note 20)			
$1-2/3 par value from continuing operations before cumulative effect of accounting changes	$4,589	$5,404	$4,296
Income (loss) from discontinued operations (Note 2)	(5)	105	349
Cumulative effect of accounting changes (Note 1)	—	(52)	(751)
Net earnings attributable to $1-2/3 par value	$4,584	$5,457	$3,894
Income from discontinued operations attributable to Class E (Note 2)	$15	$795	$444
Class H before cumulative effect of accounting change	$283	$265	$249
Cumulative effect of accounting change (Note 1)	—	—	(7)
Net earnings attributable to Class H	$283	$265	$242

Source: General Motors, annual report, 1996, p. 59

Exhibit 13.11 FORD MOTOR CO.: SEGMENTAL REPORTING WITHIN INCOME STATEMENT, 1996

CONSOLIDATED STATEMENT OF INCOME

For the Years Ended December 31, 1996, 1995 and 1994
(in millions, except amounts per share)

	1996	1995	1994
AUTOMOTIVE			
Sales (Note 1)	$118,023	$110,496	$107,137
Costs and expenses (Notes 1 and 15):			
Costs of sales	108,882	101,171	95,887
Selling, administrative and other expenses	6,625	6,044	5,424
Total costs and expenses	115,507	107,215	101,311
Operating income	2,516	3,281	5,826
Interest income	841	800	665
Interest expense	695	622	721
Net interest income/(expense)	146	178	(56)
Equity in net (loss)/income of affiliated companies (Note 1)	(6)	(154)	271
Net expense from transactions with Financial Services (Note 1)	(85)	(139)	(44)
Income before income taxes - Automotive	2,571	3,166	5,997
FINANCIAL SERVICES			
Revenues (Note 1)	28,968	26,641	21,302
Costs and expenses (Note 1):			
Interest expense	9,704	9,424	7,023
Depreciation	6,875	6,500	4,910
Operating and other expenses	6,217	5,499	4,607
Provision for credit and insurance losses	2,564	1,818	1,539
Asset write-downs and dispositions (Note 15)	121	-	475
Total costs and expenses	25,481	23,241	18,554
Net revenue from transactions with Automotive (Note 1)	85	139	44
Gain on sale of The Associates' common stock (Note 15)	650	-	-
Income before income taxes - Financial Services	4,222	3,539	2,792
TOTAL COMPANY			
Income before income taxes	6,793	6,705	8,789
Provision for income taxes (Note 6)	2,166	2,379	3,329
Income before minority interests	4,627	4,326	5,460
Minority interests in net income of subsidiaries	181	187	152
Net income	$4,446	$ 4,139	$ 5,308

Source: Ford Motor Co., annual report, 1996, p. 34

Exhibit 13.12 AT&T CORP.: REPORTING THE RESULTS OF DISCONTINUED OPERATIONS, 1996

Notes to Consolidated Financial Statements

2. Discontinued Operations

On September 20, 1995, AT&T announced a plan, subject to certain conditions, to separate into three independent, publicly held, global companies: communications services (AT&T), communications systems and technologies (Lucent Technologies Inc., "Lucent") and transaction-intensive computing (NCR Corporation, "NCR"). In April 1996 Lucent sold 112 million shares of common stock in an initial public offering (IPO), representing 17.6% of the Lucent common stock outstanding. Because of AT&T's plan to spin off its remaining 82.4% interest in Lucent, the sale of the Lucent stock was recorded as an equity transaction, resulting in an increase in AT&T's additional paid-in capital at the time of the IPO. In addition, in connection with the restructuring, Lucent assumed $3.7 billion of AT&T debt in 1996. On September 30, 1996, AT&T distributed to AT&T shareowners of record as of September 17, 1996, the remaining Lucent common stock held by AT&T. The shares were distributed on the basis of .324084 of a share of Lucent for each AT&T share outstanding.

Also announced as part of the separation plan was AT&T's intent to pursue the sale of its remaining approximately 86% interest in AT&T Capital Corporation (AT&T Capital). On October 1, 1996, AT&T sold its remaining interest in AT&T Capital for approximately $1.8 billion, resulting in a gain of $162, or $.10 per share, after taxes.

On December 31, 1996, AT&T also distributed all of the outstanding common stock of NCR to AT&T shareowners of record as of December 13, 1996. The shares were distributed on the basis of .0625 of a share of NCR for each AT&T share outstanding on the record date. As a result of the Lucent and NCR distributions, AT&T's shareowners' equity was reduced by $2.2 billion. The distributions of the Lucent and NCR common stock to AT&T shareowners were noncash transactions which did not affect AT&T's results of operations. The distribution of NCR stock completed

AT&T's strategic restructuring plan as announced on September 20, 1995.

The consolidated financial statements of AT&T have been restated to reflect the dispositions of Lucent, NCR and AT&T Capital and the planned dispositions of other businesses as discontinued operations. Accordingly, the revenues, costs and expenses, assets and liabilities, and cash flows of Lucent, NCR, AT&T Capital and other businesses have been excluded from the respective captions in the Consolidated Statements of Income, Consolidated Balance Sheets and Consolidated Statements of Cash Flows, and have been reported through the dates of disposition as "Income (loss) from discontinued operations," net of applicable income taxes; as "Net assets of discontinued operations"; and as "Net cash used in discontinued operations" for all periods presented.

Summarized financial information for the discontinued operations is as follows:

	1996	1995	1994
Revenues	$22,341	$28,945	$27,318
Income (loss) before income taxes	(236)	(4,320)	278
Net income (loss)	138	(3,066)	317
Current assets	554	17,415	
Total assets	862	34,181	
Current liabilities	230	14,787	
Total liabilities	336	26,755	
Net assets of discontinued operations	$ 526	$ 7,426	

The income (loss) before income taxes includes allocated interest expense of $45, $134 and $198 in 1996, 1995 and 1994, respectively. Interest expense was allocated to discontinued operations based on a ratio of net assets of discontinued operations to total AT&T consolidated assets.

Source: AT&T Corp., annual report 1996, p. 35. Reprinted with permission

Statement of shareholders' equity (stockholders' equity)

This statement is commonly found in annual reports but there is considerable variety of presentation. It may include the following components:

- preferred shares
- common shares (at par value or at stated value)
- additional paid in capital
- retained earnings
- treasury shares (repurchased equity)
- valuation gains and losses unrealised (marketable equity securities)
- cumulative translation gains and losses (foreign operations).

Most companies provide this information in the form of a separate primary financial statement. An example is provided by AT&T which emphasises the changes in share-owners' equity (Exhibit 13.13). Some prefer the approach of a note to the accounts.

Comprehensive income

SFAS 130, 'Statement on comprehensive income', was issued in 1997. It becomes effective in 1998 and requires that comprehensive income items which bypass the income statement should be reported in a financial statement, displayed as prominently as any other financial statement. Such items might include foreign currency translation adjustments and gains or losses on certain securities. There is no format specified for this statement of comprehensive income. A similar idea is already established in the UK with a Statement of total recognised gains and losses. The idea was discussed in the revision of IAS 1, but was not implemented.

13.7.2.4 Notes to the accounts

There are extensive requirements for notes to the accounts. The notes are not always indicated clearly on the face of the primary financial statements so that the reader is obliged on occasions to work backwards from the notes rather than forwards from the financial statements.

Particularly interesting is a relatively recent requirement of the AICPA, set out in a Statement of Position,[22] for companies to disclose significant risks and uncertainties existing in the areas of nature of operations; use of estimates in the preparation of financial statements; certain significant estimates; and current vulnerability due to concentrations of activities or markets. Another important area of disclosure is that of related party transactions where 'related parties' are subject to a wide definition.

Extensive disclosures are required regarding financial instruments and derivative financial instruments, covering many aspects of treasury management within the company. Notes to the accounts give detailed information on the costs of post-retirement benefits, including pensions. Employee stock option plans are described in the notes. Contingent losses and liabilities are reported in the notes where they are reasonably possible. If they are probable, then they must be included in the primary financial statements. SFAS 5 defines 'probable' and 'possible'. Environmental liabilities are to be disclosed, although substantial management judgement is needed in deciding the precise nature of the disclosure.

---

[22] AICPA (1995) Statement of Position, 'Disclosure of certain significant risks and uncertainties'

Exhibit 13.13 AT&T CORP.: CONSOLIDATED STATEMENTS OF CHANGES IN SHAREOWNERS' EQUITY, 1996

Consolidated Statements of Changes in Shareowners' Equity

AT&T Corp. and Subsidiaries

DOLLARS IN MILLIONS

Years Ended December 31	1996	1995	1994
Common Shares			
Balance at beginning of year	$ 1,596	$ 1,569	$ 1,547
Shares issued:			
Under employee plans	19	13	11
Under shareowner plans	8	13	8
Other	—	1	3
Balance at end of year	1,623	1,596	1,569
Additional Paid-In Capital			
Balance at beginning of year	16,614	15,825	14,324
Shares issued:			
Under employee plans	975	598	536
Under shareowner plans	434	687	424
Other	—	31	133
Preferred stock redemption	—	—	408
Dividends declared	—	(527)	—
Spin-offs of Lucent and NCR(a)	(2,380)	—	—
Balance at end of year	15,643	16,614	15,825
Guaranteed ESOP Obligation			
Balance at beginning of year	(254)	(305)	(355)
Amortization	52	51	50
Assumption by Lucent(a)	106	—	—
Balance at end of year	(96)	(254)	(305)
Foreign Currency Translation Adjustments			
Balance at beginning of year	5	145	(32)
Translation adjustments	(33)	(140)	177
Spin-offs of Lucent and NCR(a)	75	—	—
Balance at end of year	47	5	145
Retained Earnings (Deficit)			
Balance at beginning of year	(687)	687	(2,110)
Net income	5,908	139	4,710
Dividends declared	(2,132)	(1,570)	(1,940)
Other changes	(11)	57	27
Balance at end of year	3,078	(687)	687
Total Shareowners' Equity	$20,295	$17,274	$17,921

(a) THE NET IMPACT OF THE SPIN-OFFS OF LUCENT AND NCR ON TOTAL SHAREOWNERS' EQUITY WAS $2,199 MILLION.

In March 1990 we issued 13.4 million new shares of common stock in connection with the establishment of an ESOP feature for the nonmanagement savings plan. The shares are being allocated to plan participants over ten years commencing in July 1990 as contributions are made to the plan. In connection with the Lucent spin-off, $106 million of the unamortized guaranteed ESOP obligation was assumed by Lucent.

We have 100 million authorized shares of preferred stock at $1 par value. No preferred stock is currently issued or outstanding.

Source: AT&T Corp., annual report, 1996, p. 32. Reprinted with permission

13.7.2.5 Earnings per share

The FASB issued SFAS 128, 'Earnings per share' in March 1997. It was the result of an intention to simplify existing standards in the USA and make these compatible with international standards. SFAS 128 requires that entities with simple capital structures present a single figure of 'earnings per common share' on the face of the income statement, whereas those with complex capital structures should present both primary and fully diluted earnings per share.[23]

There had been criticism that the former standard, APB Opinion no 15, was arbitrary and unnecessarily complex. Although it required companies to report the primary earnings per share and the fully diluted earnings per share, in practice the disclosure note on earnings per share was often of considerable length because the earnings per share figure was reported separately for each class of share and, in each case, before and after discontinued operations. Earnings per share figures were also reported separately for income before extraordinary items, for extraordinary items alone, and for cumulative effects of accounting changes. This variety and detail may have provided an example of professionalism meeting a variety of user needs but in practice it appears to have created potential overload of information. An example of the complexity of the earnings per share note is provided in the extract from General Motors (*see* Exhibit 13.14).

Exhibit 13.14 GENERAL MOTORS: EARNINGS PER SHARE NOTE, 1996

	1996	1995	1994
Earnings attributable to common stocks (Note 20)			
$1-2/3 par value from continuing operations before cumulative effect of accounting changes	$4,589	$5,404	$4,296
Income (loss) from discontinued operations (Note 2)	(5)	105	349
Cumulative effect of accounting changes (Note 1)	—	(52)	(751)
Net earnings attributable to $1-2/3 par value	$4,584	$5,457	$3,894
Income from discontinued operations attributable to Class E (Note 2)	$15	$795	$444
Class H before cumulative effect of accounting change	$283	$265	$249
Cumulative effect of accounting change (Note 1)	—	—	(7)
Net earnings attributable to Class H	$283	$265	$242
Average number of shares of common stocks outstanding (in millions)			
$1-2/3 par value	756	750	741
Class E (Notes 2 and 20)	470	405	260
Class H	98	96	92
Earnings per share attributable to common stocks (Note 20)			
$1-2/3 par value from continuing operations before cumulative effect of accounting changes	$6.07	$7.14	$5.74
Income (loss) from discontinued operations (Note 2)	(0.01)	0.14	0.46
Cumulative effect of accounting changes (Note 1)	—	(0.07)	(1.05)
Net earnings attributable to $1-2/3 par value	$6.06	$7.21	$5.15
Income from discontinued operations attributable to Class E (Note 2)	$0.04	$1.96	$1.71
Class H before cumulative effect of accounting change	$2.88	$2.77	$2.70
Cumulative effect of accounting change (Note 1)	—	—	(0.08)
Net earnings attributable to Class H	$2.88	$2.77	$2.62

Reference should be made to the notes to consolidated financial statements.

Source: General Motors, annual report, 1996, p. 59

---

[23] Meeting *et al.* (1997)

There was at one stage a difference of opinion between the FASB and the IASC on the approach to be taken in calculating the fully diluted earnings per share. The FASB took the view that diluted earnings per share was information on past performance which had predictive value as indirect input to a predictive process. The IASC initially took the view that fully diluted earnings per share provided a forward-looking warning signal. It tried to accommodate both approaches in E 52, but after receiving comment moved towards the US position in issuing IAS 33. That in turn allowed the FASB to harmonise by issuing SFAS 128. There is now agreement on the number of shares to be used in the denominator, although differences in GAAP may still cause international differences in the numerator.[24]

13.7.2.6 Special industry standards

The FASB sets special industry standards, based on direct action by the FASB rather than the less direct approach of the UK where the ASB franks (approves) the industry's own proposals. FASB industry standards cover the oil and gas industry where there have on occasions been differences of opinion between the FASB and the SEC. The example of SFAS 69, 'Disclosures about oil and gas producing activities', is interesting because it requires disclosure of financially relevant information beyond that conventionally expected in published accounts. In particular, it requires disclosure of proven oil and gas reserve quantities, capitalised costs relating to oil and gas producing activities, costs incurred on oil and gas exploration and development activities, results of production activities, and a discounted cash flow measure of future cash flows expected from proven reserves.

Other industries covered by FASB standards include banking and thrift institutions; broadcasters; cable television companies; motion picture films; record and music; franchisors; insurance enterprises; the mortgage banking industry; real estate (property) companies; and regulated industries. These industries may also be subject to other regulatory bodies setting accounting requirements (*see* Exhibit 13.15).

The US approach in developing specific industry standards is quite different from the more general approach of the IASC. The only specialised international standards are IAS 26, 'Accounting and reporting by retirement benefit plans', and IAS 30, 'Disclosures in the financial statements of banks and similar financial institutions'.

13.7.3 Uniformity versus flexibility

Gray's classification, based on Hofstede, indicates high flexibility, By way of contrast it has been suggested[25] that US accounting shows a mixture of both finite uniformity and rigid uniformity. Finite uniformity is seen as the attempt to equate prescribed accounting methods with the relevant circumstances in generally similar situations. The example given is the rule in SFAS 13 on long-term leases where percentages are used to draw the line for capitalisation. The percentage is to some extent arbitrary but ensures comparable practice. Another example is the rule on

---

[24] Meeting *et al.* (1997), p. 90
[25] Wolk and Tearney (1997), Chapter 9

Exhibit 13.15 SOUTHERN CO.: SUMMARY OF SIGNIFICANT ACCOUNTING POLICIES, ELECTRICITY SUPPLY, 1996

> ### Notes to Financial Statements
> *Southern Company and Subsidiary Companies 1996 Annual Report*

1. Summary of Significant Accounting Policies

General

Southern Company is the parent company of five operating companies, a system service company, Southern Communications Services (Southern Communications), Southern Energy, Inc. (Southern Energy), Southern Nuclear Operating Company (Southern Nuclear), The Southern Development and Investment Group (Southern Development), and other direct and indirect subsidiaries. The operating companies — Alabama Power, Georgia Power, Gulf Power, Mississippi Power, and Savannah Electric — provide electric service in four southeastern states. Contracts among the operating companies — dealing with jointly owned generating facilities, interconnecting transmission lines, and the exchange of electric power — are regulated by the Federal Energy Regulatory Commission (FERC) or the Securities and Exchange Commission (SEC). The system service company provides, at cost, specialized services to Southern Company and subsidiary companies. Southern Communications provides digital wireless communications services to the operating companies and also markets these services to the public within the Southeast. Southern Energy designs, builds, owns, and operates power production and delivery facilities and provides a broad range of energy related services in the United States and international markets. Southern Nuclear provides services to Southern Company's nuclear power plants. Southern Development develops new business opportunities related to energy products and services.

Southern Company is registered as a holding company under the Public Utility Holding Company Act of 1935 (PUHCA). Both the company and its subsidiaries are subject to the regulatory provisions of the PUHCA. The operating companies also are subject to regulation by the FERC and their respective state regulatory commissions. The companies follow generally accepted accounting principles and comply with the accounting policies and practices prescribed by their respective commissions. The preparation of financial statements in conformity with generally accepted accounting principles requires the use of estimates, and the actual results may differ from those estimates. All material intercompany items have been eliminated in consolidation.

The consolidated financial statements reflect investments in majority-owned or controlled subsidiaries on a consolidated basis and other investments on an equity basis. Certain prior years' data presented in the consolidated financial statements have been reclassified to conform with current year presentation.

Regulatory Assets and Liabilities

The operating companies are subject to the provisions of Financial Accounting Standards Board (FASB) Statement No. 71, Accounting for the Effects of Certain Types of Regulation. Regulatory assets represent probable future revenues to the operating companies associated with certain costs that are expected to be recovered from customers through the ratemaking process. Regulatory liabilities represent probable future reductions in revenues associated with amounts that are to be credited to customers through the ratemaking process. Regulatory assets and (liabilities) reflected in the Consolidated Balance Sheets at December 31 relate to the following:

	1996	1995
	(in millions)	
Deferred income taxes	**$1,302**	$1,386
Deferred Plant Vogtle costs	171	308
Premium on reacquired debt	289	295
Demand-side programs	44	79
Department of Energy assessments	69	73
Vacation pay	77	74
Deferred fuel charges	29	49
Postretirement benefits	38	53
Work force reduction costs	48	56
Deferred income tax credits	(879)	(936)
Storm damage reserves	(32)	(23)
Other, net	114	98
Total	**$1,270**	$1,512

Source: Southern Co. annual report, 1996, p. 37

capitalisation of borrowing costs in specific circumstances. Rigid uniformity means prescribing one method for generally similar transactions. An example is SFAS 2, requiring all research and development expenditure to be reported in the income statement as incurred.

However, flexibility is evident in matters such as depreciation accounting and inventory valuation and in the separation of tax law from accounting practice.

13.7.3.1 Tax law and impact on accounting practice

Tax law and accounting law are separate but there may be situations where accountants find it convenient, or even necessary, to use the tax-based approach in the accounting statements. This reduces the flexibility available in principle. An example lies in inventory valuation and the use of LIFO (*see* section 7.3.5).

13.7.3.2 Depreciation

The definition of depreciation has a long history from ARB 43, emphasising the allocation of cost. ARB 43 specifically states that it is a process of allocation, not valuation. For income tax purposes, many companies use accelerated depreciation but this is used relatively rarely in the published accounts of listed companies. One case, showing use of accelerated depreciation as a means of dealing crudely with the additional cost of asset replacement, is the Ford Motor Company, giving the explanation set out in Exhibit 13.16.

A similar policy is found in General Motors, except that the policy continued to the reporting date, without change.

13.7.3.3 Capitalisation of borrowing costs

SFAS 34 requires that borrowing costs are normally reported through the income statement. However, in specific circumstances the interest cost may be added to the asset cost (referred to as capitalisation of borrowing costs) in order to obtain a measure of acquisition cost that more closely reflects the enterprise's total invest-ment in the asset. Capitalisation is also used so as to charge a cost that relates to the acquisition of a resource that will benefit future periods against the revenues of the periods benefited (*see* Exhibit 13.7). In the circumstances set out in SFAS 34 the capitalisation is compulsory. The types of asset to which borrowing costs may be attached are assets under construction or completed investments intended for sale or lease. In contrast, IAS 23 is permissive on capitalisation.

Exhibit 13.16 FORD MOTOR CO.: ACCOUNTING POLICIES (EXTRACT) 1996

> Property and equipment placed in service before January 1, 1993 are depreciated using an accelerated method that results in accumulated depreciation of approximately two-thirds of asset cost during the first half of the estimated useful life of the asset. Property and equipment placed in service after December 31, 1992 are depreciated using the straight-line method of depreciation over the estimated useful life of the asset.

Source: Ford Motor Co., annual report, 1996, p. 45

Exhibit 13.17 WMX TECHNOLOGIES, INC.: CAPITALISATION OF INTEREST, 1996

> ***Capitalized Interest*** Interest has been capitalized on significant landfills, trash-to-energy plants and other projects under construction in accordance with Statement of Financial Accounting Standards ('FAS') No. 34. Amounts capitalized and netted against Interest Expense in the Consolidated Statements of Income were $104,512,000 in 1994, $81,471,000 in 1995 and $73,347,000 in 1996.

Source: WMX Technologies, Inc., annual report, 1996, P. 23

13.7.3.4 Financial instruments

The FASB has taken an international lead in developing practices for reporting the complexities of financial instruments. The first stage was to focus on disclosure, dealt with in SFAS 105. That standard sets out requirements for information about the extent, nature and terms of financial instruments which carry an off-balance sheet risk of accounting loss. There is also a requirement for information on concentration of credit risk for all financial instruments, whether on or off the balance sheet.

The second phase was to concentrate on measurement, dealt with in SFAS 107. This applies to all financial instruments whether in the primary financial statements or in the notes to the accounts.

SFAS 119 takes the project further, with significant additional disclosures for derivative financial instruments such as futures, forward contracts, swaps and options. It requires disclosure of the purposes for which derivatives are held or issued, distinguishing trading purposes from others.

Meeting the requirements of SFAS 105, 107 and 119 takes up three full pages in General Motors' 1996 annual report. It is indicative of the work yet to be done in the IASC project on financial instruments and the considerable amount of information not available to readers of accounts in many other countries which have sophisticated capital markets.

13.7.4 Conservatism versus optimism

Gray's (1988) classification, linked to Hofstede's (1984) analysis, was one of optimism which is defined in his paper as a *laissez-faire*, risk-taking approach contrasting with conservatism as a cautious approach to measurement. This seems at variance with the US insistence on historical cost accounting and the refusal to allow revaluation. In Gray's paper he classifies the US as optimistic in relation to countries such as Germany and France. The sources cited date from the 1970s and early 1980s so it may be that his view of relative optimism was based on the absence in the USA of the excessive provisions found in some continental European practices prior to the implementation of the Fourth Directive. There is also mention of the practice of secret reserves, existing in continental Europe, not being found in the USA or UK.

The US picture in practice is not totally clear because the caution in banning revaluation, having a long history linked to the 1929 stock market crash, is in contrast to the reluctance to take the harder line on impairment, compared with the IASC's preference. Permitting LIFO stock valuation is probably explained more by the influence of tax law than by the influence of conservatism. Providing in full for deferred taxation could be seen as conservative, but it could also be seen as a professional approach to applying a balance sheet approach consistently. However, the view of a distinguished US academic, commenting on a draft of this section, was 'please do not even try to characterise US accounting as other than conservative. It simply is conservative to the point of being inconsistent in theory'.

13.7.4.1 Valuation of tangible fixed assets

The prohibition on revaluation of fixed assets dates from APB 6. It is consistent with the benchmark treatment of IAS 16. The prohibition extends to investment properties, some real estate companies (property companies) present historical cost accounts but provide supplementary notes on current value information.

13.7.4.2 Impairment of assets

There is more interest in reduction in the value of fixed assets, referred to as impairment. There was for some time a requirement in APB 4 that, in unusual circumstances, impairment of an asset may have occurred. There was lack of clarity as to when and by how much the impairment should be recognised. SFAS 121, 'Accounting for the impairment of long-lived assets and long-lived assets to be disposed of', requires that an impairment loss should be recognised if, and only if, the sum of the future *undiscounted* cash flows is less than the carrying amount of the asset. This has caused difficulty for the IASC core standards project because the IASC Board believes this test carries too high a risk that the recognition of impairment will be delayed. The Board's preference is to compare the *discounted* cash flows with the carrying amount, causing earlier recognition.

Where impairment is to be recognised, SFAS 121 states that the recoverable amount is fair value defined as the price for sale or purchase of the asset between willing parties. The IASC proposes, in E55, that recoverable amount should be based on the higher of net selling price and value in use. In many cases both approaches will lead to the same answer but E55 may sometimes result in a higher recoverable amount based on value in use.

Finally, SFAS 121 prohibits reversal of an impairment loss where the asset value recovers. The IASC proposes, in E55, circumstances where reversal could be permitted.

13.7.4.3 Intangible assets

'Intangible assets' are stated at historical cost *less* accumulated amortisation. The standard APB 17 prescribes straight-line depreciation over a maximum of 40 years. Even in the case of brand names, where it might be argued that the asset life is longer, the view of the standard is that 40 years is the maximum period. All intangible assets are treated in a similar manner.

One particular example is advertising costs, which may be treated as an asset where there are demonstrable expectations of future economic benefits. An example is provided by Sears, Roebuck and Co (Exhibit 13.18). Advertising which does not meet the criteria is reported as an expense of the period.

Exhibit 13.18 SEARS, ROEBUCK AND CO.: NOTE ON ADVERTISING COSTS, 1996

> **ADVERTISING**
>
> Costs for newspaper, television, radio and other media advertising are expensed as incurred. Specialty catalog book preparation and other direct response advertising costs (printing costs and advertising inserts) are charged to expense over the expected period of future benefits. For specialty catalogs, amortization of costs occurs over the life of the catalog, not to exceed one year. For advertising inserts and other direct response advertising, the amortization period ranges from six months to five years depending on the period of future benefits. In 1996, the total cost of advertising charged to expense was $1.28 billion, compared with $1.22 billion in 1995, and $1.18 billion in 1994. The consolidated balance sheets include deferred direct-response advertising costs of $59 million at Dec. 28, 1996, $46 million at Dec. 30, 1995, and $37 million at Dec. 31, 1994, which are included in other assets.

Source: Sears, Roebuck and Co., annual report, 1996, p. 32

Under a separate standard, SFAS 2, research and development (R&D) expenditure is one instance of intangible assets where there is a strong element of conservatism that all expenditure should be reported through the income statement as incurred (SFAS 2). It has also been suggested that concern about measurement reliability led in this case to rigid uniformity. This is in contrast to IAS 9, which modifies this approach with a requirement that development costs meeting specific criteria should be capitalised. However, as noted in Chapter 6, there is continued pressure to base the international practice on expense treatment only.

13.7.4.4 Marketable securities

Marketable securities must be carried in the balance sheet at the lower of cost or market value on a portfolio basis. This is conservative in the overall approach, but less conservative in permitting the loss on one investment to be set against a gain on another. Current and non-current investments must be separated. Reductions in value of the current investment portfolio must be taken through the income statement, but those in relation to non-current investments are taken to a separate component of shareholders' equity. SFAS 107 requires disclosure of the fair value of financial instruments where practicable. The IASC has experienced considerable criticism and debate in the course of its work in this area, but appears to be pursuing the aim of valuing all marketable securities at fair value, measured as current value.

13.7.4.5 Inventory and long-term contracts

Valuation of inventory is covered in ARB 43 (1953), requiring the lower of cost or market value. Cost may be determined using a range of techniques which include FIFO, LIFO and average cost. 'Market value' is defined as current replacement cost subject to an upper limit of net realisable value and a lower limit of net realisable value *less* a normal profit margin. IAS 2 differs in requiring the lower of cost and net realisable value. US influence caused the retention of LIFO as an allowed alternative in IAS 2. Around two-thirds of US companies use LIFO (*see*, for example Sonoco, Exhibit 13.19). A strong factor is that the Internal Revenue Service (IRS) requires that if LIFO is used for tax purposes it must be used for financial reporting purposes.

Accounting for long-term contracts is dealt with in ARB 45 (1955). Both percentage of completion and completed contract methods are permitted, although there is a preference expressed for the former. IAS 11 requires percentage of completion.

13.7.4.6 Deferred taxation

Consistent with the balance sheet approach of the FASB's conceptual framework, SFAS 109 requires the deferred taxation liability to be accounted for on the basis of the full liability which the enterprise will eventually have to meet. A change in the expected liability will result in an expense in the income statement. The move from the earlier APB 11, based on the matching of income and expenses in any accounting period and having little regard to the resulting balance sheet figure, reflects the FASB's intention to move to a balance sheet approach.

13.7.5 Secrecy versus transparency

Gray's (1988) classification of US accounting as highly transparent is supported by the extensive disclosure requirements imposed by the SEC, as well as those of the FASB standards. However it must be remembered that the SEC regulates only listed companies and there are many more unlisted companies in the USA about which much less is known. Research evidence suggests that there is voluntary disclosure by US multinational companies, although less extensive than the voluntary disclosures provided by UK multinational companies.[26] Multinational US companies might reply that they already disclose more under compulsion. Specific elements of secrecy remain in off-balance sheet transactions which are not regulated by any particular standard. On the other hand, the move towards openness and informativeness is reinforced by the AICPA in the work of the Jenkins Committee.

13.7.5.1 Basic information package

The requirements of the SEC are considerable, and the most convenient starting point is the basic information package (BIP). The five classes of information in the BIP are:

Exhibit 13.19 SONOCO: NOTES TO THE CONSOLIDATED FINANCIAL STATEMENTS, 1996

> **Inventories ($000s)**
>
> **Inventories are stated at the lower of cost or market**. The last-in, first-out (LIFO) method was used to determine costs of approximately 38% of total inventories in both 1996 and 1995. The remaining inventories are determined on the first-in, first-out (FIFO) method.
>
> If the FIFO method of accounting had been used for all inventories, the totals would have been higher by $12,043 in 1996 and $12,084 in 1995.

Source: Sonoco, annual report, 1996, p. 37

---

[26] Meek *et al.* (1995)

- Market price of, and dividends on, common equity, and related security matters
- Selected financial data
- Management's discussion and analysis (MD&A)
- Audited financial statements and supplementary data
- Other information.

The information must be presented in its entirety to the SEC, but there are various ways of achieving this. It may all be included in a form 10-K report, which is then a document of considerable length (as much as 100–200 pages) and generally uninteresting appearance (one font of type and no illustrations or graphics). Alternatively companies may choose to present some or most of the BIP in the annual report to shareholders, with a much reduced form 10-K in which there is a reference to portions of the annual report and the statement for the annual meeting, which are to be read as part of the 10-K filing. Some information required for the 10-K does not normally appear in the annual report, such as lists of legal proceedings being taken against the company, detailed descriptions of the business and detailed description of land and buildings held by the company.

Other information may be included in the proxy statement which accompanies the notice to shareholders convening the annual general meeting. In particular, there is more about directors – their remuneration package ('compensation'); the report of the remuneration committee; information on related-party transactions; and share performance over a period of time. An example is provided by Wal-Mart Stores (Exhibit 13.20).

It is thus essential for the interested reader to request the annual report, the 10-K filing and the proxy statement in order to have the benefit of the full BIP intended by the SEC. The main features of each section of the BIP are as follows:

Market price of, and dividends on, common equity, and related security matters

This provides investors with information including the markets in which the stock is traded, the quarterly share price for the past two years, the approximate number of ordinary shareholders, and the frequency and amount of dividends paid over the past two years.

Selected financial data

This is intended to highlight key items including the net sales or operating revenue, income or loss from continuing operations, income (in total and per share) and total assets.

Management's discussion and analysis

The MD&A is explained in more detail in the next section.

Audited financial statements and supplementary data

The company must present income statements and statements of cash flow in respect of the current period and the previous two years. Balance sheets must be presented at the year-end and for the previous year-end. Notes to the accounts are also required.

Exhibit 13.20 WAL-MART STORES, INC.: PROXY STATEMENT (EXTRACTS), 1996

EXECUTIVE COMPENSATION

Summary Compensation Table: This table shows the compensation during each of the Company's last three fiscal years of Wal-Mart's Chief Executive Officer and four other most highly compensated executive officers based on compensation earned during the fiscal year ended January 31, 1997.

Name and position	Fiscal year ended Jan. 31.	Salary ($)(1)	Incentive Payment ($)(2)	Other annual compensation ($)(3)	Restricted stock awards ($)	Number of securities underlying options	LTIP payouts ($)	All other compensation ($)(4)
David D. Glass	1997	1,085,000	377,580	71,363	0	135,625	0	40,436
President and Chief Executive Officer	1996	1,035,000	0	66,759	0	66,064	0	40,359
	1995	985,000	0	61,443	0	64,590	0	14,089
Donald G. Soderquist	1997	860,000	299,280	0	0	89,583	0	30,866
Vice Chairman and Chief Operating Officer	1996	830,000	0	0	0	52,979	0	29,119
	1995	790,000	0	0	0	51,803	0	27,949
Joseph S. Hardin, Jr.	1997	560,000	139,440	0	0	58,333	0	20,376
Executive Vice President	1996	537,885	0	0	0	47,126	0	19,415
	1995	500,000	0	0	0	29,670	0	17,712
Bob L. Martin	1997	500,000	87,000	23,708	0	52,083	0	18,011
Executive Vice President	1996	450,000	0	0	0	40,000	0	15,886
	1995	400,000	0	0	0	23,736	0	14,182
Paul R. Carter	1997	470,000	163,560	36,124	0	48,958	0	17,675
Executive Vice President	1996	470,000	0	34,525	0	27,000	0	22,192
	1995	470,000	0	30,758	0	27,738	0	26,946

Annual compensation — Long-term compensation (Awards / Payouts)

(1) This column includes compensation earned during the fiscal year but deferred under agreements with Wal-Mart.

(2) Incentive payments shown in this column relate to performance under the Management Incentive Plan during the January 31, 1997, fiscal year but were paid during the January 31, 1998, fiscal year.

(3) These amounts are incentive payments on amounts deferred under the Officer Deferred Compensation Plan. These amounts do not include the value of perquisites or other personal benefits because they do not exceed the lesser of $50,000 or 10% of the total annual salary and bonus for any named executive officer.

(4) "All other compensation" for the fiscal year ended January 31, 1997, includes Company contributions to Wal-Mart's Profit Sharing and Supplemental Executive Retirement Plans, above-market interest credited on deferred compensation, and term life insurance premiums paid by Wal-Mart for the benefit of each officer.

Exhibit 13.20 continued

STOCK PERFORMANCE GRAPH

This graph shows the yearly percentage change in cumulative total shareholder return on Wal-Mart stock during the last five fiscal years ended January 31, 1997. The graph also shows the cumulative total returns of the S&P 500 Index and the published retail industry index. The comparison assumes $100 was invested on January 31, 1992, in Wal-Mart stock and in each of the indices shown and assumes reinvestment of dividends.

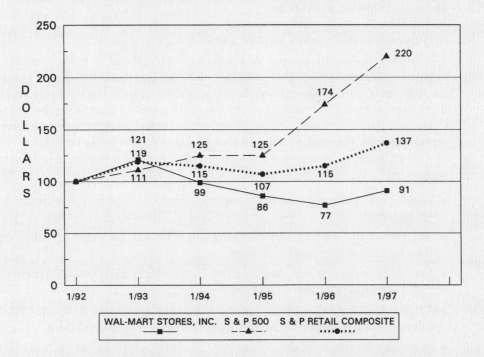

WAL-MART STORES, INC.   S & P 500   S & P RETAIL COMPOSITE

INTEREST OF MANAGEMENT IN CERTAIN TRANSACTIONS

During the fiscal year ended January 31, 1997, Stan Kroenke, a director, held interests in shopping center developments which leased space to Wal-Mart for 43 stores and Sam's Club locations. Total rents and maintenance fees paid by Wal-Mart under these leases for the fiscal year were $25,573,948. Mr. Kroenke's interest in the amounts paid was $17,968,597. We believe that rents and fees paid for this leased space are competitive with amounts that would be paid to a third party to lease similar space.

Additionally, during the fiscal year Wal-Mart paid the Kroenke/THF Utility Co., a utility company in which Mr. Kroenke has an ownership interest, $383,600 for utility services provided to two stores. Mr. Kroenke's interest in the amounts paid was $140,666.

Frank Robson, the brother of Helen R. Walton, a beneficial owner of more that 5% of Wal-Mart stock, held various ownership interests in nine store locations leased by Wal-Mart. The Company paid rents and maintenance fees of $2,688,674 under the leases for the fiscal year ended January 31, 1997. We believe that the rents and maintenance fees paid under the leases is competitive with amounts that would be paid to a third party to lease similar space.

Alice Walton, a beneficial owner of more that 5% of Wal-Mart stock, has an indirect interest in U.S. Housewares Corporation. A wholly owned subsidiary of U.S. Housewares Corporation sold $5,147,186 in consumer products to the Company during the fiscal year ended January 31, 1997. We believe that these transactions were competitive with amounts that would be paid to third parties in similar transactions.

Source: Wal-Mart Stores, Inc., annual report, 1996, pp. 4–5, 9

Other information

This is quite substantial, and covers a brief description of the business; major operating developments such as acquisitions of assets or bankruptcies of parts of the organisation; segment information; description of major properties currently owned; description of major active legal proceedings; information about management such as background, remuneration, and major transactions between management and the company; and selected industry-specific disclosures, such as for banking, insurance and other regulated industries.

13.7.5.2 Management discussion and analysis

The management discussion and analysis (MD&A) is a report required by Regulation S-K of the SEC. The full title is the 'Management's discussion and analysis of financial condition and results of operations'. It is one of the most important disclosures made by the company. The full version will in many cases be printed in the annual report. Some companies give an edited summary in the financial report, referring the reader to the 10-K registration for the fuller version.

A flexible format is permitted for the MD&A, but the following five items must be covered:

- Specific information about the company's liquidity, capital resources and results of operations
- The impact of inflation and changing prices on net sales and revenues and on income from continuing operations
- Material changes in line items of the consolidated financial statements compared with the prior-period amount
- Known material events and uncertainties that may make historical financial information not indicative of future operations or future conditions
- Any other information the company believes necessary for an understanding of its financial condition, changes in financial condition, and results of operations.

Although a flexible format is permitted, practice has tended to converge on repetitive and stereotyped paragraphs where the US-resident companies do not always score as highly as foreign registrants seeking to make their mark.[27]

The reference to 'future operations and future conditions' reflects a desire of the SEC to give a forward-looking aspect to the MD&A. The encouragement to give forward-looking information is backed by a 'Safe Harbor' Law which is intended to protect forward-looking statements made in good faith. However, in practice there is considerable fear of legal action where a company makes a forward-looking statement which is subsequently contradicted by events. The Jenkins Committee of the AICPA (13.7.5.6) declined to make recommendations on provision of forward-looking information until the legal position about such information was clarified.

13.7.5.3 Segment reporting

In June 1997 the FASB issued SFAS 131 'Disclosures about segments of an enterprise and related information'. It superseded SFAS 14, which had for some years required

---

[27] Collins *et al.* (1993)

segmental disclosure of turnover, profits and assets analysed by industry and geographical segments. SFAS 14, in turn, had been prompted by earlier requirements of the SEC in relation to reports filed on form 10-K. The move to SFAS 131 was prompted by an emerging debate on the definition of segments. The view in the USA and Canada has been that the enterprise should be allowed to base segments on the organisational structure of the enterprise, even where such segments cover more than one industry or geographical area. The IASC had, at one stage in its discussion, preferred to concentrate on diversity of industry and geography which requires segmental analysis on this basis. The resulting revision of IAS 14 was a compromise which accommodated the position in SFAS 131, but left some flexibility for other countries which prefer the approach based on geographical and industry-based risk and reward. The reason given by FASB for requiring companies to disclose segment data based on how management makes its decisions was that this was a response to requests from analysts for better information about segments.

13.7.5.4 Frequency of reporting

In addition to the annual report, the SEC requires listed companies to produce quarterly reports. Interim reporting is covered by APB 28. US interim reports usually include both the current interim period and a cumulative year-to-date period, together with comparative figures for the previous year. Each interim period is viewed as an integral part of the annual period. This means that while operating cost and revenues will generally be reported in the interim period to which they relate, discretion exists to allocate other costs across interim periods. When APB 28 was issued there was a dissenting view that it was not sufficiently strict in its guidance on allocation to interim periods. The IASC has indicated in E 57 a general principle of the 'year-to-date' approach, where the events of the interim period are reported as they occur.

Under APB 28 the cumulative effect of a change in accounting principle is always included in net income of the first interim period of the company's accounting year, regardless of when the accounting change occurred. The IASC indicates in E 57 a preference for restatement of the comparative figures for the corresponding previous period so that accounting changes do not appear in any one interim period.

13.7.5.5 Off-balance sheet transactions

There is no single standard in the US which deals with off-balance sheet transactions in general terms. Similarly, the IASC has no specific standard on the subject. Various separate FASB standards address specific issues such as sale and repurchase of products and sale of real estate with conditions attached. Disclosures are required about some long-term obligations which establish commitments to future cash outflows. These and other specific standards restrict the scope for off-balance sheet transactions in particular situations.

However, there is a more flexible approach to consolidation of subsidiary companies which does leave scope for assets and liabilities remaining off-balance sheet. The usual condition for establishing that control exists is ownership of a majority shareholding. There is no concept of 'dominant interest' or of entities which closely resemble subsidiaries (quasi-subsidiaries), although the FASB has a long-term project in progress. Also, as mentioned earlier, joint ventures are generally reported using equity accounting where the investment appears as a single line item. Proportional consolidation is rare.

13.7.5.6 The Jenkins Report

The AICPA formed a Special Committee on Financial Reporting in 1991, chaired by E. L. Jenkins, to address two questions:

- What information should companies provide to investors and creditors?
- To what extent should auditors be associated with that information?

The work of the Jenkins Committee was part of the AICPA's broad initiative to improve the value of business information and the confidence of the public in that information. Extensive research was undertaken to ascertain the views of investors and creditors. The Jenkins Committee, reporting in 1994,[28] found that a great deal was right with the present state of business reporting in the USA. However, the criticisms offered by users of business reports led to the identification of high-priority areas for improvement. Key recommendations were that, to meet users' changing needs, business reporting must:

- provide more information with a forward-looking perspective, including management's plans, opportunities, risks and measurement uncertainties
- focus more on the factors that create long-term value, including non-financial measures indicating how key business processes are performing
- align information reported externally better with the information reported to senior management to manage the business.

The report also recommended that participants in the business reporting process must do a better job of anticipating change by:

- focusing on information needs of users and finding cost-effective ways of aligning reporting with those needs
- developing and maintaining a comprehensive model of business reporting reflecting the kind of information that users need
- adopting a longer-term focus by developing a vision of the future business environment and users' future needs for information.

The Jenkins Committee designed and illustrated a comprehensive model of business reporting, based on revising the primary financial statements and the MD&A. It was incremental rather than revolutionary, and the report noted that the practical investigation focused on immediate rather than longer-term information needs. That reflected the concern of users with current practice and current problems.

Jenkins noted that the current legal environment in the USA discouraged companies from disclosing forward-looking information and recommended that companies should not expand reporting of forward-looking information until there were more effective deterrents to undesirable legal actions.

---

[28] AICPA (1994)

Taking similar themes to those of the Jenkins report, the Association of Investment Management and Research (AIMR) published a position paper (AIMR, 1993). Subsequently the FASB issued an Invitation to Comment (FASB, 1996a) on both papers, so that the consultation might assist the FASB in deciding how best to proceed in addressing these two sets of recommendations.

13.8 EMPIRICAL STUDIES

13.8.1 Classification studies

In Chapter 4 it was shown that Mueller (1967) classified the USA as an independent discipline system where accounting is seen as a service function derived from business practices and characterised by the use of professional judgement (section 4.4.1). Nobes (1984) classified US accounting as micro-based, founded in business practice, pragmatic, of British origin but having subsequently developed a characteristic US influence applicable beyond the USA itself (Exhibit 4.7). Frank and Nair (1980) classified the USA with Canada, Japan, Mexico, Panama and the Philippines on the basis of measurement (Exhibit 4.10) but with Canada, Mexico, the Netherlands, Panama and the Philippines on the basis of disclosure (Exhibit 4.11). Using more recent survey data, Salter and Doupnik (1992) (Exhibit 4.8) classified the USA as micro-based and in a group dominated by characteristics of a well developed capital market, an attitude to uncertainty which differed from that of the UK, the Netherlands or Australia (also micro-based) and a legal system which also distinguished it from the UK, the Netherlands or Australia.

13.8.2 Comparability measures

Research studies measuring relative comparability were explained in Chapter 3. As the SEC is one of the main regulators, requiring other companies to reconcile their accounting practices with those of the USA, the studies measuring comparability have tended to do so relative to the US as a benchmark.[29] The conclusions from such studies may nevertheless be reversed to indicate that US GAAP are, for example, more conservative than UK GAAP but apparently less conservative than accounting practices in Germany.

A study of financial reporting in North America[30] found that of 121 Canadian companies reconciling their profit to US GAAP, 71 (59%) reported that Canadian income was greater than US net income and 50 (41%) reported that Canadian net income was less than US net income. Of six Mexican companies providing a reconciliation, all reported that Mexican net income was greater than US net income.

It appears that the SEC insistence on the preparation of a reconciliation to US GAAP (except by Canadian companies) may partly reflect a concern for insufficiently conservative accounting practices, as well as a desire to see extensive disclosure.

---

[29] Weetman and Gray (1990, 1991)
[30] Joint study (1995)

13.8.3 Harmonisation studies

Research studies into harmonisation are explained in Chapter 3. Harmonisation studies based on empirical data have tended to focus on EU countries. Comparative studies have been published as the output of professional bodies, such as comparing the USA with Canada and Mexico,[31] or the USA with the UK.[32] The Routledge/ICAEW series[33] on European Financial Reporting provided, in each volume, a brief comparison of the particular country with accounting in the USA.

13.9 SUMMARY AND CONCLUSIONS

In this chapter you have seen how characteristics of accounting principles and practice in the USA are related to the predictions made by Gray (1988) and others based upon analysis of cultural factors. Using the scores developed by Hofstede (1984), Gray's method of analysis may be used to predict that the accounting system in the USA will be characterised by strong professionalism, strong flexibility, strong conservatism and strong transparency. The strong professionalism is embedded in the historical development of the accountancy profession and the responsibility taken by the profession for setting accounting standards. Statutory control is a reserve power but is rarely implemented in practice. Flexibility is seen in the lack of prescribed formats of presentation and the separate existence of tax law and accounting law. Insistence on historical cost would place the USA in a highly conservative category, but other aspects of detail in practice give glimpses of practices which are not always directed towards conservatism. Transparency is seen in the very extensive disclosures required by law and practice, particularly in the basic information package required by the SEC of all listed US companies.

QUESTIONS

Business environment (13.2)

1 To what extent does the business environment of the USA provide clues as to possible influences on accounting practices?

Early developments in accounting (13.3)

1 To what extent do early developments in accounting practice indicate the likely directions of professionalism/statutory control; uniformity/flexibility; conservatism/optimism; and secrecy/transparency in current practice?

Institutions (13.4)

1 How does the political and economic system of the USA fit into the classifications described in Chapter 1?

---

[31] Joint study (1995)
[32] Coopers and Lybrand Deloitte (1990)
[33] McLeay, S. and Archer, S., *European Financial Reporting*, series published in the early 1990s by Routledge in association with the Institute of Chartered Accountants in England and Wales

2 How does the legal system of the USA fit into the classifications described in Chapter 1?

3 How does the taxation system of the USA compare to the descriptions given in Chapter 1?

4 How does the corporate financing system of the USA compare to the descriptions given in Chapter 1?

5 How does the accounting profession in the USA compare to the descriptions given in Chapter 1?

6 How do the external influences on accounting practice in the USA compare to those described in Chapter 1?

7 Which institutional factors are most likely to influence US accounting practice?

Societal culture and accounting sub-culture (13.5)

1 What is the position of the USA relative to the UK and continental European countries, according to Hofstede's 1984 analysis (Chapter 2)?

2 What are the features of US societal culture identified by Hofstede which led Gray (1988) to his conclusions regarding the likely system of accounting in the USA?

3 What is the position of the USA relative to Japan, Australia and Malaysia, according to Hofstede's (1984) analysis (Chapter 2)?

IASs (13.6)

1 In which areas does accounting practice in the USA depart from that set out in IASs?

2 For each of the areas of departure which you have identified, describe the treatment prescribed or practised in US accounting, and identify the likely impact on the income and shareholders' equity of moving from US GAAP to the relevant IASs.

3 What explanations may be offered for these departures from IASs, in terms of the institutional factors described in the chapter?

4 What are the most difficult problems facing accounting in the USA if it seeks harmonisation with the IASC core standards programme?

Professionalism/statutory control (13.7.2)

1 Identify the key features supporting a conclusion that professionalism, rather than statutory control, is a dominant characteristic of US accounting.

2 Explain which institutional influences cause professionalism, rather than statutory control, to be a dominant characteristic of US accounting.

3 Discuss whether a classification of strong professionalism is appropriate for the 1990s.

Uniformity/flexibility (13.7.3)

1 Identify the key features supporting a conclusion that flexibility, rather than uniformity, is a dominant characteristic of US accounting.

2 Explain which institutional influences cause flexibility, rather than uniformity, to be a dominant characteristic of US accounting.

3 Discuss whether a classification of strong flexibility is appropriate for the 1990s.

Conservatism/optimism (13.7.4)

1 Identify the key features supporting a conclusion that optimism, rather than conservatism, is a dominant characteristic of US accounting.

2 Explain which institutional influences cause optimism, rather than conservatism, to be a dominant characteristic of US accounting.

3 Discuss whether a classification of strong optimism is appropriate for the 1990s.

Secrecy/transparency (13.7.5)

1 Identify the key features supporting a conclusion that transparency, rather than secrecy, is a dominant characteristic of US accounting.

2 Explain which institutional influences cause transparency, rather than secrecy, to be a dominant characteristic of US accounting.

3 Discuss whether a classification of strong transparency is appropriate for the 1990s.

Empirical studies (13.8)

1 What is the relative position of the USA as indicated by research studies into classification, comparability and harmonisation?

REFERENCES

AICPA (1973) *Objectives of Financial Statements: Reports of the Study Group on the Objectives of Financial Statements.* American Institute of Certified Public Accountants, New York.

AICPA (1994) *Improving Business Reporting – A Customer Focus: Meeting Information Needs of Investors and Creditors, Comprehensive Report of the Special Committee on Financial Reporting.* New York: American Institute of Certified Public Accountants (The Special Committee was chaired by Edmund L. Jenkins, partner in Arthur Andersen).

AICPA (1995) Statement of Position, 'Disclosure of certain significant risks and uncertainties'. New York: American Institute of Certified Public Accountants.

AIMR (1993) *Financial Reporting in the 1990s and Beyond.* New York: Association of Investment Management and Research.

Cairns, D. (1997) 'The future shape of harmonisation: A reply', *The European Accounting Review*, 6(2), 305–48.

Charkham, J.P. (1994) *Keeping Good Company: A Study of Corporate Governance in Five Countries* Oxford: Clarendon Press.

Choi, F.D.S. and Mueller, G.G. (1992) *International Accounting*, 2nd edn. Englewood Cliffs, NJ: Prentice-Hall.

Collins, W., Davie, E.S. and Weetman, P. (1993) 'Management discussion and analysis: An evaluation of practice in UK and US companies', *Accounting and Business Research*, 23(90), 123–37.

Coopers and Lybrand Deloitte (1990) *Accounting Comparisons: UK/USA*. London: Coopers & Lybrand Deloitte.

Davies, M., Paterson, R. and Wilson, A. (1997) *UK GAAP*, 5th edn. London: Macmillan/Ernst and Young.

Doupnik, T.S. and Salter, S.B. (1993) 'An empirical test of a judgemental international classification of financial reporting practices', *Journal of International Business Studies*, 24(1), 41–60.

Fabozzi, F.J. and Modigliani, F. (1996) *Capital Markets: Institutions and Instruments*, 2nd edn. Englewood Cliffs, NJ: Prentice-Hall.

FASB (1996a) *Invitation to Comment – Recommendations of the AICPA Special Committee on Financial Reporting and the Association for Investment Management and Research*. London: Financial Accounting Standards Board.

FASB (1996b) *The IASC–US Comparison Project: A Report on the Similarities and Differences between IASC Standards and US GAAP*. London: Financial Accounting Standards Board.

Flower, J. (1997) 'The future shape of harmonisation: The EU versus the IASC versus the SEC', *The European Accounting Review*, 6(2), 281–303.

Gray, S.J. (1988) 'Towards a theory of cultural influence on the development of accounting systems internationally', *Abacus*, 24(1), 1–15.

Hofstede, G. (1984) *Culture Consequences: International Differences in Work-Related Values*. Beverly Hills, CA: Sage Publications.

Horngren, C.T, Sundem, G.L. and Elliott, J.A. (1996) *Introduction to Financial Accounting*. Englewood Cliffs, NJ: Prentice-Hall.

IASC (1996) *Annual Review*. London: International Accounting Standards Committee.

Joint study (1995) *Financial Reporting in North America*, undertaken by the Canadian Institute of Chartered Accountants, the Instituto Mexicano de Contadores Públicos, AC, and the Financial Accounting Standards Board of the United States, assisted by KPMG Peat Marwick LLP and published jointly.

Kubin, K. (1993) 'Group accounting in the United States of America', in Gray, S.J. Coenenberg, A.G. and Gordon, P.D. *International Group Accounting – Issues in European Harmonisation*. London: Routledge.

Meek, G.K., Roberts, C.B. and Gray, S.J. (1995) 'Factors influencing voluntary annual report disclosures by US, UK and continental European multinational corporations', *Journal of International Business Studies*, Third Quarter, 555–72.

Meeting, D.T., Law, D.B. and Luecke, R.W. (1997) 'Simplifying EPS', *Journal of Accountancy*, August, 61–70.

Mueller, G.G. (1967) *International Accounting*. London: Macmillan.

Nair, R.D. and Frank, W.G. (1980) 'The impact of disclosure and measurement practices on international accounting classifications', *Accounting Review*, July, 426–50.

Nobes, C.W. (1984) *International Classification of Financial Reporting*. London: Croom Helm.

Nobes, C. (1995) 'Financial reporting in North America', in Nobes, C. and Parker, R. *Comparative International Accounting*, 4th edn. Englewood Cliffs, NJ: Prentice-Hall.

North, D.C. (1974) *Growth and Welfare in the American Past: A New Economic History*. Englewood Cliffs, NJ: Prentice-Hall.

OECD (1996). *Economic Surveys 1995/96*. Paris: Organization for Economic Co-operation and Development, 118–21.

Salter, S.B. and Doupnik, T.S. (1992) 'The relationship between legal systems and accounting practices: A classification exercise', *Advances in International Accounting*, 5, 3–22.

499

Salter, S.B., Roberts, C.B. and Kantor, J. (1996) 'The IASC comparability project: A cross-national comparison of financial reporting practices and IASC proposed rules', *Journal of International Accounting and Taxation*, 5(1), 89–111.

Starr, R. and Donin, R. (1979) *Doing Business in the United States – An Executive's Guide.* London: Oyez Publishing.

Sudarsanam, P.S. (1995) *The Essence of Mergers and Acquisitions*. Englewood Cliffs, NJ: Prentice-Hall.

Weetman, P. and Gray, S.J. (1990) 'International financial analysis and comparative corporate performance: The impact of UK versus US accounting principles on earnings', *Journal of International Financial Management and Accounting*, 2(2/3), 111–29.

Weetman, P. and Gray, S.J. (1991) 'A comparative international analysis of the impact of accounting principles on profits: The US versus the UK, Sweden and the Netherlands', *Accounting and Business Research*, 21(84), 363–37.

White, G.I., Sondhi, G.I. and Fried, D. (1994) *The Analysis and Use of Financial Statements.* New York: John Wiley.

Wolk, H.I. and Tearney, M.G. (1997) *Accounting Theory: A Conceptual and Institutional approach*, 4th edn. Cincinnati: South-Western College Publishing.

Journals/professional magazines

The *Financial Times* (UK)

The Accountant (UK)

OECD, *Economic Surveys*. Paris: Organization for Economic Co-operation and Development.

Chapter 14

Hungary

14.1 INTRODUCTION[1]

The history of Hungary in the nineteenth and twentieth century is one of political turbulence at least equal to, and probably beyond, that of other European countries studied in this book. Hungary emerged from the Austro-Hungarian empire in the late 1800s but retained close economic links with Austria and Germany; the country suffered reduction in territory and population after the First World War, faced Soviet communist dominance for 40 years after the Second World War and finally moved under a new political regime to a free market economy and a desire to establish membership of the European Union (EU).

Accounting during the nineteenth century and up to 1948 was influenced by western European practices. From 1948 to 1988 the accounting practices developed within a framework of the requirements of a centrally planned economic system. The transition to a market economy from 1989 onwards required new accounting practices for external reporting and an indication of the desire to align with the EC Directives and acceptable international practice. An association agreement with the EU has existed since 1995. This means that western European companies can move production of components or finished goods to Hungary and yet sell on EU markets without incurring heavy import taxes. Hungary is scheduled to become one of the first eastern European countries to achieve full membership of the EU.

The Accounting Law of 1991 came into force in 1992. The Accounting Law was designed to dovetail with the desire to join the EU, the need to seek foreign partners in joint ventures, the need for a new type of information in privatised businesses and many other aspects of the move towards a market economy

The introduction of a new law to meet the needs of a new political and economic system is a significant phenomenon and this chapter therefore reports some research findings concerning that new experience, as perceived by Hungarian nationals and by foreign persons working in Hungary at the time.

---

[1] Borda (1995), p. 1397

14.2 THE COUNTRY

There was a negative rate of growth of gross domestic product (GDP) over the period 1985 to 1995, indicating the problems which the economic system has faced, a fall particularly marked after 1989 (*see* Exhibit 14.1). The general standard of living may be assessed by comparison with the statistics given for Germany (Chapter 9). GDP per head in Hungary is less than one-sixth that of Germany, life expectancy is marginally lower and the average household size is higher at 2.7 persons, compared with 2.5 for Germany. Unemployment at 1996 stood at 10.7%, comparable to 1995, but real wages declined by 3.6% in 1996.[2]

14.2.1 Geography

Hungary is located in the centre of Europe, surrounded by the Carpathian Mountains and the Alps. It is landlocked and shares its borders with Slovakia, Ukraine, Romania, Yugoslavia, Croatia and Slovenia and Austria. Much of the country is lowland. The main waterway is the Danube and there are many natural and artificial lakes. Geothermic energy is abundant below the surface of the Earth's crust, giving rise to thermal waters used for curative bathing and drinking.

The population of Hungary is not large at 10 million but over 250 million people live within a 1,000 km radius of Budapest. It is therefore seen not only as a country where business may be transacted internally but also as a business route to eastern Europe and the Russian federation.[3]

14.2.2 Economic indicators

Exhibit 14.1 HUNGARY: COUNTRY PROFILE, TAKEN FROM EIU STATISTICS

Population	10.1 m.	
Land mass	93,030 sq.km	
GDP per head	US $4,169	
GDP per head in purchasing-power parity	24	(USA=100)
Origins of GDP:	%	
Agriculture	7.3	
Industry	37.5	
Services	55.2	
	%	
Real GDP average annual growth 1985–95	–0.9	
Inflation, average annual rate 1989–96	24.4	

Source: *The Economist Pocket World in Figures 1998 Edition*, The Economist (1997)

---

[2] Web page of Hungarian Ministry of Trade and Industry (September 1997)
[3] Krieglsteiner (1996), p. 37

More than half of GDP is created by service industry. Agriculture makes a higher percentage contribution than it does in some EU member countries but this does not indicate an agricultural economy. In manufacturing industry there is some reliance on machinery and transport and on agriculture and food processing, but there is also diversification across 50% of the manufacturing sector.

Inflation was high at 24.5% on the average over the period 1989–95, and consumer prices rose comparably. However, the country still offered significantly lower operating costs in some sectors than those found elsewhere in Europe. There is a highly skilled labour force, whose wages are perhaps one-tenth of those in Germany and Austria, both significant trade partners. The incoming socialist government started an austerity programme in March 1995, based on cutting spending, devaluing the currency and shifting resources into exports. This appeared to bring the economy under better control, and experts forecast inflation at 15.5% for 1998.[4]

Unemployment remains high (10% in 1997) but there is a flourishing unrecorded economy because some business people will not declare their profits and the wages they are paying to employees. Payroll taxes, wage flexibility and job protection laws are seen as inhibiting economic development.

The main export destination is Germany, followed by Austria, Italy and Russia. Imports show a similar relative importance of source countries – in 1995, trade with Germany, both in exports and imports, was three times that of Austria, the next country in the list.

It is clear that the markets of the EU could be very attractive to Hungary in full membership. The trade balance is negative, with visible imports exceeding exports by US$2.3 billion in 1995 and US$2.6 billion in 1996. There is also a net outflow of invisibles, so that the overall current account balance is negative. Foreign debt is a high percentage of GDP.

Foreign inward investment is essential to the development of business in Hungary.[5] Between 1990 and 1994, the country attracted US$8.485 billion in foreign investment, an amount greater than that invested in all other eastern European countries combined. A similar amount was received between 1994 and 1997. Taking foreign inward investment as a whole (e.g. joint ventures, privatisation, establishing branches and subsidiaries), the largest amount by country is derived from the USA, with Germany second.[6] The country is seen as providing a relatively stable environment within which to conduct business. In particular the association agreement gave US manufacturers a low-cost base from which to export to EU countries.

More particularly, foreign investment in privatisation of Hungarian companies has been dominated by German companies, providing 36% of the amount invested in the period 1990–1995.[7] Second has been the USA (19.4%) and third France (13.84%). Other countries participated in privatisation at less than 10% each.

---

[4] *Finanical Times* survey, *World Economy and Finance*, Part II, 19 September 1997, p. 31
[5] Krieglsteiner (1996), pp. 36–9
[6] Krieglsteiner (1996), p. 36 citing *Accountancy* (August 1995), p. 30
[7] Canning and Hare (1996), Table 7

14.3 OVERVIEW OF ACCOUNTING REGULATIONS[8]

14.3.1 Early accounting law

The first company law in Hungary was the Commercial Law of 1875.[9] Further laws followed in the early twentieth century, so that the legal standards of business in Hungary conformed to accepted European practices in general. The present-day chart of accounts in Hungary may be traced to the influence of Schmalenbach in Germany (1927).[10] Because Hungary was under Soviet domination in the late 1940s and 1950s it did not develop management accounting practices as happened in western European countries. In the Soviet system, central planning dictated the accounting approach.

While direct central control was in place, the role of accounting was to provide data on the economic activities of enterprises, to measure achievement of planned targets and to provide information for aggregation across the sector and across the national economy. Accounting was essentially serving the macroeconomic needs of government rather than the microeconomic needs of enterprises. In particular, accounting could not provide information for management decision making. There was no external ownership and so no concept of accountability to the owners of the enterprise.

For macroeconomic aggregation to be successful, strict rules of bookkeeping were necessary. Before 1992 the Ministry of Finance regulated the bookkeeping systems through the General Compulsory Scheme of Accounts. Strict formats of accounts were applied and a uniform chart of accounts was used. Regulation applied to the basic system of documentation, the system of tracing production costs, the principles of financial statement preparation, valuation methods and disclosure of information

The result was a separation of reporting and planning. Reporting was seen as a bookkeeping task under strict rules while planning was seen as making adjustments to the shortfalls of previous plans at a national level. When it came down to details of accounting practice, the effect of state regulation prior to the new Law was seen in the particular areas of bookkeeping, balance sheet preparation, stocktaking, cost calculations, handling cash accounts and the connection of tax laws with accounting. That kind of control was needed to facilitate the provision of summarised accounting information,[11] but did not necessarily ensure its usefulness or accountability.

14.3.2 The introduction of consolidated accounting

The Seventh Directive was not implemented in Hungary until 1994. Before the Accounting Law 1991, consolidation was not used. Taking as a basis for analysis the list of options in the Seventh Directive,[12] it has been shown that, for 36

---

[8] Borda (1995), pp. 1397–1404
[9] Borda (1995), p. 1397
[10] Borda (1995), p. 1400
[11] Coopers and Lybrand (1992), p. 71
[12] Krieglsteiner (1996), pp. 94–5

options Hungary was in accordance with Germany and the UK; for a further ten options Hungary was in accordance with Germany alone; for another eight Hungary was in accordance with the UK alone; and in two situations Hungary took an individualistic approach. For a final seven options it was not clear how the Hungarian practice matched others.

The main method of consolidation is acquisition accounting. It may use either the book value method or the current value method. The book value method compares the book values in the individual balance sheets with the cost of the investment. Any excess of cost over book value must be allocated to the relevant balance sheet headings in proportion to the shares held. Any amount remaining is recorded as goodwill and amortised over a period not greater than 15 years. If the cost is greater than book value, the difference must first be allocated to assets and liabilities and any remaining credit balance must be recorded as a consolidation difference on the liability side of the balance sheet. Under the current value method, the cost of the investment is compared with the updated values of net assets. There can never be negative goodwill because there is a requirement that the proportional net equity of the subsidiary must not exceed the cost of the investment.[13]

In the consolidated profit and loss account, intercompany transactions are eliminated. Minority interest is a deduction in arriving at group profit. For consolidation of jointly managed enterprises the proportional consolidation method may be used.

14.3.3 Method of introducing the law

The Hungarian law on group accounting was introduced under considerable pressure of time.[14] Business failures and the bankruptcy of a major bank in 1992 led to the conclusion that the picture would be clearer if subsidiaries were consolidated. A development team was set up at the end of 1992 involving the German affiliate of a leading international accountancy firm as consultants. The role of the consultants was to explain the Seventh Directive but not to impose the German approach to implementing it. They recommended that detailed instructions would be required because Hungarian accountants were used to having meticulous guidance. The law was effective from 1994 but the first year of practical implementation was 1995 and there was little software in place, so that the exercise was largely manual.

14.3.4 Problems of change

Some of the unexpected problems of consolidating for the first time include not knowing precisely what the list of subsidiaries comprises. Where there is a lack of clear agreements between companies which have worked together for some years, it may not be possible to match the relationship to a definition. The unexpected problems also included lack of access to information where, for example, a Hungarian company had a Russian subsidiary. Some companies in Hungary have

---

[13] Borda (1995), p. 1430
[14] Krieglsteiner (1996), pp. 96–100

regarded consolidated accounting as an additional burden because it does not affect tax payable or dividend policy. Where Hungarian companies are themselves subsidiaries of a larger group the Hungarian accountants may not trouble themselves to understand the consolidation process. Intra-group transactions may cause complications in disentangling them.[15]

14.4 INSTITUTIONS

There is general introduction in Chapter 1 to the impact of institutions on accounting practice. This section expands on that work in relation to Hungary. In particular, for Hungary it is essential to understand the very significant changes in the political and economic systems which took place from 1988 onwards.

14.4.1 Political and economic system[16]

Political change took place across central Europe in the late 1980s. The collapse of Soviet-dominated communist governments affected countries across eastern Europe, including Hungary.[17] At the end of the 1980s, Hungary made a major change from being a centrally run economy to one dominated by the free market.[18] The first post-socialist government, led by the centre-right Hungarian Democratic Forum, initiated a policy of privatisation[19] but the direction of policy on privatisation moved from a decentralised approach to one of centralised privatisation. The initial goals had been expressed in economic terms; they were gradually modified towards political aims. A new coalition government, comprising the Hungarian Socialist Party and the Alliance of Free Democrats, took office in 1994. Its aim was to accelerate privatisation and encourage the development of commercial firms rather than state-run organisations. The progress of legislation was slow from the initial enabling law of 1989 but the Privatisation Act was eventually passed in 1995, amalgamating the State Property Agency and the State Holding Company. The Act included considerable bureaucratic control of privatisation transactions; cash sales are permitted, but there is also leeway for preferential schemes supporting employees and small domestic investors.

The history of the privatisation developments is a useful illustration of the retention of political control of the economic system within the overall move towards free markets. However there are aspects of Hungarian culture which predate the communist takeover of the 1940s and those historical aspects have survived to influence legislation and economic affairs and may be seen to have an influence on accounting practice in particular. The development of commerce and business in the late nineteenth and into the early twentieth century was influenced by close links with Austria and Germany. After the First World War, Hungary lost two-thirds of its territory and three-fifths of its population; it was then helped by Germany in developing new industrialisation. After the Second World War, it became subject to 40 years of Soviet communism until 1989.

---

15 Interview research reported by Krieglsteiner (1996), pp. 96–100
16 Borda and McLeay (1996), pp. 117–20
17 Garrod and McLeay (1996), Chapter 1
18 Borda and McLeay (1996), pp. 117–20
19 Canning and Hare (1996)

14.4.1.1 Central planning

Communist approaches to the economic system were imposed on Hungary from the onset of the People's State in 1949. Central planning dominated in the 1950s and 1960s. Although the fall of the communist government was the trigger for the major change from a centrally run economy, the change was not instantaneous. The New Economic Mechanism of 1968 had tried to ensure the achievement of the central plan through financial incentives. After 1968, companies could retain part of their profit, calculated at 60% of the depreciation charge. There was cessation of directive planning and tax reform, together with price reform and the removal of some price controls. At the same time, companies were regulated through profit as a measure of efficiency, a basis of performance evaluation and a criterion for allocation of resources. In 1980, competitive pricing was introduced in part, replacing the 'cost plus' approach taken by the Ministry of Finance, intended to encourage companies to make domestic prices competitive with export prices so that they were not achieving higher prices on the domestic market.[20] Reform in the 1980s also looked to decentralisation of the industrial base and encouragement of smaller more entrepreneurial businesses.

The New Economic Mechanism proved to have weaknesses through difficulties in foreign trade, problems of the national economy and government budget deficits. In 1987, a form of competitive capitalism was introduced whereby an entrepreneurial approach would be encouraged and the risk of bankruptcy would become a real one.[21] Reorganisation of the state bank in 1987 into a two-tier system led to a central bank and commercial banks. The commercial banks were expected to be managed in an entrepreneurial manner, this created the potential for bankruptcies, but generally bad debts were concealed because the government continued to subsidise the loss-making state-owned ventures. Unemployment was unacceptable and so employees made redundant continued to be paid during a period of job search.

14.4.1.2 The free market system

In this context of the failure of economic development in Hungary up to 1989, the major transition to a free market system, with reform of business ownership, was put in train. The political changes of 1994 brought in a socialist government but it remained committed to the free market system. Reforms in the 1990s have involved the banking system, foreign investment and the use of joint ventures, privatisation, and the capital markets. The slowest change has perhaps been that of privatisation, particularly in relation to the utility companies and others of national strategic importance.

Stabilisation measures were introduced by the Hungarian government in March 1995 with the aim of improving external and internal equilibrium by 1997. The focus of government policy became economic growth and the curbing of inflation, with action taken to devalue the forint and adopt a package of measures to shift resources from domestic consumption to export. As a result of the stabilisation

---

[20] Borda and McLeay (1996), p. 119
[21] Borda and McLeay (1996), p. 119

measures, the deficit in the balance of trade declined and net external debt was reduced. Growth from 1997 was planned to be driven by an increase in exports and a growth in investment, and a target of single-digit inflation was set for 1999.[22]

14.4.2 Legal system[23]

It should be noted that it is difficult to specify a date for Hungarian legislation because there is frequently a time lag between adoption by the legislature and effective implementation. The following section will concentrate on implementation, but will give both dates where possible. In 1989, Hungary began establishing the legal framework necessary to meet European standards of business practice. The Companies Act introduced in 1988 was put into practice in 1989, along with a law on Business Associations, and a law on Investment by Foreigners in Hungary. Previous laws regulating wages were abolished.[24]

The law on privatisation was set out in the Transformation of Business Organisations and Companies Law 1989. A Valuation Decree established the principles of initial pricing of shares and valuation of net assets; a State Property Agency was established to ensure that state assets were sold at fair prices. As the 1990s progressed, further organisations were set up under legislation to implement privatisation.

The insolvency Law of 1991 was put into effect in 1992 and amended in 1993. General principles of insolvency were already in place, but the procedures for taking action on bankruptcy were tightened so that automatic liquidation takes place if the debtor and creditor cannot reach agreement within 90 days.[25]

Laws were also passed in 1991 to set up a two-tier banking system (National Bank of Hungary Law 1991 and Commercial Banks and Banking Activities Law 1991). A general scheme of classification by legal system, as proposed by Salter and Doupnik (1992), does not include the former socialist countries of eastern Europe but the text on which their work is based (David and Brierley, 1985) identifies a separate family of socialist laws. These formerly belonged to the Romano-Germanic System and therefore preserve some of those characteristics. The Hungarian legal system has parallels to the Germany approach.

14.4.2.1 Forms of business organisation[26]

The Companies Act implemented in 1989 established the public limited company (abbreviated as Rt) and the private limited company (abbreviated as Kft), resembling respectively the German AG and GmbH forms. The Kft had been regulated previously by a law dating from 1930.

Many aspects of the operations of these companies resemble those found in Germany. All Rts and any Kfts with more than 200 employees are required to appoint a supervisory board which includes employee representatives. Growth in the number of Rts and Kfts was rapid under the new economic system (*see* Exhibit 14.2).

---

[22] Web pages of the Hungarian government ministries (September 1997)
[23] Borda and McLeay (1996), pp. 120–3
[24] Borda and McLeay (1996), p. 120
[25] Borda and McLeay (1996), p. 123
[26] Borda and McLeay (1996), pp. 120–1; KPMG (1990)

Exhibit 14.2 HUNGARY: GROWTH IN PUBLIC AND PRIVATE LIMITED COMPANIES, 1989–96

Type of company	31 Dec 1989	Registered at 31 Mar 1994	1996
Public limited company	307	2,588	3,536
Limited company	4,485	77,015	122,044
State enterprises	2,399	943	456

Source: Adapted from National Bank of Hungary, *Monthly Report*, 4/5, 1994, reported in Borda and McLeay (1996), Web page of Ministry for Finance and Industry (1996 column).

Formation of joint ventures was facilitated by the Law on Investment by Foreigners in Hungary (1988). A permit from the Ministries of Finance and Trade is required only where the foreign party wishes to acquire a controlling interest. A foreign individual may own a majority stake in a Hungarian company, and there is protection under the law for the interests of the foreign investor.

14.4.2.2 The Accounting Law[27]

The Accounting Law 1991 was written with the intention of being compatible with the Fourth and Seventh Directives. Its purpose is to ensure the production of information that is sufficiently comprehensive and accurate to present a true and fair view of the profit or loss of the period, the net assets and the financial position. The law defines requirements for reporting and bookkeeping and basic principles of accounting. There are rules for independent auditing and for publication of financial statements. The Accounting Law 1991 implemented the Fourth Directive and, in s. 8, contained the provisions for implementing the Seventh Directive. An amending law taking effect in 1994 corrected some details of the 1991 Law and brought forward the effective implementation of the consolidated reporting requirements.

The Accounting Law did not adopt all aspects of the Fourth Directive, some being left for subsequent attention. The apparent deviations are listed in Exhibit 14.3. Valuations of securities may not be written down where there is a short-term fluctuation. There is some reluctance to account for a participating interest under equity accounting, and the limit is higher than that allowed by the EU. Provisions are established with some restrictions on what may be included. There are some detailed differences in foreign currency translation of cash balances. Provisions for doubtful debts are restricted, itemised recording of inventory is required and segmental information is not a condition. These differences relate to the lingering effects of past practice, which will be explained later in the chapter.

---

[27] Borda (1995), p. 1405

Exhibit 14.3 APPARENT DEVIATIONS FROM REQUIREMENTS OF THE FOURTH DIRECTIVE

Item	Hungarian Accounting Law, 1991	Fourth Directive
Valuation of securities and investments	Securities and investments are carried at cost A write-down is not allowed unless the market value is below cost for one year (para. 33)	Article 31 contains general principles of valuation which would not allow an investment to be carried at cost where there was a foreseeable loss
Participating interest	In the various aspects where a significant influence creates a requirement for further disclosures, the Law states that a significant influence is a holding of more than 25% (para. 60)	Article 43 stipulates that member states cannot fix this limit at more than 20%
Provisions	The Law lists the type of provisions which may be utilised Provisions for expected losses can be created only for doubtful receivables which are overdue at the year-end and which remain unpaid at the preparation date Provisions for expected obligations can be used only for guarantees defined by law, while other types of provisions are allowed only for insurance companies and institutions (para. 27)	Article 20 requires provisions for all items which at the date of the balance sheet are either likely to be incurred or certain to be incurred but uncertain as to amount or as to the date on which they will arise Member states may authorise further provisions, within guidance provided by the Article, but there is no authority to restrict the list of provisions
Valuation of current assets	The Law requires that foreign exchange cash balances be carried at the lower of the year-end balance and the original HUF book value The Law requires that foreign currency-denominated receivables are valued at the amount of HUF received if paid between the balance sheet date and the preparation date If the receivable is unpaid then it is valued at the lower of the HUF value at the balance sheet date and the original HUF at the invoice date (para. 32)	Article 39 requires, as a general principle, that current assets are to be valued at the lower of cost or market value at the balance sheet date Under Article 39(1)(c) member states may permit exceptional value adjustments where, on the basis of a reasonable commercial assessment, these are necessary if the valuation of these items is not to be modified in the near future because of fluctuations in value
Doubtful accounts receivable	The Law permits provisions only for doubtful accounts receivable which are overdue at the year end (para. 27)	Article 39 has a wider scope for provision, as explained above

Exhibit 14.3 continued

Item	Hungarian Accounting Law, 1991	Fourth Directive
Inventory	The Law requires itemised recording of inventory (para. 42) and recording at the lower of cost or market value for each item	Article 39 does not specify itemised valuation, but lower of cost or market value is required
Segmental information	The Law does not require the disclosure of segmental information	Article 43(8) specifies segmental disclosures

Source: Boross *et al.* (1995), Table 4, *The European Accounting Review*, Vol 4, No 4, pp. 713–37

14.4.2.3 Change in accounting law

In several areas advantage has been taken of the options available in the Directive (Exhibit 14.4). The lack of opportunity for revaluation of fixed assets and the requirement for cost rather than equity accounting both show a conservative attitude to valuation which is found in other countries where fiscal and accounting profit go hand in hand. The lack of any reference in the law to deferred tax accounting could be taken to provide further evidence of the continuing influence of fiscal policy on accounting practice. However, the payment of tax takes place frequently during the year so that the concept of deferral does not in practice arise.

Exhibit 14.4 CHANGES IN ACCOUNTING PRACTICE UNDER 1991 LAW

Subject	Former practice	New Accounting Law
Balance sheet categories	No distinction of long-term or short-term assets and liabilities, other than fixed assets	Long-term and short-term assets and liabilities distinguished
Tangible fixed assets	Recorded at cost, no provision for diminution in value, other than depreciation which was in accordance with taxation authority rules	Recorded at lower of purchase price (or production cost) and net realisable value. Value must not exceed historical cost. Depreciation can differ from taxation depreciation, rates to be determined by the company but must be realistic
Materiality	Fixtures, fittings and equipment with value less than HUF 50,000 were reflected in stock, written down by 50% when put into use and 50% on disposal	Fixtures, fittings and equipment with value less than HUF 20,000 may be written off on acquisition

511

Exhibit 14.4 continued

Subject	Former practice	New Accounting Law
Intangible assets	Record at cost, no amortisation	Capitalise only where acquired from third party, amortise over specified periods, depending on nature of asset (e.g. goodwill over 5–15 years)
Investments	Record at cost	Consolidate if holding exceeds 50%; equity accounting for 25% or more
Inventory	Record at cost: retail stock at selling price No provision for obsolescence	Record at lower of cost and net realisable value
Receivables	Record at cost No provision for bad or doubtful debts Permission of court required to write off accounts	Record at cost Provide for doubtful debts
Deferred taxes	No provision; accounting and taxable income were the same	No specific guidance in the legislation, but timing differences will arise because provisions for obsolete inventory and doubtful debts can be deducted for tax purposes only if written off the books
Foreign currency	Year-end rate for all amounts except contribution to capital, which is at historical rate	Translate at lower of historical and year-end rates

Source: Boross *et al.* (1995), Table 1 (adapted), *The European Accounting Review*, Vol 4, No 4, pp. 713–37

One interesting aspect of the Accounting Law 1991 is its attention to detail beyond that required by the Directives and particularly the preservation of the importance of the bookkeeping process and the chart of accounts from an earlier period. Particular aspects of the law which show emphasis on the bookkeeping process are set out in Exhibit 14.5.

In a research paper discussing influences on the accounting law, the views of accountants on the derivation of the new law were sought.[28] In particular, they were asked which aspects of the 1991 law were perceived as being influenced by past practice (Exhibit 14.6).

There appears to be a strong element of the past in the present Hungarian law, which could be dismissed as being nothing worse than bureaucratic and time-consuming, but could go further in distorting the ability of accounting statements to represent the economic substance of transactions. The influence of the book-keeping system is a particular factor reflecting the culture and history of Hungary

---

[28] Boross *et al.* (1995)

Exhibit 14.5 ASPECTS OF 1991 LAW SHOWING EMPHASIS ON THE BOOKKEEPING PROCESS

Para.	*Provision*
7	All entrepreneurs keeping double entry books must prepare annual reports
10(3)	If the mode of bookkeeping changes then the reporting obligations also change
12	Specifies who must use double entry, who should use single entry, and who has the choice
15	Accounting principles govern bookkeeping and accounts preparation
16	Closing date for double entry bookkeeping is 31 December
Appendix 2	Capitalised value of own work done is at prime cost only

Source: Boross *et al.* (1995), Table 2, *The European Accounting Review*, Vol 4, No 4, pp. 713–37

Exhibit 14.6 ASPECTS OF 1991 LAW PERCEIVED AS BEING INFLUENCED BY PAST PRACTICE

Item identified
• Strict regulation that 31 December is the year-end date
• Regulations that are too restrictive, e.g. low-value software has to be considered as a fixed asset
• Certain tax aspects
• Continued use of the chart of accounts
• The requirement for certifying the company reports was introduced in stages and is an influence of the past
• Not as flexible as western regulations
• Items such as formation and usage of capital and retained earnings; interpretation of maintenance work are taken from the old law
• Provisions not fully allowed for tax purposes. Attitudes to expensing/allowances are affected by bureaucratic rules

Source: Boross *et al.* (1995), Table 8, *The European Accounting Review*, Vol 4, No 4, pp. 713–37

which could be contrasted with the different culture and history of countries where the accountants would be more used to regarding the bookkeeping system as the servant of the financial statements rather than the master. The influence of fiscal policy, with its domestic orientation, could be in conflict with the needs of entrepreneurs to raise finance in the international markets.

There are considerably detailed rules on preparation of financial statements. Appendix 2 to the Law, for example, contains 26 regulations relating to items in the profit and loss account, of which the following is typical:

8. The invoiced and paid price under a contract which does not include deductible general turnover tax for material-type services (travelling, forwarding, loading, packaging, leasing, commission work, external maintenance of assets not qualified as overhauling, postal services) used or [performed] during the calendar year shall be shown as costs of material-type services.

The law has compromised between the old system and the needs of the new market economy by preserving a prescribed minimum obligation in respect of publication (presentation to the general meeting and lodgement at the Court of Registration) but also allowing more detail according to the needs of the entrepreneur, owner or creditor. This could give rise to a concern that if the needs of the new market participants are not specified in the law, they will not be met on a voluntary basis unless the company is specifically seeking new finance. At other times, the company will concentrate on compliance with the minimum requirements as set out in the law.

Although some of the more idiosyncratic valuation methods have been eliminated and the formal link with taxation regulations severed, the law contains no positive guidance in directing companies to meet the needs of the new market economy; it merely allows them to find their own methods of doing so, should they wish.

14.4.2.4 Consulting with interest groups

It has been stated that the provisions of the new accounting law were worked out by the accounting department of the Ministry of Finance, taking into consideration the opinions of future users of accounting information such as the Union of Entrepreneurs, Chamber of Commerce, managers of enterprises, the World Bank, academics, experts from the international accountancy firms, foreign and domestic accounting and auditing associations and the worldwide accounting profession.[29]

The Accounting Law established a National Accounting Board, comprising experts in the field, whose duties were stated to include setting accounting standards and making recommendations to the Ministry of Finance. It is intended that eventually this Board will become a generally acknowledged professional body of experts, independent of government.[30]

The survey in 1993 asked accountants in Hungary which factors were perceived to have influenced the preparation of the Accounting Law 1991. The responses are indicated in Exhibit 14.7.

14.4.2.5 Learning about change

Many useful books and articles were published about the Accounting Law 1991, in order to help the change take place. In particular the originators of the law published the first volume of a series of 'Blue Books' on the Accounting Law and the Annual Report.[31] These books explained the Law and the Annual Report, setting out the text of the law together with supplementary explanation. Because these books were issued by the originators of the law, they were associated with the law

---

[29] Borda (1992), p. 947
[30] Borda and McLeay (1996), p. 128
[31] Nagy (1991)

Exhibit 14.7 FACTORS PERCEIVED BY HUNGARIAN ACCOUNTANTS TO HAVE INFLUENCED THE 1991 LAW, RANKED IN ORDER OF IMPORTANCE

Very strong influence

- Fiscal policy and tax collecting
- Move to EC membership

Moderately strong influence

- Need to attract foreign capital investment
- Experts from international accountancy firms
- World Bank
- Government need for statistical data

Weaker influence

- The Association of Hungarian Auditors
- Requirements of shareholders
- Requirements of creditors
- Development of a Stock Exchange
- Union of Entrepreneurs
- Chamber of Commerce
- Managers of enterprises
- Academics

Source: Boross *et al.* (1995), Table 10, *The European Accounting Review*, Vol 4, No 4, pp. 713–37

to the extent that the supplementary explanations are regarded by some readers as being part of it. The English-language guides[32] published by international accountancy firms contained supplementary explanations similar to those found in the Blue Books.

As a result of ambiguities discovered when the law became operational, some modifications were made in 1994.[33] The Seventh Directive was not implemented in Hungary until 1995.

14.4.3 Taxation system[34]

Tax law is separate from accounting law. Personal income tax and value added tax were introduced in Hungary as new taxes in the tax law of 1988. Basic principles of the taxation of business profit were also established in the 1988 law.

---

[32] Published by Coopers and Lybrand, for example
[33] Nagy (1994)
[34] KPMG (1990); Koltay (1992)

14.4.3.1 Taxable profit[35]

Companies pay corporation tax. The basis of assessment of business profit is the profit reported in the balance sheet of the taxable entity, and that reported profit is modified by adjustments specified in the tax law. Losses may be carried forward for two years. There are special tax allowances for joint ventures, and special tax allowances are also given to specific activities which the government wishes to encourage. Self-assessment is in place, so that companies must calculate and declare the amount of tax they are due to pay.

14.4.3.2 Tax on distributions[36]

Specific categories of income are taxed under special rules. Dividends are taxed at a relatively low flat rate (compared with a progressive rate of income tax generally). A withholding tax is applied to payments made by a Hungarian resident to a non-resident in respect of some types of income but no withholding tax is applied to dividends paid to corporate investors. Dividends paid to individuals may be subject to withholding tax. There are double tax treaties with a considerable number of countries.

14.4.3.3 Past influence of tax on accounting

It has been explained that the government, in the period before economic reform, encouraged the showing of unreal profit in financial statements because this could increase the state budget tax receipts.[37] The concept of ownership interest was absent so that there was no problem if a company paid tax on the basis of a profit which did not exist. It has been suggested that this influence may be traced forward[38] into those aspects of the new law which differ from EC Directives. Inventory valuation, for example, under the new law is restricted in the variety of permissible methods because there is a government concern that allowing valuation alternatives could reduce the state budget cash receipts. Similarly,[39] writing off cumulative bad debts, writing off obsolete inventories and using accelerated depreciation methods would lower state cash receipts derived from taxation.

Prior to the new Accounting Law, part of the accounting regulation was included in the entrepreneurial income tax law.[40] Disentangling the accounting law from the tax law has meant changes in the structure of expenses; the range and amount of accountable expenses; and taking to profit and loss account items that might previously have been taken directly to reserves for tax reasons. However the formal disentanglement has not necessarily removed the practical interaction of tax and accounting matters (*see* discussion below).

---

[35] Rooz *et al.* (1996)
[36] Coopers and Lybrand International Tax Network (1995)
[37] Borda (1992), p. 962
[38] Borda (1992), p. 962
[39] Borda (1992), p. 957
[40] Coopers and Lybrand (1992), p. 74

14.4.4 Corporate financing system

14.4.4.1 Equity investors[41]

The Budapest Commodity and Security Exchange (BSE) was established in 1864. It ceased to operate under communist rule but was the first eastern European exchange to reopen in 1990. The supervisory authority is the Hungarian Banking and Capital Market Supervision (HBCMS). The legal framework is laid down in the Securities Act 1990. The BSE council is entrusted with the approval and amendment of the day-to-day rules.[42] Establishing a stock exchange requires other economic reforms which may not happen immediately. The currency has to be fully convertible and the national economy has to be stable, with inflation and interest rates under control. These factors were not brought under control at the start of the 1990s, and so the effective operation of the market was delayed. There has been an expansion of listings on the Budapest stock exchange (see *The LGT Guide to World Equity Markets 1997*). Listings of companies between 1992 and 1996 doubled from 23 companies in 1992 to 45 companies in 1996. Market value of the companies listed increased far more rapidly, from 47.2 billion forints in 1992 to 852.5 billion forints in 1996.

As explained elsewhere in this chapter, effective implementation of privatisation was delayed until the mid-1990s. Direct foreign investment (FDI) has been directed more towards investment through the banking system and through bond issues on the securities market.

The BSE has contributed to the requirements for accounting information by requiring disclosure of certain types of information. Companies seeking a listing must provide a detailed prospectus, approved by the HBCMS. There are two listing categories on the BSE, based on size, and once listed a company must conform to specific disclosure requirements. Category A companies must file quarterly reports with the BSE and Category B must file semi-annual reports. There are time limits on filing. The annual report containing the audited accounts must be filed with the BSE.[43] The Stock Exchange encourages submission of accounts prepared in accordance with International Accounting Standards.[44]

In 1996 the Hungarian stock market index (BUX) rose 125% in dollar terms as compared with 59% for the corresponding Warsaw index and 20% for Prague. This reflected the strict fiscal and monetary policies put in place in 1995.[45] Increased foreign participation in the market contributed to greater liquidity and a higher trading volume. At the end of 1996 there were 45 traded stocks, but trading was heavily concentrated among a small number of those stocks. Daily share turnover during 1996 was substantially higher than in 1995 but remained low by international comparisons.[46] About 85% of the market's free float is held by foreigners.[47]

---

[41] Borda and McLeay (1996), pp. 123–4; Arthur Andersen & Co (1991)
[42] LGT (1997), p. 212
[43] LGT (1997), pp. 214–15
[44] Arthur Andersen (1991), p. 37
[45] *Financial Times, FT 500 Survey*, 24 January 1997, p. 16
[46] Coopers and Lybrand web site, *International Briefings – Central Europe*
[47] LGT (1997), p. 210

14.4.4.2 Top companies

From the *Financial Times FT 500*[48] annual survey there are three Russian companies as the only eastern European companies in the top 500 world companies, measured by market capitalisation. However, a separate list is provided for the eastern Europe top 50 companies. Three Hungarian companies were listed in the top 50 eastern European companies at January 1998. The highest eastern European company at that date was Gazprom, a Russian company, ranked 91 in the world and 23 in Europe. The Hungarian companies are MOL (market capitalisation at January 1998 $2,150m), ranked 455 in Europe and 17 in Eastern Europe, Richter Gedeon ($1,964m), ranked 477 in Europe and 19 Eastern Europe, and OTP Bank ($885m), ranked 32 in Eastern Europe.

The data in Exhibit 14.8, showing the top ten Hungarian companies by market capitalisation, was extracted from Datastream towards the end of 1997. The market capitalisation is measured in pounds sterling (converted from forints).

Exhibit 14.8 TOP TEN LISTED HUNGARIAN COMPANIES, 1997

	Name	*Market cap £m (Sept 97)*	*Rank in eastern Europe (Jan 98)*	*Sector*
1	MOL Magyar	1,248	17	Oil international
2	Richter Gedeon	1,061	19	Drugs and pharmaceuticals
3	OTP Bank	516	32	Commercial banks
4	Borsodchem	249	–	Other
5	Egis	34	–	Drugs and pharmaceuticals
6	Graboplast	171		Textiles
7	Danubius Hotel & Spa	136		Hotels
8	Pannonplast	122		Diversified industrial
9	Pick Szeged	119		Food production
10	Prímagáz Hungária	113		Gas distribution

Source: Datastream (1997)

14.4.4.3 Privatisation[49]

Although privatisation was a stated policy of the post-socialist government, there had already been a considerable expansion in private enterprise activity after 1982, and the change in direction of the policy on privatisation was in reaction against earlier spontaneous privatisation. There was more than one view on the mechanism of privatisation. At least initially, voucher privatisation was rejected,

---

[48] *Financial Times, FT 500 Survey*, 22 January 1998
[49] Benkó and Török (1997), p. 77

and there was also privatisation through stock market flotation, foreign acquisition, purchase bid and self-privatisation.[50] The following case studies indicate the practicalities of privatisation.

Case study 14.1

MOL MAGYAR

The largest listed company, MOL Magyar, is a privatised oil and gas company, and it provides an interesting case study on the approach to privatisation. The government wished the company to remain an integrated company, despite its size. In August 1995 the government announced that 35% of the shares of the company would be sold, with 33% being made available for international placement and the remaining 2% for Hungarian domestic investors through the BSE, a further 3% would be offered to employees. Separately, five gas distribution companies were offered for sale by tender. The employee share sale and the private placement were completed by November.

Competition for the gas distribution companies came from the UK, France, Germany and Italy. Tenders were invited for 50% plus one share. The bidder who won the highest region was not permitted to acquire any other. No single bidder could acquire more than two of the other regions. The largest company went to an Italian bidder, two more to France and one to Germany. The final company was bid for a second time and acquired by a German consortium.

Case study 14.2

RICHTER GEDEON AND EGIS

Richter Gedeon is a pharmaceutical company founded in 1901. In September 1994 the company raised $68 million through an international share offer. The State Holding Agency retained 62.5%. There is no joint venture link with any foreign investor.[51] Egis is another pharmaceutical company, founded in 1912. In 1993 the European Bank for Reconstruction and Development (EBRD) acquired a 30% ownership stake in the company. A public offer sold further shares and the State Asset Management Company reduced its stake to 28%.[52]

---

[50] We are grateful to Professor Derek Bailey for this observation
[51] Benkó and Török (1997), p. 116
[52] Benkó and Török (1997), pp. 116–17

Case study 14.3

PANNONPLAST

Pannonplast was privatised by first reorganising it as a holding company. The management initiated the change, so as to present the company in a focused manner which would attract professional investors. The company is regarded as having been successful in this strategy.[53]

14.4.4.4 Bank lending

Since 1987, there has been a two-tier banking system in Hungary with a central bank and a commercial banking sector. Most banks remain in state ownership, with a small number of joint venture banks. Commercial banks, specialised banks and financial institutions are sources of finance and financial services. Bank legislation is based on the EU Banking Directives. The central bank has responsibility for monetary policy.

14.4.4.5 International financing[54]

In creating a market economy and establishing a capital market, Hungary has looked to foreign investment to provide working capital for businesses as well as longer-term investment in fixed assets. The facility to establish joint ventures existed from 1972 but there were many administrative barriers and no real outside interest was shown until the laws enacted in 1988 and 1989 gave easier access, and some protection, to foreign inward investment. A foreigner may acquire a stake in an existing operating company, or found a new joint venture, or establish a wholly owned venture located in Hungary. Particular interest has been shown in telecommunications, the processing industry, electricity and gas service, retail trade and the banking sector.

Incentives have been made available to encourage FDI. These include investment tax preferences; regional and other tax preferences; special concessions on dividend tax; concessions on research and development expenditure being used to reduce the tax base; depreciation write-off at special rates; and some direct subsidies.[55]

14.4.4.6 Joint ventures

Joint ventures are particularly interesting from an accounting viewpoint. As already mentioned, the law changed from 1989 to encourage foreign investment in joint ventures. By the end of 1995, the Ministry of Industry, Trade and Tourism indicated that foreign owned and joint venture companies, totalling some 25,000, were estimated to account for around 25% of privately owned entrepreneurial assets and to produce 70% of Hungary's export income.[56]

---

[53] Benkó and Török (1997), p. 54
[54] KPMG (1990)
[55] Web page of the Hungarian Ministry of Industry, Trade and Tourism (September 1997)
[56] Quoted in Canning and Hare (1996), section 5.3

14.4.5 The accounting profession[57]

The profession has historically been that of the auditing profession, out of which accounting has emerged.

14.4.5.1 Professional body

The Association of Hungarian Auditors was founded in 1932. During the years of central planning the association was not active because external audit was not featured. In the 40 years of central planning the accounting function was that of bookkeeper. The Association re-established itself, and from 1987 is a member of the International Federation of Accountants (IFAC).

A change of name to the Hungarian Chamber of Auditors took place in 1991. Decrees in 1992 defined a process for qualifying as a chartered accountant, setting out requirements based on the EU Eighth Directive. Essential conditions are a university degree, further examinations leading to an award by the Ministry of Finance, and four years' practical experience. Achievement of the qualification allows the person to be employed as a statutory auditor.

14.4.5.2 Learning the new system[58]

Those who had acquired their qualifications under the old system found that they had to attend courses and think about what change would mean for their profession and their individual careers. The success of the law would depend significantly on how well the individuals reacted to the changing requirements imposed on the accounting profession, and how adequate the re-education process was. In 1991 and 1992 various state and private organisations ran courses on the law. Two of the most popular courses were those organised by the Ministry of Finance and by the local authorities, the ten-day courses of the Ministry were attended by more than 10,000 accountants and auditors, while the shorter courses of the local authorities were attended by 12,000 people. The international accounting firms also organised courses.

14.4.6 External influences

The political history of Hungary contains various periods of independence, conquest, alliances, and new independence, all of which have in turn influenced strongly the practice of accounting in Hungary. For a period of 40 years to the end of the 1980s, accounting in Hungary was influenced by socialist politics and economics.[59] A more long-standing link with Austria and Germany, and the continuing trade links with these countries, show in those aspects of accounting practice which were embedded before the influx of socialism and in the options which the Hungarian legislators have favoured in more recent implementation of the EU Directives.

In the period of developing a market economy in the 1990s, Hungary has received a wide range of external advisers from western Europe, advising on

---

[57] Borda (1995), pp. 1404–5
[58] Illés *et al.* (1996)
[59] Bailey (1988)

accounting practices and accounting education. One example of educational initiatives lies in the education links established by the UK government through aid under the 'Know-how fund'. International accountancy firms have established a presence in Budapest and are advising Hungarian companies on implementing accounting practices acceptable to EU countries. These accountancy firms produce detailed manuals which soon become guides to established practice.[60]

14.5 SOCIETAL CULTURE AND ACCOUNTING SUBCULTURE

Hofstede (1984) (see Chapter 2) did not apply his analysis of cultural dimensions to eastern Europe. Consequently Gray's (1988) analysis (Chapter 4) does not cover these countries either. It may be too early in the development of accounting practice in Hungary to attempt such a classification based on tradition. It could be speculated that the strong Germanic influence prior to the communist period and the continued strength of economic links with Germany under the free market economy might lead to an expectation that Hungarian accounting practices would converge on the classifications given to Germany. However, features like conservatism in accounting practice remain under government regulatory influence because of economic factors such as the problems of extensive bankruptcies. In general, there are indications that the political system has sought to retain central control of processes such as privatisation so that there have been conflicting signals in the stated desire for a free market economy and the political desire to oversee the process.

In the transition from a former socialist economy and administration, Jaruga (1990) identified Hungary and Poland as former socialist countries which have led the move from a very rigid uniform accounting system under administrative commands to a more adaptive and flexible approach under the influence of economic reforms and democratisation. Jaruga specified four features, existing before reforms in the formerly socialist countries, as being influential on the development of accounting practice. These were the budget (locating Hungary at the end of the spectrum where the state budget had undertaken less of a redistributive role); joint ventures (relatively well known in Hungary); the control function orientation; and increases in management accounting applications. The control function orientation had a macro-economic effect in leading to the uniform plan of accounts and uniform basic accounting principles and a micro-economic effect in that the chief accountant of an enterprise had a role which was mainly focused on financial control on behalf of the Ministry of Finance.

The exploration of overall attitudes shows a distinction according to industry type, with manufacturing industry showing, in general, a stronger adherence to the former practices and service businesses and trading companies showing more evidence of applying the new techniques. It may be that manufacturing industry continues to apply traditional methods of management (and it should be noted that the state sector is likely to be greater in manufacturing, so influencing managerial methods). It is unlikely that accounting change would take place without a

---

[60] *See*, for example, Coopers & Lybrand (1992)

change in the underlying management practices. Research into accounting change is inevitably tied to investigation of management change, and it may be that management has not yet evolved fully to meet the new market conditions.

It has been found in interview-based survey that the attitudes of financial managers repeatedly indicate a desire for the simplest method subject to the constraint of meeting the needs of the business.[61] To some extent, this could be indicative of a size effect because it would normally be the smaller businesses which would look for a choice requiring minimum change. Surveys also show that professional satisfaction is important to employees. However, satisfying the needs of employees does not have to be constrained by company size if it is related to the need of many Hungarian families to take on two jobs of work in order to maintain a decent standard of living. Professional satisfaction may be important, but may have to be weighed against the pragmatism of supporting a family.

It is important to note that, where managerial needs are seen to require it, the more demanding option will be selected notwithstanding the extra work it necessitates. At the same time, financial managers do not espouse change for its own sake – where the old practice is seen to have usefulness for management purposes, it is retained, and there is evidence that this is strongest in manufacturing companies. The value seen in the old practices is predominantly that of usefulness in management. Where change has not taken place, it is rarely a desire to keep up the traditional practice. If there is an inhibiting factor, it is perhaps that the software available has lagged behind the changes in business practice.

14.6 ACCOUNTING REGULATIONS AND THE IASC

The Accounting Law 1991 was drawn up to meet the requirements of the EU Fourth Directive. Modification in 1995 took account of the Seventh Directive. To the extent that IASs are close to the directives this necessarily brought Hungarian accounting practice into the arena of compliance with the disclosure aspects of some IASs. There are several areas where the Hungarian law is silent and so there is no immediate comparison with IASs. Exhibit 14.9 sets out the current position in relation to IASs.

At September 1997, the IASC had identified six Hungarian companies which referred to the use of IASs in their financial statements (Exhibit 14.10).[62]

Examples are set out in Exhibit 14.11 from two of the major listed companies which refer in their accounting policy notes to the use of IASs. Graboplast includes a full set of accounts under IASs, rather than under Hungarian standards, in its English-language version. It does, however, provide a comparison of selected accounting measures under Hungarian accounting standards and IASs (Exhibit 14.12) in its summarised annual report. A full reconciliation is provided in the consolidated financial statement (Exhibit 14.13).

---

[61] Illés *et al.* (1996)
[62] Web pages for IASC

Exhibit 14.9 COMPARISON OF ACCOUNTING PRACTICES IN HUNGARY WITH REQUIREMENTS OF IASs: KEY SIMILARITIES AND DIFFERENCES

IAS	Subject of IAS	Practice in Hungary	Ref
Disclosure and presentation			
	General aspects consolidated in IAS 1 (revised)		
IAS 1	Fair Presentation	'Realistic' report plus notes for 'true' picture	7.2.4
	Disclosure of Accounting Policies (former IAS 1)	Generally in agreement	
	Information to be Disclosed in Financial Statements (former IAS 5)	Generally in agreement	7.3.4
	Presentation of Current Assets and Current Liabilities (former IAS 13)	Generally in agreement	
	Specific aspects		
IAS 7	Cash Flow Statements	No specific requirement	
IAS 8	Net Profit or Loss for the Period, Fundamental Errors and Changes in Accounting Policies	Extraordinary items disclosed separately	7.3.2
IAS 14	Reporting Financial Information by Segments	Not dealt with in legislation	
IAS 24	Related Party Disclosure	Generally not required; some details required on transactions with directors	
IAS 33	Earnings per Share	No specific requirement	
IAS 34	Interim Financial Reporting	Required by Stock Exchange, less detailed than IAS	
Asset recognition and measurement			
IAS 2	Inventories	More flexible than IAS	7.3.5
IAS 4	Depreciation Accounting	Generally in agreement	7.3.3
IAS 16	Property, Plant and Equipment	Generally in agreement; revaluation not permitted	
IAS 23	Borrowing Costs		
IAS 25	Accounting for Investments	More conservative than IAS 25	
IAS 9	Research and Development costs	To be stated in directors' report	
IAS xx	Intangible Assets		
Liability recognition and measurement			
IAS 10	Contingencies and Events Occurring After the Balance Sheet Date	Generally in agreement; post balance sheet events reported in directors' report	4.2.3 7.4.1
IAS 12	Income Taxes	Not dealt with in legislation	
IAS 17	Leases	Not dealt with in legislation – all treated as operating leases	6
IAS 19	Employee Benefits	Contributions reported as incurred	
IAS 32	Financial Instruments: Disclosure and Presentation	Not dealt with in legislation	
Recognition of economic activity			
IAS 11	Construction Contracts	Not dealt with in legislation	
IAS 18	Revenue	Recognised when performance is completed and there is reasonable assurance of collectibility	
IAS 20	Accounting for Government Grants and Disclosure of Government Assistance		

Exhibit 14.9 continued

IAS	Subject of IAS	Practice in Hungary	Ref
Measurement			
IAS 15	Information Reflecting the Effects of Changing Prices	Not dealt with in legislation	
IAS 29	Financial Reporting in Hyperinflationary Economies	Not applied; government policy for control of inflation rate	
Group accounting			
IAS 21	The Effects of Changes in Foreign Exchange Rates	Specific rules on translation of liabilities and receivables	
IAS 22	Business Combinations	Has adopted Seventh Directive	3.2
IAS 27	Consolidated Financial Statements and Accounting for Investments in Subsidiaries	Has adopted Seventh Directive	3.2
IAS 28	Accounting for Investments in Associates	Equity accounting not used	7.3
IAS 31	Financial Reporting of Interests in Joint Ventures	Proportional consolidation permitted	7.3.6

Note: This exhibit should be read in conjunction with Exhibit 14.4, making comparison with the Fourth Directive

Exhibit 14.10 HUNGARIAN COMPANIES REFERRING TO USE OF IASs IN THEIR FINANCIAL STATEMENTS

Name	Rank in Hungarian stock exchange, by market capitalisation
Borsod Chemical Rt	4
Fotex	23
Global	17
Goldsun	Not available
Graboplast	6
Magyar Tavkozlesi Rt	Not available
Primagaz	10
Styl Ruhar	24

As a different approach, Prímagáz provides full and separate accounting statements and notes under both IASs and Hungarian accounting standards. It also provides a detailed reconciliation of all major balance sheet and income statement items for each set of accounting standards (Exhibit 14.14). A Financial Highlights page in the annual report of Prímagáz gives prominence to the IAS measures of key accounting items.

Exhibit 14.11 GRABOPLAST AND PRÍMAGÁZ: ACCOUNTING POLICY NOTES, 1996

Graboplast Rt. and Subsidiaries
Notes to Consolidated Financial Statements
December 31, 1996

2. **Significant accounting policies**

Accounting convention

Graboplast Rt. and its subsidiaries maintain their official accounting records and prepare their financial statements for domestic purposes in accordance with the accounting regulations of Hungary. The accompanying financial statements have been prepared in accordance with International Accounting Standards and, as a consequence, reflect adjustments not recorded in the Hungarian statutory records including leases, deferred leases and negative goodwill.

◗ Notes to the financial statements for the year ended 31 December, 1996

1. General
(a) Basis of preparation of the financial statements
The financial statements have been prepared on the historical cost basis of accounting and in compliance with International Accounting Standards ("IAS").
In common with all other Hungarian businesses, the Company maintains its accounting, financial and other records in accordance with local statutory requirements. In order to present financial statements which comply with IAS, appropriate adjustments have been made to the local statutory accounts. These adjustments are summarised in the Appendix.

Source: Graboplast Rt, annual report, 1996, p. 6 and Prímagáz Hungária Rt, annual report, 1996, p. 15

Exhibit 14.12 GRABOPLAST: FINANCIAL HIGHLIGHTS STATEMENT, 1996

According to Hungarian Accounting Standards:		1995	1996
Net sales	HUF million	11,591	**15,059**
Operating income	HUF million	842	**1,875**
Income before income taxes	HUF million	611	**1,747**
Net income	HUF million	501	**1,397**

According to International Accounting Standards:		1995	1996
Net sales	HUF million	9,531	**14,724**
Operating income	HUF million	920	**2,067**
Income before income taxes	HUF million	695	**1,925**
Net income	HUF million	599	**1,596**

Source: Graboplast Rt, annual report, 1996, p. 3

Exhibit 14.13 GRABOPLAST: RECONCILIATION OF NET INCOME FROM HUNGARIAN
STATUTORY ACCOUNTS TO IASs, 1996

Graboplast Rt. and Subsidiaries
Notes to Consolidated Financial Statements
December 31, 1996
(All amounts of HUF millions, unless otherwise noted)

**22. Reconciliation of Net Income from the Hungarian Statutory Financial
Statements to the Accompanying Consolidated Financial Statements**

	1996	1995
Profit after taxation per Hungarian Statutory accounts	1,408	507
Change in general provision against slow moving stock	(50)	(20)
Net of Foreign currency revaluation	(21)	71
Share issurance costs	95	71
Write off intangibles	0	(36)
Lease adjustments	37	40
Amortisation of goodwill	91	44
Elimination of pre acquisition profits	0	(81)
Provision for environmental damages	(50)	0
Interest on share issue	81	0
Write back of assets previously written off	58	0
Forgiveness of liability	(53)	0
Write off intangibles in HAL	40	0
Written off in IAS previous years	0	0
Tax penalties	(40)	0
Other	0	3
Profit after taxation	1,596	599

Source: Graboplast Rt, annual report, 1996, p. 18

The first task of accounting developments in Hungary is to achieve acceptability in
the EU in the context of meeting the requirements of EU Directives. The focus on
IASs may become greater as the capital market develops but initially the country is
reliant on direct inward investment which is attracted by the potential for links
with EU countries.

Exhibit 14.14 PRÍMAGÁZ: RECONCILIATION OF IASs AND STATUTORY ACCOUNTS, 1996

◼ Appendix · Reconciliation of IAS and statutory accounts

In common with all other Hungarian businesses, the Company maintains its accounting, financial and other records in accordance with local statutory requirements. In order to present financial statements which comply with IAS, appropriate adjustments have been made to the local statutory accounts. These adjustments are summarised as follows:

(a) Summary balance sheet as at 31 December, 1996

HUF'm

	IAS Accounts	(i)	(ii)	Note (iii)	(iv)	(v)	(vi)	Statutory Accounts
Fixed assets								
Operational	8,499	-		(810)	(100)	-	-	7,589
Financial	48	19	-	-	110	-	-	177
	8,547	19		(810)	10	-	-	7,766
Current assets								
Inventories	1,196	-	-	-	-	-	-	1,196
Receivables and prepayments	1,605	-	-	-	118	-	8	1,731
Cash	2,653	-	-	-	-	(1,033)	-	1,620
	5,454	-	-	-	118	(1,033)	8	4,547
Liabilities								
Provisions	(616)	616	-	-	(118)	-	-	(118)
Other liabilities and accruals	(5,146)	-	-	-	-	30	(10)	(5,126)
Deferred income	(176)	-	176	-	-	-	-	-
	(5,938)	616	176	-	(118)	30	(10)	(5,244)
Net assets	8,063	635	176	(810)	10	(1,003)	(2)	7,069
Represented by:								
Share capital	3,600	-	-	-	-	-	-	3,600
Premium on share capital increase	1,716	-	-	-	-	-	-	1,716
Retained earnings (profit reserve)	2,747	635	176	(810)	10	(1,003)	(2)	1,753
	8,063	635	176	(810)	10	(1,003)	(2)	7,069

Exhibit 14.14 continued

◗ **Appendix - Reconciliation of IAS and statutory accounts**
(continued)

(b) Summary statement of income for the year ended 31 December, 1996

HUF'm

	IAS Accounts	(vii)	(viii)	Note (ix)	(x)	(xi)	Statutory Accounts
Sales and other revenues	17,629	-	-	-	-	183	17,812
Cost of sales	(9,890)	-	-	50	-	(1,681)	(11,521)
Gross profit	**7,739**	**-**	**-**	**50**	**-**	**(1,498)**	**6,291**
Operating expenses							
Wages and Salaries	1,707	-	-	-	-	9	1,716
Depreciation	569	-	(8)	488	-	(10)	1,039
Other operating expenses	3,091	-	-	(50)	-	(1,256)	1,785
Total	**5,367**	**-**	**(8)**	**438**	**-**	**(1,257)**	**4,540**
Operating profit	**2,372**	**-**	**8**	**(388)**	**-**	**(241)**	**1,751**
Result of financial activities							
Interest income	125	-	-	-	-	(13)	112
Interest expense	(507)	-	-	-	-	41	(466)
Other financial items	62	-	-	-	(256)	-	(194)
Total	**(320)**	**-**	**-**	**-**	**(256)**	**28**	**(548)**
Extraordinary items	**(9)**	**-**	**-**	**-**	**-**	**13**	**4**
Income before tax	**2,043**	**-**	**8**	**(388)**	**(256)**	**(200)**	**1,207**
Corporation tax	(473)	277	-	-	-	-	(196)
Net income	**1,570**	**277**	**8**	**(388)**	**(256)**	**(200)**	**1,011**

▶

Exhibit 14.14 continued

◾ Appendix - Reconciliation of IAS and statutory accounts

(continued)

(c) Notes

(i) Non-allowable provisions

1. *Financial fixed assets - 19 million*

    Included within assets contributed from the three gas supply companies upon the formation of the Company on 1 May, 1992 were loans to employees with a face value of HUF 29 million. Amounts are due within 25 years and bear no interest. The original provision, made in full against the face value of the loans in the 1992 accounts, has been reduced by amounts received in the meantime.

2. *Other provisions - 616 million*

    See note 13. for analysis.

(ii) Deferred income

See note 15.

(iii) Net book value of working stock of cylinders

Under local accounting regulations assets with an individual gross value of less than HUF 20,000 are depreciated in full in the year of purchase. However, due to their substantial combined value, under the IAS convention cylinders are depreciated over their estimated useful lives.

(iv) Reclassifications

1. *Reclassification of goodwill portion of investment in Alfagas Kft. - 110 million gross value and relating to 10 million depreciation (see note: iv.and xi)*

2. *Bad debt provision - 118 million*

    Trade debtors are stated net of provisions for doubtful amounts.

(v) Foreign exchange gain

Cumulative unrealised exchange gains on ECU bank deposits which are not recognised under local statutory accounting regulations.

(vi) Other

Reclassifications and exchange differences of items.

(vii) Non-allowable provisions

Corporation tax -277 million

(viii) Deferred income

Sales related & other operating expenses - 8 million

Reclassification of depreciation and deferred income on assets purchased from 100% government grant.

(ix) Cylinders

See note (iii) above.

1. *Cost of sales - 50 million*

    Net book value of cylinders sold to customers.

2. *Depreciation - 488 million*

    Cylinders purchased during the year (written off in full in statutory accounts) less depreciation applied to working stock of cylinders under IAS.

(x) Foreign exchange gain

Unrealised exchange gains on ECU bank deposits during the year which are not recognised under local statutory accounting regulations and realised exchange gains on ECU capital deposits accounted for as capital reserves.

(xi) Other

Reclassifications of items due to differing disclosure formats of accounts, reversals of prior year non-allowable accruals.

Source: Prímagáz Hungária Rt, annual report, 1996, pp. 22–4

14.7 THE ACCOUNTING SYSTEM

14.7.1 Current regulation

In discussing detail of particular aspects of accounting practice in Hungary, this section will draw on two surveys reported in research papers. The first, referred to as 'the 1993 survey', was a pilot project based on only 14 accountant respondents.[63] The second, referred to as 'the 1994 survey', was a larger scale survey of those who prepare accounts and those who observe the process.[64]

When respondents in the 1993 survey were asked what significant differences they perceived between the Accounting Law 1991 and previous practice, they answered as shown in Exhibit 14.15.

Exhibit 14.15 1991 LAW AND PREVIOUS LAW: PERCEPTIONS OF SIGNIFICANT DIFFERENCES (1993)

Item identified
● Valuation rules: – Bad debts, year-end valuations   – Provisions, asset values   – Carry forward tax losses   – Stock write-offs   ● New emphasis on principles   ● Closer to European standards and Directives   ● Gives greater independence of decisions on accounts preparation   ● Intended to encourage market economy, but constrained in practice by tax law

Source: Boross *et al.* (1995), *The European Accounting Review*, Vol 4, No 4, pp. 713–37

All these themes will be explored further in the next four sections, which follow Gray's (1988) classification system.

14.7.2 Professionalism versus statutory control

The Accounting Law 1991 introduced the potential for choice in accounting which had not previously existed in the working lives of accountants practising at that time. Accountants were aware that they would in future face accounting choices, some of which would be very important. Responses to the 1994 survey showed the relative perceptions set out in Exhibit 14.16.

---

[63] Boross *et al.* (1995)
[64] Illés *et al.* (1996)

Exhibit 14.16 ACCOUNTANTS' PERCEPTIONS OF IMPORTANT ACCOUNTING CHOICES FACED IN THEIR WORK (1994)

Accounting issue	Number of respondents mentioning this issue
Type of profit and loss account format	14
Depreciation policy	13
Stock valuation	7
Reserves	6
Cost of own production	4
Valuation of debtors	4
The after-calculation	3
Accounting by cost centre	2
Ordinary and extraordinary items	1

Source: Illés *et al.* (1996), Table 2, *The European Accounting Review*, Vol 5, No 3, pp. 523–43

The findings of the 1994 survey were that an existing practice will continue where it is found to be useful in the management of the business, notwithstanding that additional work may be required by the previous method. That suggests an element of professionalism among those practising accounting.

It has been suggested[65] that, under the free market approach, a practitioner seeking to act in the spirit of the law was required to forget the old philosophy of regularity and identify with the philosophy of true and fair value. Within the framework of global rules, the accountant using the law was required to analyse the situation, make the best decision and justify the choice where necessary. Finally the accountant using the law had to be aware that loosening the ties with the tax law could be advantageous to the company, even if it meant more work for the accountants.

14.7.2.1 Requirement for micro-economic information

Once the free market economy had been put in place, accountants had to think, almost for the first time, about meeting the needs of the users of accounting information in a particular enterprise. Respondents to the 1993 survey were asked who they thought would be the principal users of financial statements. The relative importance is measured by the frequency with which each category was mentioned over the total responses (*see* Exhibit 14.17).

It is clear that the introduction of a law to serve the free market did not instantly lead to a change from the perceived importance of the state as a user of accounting information.

When asked about the perceived needs of users of company accounts, respondents in the 1993 survey provided a range of ideas (*see* Exhibit 14.18). The mix of ideas indicates an awareness of the competitive market but also a link to the former macroeconomic purposes of accounting.

---

[65] Illés *et al.* (1996)

Exhibit 14.17 PERCEIVED USERS OF ACCOUNTING INFORMATION (1993) (RANKED IN ORDER OF PERCEIVED IMPORTANCE IN RELATION TO THE 1991 LAW)

Perceived user	Frequency of mention
State regulatory authorities	13
Banks	10
Private owners	9
Intending investors	8
Employees	4
Customers	3
Credit reference agencies	2
Suppliers	1
Competitors	1
No response	1

Source: Boross *et al*. (1995), Table 11, *The European Accounting Review*, Vol 4, No 4, pp. 713–37

Exhibit 14.18 ACCOUNTANTS' PERCEPTIONS OF NEEDS OF THOSE USING COMPANY ACCOUNTS (1993)

- State authorities; all governmental decisions on economic policy might depend on this information. Also tax authorities, in order to forecast tax revenues
- Banks; to monitor credit-worthiness of customers
- Private owners and intending investors
  - Intending investors, in order to base their decisions on most up-to-date and reliable information
  - Investors, to monitor the after-tax performance of their investments
  - Accounting and management, e.g. for supervisory committee, board of directors
  - Ownership, capital, profit distribution and investment
  - Privatisation, investors, banks, merchant banks, IMF/EBRD
- Suppliers, as to the credit-worthiness of their customers
- Competitors, to check on profitability across the industry.

Source: Boross *et al*. (1995), Table 12, *The European Accounting Review*, Vol 4, No 4, pp. 713–37

14.7.2.2 Taking inventory of all assets

Prior to the Accounting Law 1991 it was compulsory to take a physical inventory of all assets each year, for the purpose of preparing the annual balance sheet. The new Law permitted, but no longer required, a full physical inventory of all assets (para. 42).

In the 1994 survey there were indications that that taking full annual inventory remained a widely used practice. There was a distinct preference for the greater accuracy available using actual inventory, the reasons put forward being giving a true and fair view; truth and protection of the assets; most relevant for the operating conditions; tradition and stewardship. The emphasis on the true and fair view was particularly strong in these responses, although this might require further probing as to the understanding of 'true and fair'.

14.7.2.3 Approaches to costing

The professional attitude of making a reasoned choice was applied to cost classification where some companies confirmed in the 1994 survey that they had continued the former practice of taking first the cost centre and second the cost type because it gave more management information where divisional profitability was required. Others said that one method of cost classification would suffice and that cost type alone was sufficient for small companies and was widely used. Software availability may have been a factor inhibiting change.

14.7.2.4 'True and fair' view

Although the Accounting Law has been based on the EU Fourth Directive, the concept of a true and fair view has not been included in such words. The Act requires a 'realistic' report and reliance is placed on the notes to complete a 'true' picture. The principle of truth is one of the generally accepted accounting principles listed in the legislation.[66]

14.7.3 Uniformity versus flexibility

Respondents to the 1994 survey were asked whether choice in accounting matters was helpful to the readers of annual reports. There were 23 positive responses and 13 negative. The negative responses were supported in particular cases with reasons such as:

● method and choice cannot be identified from the published annual report (3)
● most readers do not care about the company's choice; only professionals are interested (2)
● readers might not understand the choice; it has to be explained (2)
● stock exchange news is more useful (1)
● it would be better to follow straightforward regulations (1).

Those who gave negative or nil response replies were found to be spread across the entire spectrum of change revealed by the study, so their view on users did not appear to be a factor which, in itself, relates to the extent of change or choice.

It has already been shown that where the Fourth Directive allowed options, Hungary took some options which allowed it to continue to apply former business practice (*see* Exhibit 14.19).

14.7.3.1 Relationship between tax law and accounting law

It has been explained that tax law and accounting law are separate. However, in the accounts of individual companies accountants may decide to use the tax-based approach in order to avoid unnecessary extra work. In the 1994 survey there was a

---

[66] Borda (1995), p. 1424

Exhibit 14.19 APPLICATION OF THE FOURTH DIRECTIVE WHERE OPTIONS EXIST

Item	Hungarian Law	Fourth Directive
Valuation of fixed assets	Revaluation is not permitted	Article 32 prescribes historical cost valuations; Article 33 permits, but does not require, alternative valuation rules
Equity accounting for a participation where there is a significant influence	The valuation method used is the lower of cost or market (para. 31) subject to the market value being below cost for at least one year (para. 33)	Article 59 permits, but does not require, equity accounting
Deferred taxation accounting	The law makes no regulation regarding deferred taxation Reported income and taxable income are required to be the same	Article 43(11) requires disclosure of deferred taxation, where this is material

Source: Boross *et al.* (1995), Table 3, *The European Accounting Review*, Vol 4, No 4, pp. 713–37

range of views on the relationship between tax law and accounting law. Although respondents indicated awareness that tax law and accounting law were separate, they also said that while the new law appeared flexible the tax laws in practice limited that freedom. The company may choose to produce different statements of profit for accounting and for tax purposes, but time may be saved if the accounting choice lies within the bounds of tax acceptability. It was not clear how frequently they made the accounting choice which was closest to the tax rule.

14.7.3.2 Extraordinary items

Before the Accounting Law 1991, extraordinary items were credited or debited directly to accumulated equity, where permitted by the rules. Under the 1991 Law the profit and loss account formats allows extraordinary events to be reported. However there is no specified method of calculation (para. 49) and the definition is not specific in the law. Those preparing accounts must use their judgement consequently. In the 1994 survey, the respondents' explanation of accounting choice gave a strong impression of taking each transaction separately and evaluating its circumstances rather than applying some standard percentages or other rules of thumb to a base figure such as reported profit. There were some indications that respondents used the tax rules as a guide to accounting practice.

Although the Accounting Law 1991 specifies no particular approach to determining what is an extraordinary item, there is guidance in the Blue Book. As explained earlier, some Hungarian accountants treat this guidance as being effectively part of the 1991 Law. The Blue Book guidance is that the extraordinary item should be considered in the context of its size, value and frequency, and of the company's previous experience. In the 1994 survey there appeared to be knowledge of the Blue Book's recommendation but a general belief that it comprised part of the 1991 Law.

14.7.3.3 Depreciation

Prior to the Accounting Law 1991, depreciation rates were prescribed centrally. Under the Accounting Law companies were permitted to have their own accounting policy (paras 37–38). Tax law continued to specify depreciation policy to be applied for tax accounts.

In the 1994 survey it was suggested that having a separate accounting policy, different from the policy which follows the tax law, would be appropriate only to large companies and foreign joint ventures. Some commented on the practical problems of having an accounting policy differing from the tax law. Of the financial managers, 15 chose an accounting policy which corresponded to the tax law, 13 had an accounting policy which did not follow the tax law and one did not respond. Those keeping close to the tax law gave reasons such as

- our activity does not require any other policy (5)
- any other policy would be extra work (1)
- we are happy with the tax law (1).

Those who had their own accounting policy also had positive reasons:

- influence of foreign partner (3)
- defined by holding company (1)
- variety of machinery (1).

Four acknowledged that having an accounting policy which differed from the tax law did give rise to practical difficulties. Perhaps unsurprisingly no one raised the question as to whether following the tax rules might be in conflict with a true and fair view.

The distribution of answers, in relation to preparation of the statutory financial statements, led to the conclusion that there was to some extent a size effect, with 10 out of 11 small and medium-sized companies (SMEs) tending to follow the tax law. However, the larger companies were split equally, some following the tax law and others devising their own policy. There was also an indication of an international influence, with four out of five such companies showing their policy influenced by the foreign partner or parent. The responses also indicated that relative ease and convenience was a factor.

14.7.3.4 Formats[67]

The type of report required of a company depends on its size and the method of bookkeeping. Where a company uses double entry bookkeeping and meets various size criteria it must produce an annual report comprising a balance sheet, profit and loss account, notes to the accounts and a business report. Companies which

---

[67] Borda (1995), pp. 1408–21

use double entry bookkeeping but fall below the size criteria for compulsory double entry bookkeeping may produce a simplified annual report. Entrepreneurs in relatively small businesses who keep single entry books must prepare a simplified balance sheet.

Formats prescribed in the Accounting Law are based on the Fourth Directive, as explained below.

Profit and loss account

The profit and loss account may use either the total cost model or the cost of sales model (para. 44; Appendix 2). If the cost of sales model is used then the functional approach is taken where manufacturing costs, marketing costs and general administration costs are detailed. Introduction of these two formats initially caused some confusion because the previous practice had placed great emphasis on detailed cost accounting. In particular, companies were obliged to account for cost by cost centre and by type of cost. Under the 1991 Law, it became sufficient to account by type of cost alone, but because of the tradition of detailed practice in costing, some large organisations continued to produce both formats of profit and loss account.

In the 1994 survey it appeared that total cost method was more often used, and was satisfactory, for small business and for non-manufacturing businesses. There was a perception that the total cost method showed the scale of activity while the cost of sales approach showed realised costs and profits. Where companies used only one method they tended to favour total costs, giving reasons such as relative ease of preparation and adequacy for the needs of the business. An example of the 'total cost method' income statement as required by Hungarian statute, is given by Prímagáz (*see* Exhibit 14.20).

Balance sheet

The formats used under the Accounting Law 1991 are acceptable under the Fourth Directive and quite different from those prepared previously. A horizontal balance sheet is required. An example of a balance sheet conforming to the Accounting Law format is given by Prímagáz (*see* Exhibit 14.21).

14.7.3.5 Stock valuation

Prior to the Accounting Law 1991, there were considerable rules in place for management accounting purposes. These were designed to achieve uniformity and to meet the needs of macro-economic information. The 1991 Law provided liberalising provisions incorporating the flexibility of western European practice; however, the management accounting methods remained in use, within the new law, as a basis for stock valuation in financial accounting.

In relation to the manufacturing cost of self-manufactured inventories, a method known as the 'after-calculation' was compulsory under previous practice. This involved accounting initially on the basis of a budgeted cost and subsequently making adjustments for actual costs. Under the Accounting Law 1991 (paras 35, 36), a choice of method is now permitted, with the aim of reporting the actual cost.

Exhibit 14.20 PRÍMAGÁZ: STATEMENT OF INCOME AND RETAINED EARNINGS USING TOTAL COST METHOD, 1996

■ **Statement of income and retained earnings for the year ended 31 December, 1996** (Hungarian statutory accounts)

DESCRIPTION	lines	1995	HUF'000 1996
01 Domestic sales revenues		12,256,587	17,635,982
02 Export sales revenues		12,412	30,909
03 Net sales revenues	(01+02)	12,268,999	17,666,891
04 Other revenues		162,509	144,861
05 Capitalised value of self-manufactured assets		3,264	510,759
06 Change in self-manufactured inventories		2,899	14,783
07 Capitalised value of own performance	(05+06)	6,163	525,542
08 Raw material costs		6,751,887	949,870
09 Value of material-type services used		982,018	1,267,838
10 Purchase price of goods sold		634,968	9,988,682
11 Value of subcontractors' work		61,634	326,450
12 Material-type expenditures	(08+09+10+11)	8,430,507	12,532,840
13 Wage costs		938,300	1,135,359
14 Other payments to personnel		86,325	96,661
15 Social insurance contribution		406,899	484,010
16 Payments to personnel	(13+14+15)	1,431,524	1,716,030
17 Depreciation charge		305,106	1,038,630
18 Other costs		493,500	797,260
19 Other expenditures		298,420	501,149
20 Trading profit	(03+04+07-12-16-17-18-19)	1,478,614	1,751,385
21 Interest received and interest-related revenues		121,705	112,084
22 Dividend and profit-sharing received		-	-
23 Other revenues from financial transactions		105,044	11,662
24 Revenues from financial transactions	(21+22+23)	226,749	123,746
25 Paid interest and interest-related payments		333,428	466,446
26 Write-off of financial investments		-	-
27 Other expenditures on financial transactions		107,933	205,238
28 Financial transaction expenditures	(25+26+27)	441,361	671,684
29 Net financial result	(24-28)	(214,612)	(547,938)
30 Profit before tax and extraordinary items	(±20± 29)	1,264,002	1,203,447
31 Extraordinary revenues		530	14,353
32 Extraordinary expenditures		1,681	10,576
33 Net extraordinary items	(31-32)	(1,151)	3,777
34 Pre-tax net profit	(±30±33)	1,262,851	1,207,224
35 Tax charge		257,447	196,293
36 After tax profit	(34-35)	1,005,404	1,010,931
37 Use of acc. profit reserve for dividends & profit-sharing		-	-
38 Dividend and profit-sharing paid (approved)		480,000	630,000
39 Balance sheet net profit figure	(±36+37-38)	525,404	380,931

Source: Prímagáz Hungária Rt, annual report, 1996, p. 28

Exhibit 14.21 PRÍMAGÁZ: BALANCE SHEET CONFORMING TO HUNGARIAN STATUTORY ACCOUNTS, 1996

◨ Balance sheet as at 31 December, 1996 after proposed dividend
(Hungarian statutory accounts)

		ASSETS	lines	1995	HUF'000 1996
01	A)	**Invested assets**	(02+09+16)	**5,417,436**	**7,766,076**
02	I.	**Intangible assets**	(03 to 08)	**7,758**	**7,429**
03		Right of pecuniary value		-	-
04		Goodwill		-	-
05		Intellectual property		7,758	7,429
06		Capitalised value of research and development		-	-
07		Capitalised value of original contribution/restructuring		-	-
08		Value adjustment of intangible assets		-	-
09	II.	**Tangible assets**	(10 to 15)	**5,365,427**	**7,581,005**
10		Real property		1,690,791	2,314,638
11		Technical equipment, machinery, vehicles		2,417,440	3,924,288
12		Other equipment and fittings		195,011	186,991
13		Investments (work in progress)		982,270	1,153,359
14		Advance payments made towards investments		79,915	1,729
15		Value adjustment of tangible assets		-	-
16	III.	**Financial investments**	(17 to 21)	**44,251**	**177,642**
17		Profit-sharing		-	124,176
18		Securities		-	-
19		Loans		44,251	53,466
20		Long term bank deposits		-	-
21		Value adjustment of financial investments		-	-
22	B)	**Current assets**	(23+30+36+40)	**3,437,301**	**4,538,274**
23	I.	**Inventories**	(24 to 29)	**723,167**	**1,196,421**
24		Raw materials and cumsumables		353,022	637,715
25		Goods for resale		323,878	498,586
26		Advance payments made towards inventories		856	310
27		Livestock		-	-
28		Raw materials and work in progress		2,679	-
29		Finished products (filled gas)		42,732	59,810
30	II.	**Receivables**	(31 to 35)	**1,215,857**	**1,721,545**
31		Accounts receivable from supply of goods		1,064,077	1,458,697
32		Draft receivables		-	-
33		Unpaid issued capital		-	-
34		Claims against founding members		-	-
35		Other receivables		151,780	262,848
36	III.	**Securities**	(37 to 39)	**-**	**-**
37		Bonds bought for sale		-	-
38		Own shares, share quotas, shares bought for sale		-	-
39		Other securities		-	-

▶

Exhibit 14.21   continued

▶ Balance sheet as at 31 December, 1996 after proposed dividend
(Hungarian statutory accounts)
(continued)

		ASSETS	lines	1995	1996
40	IV.	**Liquid assets**	(41 to 42)	**1,498,277**	**1,620,308**
41		Cash, cheques		241,957	9,701
42		Bank deposits		1,256,320	1,610,607
43	C)	**Pre-paid expenses**		**21,948**	**9,079**
44		**Total**	(01+22+43)	**8,876,685**	**12,313,429**

		SOURCES (LIABILITIES)		1995	1996
45	D)	**Equity**	(46 to 51)	**4,278,321**	**7,069,127**
46		Issued capital		3,200,000	3,600,000
47		Capital reserve		115,042	2,131,562
48		Accumulated profit reserve		437,875	956,634
49		Evaluation reserve		-	-
50		Losses carried forward from previous years		-	-
51		Balance sheet profit figue after taxation		525,40 ⁎	380,931
52	E)	**Provisions**	(53 to 55)	**19,102**	**117,919**
53		Provisions for expected losses		19,102	117,919
54		Provisions for expected obligations		-	-
55		Other provisions		-	-
56	F)	**Liabilities**	(57+64)	**4,438,316**	**4.664,270**
57	I.	**Long term liabilities**	(58 to 63)	**1,855**	**-**
58		Investment and development loans		-	-
59		Other long term credits		-	-
60		Long term loans		-	-
61		Debts on the issue of bonds		-	-
62		Obligations to founders		1,855	-
63		Other long term liabilities		-	-
64	II.	**Short term liabilities**	(65 to 70)	**4,436,461**	**4,664,270**
65		Advance payments received from purchasers		30,794	13,970
66		Creditors (from purchase of goods and services)		720,965	751,275
67		Overdraft debts		-	-
68		Short term debts		2,987,402	3,145,413
69		Short term loans		-	-
70		Other short term liabilities		697,300	753,612
71	G)	**Accrued expenses**		**140,946**	**462,113**
72		**Total**	(45+52+56+71)	**8,876,685**	**12,313,429**

Source: Prímagáz Hungária Rt, annual report, 1996, pp. 29–30

Where the trading stocks of a business are purchased at different prices, under former practice the average price was compulsory; under the Accounting Law 1991 (para. 35) a range of methods is now permitted.

The 1994 survey indicated strong signs of continued use of the 'after-calculation'. Reasons given were that the after-calculation provides the real costs of production and is most suitable for the needs of the business. These responses were mainly from manufacturing companies, but also included large enterprises. It appears that enterprises will continue to use the practice existing before the 1991 Law where it remains a permitted practice and where it is seen to be of particular value to management despite the fact that the alternative would require less effort.

Turning to the price at which stocks of materials are valued, in the 1994 survey it was noted that average pricing remained widely used. The managers of the enterprises were broadly in agreement that relative ease and convenience of working was a reason for continuing to use average price. Of the models implicitly made available under the Law, HIFO (highest-in-first-out) was used in several cases, and justified in terms of frequent changes of inventory, changes of suppliers, simplicity and relevance of the price used. A smaller number of respondents used FIFO and a few used their own variations on purchase price. Advisers who were working with international accountancy firms suggested that FIFO (first-in-first-out) was the preferred approach of their clients.

14.7.3.6 Joint venture accounting[68]

Proportional consolidation may be used for joint ventures. The international accounting standard IAS 31 has proportional consolidation as the benchmark treatment and so is stronger in emphasis. In Hungary, there is an element of professional choice between equity accounting and proportional consolidation.

14.7.4 Conservatism versus optimism

One of the greatest changes to Hungarian accounting in adopting the EU Fourth Directive was the application of the concepts of going concern, prudence and realisation. Previously the concept of prudence was not applied, but under the Accounting Law 1991 all foreseeable risks and losses were required to be considered as income-reducing factors even if they became known after the accounting date (31 December) but prior to preparation of the accounts.

Although accrual accounting existed previously, it applied only at the year-end and only for those invoices received in January following. The 1991 Law required that foreseeable liabilities should be accrued (applying the principle of coherence).

The apparent deviations from the Fourth Directive (*see* section 14.4.2.2 and Exhibit 14.3) are even more interesting to the UK observer, because they indicate a lack of conservatism in excluding items which would be provisions under the more usual conventions of prudence.

A further indication of lack of conservatism may be seen in the treatment of all leases as operating leases. This is not a Fourth Directive matter, but contrasts with the IAS position of recognising, on the balance sheet, the liability on a finance lease.

[68] Rooz *et al.* (1996)

14.7.4.1 Provisions for liabilities and losses

Prior to the Accounting Law 1991 reserves were not permitted. Under the 1991 Law (Appendix items E1; E2, para. 27) reserves are now permitted in the balance sheet format. There are no rules in the Law as to the method of calculation. It is also permitted under the 1991 Law to make provisions for losses and liabilities, but there are no detailed rules as to how this should be carried out.

From the 1994 survey it was evident that tax law was an influential factor but the full extent could not be determined because of the number of respondents who did not give a clear reason for the policy chosen. To research this issue more clearly it would be necessary to know what amount of provision would be allowed under tax law and what amount had been provided under the company's discretion. The relative materiality might be a stronger indication of how far financial managers will in fact exercise discretion independent of the tax consequences.

14.7.4.2 Doubtful debts

Under the previous legislation it was not permitted to make provision for doubtful debts. It is now permitted where specified conditions are met, but the provision must be disclosed as a specific reserve rather than as a reduction in the asset. The international accounting practice is to set the provision as a deduction from the asset. The reason for what appears a less prudent practice in Hungary was the regulators' fear of disclosing the true extent of bankrupt businesses as the new economic system found its feet.

14.7.5 Secrecy versus transparency

Exhibit 14.3 indicates a reluctance to disclose sensitive information in relation to segments and a lack of transparency over investments when the holding is 25% or less.

A further indication of lack of transparency may be seen in the treatment of all leases as operating leases. This is not strictly a Fourth Directive matter, but contrasts with the UK position of recognising, on the balance sheet, the liability on a finance lease. Publication is required by law but in practice the information may not be readily available. Notes to the accounts are required under the Law, and there is a requirement to report extraordinary items through the profit and loss account but flexibility as to what is classified as 'extraordinary'.

14.7.5.1 Publication of accounts

The Accounting Law 1991 contains requirements for publication of accounts. The full report is lodged at the Court of Registration, with a requirement of the law that the balance sheet be handed in to the Court of Registration by 31 May following the December year-end. There is a copy at the headquarters of the company, and, on request, the company must show the full report to an enquirer. It should be noted that 'publication' means that the annual report will be published in a national newspaper. Publication of the whole or part of the notes is not necessary if, according to the auditor, the information shown in the balance sheet and in the income statement is sufficient for a clear assessment of the entity's results and financial position (para. 72). This includes publication in a newspaper.

In the 1994 survey, respondents were asked whether those who read the annual report published in the newspapers would understand how much choice had taken place. Negative answers were given by 35 respondents, some of whom went on to say that the published financial statements would be useful only when read with the notes.

14.7.5.2 Notes to the accounts[69]

Notes to the accounts contain the additional information necessary for providing a true and fair view. They contain both numerical data and explanatory text. The notes include disclosure of accounting policies adopted by the company where discretion exists under the law, and contain the type of detail found in the annual reports of western European companies.

14.7.5.3 Business report[70]

The law requires a business report which reviews the company's business and its development. It must refer to any significant events that took place after the balance sheet date. The business report will also report on matters such as the R&D policy of the company and on purchase by the company of its own shares.

14.8 EMPIRICAL STUDIES

Chapter 3 sets out research methods for measuring comparability and harmonisation. Chapter 4 explains approaches to classification. Hungary has not been included in any of the empirical studies concerned with classification. It would, prior to the late 1980s, have been classed as eastern European and there have been many publications on eastern European accounting which have made contrasts within that group, such as Hare (1987), Bailey (1988) and Jaruga (1990).

14.9 SUMMARY AND CONCLUSIONS

In this chapter you have seen how characteristics of accounting principles and practice in Hungary may be related to the framework of analysis created by Gray (1988) and others based upon analysis of cultural factors. Although Gray did not include Hungary in his classification, it is reasonable to predict that accounting in Hungary might be classified in a manner similar to that of Germany, which is characterised by moderate professionalism, marginal uniformity, marginal conservatism and strong secrecy. As the Accounting Law in Hungary began to operate in 1991, conservatism might be classed as relatively high, because of regulatory constraints imposed by a weak economy. There is a strong body of statutory control, but choice is permitted and there is evidence of professionalism in the exercise of that choice. Uniformity is strong in matters such as the bookkeeping rules, but there is flexibility under the law within the overall guidance of the Fourth and Seventh Directives. Secrecy has been high, and it is the importance of attracting foreign capital which has started to break down some of the secrecy barriers. Accounting practice has altered in the 1990s mirroring economic and political change and is moving closer to EU practice while retaining some specifically Hungarian aspects.

[69] Borda (1995), p. 1419
[70] Borda and McLeay (1996), p. 132

■ QUESTIONS

Business environment (14.2)

1 To what extent does the business environment of Hungary provide clues as to possible influences on accounting practices?

Early developments in accounting (14.3)

1 To what extent do early developments in accounting practice indicate the likely directions of professionalism/statutory control; uniformity/flexibility; conservatism/optimism; and secrecy/transparency in current practice?

Institutions (14.4)

1 How does the political and economic system of Hungary fit into the classifications described in Chapter 1?

2 How does the legal system of Hungary fit into the classifications described in Chapter 1?

3 How does the taxation system of Hungary compare to the descriptions given in Chapter 1?

4 How does the corporate financing system of Hungary compare to the descriptions given in Chapter 1?

5 How does the accounting profession in Hungary compare to the descriptions given in Chapter 1?

6 How do the external influences on accounting practice in Hungary compare to those described in Chapter 1?

7 Which institutional factors are most likely to influence Hungarian accounting practice?

Societal culture and accounting subculture (14.5)

1 What features of societal culture and accounting subculture might be identified if the work of Hofstede (1984) (Chapter 2) and the analytical system used by Gray (1988) (Chapter 4) were to be repeated today in analysing Hungary?

2 What position might emerge in such an analysis if Hungary today were compared with Germany and the UK? Give reasons for your answer.

IASs (14.6)

1 In which areas does accounting practice in Hungary depart from that set out in IASs?

2 For each of the areas of departure which you have identified, describe the treatment prescribed in Hungarian accounting and identify the likely impact on the income and shareholders' equity of moving from Hungarian GAAP to the relevant IAS standards.

3 What explanations may be offered for these departures from IASs, in terms of the institutional factors described in the chapter?

4 What are the most difficult problems facing accounting in Hungary if it seeks harmonisation with the IASC core standards programme?

EU membership (14.7 and 14.4.2)

1 What have been the most significant changes in accounting practice in Hungary arising from the Fourth and Seventh Directives?

2 Which factors make it relatively easy or relatively difficult for Hungarian accounting practices to harmonise with those of other European countries?

Professionalism/statutory control (14.7.2)

1 Identify the key features supporting a conclusion that statutory control is the dominant characteristic but that professionalism is starting to make an appearance in Hungarian accounting.

2 Explain which institutional factors influence statutory control and which influence professionalism in Hungarian accounting practice.

Uniformity/flexibility (14.7.3)

1 Identify the key features supporting a conclusion that uniformity is the dominant characteristic but that flexibility is starting to make an appearance in Hungarian accounting.

2 Explain which institutional factors influence uniformity and which influence flexibility in Hungarian accounting practice.

Conservatism/optimism (14.7.4)

1 Identify the key features supporting a conclusion that past practice has been ambivalent on conservatism but that an approach closer to that of EU countries is starting to make an appearance in Hungarian accounting.

2 Explain which institutional factors influence conservatism and which influence optimism in Hungarian accounting practice.

Secrecy/transparency (14.7.5)

1 Identify the key features supporting a conclusion that secrecy is the dominant characteristic but that transparency is starting to make an appearance in Hungarian accounting.

2 Explain which institutional factors influence secrecy and which influence transparency in Hungarian accounting practice.

REFERENCES

Arthur Andersen (1991) *The Budapest Stock Exchange: The path to a successful flotation.* London: Arthur Andersen & Co.

Bailey, D. (1988) *Accounting in Socialist Countries.* London: Routledge.

Benkó, T. and Török, E. (1997) 'MOL Ltd (Hungarian Oil and Gas)', Chapter 5 in Bógel, G., Edwards, V. and Wax, M. *Hungary since Communism.* London: Macmillan Business, 77.

Borda, M. (1995) 'Hungary', in Alexander, D. and Archer, S. *European Accounting Guide.* 2nd edn. New York: Harcourt Brace.

Borda, M. (1992) 'Hungary', in Alexander, D. and Archer, S. *The European Accounting Guide.* London: Academic Press.

Borda, M. and McLeay, S. (1996) 'Accounting and economic transformation in Hungary', Chapter 7 in Garrod, N. and McLeay, S. (eds) *Accounting in Transition: The implications of political and economic reforms in Central Europe*. London: Routledge.

Boross, Z., Clarkson, A.H., Fraser, M. and Weetman, P. (1995) 'Pressures and conflicts in moving towards harmonisation of accounting practice: The Hungarian experience', *European Accounting Review*, 4(4), 713–37.

Canning, A. and Hare, P.G. (1996) 'Political economy of privatisation in Hungary: A progress report', *CERT Discussion Paper*, 96/13, Centre for Economic Reform and Transformation, Heriot-Watt University, Edinburgh.

Coopers and Lybrand (1992) *New Hungarian Accounting Law*. Budapest: Láng Kiado.

Coopers and Lybrand Tax Network (1995) *1995 International Tax Summaries: A guide for planning and decisions*. New York: John Wiley.

David, R. and Brierley, J. (1985) *Major Legal Systems of the World Today*. London: Stevens.

Doupnik, T.S. and Salter, S.B. (1993) 'An empirical test of a judgemental international classification of financial reporting practices', *Journal of International Business Studies*, 24(1), 41–60.

Garrod, N. and McLeay, S. (1996) 'The accounting implications of political and economic reform in central Europe', Chapter 1 in Garrod, N. and McLeay, S. (eds) *Accounting in Transition: The implications of political and economic reforms in Central Europe*. London: Routledge.

Gray, S.J. (1988) 'Towards a theory of cultural influence on the development of accounting systems internationally', *Abacus*, 24(1), 1–15.

Hare, P.G. (1987) 'Economic reform in Eastern Europe', *Journal of Economics Survey*, 1, 25–58.

Hofstede, G. (1984) *'Culture Consequences: International Differences in Work-related Values*. Beverly Hills, CA: Sage Publications.

Illés, K., Weetman, P., Clarkson, A.H. and Fraser, M. (1996) 'Change and choice in Hungarian accounting practice', *European Accounting Review*, 5(3), 523–43.

Jaruga, A.A. (1990) 'Accounting functions in socialist countries', *British Accounting Review*, 22(1), 51–77.

Krieglsteiner, C. (1996) *Group Accounting in an Eastern European Country (Hungary) – influences of German, UK and IAS accounting practice*, Masters degree thesis, Heriot-Watt University, Edinburgh.

Koltay, J. (1992) 'Tax reform in Hungary', reprinted in Halpern, L. and Wyploz, C. (eds.) (1998), *Hungary: Towards a Market Economy*. Cambridge: Cambridge University Press (for the Centre for Economic Policy Research).

KPMG (1990) *Investment in Hungary*. Budapest: KPMG Reviconsult Auditing and Consulting LLC.

LGT (1997) *The LGT Guide to World Equity Markets 1997* (ed. Rathborne, D.) London: Euromoney Publications and LGT Asset Management, 210–15.

Nagy, G. (1991) 'A Számvileli törvény és az Eves Beszámoló', The Accounting Law and the Annual Report. Budapest: Saldo. [Referred to as *The Blue Book*.]

Nagy, G. (1994) 'A Számvitelröl szóló törvény mó dositása' [The modification of the Accounting Law], *Számvilel és Konyvvizsgálat* [Accounting and Auditing], September.

Piesse, J. (1993) 'The transition to a new system of accounting: The case of Hungary', *Journal of European Business Education*, 2(2), 19–29.

Rooz, J., Sztano, I. and Sztano, F. (1996) 'The regulation of joint ventures in Hungary', *European Accounting Review*, 5(1), 115–147.

Salter, S.B. and Doupnik, T.S. (1992) 'The relationship between legal systems and accounting practices: a classification exercise', *Advances in International Accounting*, 5, 3–22.

Newspapers and professional journals/magazines

The *Financial Times*, UK; includes an annual survey entitled the *Financial Times 500*, issued 22 January 1998.

Chapter 15

Japan

15.1 ## INTRODUCTION

Despite the international preeminence of Japanese corporations, it is often difficult for a non-Japanese report reader to discover the measurement or disclosure practices of the typical Japanese company. The most obvious reason for this is the problem of language – while most large Japanese companies, including many not listed on any overseas stock markets, produce English-language annual accounts and reports, these are different from the Japanese reports.[1]

Unlike the statutory Japanese reports, they are normally glossy documents full of photos and graphics with a PR-style review of activities. More importantly, the financial statements are not identical. They may contain different information, additional notes may be disclosed and other information given in the Japanese accounts is not provided. Japanese financial statements also look somewhat different from UK or US financial statements which can confuse the unsophisticated user. Companies therefore recast their financial statements to make the English-language versions look more like a typical set of US financial statements. This does not affect the reported earnings or equity figures, but many items in the accounts will be re-ordered or re-classified. For example, Mazda Motor Corporation states that:

> Mazda Motor Corporation (the 'Company'), a Japanese company, maintains its records and prepares its financial statements in yen in accordance with accounting principles generally accepted in Japan.
>
> The accompanying consolidated financial statements have been translated from the financial statements that are prepared for Japanese domestic purposes in accordance with the provisions of the Securities and Exchange Law of Japan. The statements have been filed with the Minister of Finance of Japan.
>
> In preparing the accompanying financial statements, certain reclassifications have been made and some information, including the statements of shareholders equity and cash flows, has been added to facilitate understanding by readers outside Japan.
>
> *Source*: Mazda Motor Corp. Annual report, 1997

The main problem for the non-Japanese reader will be understanding an unfamiliar set of GAAP. A number of companies, especially those listed in

---

[1] Nakanishi (1987)

the USA, therefore adjust the Japanese accounts to reflect US GAAP which is also then used as a basis for the audit. As illustrated in Exhibit 15.1, from Kubota Corporation, this can involve a substantial number of adjustments. This is a form of restatement and it is not always possible to restate the figures without resorting to various estimates and assumptions, as recognised by Hitachi (*see* Exhibit 15.2).

Whichever approach is used, the figures and formats will not be identical to the Japanese-language accounts and, where different accounting rules are used, companies do not generally quantify the impact on reported figures. The English-language version of the accounts will also report the latest year's results in US dollars using a 'convenience translation'. In other words, the yen figures are simply converted into dollars at the exchange rate ruling at the balance sheet date.

Exhibit 15.1 KUBOTA CORP.: USING US GAAP IN THE ENGLISH-LANGUAGE REPORT (EXTRACTS), 1996

Kubota Corporation, 1996

Notes to the Accounts.
The consolidated financial statements, stated in Japanese yen, reflect certain adjustments, not recorded on the books of account of Kubota Corporation (the "Company") and subsidiaries (collectively the "Companies"), to present these statements in accordance with accounting principles generally accepted in the United States of America ("US GAAP") with the exception of Statement of Financial Accounting Standards ("SFAS") No. 115 . . . The principal adjustments include: (1) accounting for foreign currency translations, (2) valuation of inventories, (3) accounting for short-term and other investments, (4) accrual of certain expenses, (5) accounting for retirement and pension plans, (6) recognition of deferred income taxes on temporary differences and tax loss carryforwards, (7) recognition of warrant values, and (8) accounting for stock dividends approved by shareholders in prior years at market value.

Audit report
We conducted our audits in accordance with auditing standards generally accepted in the United States of America.

Certain information required by Statement of Financial Accounting Standards ("SFAS") No. 14, "Financial Reporting for Segments of a Business Enterprise", has not been presented in the accompanying consolidated financial statements. In our opinion, presentation of segment information concerning the Company's operations is required for a complete presentation of the Company's consolidated financial statements.

The Company has not accounted for its investments in securities, for the years ended March 31, 1996 and 1995, in accordance with SFAS No. 115, "Accounting for Certain Investments in Debt and Equity Securities". The Company has continued to apply the lower of cost or market method as in SFAS No.12, "Accounting for Certain Marketable Securities" which was superseded by SFAS No. 115. In our opinion, adoption of SFAS No. 115 to the Company's 1996 and 1995 consolidated financial statements is required by accounting principles generally accepted in the United States of America.

Exhibit 15.1 continued

In our opinion, except for the omission of segment information and the effect on the 1996 and 1995 consolidated financial statements of the departure from SFAS No. 115 as discussed in the preceding paragraphs, such consolidated financial statements present fairly, in all material respects, the financial position of Kubota Corporation and subsidiaries as of March 31, 1996 and 1995, and the results of their operations and their cash flows for each of the three years in the period ended March 31, 1996 in conformity with accounting principles generally accepted in the United States of America.

Our audits also comprehended the translation of Japanese yen amounts into US dollar amounts and, in our opinion, such translation has been made in conformity with the basis stated in Note 1. Such United States dollar amounts are presented solely for the convenience of readers outside Japan.

Source: Kubota Corp., annual report, 1996

Exhibit 15.2 HITACHI LTD: USING US GAAP IN THE ENGLISH-LANGUAGE REPORT (EXTRACTS), 1996

Hitachi Ltd 1996

Notes to the Accounts

Hitachi Ltd (the Company) and its domestic subsidiaries maintain their books of account in conformity with the financial accounting standards of Japan, and its foreign subsidiaries in conformity with those of the countries of their domicile.

The consolidated financial statements presented herein have been prepared in a manner and reflect the adjustments which are necessary to conform them with United States generally accepted accounting principles. Management of the Company has made a number of estimates and assumptions relating to the reporting of assets and liabilities and the disclosure of contingent assets and liabilities to prepare these financial statements. Actual results could differ from those estimates.

Audit report

. . .

In our opinion, except for the effects of not stating investments in certain debt and equity securities at fair value and reporting the resulting net unrealized holding gain in a separate component of stockholders' equity as of March 31, 1996 and 1995, as discussed in the third paragraph of this report, and except for the omission of segment information, as discussed in the preceding paragraph, the consolidated financial statements referred to in the first paragraph above present fairly, in all material respects, the financial position of Hitachi Ltd and subsidiaries as of March 31, 1996 and 1995, and the results of their operations and their cash flows for each of the years in the three-year period ended March 31, 1996 in conformity with United States generally accepted accounting principles.

Source: Hitachi Ltd, annual report, 1996

15.2 THE COUNTRY

Japan is made up of a number of islands off the coast of China. Much of the land is extremely mountainous and the population resides in the densely populated coastal areas. As can be seen from the figures in Exhibit 15.3, Japan is a highly successful country, with an average *per capita* gross domestic product (GDP) of nearly US$40,000 in 1996, the third highest of any country.[2]

One of the continuing debates in accounting centres around the role of accounting in economic development. Many people argue that if a country is to be economically successful it must have an appropriate accounting system. As we saw above, considerable interest has been shown as to what type of accounting system is most appropriate to a country. Japan is interesting because it imported much of its accounting system, and there is continuing debate over the appropriateness of some of its regulations.

Japan has achieved remarkable growth since the Second World War. It is a highly industrialised and urbanised country that is dependent for its economic success on large international companies. Much of its success is built on trade, with the country being the home of some of the top consumer products companies in the world. Japan has relied extensively upon exports, resulting in a large balance of payments surplus. Outward investment has always been more important than inward investment, with Japan having successfully restricted imports and inward investment in the past. While this situation is beginning to change, outward foreign investment was, in the early 1990s, up to 15 times greater than inward investment (*see* Exhibit 15.4).

Japan has a long history of importing ideas from other countries and, as will be discussed below, this includes accounting principles. Foreign influences can be seen in both the regulatory system and in the rules and practices adopted.

| Exhibit 15.3 | JAPAN: COUNTRY PROFILE, TAKEN FROM EIU STATISTICS |

Population	125.1 m.	
Land mass	377,727 sq.km	
GDP per head	US $39,687	
GDP per head in purchasing power parity	82	(USA=100)
Origins of GDP:	%	
Agriculture	2.1	
Industry	38.3	
Services	59.6	
	%	
Real GDP average annual growth 1985–95	3.1	
Inflation, average annual rate 1989–96	1.5	

Source: The Economist Pocket World in Figures 1998 Edition, The Economist (1997), p. 154

---

[2] *The Economist* (1997), p. 24; the two countries with the highest GDP per head are Luxembourg and Switzerland

Exhibit 15.4 JAPAN: EXTERNAL RELATIONS, 1996

Inward direct investment (US$ billion) (1951–93) from:	USA	Netherlands	Switz.	UK	Germany	Canada
	12.2	2.3	2.0	1.4	1.4	1.3

Outward direct investment (US$ billion) (as at 1994) to:	USA	UK	Australia	Netherlands	Indonesia	HK
	177.1	31.7	22.7	18.4	15.2	12.7

		%		%		%
Main export destinations:	USA	27.3	South Korea	6.2	Taiwan	6.5
Main import origins:	USA	22.4	China	10.7	South Korea	5.1

Source: Steven (1996); *The Economist* (1997)

15.3 OVERVIEW OF ACCOUNTING REGULATIONS

The Japanese regulatory system is similar to that of many of the code-based European countries. Both the Ministry of Justice and the Ministry of Finance play an important role in regulating accounting. While the stock market is important, it does not regulate corporate disclosures itself. Instead, this role has been subsumed into the Ministry of Finance. The tax authorities also have an important indirect influence on regulations and the accounting profession is relatively unimportant. There is no independent standard setting body; the profession and the business community are instead represented through advisory committee membership.

The earliest regulations took the form of Commercial Code regulations administered by the Ministry of Justice. These apply to all companies. While there is no code of accounts, these rules are relatively uniform and conservative. The most important objective is to protect creditors, and the single-entity financial statements are considered to be the more important set of financial documents.

The Ministry of Justice administers the Securities and Exchange Law. This sets down regulations which must be followed by all listed companies. Much of the Ministry's work in this regard has been passed down to the Business Accounting Deliberation Council. While this may appear to be quite similar to the standard setting bodies of countries like the UK or USA, it has certain important differences. In particular, it is less independent of the government – its members are appointed by the ministry and bureaucrats play an important role in initiating and guiding new rules through the legislative process. In the past, Japan has been little influenced by the IASC or practices in other countries. However, there are increasing moves being made to increase the level of international harmony and to introduce new standards that are more compatible with international standards.

15.4 INSTITUTIONS

15.4.1 Political and economic system

Japan has a liberal-democratic parliamentary system of government and government–business relations may be characterised in terms of co-operation. The government is actively involved in regulating and guiding businesses. A noticeable feature of this system is the bureaucracy, which is far more important and influential than it is in most western democratic societies. Ministerial officials draft legislative bills, brief parliamentary committees and commissions of enquiry and present bills personally to Parliament (the Diet). Particularly important for business is the powerful Ministry of International Trade and Investment (MITI) which, while less influential than many western authors claim, has played a significant role in managing the corporate sector. Also important is the powerful employers' federation, the *Keidanren* which, while not a formal part of the political or government system, plays an important role in influencing government–business relationships and the regulation of business, including the regulation of accounting.

One of the most important features of the economic system that affects accounting is the way in which business is organised. Japanese trade was dominated in the last century by powerful trading houses which formed the basis of the *zaibatsu* (large financial combines). These groups were broken up after the Second World War and, in an attempt to stop them re-forming, the 1946 Anti-monopoly Law (modelled on US laws) prohibited holding companies. However, it is not so easy to regulate business behaviour and the zaibatsu have been largely replaced by keiretsu. Lacking a holding company, the keiretsu tend instead to be quite loose networks of related companies which are centred around a bank, trading company (sogo shosha) or large manufacturing company. The largest of these is the DKB group centred around the Dai-Ichi Kangyo Bank (*see* Exhibit 15.5). Typically, the size of shareholdings held by the lead company is small, with minority cross-holdings between group members being more important than majority share ownership. The group is also maintained through interlocking directorships and meetings of key staff. Intergroup sales and purchases are often also important and long credit terms, especially in times of financial difficulty, are not uncommon. The relationships may also be cemented by a number of other activities such as joint research and development projects.

15.4.2 Legal system

The legal system is a code-based legal system. While it has been influenced by other countries such as France and Germany it also has some unique features. Like other code law countries, business relationships are regulated by the Commercial Code (CC). The CC, being set by the Ministry of Justice, is concerned with ensuring that all parties to a contract are protected, especially lenders and other creditors. The emphasis is therefore placed upon single-entity reporting – as it is the legal entity not the group that enters into the legal contracts – and upon prudence or conservatism in reporting performance.

Exhibit 15.5 CORE OF THE DKB KEIRETSU

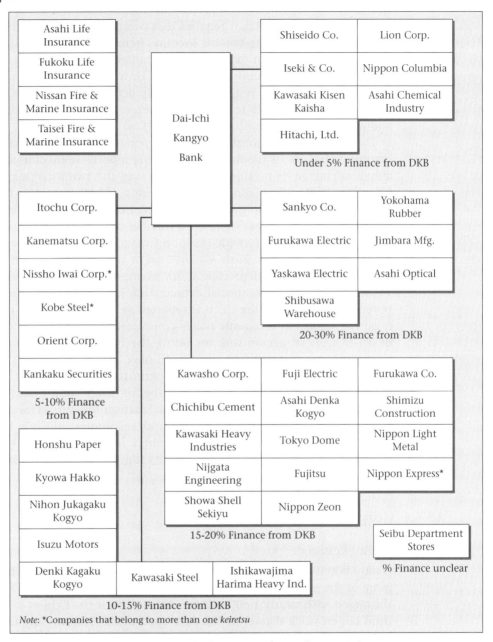

Source: Steven (1996), p. 47. Reproduced by kind permission of Macmillan Press Ltd

15.4.3 Taxation system

The Japanese corporate tax system has been described as a mixed system. It retains a German influence, seen in the relative importance of the Commercial Code in prescribing methods of tax computation, while it has also been influenced by the US system, seen in its reliance upon GAAP.

The Corporation Tax (CT) law does not contain sufficiently detailed rules to enable companies to calculate taxable income. Instead, it relies upon other sources of authority. In particular, it requires that companies use the Commercial Code as the basis for computing taxable income, hence the continental European-style rules that allowances or expenses are permitted for tax purposes only if they are also included in the published accounts. However, the Commercial Code is not exhaustive and it does not unambiguously define income. The CT law therefore also requires companies to use GAAP wherever there are no specific regulations and where it does not conflict with the CT law.

There is a clear relationship between reported income and taxable income. If a company changes its methods of calculating reportable income then it will probably also change its taxable income. However, the two income measures are not identical. While the Commercial Code and GAAP form the basis of taxable income, the CT law also prescribes a number of adjustments to reported income, expenses and allowances. There are a number of reasons for this. In particular, CT law is also designed to provide tax incentives to encourage companies to meet the government's economic goals – additional or special depreciation over and above economic or ordinary depreciation, for example, is allowed for under the Special Taxation Measures Law. Special depreciation is recognised as an expense for tax purposes, while under the CC it is reported as an appropriation of retained earnings. The impact of economic policy considerations can also be seen in a number of other areas of accounting including the further use of reserve accounting. Companies are permitted to set up a number of tax-free reserves. Some of these, such as reserves for bad debts, are permitted under both CT law and the Commercial Code. A considerable number of other tax-free reserves are instead treated as an expense under the Special Taxation Measures Law and so deducted from earnings before taxation, while under Commercial Code they are instead treated as appropriations of retained earnings. Just how common these reserves are is illustrated in Exhibit 15.6, which lists some of the reserves permitted in the Special Taxation Measurement Law.[3]

15.4.4 Corporate financing system

15.4.4.1 Stock exchange

Over 3,000 domestic companies publicly trade either equity or bonds on one or more of the eight domestic stock exchanges. The Tokyo Stock Exchange (TSE) is the largest with nearly 1,800 companies listed on it (*see* Exhibit 1.3), making it the third largest stock market in the developed world, behind only London and New York in terms of the number of companies listed. However, of these nearly 1,800 companies, there were only 67 foreign companies listed at the end of 1996 (down from 77 a year earlier).[4]

For a period in the late 1980s the TSE was the largest in the world, as measured by market capitalisation. Now, following the recession of the early 1990s and a

---

[3] Gomi (1997)
[4] Rathborne and Grosch (1997)

Exhibit 15.6 RESERVES PERMITTED IN THE SPECIAL TAXATION MEASUREMENT LAW

- Overseas investment loss reserve
- Electronic computer purchase loss reserve
- Reserve for investment loss in the free-tax zone
- Mine prospecting reserve or foreign mine prospecting reserve
- Drought reserve
- Used nuclear fuel reprocessing reserve
- Nuclear plant dismantling reserve
- Unusual accidental loss reserve for fire risks or flood damage risks
- Unusual accidental loss reserve for atomic damage risks or earthquake risks
- Reserve for expenses for change of gas calories
- Reserve for development of computer programs
- Small-venture enterprise investment loss reserve
- Metal mining pollution control reserve
- Reserve for close-down of ocean oil or gas fields
- Reserve for prevention of specified disasters
- Reserve for the expansion of railways in specific cities
- Reserve for forestation
- Reserve for construction of New Osaka International Airport
- Reserve for the improvement of intensive agriculture.

major fall in share prices,[5] it is the second largest behind the NYSE (*see* Exhibit 1.4). However, these figures are slightly misleading. The TSE has a relatively low market turnover. This is partly because many shareholdings take the form of cross-holdings and are not actively traded and partly because the personal taxation system encourages long-term shareholdings by taxing dividends at a higher rate than capital gains. Thus, on the basis of market turnover, the TSE is also smaller than London.

The more important source of finance for most companies is bank loans. In the past, these have tended to be short-term loans, although this is changing and the financing patterns of Japanese companies are beginning to resemble more closely those of US or UK companies. Most large companies tend to have close relationships with a key bank and short-term bank loans are automatically rolled over. (Note that this has the effect of making typical working capital and long-term debt:equity ratios different from what might be expected with UK or US companies.) One of the advantages of being a member of a keiretsu is that the central bank is more likely to increase lending in periods of difficulty to prevent a crisis occurring. In many countries, such as the UK, large companies typically have relationships with numerous banks, these may even compete with each other to be the first to call in their loans at the first sign of difficulty.

---

[5] For example, the NIKKEI share price index fell from an all-time high of 38,916 in December 1990 to a low of 14,390 in August 1992

15.4.4.2 Top ten companies

From the *Financial Times FT 500* annual survey there are 71 Japanese companies in the top 500 world companies, measured by market capitalisation. The top ten listed Japanese companies are shown in Exhibit 15.7.

This list shows the importance of financial institutions. There are five banks in the list and four industrial companies. However, if the list were extended to include the next tier of companies many more familiar names would appear. Hitachi, Nissan, Toshiba, NEC, Canon and Sharp, as well as a number of less well known companies such as Tokyo Electric Power and Mitsubishi Heavy Industries, would feature on any list of major international companies.

15.4.5 The accounting profession

The first institute of professional accountants was created in 1927, although the profession in its current form originates in the post-Second World War period as one of the creations of the American occupation forces. The CPA law was passed in 1948 which required accountants to be suitably trained (in a manner and at a level similar to US accountants). This led to the creation of the Japanese Institute of Certified Public Accountants (JICPA) in 1949, although it was not until 1966 that all CPAs had to be members of the JICPA.

All companies regulated by the Securities and Exchange Law – and, since 1974, large Commercial Code-regulated companies – have to be audited by a registered CPA. The profession itself is very small. As was shown in Exhibit 1.6, there are approximately 11,000 members of the JICPA. However, this figure is somewhat misleading as tax accountants do much of the work required by the CT Law and they have their own professional body and examinations. While there is some overlap in the membership of the two bodies, the tax accountants are numerically much larger (approximately six times as large). A second difference from the UK or USA is that far fewer people train as accountants and subsequently leave the pro-

Exhibit 15.7 TOP 10 LISTED JAPANESE COMPANIES, 1998

Name	*Market cap. $m.*	*Rank in world*	*Sector*
1 Nippon Telegraph & Telephone	146,139	7	Telephone companies
2 Toyota Motor Corporation	116,585	9	Automobiles
3 Bank of Tokyo-Mitsubishi	88,819	15	Commercial and other banks
4 Sumitomo Bank	47,301	54	Commercial and other banks
5 Matsushita Electric Industrial Co	38,099	69	Household durables and appliances
6 Sony Corporation	37,171	75	Household durables and appliances
7 Sanwa Bank	35,532	81	Commercial and other banks
8 Dai-Ichi Kangyo Bank	35,375	82	Commercial and other banks
9 Honda Motor	33,940	85	Automobiles
10 Fuji Bank	31,887	92	Commercial and other banks

Source: Financial Times, FT 500 Survey, 22 January 1998

fession to join commercial or financial institutions. This difference can be largely ascribed to cultural differences. Japan is famous for lifetime employment, although its importance tends to be overstated in that it applies only to larger companies and to the more skilled workforce. (Even here, most people take early retirement and then continue to work after this on a consultancy or short-term contract basis.) However, lifetime employment policies and the philosophy of group membership and loyalty to the company is far stronger in Japan than it is in most other countries – commercial and financial institutions prefer to train their own staff and place far less emphasis upon external training or professional qualifications.

The competition to enter the profession has historically been extremely intense and the success rate has correspondingly been very low. The examinations are set by the government; the first exam is an entrance exam open to all non-graduates which tests general literary ability. The second stage allows successful candidates to become junior accountants. The success rate in the second set of examinations has historically been below 10% and only about half of the successful candidates go on and pass the third and final set of examinations in their first sitting at the end of a further three years of training and practical experience.

The JICPA acts to a large extent as a trade body. The CPA examinations are controlled by the government not the Institute – and, as discussed below, the JICPA does not issue accounting standards. Instead, its role is limited to issuing opinions and advice to its members to clarify the legal accounting requirements. It also acts to maintain professional conduct and ethics and sponsors training and professional development of its members.

15.4.6 External Influences

15.4.6.1 Early influences on accounting regulations

Before the Meiji era (1868–1912), Japan was a closed country made up of some 2,000 feudal entities with political power shared between the Shogun (military leaders) and the daimyo (feudal lords). There were no formal courts or written laws, accounting was not regulated and a variety of different types of traditional bookkeeping methods were used. While some of these were extremely sophisticated, they were diary-style single-entry systems. This began to change in the 1860s and 1870s when Japan started to look to the west, to develop international trade and to learn from the experiences of other countries. Double entry bookkeeping was introduced for the first time in Japan in the Yokosuka Steel Works in 1865 where it was introduced in collaboration with French naval accountants. Particularly important was the Iwakura Mission in 1871, which included over 1,000 officials who went to Europe and the USA to see how businesses were organised and how business–government relationships were structured. Japan also began to import accounting texts from a number of countries and to employ foreign accountants to train local accountants.[6]

---

[6] Someya (1989)

The influence of the UK in this period can be seen in the work of Alexander Shand. His system was incorporated into the 1872 National Bank Act which included the requirement to prepare annual accounts which had to be examined or audited by government officials. However, continental European influences were more important. The first Draft of the Civil Code of 1878 was rejected by Japanese jurists as being too close to the French Code, from which it was largely derived. The final 1889 version clearly contained influences from French, German and British law. Similarly, the original draft Commercial Code of 1881 was drafted by a German and both the final version of the Old Commercial Code of 1890 and its amended version or the New Commercial Code of 1899 retained a strong German flavour. This legal framework remains in place, and Japanese accounting in consequence continues to retain certain continental European characteristics.

15.4.6.2 External influences on the regulation of listed companies

Significant external influences can be seen in the regulation of listed companies. Following the defeat of Japan after the Second World War, the allied occupation under the American General MacArthur set out, *inter alia,* to reform and restructure Japanese business. An important element of this was the disbanding of the 15 most powerful *zaibatsu* or large financial combines which controlled much of Japanese business and the sale of the shares of the constituent companies to the general public. For this to succeed the stock market, which was not very active, had to be reconstructed to provide external shareholders with sufficient security at an acceptable cost to make share ownership an attractive proposition. The occupation forces naturally turned to the USA to provide a model of how to do this and (in an albeit modified form) they imported and imposed the relevant US laws. One of the things required was a highly skilled and highly regarded profession of independent auditors to attest the accounts of listed companies. They therefore passed the CPA law in 1948 which as we saw above led to the creation of JICPA. The Securities and Exchange Commission (SEC), an independent body designed to oversee the securities market, was also established in the same year. However, this was disbanded in 1953 and its role transferred instead to the Ministry of Finance. Of long-term importance was the Securities and Exchange Law (SEL) of 1949, which still forms the basis of the regulation of listed companies. Also created was the Investigation Committee on Business Accounting Systems (ICBAS), an independent body charged with developing accounting standards. It began work by issuing, in 1949, two statements, the 'Working rules for preparing financial statements' and the 'Financial accounting standards for business enterprises' (also known as the Business Accounting Principles). The latter was very heavily influenced by 'A statement of accounting principles' which had been published by the American AICPA in 1938. In 1952 the ICBAS ceased to be an independent body when it was effectively made a part of the Ministry of Finance; it also changed its name to the Business Accounting Deliberation Council (BADC). While the power to regulate accounting had therefore passed from independent bodies to the government and the bureaucracy, the BADC retains an important advisory role.

15.4.7 The introduction of consolidated accounting

Many specific accounting rules also show the influence of foreign practices. Consolidated accounting provides a particularly good illustration of the conscious importing of a foreign practice by the Japanese themselves because local or domestic practice was considered inferior. Until the 1960s, consolidated accounts were not produced. However, the 1960s and 1970s were marked by a number of high profile bankruptcies which were either caused by, or made worse by, profit manipulation which remained undetected under single-entity accounting. In addition, the oil crises of the early 1970s led to a number of mergers and takeovers with companies becoming larger and more complex. A number of Japanese companies also had to produce consolidated accounts to achieve a listing on a foreign stock exchange. Sony was the first Japanese company to list on the New York Stock Exchange (NYSE) in 1961, closely followed by Honda, Mitsubishi and Matsushita. The NYSE refused to accept single-entity accounts, and by 1973, more than 60 Japanese companies were producing consolidated accounts. Likewise, a number of US companies wanted to list in Japan and they had to gain permission from the TSE to be allowed to list when producing group or consolidated accounts instead of individual company accounts. By the end of 1973, Citicorp, Dow Chemical and First Chicago Corp. had achieved listings on the TSE on this basis.[7]

It has been argued[8] that these factors all meant that the Japanese perceived their accounts to be of a lower quality or status than those of companies from many other countries. This prompted them to consider the introduction of consolidated accounts, which were eventually required for all listed companies in 1977. The 1977 rules were heavily influenced by the rules of other countries, in particular the USA, despite controversy over whether or not such rules were appropriate in the Japanese context. (As discussed above, the structure of the typical Japanese group differs quite markedly from the pyramid structure based upon total or majority ownership of subsidiaries and subsubsidiaries, as is typically found in developed western countries.)

15.5 SOCIETAL CULTURE AND ACCOUNTING SUBCULTURE

15.5.1 Hofstede's cultural dimensions

When asked to describe Japan or the Japanese, the westerner will often resort to describing the Japanese journeyman working excessively long hours for a large company and then socialising with his (never her) co-workers. They may also describe the Japanese as being excessively polite, avoiding conflict if at all possible. Like all such descriptions this is at best a caricature that is both an exaggeration and a simplification. However, Japan is often described in cultural terms and cultural values or beliefs are often used to explain differences in institutions, organisations or behaviours. For example, one study[9] comparing the accounting systems of Japan and the USA sought to explain why Japan had a different approach to, and style of, accounting standards from the USA. The study offered four possible explanations (*see* Exhibit 15.8) – three of the four relate to cultural differences.

---

[7] McKinnon (1984)
[8] McKinnon (1986)
[9] Bloom *et al.* (1994)

Exhibit 15.8   POSSIBLE REASONS FOR DIFFERENCES IN JAPANESE AND US STANDARDS

Fewer and looser Japanese GAAP in contrast to US GAAP may well be attributed to the following causal factors:

a. the lack of full development of accounting practice and the accounting profession in Japan in view of the primacy of the tax law;

b. the greater sense of trust Japanese have in business relationships *vis-à-vis* Americans, who are all too familiar with fly-by-night, fraudulent firms;

c. the Japanese expectation of honouring contracts or agreements (if they cannot do so, they attempt to re-negotiate such agreements) with the result that Japan is not a litigious society;

d. the domination of a system of consensus so that specific rules, regulation, and contracts are not as important to the Japanese as to Americans.

Source: Bloom *et al.* (1994) (extract)

Exhibit 15.9 reproduces part of the table set out in Chapter 2, section 2.4, showing the scores and rankings for Japan from Hofstede's (1984) research on cultural dimensions.

Japan was ranked towards the middle of the 50 countries Hofstede looked at for both individualism and power distance. In contrast, it had relatively extreme scores on two of the measures. It was the country with the weakest nurturing score and it was ranked in seventh place in terms of its high uncertainty avoidance. These two measures tend to affect motivation in particular, and at first sight the scores appear to conflict. Weak nurturing implies the need for visible personal rewards; financial or other extrinsic measures of success are considered important and risk-taking will be well rewarded. High uncertainty avoidance implies an unwillingness to take risks, as it implies a more fatalistic view of the future and a greater reliance upon playing by the rules. The two taken together explain the importance of the group and group consciousness and belonging, coupled with a belief in wealth generation through hard work. In other words, it is important to belong to the group, or the company, and to give this your complete loyalty. In return, if you work hard and are successful you will be well treated and well rewarded.

Exhibit 15.9   JAPAN: SCORES AND RANKINGS FOR INDIVIDUAL COUNTRIES FROM HOFSTEDE'S (1984) CULTURAL DIMENSION RESEARCH

Individualism versus collectivism		*Large power distance versus small power difference*		*Strong uncertainty avoidance versus weak uncertainty avoidance*		*Weak versus strong nurturing*	
Score	*Rank*	*Score*	*Rank*	*Score*	*Rank*	*Score*	*Rank*
46	22/23	54	33	92	7	95	1

15.5.2 Culture and accounting

Exhibit 15.10 links Gray's (1988) accounting values to Hofstede's (1984) cultural dimensions and uses this to describe the expected characteristics of the Japanese accounting system.

The most important of the four dimensions for explaining the Japanese accounting system will probably be uncertainty avoidance. High uncertainty avoidance implies a reliance upon prescribed rules and little reliance upon professional judgement and relatively conservative income measurement rules. We should also expect to find relatively little emphasis placed upon information disclosure to those outside the group.

When it comes to explaining accounting standard setting, other authors have highlighted other cultural features. Particularly important appear to be the need to avoid conflict and closely related to this something that has been called the 'shame culture' of Japan.[10] A shame culture is one where individuals are motivated by the need to avoid the adverse reactions of others – in other words, values

Exhibit 15.10 LINKING GRAY'S (1988) ACCOUNTING VALUES TO HOFSTEDE'S (1984) CULTURAL DIMENSIONS IN THE MANNER PROPOSED BY GRAY

Gray's accounting values – classification	Cultural dimensions affecting the country's accounting values	Interpretation of Hofstede's scores of cultural values for Japan
Professionalism (weak)	Professionalism tends to be associated with: • Individualism • Weak uncertainty avoidance • Small power distance	Moderate individualism Strong uncertainty avoidance Moderate power distance
Uniformity (strong)	Uniformity tends to be associated with: • Strong uncertainty avoidance • Large power distance • Collectivism	Strong uncertainty avoidance Moderate power distance Moderate individualism
Conservatism (strong)	Conservatism tends to be associated with: • Strong uncertainty avoidance • Collectivism • Strong nurturing	Strong uncertainty avoidance Moderate individualism Weak nurturing
Secrecy (strong)	Secrecy tends to be associated with: • Strong uncertainty avoidance • Large power distance • Collectivism • Strong nurturing	Strong uncertainty avoidance Moderate power distance Moderate individualism Weak nurturing

---

[10] Cooke (1991)

are derived from external stimuli. As discussed above, the belief that Japanese accounting was not as good as the accounting system of other countries was one of the driving forces for introducing new consolidation standards. In addition, due to a wish to avoid conflict, harmony and concessional decision making are both important. This is important as non-governmental groups were consulted over the proposed standards, with the BADC playing an important advisory role. This can be contrasted with a 'guilt culture', as tends to be found in western countries, where individuals are motivated by internal feelings of guilt and the need to avoid such feelings – in other words values are internalised, and these guide behaviour.

It took fully 12 years and over 60 meetings of the BADC for the Ministry of Finance to issue Ordinances on consolidated accounts and another five years before they were tightened and increased in scope: the Ministry of Finance could have unilaterally imposed them as soon as requested by the Diet in 1965. It is also interesting to note that the Keidanren did not oppose the proposals from any theoretical perspective but instead argued that their implementation would be too difficult (*see* Exhibit 15.11 for a description of the process that the Ministry went through in seeking a consensus over this issue in the period up to the early 1980s).

Exhibit 15.11 REGULATIONS FOR CONSOLIDATED ACCOUNTS, 1965–81

1965	Diet requests the Ministry of Finance (MoF) to improve corporate disclosure under the Securities Exchange Law
	The MoF requests the BADC to prepare an interim report on consolidated financial statements, with the idea of improving corporate disclosure
1966	The BADC reports to the MoF and the ministry releases an Exposure Draft on Consolidation for public review
	The Keidanren reports that it supports the exposure draft in principle but that it strongly opposes the implementation of consolidation in the near future
1967	The MoF releases its 'Opinion on Consolidated Statements', which supports the introduction of consolidation
1971	Diet revises the Securities Exchange Law to require that the financial statement of important subsidiaries be attached to the parent-only statements and calls on the MoF to draft the necessary new provisions and revision clauses for the introduction of consolidation
	The BADC resumes discussion on consolidation
1975	The BADC releases financial accounting standards for consolidated financial statements
1976	The MoF issues Ordinances 27–30 operational from fiscal periods commencing 1 April 1977
1981	The MoF revises the consolidation Ordinances to make equity accounting mandatory and to tighten the materiality exclusion clause.

Source: Reprinted from McKinnon and Harrison (1985), 'Cultural influences on corporate and governmental involvement in accounting policy determination in Japan', *Journal of Accounting and Public Policy*, 4, p. 209. Reproduced by kind permission of Cambridge University Press

15.6 ACCOUNTING REGULATIONS AND THE IASC

As we saw in Chapter 5, Japan was one of the founding members of the IASC and JICPA members have been on its board ever since. However, active involvement in the work of the IASC does not guarantee compliance with IASs, and Japan has offered a good example of this. The standard setting process as set up after the Second World War was largely independent of the government. Since then, it has been successfully captured by the government and the bureaucracy so that the profession now plays a relatively minor role in setting standards. Japanese rule setters therefore have not been greatly influenced by the work of the IASC, nor felt any great need to follow their lead, although this position is beginning to change. There are many differences between Japanese accounting principles and IASs; an idea of the most important differences, as at the beginning of 1997, can be gained from Exhibit 15.12, which lists the items where Japanese GAAP differs from IASs, as identified by All Nippon Airways Co. Ltd. in their English-language annual report (note that following the introduction of new standards in late 1997, some of these differences no longer apply).

Exhibit 15.12 shows that Japanese accounting principles differ in many respects from IASs. There is some evidence that this position may be changing, and Japanese standard setters are becoming increasingly willing to consider the work of the IASC when setting domestic standards, as two quotes taken from the IASC Annual Review of December 1996 (*see* Exhibit 15.13) illustrate.

A number of Japanese companies explicitly refer to the use of IASs in their English-language consolidated statements (*see* Exhibit 15.14), and Exhibit 15.15

Exhibit 15.12 ALL NIPPON AIRWAYS CO. LTD: CONSOLIDATED ACCOUNTS (EXTRACT), 1995

The accompanying consolidated financial statements of the Company are principally prepared in conformity with accounting principles and practices generally accepted in Japan, which differ from International Accounting Standards mainly in the following respects:

(a) Consolidation and the equity method of accounting ...

(b) Tax-effect accounting ...

(c) Foreign currency translations ...

(d) Leases ...

(e) Market value information of marketable securities ...

(f) Funds in trust ...

[These are included in current assets and are short-term funds managed by trust banks, they consist mainly of marketable equity securities and interest bearing bonds.]

(g) Employees' retirement benefits ...

(h) Segment information ...

(i) Information reflecting changing prices ...

(j) Related party disclosures ...

Source: All Nippon Airways, annual report, 1995

Exhibit 15.13 JAPAN AND THE IASC: *IASC ANNUAL REVIEW* (EXTRACTS), 1996

Statement by Chairman and Secretary-General

The Secretary-General visited Japan in December 1996 and was greatly encouraged by the improving climate of opinion towards international standards there. The Japanese Prime Minister has made a commitment to liberalise the financial services industry in Japan and to undertake associated reforms. This is likely to lead to acceptance of international standards of accounting transparency within five years.

National Accounting Requirements

The Japanese Business Accounting Deliberation Council (BADC) has added to its agenda three projects on financial instruments, including adoption of a market value basis of measurement, retirement benefit costs, and research and development costs. The BADC has also indicated that its project on consolidated financial statements will give due consideration to prevailing and emerging international standards and practices.

Exhibit 15.14 JAPANESE COMPANIES REFERRING TO USE OF IASs IN THEIR FINANCIAL STATEMENTS

Company	Rank in Japan	Rank in world
Dai-Ichi Kangyo Bank	7	22
Fujitsu	35	160
Kirin Brewery Co.	53	258
Sakura Bank	11	58
Sanwa Bank	8	23
Sasebo	–	–
Toray Industries	78	368

describes the extent to which Japanese regulations are currently in harmony with IAS standards.

15.7 THE ACCOUNTING SYSTEM

15.7.1 Professionalism versus statutory control

15.7.1.1 The Commercial Code

Statutory control is far more important than professional control. Accounting is regulated by both the Ministry of Justice and the Ministry of Finance, while JICPA only plays an indirect role, being represented on the BADC which issues standards under the auspices of the Ministry of Finance. It also publishes guidelines paraphrasing and explaining statutory requirements.

The first body to be actively involved in accounting regulation was the Ministry of Justice through the Commercial Code, which applies to all companies, whether

Exhibit 15.15 COMPARISON OF ACCOUNTING PRACTICES IN JAPAN WITH REQUIREMENTS OF IASs: KEY SIMILARITIES AND DIFFERENCES

IAS	Subject of IAS	Practice in Japan	Ref
Disclosure and presentation			
	General aspects consolidated in IAS 1 (revised)		
IAS 1	Fair presentation	Generally in agreement	7.2
	Disclosure of Accounting Policies	Generally in agreement	
	Information to be Disclosed in Financial Statements	Generally in agreement	
	Presentation of Current Assets and Current Liabilities	Generally in agreement	
	Specific aspects		
IAS 7	Cash Flow Statements	Required from 1997	7.4.2
IAS 8	Net Profit or Loss for the Period, Fundamental Errors and Changes in Accounting Policies	Generally in agreement	
IAS 14	Reporting Financial Information by Segments	Generally in agreement	7.4.3
IAS 24	Related Party Disclosure	Little information until 1997	7.4.5
IAS 33	Earnings per Share	Generally in agreement	
IAS 34	Interim Financial Reporting	Generally in agreement	
Asset recognition and measurement			
IAS 2	Inventories	More choice	7.2.3
IAS 4	Depreciation Accounting	Tax rules dominate	7.2.2
IAS 9	Research and Development costs	Generally in agreement	
IAS 16	Property, Plant and Equipment	Revaluation not allowed	7.3.2
IAS 23	Borrowing costs	Generally in agreement	
IAS 25	Accounting for Investments	Generally in agreement	7.3.2
IAS xx	Intangible Assets		
Liability recognition and measurement			
IAS 10	Contingencies and Events Occurring After the Balance Sheet Date	Generally in agreement	
IAS 12	Income Taxes	Deferred tax not a major issue	7.2.1
IAS 17	Leases	Generally in agreement	7.3.2
IAS 19	Employee Benefits	New standard expected 1998	
IAS 32	Financial Instruments: Disclosure and Presentation	New standard expected 1998	
Recognition of economic activity			
IAS 11	Construction Contracts	Generally in agreement	
IAS 18	Revenue	Generally in agreement	
IAS 20	Accounting for Government Grants and Disclosure of Government Assistance	Generally in agreement	
Measurement			
IAS 15	Information Reflecting the Effects of Changing Prices	Not found	
IAS 29	Financial Reporting in Hyperinflationary Economies	Not relevant	
Group accounting			
IAS 21	The Effects of Changes in Foreign Exchange Rates	Generally in agreement	7.3.4

Exhibit 15.15 continued

IAS	Subject of IAS	Practice in Japan	Ref
IAS 22	Business Combinations	Generally in agreement	
IAS 27	Consolidated Financial Statements and Accounting for Investments in Subsidiaries	Generally in agreement	7.4.2
IAS 28	Accounting for Investments in Associates	Generally in agreement	
IAS 31	Financial Reporting of Interests in Joint Ventures	Generally in agreement	

publicly listed or not. The Commercial Code of 1899 required all companies to produce five documents:

- an inventory (no longer required)
- a balance sheet
- an income statement
- a business report
- proposals regarding profit distribution and reserve accounts.

These documents have to be audited by a statutory auditor, who does not have to be a CPA. This audit is primarily concerned with ensuring that no fraud has taken place rather than attesting to the 'correctness', 'truthfulness' or 'fairness' of the published accounts. It can be more appropriately thought of as being akin to an internal audit rather than an independent external audit.

The Commercial Code was very largely of Germanic origin, although later amendments have reflected Anglo-American influences. Emphasis was originally placed upon the inventory of assets and liabilities which had to be presented to the annual general meeting. The balance sheet had originally to be created from this inventory, rather than being derived from the original books of account. This reflected the legalistic background of the Commercial Code. The Commercial Code does not include many detailed accounting rules, these instead being prescribed in legal Ordinances which contain detailed rules regarding the form and content of the prescribed statements. The Commercial Code does not include any requirements for consolidated accounts which are instead required under the Securities and Exchange Law (SEL).

15.7.1.2 The Securities and Exchange Law

The Ministry of Finance plays a vital role in regulating listed companies. All listed companies are required, under the SEL, to file audited registration documents and annual and semi-annual accounting reports with both the Stock Exchange and the Ministry of Finance. These documents have also, since 1961, been available for purchase by private individuals. The registration documents and the annual report contain similar information including a balance sheet, income statement, statement of appropriations and various supporting schedules or notes. These documents are in addition to those required under the Commercial Code. The prescribed form and content are more detailed and the requirements are designed less for creditor protection – the needs of shareholders predominate. This means that the SEL accounts include additional disclosures and items may be classified somewhat differently. However, as far as the parent company accounts are concerned, the Commercial Code accounts and the SEL accounts should give the same net income and shareholders' equity figures. These statements have to be audited by a registered independent CPA rather than by the statutory auditors.

15.7.1.3 The Business Accounting Deliberation Council

The only standard setting body is the Business Accounting Deliberation Council (BADC) which is an advisory body of the Securities Bureau of the Ministry of Finance. The profession, in the form of JICPA, is represented on this body, as are academics and representatives from the business community (the Keidanren, banks and commercial corporations), the TSE, the Securities Analysts' Association and various other interested parties. All members are appointed by the Ministry of Finance, which also provides the funding.

The BADC has issued a number of standards including:

- 'Financial accounting standards for business enterprises' (first issued in 1949 and amended a number of times since then)
- 'Financial accounting standards on consolidated financial statements (June 1975 and later amendments, revised June 1997)
- 'Standards for the preparation of interim financial statements'
- 'Accounting standards for foreign currency translation'.

It has also issued a number of interpretations concerned, *inter alia*, with the problems of reconciling financial accounting standards with Commercial Code and tax law requirements.

In mid-1996 the BADC changed its structure and recognised the growing need to introduce a number of standards to bring Japanese accounting more in line with international practices. Thus, it no longer looks at one issue at a time but has created a number of subcommittees to work on several standards simultaneously, the first four of these being consolidation; pensions; R&D; and financial instruments.

While standards are issued under the SEL regulations, and so have to be complied with by all listed companies, they affect far more companies than the 3,000 or so that fall under the SEL. Their wider significance can be seen in the description of the role played by accounting standards as provided in the foreword to the original 1949 version of 'Financial accounting standards for business enterprises' (reproduced in Exhibit 15.16). This shows that the standards seek to codify GAAP, which the tax law requires all companies to follow, even if they are not regulated by the SEL.

15.7.2 Uniformity versus flexibility

The Commercial Code does not contain a complete code of accounts (as, for example, seen in France), and in many areas there are no requirements – or, where they exist, they allow companies a wide choice of acceptable methods. However, the accounting system can still best be described as a uniform system of account-

Exhibit 15.16 SETTING OF FINANCIAL ACCOUNTING STANDARDS FOR BUSINESS ENTERPRISES

1. *Financial Accounting Standards for Business Enterprises* is the summary of the accounting conventions which have been generally accepted as fair and proper. It should be followed by all business enterprises, even if it has no statutory binding force.

2. *Financial Accounting Standards for Business Enterprises* is what Certified Public Accountants should follow when they audit financial statements under the Certified Public Accountant Law and the Securities and Exchange Act in Japan.

3. *Financial Accounting Standards for Business Enterprises* should be highly regarded when the law and ordinance affecting business accounting, such as the Commercial Code or the tax law, are enacted, amended, or abolished in the future.

Source: Taken from Hirose (1987), p. 35

ing in the sense that the rules have to be applied in the prescribed ways. Thus, the concept of 'true and fair' is not found in Japan. The audit report instead states that the financial statements 'present fairly . . . in conformity with accounting principles generally accepted in Japan consistently applied during the period'. As we have seen above, these GAAP are codified in many different places – the Commercial Code, the SEL and the Tax laws. All of these sources of GAAP are laws or Government Ordinances, and have to be followed without any possibility of overriding them to produce more useful or relevant information.

15.7.2.1 Deferred tax

In many areas where a company has a choice of methods, the final choice of which method to use will not be guided by a consideration of the needs of external shareholders. Instead, the potential impact on taxable income will be of prime concern. The importance of the tax rules can be seen in the treatment of deferred taxation. In the single-entity Commercial Code accounts, deferred taxation is simply not an issue – it does not exist, it can instead exist; in the consolidated accounts. However, IAS 12 is often not followed and deferred tax is not recognised.

15.7.2.2 Depreciation

There are a number of areas where the choice of methods available to a company are surprisingly large, and depreciation is one of these. Depreciation may be calculated by either straight-line or reducing-balance methods. However, because of the tax implications, reducing-balance methods are more popular than they are in most countries. For example, Toyota (annual report, 1997) states that:

Property, plant and equipment and depreciation
Property, plant and equipment are stated at cost. Depreciation of property, plant and equipment is computed principally by the declining balance method in accordance with provisions of the tax code. Further depreciation of buildings and structures and of machinery and equipment is carried out for assets of the Parent up to the residual value of the assets.

IAS 16 requires companies to use the depreciation method that is most appropriate for that particular asset given the pattern of economic benefits consumed over time, rather than choosing a method that minimises the taxes payable. This means that companies will not follow the requirements of IAS 16 with regard to the choice of depreciation method. The Japanese, however, do recognise a conflict between tax and accounting when it comes to additional depreciation as permitted in the Special Taxation Measures Law. As we saw above (section 15.4.3), this extra non-economic depreciation is shown in the published accounts as an appropriation of earnings rather than as an expense of the period.

15.7.2.3 Inventory

A wide range of choices is also permitted for inventory valuation. These include not only FIFO and weighted average, but also LIFO, simple average, specific identification and latest purchase price methods. Companies are therefore allowed to use the benchmark methods laid down in IAS 2 and the permitted alternatives plus other methods, so that in practice companies may not follow the IAS in this area. However, average costs – either simple or weighted – tend to be used very frequently, certainly they are far more common than they are in most other countries. For example, turning again to Toyota, the annual report states that:

> **Inventories**
> Inventories of the Parent are stated principally at cost, as determined by the periodic average method. Inventories of consolidated subsidiaries are stated principally at cost, as determined by the specific identification method or the LIFO method.

15.7.2.4 Consistency

While audit reports state that accounting principles have been 'applied consistently', the concept of consistency is given much less prominence in Japan than it is in most other countries. There is thus a greater tendency for companies to change their accounting methods when such changes are permitted and when they improve the position of the company. Exhibit 15.17 reproduces the description of accounting changes made by Japan Airlines. Each of these changes reduced reportable losses and, while each change could be justified, none was due to changes in accounting laws.

15.7.3 Conservatism versus optimism

As we have seen, the Commercial Code rules were developed with creditor protection in mind. The SEL rules have much more of a stock market orientation, although the impact on reported figures should not be overstated. The two sets of requirements result in the same earnings and equity figures for single-entity accounts.

15.7.3.1 Reserves

The most obvious indication of the creditor protection orientation of the Commercial Code is the existence of statutory reserves. Companies have to transfer an amount equal to at least 10% of cash dividends and bonuses for officers, directors and auditors to a legal reserve each year until that reserve amounts to at least 25% of legal capital. This is a non-distributable reserve. Also designed to protect creditors are

Exhibit 15.17 JAPAN AIRLINES: CHANGES IN ACCOUNTING POLICY (EXTRACT), 1995–6

3. CHANGES IN ACCOUNTING POLICY.

a. Effective April 1, 1993, the Company changed its method of accounting for bond issuance expenses, which had previously been charged to income when incurred, to capitalizing and amortizing these over a period of three years. As a result of this change, bond issuance expenses of ¥2,128 million were capitalized for the year ended 31 March, 1994. The effect of this change was to decrease the loss before minority interests, income taxes and equity in earnings of unconsolidated subsidiaries and affiliates for the year ended March 31, 1994 by ¥1,419 million.

b. Effective April 1, 1994, the Company discontinued the policy of providing for deferred income taxes on special depreciation in accordance with the Special Taxation Measures Law and the Commercial Code of Japan. The effect of this change was to decrease the net loss for the year ended March 31, 1995, by ¥4,108 million.

c. Effective April 1, 1995, the Company changed its method of accounting for depreciation expenses related to ground property and equipment to the straight-line method from the declining-balance method. The effect of this was to decrease operating expenses and operating loss for the year ended March 31, 1996 by ¥10,974 million ($103,528 thousand) and to decrease the loss before minority interests, income taxes and equity in earnings of unconsolidated subsidiaries and affiliates for the year ended March 31, 1996 by ¥10,915 million ($102,971 thousand).

Source: Japan Airways, annual report, 1995–6

rules with respect to the maximum amounts that can be paid out as interim and final dividends. Companies often also reduce distributable reserves by making relatively large transfers from distributable to appropriated non-distributable reserves. Particularly important are transfers with respect to retirement payments, warranties and repairs. Companies will also take full advantage of any tax provisions, as discussed above in section 15.4.3. For example, Toyota states that:

Shareholders' equity
Under the Japanese Commercial Code, amounts equal to at least 10% of the sum of the cash dividends paid by the Parent and its domestic subsidiaries must be set aside as a legal reserve until that reserve equals 25% of common stock. The legal reserve may be used to reduce a deficit or may be transferred to common stock by taking appropriate corporate action.

In consolidation, the legal reserves of consolidated subsidiaries are accounted for as retained earnings.

15.7.3.2 Valuation rules – tangible assets

The accounting system is a strict historical one with all fixed assets accounted for at cost. The allowed alternative in IAS 16 of revaluation of assets is not permitted.

Inventories should be valued at cost or the lower of cost or market value. 'Market value' is more liberally interpreted in Japan than in IAS 2: it can mean either replacement cost or net realisable value. A similar rule also applies to marketable securities, with both being marked down below cost whenever the fall in market price is considered to be more than a temporary fall in value. The importance of conservatism can be seen in the choice of method used to value securities. Each security is considered separately and marked down if required. This tends to result in more frequent mark-downs than under the alternative approach of valuing the entire portfolio and comparing this with its historical cost. This treatment is therefore in accordance with IAS 25, which allows marketable securities to be valued at either the historical cost (written down if necessary) or at a revalued amount.

Until very recently, the permitted treatment of leases was permissive and IAS 17 was not followed. The treatment was usually based upon legal ownership and only a finance lease that transferred legal ownership had to be treated as a finance lease. Standard changes in 1997 introduced two options: companies can follow the traditional approach or they can adopt the approach taken by IAS 17. However, relatively few companies took the option of following IAS 17 and, at least in the first year of the new standard, approximately 85% of Japanese companies still adopted the traditional approach.

15.7.3.3 Valuation rules – intangible assets

Goodwill is accounted for only if it is acquired. Internally generated goodwill cannot be capitalised. Acquired goodwill should be capitalised and depreciated over its life. However, the Commercial Code sets a maximum limit of five years. For goodwill on consolidation, companies must, from mid-1997, depreciate over 20 years instead.

Five years is still the maximum period over which R&D can be written off. However, it is common to find that all R&D expenditures have instead been expensed.

15.7.3.4 Foreign currency translation

Until recently, Japan did not follow IAS 21 with respect to the translation of foreign currency statements. Instead of requiring the use of the closing-rate method, Japan was unique in using a modified form of the temporal method. The standard has now been changed so that the current rate is generally applied and current Japanese practice is now similar to that required in IAS 21, although there are still some minor differences between the treatment of assets and liabilities. This can be seen in the description offered by Mazda Motor Corp. (annual report, 1997):

Translation of foreign currency financial statements
In connection with consolidation, foreign currency financial statements are translated into yen in the following manner:

Until 1996, balance sheet accounts were translated at the rate of exchange in effect at the balance sheet date, except for inventories and property, plant and equipment, which were translated at the rate of exchange at the date of acquisition. Revenues and expenses were translated at the average rate of exchange during the year, except for depreciation, which was translated at the rate of exchange at the date of acquisition. Net income and retained earnings were translated at the rate of exchange in effect at the balance sheet date. Translation differences derived from the translation of retained earnings were charged or credited to retained earnings directly. Translation differences derived from the statement of income were reflected therein.

Effective April 1, 1996, the Company translates assets and liabilities at the rate of exchange in effect at the balance sheet date: revenues, expenses and net income at the average rate of exchange during the year; and retained earnings at the historical exchange rate in accordance with newly amended foreign currency transaction standards.

Translation differences are shown as other assets in the consolidated balance sheet.

15.7.4 Secrecy versus transparency

15.7.4.1 Information disclosure

As we have seen, Japan has imported many of its regulatory structures and accounting rules. However, many features of Japanese society are quite different from those of other countries. Thus, despite a complex system of accounting regulation, there is relatively little emphasis on – or demand for – information disclosure in general purpose annual reports. Debt financing has traditionally been more important than equity financing and the debt providers (the banks) have not required external financial statements as they are able to demand whatever information they require. Other keiretsu members likewise have a variety of formal and informal ways of obtaining the information they want. Thus the need for external monitoring via audited annual accounts has been largely replaced by other corporate governance systems. For example, one study of the role of non-executive directors[11] concluded that bankers and other representatives of groups with intercorporate relationships are often appointed in times of financial difficulty and that these board members are important in monitoring and disciplining corporate behaviour. This behaviour is congruent with the culture of the country. Group consciousness and interdependence leads to relatively high levels of mutual trust, so there is less of a perceived need to externally monitor corporate behaviour.

Patterns of financing, group structures and keiretsu membership and cultural values all mean that the annual reports, while providing the information required by law, tend not to go any further by providing extensive amounts of voluntary information.

15.7.4.2 Consolidation

The question of secrecy versus openness covers more than the issue of the voluntary disclosure of information; it also covers mandatory disclosures. The Commercial Code is not overly concerned with the disclosure of information. For example, it does not require any consolidated accounts, which are regulated only by the SEL. The SEL requirements also tend to err on the side of secrecy rather than openness. One of the most important differences between Japanese and IASC requirements concerns the issue of what is included in group accounts. Under IAS 27, subsidiaries are excluded from consolidation only in certain extremely restrictive and limited cases. In contrast, the Japanese requirements have been extremely lenient in this respect. We saw earlier in this chapter how the rules for consolidation were contentious and initially were not supported by the Keidanren. This meant that the rules when first introduced were something of a compromise and allowed subsidiaries to be excluded if they were not material. In this context, 'material' was defined as being less than 10% of both the combined assets and sales of the parent and the consolidated subsidiaries. Earnings were not included in the definition of materiality, as it would have made the requirements too restrictive and far fewer companies would have benefited from them. This exclusion clause was perhaps too successful in reducing the impact of the consolidation

---

[11] Kaplan and Minten (1994)

requirements. The Ministry of Finance estimated that only 27% of all subsidiaries were actually consolidated in 1979/80, most of the rest being excluded because of liberal interpretation of the materiality exclusion clause. The materiality exclusion clause was tightened in 1981, when a 10% income criterion was also added, this meant that many more subsidiaries had to be consolidated. However, Japanese companies still continued to exclude many subsidiaries from consolidation that would be consolidated under IAS 27, as can be seen from the accounting policy of Nippondenso (for year-ended March 31, 1996):

> *Principles of Consolidation*
> The Company has 86 majority-owned subsidiaries as of March 31, 1996 (82 for 1995 and 80 for 1994). It changed the consolidation scope and applied the equity method for the first time on January 1, 1995 due to revised requirements of the Japanese Securities and Exchange Law. The consolidated financial statements include the accounts of the Company and 21 significant subsidiaries (21 for 1995 and 12 for 1994) and reflect 1 non-consolidated subsidiary and 7 associate companies (company ownership 20% to 50%) under the equity method (8 for 1995 and none for 1994). The remaining 64 (60 for 1995 and 68 for 1994) subsidiaries, whose combined assets, net sales, and net income in the aggregate are not material to the related consolidated totals, have not been consolidated or subject to the application of the equity method.

The latest standard issued in June 1997, has introduced guideline materiality criteria of between 3% and 5%. It has also made a number of other changes to the standard to bring it nearer to IAS 27. In particular, it has changed the definition of a subsidiary. Previously, the definition was based exclusively upon ownership, now, the concept of control has also been introduced into the definition.

15.7.4.3 Segment information

The audit reports of Kubota Corporation and Hitachi Ltd (shown in Exhibit 15.1 and 15.2), both referred to the omission of segment information as required in the USA under FAS14. Until recently, this was a common omission in Japanese reports. Japanese companies were not required to produce any segmental information until 1990, when requirements to disclose segment sales and income data were introduced. These requirements were considerably increased in 1996, and companies will now produce information comparable to that required by IAS 14 (*see* Exhibit 15.18).

15.7.4.4 Funds flow statements

Consolidated funds flow statements which meet the requirements of IAS 7 are produced by most companies that provide English-language reports. These were voluntary statements, but the new consolidation standard of 1997 changed this as it requires all companies to produce such a funds flow statement. Before this, all companies had to produce some funds flow information for the current and past years and also forecasted for the next six months. This statement was not in a form compatible with the IASC requirements and was not generally translated into English or provided in the foreign-language report and accounts.

15.7.4.5 Related-party disclosure

There are a number of other areas where Japanese disclosure requirements are less than those of the IASC. One particularly interesting example of this was related

Exhibit 15.18 MAZDA MOTOR CORPORATION: SEGMENT INFORMATION, 1997

5. Segment Information

The Company and its consolidated subsidiaries are primarily engaged in the manufacture and sale of passenger and commercial vehicles, and net sales, operating income (loss) and identifiable assets related therewith have exceeded 90% of consolidated net sales, consolidated operating income (loss) and total identifiable assets, respectively. Accordingly, information by industry segment is not shown.

A summary of net sales and operating income (loss) by geographic area for the years ended March 31, 1997, 1996 and 1995, follows:

In accordance with the change in the provisions of the Securities and Exchange Law of Japan, the Company began to disclose identifiable assets information from 1996.

Millions of yen

1997	Japan	Other areas	Total	Elimination or corporate	Consolidated
Net sales:					
Outside customers	¥1,355,239	¥538,961	¥1,894,200	¥ —	¥1,894,200
Inter-area	154,903	11,675	166,578	(166,578)	—
Total	1,510,142	550,636	2,060,778	(166,578)	1,894,200
Costs and expenses	1,509,352	549,026	2,058,378	(164,489)	1,893,889
Operating income (loss)	¥ 790	¥ 1,610	¥ 2,400	¥ (2,089)	¥ 311
Total identifiable assets	¥1,171,619	¥284,143	¥1,455,762	¥ (38,355)	¥1,417,407

1996	Japan	Other areas	Total	Elimination or corporate	Consolidated
Net sales:					
Outside customers	¥1,368,754	¥474,138	¥1,842,892	¥ —	¥1,842,892
Inter-area	164,971	10,739	175,710	(175,710)	—
Total	1,533,725	484,877	2,018,602	(175,710)	1,842,892
Costs and expenses	1,542,030	483,623	2,025,653	(174,625)	1,851,028
Operating income (loss)	¥ (8,305)	¥ 1,254	¥ (7,051)	¥ (1,085)	¥ (8,136)
Total identifiable assets	¥1,214,583	¥182,031	¥1,396,614	¥ (28,428)	¥1,368,186

1995	Japan	Other areas	Total	Elimination or corporate	Consolidated
Net sales:					
Outside customers	¥1,602,271	¥601,858	¥2,204,129	¥ —	¥2,204,129
Inter-area	194,011	13,501	207,512	(207,512)	—
Total	1,796,282	615,359	2,411,641	(207,512)	2,204,129
Costs and expenses	1,824,128	613,204	2,437,332	(208,343)	2,228,989
Operating income (loss)	¥ (27,846)	¥ 2,155	¥ (25,691)	¥ 831	¥ (24,860)

Thousands of U.S. dollars

1997	Japan	Other areas	Total	Elimination or corporate	Consolidated
Net sales:					
Outside customers	$10,929,346	$4,346,460	$15,275,806	$ —	$15,275,806
Inter-area	1,249,218	94,153	1,343,371	(1,343,371)	—
Total	12,178,564	4,440,613	16,619,177	(1,343,371)	15,275,806
Costs and expenses	12,172,193	4,427,629	16,599,822	(1,326,524)	15,273,298
Operating income (loss)	$ 6,371	$ 12,984	$ 19,355	$ (16,847)	$ 2,508
Total identifiable assets	$ 9,448,540	$2,291,476	$11,740,016	$ (309,314)	$11,430,702

International sales of the Company and its consolidated subsidiaries for the years ended March 31, 1997, 1996 and 1995, amounted to ¥1,144,292 million ($9,228,161 thousand), ¥1,025,599 million and ¥1,393,445 million, respectively, and accounted for 60.4%, 55.7% and 63.2%, respectively, of the consolidated net sales.

International sales include exports by the Company and its domestic consolidated subsidiaries as well as sales by overseas consolidated subsidiaries.

Source: Mazda Motor Corp., annual report, 1997, p. 32

party information, as required by IAS 24. It was argued in Chapter 2 (section 2.3.2) that related-party disclosure requirements tended to reflect the cultural values or beliefs of a country and Appendix 2.1 provided details of the related party disclosure requirements in Tanzania and the UK. The evidence from Japan also supports the link between culture and disclosure requirements in this area. As argued above, Japan may be characterised by strong group consciousness and it is noticeable that until very recently there were no requirements with respect to the disclosure of related-party transactions.

15.8 EMPIRICAL STUDIES

This chapter has shown that in many respects, Japanese accounting is quite unique. The early continental European (especially German) influences are still important, reflected in the importance of the Commercial Code and its creditor orientation. In contrast, the SEL bears many traces of its roots in the US system of regulation. However, neither German nor US rules or institutions have been adopted wholesale and the imports have been adapted and changed over time to reflect local influences. The system thus reflects a mixture of quite disparate influences. Indeed, it is not even really correct to talk of 'Japanese accounting': instead, there is 'Commercial Code accounting', 'SEL accounting' and 'English-language accounting'. While all three have some common features, others are quite different in the three systems. This means that it is difficult to describe or to categorise Japanese accounting.

15.8.1 Classification studies

Different classification studies have grouped Japan alongside either Germany or the USA. In Chapter 4 we saw that Mueller (1967) classified Japan alongside Germany (section 4.4.1), a result also supported by the empirical work of Nobes (1984) (*see* Exhibit 4.7). However, Nair and Frank (1980) found that it clustered into a group alongside the USA when they looked at measurement issues (*see* Exhibit 4.10), a result that Nobes had also initially hypothesised, while there was slightly more evidence that it was similar to Germany with respect to disclosures (*see* Exhibit 4.11).

One reason for these conflicting results may be because the studies have used different data sources. As we have seen above, the Commercial Code was influenced by Germany so that studies using Commercial Code-based accounts will not surprisingly cluster Japan alongside Germany. The SEL has instead been greatly influenced by the USA, so it would not be very surprising to find that studies using the consolidated accounts of listed companies tended instead to group Japan alongside the USA. With the English-language reports often being different from the Japanese reports, and SEL and Commercial Code reports differing from each other, especially as regards disclosures, it is often impossible to know exactly what has been classified.

15.8.2 Comparability measures

The alternative way of examining differences, by using a quantified measure such as the comparability index, is very difficult to do in Japan. As we have seen, there is no need for Japanese companies to provide a reconciliation to US GAAP – it can instead use US GAAP in its English-language accounts if it wishes. Cooke (1993) tried to replicate the Weetman and Gray (1990) work on differences in accounting earnings as measured by the comparability index (as discussed earlier in Chapter 3, section 3.4.2). However, of the 19 Japanese companies that were listed in the USA and so had to report using US GAAP, only five provided quantified details of the impact of using US GAAP, and only one of these was a full reconciliation statement. From this very limited sample Cooke concluded that Japanese GAAP tended to result in more conservative earnings figures, but he was not able to quantify satisfactorily the size of most of the differences.

15.8.3 Price/earnings comparisons

Some indication of the impact of accounting differences can be seen in the differences in the price/earnings ratios of Japanese companies and other companies. Price/earnings ratios will differ across countries for either (or both) of two reasons: the accounting rules may be different so reported earnings are different, or there may be economic reasons why people in one country are willing to pay more for the same earnings stream. The price/earnings ratios of Japanese companies have generally been higher than those of other countries (*see* Exhibit 15.19, which compares the P/Es of Japanese and US companies for the period 1984–93).

Several studies have tried to adjust reported Japanese figures for differences in accounting rules to see if this explains the differences in P/E ratios. Unfortunately, they have not all reached the same conclusions – perhaps not too surprising since they used different samples of companies over different time periods and adjusted for different accounting items using different techniques. The three most common adjustments made were for the greater use of accelerated depreciation; the greater use of reserves; and the greater use of the materiality exclusion clause when consolidating. In addition, many researchers have adjusted for the greater prevalence of equity cross-holdings which increases market capitalisation. These adjustments have generally had the effect of substantially reducing the Japanese reported P/E ratios.

Exhibit 15.19 PRICE/EARNINGS RATIOS, JAPANESE AND AMERICAN COMPANIES, 1984–93

Year	Japan P/E for NRI 350 industrials	USA P/E for S&P 400 industrials
1984	26.3	10.38
1985	30.4	15.39
1986	55.6	18.73
1987	50.7	14.09
1988	52.6	12.40
1989	56.2	15.40
1990	32.4	15.90
1991	33.4	29.40
1992	50.8	26.10
1993	75.1	24.60

Source: Brown *et al.* (1997), p. 7.3

However, most studies found that the adjusted P/E ratios were still significantly higher than US P/E ratios.[12] Various reasons have been suggested for why Japanese P/E ratios are still relatively high; for example, that they reflect the impact of historical costs. As we have seen, Japan has a system of strict historical costs, as does the USA. However, Japanese land and building prices have generally increased at a faster rate than have US prices, so that land and buildings will be more seriously undervalued. This means that secret reserves are generally larger in Japanese accounts. There may also be differences in the capital markets, with Japanese investors requiring lower rates of return and therefore being willing to pay more for the same income stream than will investors from other countries. Finally, it may be that Japanese companies are a better investment prospect than companies from other countries because, on average, they have better growth and earnings prospects.[13]

15.9 SUMMARY AND CONCLUSIONS

In this chapter you have seen how the accounting principles and practices of Japan are related to the predictions made by Gray (1988), based upon analysis of cultural factors. Using the scores developed by Hofstede (1984) which suggested that the most important cultural dimension for accounting was Japan's strong uncertainty avoidance, Gray's work can be used to predict that the Japanese accounting system will be one that can be described as exhibiting strong statutory control, is uniform rather than flexible, is relatively conservative and is relatively secretive. Many of these predictions have been supported by the analysis of practices in Japan. Japan has a relatively weak profession, the legal system is a code law one and the Commercial Code is used to regulate all businesses. The Commercial Code contains a number of rules which apply to all companies, the regulations emphasise creditor protection and require relatively few disclosures. However, many areas of accounting are not covered by the Commercial Code, many of the more important regulations that affect listed companies being the result of the Securities and Exchange Law (SEL). The taxation system is largely based upon accounting GAAP; however, there are quite a number of areas where the taxation rules have an impact upon accounting and financial reporting practices – in particular, they mean that companies typically set up and disclose far more special reserves than they would otherwise.

Japan has imported many of its institutions from overseas. Many of the early accounting laws were imported from Europe, in particular Germany. Following the Second World War, new regulations and regulatory structures were introduced based upon the US system, although these have been modified to reflect Japanese influences. The Japanese accounting system has therefore been categorised alongside both the USA and Germany.

More recently, Japan has begun to look towards other countries when developing its standards. While many of its practices have been quite different from IASC standards, the IASC is becoming more influential, and this is likely to continue with Japan moving more towards internationally acceptable GAAP. Whether or not it will end up with a system that is essentially compatible with the IASC or not remains to be seen.

---

[12] Brown *et al.* (1997)
[13] Brown *et al.* (1997)

■■■■ **QUESTIONS**

Business environment (15.2)

1 To what extent does the business environment of Japan provide clues as to possible influences on accounting practices?

Early developments in accounting (15.3)

1 To what extent do early developments in accounting practice indicate the likely directions of professionalism/statutory control; uniformity/flexibility; conservatism/optimism; and secrecy/transparency in current practice?

Institutions (15.4)

1 How does the political and economic system of Japan fit into the classifications described in Chapter 1?

2 How does the legal system of Japan fit into the classifications described in Chapter 1?

3 How does the taxation system of Japan compare to the descriptions given in Chapter 1?

4 How does the corporate financing system of Japan compare to the descriptions given in Chapter 1?

5 How does the accounting profession in Japan compare to the descriptions given in Chapter 1?

6 How do the external influences on accounting practice in Japan compare to those described in Chapter 1?

7 Which institutional factors are most likely to influence Japanese accounting practice?

Societal culture and accounting subculture (15.5)

1 What is the position of Japan relative to the UK, the USA and Germany, according to Hofstede (Chapter 2)?

2 What are the features of Japanese societal culture identified by Hofstede which led Gray to his (1988) conclusions regarding the likely system of accounting in Japan?

3 What is the position of Japan relative to the UK, the USA and Germany, according to Hofstede's analysis?

IASs (15.6)

1 In which areas does accounting practice in Japan depart from that set out in IASs?

2 For each of the issues identified above:

- Describe the treatment prescribed in Japanese GAAP.

- Identify the likely impact on income and shareholders' equity of moving from Japanese GAAP to the relevant IAS standards.

3 What explanations may be offered for these departures from IASs, in terms of the institutional factors described in the chapter?

4 What are the most difficult problems facing accounting in Japan if it seeks harmonisation with the IASC core standards programme?

Professionalism/statutory control (15.7.1)

1 Identify the key features supporting a conclusion that statutory control, rather than professionalism, is a dominant characteristic of Japanese accounting.

2 Explain which institutional influences cause statutory control, rather than professionalism, to be a dominant characteristic of UK accounting.

3 Discuss whether a classification of strong statutory control is appropriate for the 1990s.

Uniformity/flexibility (15.7.2)

1 Identify the key features supporting a conclusion that uniformity, rather than flexibility, is a dominant characteristic of Japanese accounting.

2 Explain which institutional influences cause uniformity, rather than flexibility, to be a dominant characteristic of Japanese accounting.

3 Discuss whether a classification of strong uniformity is appropriate for the 1990s.

Conservatism/optimism (15.7.3)

1 Identify the key features supporting a conclusion that conservatism, rather than optimism, is a dominant characteristic of Japanese accounting.

2 Explain which institutional influences cause conservatism, rather than optimism, to be a dominant characteristic of Japanese accounting.

3 Discuss whether a classification of strong conservatism is appropriate for the 1990s.

Secrecy/transparency (15.7.4)

1 Identify the key features supporting a conclusion that secrecy, rather than transparency, is a dominant characteristic of Japanese accounting.

2 Explain which institutional influences cause secrecy, rather than transparency, to be a dominant characteristic of Japanese accounting.

3 Discuss whether a classification of strong secrecy is appropriate for the 1990s.

Empirical studies (15.8)

1 What is the relative position of Japan as indicated by research studies into classification, comparability and harmonisation?

2 Discuss whether this relative position is appropriate for the 1990s.

REFERENCES

Bloom, R., Long, S. and Collins, M. (1994) 'Japanese and American accounting: Explaining the differences', *Advances in International Accounting*, 6, 265–84.

Brown, P.R. and Stickney, C.P. (1992) 'Instructional case: Tanaguchi Corporation', *Issues in Accounting Education*, 7(1), 57–79.

Brown, P.R., Soybel, V.E. and Stickney, C.P. (1997) 'Achieving comparability of US and Japanese price–earnings earnings', in Choi, F.D.S. (ed.) *International Accounting and Finance Handbook*. 2nd edn. New York: John Wiley, 7.1–7.18.

Cooke, T.E. (1991) 'The evolution of financial reporting in Japan: A shame culture perspective', *Accounting, Business and Financial History*, 1(3), 251–77.

Cooke, T.E. (1993) 'The impact of accounting principles on profits: The USA versus Japan', *Accounting and Business Research*, 23(92), 460–76.

The Economist (1997) *Pocket World in Figures 1998 Edition*. London: Profile Books

Gomi, Y. (1972) *Guide to Japanese Taxes 1997–98*. Tokyo: Zaikei Shoho Sha.

Goto, F. (1987) 'Influence of tax accounting', in Choi, F.D.S. and Hiramatsu, K. (eds) *Accounting and Financial Reporting in Japan*. London: Van Nostrand Reinhold.

Gray, S.J. (1988) 'Towards a theory of cultural influence on the development of accounting systems internationally', *Abacus*, 24(1), 1–15.

Hirose, Y. (1987) 'The promulgation and development of financial accounting standards in Japan', in Choi, F.D.S. and Hiramatsu, K. (eds) *Accounting and Financial Reporting in Japan*. London: Van Nostrand Reinhold.

Hofstede, G. (1984) *Culture's Consequences: International Differences in Work-related Values*. Beverley Hills, CA: Sage Publications.

Kaplan, S.N. and Minten, B.A. (1994) 'Appointment of outsiders to Japanese boards: Determinants and implications for managers', *Journal of Financial Economics*, 36, 225–58.

McKinnon, J.L. (1984) 'Application of Anglo-American principles of consolidation to corporate financial disclosure in Japan', *Abacus*, 20(1), 16–33.

McKinnon, J.L. (1986) *The Historical Development and Operational Form of Corporate Reporting Regulations in Japan*. New York: Garland Publishing.

McKinnon, J.L. and Harrison, G.L. (1985) 'Cultural influence on corporate and governmental involvement in accounting policy determination in Japan', *Journal of Accounting and Public Policy*, 4, 201–23.

Mueller, G.G. (1967) *International Accounting*. London: Macmillan.

Nair, R.D. and Frank, W.G. (1980) 'The impact of disclosure and measurement practices on international accounting classifications', *Accounting Review*, July, 426–50.

Nakanishi, S. (1987) 'Financial reporting by Japanese companies overseas', in Choi, F.D.S. and Hiramatsu, K. (eds) *Accounting and Financial Reporting in Japan*. London: Van Nostrand Reinhold.

Nobes, C.W. (1984) *International Classification of Financial Reporting*. London: Croom Helm.

Rathborne, D. and Grosch, J. (eds) (1997) *The LGT Guide to World Equity Markets 1997*. London: Euromoney Publications.

Someya, K. (1989) 'Accounting "revolutions" in Japan', *The Accounting Historians' Journal*. 16(1), 75–86.

Steven, R. (1996) *Japan and the New World Order: Global Investments Trade and Finance*, London: Macmillan.

Weetman, P. and Gray, S.J. (1990) 'International financial analysis and comparative corporate performance: The impact of UK versus US accounting principles on earnings', *Journal of International Financial Management and Accounting*, 2(2/3), 111–29.

Chapter 16

China

INTRODUCTION

China has become a major economic force in the last few years. With nearly one-quarter of the world's population, China has experienced remarkable growth since it began to liberalise its economy in 1979. If current trends continue, it is forecast that China will become the third largest economy in the world by the year 2000 and the largest by 2020.[1] Since 1979 annual GDP growth has easily exceeded that of any of the 'Asian tiger' economies (at an annual real growth rate of 9%). This has been accompanied by rapid increases in international trade and inward investment through a variety of vehicles including bonds, equity investment and joint ventures. As we will see in this chapter, this has been accompanied by a massive restructuring of China's economic system including its financial institutions and accounting system. New accounting laws, largely based upon IASs, are still being introduced and the accounting system is currently undergoing substantial changes.

This means that the emphasis in this chapter will be slightly different from some of the others. The current accounting system can be understood only if you first understand the key features of the previous system, which was very different from that of any western capitalist country. This chapter will therefore describe the system of accounting that was in place before the current accounting reforms began. The new accounting rules have been introduced in a piecemeal manner over the last decade and many new standards are still to be implemented. This chapter therefore also devotes less space to describing the current system and rules than do most of the other country chapters.

16.2 **THE COUNTRY**

Exhibit 16.1 provides some details about China. What is perhaps most striking is the sheer size of the country and its population. This means that it is a country of contrasts – much of the coastal area is highly industrialised and economically successful, with the population having a rapidly rising standard of living. There are also parts of the hinterland that have been little affected by recent political and economic changes where the rural population barely ekes out a subsistence existence.

---

[1] World Bank forecast, reprinted in Firth (1996)

Exhibit 16.1 CHINA: COUNTRY PROFILE, TAKEN FROM EIU STATISTICS

Population	1,220.2 m.	
Land mass	9,560,900 sq.km	
GDP per head	US $610	
GDP per head in purchasing-power parity	11	(USA=100)
Origins of GDP:	%	
Agriculture	20.5	
Industry	49.2	
Services	30.3	
	%	
Real GDP average annual growth 1985–95	9.5	
Inflation, average annual rate 1989–96	11.3	

Source: The Economist Pocket World in Figures 1998 Edition, The Economist (1997), p. 116

Recent years have witnessed much debate in the western press about just how successful China has been in restructuring its economy. With such a large country it is difficult to get accurate data, and government statistics are often woefully inadequate. From Exhibit 16.1, we can see that *per capita* gross domestic product (GDP) was only US$610 in 1996, implying that China is still a very poor country. However, this figure is somewhat misleading. With a large rural population (more than 70% of the population living in rural areas) much production is for personnel consumption and so is excluded from official statistics. Based upon consumption patterns (for example, a majority of the urban population have colour TVs and washing machines) and life expectancies, it is estimated that the real GNP is anything up to four times greater than the official statistics, placing China on a par with countries such as Thailand or Turkey.

The size of the country obviously makes it much more difficult to modernise and reform the economy. Some smaller Asian economies such as Singapore were able to rapidly develop by pursuing a policy of export-led growth. The sheer size of China rules out reliance upon such strategies, and instead it must develop mainly through internal growth.

The size of the country also means that it is more difficult to administer and co-ordinate economic policies. While centralised control of the economy has been of prime importance, in practice the system is often far from uniform. Many of the economic reforms have been applied in a piecemeal fashion. Institutions have been allowed to grow and develop in response to market needs and government control or regulation has often followed, not preceded, market developments. Different parts of the country have been subject to different rules and various government ministries have imposed different sets of rules on the enterprises and institutions under their control. One example of this is Hong Kong. As from 1 July 1997, Hong Kong returned to the control of China, and China has promised that it will remain as a market-led capitalist system for at least the next 50 years – the 'one country, two systems' policy. That China felt able to do this and that it was prepared to live with such apparently different economic systems co-existing alongside each other is not as remarkable as might at first appear. In an attempt to modernise and increase economic welfare, many of the economic structures of mainland China had already been 'westernised'. In addition, China already had experience of running four Special Economic Zones (SEZs) in the coastal region where the economic rules were already far more liberal than those that applied elsewhere in the country.

16.3 INSTITUTIONS

16.3.1 Political and economic systems

When the communist party came to power in 1949, the most important task facing it was to achieve rapid socio-economic development without depending in any way on the advanced capitalist nations. The only model then available was the Soviet one, which was imported with almost no major changes. Thus, Soviet-style economic and political institutions were introduced including centralised planning via a series of five-year plans.

The 1949 revolution resulted in the public ownership of all enterprises. Public ownership existed in two forms: state enterprises and collectives. Collective enterprises were owned by the people who operated them. State enterprises were held by the state and owned ultimately by the entire population. State ownership was considered to be the ideal, and collectives were generally converted into state enterprises once they reached a certain size. The government was the main, if not the sole, user of financial statements. The economy was run by means of a compulsory comprehensive economic plan – perceived demand was converted into specific production targets for each enterprise. Capital, labour, equipment and materials were all allocated to enterprises on the basis of production targets. Similarly, prices and customers were strictly controlled via the plan. The only role for accounting was therefore to provide information to the government for planning purposes, for resource allocation decisions and for monitoring of the plan. Each state enterprise can perhaps be best thought of as being equivalent to a cost centre in a typical western commercial organisation. There was therefore no real system of external financial reporting as it is commonly understood. Instead, enterprises had to produce uniform statements describing, *inter alia*, their past production levels and cost data.

Starting in 1949, the Chinese leadership attempted to introduce a more uniquely Chinese system. This was seen in the Great Leap Forward of 1958–9 and it culminated, most disastrously, in the Cultural Revolution of 1966–76. The Cultural Revolution attempted to ensure that the country retained its socialist nature – in particular, market structures were not to be introduced and no class system was to be allowed to develop. The attempt to prevent a bureaucratic elite developing by, *inter alia*, forcing intellectuals to undertake manual labour and the creation of revolutionary committees of workers to run their factories, resulted in a major collapse of the economy. Following the death of Mao in 1976 the 'Maoist model' was heavily criticised and a new model of socialist development based upon market-orientated principles and institutions began to be created under the leadership of Deng Xiaoping.[2]

Market socialism is a difficult thing to achieve as it involves maintaining the political system and the position of the present political leadership while also undertaking major changes to the economic system. It is difficult to restructure the economy without also calling into doubt the legitimacy and effectiveness of the political system and politicians who ran the previous socialist economic system. This is one of the major reasons why China is adopting a process of piecemeal economic reforms. It also helps to explain why the process is far from smooth and why, at times, political considerations mean that the economic reforms have stalled.

During the initial period of reform the emphasis was mainly on agriculture and the commune system was dismantled. Some reforms were also made in the commodity markets, with state enterprises being allowed to sell some of their output independently and keep some of their income; some goods were removed from price controls and some private businesses were allowed. Some enterprises were also allowed to raise foreign currency loans and to keep a proportion of any foreign currency that they earned.

From the mid-1980s greater emphasis has been placed on state enterprise reforms. This encompasses a large number of different areas: the finance system has been reformed with commercial banks taking over some of the roles of the central bank, foreign exchange markets have been established, as have stock markets (see below) and even agricultural products and metals futures markets. Many more, but not all, goods are now traded at market prices and most enterprises are increasingly free to trade in the marketplace. However, the process is still far from complete. Many large state enterprises are not able to operate profitably. Forcing them into a free market would lead to a large number of bankruptcies and increased unemployment. This is politically unacceptable and it acts as a major brake on the speed of movement towards freeing all enterprises from state control.

16.3.2 Legal system

It is not much of an exaggeration to say that China did not have a legal system, at least in the sense that it is understood in the west, before the current reforms began. During the period of communist control, the legal system was increasingly seen simply as another tool for the social control of society. Emphasis was placed upon maintaining political control and social order. Other objectives, such as guaranteeing personnel liberties or ensuring the smooth functioning of the economy, were ignored. Legal reform has thus also been an important feature of the last two decades. Economic reforms can be successful only if suitable legal controls and protections are developed in parallel with the new market structures. A complete system of contract and commercial law therefore had to be developed almost entirely from scratch. While there have been a significant number of new codes and statutes introduced, the process is still far from complete.

There are three different levels of legislative power, and accounting has been regulated by institutions at all three levels. Laws are set by the National People's

---

[2] White (1993)

Congress. Below this is the State Council, which issues administrative rules and regulations. Finally, national ministries and commissions issue directives and regulations for the particular industries or enterprises under their control. In the past, different accounting systems have been employed by different industries and the various ministries have imposed different accounting rules. Recent legal moves have therefore not only involved a move away from the traditional fund-based system towards a westernised system, but have also increasingly dismantled industry-specific regulations and moved towards imposing uniform rules on all commercial enterprises, whether foreign owned, joint ventures, equity financed or government owned.

16.3.3 Taxation system

Until the economic reforms began, enterprises were not taxed on their profits or surpluses – all of these were transferred to the state. Starting in 1979, some enterprises were allowed to keep some of their surpluses which, since 1983, have been taxed. Given that the surplus earned was largely outside the control of the enterprise, being dependent instead upon the centralised plan and the amounts of funds given to the enterprise, each enterprise was initially taxed at a different rate. From 1984, this system was simplified and a uniform flat rate tax of 55% was applied to all state enterprises.[3]

Enterprises with foreign investments were treated rather differently. A series of laws were passed starting in 1980, which established the tax structure for these enterprises. Taxable profits were generally the same as reportable profits, although there were some differences. Enterprises were given a number of tax incentives while some items were not deductible for tax purposes. Loss carry-forwards were also allowed. From 1994, the enterprise taxation system has been considerably simplified. State enterprises are now taxed in the same way as other enterprises and the number of different types of taxes substantially reduced. More important for accounting is the fact that there has been a de-coupling of tax and accounting. The financial reporting rules may now differ from the rules used to compute taxable earnings. This means that the influence of the tax rules on financial reporting is likely to decrease over time as new financial accounting rules can be introduced without being constrained by their impact upon tax revenues.

16.3.4 Corporate financing system

One of the most important differences between the economic reforms of China and those of most of eastern Europe has been the greater emphasis that China has placed upon establishing a suitable financial infrastructure. Thus, rather than starting by privatising companies and hoping that stock markets and other necessary financial institutions would then develop naturally as they were needed, China instead began much of its economic reforms at the other end, by setting up the required financial institutions. One of the most important of these institutions is a stock market. If companies are no longer to be financed by the government then

---

[3] Blake and Gao (1995)

there needs to be an active and efficient market in which they can raise public debt and equity.

While there was a stock market in China prior to the communist revolution, it was closed down in 1949 and it was not until the 1980s that moves began to reestablish capital markets. Treasury bonds were first sold to public enterprises in 1981 while, in 1984, state owned enterprises also started issuing bonds. This was rapidly followed by a number of other developments such as the bond credit rating service of the People's Bank of China, a nationwide computerised bond trading network (the Securities Trading Automated Quotations System, STAQS) and foreign currency-denominated commercial and treasury bonds.

A number of commercial enterprises also started issuing shares in 1984. The Shenzhen stock market opened unofficially on 1 December 1990 and the Shanghai Securities Exchange soon after. The number of companies making equity issues initially increased only slowly. By the time Shenzhen stock market officially opened in mid-1991, it had only five listed companies which had increased to 17 by mid-1992. However, the demand for shares was almost limitless. Individuals had to buy application forms before purchasing shares and such was the demand that over 1 million people gathered in Shenzhen at one point in 1992 to buy these application forms. By June 1997, 301 companies were listed in Shanghai and only slightly fewer (273) in Shenzhen. These companies listed and traded in local currency shares available only to Chinese nationals – the so-called A-shares.

By the end of 1991 the Shanghai exchange also began to list a number of Chinese companies that traded US dollar-denominated B-shares while the Shenzhen exchange dealt in Hong Kong dollar-denominated H-shares. By the end of March 1997, there were 87 companies with these shares. They are designed to attract foreign investors. Foreign shareholders cannot gain control of local enterprises and no single investor can acquire more than 5% of an enterprise's share capital without central bank permission. While these shares proved to be very popular with non-Chinese investors, a number of other companies instead decided to list on foreign stock markets. The first companies to list on the Hong Kong and New York markets both gained a listing in October 1992; since then, a number of other companies have listed equity or bonds in these two markets. In the six months leading up to the Chinese takeover of Hong Kong on 1 July 1997, the most active sector of the Hong Kong stock market was the so called 'red-chip' companies.

By the end of 1996, 15 Chinese companies were listed with so-called H-shares on the Hong Kong stock exchange and a further five had listed N-shares on the New York stock exchange (NYSE). There were also plans under way for Chinese companies to list on both the London and Singapore stock exchanges.[4] Exhibit 16.2 lists the eight Chinese companies listed on the NYSE as at October 1997. All of these companies have listed ADRs and have used their listings to raise new capital.

Foreign investors wishing to invest in Chinese companies can also invest in a number of investment funds. By the end of 1996, there were at least 40 funds based in a number of countries including the UK, the USA, Japan, France and Switzerland which specialise in investing in this part of the world.[5]

---

[4] Rathborne and Grosch (1997)
[5] Rathborne and Grosch (1997)

Exhibit 16.2 CHINESE COMPANIES LISTED ON THE NYSE, OCTOBER 1997

Company	Industry	Listed
Beijing Yanhua Petrochemical	Petrochemicals	June 1997
China Eastern Airlines	Passenger airline	February 1997
China Southern Airlines	Commercial airline services	July 1997
Guangshen Railway	Rail transportation	May 1996
Huaneng Power International	Holding co./Power plants	October 1994
Jilin Chemical Industrial	Chemical products	May 1995
Shandong Huaneng Power Development	Electricity generation	August 1994
Shanghai Petrochemical	Petrochemical production	July 1993

Source: www.nyse.com, 28 October 1997

16.3.5 Accounting profession

As might be expected, one of the problems that China is facing is the extreme shortage of qualified accountants. Until the reforms began all that was required at the enterprise level was people who could follow the prescribed systems and record the required transactions. The only professional accountants were the 10,000 or so who had qualified before the communist revolution.[6]

The Accounting Society of China (ASC) was the first accounting body to be set up after the beginnings of the reforms, in January 1980. The ASC is an academic body which seeks to foster education and research. It was the first body to become involved in standard setting when, in 1987, it formed a committee to establish a conceptual framework and promote accounting standards. Its work was superseded by Ministry of Finance initiatives when the ministry formed a similar working group. This was the first stage in setting and enforcing authoritative standards.

The main accounting professional body, the Chinese Institute of Certified Public Accountants (CICPA), was set up in 1984. Government influence can be seen most obviously in its membership, with the Chair of CICPA being the Ministry of Finance Vice-Minister in charge of accounting affairs. Following merger with the Association of Certified Public Accountants (ACPA) in 1996, the membership rose to approximately 58,000 (1 per 20,000 or so of population in comparison to the UK at 1 per 400) (*see* Exhibit 1.6).

While the CICPA does not set accounting standards, it has issued a number of important guidelines or codes of conduct on professional ethics, education and training which all of its members are expected to follow. The government has recently set a target that all enterprises of sufficient size should be audited by qualified CPAs by the year 2000. Selected state enterprises started to be independently audited by qualified CPAs in 1997. Following these initiatives, the CICPA has started to issue its own 'Independent Auditing Standards'. These are generally consistent with IFAC standards. Exhibit 16.3 reproduces the audit report of

---

[6] Blake and Gao (1995)

the Guangzhou Shipyard International Co. (GSI). This report with its reference to 'Independent auditing standards' of China, the 'Accounting Standards for Enterprises' and 'fair view of the state of affairs' can be compared with the Hong Kong audit report for the same company as shown in Exhibit 16.4. (This company is listed in Shanghai and Hong Kong and reports its results using both sets of requirements.) As can be seen, the Hong Kong-based audit report instead talks of 'accounting principles generally accepted' in Hong Kong, Hong Kong Statements of auditing standards and Companies Ordinance while the opinion of the auditors refers to the 'true and fair view', as imported from UK law.

The CICPA also assists the Ministry of Finance in organising the national CPA

Exhibit 16.3 GSI: CHINESE-BASED AUDIT REPORT, DECEMBER 1996

China Guangzhou
Guangzhou Shipyard International Company Limited

We have been appointed by the Company to conduct an audit of the balance sheet as at December 31, 1996 and the profit statement and the statement of changes in financial position for the year then ended. The management of the Company shall be responsible for the truthfulness of the above-mentioned financial statements and our responsibility is to form an opinion on these financial statements based on our audit.

We conducted our audit in accordance with the provisions of 'Independent Auditing Standards for Certified Public Accountants in the People's Republic of China', and based on the specific circumstances of the Company, we have reviewed the compliance of the internal control system, the authenticity of the accounting records and carried out other auditing procedures considered necessary

In our opinion, the financial statements attached to this report which have been prepared in accordance with the 'Accounting Standards for Enterprises' and other relevant financial and accounting regulations of the State, give a fair view of the state of affairs, the operating results and the changes in financial position of the Company for the year. The accounting policies as well as the classification and presentation of items in the financial statements are consistent with those adopted in the previous years

Yangcheng Certified Public Accountants
China Certified Public Accountants
Chen Xiong yi, Huang Wei Cheng

3rd March 1997

Source: GSI, Report of PRC auditors, 1996, p. 42

exams and in approving the registration of CPAs. The 1993 Law of Certified Public Accountants gave the Ministry of Finance power to supervise CPAs, auditing firms and accountancy bodies. It was also made responsible for developing the national CPA exams and authorising the establishment of CPA firms.

Exhibit 16.4 | GSI: HONG KONG-BASED AUDIT REPORT, DECEMBER 1996

To the members of
Guangzhou Shipyard International Company Limited

(incorporated in the People's Republic of China with limited liability)

We have audited the financial statements set out on pages [85] to [126] which have been prepared in accordance with accounting principles generally accepted in Hong Kong.

Respective responsibilities of directors and auditors

The directors are required to prepare financial statements which give a true and fair view. In preparing financial statements which give a true and fair view it is fundamental that appropriate accounting policies are selected and applied consistently.

It is our responsibility to form an independent opinion, based on our audit, on those financial statements and to report our opinion to you.

Basis of opinion

We conducted our audit in accordance with Statements of Auditing Standards issued by the Hong Kong Society of Accountants. An audit includes examination, on a test basis, of evidence relevant to the amounts and disclosures in the financial statements. It also includes an assessment of the significant estimates and judgements made by the directors in the preparation of the financial statements, and of whether the accounting policies are appropriate to the circumstances of the Company and the Group, consistently applied and adequately disclosed.

We planned and performed our audit so as to obtain all the information and explanations which we considered necessary in order to provide us with sufficient evidence to give reasonable assurance as to whether the financial statements are free from material mis-statement. In forming our opinion we also evaluated the overall adequacy of the presentation of information in the financial statements. We believe that our audit provides a reasonable basis for our opinion.

Opinion

In our opinion, the financial statements give a true and fair view of the state of affairs of the Company and the Group at 31 December 1996 and of the Group's profit and cash flows for the year then ended and have been properly prepared in accordance with the disclosure requirements of the Hong Kong Companies Ordinance.

COOPERS & LYBRAND
Certified Public Accountants
Hong Kong

Source: GSI, Report of the international auditors, 1996, p. 84

16.3.6 External influences

Accounting in China has a very long history. Both accounting and auditing systems were highly developed, at least as regards the recording of economic and financial transactions, more than 2,000 years ago. Indeed, the emergence of the first form of accounting can be traced back to the Shang Dynasty (1500–1000 BC). However, accounting failed to develop rapidly after this due at least partially to domestic political upheavals. Thus, until the early part of this century single-entry bookkeeping predominated. Western accounting methods began to be imported into the country in the 1920s although they were still relatively underdeveloped when the People's Republic of China (PRC) was formed in 1949.

With the change to a communist system, China adopted wholesale the Soviet system of accounting. Despite attempts at developing a unique Chinese political and economic system, both during the period of the Great Leap Forward (1958–9) and the Cultural Revolution (1966–76), the accounting system remained largely unchanged until economic liberalisation began in the late 1970s.

China is now attempting to find a unique development path combining social-ist social structures with capitalist markets. This has involved major changes in the ways in which enterprises are organised with the introduction of profit measures and private ownership. This means that the accounting system has also had to be radically restructured, starting virtually from scratch. This has encompassed all aspects of accounting, including not only financial accounting and reporting by both domestic enterprises and foreign joint ventures, but also stock market regula-tions, auditing regulations and accounting education.

As discussed in Chapter 1, it is obviously neither feasible nor sensible to develop a brand new accounting system without reference to the models established else-where. This has meant that China has now begun to import western accounting rules as exemplified by, in particular, International Accounting Standards (IASs). These are being deliberately imported into China by the Chinese authorities rather than being imposed by more powerful players. They are therefore not being imported wholesale without modification; instead, they are being used as a blueprint and are being modified to match more closely the unique environment of China.

16.4 SOCIETAL CULTURE AND ACCOUNTING SUBCULTURE

16.4.1 Confucianism

The culture of China is one of the reasons why accounting remained relatively underdeveloped before the Communist Revolution. Confucianism has traditionally been an important influence in China. It is very much the product of an agricultural society with a pronounced anti-commerce bias. Under this philosophy, peasants are considered the producers of wealth, providing both food and other essential raw materials, while merchants are regarded as being non-productive or even parasites on the peasants. All commercial activities, including accounting, were therefore ascribed a low status and little interest was shown in their development.

Following the foundation of the PRC, Confucianism was heavily criticised as a feudal philosophy and attempts were made to remove its influence. However, it is not easy to change people's beliefs and attitudes and it has remained a significant influence on the Chinese culture.

16.4.2 Hofstede's cultural dimensions

Hofstede did not include China in his (1984) study. However, it might be expected that China would group alongside the South-east Asian countries that were

Exhibit 16.5 HONG KONG: SCORES AND RANKINGS FROM HOFSTEDE'S CULTURAL DIMENSION RESEARCH

Individualism versus collectivism		Large power distance versus small power distance		Strong uncertainty avoidance versus weak uncertainty avoidance		Low nurture versus high nurture	
Score	Rank	Score	Rank	Score	Rank	Score	Rank
25	37	68	15/16	29	49/50	57	28/19

included and in particular Hong Kong. Hofstede's findings with respect to Hong Kong are reproduced in Exhibit 16.5.

While the South-east Asian countries did not cluster together on all four dimensions, they were the only ones to cluster into a large power distance, weak uncertainty avoidance group.

It might be argued that Hofstede's work was based upon questions derived in a western setting and as such it might not be useful in explaining or measuring Chinese culture. A later study[7] explored this issue, it used a very similar methodology but derived the initial questions or value statements from Chinese rather than western scholars. These value statements were then presented to university students from 22 countries. Four underlying cultural dimensions were found. Three of these are significantly related to Hofstede's dimensions of individualism, power distance and nurturing. However, Hofstede's fourth dimension, uncertainty avoidance, was not found to be relevant while a new dimension of 'Confucianism work dynamism' was instead found to be important. In later work, Hofstede called this dimension 'long-term versus short-term orientation'; China tends towards a long-term orientation, placing a high value upon thrift and perseverance.

16.4.3 Cultural values and accounting

As we saw in Chapter 2, cultural values are likely to impact upon accounting. However, it is not immediately obvious how China's particular combination of values will have an impact. As argued by Gray (1988) and shown in Exhibit 16.6, countries with a large power distance should tend to have a uniform, secretive accounting system with a low level of professionalism. In contrast, countries with weak uncertainty avoidance will instead tend to be characterised by a lack of uniformity, relative openness and a high level of professionalism. Which of these two scenarios is more likely therefore depends upon the other features of the country and its culture.

China may also characterised by its relative lack of economic development (a variable that is important for accounting, but was ignored by Gray) and its history of extensive state control. It is also relatively collective, so that individualism is not

---

[7] Hofstede and Bond (1988)

Exhibit 16.6 LINKING GRAY'S ACCOUNTING VALUES TO HOFSTEDE'S CULTURAL DIMENSIONS, IN THE MANNER PROPOSED BY GRAY

Cultural dimensions affecting the country's accounting values	
Professionalism tends to be associated with: ● Individualism ● Weak uncertainty avoidance ● Small power distance	Statutory control tends to be associated with: ● Collectivism ● Strong uncertainty avoidance ● Large power distance
Uniformity tends to be associated with: ● Strong uncertainty avoidance ● Large power distance ● Collectivism	Flexibility tends to be associated with: ● Weak uncertainty avoidance ● Small power distance ● Individualism
Conservatism tends to be associated with: ● Strong uncertainty avoidance ● Collectivism ● High nurture	Optimism tends to be associated with: ● Weak uncertainty avoidance ● Individualism ● Low nurture
Secrecy tends to be associated with: ● Strong uncertainty avoidance ● Large power distance ● Collectivism ● High nurture	Transparency tends to be associated with: ● Weak uncertainty avoidance ● Small power distance ● Individualism ● Low nurture

important and it has a long-term orientation. All of these variables imply that, where there is a conflict between large power distance and small uncertainty avoidance, large power distance will be the more important of the two. The accounting system should be characterised by its low professionalism, high uniformity and high secrecy. This implies that the system should be one in which government or legal control is important, with uniform accounting regulations or even accounting plans. The long-term orientation of people should also favour conservatism and a relatively cautious approach towards the introduction of new rules, ideas and concepts.[8]

16.5 ACCOUNTING REGULATIONS AND THE IASC

16.5.1 Accounting regulations before the reforms

Prior to the reforms accounting regulations, known as the Uniform Accounting Regulations (UAR), were set either directly by the Department of Administration of

---

[8] Chow *et al.* (1995)

Accounting Affairs (a part of the Ministry of Finance) or, in the case of specific industries, by the ministry responsible for that industry and then approved by the Ministry of Finance. The UAR were a system of many uniform plans, each consisting of detailed rules or regulations covering both costing and financial reporting matters. Accounting was controlled by the Ministry of Finance, as it was seen as just one of the many tools available to ensure the efficient functioning of businesses.

The system was a uniform one, with enterprises having to follow detailed regulations. This may be seen in the treatment of depreciation, for example, with only straight-line depreciation being permitted for most enterprises (Chinese–foreign joint ventures followed more permissive regulations). Approved useful lives were promulgated and enterprises were allowed to use different depreciation rates only if they had prior approval. However, while the accounting rules were detailed and rigidly imposed, different systems were developed for enterprises in different sectors or industries, for enterprises with different ownership structures and for enterprises with different budgetary statuses.

The most obvious example of differences across enterprises relates to bookkeeping, with three slightly different systems being used. The debit/credit system was typically used in state owned industrial enterprises, joint ventures and international trade companies. During the Cultural Revolution this system was often replaced by the increase/decrease method which continued to be used by many commercial enterprises. Finally, the receipt/payment method was employed by many banks as well as some collectives and budgetary government units.

Another, more important, difference from western accounting concerned the use of fund accounting. This is not a type of funds flow statement but rather a way of categorising accrual-based assets and liabilities. The balance sheet categorised both assets and liabilities on the basis of their function. This practice originated because of the need to control the activities of enterprises to ensure that they met the national plan. Three categories were used: fixed funds; current funds; and specific funds. Fixed funds were similar to fixed assets in that they included the physical assets of the enterprise used by labour to generate output. However, intangible assets were not included and land was also generally excluded. Land is seen as belonging to the people and therefore it cannot be owned by an enterprise, although increasingly, rights to use land were valued and traded. This practice still continues – for example, Guangzhou Shipyard International (GSI) states that: 'Land use rights are amortised evenly over the useful lives of 50 years . . . Included is land use right of RMB X,000 and this is not yet subject to amortisation as the operations have not commenced.'

Current funds represented those goods and materials, including cash and accounts receivable, which are continuously circulated by the enterprise and any assets below a stipulated value or with a life of less than one year. Specific funds were special-purpose funds which could be used only for certain specified purposes such as employee welfare, research and development (R&D), or fixed asset overhaul and renovation. Funds were obtained from bank loans, from state appropriations – and, from the early 1980s, from retained profits. However, irrespective of the source of funds, they had to be classified as fixed, current or special and could be applied only in that way – the principle of a 'specific fund for a specific purpose'. Exhibits

Exhibit 16.7 FUNDS EMPLOYED BY STATE INDUSTRIAL ENTERPRISES, 1987

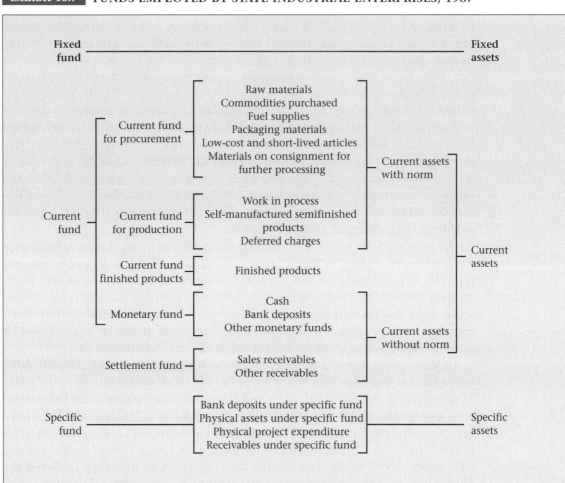

Source: Songnian and Jiafu (1987), p. 12. Reproduced by kind permission of the University of Texas at Dallas, Center for International Accounting Development

16.7 and 16.8 show the types of funds employed by industrial enterprises and the sources of these funds, while Exhibit 16.9 presents a simplified balance sheet.

While the concept of fund accounting is not one that is found in western accounting, many of the underlying principles were the same – each is based upon concepts of accrual accounting, historical costs, going concern and consistency. However, Chinese accounting had no concept of conservatism; it was also a uniform system with no concept of 'true and fair'.

Income was calculated in a somewhat different way. Reflecting the state control of the economy, it was calculated after a number of appropriations which would be treated as profit distributions in western companies (see Exhibit 16.10). Indeed, the current system retains some element of this with transfers from profits to statutory public welfare funds as can be seen in Exhibit 16.11 which gives GSI's accounting policy note explaining its profit distribution policy. Administration and workshop expenses were also treated as product costs. This was an important difference

Exhibit 16.8 FUND SOURCES OF STATE INDUSTRIAL ENTERPRISES, 1987

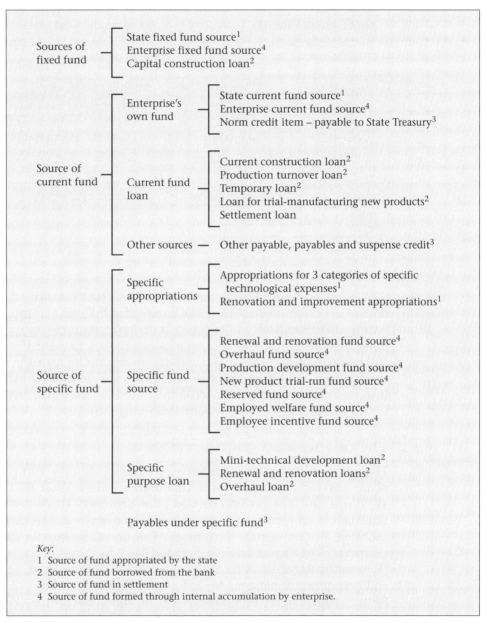

Key:
1 Source of fund appropriated by the state
2 Source of fund borrowed from the bank
3 Source of fund in settlement
4 Source of fund formed through internal accumulation by enterprise.

Source: Songnian and Jiafu (1987), p. 15. Reproduced by kind permission of the University of Texas at Dallas, Center for International Accounting Development

because many enterprises were producing to centralised plans and stock-piling unsaleable inventory. Including such expenses as product costs meant that they were not being charged to the income statement but instead appearing as assets in the balance sheet. Not having any overriding principle of conservatism meant that this practice could continue for long periods.

Exhibit 16.9 EXAMPLE OF A SIMPLIFIED BALANCE SHEET

Application of funds			Sources of funds		
Fixed assets		xx	Fixed funds		xx
Current assets			Current funds		
Current fund for procurement	xx		State current fund source	xx	
Current fund for production	xx		Capital construction loan	xx	
Current fund, finished product	xx		Current fund from other unit	xx	
Other current assets	xx	xx	Current fund loan	xx	xx
Specific assets		xx	Specific fund		xx
Total fund applications		xx	Total fund sources		xx

Source: Songnian and Jiafu (1987), p. 20. Reproduced by kind permission of the University of Texas at Dallas, Center for International Accounting Development

With the economic liberalisation of the 1980s which increased enterprises' freedom of action and with ever more enterprises investing in other enterprises, it became increasingly easy to circumvent the restrictions on the use of the different funds. Also, as enterprises became increasingly free to make their own operating and investment decisions and as private ownership increased in importance, the state had less need to dictate how enterprises should use any particular source of finance. The need to use fund accounting therefore decreased greatly, opening the way for the introduction of western accounting principles.

16.5.2 The financial accounting reforms

The reform of financial accounting can be divided into four phases.[9] The first phase involved regulations for foreign joint ventures. These regulation started, in 1979, with the 'Law on Sino-Foreign Joint Ventures'. This was little more than a statement of principles and it was followed by a series of more detailed laws. These included a joint venture income tax law and laws on contracts and foreign exchange. The first accounting-related laws were passed in March 1985, the 'Accounting Regulations for Sino-Foreign Joint Ventures' and 'Charts of Account and Accounting Statements for Industrial Sino-Foreign Joint Ventures'. Following further changes in the economic system, including the further development of foreign exchange markets, these regulations were replaced, in 1993, by 'Accounting Regulations for Enterprises with Foreign Investments' and 'Charts of Accounts and Accounting Statements for Industrial Enterprises with Foreign Investments'. The 1985 regulations were particularly important as they were the first move away from fund accounting towards international practices.

As discussed above, enterprises started to issue equity shares in 1984. Thus, the second stage of reform involved the introduction of regulations for domestic or Chinese owned public companies. This started in May 1992 when the Ministry of

[9] Roberts *et al.* (1995)

596

Exhibit 16.10 EXAMPLE OF THE FORMAT OF A TYPICAL INCOME STATEMENT

Revenue from sale of products
  of which:
    Revenue from sales of self-sold products
    Less:
      Sales tax
      Factory cost of product sold
      Selling expenses
      Technical know-how transfer charge

Profit from sales of finished products
  of which:
    Profit from sales of self-sold products
  Add
    Other sales products
    Non-operating income
  Less
    Non-operating expenses
    Tax on natural resources
    Fixed fund usage charges
    Current fund usage charges

Total net income
  Add
    Profit transferred from other units
    Deficit to be covered by budget
    Deficit to be covered by profit of later years
  Less
    Profit for repayment of capital construction loan
    Profit for repayment of specific loan
    Net profit of 'three wastes' products left to enterprise
    Processing and assembling with supplied materials from abroad
    Employee welfare and employee incentive funds sources drawn from profit
      and repaying loans
    Profit allotted to other units
    Profit for covering prior year deficits

Subtotal
  Less
    Income tax payable
    Income adjustment tax payable
    Contract fee payable
    Profit to be turned over to the state
    Profit retained by enterprise

    Unretained profit.

Source: Songnian and Jiafu (1987), pp. 26–7. Reproduced by kind permission of the University of Texas at Dallas, Center for International Accounting Development

Exhibit 16.11 GSI: PROFIT DISTRIBUTION POLICY STATEMENT, DECEMBER 1996

15. Profit Distribution

In accordance with relevant regulations and the Company's articles of association, the profit after income tax is distributed in the following sequence:

(1) Offset accumulated losses;

(2) Provide 10% for statutory surplus reserve;

(3) Provide 5–10% for statutory public welfare fund;

(4) Pay dividends of ordinary shares.

Distribution of profit after tax and payment of dividends, as recommended by the Board of Directors, have to be approved in shareholders' meeting. Interim dividends can be declared by the Board of Directors and authorized in shareholders' meeting.

Source: GSI, Notes to the financial statements, 1996, p. 56

Finance and the National Committee of Economic Structure Reform jointly promulgated 'Accounting Regulations for Share Enterprises' This was an important development as it was the first set of regulations which adopted international accounting practices for use by purely domestic enterprises.

While the 1992 laws introduced western-style financial statements it was not a very detailed set of regulations. The third and crucial reform was therefore the 'Enterprise Accounting Standard' (EAS) issued in November 1992 and effective from 1 July 1993. EAS was a major attempt both to unify the accounting systems used by different industries and to move financial accounting towards international accounting practices.

The fourth stage of reform is still taking place, and involves establishing a complete set of accounting standards. By the completion of this phase all industry-specific regulations will have been phased out and financial reporting should be regulated by a uniform and detailed set of accounting standards.

16.5.3 The enterprise accounting standard (EAS)[10]

The EAS was the first major piece of accounting legislation that applied to all enterprises irrespective of their form of ownership. It was also the first attempt to introduce regulations that applied equally to all industries rather than relying, as in the past, on industry-specific regulations. However, the move from a series of uniform fund-based accounting systems to one western-style system involves major changes for enterprises, and it would be unrealistic to expect them to be able to change quickly and easily. A number of transitional arrangements were thus set up including several voluntary industry-specific accounting systems, each based upon EAS but designed to make the move from the respective UAR as simple as possible.

[10] Tang *et al.* (1994)

The EAS involved a change in the function of financial accounting. It has been suggested that prior to the accounting reforms, financial accounting served four objectives:[11]

- to reflect, analyse and assess the implementation of the state plan
- to reflect the source of funds obtained by enterprises and the ways funds are applied, and to evaluate fund utilisation and turnover in operation
- to ensure legitimacy of the sources of funds and fund application
- to provide financial and cost information in order to improve operation and management of enterprises for greater economic benefit.

The EAS introduced the idea of reporting to all external users. Article 11 sets out the objectives of accounting information as:

> Accounting information must be designed to meet the requirements of national economic control, the needs of all concerned external users in order to understand an enterprise's financial position and operating results, and the needs of management to strengthen financial practices and administration. (Tang *et al.* 1994)

The EAS consists of ten chapters dealing not only with the objectives of financial accounting, but also accounting principles; elements of financial statements; recognition; measurement; and financial statements. The EAS therefore contains elements of a conceptual framework in that it includes general principles that should be applied by enterprises even in those areas where there are no specific rules and regulations. It also includes accounting standards or rules for specific types of transactions and events.

The four fundamental accounting principles included were:

- business entity (EAS Article 4)
- going concern (Article 5)
- accounting period (Article 6)
- money measurement (Article 7).

The general principles of accounting measurement included were:

- matching or accrual (Articles 16, 17)
- historical cost accounting (Article 19)
- the clear distinction between revenue and capital items (Article 20).

The qualitative characteristics listed were:

- faithful representation (Article 10)
- relevance (Article 11)
- comparability (Article 12)
- consistency (Article 13)
- timeliness (Article14)

---

[11] Tang *et al.* (1994)

- understandability (Article 15)
- prudence (Article 18)
- comprehensiveness (Article 21).

The regulations then go on to define the elements of financial statements (assets; liabilities; equity; revenue; expenses; profits). Recognition criteria, measurement criteria and measurement rules for specific items (including inventory, fixed assets, leases, long-term investments and intangible assets) are also provided. Finally there are disclosure requirements. (*See* Appendix 16.1 for Articles 1–21 and some of the more important of the other articles and Appendix 16.2 for a set of Chinese financial statements that meet these requirements.)

16.5.4 Accounting regulations and the IASC

China has not adopted any IASs and, given its unique environment, does not intend to adopt any in the future. However, this does not mean that IASs were or will be ignored. CICPA became a member of IFAC and the IASC in May 1997 and China became an observer at IASC Board meetings shortly afterwards. This reflects China's intention to carry on introducing internationally acceptable standards which, while not being identical to IASs, are in harmony with them.

While the principles contained in the EAS are different from the IASC's Statement of Principles in certain important respects, being generally a simpler and less sophisticated statement, they were greatly influenced by the IASC. The differences in the two can be attributed to the unique circumstances of China – a large state owned enterprise system and a system of accounting that was very different from western systems, made it impossible to adopt all of the principles endorsed by the IASC. However, while there still remain a number of significant differences between Chinese regulations and IASs, some Chinese companies voluntarily refer to their use of IASs in their financial statements (*see* Exhibit 16.12).

Exhibit 16.12 CHINESE COMPANIES REFERRING TO USE OF IASs IN THEIR FINANCIAL STATEMENTS

- Louyang Glass
- Shanghai Shangling Electric Appliances Co.
- Shanghai Petrochemicals Co.
- Shenzhen Chiwan Petroleum Supply Base Co.
- Yizheng Chemical Fibre Co.
- Zhenhai Refining & Chemical
- ZRCC

Source: IASC web page, October 1997

16.6 THE ACCOUNTING SYSTEM

16.6.1 Professionalism versus statutory control

As we have seen, the system of accounting is one which relies exclusively upon statutory control. While accounting standards are issued, they are issued by the Ministry of Finance independently of the profession; the CICPA is limited to setting auditing standards and acting as a trade organisation for exams and CPA registration. This position is probably inevitable – the state traditionally closely controlled all enterprises by a system of centralised plans and as one part of this system of control it imposed a highly regulated set of accounting plans. The state is unlikely to give up this power to a professional body unless there is a very good reason to do so. The profession is also still relatively new, small and powerless and it is currently occupied with the problems involved in meeting the new audit requirements. As such, it is unlikely to be in the position to offer a strong case for why standard setting should be devolved from the state. The interesting question is what might happen in the future. It remains to be seen whether or not, once the profession expands in size and once the full set of basic accounting regulations are in place, the system will rely less exclusively upon statutory control.

16.6.2 Uniformity versus flexibility

While the accounting system lies at an extreme position on the professionalism/ statutory control continuum, it is more difficult to place it in relation to uniformity/flexibility. The UAR was a uniform system giving enterprises no discretion on how to account for particular transactions or events. This philosophy continues into the new regulations although there are a number of areas where enterprises are given almost complete discretion over the methods to use. However, in most cases there is flexibility not because this is considered to be desirable but because the rules are new. They are being introduced in a piecemeal fashion and the EAR was not sufficiently detailed to act as a complete guide to action. The new standards should introduce far less flexible rules.

There are several areas where the rules are currently very flexible. A few examples are given below.

16.6.2.1 Revenue recognition

The general principles for revenue recognition are similar to those espoused by the IASC but they are far less detailed and offer no help in deciding whether or not revenue should be recognised in unclear situations. Thus EAS, Article 45, states that:

> Enterprises generally recognise revenue when merchandise is shipped, service is provided, money collected or the rights to collect money obtained.

In contrast, IAS 18 (revised) requires that several conditions should be fulfilled before revenues can be recognised. In the case of the sale of goods, for example, revenues should be recognised only if there is no significant uncertainty regarding the consideration that will be derived; the associated costs incurred in producing the goods; and the extent to which the goods may be returned. In addition, the standard has an extensive appendix illustrating its application in various situations.

16.6.2.2 Inventory valuation

This is perhaps the most surprising instance of extreme flexibility. While it would have been easy to impose a uniform system mandating one particular method, EAS Article 28 instead allows enterprises considerable freedom in how they account for inventory. They are permitted to use FIFO, LIFO, weighted or moving average, or specific identification methods of valuation – thus all the alternatives permitted by IAS 2, both preferred and allowed alternatives, are permitted.

Companies can use the lower of cost or market rule, although not all do so. GSI's policy is given in Exhibit 16.13.

Exhibit 16.13 GSI: ACCOUNTING POLICY FOR INVENTORIES, DECEMBER 1996

7. Inventories

Inventories of the Company are stated at cost.

(1) Raw materials and low-value consumable are stated at standard costs. The stated amount is adjusted for price variance to arrive at the actual cost at the end of month.

(2) Low-value consumable are amortized upon issuance for use.

(3) Finished products and work-in-progress are stated at actual cost.

14. Inventories and long-term contract work in progress

Inventories are stated at the lower of historic cost and net realizable value. Where the net realizable value of inventories are lower than historic cost, the book value will be adjusted with the reduction included in the profit and loss of the current period.

Income from long-term contract work in progress are account for when there is reasonable certainty as to the financial outcome of the contract and the percentage completion basis is adopted. Where it is anticipated that based on the portion completed and the portion yet to be completed in accordance with the terms of contracts will incur a loss, provision will be made accordingly.

Source: GSI, Notes to the financial statements, 1996, pp. 53 and 56

16.6.2.3 Depreciation

The permissive treatment of inventory is in marked contrast to the treatment of depreciation. The required treatment of depreciation differs from IAS 16 (revised). Enterprises are still not free to select either the most appropriate method of depreciation or the economic lives of their assets. Instead, depreciation remains essentially unchanged from the previous regulations and excess depreciation is permitted (*see* Article 30 in Appendix 16.1).

16.6.3 Conservatism versus optimism

The concept of conservatism or prudence is a new and controversial concept for most Chinese enterprises. According to EAS the 'principle of prudence should be followed in reasonably determining the possible loss and expense' (Article 18). However, prudence is still not an overriding concept and it is not universally applied. The reasons for this are twofold. First, prudence had always been regarded as a feature of capitalist accounting which could be used by management to manipulate profits and to exploit the workers. As such, criticisms of the concept used to be found in nearly all Chinese accounting textbooks until the 1980s. Second, prudence tends to result in a reduction in reported surpluses or profits. As these were handed back to the state, the introduction of prudence would have resulted in a fall in state revenues.

When the measurement rules for specific assets are considered it is clear that while the Chinese system has moved towards IASs, it is still different from IASs in certain important respects. Some of the more important differences are briefly described below.

16.6.3.1 Valuation rules – tangible assets

Looking first at fixed assets, EAS Article 30 deals with tangible assets. The recording of cost is the same as the IAS preferred treatment, namely historical costs with interest costs being capitalised if relevant, while the treatment of leased assets is based upon economic substance. The allowed alternative of revaluation is generally not permitted. The only exception to this concerns the transfer of enterprises from state control to private ownership. On transfer, such enterprises must revalue their assets to market values, but no further revaluations are permitted at later dates.

16.6.3.2 Valuation rules – intangible assets

The EAS is more all-embracing than are IASs in this area. EAS requires similar treatment for all intangible assets including patents, non-patented technology, trademarks, copyrights, rights to use sites and positive goodwill. All purchased intangible assets must be initially recorded at cost, as should all self-generated intangible assets. This requirement to account for self-generated patents, trademarks, copyrights and technology goes considerably beyond the scope of accounting requirements in most countries, and the problems of actually costing these items remains unresolved. Once the initial costs have been recorded, they must then be amortised over the periods expected to benefit, if any; otherwise they must be amortised over a period of not less than ten years (Article 31).

For example, GSI states its accounting policy in this area as:

> Intangible assets are stated at cost. Amortization is provided to write-off the cost evenly over the legal or contractual lives or, in the absence of legal or contractual lives, evenly over the useful lives. Where the useful lives of intangible assets cannot be ascertained, amortization is provided evenly over a period of no less than 10 years.

When it comes to the Hong Kong GAAP statements, GSI does not appear to capitalise or recognise any intangible assets.

16.6.3.3 Deferred assets

The Chinese regulations are also optimistic with respect to the recognition and amortisation of deferred assets. For example, GSI recognises start-up costs as a deferred asset in its Chinese financial statements. Again, these are not capitalised as an asset in its Hong Kong GAAP-based financial statements (*see* Exhibit 16.14).

Exhibit 16.14 GSI: ACCOUNTING POLICY FOR DEFERRED ASSETS, DECEMBER 1996

9. 递延资产
Deferred Assets

递延资产分类及其摊销：
Deferred assets are categorized and amortised as follows:

	发生额 Cost 人民币千元 RMB'000	已摊销额 Accumulated amortisation 人民币千元 RMB'000	合 并 Consolidated 1996 帐面余额 Net book value 人民币千元 RMB'000	剩余摊销 年限 Unamortised period 人民币千元 RMB'000
广州市万达木业有限公司 Guangzhou Masterwood Company	开办费 292	146	146	2年06月
广州市广联集装箱运输公司 Guangzhou Guanglian Transportation Company Limited	开办费 684	346	338	3年
新会市南洋船舶工业公司 Xinhui City Nanyang Shipping Company	开办费 1,848	–	1,848	–
广州永联钢结构有限公司 Guangzhou United Steel Structures	开办费 5,562	–	5,562	–
广州三龙工贸工程有限公司 Guangzhou Three Dragon Industrial Trading & Development Company	开办费 28	7	21	2年03月
广州兴顺船舶服务有限公司 Guangzhou Xingshun Ship Service Company Limited	开办费 8	–	8	–
	8,422	499	7,923	

Deferred assets represent pre-operating expenses incurred by certain subsidiaries, and subject to amortisation upon commencing of commercial production. Deferred assets of Guangzhou United Structures Limited and Guangzhou Xinshun Ship Service Company Limited are not yet subject to amortisation as these two companies are in the preliminary set up period, and Xinhui City Nanyang Shipping Industrial Company is also not subject to amortisation as the operations have not commenced.

Pre-operating expenses are amortised evenly over a period of not less than 5 years from the first month after the month of commencing operations or according to the actual period of agreement where the agreement period is less than five years.

Source: GSI, Notes to the financial statements, 1996, pp. 68–9

16.6.3.4 Investments

Prudence has also been ignored in the mandated treatment for long-term investments. IAS 25 requires companies to recognise any permanent diminution in the value of long-term investments while also permitting the use of revalued amounts as an alternative method of valuation. In contrast, EAS permits only the use of historical costs, and does not allow this figure to be written down in recognition of any permanent fall in the value of the investment (Article 29). Similar rules apply to short-term investments, which also cannot be written down below their historical costs (Article 26). This contrasts to IAS 25, which mandates the use of the lower of cost or market rule.

16.6.3.5 Inventory

The different attitude towards prudence can also be seen in the treatment of other current assets, in particular inventory. EAS Article 28 requires the use of historical cost only, while IAS 2 (revised) again mandates the use of the lower of cost or market rule. The reason for this difference is perhaps made clear when it is realised that there are large quantities of outdated inventory being held by many enterprises and writing these down to their economic values would have led to significant losses being shown.

16.6.3.6 Doubtful debts

One of the effects of introducing the concept of prudence relates to the treatment of doubtful debts with doubtful debt provisions now being required. However, judgement is circumscribed and enterprises cannot provide for doubtful debts in excess of maximum limits prescribed by state regulations. In addition, doubtful debts can be written off only when the debtor is declared bankrupt or is deceased or if the debt has been outstanding for at least three years.

For example, GSI states that: 'Provision for doubtful debts is made at 0.3% to 0.5% of the closing balance of accounts receivable.' While no policy is disclosed in the Hong Kong GAAP-based statements, the policy used would appear to be far more prudent. The total amount disclosed for accounts receivable in the Chinese GAAP consolidated balance sheet is RMB629.1 million. In the Hong Kong GAAP-based statement, the group discloses long-term receivables of RMB208.6 million and short-term receivables of RMB237.2 million.

16.6.4 Secrecy versus transparency

16.6.4.1 Required disclosures

EAS Article 57 requires enterprises to produce all the statements normally found in western annual reports:

- a balance sheet
- an income statement
- a statement of changes in financial position (or a cash flow statement)
- supporting schedules

- notes to the financial statements
- explanatory statements on financial condition.

Article 64 goes on to explain the purpose of the notes to the accounts and the information that should be included in the notes:

> Notes to the financial statements are explanatory to related items in the financial statement of the enterprise concerned so as to meet the needs to understand the contents of the statements. This should include mainly:
>
> 1. the accounting methods adopted for the current and previous accounting periods;
> 2. changes in accounting treatments between the current and prior periods, including the reasons for, and impact on the financial performance and status of the enterprise of such changes;
> 3. description of unusual items;
> 4. detailed information relating to major items listed in the accounting statements; and
> 5. any other explanations necessary to provide users with a clear view and understanding of the financial statements.

These requirements do not differ significantly from IASs, although they are generally far less detailed and lack sufficient explanation to be easily and consistently implemented.

16.6.4.2 Consolidated accounts

The lack of detail in the EAS requirements can most obviously be seen in consolidated accounts. One of the major changes that has occurred in China in the past decade or so is the increase in mergers and takeovers. Because of these economic changes, the EAS has, for the first time, required enterprises to produce consolidated statements. However, the regulations are not as detailed or as prescriptive as those laid down by the IASC. Article 63 merely states that:

> Consolidated financial statements shall be prepared by the enterprise parent which owns 50 per cent or more of the total capital of the enterprise it invested in (acts as a subsidiary) or otherwise owns the right of control over the invested enterprise. Financial statements of an invested enterprise in a special line of business not suitable for consolidation, may not be consolidated with the parent company.

Unlike the IASC, the EAS does not specify the method of accounting that should be used, whether pooling of interests or the purchase method, nor does it give any further guidance on when a subsidiary should be excluded from consolidation. This is an area that will be covered in later standards and, while they will provide more details on how to account for groups, it remains to be seen just how detailed the requirements will be.

16.6.4.3 Voluntary disclosures

As we have seen, the new requirements mark a major change from the old system. In the past, enterprises had only to report to the state and they were not expected to produce any more information than that which was required. As we saw above, the EAS has introduced the idea of reporting information useful to all external users. In addition, increasing numbers of enterprises are moving from state ownership and the numbers of listed companies is now increasing quite rapidly. These changes imply that at least some enterprises are likely to begin to disclose extra information voluntarily. However, this is likely to be a slow process and the level of voluntary disclosure by most companies is likely to remain relatively low at least for the next few years.

16.7 EMPIRICAL STUDIES

16.7.1 Classification studies

China has not been included in any of the empirical studies concerned with classifying accounting systems. If it had been included, it would have formed an extra or new group. Until the reforms began it would have grouped alongside the USSR and other eastern European countries. Since the Chinese reforms began, China has moved away from a centralised, socialist and plan-based accounting system. Likewise, the countries of eastern Europe have also been dismantling their accounting systems and replacing them with systems more akin to those in western countries. If the Chinese accounting reforms described above are compared with those of, for example, Hungary, as discussed in Chapter 14, it is clear that the reforms have taken somewhat different directions. We saw in Chapter 14 how Hungary has been heavily influenced by the EU and has implemented accounting rules designed to be in harmony with EU rules. China, in contrast, is attempting to harmonise with the IASC while adapting the standards to meet the continuing unique features of the country. While China has introduced many of the institutions that exist in free markets, state owned enterprises are still important and the state still maintains its socialist orientation with control of the economy and regulation of business being of prime importance. Thus, if China were now to be classified alongside other countries it would probably no longer form a large group with all the countries of eastern Europe; instead, it would probably form its own unique group as a country that has a system that shows the influence of international standards while still retaining some characteristics of the pre-reform system.

16.7.2 Comparability measures

We might expect the figures reported by Chinese companies to be quite different from those reported by similar companies from other countries, because of differences in the accounting rules and differences in the environment in which the companies act. As we saw above, the concept of conservatism is a new one in China. While historical costs have been used, assets have not in the past been written down below cost. To the extent that inventories are overvalued and liabilities are not recognised, Chinese profits will be relatively overstated. Similarly, R&D capitalisation and the capitalisation of self-generated intangibles and pre-operating expenses will also lead to a relative overstatement of earnings. However, there are other accounting methods used in China that will in contrast tend to reduce reported earnings. The use of LIFO, one-off fixed asset revaluations and excess depreciation charges will all reduce reported earnings. Whether the overall effect is one of reducing or increasing earnings in contrast with the equivalent UK or US firm is not obvious.

We should not generalise to all companies from the case of one firm, but as an illustration of differences, Exhibit 16.15 gives the reported figures for GSI under both Chinese and Hong Kong GAAP.

Exhibit 16.15 GSI: COMPARISON OF CHINESE AND HONG KONG GAAP-BASED FIGURES, 1993–6

| | PRC accounting standards | | | | Hong Kong GAAP | | | |
	1996	*1995*	*1994*	*1993*	*1996*	*1995*	*1994*	*1993*
Profit before tax	40.3	152.4	189.3	128.3	40.5	122.3	219.7	128.5
Profit attributable	33.3	127.0	157.3	111.2	33.3	101.3	183.1	111.2
Total assets	2724	3034	2575	1996	2533	2704	2522	2024
Total liabilities	1357	1676	1296	794	1171	1346	1218	822
EPS	.067	.257	.318	.225	.067	.205	.370	.361
Equity/Total net assets	48.6	43.4	49.3	60.1	52.3	48.7	51.3	59.3
Current ratio	1.32	1.52	1.55	2.09	1.17	1.69	1.57	2.05

16.8 FUTURE DEVELOPMENTS

As we have seen, the EAS requirements are not only different from IASs in some important respects, but they are also far less detailed. The EAS says little more on consolidation, for example, than 'consolidation is required where relevant'. This position cannot continue for too long and the Accounting Affairs Administration Department of the Ministry of Finance has set up an Accounting Standards Task Force while the Accounting Society of China has set up the Research Group on Fundamental Accounting Theory and Accounting Standards.

Plans were announced as long ago as 1994 to issue a further 30 accounting standards of three types:

- standards covering each of the accounting elements (specific assets, equity, revenue, etc)
- standards covering each financial statement, including consolidated statements
- standards for specific transactions (including foreign exchange transactions, R&D, long-term contracts, leases and hire-purchase contracts, pensions, income taxes, business combinations and special transactions of various industries including banks).

All 30 have now been issued in draft form and the first of the new standards, 'Disclosure of Related Party Relationships' came into force at the beginning of 1997. The standard is generally consistent with IAS 24 although, unlike IAS 24, it also applies to state owned enterprises. The standard is also more prescriptive than the international standard. IAS 24 does not define 'significant influence', being content to leave it up to the professional discretion of reporting entities and their auditors. The Chinese standard instead defines a related party as one which controls, directly or indirectly, at least 10% of the voting capital of the enterprise.

While this definition excludes some situations that will be included in IAS 24, it offers the advantages of being simple to understand and simple to apply in a country where the need to provide this type of information is new and where there are a limited number of qualified accountants and auditors.

While this is only one of 30 new standards, it is probable that the other standards will follow a similar model – that is, it is likely that they will all be somewhat simpler than the IASs they are based upon. This ease of use and understanding comes with a cost, increased uniformity and rigidity, so that they are less able to deal with unusual situations or special cases.

16.9 HONG KONG CHINA[12]

As discussed above, Honk Kong reverted from British control to Chinese control in July 1997 when it became a Special Administrative Region (SAR) of China. Hong Kong, or as it is now officially termed, Hong Kong China, had been acquired by the British in stages from 1842 and since then it has been economically highly successful, as can be seen if the economic data given in Exhibit 16.16 is examined.

Exhibit 16.16 HONG KONG VERSUS CHINA: COUNTRY PROFILE TAKEN FROM EIU STATISTICS

	China	*Hong Kong*	
Population	1,220.2 m.	6.1 m.	
Land mass	9,560,900 sq.km	1,075 sq.km	
GDP per head	US $610	US $23,245	
GDP per head in purchasing-power parity	11	85	(USA=100)
Origins of GDP:	%	%	
Agriculture	20.5	0.1	
Industry	49.2	16.0	
Services	30.3	83.9	
	%	%	
Real GDP average annual growth 1985–95		9.5	6.7
Inflation, average annual rate 1989–96	11.3	9.1	

Source: The Economist Pocket World in Figures 1998 Edition, The Economist (1997), pp. 116, 136

Hong Kong has succeeded not only as a trading nation but also increasingly as an important financial centre. With nearly 600 companies quoted on the Hong Kong stock market (*see* Exhibit 1.3), the stock exchange has grown rapidly in recent years, now accounting for nearly 2% of the total world market capitalisation (*see* Exhibit 1.4) making it the ninth largest stock market in the world at the end of 1995, just behind the Dutch market,[13] a remarkable achievement for a country

---

[12] Nobes and Parker (1998)
[13] *The Economist* (1997), p. 58

with a population of just 6.1 million. The economic success of Hong Kong can also be seen in its GNP – with a *per capita* GNP of over US$23,000, it is the sixteenth richest country in the world, sandwiched between Sweden and Finland.

As discussed in the Introduction to this chapter, China has promised that Hong Kong will remain as a market-led capitalist system for at least the next 50 years, the 'one country, two systems' policy. Given the tiny size of Hong Kong compared to China, the absorption of Hong Kong into China might at first sight be thought to be of little significance to China. However, as we have seen throughout this chapter, China is undergoing a profound process of change. It is introducing market-based laws and regulations and moving more and more towards a market-led capitalist system as exemplified by the economy of Hong Kong. Given the economic success of Hong Kong, it might be expected that Hong Kong will therefore be an important influence upon the rest of China. Thus, when we try to predict future changes in the Chinese accounting system, one place to look for possible influences is the Hong Kong accounting system.

The institutions of Hong Kong have all been heavily influenced by the British. This includes the legal system and corporate legislation and the accounting profession. For example, the Hong Kong Society of Accountants (HKSA) sets its examinations in conjunction with the UK-based Association of Chartered Certified Accountants (ACCA). Membership of the HKSA is also open to accountants that are professionally qualified in the USA or a number of British Commonwealth countries including Australia, Canada and South Africa as well as the UK. As in the UK, accounting is mainly regulated via statute or company law and accounting standards. Statute, in the form of the Companies Ordinance 1965, was very largely based upon the UK Companies Act 1948. Thus, it sets out basic requirements to disclose group accounts and directors' reports and details certain disclosures inside both the accounts and the directors' report. As far as accounting is concerned, the Act is very much a disclosure act and it does not include any valuation or measurement rules. Of probably greater significance are the accounting standards which have tended to fill the gap and cover most measurement issues. Also important are auditing standards, these standards are issued by the Accounting Standards Committee (ASC) and the Auditing Standards Committee (AUSC), both committees of the HKSA. Standards are thus professionally set, however, the ASC is made up not only of 'big-6' or international auditing firms employees but also members from small audit firms, industry and the stock exchange.

As in the UK prior to the ASB, these standards have no statutory or legal backing. Instead, the HKSA has made them mandatory on its members. In other words, if a company fails to comply with standards, there is no legal sanction that can be taken against the company. However, if the failure to comply is not due to the necessity to report a 'true and fair view' the auditor must qualify the accounts. Failure to issue a qualified report would mean that the auditor could, at least potentially, be held liable to professional misconduct.

Until 1993, the standards issued by the ASC were mainly local adaptations of UK standards. However, as discussed in Chapter 11, the UK has since then been increasingly influenced by EU Directives. Many of Hong Kong's companies have also become increasingly international – Exhibit 16.17 lists the Hong Kong companies listed on the NYSE.

Exhibit 16.17 HONG KONG COMPANIES LISTED ON THE NYSE, 1997

Company	Industry	Date listed
H.K. Telecommunications	Telecommunications	Dec. 1988
Tommy Hilfiger	Sportswear	Sept. 1992
Brilliance China Automotive	Auto manufacture	Oct. 1992
Ek Chor China Motorcycle	Motorcycle manufacture	June 1993
China Tire Holdings	Tyre manufacture	July 1993
Amway Asia Pacific	Distribution	Dec. 1993
Renaissance Hotel Gp.	Hotel management	Oct. 1995–Mar. 97
Asia Satellite Telecommunications	Telecommunications	June 1996
APT Satellite	Telecommunications	Dec. 1996

Source: www.nyse.com, November 1997

From 1993, the standards issued have very largely been local adaptations of IASs. Hong Kong has decided not to issue its own standards nor to uncritically accept IASs; instead, it currently reviews all IASs to assess their suitability to the particular circumstances of the country. If they are considered suitable, they are issued as local standards, adapted if necessary to meet any unique local circumstances.

16.10 SUMMARY AND CONCLUSIONS

In this chapter, you have seen described a country of contrasts. China has undergone profound changes in recent years. The economic system is still changing and the country is in the midst of introducing many new accounting standards. China has moved from a system of public ownership of all enterprises to a mixed system with increasing private ownership of both small and large companies. Many companies now freely trade their shares on both domestic and overseas stock markets. However, the economic changes are still not complete, and many parts of the economy are still owned and controlled by the state.

The communist system led to a uniform accounting system, the recent economic reforms have resulted in the introduction of new accounting laws, the most important being the Enterprise Accounting Standard 1992. However, the system can still be characterised in terms of low professionalism and high secrecy. It is rather more difficult to characterise the system in terms of conservatism and uniformity – in some areas, the system is still very rigid or uniform, in others, the system may be characterised by extreme flexibility. Similarly, while conservatism or prudence is a new concept, in some areas the system is very conservative while in other areas it is far from conservative. Finally, there is the fairly large impact of the IASC, while China is not going to introduce IASs directly, the new standards are to be based upon IASs. This is similar to the approach adopted by Hong Kong. However, it remains to be seen how different the standards will be from IASs – they will tend to be simpler and probably also more uniform. How much more simplified they will be is impossible to tell.

■ APPENDIX 16.1: ACCOUNTING STANDARDS FOR ENTERPRISES

Chapter I General provisions

Article 1. In accordance with 'The Accounting Law of the People's Republic of China', these standards are formulated to meet the needs of developing a socialist market economy in our country, to standardise accounting practice and to ensure the quality of accounting information.

Article 2. These standards are applicable to all enterprises established within the territory of the People's Republic of China. Chinese enterprises established outside the territory of the People's Republic of China . . . are required to prepare and disclose their financial reports to appropriate domestic regulatory authorities in accordance with these standards.

Article 3. Accounting systems of enterprises are required to comply with these standards.

Article 4. An enterprise shall account for all its transactions to reflect the production and operating activities of the enterprise.

Article 5. Accounting and financial reports should proceed on the basis that the enterprise is a continuing entity and will remain in operation into the foreseeable future.

Article 6. An enterprise shall account for its transactions and prepare its financial statements in distinct accounting periods. Accounting periods may be a fiscal year, a quarter, or a month . . .

Article 7. The Renminbi is the bookkeeping base currency of an enterprise. A foreign currency may be used as the bookkeeping base currency for enterprises which conduct transactions mainly in foreign currency. However, in preparing financial statements, foreign currency transactions are to be converted into Renminbi . . .

Article 8. The debit and credit double entry bookkeeping technique is to be used for recording all accounting transactions.

Article 9. Accounting records and financial reports are to be compiled using the Chinese language. Minority or foreign languages may be used concurrently with the Chinese language . . .

Chapter II General principles

Article 10. The accounting records and financial reports must be based on financial and economic transactions as they actually take place, in order to truly reflect the financial position and operating results of an enterprise.

Article 11. Accounting information must be designed to meet the requirements of national macro-economy control, the needs of all concerned external users to understand an enterprise's financial position and operating results, and the needs of management of enterprises to strengthen their financial management and administration.

Article 12. Accounting records and financial statements shall be prepared according to stipulated accounting methods, and accounting information of enterprises must be comparable and convenient to be analysed.

Article 13. Accounting methods used shall be consistent from one period to the other and shall not be arbitrarily changed. Changes and reasons for changes, if necessary, and their impact on an enterprise's financial position and operating results, shall be reported in notes to the financial statements.

Article 14. Accounting and financial reports preparation must be conducted in a timely manner.

Article 15. Accounting records and financial reports shall be prepared in a clear, concise manner to facilitate understanding, examination and use.

Article 16. The accrual basis of accounting is to be adopted.

Article 17. Revenue shall be matched with related costs and expenses in accounting.

Article 18. The principle of prudence should be followed in reasonably determining the possible loss and expense.

Article 19. The values of all assets are to be recorded at historical costs at the time of acquisition. The amount recorded in books of account shall not be adjusted even though a fluctuation in their value may occur, except when State laws or regulations require specific treatment or adjustments.

Article 20. A clear distinction shall be drawn between revenue expenditures and capital expenditures. Expenditure shall be regarded as revenue expenditure where the benefits to the enterprise is only related to the current fiscal year; and as capital expenditure where the benefits to the enterprise last for several fiscal years.

Article 21. Financial reports must reflect comprehensively the financial position and operating results of an enterprise. Transactions relating to major economic activities are to be identified, appropriately classified, and accounted for, and separately reported in financial statements.

Chapter III   Assets

Article 22. Assets are economic resources, which are measurable by money value, and which are owned or controlled by an enterprise, including all property, rights as a creditor to others, and other rights.

Article 26. . . . Marketable securities shall be accounted for according to historical cost as obtained.

Article 27. . . . Receivables and prepayments shall be accounted for according to actual amount.

Article 28. . . . All inventories shall be accounted for at historical cost as obtained. Those enterprises which keep books at planned cost or norm cost in daily accounting shall account for the cost variances and adjust planned cost (or norm cost) into historical cost periodically.

When inventories issuing, enterprises may account for them under the following methods: first-in-out, weighted average, moving average, specific identification, last-in first-out, etc.

. . . All the inventories shall be disclosed at historical cost in accounting statement.

Article 29. . . . In accordance with different situation, shares investment and other investments shall be accounted for by cost method or equity method respectively.

Article 30. . . . Fixed assets shall be accounted for at historical cost as obtained. Interest of loan and other related expenses for acquiring fixed assets, and the exchange difference from conversion of foreign currency loan, if incurred before the assets have been put into operation or after they have been put into operation but before the final account for completed project is made, shall be accounted as fixed assets value; if incurred after that, shall be accounted for as current profit or loss.

Fixed assets coming from donations shall be accounted through evaluation with reference to market price, wear and tear degree or determined the value with relevant evidence provided by contributors. Expenses incurred on receiving those donated fixed assets, shall be accounted for as the fixed assets value.

Fixed assets financed by leasing shall be accounted with reference of the way fixed assets are accounted and shall be explained in notes to the accounting statements.

Depreciation on the fixed assets shall be accounted according to state regulations. On the basis of the original cost, estimated residual value, the useful life of the fixed assets or estimated working capacity, depreciation on the fixed assets shall be accounted for on the straight-line method or the working capacity (or output) method. If approved or conforming to relevant regulations, accelerated depreciation method may be adopted.

Article 31. Intangible assets refer to assets that will be used by an enterprise for a long term without material state, including patents, non-patented technology, trademark, copyrights, right to use sites, and goodwill, etc.

Intangible assets obtained through purchase shall be accounted for at actual cost. Intangible assets received from investors shall be accounted for at the assessed value recognised or the amount specified in the contract. Self-developed intangible assets shall be accounted at actual cost in the development process.

All intangible assets shall be averagely amortised periodically over the period benefited from such expenditures and be shown with un-amortised balance in accounting statement.

Chapter IV Liabilities

Article 34. A liability is debt borne by an enterprise, measurable by money value, which will be paid to a creditor using assets, or services.

Chapter V Owners' equity

Article 38. Owners' equity refers to the interest of the investors remaining in the net assets of an enterprise, including capital of the enterprise invested in by investors, capital reserve, surplus reserve, and undistributed profit retained in the enterprise, etc.

Article 39. Invested capital is the capital fund actually invested in the enterprise by its investors, whether it be in form of cash, physical goods or other assets for the operation of the enterprise . . .

Article 40. Capital reserve includes premium on capital stock, legal increment of property value through revaluation and value of donated assets accepted, etc.

Article 41. Surplus reserve refers to the reserve fund set up from profit according to relevant government regulations.

Chapter VII   Profit and loss

Article 54. Profit is the operating results of an enterprise in an accounting period, including operating profit, net investment profit and net non-operating income.

Operating profit is the balance of operating revenue after deducting operating cost, periodic expenses and all turnover taxes, surtax and fees.

Net investment profit is the balance of income on external investment after deducting investment loss.

Net non-operating income is the balance of non-operating income after deducting non-operating expenses. Non-operating income and expenses have no direct relationship with the production operations of an enterprise.

Chapter IX   Financial reports

Article 62. Accounting statements should be prepared from the records of account books, completely recorded and correctly checked and other relevant information. It is required that they must be true and correct in figures, complete in contents and issued on time.

Article 63. Consolidated financial statements shall be prepared by the enterprise (acts as a parent company) which owns 50 per cent or more of the total capital of the enterprise it invested in (acts as subsidiary) or otherwise owns the right of control over the invested enterprise. Financial statements of an invested enterprise in special line of business not suitable for consolidation, may not be consolidated in the financial statements of the parent company.

APPENDIX 16.2: GUANGZGHOU SHIPYARD
INTERNATIONAL CO. LTD: FINANCIAL STATEMENTS
(as prepared in accordance with PRC accounting standards, December 1996)

Balance Sheets
资产负债表

(prepared in accordance with PRC accounting standards)
(根据中华人民共和国会计准则编制)
Year ended 31 December, 1996
截至1996年12月31日止年度

资产 Assets	附注 Note	合并 Consolidated		母公司 Parent Company	
		1996 人民币千元 RMB'000	1995 人民币千元 RMB'000	1996 人民币千元 RMB'000	1995 人民币千元 RMB'000
流动资产： **Current assets**					
货币资金 Cash and bank balances	1	130,234	304,402	109,245	240,745
应收帐款 Accounts receivable	2	631,655	573,527	393,694	458,016
减：坏帐准备 Less:provision for doubtful debts		-2,527	-2,294	-1,816	-1,952
应收帐款净额 Accounts receivable – net value		629,128	571,233	391,878	456,064
预付货款 Prepayments to suppliers		136,852	304,106	122,961	253,700
其他应收款 Other receivables	3	322,656	205,363	315,172	205,970
待摊费用 Deferred expenses		23,770	34,158	21,376	30,424
存货 Inventories	4	350,519	661,256	218,159	417,712
减：存货变现准备 Less:Provision for loss on realisation of assets		-800	-1,722	-800	-1,722
存货净额 Inventories - net value		349,719	659,534	217,359	415,990
流动资产合计 Total current assets		1,592,359	2,078,796	1,177,991	1,602,893
长期投资： Long – term investments					
长期投资： Long – term investments	5	28,644	31,596	154,790	156,998

Balance Sheets · 资产负债表
(prepared in accordance with PRC accounting standards)
(根据中华人民共和国会计准则编制)
(cont'd) · 续

资产 Assets	附注 Note	合 并 Consolidated		母 公 司 Parent Company	
		1996 人民币千元 RMB'000	1995 人民币千元 RMB'000	1996 人民币千元 RMB'000	1995 人民币千元 RMB'000
固定资产： **Fixed assets**					
固定资产原值 Fixed assets – cost	6	941,488	741,033	755,807	560,302
减：累计折旧 Less:accumulated depreciation		-165,643	-123,122	-125,050	-95,056
固定资产净额 Fixed assets – net value		775,845	617,911	630,757	465,246
在建工程 Construction in progress	7	235,933	233,755	189,914	220,260
固定资产合计 Total fixed assets		1,011,778	851,666	820,671	685,506
无形资产及递延资产： Intangible and deferred assets					
无形资产 Intangible assets	8	83,717	69,404	68,227	53,913
递延资产 Deferred assets	9	7,923	2,258	–	–
无形资产及递延资产合计 Total intangible and deferred assets		91,640	71,662	68,227	53,913
资产总额 Total assets		2,724,421	3,033,720	2,221,679	2,499,310

617

Balance Sheets · 资产负债表
(prepared in accordance with PRC accounting standards)
（根据中华人民共和国会计准则编制）
(cont'd) · 续

负债及股东权益： Liability and shareholder's equity	附注 Note	合 并 Consolidated		母公司 Parent Company	
		1996 人民币千元 RMB'000	1995 人民币千元 RMB'000	1996 人民币千元 RMB'000	1995 人民币千元 RMB'000
流动负债： **Current liabilities**					
短期借款 Short – term loans	10	271,659	487,207	221,000	308,209
应付帐款 Accounts payable	11	150,929	321,017	110,511	258,396
预收货款 Receipts in advance	12	245,793	440,014	226,433	416,545
应付福利费 Staff welfare payable		516	1,334	177	983
应付股利 Dividends payable		24,795	59,361	24,742	59,361
未交税金 Taxes payable	13	97,070	-52,067	48,542	-39,868
其他未交款 Other unpaid items		2,552	3,317	920	3,170
其他应付款 Other payable	14	14,276	12,775	-254,788	-222,484
预提费用 Accrued expenses		63,278	21,067	61,499	16,519
一年内到期的长期负债 Long – term liabilities	15	338,604	72,880	334,880	72,880
流动资产合计 Total current liabilities		1,209,472	1,366,905	773,916	873,711
长期负债： **Long – term liabilities**					
长期借款 Long – term loans	16	122,302	308,700	122,302	308,700
其他长期负债 Other long – term liabilities	17	25,378	341	–	–
长期负债合计 Total long – term liabilities		147,680	309,041	122,302	308,700
负债合计 Total liabilities		1,357,152	1,675,946	896,218	1,182,411

Balance Sheets · 资产负债表
(prepared in accordance with PRC accounting standards)
(根据中华人民共和国会计准则编制)
(cont'd) · 续

		合 并 Consolidated		母公司 Parent Company	
	附注 Note	1996 人民币千元 RMB'000	1995 人民币千元 RMB'000	1996 人民币千元 RMB'000	1995 人民币千元 RMB'000
少数股东权益 **Minority interests**		41,807	40,875	–	–
股东权益： **Shareholders' equity**					
股本 Capital	18	494,678	494,678	494,678	494,678
资本公积 Capital reserve	19	651,931	651,931	651,931	651,931
盈余公积 Surplus common reserves	20	85,855	79,116	85,775	79,116
其中：公益金 Including: statutory public welfare fund		31,373	34,879	31,333	34,879
未分配利润 Retained earnings	21	92,998	91,174	93,077	91,174
股东权益合计 Total shareholders' equity		1,325,462	1,316,899	1,325,461	1,316,899
负债及股东权益合计 Total liabilities and shareholders' equity		2,724,421	3,033,720	2,221,679	2,499,310

(prepared in accordance with PRC accounting standards)
(根据中华人民共和国会计准则编制)
Year ended 31 December, 1996
截至1996年12月31日止年度

项目 Item	附注 Note	合 并 Consolidated		母公司 Parent Company	
		1996 人民币千元 RMB'000	1995 人民币千元 RMB'000	1996 人民币千元 RMB'000	1995 人民币千元 RMB'000
一、主营业务收入 **Operating income**	22	2,061,349	1,833,513	1,380,646	1,049,999
减：营业成本 Less: operating cost		1,892,793	1,601,052	1,276,958	899,736
销售费用 selling expenses		3,685	17,519	602	1,142
管理费用 administrative expenses		122,607	103,319	111,361	98,140
财务费用 financial expenses	23	17,566	-25,115	-13,972	-54,851
营业税金及附加 business tax and surcharge		10,912	1,983	4,542	1,667
二、主营业务利润 **Pincipal operating profit**		13,786	134,755	1,155	104,165
加：其他业务利润 Add: other operating profit	24	23,527	15,718	21,821	11,212
三、营业利润 **Operating profit**		37,313	150,473	22,976	115,377
加：投资收益 Add: investment gains	25	2,001	1,285	15,739	36,279
补贴收入 subsidiary income		1,568	–	1,568	–
营业外收入 non - operating income	26	353	1,632	353	1,620
减：营业外支出 Less: non - operating expenses	27	1,274	3,315	971	3,148
加：以前年度损益调整 Add: adjustment on the P & L of the prior years		350	2,324	367	1,646

Profit and Profit Distribution Statement · 利润及利润分配表
(prepared in accordance with PRC accounting standards)
(根据中华人民共和国会计准则编制)
(cont'd) · 续

项目 Item	附注 Note	合 并 Consolidated		母公司 Parent Company	
		1996 人民币千元 RMB'000	1995 人民币千元 RMB'000	1996 人民币千元 RMB'000	1995 人民币千元 RMB'000
四、利润总额 **Total Profit**		40,311	152,399	40,032	151,774
减：所得税 Less: Income tax		6,874	24,845	6,736	24,755
减：少数股东损益 Less: Profit and loss of minority shareholders		141	535	–	–
五、净利润 **Net Profit**		33,296	127,019	33,296	127,019
加：年初未分配利润 Add: Retained profit at the beginning of the year		91,174	68,707	91,174	68,707
六、可分配的利润 **Distributable profit**		124,470	195,726	124,470	195,726
减：提取法定公积金 Less: Appropriation to statutory surplus reserve		3,369	12,702	3,330	12,702
提取法定公益金 Appropriation to statutory public welfare fund		3,369	12,702	3,330	12,702
七、可供股东分配的利润 **Profit distributable to shareholders**		117,732	170,322	117,810	170,322
减：已分配普通股股利 Less: Dividends on ordinary shares		24,734	79,148	24,734	79,148
八、未分配利润 Undistributed profit		92,998	91,174	93,076	91,174

Source: GSI, Annual report, 1996, pp. 43–8

▰▰▰ QUESTIONS

Business environment (16.3)

1 To what extent does the business environment of China under the communist regime provide clues as to possible influences on accounting practices?

2 To what extent do the current reforms in the business environment of China provide clues as to possible influences on accounting practices?

Early developments in accounting (16.5)

1 To what extent do early developments in accounting practice indicate the likely directions of professionalism/statutory control; uniformity/flexibility; conservatism/optimism; and secrecy/transparency in current practice?

2 To what extent do the current economic reforms indicate the likely directions of professionalism/statutory control; uniformity/flexibility; conservatism/optimism; and secrecy/transparency in current accounting practice?

Institutions (16.3)

1 How does the political and economic system of China fit into the classifications described in Chapter 1?

2 How does the taxation system of China compare to the descriptions given in Chapter 1?

3 How does the corporate financing system of China compare to the descriptions given in Chapter 1?

4 How does the accounting profession in China compare to the descriptions given in Chapter 1?

5 How do the external influences on accounting practice in China compare to those described in Chapter 1?

6 Which institutional factors are most likely to influence Chinese accounting practice?

IASs (16.6)

1 In which areas does accounting practice in China depart from that set out in IASs?

  For each of the areas of departure which you have identified, describe the treatment required or applied in China and identify the likely impact on net income and shareholders' equity of moving from Chinese accounting practice to the relevant IAS.

2 What explanations may be offered for these differences from IASs, in terms of the institutional factors described in the chapter?

3 What are the most difficult problems facing accounting in China if it seeks harmonisation with the IASC core standards programme?

Professionalism/statutory control (16.6.1)

1 Identify the key features supporting a conclusion that statutory control is a characteristic of Chinese accounting.

2 Explain which institutional influences cause statutory control to be a characteristic of Chinese accounting.

3 Discuss whether a classification of strong statutory control is appropriate for the 1990s.

Uniformity/flexibility (16.6.2)

1 Identify the key features supporting a conclusion that uniformity, rather than flexibility, is a dominant characteristic of Chinese accounting.

2 Explain which institutional influences cause uniformity, rather than flexibility, to be a dominant characteristic of Chinese accounting.

3 Discuss whether a classification of strong uniformity is appropriate for the 1990s.

Conservatism/optimism (16.6.3)

1 Identify the key features supporting a conclusion that conservatism is not a dominant characteristic of Chinese accounting.

2 Explain which institutional influences mean that conservatism is not an important characteristic of Chinese accounting.

3 Discuss whether a classification of weak conservatism is appropriate for the 1990s.

Secrecy/transparency (16.6.4)

1 Identify the key features supporting a conclusion that secrecy is a characteristic of Chinese accounting.

2 Explain which institutional influences cause secrecy to be a characteristic of Chinese accounting.

3 Discuss whether a classification of strong secrecy is appropriate for the 1990s.

■ REFERENCES

Blake, J. and Gao, S. (eds) (1995) *Perspectives on Accounting and Finance in China*. London: Routledge.

Chow, L.M., Chau, G.K. and Gray, S.J. (1995) 'Accounting reforms in China: Cultural constraints on implementation and development', *Accounting and Business Research*, 26(1), 29–49.

Firth, M. (1996) 'The diffusion of managerial accounting procedures in the People's Republic of China and the influence of foreign partnership joint ventures', *Accounting, Organisations and Society*, 21 (7/8), 629–54.

Gray, S.J. (1988) 'Towards a theory of cultural influence on the development of accounting systems internationally', *Abacus*, 24(1), 1–15.

Hofstede, G. (1984) *Culture's Consequences: International Differences in Work-Related Values*. Beverly Hills, CA: Sage Publications.

Hofstede, G. and Bond, M.H. (1988) 'The Confucius connection: From cultural roots to economic growth', *Organizational Dynamics*, 16(1), 5–21.

Nobes, C. and Parker, R.H. (1998) *Comparative International Accounting*. 5th edn. Hemel Hempstead: Prentice Hall.

Overholt, W.H. (1993) *China: The Next Economic Superpower*. London: Weidenfeld & Nicolson.

Rathborne, D. and Grosch, J. (eds) (1997) *The LGT Guide to World Equity Markets 1997*. London: Euromoney Publications.

Roberts, C.B., Adams, C.A. Woo, R.W.K. and Wu, X. (1995) 'Chinese accounting reform: The internationalisation of financial reporting', *Advances in International Accounting*, 8, 201–20.

Songnian, W. and Jiafu, Q. (1987) 'Financial accounting and reporting', in *Accounting and Auditing in the People's Republic of China*. Dallas: Shanghai University of Finance & Economics and The Center for International Accounting Development, The University of Texas at Dallas.

Tang, Y.W., Chow, L. and Cooper, B.J. (1994) *Accounting and Finance in China*. 2nd edn. Hong Kong: Longman.

White, G. (1993) *Riding the Tiger: The Politics of Economic Reform in Post-Mao China*. London: Macmillan.

Chapter 17

Egypt

This chapter has been written by Omneya H Abd Elsalam,
Lecturer, Mansoura University, Egypt

17.1 **INTRODUCTION**

From Chapter 5 you will have seen that countries adopt a number of very different approaches to standard setting and the use of IASs. Exhibit 5.14 listed the status of IASs in 67 countries. Among the approaches adopted were the use of IASs as national standards both with and without adaptation to meet any unique local circumstances. Other countries use IASs instead but add local standards in areas not covered by IASs, while another alternative is to develop the country's own standards but base them upon IASs.

This chapter looks at the approach taken to standard setting and the use of IASs in one developing country, namely Egypt. Egypt is a fairly late entrant into the standard setting process. It has only begun to set its own standards for shareholder companies in the last decade or so. As such, it was able to take advantage of the availability of IASs and did not have to make the decision either to develop its own standards independently or to follow the standards of a single country or regional grouping such as the USA or the EU.

Egypt began in the late 1980s to develop its own standards which, in most cases, were very similar to IASs. It has now moved from this position towards the more complete use of IASs. Firstly, in 1993, as a short-term measure, it required listed companies to follow IASs where there were no local regulations. More recently, in 1996, it has instead stated its intention of setting its own standards which will be explicitly based upon IASs, adapted wherever necessary to meet its local circumstances – a fairly common approach also adopted by countries such as Bangladesh, Barbados, Colombia, Jamaica, Jordan, Kenya, Poland, Thailand, Uruguay, Zimbabwe and Zambia.

17.2 **THE COUNTRY**

Egypt is a developing country (*see* Exhibit 17.1). Relatively high unemployment (at 17% in 1996) has been accompanied by an impressive growth rate of nearly 5% pa. Inflation averaged 17–21% in the period from 1987 to 1990 but fell to 8.1% (1994), 8.4% (1995) and 7.4% (1996).

Exhibit 17.1 EGYPT: COUNTRY PROFILE, TAKEN FROM EIU STATISTICS

Population	62.1 m.	
Land mass	1,000,250 sq.km	
GDP per head	US $733	
GDP per head in purchasing power parity	14	(USA=100)
Origins of GDP:	%	
Agriculture	16.3	
Industry	22.3	
Services	61.4	
	%	
Real GDP average annual growth 1985–95	4.9	
Inflation, average annual rate 1989–96	13.8	

Source: *The Economist Pocket World in Figures 1998 Edition*, The Economist (1997)

17.3 OVERVIEW OF ACCOUNTING REGULATIONS

Before the 1990s, private sector company accounting was very largely unregulated, the exceptions to this being some minor guidelines or rules included in the Egyptian charter issued in 1958 and the Companies Act (CA) of 1981. In the public sector, the Uniform Accounting System 1966 (UAS) required application of specific concepts, terms, definitions, accounting principles and standard forms.

In 1992, the Egyptian Institute of Accountants and Auditors (EIAA) completed the preparation of 20 Egyptian standards (ESs). These standards were presented and discussed in public at a number of seminars held under the supervision of the EIAA and were recommended by the Institute for use in practice.

In 1993, the Executive Regulations (ERs) of the Capital Market Law (CML) (1992) were issued. These included a statement requiring listed companies to use IASs in all those areas where the CML is silent. All listed companies had to meet these requirements by October 1995. In 1997 a ministerial decision obliged all shareholder companies, whether listed or not, to follow the IASs.

17.4 INSTITUTIONS

17.4.1 Political and economic system

Egypt has moved, in the 1990s, towards privatisation and a free market economy after nearly 30 years of socialism (*see* Exhibit 17.2).

17.4.2 Business organisations and the law

Joint stock companies (also called shareholder companies) may issue shares to the public. Limited liability companies are private companies and have restrictions on share transfer (similar to the German GmbH or the UK Ltd company). Egyptian companies face various forms of regulation of financial disclosure. All private sector

Exhibit 17.2 MAIN ECONOMIC DEVELOPMENTS

Pre-1956	Large private ownership sector
1956–1973	Large public sector and central planning by the State
1974–1989	Open Door Policy – encouragement of foreign investment
1990–present	Privatisation programme including the revitalising of the country's stock exchange

companies must comply with the Companies Act (CA) 1981. If they are listed on the Stock Exchange they must comply also with the CML. The CML requires compliance with IASs in any area not specifically mentioned in the CML or its ERs. Public sector companies must apply the UAS. If listed they must also comply with the CML. The CA includes some guidelines for accounting practice. However, they are neither comprehensive nor specific[1] and they do not provide a definitive set of accounting standards which should be followed by companies. The Act was issued in a period when the Capital Market was less important, and market pressures for adequate information disclosure were much lower, than in most developed countries.[2] As a result, the level of disclosure required by the CA is now inadequate.[3]

The new Capital Market Law (1992) and its Executive Regulations (1993) are very important as they attempt to increase awareness of, and confidence in, the benefits of investments in securities and so attract back Egyptian capital invested abroad, estimated at between $40 billion and $70 billion.[4] Also, they include the first mandatory comprehensive disclosure package for listed companies in Egypt.

17.4.3 The taxation system

Companies are liable for corporate income tax if they operate in Egypt. Taxable income comprises total revenue, including gains from the sale of fixed assets, minus legitimate business expenses. There is relief for losses brought forward. There are exemptions for companies located in tax-free zones and for companies given a tax holiday under various incentive schemes. Generally, the tax authorities accept the accounting figures in respect of depreciation, stock valuation and business expenses.

17.4.4 The Egyptian stock exchange

In the 1950s, the Cairo exchange was the fifth most active market in the world.[5] However, after the nationalisation laws in the late 1950s and early 1960s, stock exchange activities decreased dramatically.

---

[1] El Halawany (1993)
[2] Tawfic (1992)
[3] El Halawany (1993)
[4] Brindle (1993)
[5] *Ibid.*

In the early 1970s, the Open Door Policy, resulting from a change of government, was followed by a resurgence of listings.[6] However, the volume of trading in the stock exchange remained small because most of the listings were closed companies which were mainly formed between relatives and friends with no intention of raising funds externally. From 1992 such companies were excluded from official tables in the stock exchange. Another major constraint during the 1970s was the tax of up to 40% on investment income from securities, compared with no tax on bank interest received. A new tax law and Companies Act were issued in 1981. To encourage investment, the tax law exempted *listed* joint stock companies from tax on profits in a range not exceeding the interest rate determined by the Central Bank of Egypt. This exemption is still present under the new unified tax law issued in 1993.

The number of companies registered in the Capital Market increased from 112 companies in 1983 to 674 at the end of 1994,[7] mainly through growth in the number of joint stock companies. In the six months after issuing the CML, there was a great increase in the volume of shares exchanged, the number of transactions and the market value of stock. Capitalisation rose from E£27.4bn in 1995 to E£48.1bn in 1996 and annual turnover rose from E£3.8bn in 1995 to E£10.8bn in 1996.[8] There were one million investors in 1996, compared with only 25,000 three years earlier.[9]

17.4.5 Charter of the accounting and auditing profession

The fifth division of Article 5 of the 1958 Charter of the Accounting and Auditing profession states that the auditor has to examine whether the company has applied generally accepted accounting principles. While GAAP has never been defined or determined formally, it is taken to include the following:

- recording fixed assets at their historical cost;
- depreciating fixed assets adequately according to their nature;
- applying the general methods for valuing inventory – either cost or the lower of the cost and the market price. Companies are allowed to use other methods for special reasons. In all cases there has to be consistency in the method of valuation;
- in the calculation of the debtors balance, relevant provisions have to be deducted;
- the accruals basis has to be followed in determining revenues and costs of the period;
- the enterprise is normally viewed as a going concern. Profits or losses and the valuation of assets and liabilities must be based on this assumption except in cases of combination and liquidation;
- preparing the balance sheet and the final accounts on the assumption that the value of the money unit is stable (this means that there is no inflation accounting);
- following the conservatism policy which means any unrealised profits are not taken into account. At the same time any expected losses have to be considered

---

[6] El Henaway (1995)
[7] Inceler (1994)
[8] At the end of 1995 the exchange rate was approximately E£3.4 = US$1.00
[9] *FT Survey*, Egypt, 13 May 1997, p. 4

by making adequate provisions. For long term construction enterprises the amount of profit of the year is estimated, based on a percentage of completion of the work and making adequate provision for expected losses.

17.4.6 External influences

The influence of the UK Companies Act 1948 may be seen in the Egyptian Companies Act of 1954 and the Charter of the Accounting and Auditing Profession (1958). Those who drafted the charter had the experience of a UK education. The influence of the French Plan Comptable Général may be seen in the Uniform Accounting System (1966).

17.5 SOCIETAL CULTURE AND ACCOUNTING SUB-CULTURE

Hofstede (1984) ranked Arab countries as one region (*see* Chapter 2). He measured collectivism, large power distance, strong uncertainty avoidance and a mid-point of nurture. Using Gray's (1988) analysis, this would lead to a prediction of statutory control, uniformity, conservatism and moderate secrecy.

17.6 ACCOUNTING REGULATIONS AND THE IASC

Mandating the use of IASs may have confused many people, especially local Egyptian accountants who may not know whether their practice is compatible with or similar to the IASs. Before 1992 there was no great interest in knowing the IASs, largely because of the economic environment and the prevalence of public sector companies which were required to apply the Uniform Accounting System.

Many companies have contacted the Capital Market Authority asking for an approved Arabic translation of the IASs. A number of auditors who are members of the Central Auditing Agency team have expressed their concerns in their audit reports, stating that the Arabic translation of the IASs is not approved as required by the Law in Egypt (*see* Exhibit 17.3). It appears that there is no official translation available in Egypt, although the IASC has given copyright permission to the Egyptian Society of Accountants and Auditors (ESAA). The ESAA is a professional body member of the IASC.

In May 1996 a Ministerial decision (No 323 of 1996) was issued stating the intention to form a permanent national committee for issuing Egyptian accounting standards in the context of the IASs, after adapting them to suit the Egyptian environment. The Committee is chaired by the chairman of the CMA. Its membership includes representatives of many important organisations such as:

The Central Auditing Agency (CAA)
The Egyptian Institute of Accountants and Auditors (EIAA)
The Egyptian Association for Costs
The Egyptian Association of Accountants and Auditors (EAAA)
The Syndicate of Accountants and Auditors
The General Authority for investment
The Central accounting department of the CMA.

An example of the work of the Committee is described in Exhibit 17.4.

| Exhibit 17.3 | AUDIT REPORT OF A LISTED COMPANY |

Central Auditing Agency

Audit Report on the financial statements of the Company at 31 December 1995, according to the requirements of the Capital Market Law

We have audited the financial statements of the Company, SAE, which was formed under the Investment Law 43 of 1973, which was replaced by Law 230 of 1989.

The details of the financial statements are:
    Balance sheet at 31 December 1995 with the amount of E£744 million
    Income statement of the year then ended, with a net profit of E£280 million
    Statement of sources and use of funds
    Statement of proposed distribution of profit

These statements were prepared by the company, according to the requirements of the Executive Regulations of the Capital Market Law 95 of 1992, and are the responsibility of the company's management. Our responsibility is to express an opinion on these financial statements based on our audit. We conducted our audit according to generally accepted principles.

The company keeps proper financial accounting records which include all that is required by the law and by the statutes of the company, according to generally accepted principles. But we express our concern about the lack of an approved Arabic translation of the International Accounting Standards mentioned in statement 58 of the Executive Regulations of the Capital Market Law. Such approval is required by Law 115 of 1958 and by the Egyptian Constitution.

Except for the aforementioned, the balance sheet presents truly and fairly the financial position of the company as on 31 December 1995 and the profit and loss account reflects correctly the results of its operations for the year then ended. The information contained in the Report of the board of directors and the financial statements conforms to the requirements of the Companies Act 159 of 1981.

May 1996   Auditors' signatures and names

| Exhibit 17.4 | DEVELOPMENT OF A STANDARD FOR FINANCE LEASES |

In June 1995 Law 95 of 1995 was issued concerning finance lease contracts. The law was quite different from international practice and standards. The Law did not specify the particular conditions required for classifying a contract as a finance lease. It relied either on the use of the words 'finance lease' in the contract or on a contractual requirement of purchase at the end of the lease period (statements 2 and 5).

The Law requires the lessor to depreciate the value of the leased asset. In order to enjoy five years' exemption from tax the lessor must include depreciation in the calculation of taxable profit. The lessee may deduct only the rental charge from taxable profit. The explanatory notes are used to disclose the nature of the finance leasing contract and any rent paid or accrued. These practices are contrary to the requirements of IAS 17 (*see* Chapter 6).

In October 1996 a ministerial decree was issued, forming a special committee to set accounting rules and a standard for finance leases. Various parties were invited to participate. Egyptian correspondents of international accounting firms expressed their concern over the confusion caused by the Law and proposed changes to conform to IAS 17.

17.7 THE ACCOUNTING SYSTEM

17.7.1 Issuing standards

The International Conference of Accounting and Auditing organised by the Accounting and Auditing Division of the syndicate of Commerce Professions, which was held in Egypt in 1980, recommended the establishment of an institute to train accountants and auditors and to formulate accounting standards, auditing guidelines and professional ethics. In 1986 the report of the Second International Conference on Accounting and Auditing, organised by the Egyptian Society of Accountants and Auditors (ESAA) included the following recommendations:

1 The speedy formation of an independent board to formulate, establish and monitor the accounting standards and auditing guidelines.
2 The board should set the priorities for the issue of statements on accounting and auditing standards and should expose drafts to open discussion within the profession and by interested parties, before final approval.
3 The formulation of accounting standards issued by this board should be based primarily on the IASs after taking into consideration the local economic and social needs and the specific environment in Egypt.

In 1987 a public seminar, supervised by the newly-formed Egyptian Institute of Accountants and Auditors (EIAA),[10] was held for discussion of the first four accounting standards:

1 Disclosure of accounting policies.
2 Valuation and presentation of inventories in the context of the historical cost system.
3 Depreciation accounting.
4 Accounting for the effects of changes in foreign exchange rates.

In 1989 a further seminar was organised for the public discussion of another four standards:

5 Statement of sources and application of funds.
6 Capitalisation of borrowing costs.
7 Information to be disclosed in the financial statements.
8 Presentation of current assets and liabilities.

In 1992 a further conference discussed standards on:

9 Net profit or loss for the period, fundamental errors and changes in accounting policies.
10 Contingencies and events occurring after the balance sheet date.
11 Accounting for construction contracts.
12 Accounting for research and development activities.
13 Information reflecting the effects of changing prices.
14 Accounting for property, plant and equipment.

---

[10] The EIAA was established in 1987 as an independent entity of the Division of Accounting and Auditing of the Syndicate of Commerce Professions.

15 Accounting for government grants and disclosure of government assistance.

16 Accounting for business combinations.

17 Consolidated financial statements.

18 Related party transactions.

19 Accounting for investments.

20 Revenue recognition.

Despite the independent process of standard setting, scrutiny of the standards soon reveals similarities to International Accounting Standards. A detailed comparison between the ESs and the IASs in place at the time of issue of the ESs reveals:

1 a group of IASs (14 standards), fully comparable to the ESs (*see* Exhibit 17.5);

2 another group of IASs (six standards) comparable after minor adaptation (*see* Exhibit 17.6);

Exhibit 17.5 INTERNATIONAL ACCOUNTING STANDARDS WHICH WERE FULLY COMPARABLE TO THE CORRESPONDING EGYPTIAN STANDARDS (ESs) AT THE DATE OF THE CML (1993)

ES	IAS	Title	Effective date of IAS	Subsequent change to the IAS
1	1	Disclosure of accounting policies	1.1.75	Reformatted, effective 1.1.95
3	4	Depreciation accounting	1.1.77	Reformatted, effective 1.1.95
6	23	Borrowing costs	1.1.86	Reformatted, effective 1.1.95
7	5	Information to be disclosed in financial statements	1.1.77	Reformatted, effective 1.1.95
8	13	Presentation of current assets and current liabilities	1.1.81	Reformatted, effective 1.1.95
9	8	Net profit or loss for the period, fundamental errors and changes in accounting policies	1.1.79	Superseded by IAS 8, Dec 93 Effective date 1.1.95
10	10	Contingencies and events occurring after the balance sheet date	1.1.80	Reformatted, effective 1.1.95
11	11	Construction contracts	1.1.80	Superseded by IAS 11, Dec 93, effective date 1.1.95
12	9	Research & Development costs	1.1.80	Superseded by IAS 9, Dec 93, effective date 1.1.95
15	20	Accounting for government grants and disclosure of government assistance	1.1.85	Reformatted, effective 1.1.95
17	27	Consolidated financial statements	1.1.90	Reformatted, effective 1.1.95
18	24	Related party disclosures	1.8.86	Reformatted, effective 1.1.95
19	25	Accounting for investments	1.1.87	Reformatted, effective 1.1.95
20	18	Revenue	1.1.84	Superseded by IAS 18, Dec 93, effective 1.1.95

Exhibit 17.6 EGYPTIAN STANDARDS WITH MINOR DIFFERENCES FROM THE IASs (1993)

ES	IAS	Title	Comment on the difference	Effective date of the IAS	Further changes to the IAS
2	2	Valuation & presentation of inventories in the context of the historical cost system	Within the current asset classification 'Inventory' consists of the following items (a) raw materials, fuels, spare parts and others;: (b) unfinished products and work in progress; (c) finished products; (d) goods purchased for resale	1.1.76	1993 superseded, effective 1.1.95
4	21	The effects of changes in foreign exchange rates	Using a different definition of the 'spot rate' which is 'the exchange rate published by the authorities or dealt with in the free market'. The reason for this difference is that, prior to 1991, the exchange rate between the Egyptian pound and all foreign currencies was set by the Central Bank of Egypt. The rates were liberalised in 1991. This means that the ES has to be adapted and the phrase 'the exchange rate published by the authorities' should be omitted.	1.1.85	1993 superseded, effective 1.1.95
5	7	Statement of changes in financial position [IAS 7 later became Cash Flow Statements]	The following paragraphs were omitted from the ES: • Consolidated financial statements • Preparing the statement of changes in financial position on a consolidated basis • Accounting for investments using the equity method • How to present investments in the statement and the acquisition or disposal of subsidiaries. The possible reason for these differences is that the ES was issued in 1989 before the start of the privatisation programme. Those kinds of investment were not common in a country where the public sector dominated and there were many constraints on private sector growth. This situation has changed rapidly since 1991. The IAS was replaced by the cash flow standard in 1994, which means that the ES will have to be changed to conform with the IAS	1.1.79	1992 superseded, effective 1.1.94
13	15	Information reflecting the effects of changing prices	A sentence was added to the ES 'It is very important to encourage preparation of information reflecting the effects of changing prices'. This is because, at the time of issuing the ES, the inflation rates were relatively high. These rates were 17%–21% in the late '80s, slowing down to 8.4% in 1995 and around 7% in 1996.	1.1.83	reformatted 1995
14	16	Property, plant and equipment	All parts of the IAS relating to valuation of property, plant and equipment, using bases other than historical cost, were omitted. This is because historical cost is mandated by the Egyptian law.	1.1.83	1993 superseded, effective 1.1.95
16	22	Business combinations	The ES required an additional disclosure of the changes in the legal form of the combining firms which may affect the limits of guarantees offered to creditors which requires their approval	1.1.85	1993 superseded, effective 1.1.95

Exhibit 17.7 IASs WHICH HAD NO CORRESPONDING EGYPTIAN STANDARD, 1992

IAS	Title	Comment	Date*
12	Accounting for income taxes	Egypt has a special tax law	1979 (R)
14	Reporting financial information by segment	After nationalisation, and the consequent dominance of the public sector, financial reporting to the public was not important and therefore segmental reporting had low priority. All segment information was available to the government because the employees of the CAA have access to companies' documentation.	1983 (R)
17	Accounting for leases	Standard now in preparation	1982 (R)
19	Retirement benefit costs	Egypt has a special law for its benefit plan which is sponsored by the government.	1983 (R)
26	Accounting and reporting by retirement benefit plans	Ditto	1987 (R)
28	Accounting for investments in associates	This type of investment was not common in Egypt in the period of dominance of the public sector; but gradual change since 1991	1989 (R)
29	Financial reporting in hyperinflationary economies	Not applicable.	1983 (R)
30	Disclosures in the financial statements of banks and similar institutions	Egypt has special laws for these financial institutions.	1990 (R)
31	Financial reporting of interests in joint ventures	See comment on IAS 28.	1990 (R)

*(R) = reformatted 1995

3 a third group of IASs (nine standards) not urgent for standard setting (*see* Exhibit 17.7).

However, more recently, the CML has moved to the position of considering all IASs as being relevant for companies listed on the Egyptian Stock Exchange. Thus, it now requires all listed companies to follow IASs on all those issues where the CML is silent.

17.7.2 The impact of changes

Simply changing the laws does not mean that corporate reporting practices also change immediately. Companies may be relatively unaffected in either of two situations. Firstly, companies may have voluntarily reported using IASs or have used other internationally acceptable GAAP prior to the new regulations. They may have done this if they have foreign users of accounts. Secondly, those companies

Exhibit 17.8 FINANCIAL STATEMENT DISCLOSURE

Company A: Public company, business sector	
Before	Directors' report include voluntary information Central Auditing Agency report UAS based financial statements Brief notes to the accounts
Transition	Significant increase in notes
After	Extra information including IAS based cash flow statement and performance review
Company B: Public company, business sector	
Before	Directors' report Central Auditing Agency report UAS based financial statements
Transition	IAS based cash flow statement Extra notes to accounts
After	Three sets of accounts – UAS, CML and CA
Company C: Formed under the Investment Law	
Before	Directors' report CA based financial statements (B/S, P&L, funds statement) Brief notes
Transition	Additional set of accounts – according to CML
After	More detailed Directors' report More detailed notes
Company D: Formed under the Investment Law	
Before	Directors' report Central Auditing Agency report CA based financial statements (B/S, P&L, distribution account)
Transition	Additional set of accounts – according to CML
After	No further changes
Company E: Formed under Investment Law – 52% foreign parent, 38% Government owned	
Before	Directors' report Central Auditing Agency and private auditors' reports B/S, P&L, no explanatory report
Transition	No change
After	No change

which did not apply the IASs before these became mandatory may intially lack knowledge of the IASs, or may not think the IASs to be important, or may have no external users of their accounts (e.g. a closed company).

No discussion of accounting change can be complete without also looking at actual corporate reporting practices. Unfortunately, this is difficult to do in a developing country such as Egypt as no recent surveys of reporting practice exist. These annual reports should be obtained from the Capital Markets Authority (CMA). At present a brief version of the annual report is shown on the computer system of the CMA and is readily available. However, the full version of the report is filed in the archive and retrieval is time consuming for the staff of the CMA. Obtaining the full version requires a personal visit. However, some idea of the nature of changes that have happened can be seen from an analysis of a representative group of five companies (*see* Exhibit 17.8). In each case, the 1992 annual report (*before change*), is then compared to the annual reports issued in 1993 and 1994 (*transition period*) when the CML was not fully mandatory, and the 1995 report (*after change*), for which the CML was mandatory. Some fairly significant changes were made by four of the five companies. This included not only the provision of additional notes and cash flow statements, but also in three cases (Companies B, C and D), the addition of a competely new set of accounts.

It is particularly note-worthy, in the five annual reports reviewed, that, before the new requirements were introduced, many items that are commonly found in corporate reports from western developed countries were not provided by these companies. Since then, the level of disclosure has clearly increased significantly. However, there are still a number of items that are not disclosed that are likely to be relevant to the companies concerned and of interest to the readers of the annual report, such as provision for doubtful debts, current value of land, and separate identification of secured and unsecured loans. Disclosures have developed further since 1995.

17.7.3 Gray's (1988) accounting values

Statutory control remains strong and influences the attitudes towards factors which might introduce professionalism. Because of the history of statutory regulation it is seen that companies primarily take notice of matters mandated by law. When the Egyptian standards, mainly based on IASs, were issued in 1992 they were discussed and recommended by the EIAA but not applied by companies. When the CML made compliance with the IASs mandatory, companies complied.

Uniformity is most evident in the Uniform Accounting System which still applies to public sector companies. Private sector accounting was less regulated and allowed scope for management discretion until 1992. From 1992 the situation changed and the ministerial decree of 1996 has stated the intention of requiring IASs to be observed by all shareholder companies, whether or not these are listed.

Conservatism may be seen in the requirement of the Charter that historical cost be applied and in its recommendation to consider unrealised losses but not unrealised profit.

There has been a strong tradition of secrecy, supported by attitudes to tax law and the strength of family-owned companies. Now there is greater pressure on listed companies to disclose more information. The full accounts of a public sector company may be as long as 200 pages, while 50 pages is not untypical for a share-holder company.

17.8 SUMMARY AND CONCLUSIONS

This chapter has described the introduction of a series of accounting regulations for companies in Egypt. The country could have adopted any one of a number of different approaches to standard setting, each of which has its own strengths and weaknesses. At one extreme, it could have developed its own standards without reference to other countries. This would be a very expensive and time consuming alternative. It would also seem extremely unwise to ignore the experience and knowledge of other countries. While each country has some unique features and circumstances, no country is so unique that it cannot learn from others.

Given the urgent need for a set of acceptable standards to encourage the revitalisation of the stock market, the obvious place to start was with IASs. Thus, a series of 20 standards was issued by the profession from 1987 to 1992, based upon extant IASs. As shown in the exhibits, most of these standards were compar-able to IASs. Six IASs had to be modified slightly due to unique legal circumstances (e.g. strict historical cost accounting) or economic circumstances (e.g. exchange rate setting by the central bank, relatively high inflation rates). A further nine IASs were considered not to be a priority in the first instance, mainly because of differences in the institutional arrangements in place in the country (e.g. differences in pension arrangements and the relative lack of leases, tax law). Since then, the importance of IASs has increased greatly, and the capital market has mandated their use in all areas not covered by the CA and CML. However, it must be recognised that Egypt will continue to have its own unique institutional arrangements such that specific international standards may not be appropriate either in full or in certain respects. Thus, after a decade of experience with setting standards for shareholder companies, Egypt has reached what may, at least for the time being, be seen as a final position with regard to standard setting, a position which means that the country can benefit from the knowledge, skills, and experience of the IASC while not having to accept all its standards if they are inappropriate to the country, whether due to differences in the economic or legal environment or because of any other unique circumstances. Thus, Egypt has joined a fairly large and diffuse group of countries that sets its own standards which will be explicitly based upon IASs. It will seek in the future to ascertain the acceptability of all IASs. Where necessary they will be modified before being introduced into the country.

QUESTIONS

1 What factors led Egypt to begin to set accounting standards for shareholder companies in the 1980s?

2 In which areas do the accounting standards of Egypt depart from those set out in the equivalent IASs?

3 What institutional factors help to explain these differences?

4 In which areas did Egypt decide it was not urgent to introduce a standard based upon IASs?

5 What institutional factors help to explain these decisions?

6 Do you think Egypt was correct in mandating the use of IASs in all those areas where there were no local regulations? Explain your answer.

7 On the basis of the information contained in Exhibits 17.3 and 17.4, do you think the new accounting regulations can be considered a success? Explain your answer.

REFERENCES

Brindle, S. (1993) 'Stock Exchange: marketing the market', *Business Monthly*. Cairo, June.

Deloitte Touche Tohmatsu International (1995) 'Egypt', *International Tax and Business Guide*. New York.

Economist (1997) *Pocket World in Figures 1998 Edition*. London: The Economist.

El Halawany, Y.A. (1993) 'The importance of accounting disclosure for the Capital Market', paper presented at the Second Conference of the Scientific Association of Accounting, Systems and Auditing, *Horizons of Accounting Developments in Egypt*. Cairo, 24–25 April (paper in Arabic).

El Henawy, M.S. (1995) 'Reviewing the Egyptian Capital Market', *A Supplement of the Economic Ahram Magazine*, 13 February (paper in Arabic).

Gray, S.J. (1988) 'Towards a theory of cultural influences on the development of accounting systems internationally', *Abacus*, 24(1), 1–15.

Hofstede, G. (1984) *Culture's Consequences: International Differences in Work-Related Values*. Beverly Hills, CA: Sage Publications.

Inceler, K.H. (1994) 'Financial structure of Egypt', *Journal of Economic Co-operation among Islamic Countries*, 15(3–4), pp 45–82.

Tawfic, M.S. (1992) 'The role of accounting standards in supporting the capital market and reforming the accounting approach to fulfilling the needs of investors'. Paper presented at the conference of the All Egyptian Bank, Cairo, 29 February–3 March.

Part 3

REACTIONS TO INTERNATIONAL DIVERSITY IN FINANCIAL REPORTING SYSTEMS

Introduction to Part 3

After having read the first two parts of this book, you should be familiar with a number of different financial accounting systems. You will have seen that while there are a number of identical or very similar practices across various countries, there are also a number of practices that are quite dissimilar. From reading the first two chapters you should have gained an appreciation of why differences exist internationally. Each country chapter will then have given you an understanding of the specific institutional and cultural factors that are most important in explaining and understanding financial accounting practices in that country.

You will also have seen the increasing efforts made by various international bodies, in particular the International Accounting Standards Committee, to encourage increased international harmonisation. However, it is also clear from all the material that you have read so far that this process is far from complete. Indeed, given the different institutional and cultural factors, some of the differences will prove very difficult, if not impossible to eliminate, at least for the foreseeable future.

By this stage, you are perhaps asking yourself the obvious questions 'So what?' or 'What are the implications of all of this?'. It is to this type of question that the final part of this book addresses itself. All companies with any international operations and all users of their financial statements will be affected by differences in accounting practices internationally – or what we might term accounting diversity. Accounting diversity can impose extra direct costs on companies. To the extent that companies have to report in multiple jurisdictions, they may have to report under a number of different sets of rules, increasing their accounting and information production costs. If instead, they continue to use domestic rules and follow normal domestic practices, the information reported may be unfamiliar to foreign users, leading to a number of indirect costs to the company. Foreign users will be faced with additional processing costs, as they now have to cope either with unfamiliar types of information or with familiar types of information that are produced in unfamiliar ways. These extra information processing costs will make foreign users less willing to enter into transactions with the company. This will increase costs to the company – it may have to pay more for capital or offer suppliers and customers better terms. Indeed, at the extreme, if foreign users cannot understand the information provided, they may refuse to enter into any transactions with the company at all.

Chapter 18 looks at companies and how international diversity impacts upon a wide range of corporate decisions. Whenever a company has to report under a different set of rules or whenever it reports to users unfamiliar with its domestic reporting package, it will be influenced by accounting diversity and may behave differently because of this. One of the main decisions that will be affected is the decision about where to raise capital or what stock markets to list on. This is the area that Chapter 18 concentrates upon. It starts by looking at the costs of listing – how and why multiple listings are more expensive than listing only on the domestic stock exchange. It then turns to the obvious question of why, given the extra costs involved, do any companies list on foreign stock exchange(s)? While some companies list in a large number of countries, the two countries that have attracted the largest number of foreign registrants are the UK and the USA. Accordingly, the chapter moves on to look at the requirements facing foreign companies in the UK and the USA and examines the pattern of listings in each country. Finally, a review of empirical work in this area shows that while accounting differences are important, they are not the only factor that helps to explain listing behaviour. Indeed, the evidence presented shows that there has been a significant increase in the number of companies listing on the New York Stock Exchange in recent years despite it having the most stringent disclosure and measurement rules for foreign companies of any stock exchange in developed countries.

The final chapter, Chapter 19, turns to look instead at investors. It explores two issues – firstly, how do investors cope with international diversity? and, secondly, how, if at all, do companies change their reporting package when reporting to foreign investors?

Just as it is not immediately obvious why a company might want to raise equity capital in foreign countries, it is not immediately obvious why investors would want to invest in foreign companies. This is therefore the first issue that Chapter 19 explores. It starts by looking at the reasons why investors should invest in foreign, as well as domestic, companies and it looks at the types of investment strategies they can adopt when choosing a portfolio of foreign shares. The chapter then looks at a number of empirical studies that seek to discover how investors in practice choose between companies from different countries. The academic research done shows that some investors are affected by accounting diversity and they adopt a variety of different strategies to cope with this diversity. These are all explored in the chapter. The chapter ends by describing and offering a number of examples of the different disclosure strategies adopted by companies. These range all the way from nothing through to translation of the language used, translation of the currencies reported, reformatting of the statements, reporting using foreign GAAP, to even, in a few cases, changing the policies used or the information provided to domestic users, so producing a single set of financial statements that can be understood by both domestic and foreign users.

The specific learning outcomes of each chapter are given at the beginning of each chapter, but by the end of this final part of the book, you should be able to:

- understand the costs and benefits to companies of listing on foreign stock markets
- understand the costs and benefits to investors of investing in foreign companies
- be aware of the investment strategies that investors may adopt to cope with accounting diversity
- be aware of the reporting strategies that companies may adopt to reduce accounting diversity.

Chapter 18

Stock market listing behaviour

PURPOSE OF THE CHAPTER

In the previous chapters in this book we have looked at the accounting practices of companies from a number of different countries. We have seen that, despite the efforts of the IASC, many differences still exist. These differences are likely to affect both users and preparers of financial statements.

This chapter concentrates upon one important corporate decision that can be affected by international accounting differences – where to list or which stock markets to raise capital on.

Learning objectives

After reading this chapter you should be able to:

● Understand the additional costs of listing on foreign stock markets.

● Understand the reasons why companies might list on foreign stock markets.

● Evaluate published research seeking to explain the foreign stock market listing choices of companies

It is obviously more expensive to list on more than one stock market. Some of these additional costs are described and the possible reasons for wanting a foreign listing are explored. The chapter then looks at the listing behaviour of companies. The London and New York stock exchanges are looked at in detail. Their listing requirements are described and the pattern of listings of foreign companies on each is explored. The empirical research on listing location choice is then reviewed to see whether or not there is any evidence that the choice of listing location is affected by differences in countries' accounting regulations.

18.2 **ADDITIONAL COSTS OF FOREIGN LISTINGS**

Selling shares in a foreign country can often be very expensive. There will always be extra direct costs – various registration and listing charges have to be paid and these can be substantial. However, these may be the least of the extra costs incurred. There will often be other costs caused by differences in the regulatory systems:[1]

---

[1] Hanks (1997)

- different underwriting practices
- different registration and regulatory requirements
- different initial and continuing disclosure requirements
- different control and oversight systems with respect to share dealing practices
- different clearance and settlement procedures.

This may mean that the company has to plan and organise share issues in different countries in quite distinct ways. Different accounting and reporting systems may also be necessary and extra auditing costs may be incurred.

Once a company has done all this and has managed to issue shares in more than one market, it will be faced with further additional costs if it wants to keep an active presence in the foreign market. If it fails to maintain investor interest there may be substantial share flowback – the shares that were initially issued in the foreign market will be sold back to domestic shareholders. This happened, for example, with some of the UK privatisation issues such as British Telecom, with many of the shares that were initially issued in the USA finding their way back to the UK fairly soon after issue.[2] To prevent this happening the company will have to maintain an active investor relations department in the foreign country. This department will be responsible for keeping the press, financial analysts and stock-brokers well informed about the company. Without this, there is unlikely to be much press or analyst interest and therefore less interest by ordinary shareholders. Similarly, the interest and loyalty of institutional investors may have to be actively managed. The company will need to organise systematically such measures as company briefings and meetings with financial analysts. This will obviously be far easier and more successful if there is a well organised local investor relations department to manage the relationships.

As discussed throughout this text, there are often different financial reporting requirements and practices in different countries. Companies seeking a listing in a foreign stock market may have to comply with local listing rules regarding financial reporting. Alternatively, while they might not be forced by law or stock market requirements to follow local rules, they may still feel the need to do so. Local investors may be unwilling to invest in their shares if the company does not produce reports of a similar type and quality to those produced by local companies. This can result in substantial extra direct and indirect costs. Direct costs are fairly easy to quantify – any extra information production, dissemination and auditing costs. In most cases these will be relatively small, but in those cases where the company's existing information systems have to be redesigned to pick up or process different information there may be very substantial one-off setting up costs. Indirect costs are very much more difficult, if not sometimes impossible, to quantify, and they can be very much larger than the direct costs.

The provision of any extra information has the potential to induce extra political costs and competitive disadvantage costs. Political costs may arise when the new information causes the perceptions of employees, the general public, pressure groups or the government to change. For example, the company may report

---

[2] Tondkar *et al.* (1989)

higher earnings under foreign GAAP, thus changing perceptions regarding the extent to which the company is exploiting its market position or its labour force. Such changing perceptions may mean that the company is faced with a more difficult operating climate – employees, customers, local communities and the government might become more suspicious and less co-operative. At the extreme, the government might be more likely to restrict the company's freedom of action by imposing price controls or other restrictions on its activities. Competitive disadvantage costs arise when a company is made to disclose information that is of value to its competitors. This could happen when a company is forced by foreign reporting requirements to disclose information that is not disclosed by other domestic companies. Examples might include requirements to disclose detailed segment information, research and development and advertising expenditures, or environmental contingencies information.

Often of more universal importance is the impact upon shareholders. Many investors are fairly unsophisticated in the sense of not having a good understanding of different accounting practices. It is often difficult to grasp why and how two different income statements, each purporting to show a 'true and fair' view or similar, can result in two very different earnings figures. How can there be two 'true and fair' views or two 'correct' views? Reporting two sets of quite different figures, even when the reasons and differences are explained in a reconciliation statement, may be misunderstood by many investors. At best, it may increase the apparent uncertainty faced by the investor – 'if the company does not know how it has done, then how can I know how it has done?'. At worst, it may induce the feeling that something is seriously wrong – 'if the company can produce such different figures for the same things then perhaps neither is correct, therefore I cannot trust what it tells me'. Investors may therefore be less willing to invest in a company that produces two sets of very different figures.

Political costs will generally be incurred only if foreign GAAP reporting results in larger earnings or the disclosure of particularly sensitive information. In contrast, investor resistance or reluctance to invest can occur whenever the two sets of figures are different. It does not matter if earnings are increased or decreased; all that matters is that they have changed.

18.3 BENEFITS OF FOREIGN STOCK MARKET LISTING

Given these sometimes substantial costs of listing, companies may be reluctant to seek listings in foreign countries. However, as we saw in Chapter 1 (Exhibit 1.3), some stock exchanges have a substantial number of foreign companies listed. London, New York and NASDAQ, Amsterdam, Luxembourg and Switzerland each have over 200 foreign listed companies. Some of these listings are important, with many shares being traded each year, while others are relatively unimportant, with very few shares being traded. Similarly, different companies seek foreign stock market listings for different reasons and companies may list in different countries for different reasons. A number of motives for foreign listing have been suggested.

18.3.1 Public share offerings

Exhibit 18.1 provides some details of the listings of three large Scandinavian companies. This shows their reliance upon foreign stock exchanges as sources of equity financing. (Note that while these are three of the largest companies in Scandinavia, they are not unique and many other companies could have been chosen as illustrations.) In each case, more shares are traded or owned by foreign investors than by domestic investors.

Exhibit 18.1 SELECTED SCANDINAVIAN COMPANIES: LISTING PATTERNS 1996–7

VOLVO (Sweden)
Listing of Volvo shares: market, year of listing and volume traded (1996)

Stockholm	1935	340.1 m.
London	1972	301.0 m.
Frankfurt am Main, Dusseldorf, Hamburg	1974	not significant (n/s)
Paris	1984	n/s
USA (NASDAQ)	1985	83.0 m.
Brussels, Antwerp	1985	n/s
Tokyo	1986	n/s
Zurich, Basle, Geneva	1987	n/s

NOKIA (Finland)
Listing of Nokia shares: market, year of listing and volume traded (1996)

Helsinki	1915	165.4 m.
Stockholm	1983	39.3 m.
London	1987	258.6 m.
Paris	1988	0.8 m.
Frankfurt	1988	18.5 m.
NYSE	1994	277.7 m.

NORSK HYDRO (Norway)
Listing of Norsk Hydro shares: market and ownership structure (September 1997)

Exchanges	*Ownership pattern*	*%*
	Norway state	50.00
Oslo	Norway private	17.58
NYSE	USA	12.40
London	UK	8.24
Paris	France	2.26
Zurich, Basle, Geneva	Switzerland	1.79
Frankfurt, Dusseldorf, Hamburg	Germany	1.46
Stockholm	Sweden	0.77
Amsterdam	Others	4.60

Source: Volvo, annual report and accounts or www.volvo.se, 1996; Nokia, annual report or www.nokia.com, 1996; www.hydro.com, 1997

The need to raise additional finance is a particular problem for large companies located in countries with relatively small stock markets. The local stock market in many countries is too small and/or too illiquid to absorb very large public share offerings. Thus these companies, if they want to raise equity finance, have to go to foreign stock market(s). They have little or no choice in this matter. However, this option is not available to all companies. Whether or not a foreign company can and will raise money in any particular stock market and whether or not foreign investors can and do enter a stock market depends upon the extent to which stock markets are integrated or segmented.

Stock markets can be completely segmented. Here, foreign investors are unable to invest in the local market and/or foreign companies are unable to list in the local market. This is usually the result of government-imposed restrictions. The popularity of measures to restrict entry to domestic stock markets has decreased greatly in recent years and many barriers have been dismantled. However some countries, especially developing ones, still have government-imposed restrictions. These can take various forms including foreign currency controls and the blanket prohibition of foreign ownership of companies.

At the other extreme, stock markets can be completely integrated. Investors from all countries will have equal access to all securities and foreign companies can list freely without incurring more transaction costs than do domestic companies. Foreign and local markets will therefore be equally accessible. Investors and companies will not mind where they invest as the costs will be the same and there will be no advantages in gaining a foreign listing. If investors want to invest in a foreign company they will not mind whether they buy shares in its domestic market or whether instead the company has a listing on their local stock exchange.

Obviously, stock exchanges across different countries are not completely integrated. While the EU, for example, has successfully dismantled many barriers to free trade and capital movements, the various stock exchanges in the EU use different languages and, at least until the Euro is up and running, different currencies. Both of these make it more difficult and more expensive for an investor from one EU country to invest in the stock market of another EU country. In section 18.2, we saw that there will often also be other additional costs for the company and the investor in trading on a foreign stock market. Most stock markets are therefore partially segmented. Foreign investors and/or companies can trade on foreign markets but they face additional transaction costs or restrictions that are not faced by domestic investors and/or companies. Companies will often find it cheaper to issue their stock on foreign markets rather than relying upon foreign investors buying their shares on its domestic exchange. In most cases, if a company wants to attract substantial numbers of foreign investors it will have to go to them – the transaction costs faced by the company entering a foreign stock market will be less than the aggregate transaction costs incurred by large numbers of foreign investors all entering the domestic stock exchange.

Exhibit 18.1. provides some anecdotal evidence illustrating the importance of foreign stock markets as a source of finance. More of Volvo's shares are traded in foreign countries than in Sweden, while more than three times as many of Nokia's shares are traded outside Finland than are traded on the Helsinki market. Similarly, Norsk Hydro has nearly twice as much of its stock owned by foreign investors than by Norwegian non-state investors.

18.3.2 Other types of share issues

While many companies list on foreign markets to raise finance through a public offering of their shares, there are other reasons why companies might want a foreign listing(s). One of the most publicised foreign listings in recent years was Daimler–Benz's listing on the NYSE in 1993 – the first German company to list there. Four years later it had still not raised any new finance on the NYSE. If Exhibit 18.1 is looked at again, it is fairly obvious that Volvo is listed in four countries where the number of its shares traded is not significant. Norsk Hydro lists in five countries which each account for less than 5% of its total share ownership. In these cases, the listings were probably for reasons other than raising capital for the parent company.

Increasingly, companies issue shares to their employees. Director share options and share-based employee pay schemes are becoming increasingly popular. They are seen as a way of ensuring the long-term loyalty and commitment of the workforce and they may also be tax-efficient. While companies obviously hope that most employees will not sell their shares, they must be given the opportunity to do so. If a company wants to extend these schemes to cover foreign employees they may have to list in the foreign country so that employees have a local market in which they can trade their shares. A company may also wish to issue shares, not for cash, but to finance or partially finance acquisitions. Again, if it wishes to offer shares for foreign takeovers, it may have to provide these potential shareholders with the opportunity to sell their shares in their local stock market(s).

Similarly, a large foreign ownership may help to protect the company from itself being taken over. Foreign ownership can make takeovers more difficult and more expensive to organise, while shareholders in countries such as Germany, with no history or culture of hostile takeovers, might be less willing to sell their shares to such bidding companies.

18.3.3 Share listing as a signalling device

There are several other potential benefits of a local listing.[3] It may provide the company with extra publicity, which in turn encourages brand recognition and customer loyalty. It may also signal to customers and potential customers the long-term commitment of the company to the country. Again, this may lead to increased sales. Foreign listings may also signal that the company is now a major international player and may therefore increase the company's prestige.

A local listing may also change the perceptions of other groups such as local communities, governments and local authorities and pressure groups. A local listing might therefore help to improve the operating climate facing the company. The political benefits of a local listing may be particularly great in countries that are economically or politically more unstable. The company will also want to reduce its risk in these countries, and one way to do this is to ensure that local operations are financed locally. A local listing will mean that the local affiliates can be financed in a more balanced way by local equity as well as local debt. This can

---

[3] Radebaugh *et al.* (1995)

be important in reducing the exchange rate or currency risk faced by a company. If all shareholders are situated in the parent's country, the foreign subsidiary's earnings will have to be converted into the parent currency before dividends are paid. Having local shareholders avoids this need to convert currencies, as local earnings can be used to pay local currency dividends.

18.4 LISTING BEHAVIOUR OF COMPANIES

18.4.1 General listing patterns

While there is plenty of anecdotal evidence regarding the importance of foreign stock market listings, there has been relatively little work looking at the behaviour of individual companies in any consistent way, and what evidence there is is often dated. However, it still provides a useful idea of the listing behaviour of companies. One such study[4] looked at the listing of EU companies on all the major European and American exchanges in June 1989. 290 EU companies were quoted on at least one foreign exchange (*see* Exhibit 18.2).

Seven of the then 12 EU countries had stock markets with at least one non-domestic EU company listing. Denmark, Italy, Greece, Spain and Portugal had no non-domestic EU companies listed and no companies from Ireland, Greece or

Exhibit 18.2 STOCK MARKET LISTING BEHAVIOUR OF EU COMPANIES, 1989

| Exchange | Country of domicile | | | | | | | | | | | Total |
	UK	Ger.	Neth.	Belg.	Fr.	Lux.	Ire.	Den.	It.	Gre.	Sp.	
London	–	9	15	–	7	1	–	7	1	–	4	44
Germany	42	–	25	3	20	–	–	2	8	–	12	112
Amsterdam	19	10	–	6	3	4	–	1	3	–	–	46
Brussels	18	8	21	–	11	–	–	–	3	–	–	61
Paris	22	7	4	2	–	–	–	–	1	–	4	40
Luxembourg	7	6	3	8	2	–	–	2	–	–	–	28
Ireland	6	–	–	–	–	–	–	–	–	–	–	6
Scandinavia	1	–	–	–	2	1	–	1	–	–	–	5
Switzerland	19	35	21	6	11	–	1	2	3	2	5	105
Austria	2	17	6	–	–	–	–	–	1	–	–	26
USA	66	1	11	–	3	–	2	1	3	2	7	96
Total number of companies	114	36	44	17	34	5	3	10	8	2	17	290

Source: Gray *et al.* (1994)

---

[4] Gray *et al.* (1994)

Portugal were listed on any other EU exchanges. Some of the findings were unexpected. For example, only 44 EU companies were quoted in London while only 30 non-UK companies were quoted in the USA. In contrast, the German exchanges had 112 EU companies listed and the Swiss had 105, Brussels 61 and Amsterdam 46.

While the USA was the most popular listing choice for UK companies, Germany was also relatively popular. Germany was also the favoured choice of Dutch, French, Italian and Spanish companies. In contrast, German companies appeared to prefer to list in Switzerland or Austria – both German-speaking countries – rather than listing in other EU states.

We saw in Chapter 1 (Exhibit 1.3) that the two stock markets with the most foreign company listings are London and New York. These two markets are interesting not only because of their importance to foreign companies but because they have taken very different approaches towards the regulation of foreign companies. Because of their importance and because they illustrate such different approaches, this chapter continues by looking at the listing requirements in these two countries.

18.4.2 The London Stock Exchange (LSE)

18.4.2.1 LSE Listing requirements

The listing requirements of the LSE are influenced by the EU. The EU has issued several Directives on listing which, like the accounting Directives discussed in Chapter 7, have had to be incorporated into the laws of all EU member states. EU legislation in this area has been based upon the concept of 'competition among rules'. As we saw in the country chapters, the EU has not harmonised the very different regulatory and legal systems. Instead, EU Directives set out an acceptable minimum set of regulations. Countries therefore have to recognise the rules and regulations of other member states as being 'equivalent', even when the local rules that apply to domestic companies are more onerous. This principle of mutual recognition means that countries should set rules only if they are clearly justifiable. If local rules are unduly onerous then domestic companies will be seen to suffer in comparison to other EU companies.

Several directives are particularly relevant to the harmonisation of stock exchanges in the EU.[5] See Exhibit 18.3 for details of these.

Exhibit 18.3 EU STOCK EXCHANGE DIRECTIVES, 1979–90

1979 79/279/EEC	Co-ordinate conditions for admission of securities.
1980 80/390/EEC	Co-ordinate information in prospectuses
1982 82/121/EEC	Publication of half-yearly reports
1987 87/345/EEC	Mutual recognition of listing prospectuses
1989 89/298/EEC	Prospectus used for simultaneous public offer all EU states
1990 90/211/EEC	Allow single document for listing and public offers

---

[5] Scott-Quinn (1994)

The first of these directives, in 1979, established minimum conditions for the admission of securities to a stock market listing. In the following year a second Directive co-ordinated the requirements for the publication of listing particulars. The third, in 1982, set disclosure requirements for interim statements of listed companies. These three Directives had relatively little impact on the London or Paris exchanges. However, they led to significant increases in the disclosure requirements of a number of exchanges including the Amsterdam and the German exchanges.[6] The 1987 Directive was particularly important, as it was the first one to introduce the concept of mutual recognition. It ensured that member states recognised all prospectuses issued by companies listed on any EU member state's exchange as long as the prospectus was approved by the authorities in that country.

Full mutual recognition can be seen clearly in the listing requirements of the LSE. The LSE accepts all documents that have been approved by any competent authority in another EU member state if they are in English or if a certified translation is provided. In addition, its listing requirements are such that it accepts all accounts 'prepared and independently audited in accordance with standards appropriate for companies of international standing and repute'. This would automatically include accounts drawn up under US GAAP or IASs. Other standards are considered on a case-by-case basis.

18.4.2.2 Listing of foreign companies on the LSE

The London Stock Exchange had a position of international prominence by the turn of the last century. It helped to finance business in much of the British Commonwealth (particularly important was the financing of the South African mining industry) and other parts of the world. For example, up until the mid-1880s much of the US insurance industry, agriculture and railways were financed from London. The importance of the London market can be seen in the example of another US industry, brewing. By 1886 15 American breweries were listed in London[7] (*see* Exhibit 18.4).

The number of foreign companies listed in London dropped in the early part of this century. As the stock markets of other countries grew there was less need to raise finance overseas; companies now tend to list on their domestic stock market in preference to listing on foreign markets. In a relatively few cases, companies will list simultaneously on more than one market – for example, when British Telecom and British Gas were first privatised, the share sales were considered to be too big for the LSE and they listed simultaneously in both London and New York.

A study by Gray and Roberts (1997) looked at all foreign companies with full listings of equity shares (not debt) on the LSE at the end of 1994. They looked at when the companies were first listed, where they came from and what industries they operated in. The number of companies seeking a new listing increased each year, reaching a peak of new listings per annum in the mid-1980s and declining since then (with 63 of the sample companies having listed during the period 1980–4, 58 in 1985–9 and 34 in 1990–4). The 293 companies identified came from 26 countries. Over one-third (108) came from the USA and 63 came from South

---

[6] Tondkar *et al.* (1989)
[7] Reckitt (1953)

| Exhibit 18.4 | AMERICAN BREWERIES REGISTERED ON THE LSE, 1896 |

Company	Date of registration
Bartholomay Brewing Co., Rochester NY	April 1889
St Louis Breweries	Dec. 1889
City of Chicago Brewing & Malting Co.	June 1890
San Francisco Breweries	Unknown
City of Baltimore United Breweries	Nov. 1889
Milwaukee & Chicago Breweries	Dec. 1890
United States Brewing Co.	May 1889
New York Breweries	Aug. 1889
New England Breweries	March 1890
Denver Breweries	June 1889
Cincinnati Breweries	Oct. 1889
Springfield Breweries	March 1890
Washington Breweries	April 1888
Indianapolis Breweries	Nov. 1889
Chicago Breweries	April 1888

Source: Reckitt (1953), p. 31

Africa, while Australia, Bermuda, Canada, Japan and Sweden all had ten or more companies listed on the LSE. The South African companies had generally listed much earlier than had the companies from other countries. This reflects the historical links between the UK and South Africa and the importance of British finance in the development of South African mining. In contrast, the majority of the US companies listed during the 1980s. This was partly due to the break-up of the large telecommunications companies and the creation of a number of smaller companies, known as 'Baby Bells', partly due to the international expansion of US business at this time and probably partly due also to fashion or 'follow-my-leader' behaviour by companies. European companies have a long history of listing in London – Royal Dutch Petroleum and Unilever from the Netherlands both listed in the 1940s, SKF and Electrolux from Sweden in the 1950s and Thyssen, Bayer and Hoechst from Germany in the early 1960s. The 1990s has seen listings mainly from Europe (9), Japan (5), India (4) and Bermuda (6). More recent listings are also much more likely to have come from the service or the utilities sectors while until the 1980s most foreign listings operated in either the mining or manufacturing sectors.

18.4.3 The USA

18.4.3.1 American Depository Receipts (ADRs)

Most foreign companies trade their shares in the USA through American Depository Receipts (ADRs). Rather than dealing in shares denominated in their own currency they repackage their shares as ADRs. These are popular as the sale and purchase procedures are simplified and dividends are paid in US currency. There are various different types of ADRs (*see* Exhibit 18.5).

Exhibit 18.5	TYPES OF ADRs
Level One	Trade over-the-counter (OTC) Not comply with full reporting requirements
Level Two	Trade on stock exchange or NASDAQ Full registration procedures Exempt from some filing requirements
Level Three	Allows issuance of new shares Full registration and reporting requirements
Rule 144A	DR placed and traded only among Qualified Institutional Buyers Not comply with full reporting requirements
Global DR	DR structured as combination of Rule 144A private placing and public offering outside USA SEC registration not required
Side-by-side ADR	Level one ADRs that trade concurrently with Rule 144A ADRs

Source: Citibank (1997)

ADRs can be sponsored or unsponsored. Sponsored ADRs are administered by one bank only which has been appointed by the issuer. In contrast, unsponsored ADRs allow more than one bank to carry out depository services. Such ADRs usually trade on the over-the-counter (OTC) market and cannot be traded on any stock market.

The easiest and cheapest of these various ADRs are level one ADRs and Rule 144A offerings. Issuers of level one ADRs need only file their home country reports with the Securities and Exchange Commission (SEC). However, these ADRs cannot be traded on any US stock market or NASDAQ. Trade can take place only on the electronic bulletin board or the so-called 'pink sheets'. This market tends to be characterised by its expense and trading margins are typically large. However, it is still an important market. On average, approximately 55 million shares were traded each day in 1995.[8] Similarly, Rule 144A offerings cannot be traded on any stock market. Instead, the shares can be offered only as a private placing to a qualified institutional investor. The advantage to the issuing company is again that it avoids the disclosure rules involved in a stock market listing.

A non-US company can go further and issue Level Two or Level Three ADRs on any stock market or on NASDAQ. In these cases, the SEC is very much in favour of a 'level playing field' – in other words, US investors must not be less protected when investing in a foreign company than when investing in a domestic company and US companies must not be disadvantaged in comparison to foreign firms when seeking equity finance. This means that the same measurement and disclosure rules should apply to foreign and domestic companies. However, foreign companies that qualify as foreign issuers[9] (if a majority of shareholders, directors, assets or business is American, the company is treated as a domestic issuer) can opt

---

[8] Bayless *et al.* (1996)
[9] Hertz *et al.* (1997)

for Level Two ADRs and take advantage of certain concessions with respect to the information required and the measurement rules used. The SEC has introduced various formal rules over recent years that relax the reporting requirements and it also issues case-by-case waivers or non-action letters that agree not to enforce certain disclosure rules for a particular company. Without both of these, the US domestic disclosure and reporting requirements would be considered to be too onerous by many companies who would therefore not list in the USA.

The main requirement is to file the annual Form 20-F which contains much of the information commonly found in annual financial reports and statements as well as other items of information, in particular details of the shares or securities registered (*see* Exhibit 18.6).

Exhibit 18.6   INFORMATION TO BE INCLUDED IN FORM 20-F

Part I
- Description of business
- Description of property
- Legal proceedings
- Control of registrant
- Nature of trading market
- Exchange controls and other limitations affecting security holders
- Taxation
- Selected financial data
- Management's discussion and analysis of financial condition and results of operations
- Directors and officers of registrant
- Compensation of directors and officers
- Interest of management in certain transactions

Part II
- Description of securities to be registered

Part III
- Defaults upon senior securities
- Changes in securities and changes in security for registered securities

Part IV
- Financial statements and exhibits

Foreign registrants do not have to use US accounting principles, but may instead report using any non-US accounting principles providing they are based on a 'comprehensive body of accounting principles'. While this is not defined, SEC staff have indicated that this is taken to include the principles followed in all OECD member countries as well as IASC standards.[10] If this is done, the company

---

[10] Hertz *et al.* (1997)

must present, in its notes, a reconciliation statement. This must explain the material differences between the accounting principles, rules and methods used and US GAAP. The differences should be quantified so that net income, balance sheet equity and earnings per share are reconciled for the present and past year. Exhibit 3.1 reproduced the reconciliation statement of British Telecom which illustrates these requirements.

In 1994 the SEC introduced several further concessions for foreign registrants. Most importantly, it effectively endorsed IAS 7 when it exempted companies who produced cash flow statements under IAS 7 from having to provide a reconciliation to US GAAP. It also permitted foreign issuers to use IAS 21 for operations in hyperinflationary countries and many of the requirements of IAS 22 for business combinations can be used without providing a reconciliation statement.[11]

If the foreign company wishes to list its shares then it can file under item 17 of Form 20-K. Under this, the company need not provide disclosures required of US companies if the same information is not required under domestic rules. In particular, this often means that they do not have to produce detailed segment information nor provide details of each individual director and officer's remuneration. However, if they wish to make a public offering for sale (Level Three ADRs) they have to provide all material information required by US rules.

18.4.3.2 ADR issues[12]

The number of companies issuing ADRs has increased greatly in the last decade. At the end of 1990 there were 812 programmes, while by the end of 1996 this had grown to 1,733 including 252 companies from 48 countries which launched new ADRs in 1996. Of these, a slight majority (51%) came from emerging market countries.

A small number of ADRs account for the majority of the trades conducted. Between 1992 and 1996 a total of only 20 listed ADRs accounted for 66% of the aggregate value of ADR trading on US exchanges (*see* Exhibit 18.7).

18.4.3.3 Listing of foreign companies on the NYSE

While relatively few foreign companies have listed in London since 1990, the same cannot be said for New York. New York now has more foreign companies listing on it than does any other stock market, which marks a recent and significant change in listing behaviour.

As at the end of September 1997, NYSE had 329 foreign companies listing common shares. Exhibit 18.8 provides a list of all countries that are home to at least five registrants.

It is interesting to see the differences between this list and the pattern of companies listed in London. As might be expected, far more Central and South American companies are listed on NYSE than on London. In contrast, NYSE has only one South African company and fewer Scandinavian companies than are listed in London.

The far more significant difference between the two markets lies in the timing of the listings. NYSE has a few companies that have maintained listings from the

---

[11] Hanks (1997)
[12] Citibank (1997)

Exhibit 18.7 THE TOP 20 LISTED ADR PROGRAMMES, 1992–6

Issuer	Country	Value US trading 1992–6 $billion
Telefonos de Mexico	Mexico	174.5
Royal Dutch Petroleum	Netherlands	108.5
British Petroleum	UK	56.8
LM Ericsson	Sweden	53.2
Glaxo Wellcome	UK	45.9
Hanson	UK	37.3
Unilever	Netherlands	34.6
Vodafone Group	UK	29.7
Telebras	Brazil	28.9
Reuters	UK	28.5
Nokia	Finland	27.4
YPF	Argentina	22.8
Grupo Televisa	Mexico	19.9
Philips	Netherlands	16.3
The News Corp.	Australia	16.1
CTC	Chile	15.7
Teva Pharmaceutical	Israel	15.2
Telefonica Nacional de España	Spain	13.5
Telefonica de Argentina	Argentina	13.2
Repsol	Spain	12.7
Total		771.9

Source: Citibank (1997)

Exhibit 18.8 NUMBER OF NON-US CORPORATE ISSUERS ON THE NYSE, SEPTEMBER 1997

Country	No. registrants	Country	No. registrants
Argentina	11	Australia	10
Bermuda	8	Brazil	6
Canada	62	Cayman Islands	5
Chile	20	France	10
Germany	6	Hong Kong	6
Italy	11	Japan	11
Mexico	26	Netherlands	15
Norway	6	People's Republic of China	8
Spain	7	UK	48

Source: www.nyse.com, as at October 1997

1950s or earlier such as Alcan Aluminium and Canadian Pacific from Canada, KLM and Royal Dutch Petroleum from the Netherlands and Shell Transport & Trading from the UK. However, the majority of the listings have occurred in the last few years. Indeed nearly one-third of foreign registrants have listed since the beginning of 1996, with 62 listing in 1996 and 43 listing in the first eight months of 1997.

Only a minority of these companies have gone all the way and issued full public offerings on the NYSE. Of the 329 companies listed, only 95 have made public offerings. Again, the number of public offerings is rapidly increasing with 32 being made in 1996 and 25 in the first eight months of 1997. The majority of companies from South and Central America and from various mainland European countries such as the Netherlands, France, Italy and Spain and all the Chinese and Hong Kong companies have made public offerings, suggesting that the need for funds was the main reason for seeking a listing. In contrast, relatively few of the companies from Australia, Canada, Japan and the UK have made public offerings, suggesting that the decision to list may not have been driven by a need for new funding. As discussed above, these companies may have sought a listing for a number of other reasons.

18.5 EMPIRICAL RESEARCH INTO STOCK MARKET LISTING CHOICES

Several studies have looked at the factors that help to explain listing choices or where and why companies list on foreign stock exchanges. One of the first of these studies was by Saudagaran (1988), who tested four hypotheses. These were that the likelihood that a company has a foreign listing is a function of:

- the relative size of the company in its domestic stock market (capitalisation or market value of company's equity to total market capitalisation)
- importance of foreign sales (foreign sales to total sales)
- importance of foreign investment (investment in foreign countries as a proportion of total investment)
- importance of foreign employees (employees in foreign countries as a proportion of total employees).

Looking at 223 companies with shares listed in at least one of eight foreign countries, the study found support for the importance of the company in its domestic local stock exchange and the importance of foreign sales. It failed to find any support for the other two hypotheses (foreign investment and foreign employees).

Later studies have looked instead at the importance of disclosure levels in different countries. Biddle and Saudagaran (1989), using a similar sample, found support for the hypothesis that companies tend to be indifferent across exchanges with levels of disclosure that are less than domestic disclosure levels. In contrast, they are progressively less likely to list on exchanges in countries with higher disclosure levels. In other words, if a country wants to attract foreign companies to its stock exchange, there appears to be no benefit in demanding less disclosure than foreign markets demand. However, demanding higher disclosure levels will prevent foreign companies listing. Alternative explanations of listing behaviour were also considered – the importance of industry membership; geographic location (whether located in the same geographic area or not); importance of country of listing as an export market (industry exports to country as proportion of industry exports to all sample countries); and the relative importance of the company to its domestic stock market. Even when all of these alternative explanations were also taken into account, disclosure levels still helped to explain listing choice. These results were confirmed by a later study (Saudagaran and Biddle, 1995), which looked at the listing behaviour of 459 multinational companies from the same eight countries (Canada, France, Germany, Japan, Switzerland, the UK and the USA) in 1992.

Again, they applied the model to each of the countries to see if the variables were significant in explaining whether or not the sample foreign companies listed in various countries. They ran eight regression equations – one for each country. They found that the disclosure variable was significant in explaining listing behaviour more often than were any of the other variables. In particular, the disclosure level was found to be significant in explaining listing choices with respect to six of the eight countries. The importance of international trade was significant for five countries and the need for capital was significant for four.

While these are interesting results, some care should be taken in interpreting them. It should not be assumed that the results will always hold across all countries and all time periods. This type of study suffers from two serious limitations. First, it looks only at the position at one point of time. It tries to explain the decision to list – a decision that may have been taken many years earlier – by looking at contemporary economic, corporate and accounting factors. Once a company has listed in a market it will often not reconsider the decision very often. If it does consider delisting, the factors considered may be quite different from those that drove the company to originally list. There may therefore be little or no relationship between current economic, accounting and corporate characteristics and those that applied at the time of the original listing. Secondly, these studies have looked only at certain countries. The decision to list will be dependent upon characteristics of the foreign market, the company itself and the political and economic environment of the domestic or home country. It may be that companies from other countries that were not considered have quite different reasons for seeking foreign stock market listings.

One other study (Gray and Roberts, 1997) suggests that the factors determining listing choices may differ across companies from different countries. Gray and Roberts instead tried to explain the number of registrants from each foreign country that were listed on the LSE in 1994. They ran a regression with the dependent variable being number of companies listed from country *x* and the independent variables being:

- disclosure level (more or less than UK)
- size of economy (GDP)
- economic development of country (*per capita* GDP)
- importance of national stock market (market capitalisation to GDP)
- trade with the UK (exports and imports to UK as a proportion of all exports and imports of country)

- level of domestic investment (domestic investment to GDP)

- cultural affinity to the UK (English-speaking, EU member or British Commonwealth member).

While the model was relatively successful in explaining the number of foreign registrants (adjusted R^2 of 61%) Gray and Roberts found no evidence to suggest that disclosure levels were significant. Instead, the only factors that helped to explain the number of companies listed were GDP, stock market capitalisation and domestic investment rates. More companies were listed from countries that were large, had relatively important stock markets and high needs for capital as measured by domestic investment levels.

18.6 SUMMARY AND CONCLUSIONS

This chapter has looked at the listing behaviour of companies. Taking as its starting point the evidence presented in Chapter 1 (Exhibit 1.3) that shows that many companies list on foreign exchange(s) the chapter looked at the reasons for this. It was shown that, in many cases, companies have to list on a larger exchange if they want to raise a large amount of equity capital. This is especially the case for companies from relatively small countries or countries with relatively inactive stock markets. However, this can be a problem for any company seeking a great deal of capital – as seen, for example, in a number of privatisation issues from many countries including the UK. Many companies list on foreign exchanges for a number of other reasons including risk management, issuing shares to employees and for takeovers, and signalling to customers, the general public or governments.

Given the importance of the UK and USA to foreign registrants, the chapter went on to look at the LSE and the NYSE. The USA demands the highest level of disclosure from foreign companies – requiring, for example, a reconciliation statement explaining differences from US GAAP. The problems of this in terms of direct and indirect costs were discussed and the ways in which the USA has reduced these costs by allowing a variety of different methods of selling of shares were also looked at.

Finally, the evidence on stock market listing behaviour was considered. It is difficult to interpret the often different results of these studies. There is clear evidence that differences in listing requirements have been important; however, this is not the only consideration and given the rapidly increasing importance of the USA to foreign companies and the rapidly increasing number of foreign companies raising new equity finance in the USA, the extra disclosure costs do not appear to be an insurmountable barrier.

As discussed earlier, the IASC is being supported in its work by IOSCO which is hoping for a set of international accounting standards that will be acceptable to all major stock markets for annual or on-going reporting purposes. IOSCO is similarly concerned with initial listing requirements. In autumn 1997, an IOSCO working party issued a consultative document 'International disclosure standards for cross-border offerings and initial listings by foreign issuers'. Obviously, these moves towards increased harmonisation have the potential to reduce the costs of foreign listings and this should mean that the number of foreign listings will continue to grow. Any such reduction in listing costs will have the greatest impact on those stock markets that are currently the most expensive to list on. The USA is the country with the highest or most stringent reporting requirements for foreign registrants, thus to the extent that IOSCO succeeds in removing these differences, the USA is likely to continue to see the greatest growth in the number of foreign registrants.

QUESTIONS

1 Why do companies list on foreign stock markets?

2 What are likely to be the main additional direct costs incurred by a company seeking a listing on a foreign stock market?

3 What are likely to be the main additional indirect costs incurred by a company seeking a listing on a foreign stock market?

4 What actions might a company have to take to ensure that it maintains a large active shareholder base in a foreign country?

5 Which types of companies are particularly likely to seek a listing on a foreign stock market?

6 Does the evidence of foreign listing behaviour in the USA support your answer to Question 5?

7 Does the evidence of foreign listing behaviour on EU stock markets support your answer to Question 5?

8 If a company wanted to trade its shares in the USA, what alternative methods are available to it? What would you advise it to do?

9 What does the empirical research tell you about the factors that affect a company's choice of where to list?

10 If you wanted to empirically test for the factors that affect a company's choice of where to list, how would you go about getting the information you needed? What problems do you think you would encounter?

REFERENCES

Bayless, R., Cochrane, J., Harris, T., Leisenring, J., McLaughlin, J. and Wirtz, J.P. (1996) 'International access to US capital markets – An AAA forum on accounting policy', *Accounting Horizons*, 10(1), 75–94.

Biddle, G.C. and Saudagaran, S.M. (1989) 'The effect of financial disclosure levels on firms' choices among alternative foreign stock exchange listings', *Journal of International Financial Management and Accounting*, 1(1), 55–87.

Citibank (1997) *Citibank Depositary Receipt Universal Issuance Guide*. New York: Citibank.

Gray, S.J., Meek, G.K. and Roberts, C.B. (1994) 'Financial deregulation, stock exchange listing choice, and the development of a European capital market', in Zimmerman, V.K. (ed.) *The New Europe: Recent Political and Economic Implications for Accountants and Accounting*. Urbana–Champaign, IL: Center for International Education and Research in Accounting, University of Illinois.

Gray, S.J. and Roberts, C.B. (1997) 'Foreign company listings on the London Stock Exchange: Listing patterns and influential factors', in Cooke, T.E. and Nobes, C.W. (eds) *The Development of Accounting in an International Context*. London: Routledge.

Hanks, S. (1997) 'Globalization of world financial markets: Perspective of the US Securities and Exchange Commission', in Choi, F.D.S. (ed.) *International Accounting and Finance Handbook*. 2nd edn. New York: John Wiley.

Hertz, R.H., Dittmar, N.W., Lis, S.J., Decker, W.E. and Murray, R.J. (1997) *The Coopers and Lybrand SEC Manual*. 7th edn. New York: John Wiley.

Radebaugh, L.H., Gebhart, G. and Gray, S.J. (1995) 'Foreign stock exchange listings: A case study of Daimler–Benz', *Journal of International Financial Management and Accounting*, 6(2), 158–92.

Reckitt, E. (1953) 'Reminiscences of early days of the accounting profession in Illinois: Illinois Society of Certified Public Accountants', reprinted in Zeff, S.A. (ed.) *The US Accounting Profession in the 1890s and Early 1900s*. New York: Garland Publishing, 165–314.

Saudagaran, S.M. (1988) 'An empirical study of selected factors influencing the decision to list in foreign stock exchanges', *Journal of International Business Studies*, Spring, 101–27.

Saudagaran, S.M. and Biddle, G.C. (1995) 'Foreign listing location: A study of MNCs and stock exchanges in eight countries', *Journal of International Business Studies*, 26(2), 319–42.

Scott-Quinn, B. (1994) 'EC securities markets regulation', in Steil, B. (ed.) *International Financial Market Regulation*, Chichester: John Wiley, 121–66.

Tondkar, R.H., Adhikari, A. and Coffman, E.N. (1989) 'The internationalisation of equity markets: Motivations for foreign corporate listing and filing and listing requirements of five major stock markets', *International Journal of Accounting*, Fall, 143–63.

Chapter 19

Corporate reporting policies

19.1 PURPOSE OF THE CHAPTER

Chapter 18 explored the issue of why companies raise equity finance on overseas stock exchanges and how they choose between competing exchanges. While in the past it has only been the largest of companies that have tended to go to foreign markets, this is a practice that is likely to continue to increase over the next few years. As we saw in Chapter 5, one of the main pressures on the IASC is IOSCO and its demand for a set of international accounting standards that can be used for international listing purposes. If one set of international standards is accepted by all of the major stock exchanges, the costs of listing internationally should decrease and the number of companies listing on foreign exchanges increase. However, as we have also seen throughout this book, there are and there will still continue to be some substantial differences between the accounting practices – both mandatory and voluntary – found in different countries. This chapter therefore looks at international investors and explores their reactions to diversity of accounting practices. It also looks at the approaches that companies can take to reporting to investors and other users of their accounts that are unfamiliar with the company's domestic GAAP.

Learning objectives

After reading this chapter you should:

- Understand why investors might want to invest in foreign companies.
- Be aware of the different approaches that investors can take to choosing which foreign companies to invest in.
- Be aware of the reasons why the demand for and supply of foreign equities is likely to continue to increase
- Understand the different approaches that companies can take when reporting to foreign users and understand the factors that affect corporate reporting decisions.

The chapter begins with a brief review of the discussion in Chapter 3 of the sources of differences in accounting practices internationally. It then looks at investors and explores the reasons why they might want to invest in foreign companies and how they might use (or not use) financial statement information in their investment decision making. While investors are an important user group, others are often also interested in the financial statements of foreign companies. The chapter therefore continues by looking at other users of financial statements, the sorts of decisions they might want to take and their use of financial statement information. Finally, the chapter examines the different approaches that a company can take to reporting to its foreign statement users.

19.2 ACCOUNTING DIFFERENCES ACROSS COUNTRIES

In the individual country chapters, we saw many cases of standards that permit a choice between alternatives. As we saw in Chapter 6, many of the IASC standards also allow two or even more alternatives. Even if all companies followed IASC standards, companies from different countries might still systematically choose different alternatives. Chapters 1 and 2 suggested a variety of reasons for this – for example, in some countries the choice of accounting method for external reporting purposes affects taxable income; in other countries it does not. If everything else is the same, companies are more likely to choose to use measurement rules that minimise reported income in those countries where taxable income is also affected.

There are other areas that are not regulated at all in certain countries. Many disclosures are made voluntarily. Information on employees, environmental impacts and forecast information, for example, are almost always provided voluntarily. Voluntary information disclosure may also include more detailed analysis of items which are required, such as fixed asset values, intangible assets, pensions, contingencies or segmental analysis. Some information on all of these will be legally required in most countries, but there are considerable differences in terms of how much information is required. In these areas, companies are free to provide more information than the legally required minimum amount. There are also some measurement-related issues that are not regulated at all in some countries, giving companies complete freedom in deciding upon the measurement methods to use. This includes areas such as foreign currency translation methods and leases.

Even when the rules are the same, normal or typical practice may differ across countries. Identical rules may be interpreted in different ways. How prudent should companies be when interpreting what 'reasonably certain' means, for example? This is required when assessing whether or not an asset meets the recognition criteria laid down in the IASC framework. We saw in Chapter 2 how culture can affect the actions of individuals, including accountants. This is one important reason why the same terms may be interpreted and applied in consistently different ways in different countries.

This means, as we saw in Chapter 3, that companies from different countries can often present exactly the same events in quite different ways and the resultant income statement and balance sheet figures can be quite different.

The impact of accounting differences on the reported figures has been discussed in each of the individual country chapters. These have provided an indication of the often significant differences between reported figures because of differences in accounting practices, and Exhibit 19.1 provides further evidence on this. Exhibit 19.1 shows the results of the Simmonds and Azières (1989) simulation study of a multinational company reporting under the GAAP of seven EU member states.

Exhibit 19.1 THE IMPACT OF ACCOUNTING DIFFERENCES IN THE EU

	Minimum net profit	Maximum net profit	Most likely net profit	Most likely net assets	Rate of return %
Belgium	90	193	135	726	18.6
France	121	160	149	710	21.0
Germany	27	140	133	649	20.5
Italy	167	193	174	751	23.2
Netherlands	76	156	140	704	19.9
Spain	121	192	131	722	18.2
UK	171	194	192	712	27.0

As can be seen, there is a large range of 'most likely' figures across the seven countries. Net profit varies from a high of 192 million ECU in the UK to a low of 131 million in Spain while net assets similarly vary from 751 million in Italy to 649 million in Germany. This means that the reported rate of return typically varies from the UK at 27.0% to Spain at only 18.2%. However, the differences in the possible range of figures reported is perhaps even more interesting. It is particularly noticeable that the minimum profit figure under UK GAAP is 171 million and under Italian GAAP 167 million, figures that are higher than the most optimistic figures reported under French, German and Dutch GAAP.

19.3 POSSIBLE APPROACHES TO INTERNATIONAL EQUITY INVESTMENT

19.3.1 Why invest internationally?

Reading through this book you may have been given the impression that the sensible investor should not invest in foreign companies or foreign stock markets. We have seen how accounting differs across countries, and that many if not most of these differences are not random but are explainable and, given sufficient disclosure, are also measurable. However, the empirical studies discussed in Chapter 3 and throughout Part 2 also show that the level of disclosure is not high enough and the differences not systematic enough, nor consistent enough, to allow users to predict accurately the impact of accounting differences upon any particular company. We have also seen how different equity transaction methods, different currencies and different languages all make it more difficult and more expensive to invest in foreign markets.

Despite these considerations, there are clear benefits to investing in foreign companies and foreign markets. For example, if an investor had invested $1,000 in the US market in 1985 she would have an investment worth $3,818, ten years later. If the investment had been made in the Thailand market instead it would have been worth $16,212, or $23,209 in Mexico, $48,023 in the Philippines or

$64,707 in Chile.[1] However, this is past history. An investor deciding now to invest in Chile might instead find in ten years' time that this was the worst decision she could have taken. Which stock markets have been particularly good or bad investments in the past is not relevant today. What is relevant is the fact that stock markets have not all moved together – in any one period, some stock markets will be doing well and others will not be doing so well.

A wise investor investing in their domestic stock market would not invest in only one or two companies. No investor can consistently pick winners, as it is not simply a case of predicting which companies will do well in the future and which will do badly. To be successful in picking companies, investors must make better or more accurate predictions than do other investors. While they might choose well and make a lot of money, they might equally well choose badly and lose money instead. It is well established that, over time, all investors can hope is that they do as well on average as the market does. The semi-strong form of the efficient market hypothesis generally holds in active stock markets of developed countries. Share prices react quickly and correctly to all new information and no investor is able to consistently outguess the market. Investors should invest in a well diversified portfolio of shares. This allows them to minimise their risk for any given level of return (or maximise their expected return for any given level of risk). At least in theory investors should diversify across all available shares and invest in the market portfolio. In practice, if they choose different types of companies, a well diversified investment in 12 or so stocks should be sufficient to gain most of the benefits available from diversification. Diversification brings benefits because the returns made from different equities are less than perfectly correlated. While some companies might be doing particularly well with rising share prices, other companies will instead be performing less well than expected.

Similar considerations apply to international investing. The returns from different stock markets are less than perfectly correlated with each other. Exhibit 19.2 reports the correlations between the annual returns from eight major equity markets for the period 1982–92.

Exhibit 19.2 ANNUAL INTERMARKET RETURN CORRELATIONS, 1982–92

	France	UK	Japan	Germany	Switz.	Canada	Australia
USA	0.57	0.63	0.44	0.41	0.58	0.81	0.51
France		0.56	0.53	0.65	0.64	0.39	0.34
UK			0.51	0.38	0.45	0.52	0.53
Japan				0.30	0.30	0.30	0.30
Germany					0.75	0.27	0.22
Switz.						0.43	0.35
Canada							0.56

Source: Gastineau *et al.* (1993), quoted in Fabozzi and Modigliani (1996), p. 323

[1] Melton (1996), p. 28

As can be seen from Exhibit 19.2, all the stock markets are positively correlated – they tend to move together as the performances of different economies are inter-related due to trade and capital flows between countries. All of the correlations are reasonably large. The two stock markets that have performed most alike are the USA and Canada (0.81). Given the economic closeness of these two countries, this is not surprising. In contrast, the two stock markets in Exhibit 19.2 with the most dissimilar performance have been Australia and Germany (at 0.22) followed by Canada and Germany (at 0.27). These are countries with relatively few trade or economic links. There are a number of reasons why none of the stock markets are perfectly correlated (i.e. correlation of 1.0). Different economic and political poli-cies, different trade patterns, industrial structures, corporate policies and investor behaviour all mean that companies in different countries will tend, on average, to perform somewhat differently. In any one period companies from one country will tend to perform relatively well, but in other periods, companies from other coun-tries will instead tend to perform better.

There will be substantial benefits from investing in foreign companies simply because stock markets are less than perfectly correlated. There will often also be additional diversification benefits available because investors can now invest in different types of companies or different industries. For example, a UK investor wanting to invest in an auto-manufacturer could not invest in a UK auto-manufac-turer but might instead decide to invest in a German company. A German investor wanting to invest in a large drinks company would also have to look abroad and would have a choice of UK companies to invest in. Exhibit 19.3 lists the industrial sectors of each of the 50 largest companies from the UK, Germany, the USA and Japan. This gives a good idea of differences in the industrial composition of the major companies in these countries.

Exhibit 19.3 SECTORIAL DISTRIBUTION OF THE MAJOR COMPANIES, SELECTED COUNTRIES, 1997

	UK	Germany	USA	Japan
Financial sector	18	11	16	15
Oil and gas	3	3	7	2
Metals and mining	2	5	–	5
Communications	2	–	7	1
Utilities	3	5	5	7
Chemicals and pharmaceuticals	2	5	2	1
Electronics	1	3	1	7
Engineering	–	12	3	4
Transport	7	2	1	2
Breweries	4	–	1	–
Retail	5	2	4	–
Other	3	2	3	6

Source: The Times 1,000, 1997 (1996)

When deciding upon a suitable investment strategy an investor could decide to invest in only one industry but to choose companies from across many countries. Alternatively, they might decide to invest in only one country but to choose companies from across many industries. Of these two alternatives, the less risky strategy is the first, to invest in one industry throughout the world.[2] In other words, the price movements of shares are more dependent upon the average performance of the stock exchanges they are listed on than upon the average performance of the industries that they operate in.

The best investment strategy would be to invest across both industries and countries. One of the earliest studies of the benefits of international diversification[3] calculated that a well diversified international portfolio would be typically only half as risky as a similar sized portfolio of US shares. Investors from smaller countries or countries with smaller or less active stock markets would tend to gain even more from international investment.

It is becoming increasingly cheap and easy for investors to invest in foreign stock markets. The simplest way for the ordinary investor to do this is through investing indirectly in foreign markets by buying unit trusts or other similar investments which themselves invest in foreign markets. Exhibit 19.4 lists just some of the types of funds that UK investors can buy, all of which in turn invest in foreign equities and all of which can be bought on the LSE in local currency.

Exhibit 19.4 UK FUNDS INVESTING IN FOREIGN EQUITIES, SELECTED COUNTRIES AND COUNTRY GROUPS, 1997

Regional funds	Europe, North America, Pacific Basin, Latin America, South-East Asia
Country funds	Australia, Hong Kong, New Zealand, Switzerland, Thailand
Growth funds	American, Asian, German, Latin American growth
Small company funds	American, Japanese, Pacific small companies
Others	Emerging markets, Overseas large companies, World-wide recovery, US emerging companies

Source: *The Times*, November 1997

This means that individuals or private small investors need not invest directly in the shares of foreign firms. They do not therefore have to bother with the costs and inconvenience of dealing in different currencies or languages. Instead, all they need do is decide which type of domestic fund they wish to invest in and then choose among the alternative funds. In these cases, the decision is not based upon individual company's financial statement information but is based upon economic data and information about the performance and costs of the competing funds.

---

[2] Heston and Rouwenhorst (1994)
[3] Solnik (1974)

However, this does not mean that financial statement information is not used by stock market participants – the investment funds must decide upon suitable companies to invest in. Professional fund managers and analysts will need to compare companies from different countries. The next section therefore looks at the alternative investment strategies that can be adopted by anyone, whether an individual investor or professional fund manager, wishing to invest directly in equities from different countries.

19.3.2 Passive investment strategies

Three different strategies have been identified which investors can use to cope with accounting diversity.[4] At one extreme, investors may decide not to rely upon company specific information at all. Instead, they could adopt a passive or index-based strategy. In the international arena this would involve deciding how much to invest in each country on the basis of non-accounting factors. Factors considered might include relative GNP, past and forecast country growth rates and the size of the stock market. The investor would then choose a portfolio of shares inside each country that mirrored or represented the country's total stock market. The objective is to match the returns of each of the world's stock market and therefore the returns of the global market, rather than to outperform it. Passive investment strategies are being used increasingly by US and UK institutional investors investing in their domestic stock markets. It was initially developed as a way of reducing transaction costs as it involves less share trading. Shares are only bought or sold when the portfolio no longer adequately mirrors the market due to changes in the market caused by such factors as new issues, mergers and takeovers. These types of portfolios are often called 'trackers' or 'tracker funds', because they are designed to mirror or track the market.

Because passive investment strategies reduce the need to analyse financial statements, they can also be a useful response to problems of lack of accounting information or lack of understanding of the accounting information provided. They may therefore be particularly useful for investors wishing to diversify into international markets. However, even if passive investment strategies are adopted, some financial statement information may need to be used to help in choosing a portfolio that is adequately diversified.

If UK investment funds are looked at, then the majority of investment funds available for purchase by the general public adopt various active investment strategies and attempt to outperform the market. However, a number of tracking funds are available. These include a number of international tracking funds that invest either regionally (e.g. in Europe or North America) or internationally in all major stock markets.

19.3.3 Active investment strategies

The opposite approach is to adopt an active investment strategy based, at least partially, on accounting information. Here, investors try to assess whether or not a

---

[4] Choi and Levich (1997)

company will be a good investment. They will use accounting information as well as other information (economic information including forecasts, company information from newspaper reports and stockbroker reports and possibly company visits) to assess the strength and weaknesses of companies and their management and the companies' likely future prospects. Using all of this information they will buy or sell shares whenever they have new information or whenever market conditions change in an attempt to 'beat the market' or to do better than they could by adopting a passive investment strategy.

There are two different ways or approaches to using foreign GAAP-based financial statements. First, the user might restate the figures provided into a more familiar set of accounting principles. This would mean that the figures could then be more easily compared with the figures provided by companies from other countries; this is one of the main rationales behind the reconciliation statements discussed in Chapter 3. However, in this case, it is the user that is producing the reconciliation statements rather than the company itself, and this approach is based upon the assumption that stock markets are reasonably well integrated. The investors then choose the best companies to invest in internationally irrespective of their home country. Companies from different countries can then be compared one with the other – 'Is the company a good investment compared to alternative investments from other countries?'

The second approach is to become familiar with various foreign GAAP and then to use a local perspective when analysing foreign financial statements. This approach is often called a 'multiple principles capability'; it is premised upon the opposite assumption, that markets are not integrated but are segmented. It assumes that companies can be usefully compared only with other companies from the same country and a company's performance should therefore be assessed only in the context of the local market – 'Is the company a good investment inside that market or not?'

19.3.4 Mixed investment strategies

An intermediate investment strategy is also possible which adopts aspects of both a passive and an active approach. This would involve adopting a passive strategy and using an index approach for all of those countries or industries where the investor has insufficient information or where the available information is based upon unfamiliar accounting rules. Where investors are familiar with the information provided and sufficient disclosures are made, they would instead adopt an active investment strategy.

19.4 EMPIRICAL EVIDENCE ON SHAREHOLDERS' INVESTMENT STRATEGIES

Relatively few studies have looked at how investors actually manage in a world of accounting diversity. One of the most interesting studies in this area is by Choi and Levich (1990). They interviewed 52 market participants in the UK, the USA, Japan, Germany and Switzerland. Nearly half of the interviewees stated that their decisions were affected by accounting diversity (*see* Exhibit 19.5). For some of the other interviewees there were second-order effects. While the decisions made did not change, decisions were made in a different way.

Exhibit 19.5 IMPACT OF ACCOUNTING DIVERSITY ON MARKET PARTICIPANTS, FINDINGS OF CHOI AND LEVICH (1990)

Question: Does accounting diversity affect your capital market decisions?				
	Yes	*No*	*N/A*	*Total*
Investors	9	7	1	17
Issuers	6	9		15
Underwriters	7	1		8
Regulators	–	8		8
Raters and others	2	1		3
Total	24	26	1	51

Source: Choi and Levich (1990), p. 127

Exhibit 19.6 describes how 17 investors interviewed were affected by accounting diversity. Nearly all of those affected (nine) found it more difficult to make assessments of security values or returns while the majority also found that differences in both measurement rules and disclosure practices affected the types of companies they invested in. Of these nine investors, seven attempted to either formally or informally restate the accounts into more familiar GAAP.

Exhibit 19.6 IMPACT OF ACCOUNTING DIVERSITY ON INVESTORS, FINDINGS OF CHOI AND LEVICH (1990)

Impact	*Due to GAAP differences*	*Due to disclosure differences*
Geographic spread of investments	3	3
Types of companies selected	6	7
Information processing costs	5	2
Assessment of security returns or valuation	8	8

Source: Choi and Levich (1990), p. 129

Two different approaches were identified in the sample of investors who said that they were not affected by accounting differences. Half of them used a multiple principle capability. They were able to adopt a local perspective, they were familiar with local GAAP and were able to understand the financial statements and place them in the correct context. Most of the other investors instead used non-accounting information and did not rely upon the local GAAP statements. A variety of different approaches was used, including a dividend valuation model, which valued the investments on the basis of discounted expected future dividends. An alternative method used was to decide how much to invest in a country on the basis of economic models, then to invest in particular companies inside each country on the basis of other criteria. Such investors either attempted to create a balanced portfolio inside each country or invested in the market leaders in each key sector of the economy.

In a later survey, Choi and Levich (1996) questioned 400 European institutional investors, 97 of whom replied. Two-thirds of these placed high reliance upon accounting information when selecting foreign equities and only four did not use accounting information at all. 85% of the respondents compared investments across countries rather than deciding upon the amount to invest in each country and then selecting from among potential investment targets inside it. When asked about accounting differences, only 23% of the respondents replied that differences in the quality of financial reporting limited their investments in Europe and 14% cited accounting differences as a reason for limiting investments. (Liquidity, currency and market risks were all mentioned by at least 40% of the sample.) This suggests that accounting differences are not very important. However, nearly half (42.3%) of the respondents said that they might increase their investment in Europe if a common set of accounting and reporting concepts were introduced. These respondents were equally divided on whether they would prefer IAS or US GAAP disclosures.

The respondents were also asked about how they dealt with differences in accounting principles and disclosure practices. The findings are reproduced in Exhibit 19.7.

Exhibit 19.7 DEALING WITH DIFFERENCES IN ACCOUNTING PRINCIPLES AND DISCLOSURE PRACTICES, 1996

	No. of Respondents	%
Differences in accounting principles:		
Place higher weight on other information	64	66.0
Restate foreign accounts	49	50.5
Use information and analysis from investment advisory services	41	42.3
Attach a low weight to accounting information	10	10.3
Differences in disclosure practices		
Visiting company to collect information	46	47.4
Assigning higher risk rating to company	44	45.4
Attending company road shows	42	43.3
Avoiding investment in companies with less disclosure	34	35.1
Requiring higher expected returns from companies with fewer disclosures	26	26.8
No answer	13	13.4

Source: Choi and Levich (1996), pp. 294–5

673

Two different approaches were taken when the accounting principles were different. Respondents either placed more emphasis upon other information, including the services of investment advisors, or attempted to restate the figures using more familiar GAAP. Again when the disclosure practices were different, two approaches were taken. Respondents either sought more information or they changed their investment strategies to cope with the increase in uncertainty.

19.5 CHANGES IN INVESTOR PROFILES

We argued in Chapter 18 that more and more companies have begun to raise equity finance in foreign stock exchanges over the last few years. This growth in foreign listings shows no evidence of declining and instead is likely to continue for at least the next few years. Many countries are in the middle of privatisation programmes and many very large companies from a variety of countries will be seeking large sums of equity finance in the next few years. Other companies will doubtless be tempted to issue shares internationally as the costs fall as international harmonisation increases and the extra disclosure and accounting costs decrease. This supply-side increase in equities should be accompanied by demand-side changes, with increasing demand by investors for foreign equities.

It is argued that the demand for equity investments will increase in general in the foreseeable future. There are also likely to be some changes in the composition of the demand, with demand for foreign equity investments, in particular, increasing. A number of reasons have been suggested for this.[5]

19.5.1 Pension schemes

Many countries have unfunded or underfunded pension schemes rather than funded schemes. (A funded scheme is one where the contributions of employees and employers are invested to earn returns that are then used to pay those employees' pensions when they become pensioners.) It is estimated that only about one in four EU employees are in funded pension schemes and private sector funded schemes currently account for just 7% of all pension payouts. In contrast, unfunded pension liabilities account for an average of 145% of EU countries' GDP. Of the funded schemes that do exist, the proportion of their funds invested in equities also varies greatly from a high of more than 80% in the UK to only 30% in the Netherlands or 10% in Germany. Given the pressures on governments and the state sector, it is probable that most countries will see moves away from government-based pension schemes and away from unfunded schemes to private sector funded schemes. Similarly, these schemes are likely to invest more of their funds in equities and will become more and more similar to UK funded schemes with their heavy reliance upon equity investment. If this happens, it is estimated that pension funds' total asset base in the EU might rise from around 1,100 billion ECU in 1997 to 10,200 billion ECU, at today's prices, by the year 2,020.

---

[5] Price Waterhouse (1997)

19.5.2 Privatisation

Secondly, large privatisation programmes have tended to attract foreign investors; international investors bought nearly two-thirds of all privatisation issues in 1995. With privatisations continuing to increase in the next few years, the importance of foreign investors is also likely to increase.

19.5.3 Diversification

Thirdly, the benefits of international diversification are beginning to be more and more understood. As this happens both institutional and individual investors will increasingly be looking to invest a higher proportion of their funds in foreign equities. It has been estimated that US fund managers need to increase the percentage of funds held outside the USA from the current level of 8% to nearer 20% if they wish to obtain the optimal risk–reward payoffs. Similarly, Japan has relaxed its rules to allow its pension funds to invest more in overseas equities.

These likely changes in the demand for, and supply of, equities will have different impacts in different countries. To see which countries will be most affected, and how they will be affected, it is necessary to return to the issue of differences in corporate financing systems, as discussed in Chapter 1, section 1.6. We saw in Chapter 1 examples of countries with very different corporate financing patterns. While retained earnings is usually the most important source of corporate finance, some countries rely more upon debt for external or new funding and others rely more upon equity finance. This is reflected in differences in the relative size or importance of stock markets. As we also saw in section 1.6, there are also significant differences across countries in terms of the pattern of equity ownership – whether equity is predominantly owned by private shareholders, by financial institutions or by other non-financial corporations.

Based upon these differences, two types of financial systems have been identified. As illustrated in Exhibit 19.8, these may be termed 'control-orientated' and 'arm's-length' financial systems.[6]

Other authors have instead discussed similar differences in terms of two different forms of capitalism, namely the 'Anglo-American model' and the 'Rhenish model', otherwise called the Germanic or continental European model.[7]

As with any such simple categorisation, the divide between the two systems is not always clear-cut and the distinction is often not as rigid or as unchanging as is suggested. In practice, there is the beginning of a convergence of the two systems. While UK and US capital markets can be characterised by the relatively greater importance of outside shareholders and by relatively greater interest in short-term financial results, many of the larger companies are actively engaged in promoting and building long-term relationships with their various stakeholders, so reducing the differences between 'outsiders' and insiders'. Similarly, many companies in countries such as Germany, France or Japan, all members of the continental European group, are coming to rely more upon outside shareholders for finance and so are becoming more concerned with increasing shareholder value.[8]

---

[6] Berglof (1997)
[7] Albert, quoted in Price Waterhouse (1997)
[8] Price Waterhouse (1997)

Exhibit 19.8 FINANCIAL SYSTEMS AND CAPITAL STRUCTURE

	Type of financial system	
	Control-orientated	*Arm's-length*
Share of control-orientated finance	High	Low
Financial markets	Small, less liquid	Large, highly liquid
Share of all firms listed on exchanges	Small	Large
Ownership of debt and equity	Concentrated	Dispersed
Investor orientation	Control-orientated	Portfolio-orientated
Use of mechanisms for separating control and capital base	Frequent	Limited (often by regulation)
Dominant agency conflicts	Controlling vs. minority shareholders	Shareholder vs. management
Role of board of directors	Limited	Important
Role of hostile takeovers	Very limited	Potentially important

Source: Berglof (1997)

These changes affect financial reporting in a number of ways. We have discussed throughout this book the increasing international harmonisation of financial reporting methods. However, there are still substantial differences between the accounting rules of different countries, and companies who wish to list on foreign stock markets may have to report using these foreign rules. Alternatively, increasing numbers of foreign investors that are unfamiliar with domestic GAAP may cause companies to look voluntarily for reporting methods that they can better understand. The increasing importance of independent or outside shareholders, including institutional investors, also means that companies are increasing the amount of information that they voluntarily report. This involves not just financial disclosures but also non-financial or narrative disclosures. This move towards increasing information disclosure may also be seen as a response to the needs of various non-shareholder groups.

19.6 USERS OF FINANCIAL STATEMENTS

It is not just shareholders or investors that may want to use corporate financial statements. While investors are one of the most important groups that a company will want to report to, a wide range of other report users can also be identified. An early and influential report of the UK standard setting body[9] identified seven user groups (*see* Exhibit 19.9).

While we have concentrated upon foreign equity investors so far in this chapter, many companies also have foreign financial statement users belonging to each of the other groups listed in Exhibit 19.9. Many of the motives for raising debt or loans in foreign countries will be the same as the motives for raising foreign equity.

---

[9] ASSC (1975)

Exhibit 19.9 USERS OF CORPORATE REPORTS, AS IDENTIFIED BY *THE CORPORATE REPORT* (1975)

Equity-investor group:	Existing and potential shareholders
Loan creditor group:	Debentures, loan stock, long- and short-term loan providers
Employee group:	Existing, past and potential employees
Analyst–advisor group:	Financial analysts, stockbrokers, trade unions, journalists, etc.
Business contact group:	Customers, suppliers, competitors
Government:	Taxation, supervision commerce and industry, local authorities
Public:	Consumers, tax payers, local community, environmental groups, etc.

Some companies may raise foreign loans, as they see this as a way of reducing the costs of capital. This may be part of an active treasury management policy designed to minimise costs – or, in some cases, even as part of a strategy to actively speculate on foreign currency markets.[10] Other companies will raise foreign debt as a way of reducing risk. As with equity, if debt is raised in the same countries as the money is invested, the company can use local currency earnings to repay the debt. If instead debt is raised in one country and employed in another, the company will have to convert its earnings into a different currency before they can be used to repay the debt, and may therefore be adversely affected by exchange rate changes.

Virtually all large companies have to source some of their supplies from foreign suppliers and similarly sell some of their outputs in foreign markets. Most companies, whether manufacturing or service sector companies, go further than this and also operate overseas.[11] This means that foreign customers, suppliers, employees, governments, local communities and various special interest and pressure groups are all likely to be interested in the activities of, and performance of, the company.

Some of the groups identified in Exhibit 19.9 can demand whatever information they want. Governments, stock markets, large loan or debt providers and important customers and suppliers may all be able to demand the information they want. However, providing extra information is not costless and if any of these groups demands a great deal of information they may find that foreign companies are not prepared to trade with them or operate in their countries. In other cases the users cannot or will not impose specific reporting or measurement requirements on foreign companies. Instead, companies are free to decide the extent to which they will meet the specific needs of foreign users. A number of alternative

---

[10] Discussion of this issue is outside the scope of this text, but useful texts in this area include Buckley (1992), Demirag and Goddard (1994) and Holland (1993)

[11] Again, the reasons why companies become international are outside the scope of this text, but useful texts in this area include Caves (1996), Dunning (1988) and Pitelis and Sugden (1991).

strategies are available to a company, ranging from doing nothing to producing statements that are the same as those generally produced by domestic companies. These different alternatives are all briefly examined below.

19.7 METHODS OF REPORTING TO FOREIGN USERS

19.7.1 Foreign-language statements

Obviously, companies could just ignore the fact that many users are from other countries and are used to different accounting methods, different types of narrative disclosures, different currencies and perhaps even different languages. They could design their financial statements and annual reports for domestic users and then make these available to all foreign users as well. This would involve no extra direct costs, but there may be substantial indirect or hidden costs in this approach. If potential lenders cannot even understand the language in which the reports are written they are far less likely to lend the company money. An approach adopted by many companies is therefore to translate their annual reports and accounts into foreign language(s). This might be just an abridged report (typically the financial statements, the accounting policies, the Chair's statement and a very brief overview of activities) or a complete word-for-word translation of the entire annual accounts and report. Most large European companies produce complete English-language versions of their annual report including all the narrative disclosures. Indeed, quite a number of European companies produce their complete annual accounts and reports in several languages, while others instead produce a simplified or cut-down version in several languages. Increasing numbers of companies that provide information on the World Wide Web are also providing this information in more than one language.

The only costs involved in translating the statements are the cost of translation and any additional printing costs. However, these can sometimes be quite substantial as relatively small print runs may be involved (the French company PSA Peugeot Citroen, for example, which trades in London on SEAQ and in NYSE on the OTC market, printed only 5,000 copies of its 1995 English-language statements). This alternative involves no extra information production or report design costs as exactly the same figures are reported and no new documents designed. It is therefore an acceptable method of reporting to foreign users if:

● the foreign users are relatively unimportant, or
● the foreign users of the financial figures are knowledgeable, or
● the accounting and reporting systems of the two countries are very similar to each other.

If there are relatively few foreign users or they are relatively unimportant, it will not be worth spending any more on any of the more expensive alternative ways of reporting to foreign users – the additional costs would outweigh the advantages. Alternatively, the foreign readers may be very knowledgeable about the differences in the accounting systems internationally. As we saw in section 19.4 above, some investors are able to adopt a multiple principle capability and are able to cope with differences in accounting methods. Here, there would be no advantages to the company in using other more sophisticated but more expensive reporting methods. Finally, there may be little point in doing more if there are few material differences between domestic and foreign GAAP statements.

19.7.2 Convenience translations

So far, we have discussed the translation of the words into a more familiar language. Even when this is done, users may still be confused by the use of a different or unfamiliar currency. While this is obviously less likely to be a problem, the use of a different currency can make it much more difficult to get an accurate impression of what is going on. Some companies therefore go one stage further and also translate the currency they report in – the 'convenience translation', so called as it is not a complete method of foreign currency translation, such as the closing rate or temporal method. Instead, all the figures, both the current year and past year(s), are translated at one exchange rate. The purpose and limitations of a convenience translation are discussed in Exhibit 19.10, which reproduces the description of convenience translations as provided by a Korean company, Ssangyong Cement.

Exhibit 19.10 SSANGYONG CEMENT INDUSTRIAL CO. LTD: ACCOUNTING POLICY DESCRIBING CONVENIENCE TRANSLATION, 1994

> ### 3. United States Dollar Amounts
>
> *The Company operates primarily in Korean won and its official accounting records are maintained in Korean won. The U.S. dollar amounts are provided herein as supplementary information solely for the convenience of the reader. For both 1994 and 1993, all won amounts are expressed in U.S. dollars at the rate of ₩788.7:U.S.$1, which was the prevailing rate on December 31, 1994. This presentation is not in accordance with either Korean or United States accounting principles, and should not be constructed as a manifestation that the won amounts included in the financial statements could be converted or settled in U.S. dollars at ₩788.7:U.S.$1 or any other rate.*

Source: Ssangyong Cement, annual report, 1994, p. 45

Another example of a convenience translation is provided by Hanson plc. This UK conglomerate was, before it de-merged into its constituent businesses, very dependent upon the US market. It had significant numbers of American shareholders and made more of its sales in the USA than in the UK. It therefore provided a convenience translation of its UK GAAP based balance sheet and income statement. This convenience translation was somewhat unusual as the balance sheets (current and comparative year) were both translated at the closing exchange rate or the exchange rate at the date of the latest balance sheet, while the income statements was translated at the average rate for the year (*see* Exhibit 19.11).

Exhibit 19.11 HANSON PLC: CONVENIENCE TRANSLATION OF AN INCOME STATEMENT, 1995

TRANSLATION TO US DOLLARS
INCOME STATEMENT AND CAPITAL EMPLOYED

for the year ended September 30, 1995 (UK GAAP)

By activity	1995 Profit $ million	Sales turnover $ million	Capital employed $ million	1994 Profit $ million	Sales turnover $ million	Capital employed $ million
Chemicals	914	3,207	1,966	349	2,730	1,901
Consumer	613	5,921	(79)	585	5,440	(5)
Energy	417	2,821	5,643	325	2,552	3,495
Building materials & equipment	517	3,797	6,902	484	3,659	6,614
Trading operations	**2,461**	**15,746**	**14,432**	**1,743**	**14,381**	**12,005**
Associated undertakings	25	–	158	24	–	190
Discontinued operations	155	1,922	–	366	3,547	959
	2,641	17,668	14,590	2,133	17,928	13,154
Central expenses less property and other income	(131)	55	131	(133)	260	190
Operating results	**2,510**	**17,723**	**14,721**	**2,000**	**18,188**	**13,344**
Exceptional items	(155)			537		
Net interest expense	(334)			(363)		
	2,021			2,174		
Tax	(412)			(453)		
Net income	1,609			1,721		
Net income per ADS – diluted	$1.51			$1.62		
By geographical location						
USA	1,399	7,623	10,449	808	7,201	9,922
UK	797	7,332	3,656	693	6,708	1,806
Other	159	846	616	133	732	657
Discontinued	155	1,922	–	366	3,547	959
	2,510	17,723	14,721	2,000	18,188	13,344

The exchange rate used to translate the above figures was the average rate for the year of $1.5847 to £ in respect of profit and sales turnover and the year end rate of $1.5827 to £ for capital employed.

Source: Hanson plc, annual report, 1995

Convenience translations are relatively rarely found in European reports, but many large Japanese companies provide such statements. Exhibit 15.18 showed some of the figures provided by Mazda Motor Corp., illustrating the provision of a convenience translation for the latest year for the notes to the accounts.

It is sometimes not only the language and the currency that are unfamiliar to the foreign reader. As we have seen throughout Part 2 of this text, the format of the financial statements typically found in particular countries can be quite different.

As discussed in Chapter 7, section 7.4.4, the EU Fourth and Seventh Directives prescribed particular layouts or formats for the balance sheet and the income statement. As shown in Appendix 7.1, the directives permit companies to present both statements in either a vertical or a horizontal form. While this is a presentation issue only, and users could reproduce the alternative form of balance sheet if they wished, the same is not true of the cost categories used in the income statement. The directives allow companies to produce an income statement that analyses expenditures by type (labour, materials, etc.) or by function (cost of sales, administration, etc.). Users cannot convert the information from one form to the other. As we saw in the chapters on EU countries, different formats are more popular in some countries than others. Chapter 9, section 9.7.2.3, discussed the typical formats used in Germany. Most balance sheets are produced using the two-sided format while type of expenditure-based income statements (e.g. showing total labour costs, total depreciation) are common. In contrast, in the UK (Chapter 11, section 11.7.3.1) most companies produce a one-sided or horizontal balance sheet and an income statement with costs analysed by function. We also saw differences across non-EU countries. US balance sheets (Chapter 13, section 13.7.2.3) typically list assets from the most liquid to the least liquid, or the reverse order to that found in the UK. This is then followed by all the liabilities, which also means that net current assets are not disclosed as a separate item in the statement.

Most companies are not too concerned about these differences and do not reformat their accounts to give the information in a more familiar form. The one exception to this tends to be Japanese companies. These companies almost always reformat their accounts to present them in a form more familiar to foreign (US) readers. In many cases this is not simply a case of presenting the same information in a slightly different form, but also involves the provision of additional information. Exhibit 19.12 reproduces the description provided by Toyota Motor Corporation.

Exhibit 19.12 shows that Toyota not only present English-language statements with the latest year's figures translated into US dollars, but also reclassifies some items to make the formats similar to those used by US companies. It also presents new information in the form of additional notes and a cash flow statement.

19.7.3 Use of foreign GAAP

A company can decide to go yet a stage further and use foreign GAAP in its statements to foreign users. Whether a company will do this will depend upon the relative costs and benefits. The costs obviously depend upon whether or not this information is already available and, if it is not, how different the local and foreign GAAP are. As discussed in Chapter 18 (*see* section 18.4.3.1), the US stock markets, in SEC regulation 20-F, demand that foreign companies provide a reconciliation

Exhibit 19.12 TOYOTA MOTOR CORP.: INFORMATION ON BASIS OF PRESENTING FINANCIAL STATEMENTS, 1997

1. Basis of Presenting Financial Statements

The accompanying consolidated financial statements have been prepared in accordance with the accounting principles generally accepted in Japan from accounts and records maintained by Toyota Motor Corporation (the "Parent") and its subsidiaries. The Consolidated Statements of Cash Flows have been prepared for inclusion in these consolidated financial statements, though those statements are not required in Japan. Relevant notes have been added, and certain reclassifications of the accounts in the basic financial statements published in Japan have been made to present them in a form more familiar to readers outside Japan. These reclassifications do not affect the values of total assets, shareholders' equity, net sales, or net income.

The financial statements presented here are expressed in yen. Solely for the convenience of the reader, they have been translated into U.S. dollars at the rate of ¥124=US$1, the approximate exchange rate on the Tokyo Foreign Exchange Market on March 31, 1997. These translations should not be construed as representations that the yen amounts have been or could be converted into U.S. dollars at the rate used here or at any other rate.

In 1995, the Parent changed its fiscal year-end to March 31, from June 30, which resulted in a nine-month fiscal period ended March 31, 1995.

Source: Toyota Motor Corp., annual report, 1997, p. 39

statement. These statements start with domestic earnings and equity and list all the significant differences in GAAP. Each difference is quantified so that the total difference between local and foreign earnings and equity are explained. Exhibit 3.1 provided an example of the reconciliation statement of British Telecom. Given that companies listed in the US have to produce these statements, the additional costs of publication in the annual report are small. Exhibit 19.13 reproduces a reconciliation statement showing the difference between earnings under Chinese- and Hong Kong-based GAAP.

The benefits depend upon several factors. Some companies would argue that there are no benefits. Instead, they would argue that producing two sets of figures will increase uncertainty. However, if the users are relatively sophisticated they should be able to understand why two sets of figures produce very different earnings or equity and should not be deterred from dealing with the company. Indeed, some users are sufficiently powerful to demand statements drawn-up in familiar GAAP. For example, banks when lending large sums of money will often be able to demand whatever information they require. Similar powers are held by Governments and tax authorities. The benefits will depend not only upon the particular foreign users that are most important but also the size and number of GAAP differences. For example, many Finnish companies used to provide reconciliation statements to IAS based figures.[12] They tend no longer to do so following changes in local accounting rules which have brought Finnish practices much more into line with the EU so that the rules used are now far more familiar to foreign users.

Japanese companies in particular very often go a stage further and provide financial statements using foreign GAAP. For example, Exhibits 15.1 and 15.2 reproduce the description of the accounting policies of Kubota corporation and Hitachi corporation. Both of these companies use US GAAP in their foreign language statements.

[12] Adams *et al.* (1993)

Exhibit 19.13 RECONCILIATION STATEMENT SHANGHAI HAI XING SHIPPING CO. LTD: SHOWING DIFFERENCE IN EARNINGS UNDER CHINESE- AND HONG KONG-BASED GAAP, 1996

	29. 按照香港一般採納的會計準則和中國會計準則編制財務報表之差異	29. DIFFERENCES IN FINANCIAL STATEMENTS PREPARED UNDER HK GAAP AND PRC ACCOUNTING STANDARDS

本集團按照中國會計準則編制一份截至一九九六年十二月三十一日止年度的財務報告。分別按照中國會計準則和香港一般採納的會計準則編制財務報告的主要差異載列如下：

The Group has prepared a separate set of financial statements for the year ended 31 December 1996 in accordance with the PRC accounting statutory standards. The major differences between the financial statements prepared under PRC accounting standards and HK GAAP are set out as follows:

		截至十二月三十一日止年度 Year ended 31 December	
		1996	1995
		人民幣千元 RMB'000	人民幣千元 RMB'000
按照香港一般採納的會計準則編製的年度股東應佔溢利／（虧損）	Net profit/(loss) attributable to shareholders for the year prepared under HK GAAP	(157,465)	37,649
調整：	Adjustments:		
折舊	Depreciation charges	54,070	22,747
出售船舶溢利	Profit on disposal of vessels	65,545	25,646
壞帳準備	Doubtful debt provision	9,734	28,723
確認收入和開支的時差（已扣除去年影響）	Timing differences in recognition of income and expenses, net of prior year reversal	26,161	(27,515)
其他	Others	(34)	(378)
按照中國會計準則編製的年度股東應佔溢利／（虧損）	Net profit/(loss) attributable to shareholders for the year prepared under PRC accounting standards	(1,989)	86,872

Source: Shanghai Hai Xing Shipping Co. Ltd, annual report, 1996

19.7.4 Impact upon domestic reports

Some companies have gone even further along the road towards truly international reporting. So far we have talked of what extra or different information should be given to foreign users. One stage further along the path towards being a completely international company would be to instead ask the question – 'what information is most useful to all our readers, whatever their nationality?' While most companies do not have the luxury of deciding what rules should be used in the reports given to their local stock markets, they do have greater freedom in deciding what information is given to readers of the annual accounts. Few companies have gone this far, probably as most companies view themselves as belonging to a particular country but having important foreign operations or important foreign readers of their accounts. However, some companies have begun to move away from reporting in local GAAP but are instead using the most appropriate or useful GAAP. Exhibit 19.14 reproduces the comments made by a vice president of Holderbank, a large Swiss conglomerate company, when describing why the company decided to adopt IASs and the results of this move away from local GAAP statements to IASC-based statements.

Exhibit 19.14 HOLDERBANK, SWITZERLAND: ADOPTION OF IASs

Why did we fundamentally change the way we were handling accounting and reporting? First of all, strong developments of the Group led us to reconsider our internal management information system. We wished to introduce uniform accounting procedures understood by each subsidiary around the world. Even with a good home-made accounting system in existence, we had problems explaining our system to the outside world, especially to the financial analysts. The Swiss accounting rules did not provide a high level of transparency. A major objective was to improve information to our shareholders and to make sure that our financial statements are perceived as true and fair.

The main reason for the move to international accounting standards and not to US GAAP were as follows: IAS is an excellent common denominator for all subsidiaries operating worldwide. IAS offers some flexibility to take into account special local situations. IAS are less formal and more easily understood by non-Americans. Looking at cost benefit analysis, based on our experience, it was more efficient to introduce IAS than US GAAP. In my opinion, US GAAP is too heavily US orientated and covers far too many details which are not material to our objectives.

What are the results of the three years of experience? The financial world, investors, analysts, bankers, welcomed this move, and now our financial statements and disclosures are highly appreciated. This is also valued by the financial institutions in the US. Our discussions have shown that in the US there is not any problem in understanding our financial information.

Source: P. Wirtz, Senior Vice-President Holderbank, quoted in Bayless *et al.* (1996), p. 84

More common than this approach of Holderbank are companies which use local GAAP but choose particular options inside that or chose to account for items that are not covered by local rules in ways that are determined by consideration of international practices. We discussed in Chapter 1 (section 1.8.3) the importing of accounting practices and saw examples of a New Zealand and a Belgium company which both used US standards in areas that were not covered by local rules. We have also seen throughout the country chapters examples of companies that have used IASC standards (*see*, for example, Exhibit 8.8 on France, Exhibit 9.9 on Germany or Exhibit 15.14 on Japan). In these examples, the companies are using local GAAP but wherever possible are adopting those practices which are also consistent with international standards or international practices. This should mean that the accounts are more comparable with those of companies from other countries and are therefore more familiar to and understandable by the foreign reader. This obviously reduces the need to provide reconciliation statements or full foreign GAAP-based statements.

It is not only the financial accounts themselves that might be altered to meet the needs or expectations of foreign users, the narrative disclosures might also be altered. While there is relatively little evidence on why companies change their narrative disclosures over time, there is clear evidence that the amount of narrative information provided is tending to increase. We also saw in Chapter 3 that there is some evidence that internationally listed companies report significant different and significantly more voluntary narrative information than do domestically listed companies.

19.8 SUMMARY AND CONCLUSIONS

This chapter has taken a different perspective to that adopted in Chapter 18 when looking at the same question – what are the effects of international diversity in accounting practices? This chapter has looked at the users of financial statements and tried to answer two questions in particular. How do investors cope with accounting diversity? How can companies adapt their disclosure policies to report more useful information to foreign users?

The chapter began by reviewing some of the earlier material on sources of accounting differences and revisited the question of how material these differences are. Given the often very different figures that are produced under different GAAP, it is not immediately obvious why investors would want to cope with the additional problems and uncertainty involved in investing in foreign companies. However, we saw that the benefits can be substantial and, at least for the individual or private investor, it is getting easier and easier to invest in foreign companies indirectly through the ever-increasing number of investment funds that exist. However, this does not remove the problem of how to cope with accounting diversity – the investment trusts still have to decide which companies they should invest in. The chapter therefore looked at the somewhat limited evidence there is regarding how investors cope with accounting diversity. It clearly appears that, while some market participants are able to cope with diversity, a significant number are adversely affected. The evidence suggest that foreign investment might well increase if accounting diversity was reduced. Other investors might change their behaviour in that they currently rely less upon accounting information or require companies to meet different criteria than they would otherwise. We saw that this may well become an increasingly important problem: the demand for international investments are likely to increase and the number of companies seeking foreign listing also looks likely to increase, at least over the next few years.

All of this means that more and more companies are likely to face the question of how best to report to foreign users. We saw that a variety of alternatives exist. These vary in terms of how much information is changed to meet the needs or expectations of the foreign user, ranging from translation into foreign languages, through to translation of the currencies and account formats, through to complete statements under foreign GAAP. Which approach is taken depends upon a number of factors. How important and how sophisticated are the foreign users and how different are local accounting practices from international practices? There are distinct country approaches, with Japanese companies tending to do the most to meet the demands of foreign users. Very many Japanese companies, not just those listed on overseas stock markets, produce English-language reports, often using US GAAP. They usually also contain the types of narrative disclosures typically found in North American reports. These disclosures are provided especially for the foreign reader and are not the same as those found in Japanese reports. This is unusual, most companies from other countries will either produce exactly the same narratives in domestic and foreign reports or will report less narrative information. This does not necessarily mean that international pressures are unimportant in explaining narrative disclosures. It may instead be the case that companies take an international perspective when deciding what to voluntarily report and how to report it. They may thus change the information provided to domestic users to ensure that all users, both domestic and foreign, receive the same information.

QUESTIONS

Accounting differences (19.2)

1 Outline the main causes of the differences that exist in the accounting practices across different countries.

2 On the basis of the evidence presented in Exhibit 19.1, which EU countries tend to disclose the smallest, and which the greatest, earnings figures?

3 In which of the countries identified in Exhibit 19.1 do companies appear to have the greatest discretion with respect to reported earnings figures?

4 Do your answers in questions 2 and 3 surprise you? Explain your reasoning.

International equity investment (19.3 and 19.4)

1 Why might investors wish to invest in foreign companies?

2 Describe the composition of the optimal portfolio that an investor can invest in and describe how they might go about investing in a suitable portfolio.

3 Identify and describe the alternative investment strategies an investor can adopt when deciding which shares to invest in and, in each case, describe the role and use of financial statement information.

4 What is the possible impact of accounting diversity on international investors?

5 What strategies might an investor take to cope with accounting diversity, and in what circumstances might each strategy be optimal?

Changes in international investment (19.5)

1 Describe the reasons there are for believing that the number of companies listing on foreign stock markets are likely to increase over the next few years.

2 Which stock markets are likely to prove particularly attractive to foreign companies? Why is this?

3 Describe the reasons there are for believing that the demand for foreign equities will continue to increase over the next few years.

Corporate responses to foreign users (19.7)

1 Describe each of the main methods that a company could adopt when reporting to its foreign users.

2 Describe the relative advantages and disadvantages of each of the methods identified in your answer to Question 1.

REFERENCES

Accounting Standards Steering Committee (1975) *The Corporate Report*. London: ASSC.

Adams, C.A., Weetman, P. and Gray, S.J. (1993) 'Reconciling national with international accounting standards: Lessons from a study of Finnish corporate accounts', *European Accounting Review*, December, 471–94.

Albert, M. *Capitalism against Capitalism*, quoted in Price Waterhouse (1997).

Bayless, R., Cochrane, J., Harris, T., Leisenring, J., McLaughlin, J. and Wirtz, J.P. (1996) 'International access to US capital markets – An AAA forum on accounting policy', *Accounting Horizons*, 10(1), 75–94.

Berglof, E. (1997) 'Reforming corporate governance: Redirecting the European agenda', *Economic Policy*, April, 91–117.

Buckley, A. (1992) *Multinational Finance*. 2nd edn. Hemel Hempstead: Prentice Hall.

Caves, R.E. (1996) *Multinational Enterprise and Economic Analysis*. 2nd edn. Cambridge: Cambridge University Press.

Choi, F.D.S. and Levich, R.M. (1990) *The Capital Market Effects of International Accounting Diversity*. New York: Dow Jones–Irwin.

Choi, F.D.S. and Levich, R.M. (1996) 'Accounting diversity', in Steil, B. (ed.) *The European Equity Markets*. London: Royal Institute of International Affairs.

Choi, F.D.S. and Levich, R.M. (1997) 'Accounting diversity and capital market decisions', in Choi, F.D.S. (ed.) *International Accounting and Finance Handbook*. 2nd edn. New York: John Wiley.

Demirag, I. and Goddard, S. (1994) *Financial Management and International Business*. Maidenhead: McGraw-Hill.

Dunning, J.H. (1988) *Explaining International Production*. London: Unwin Hyman.

Fabozzi, F. and Modigliani, F. (1996) *Capital Markets: Institutions and Instruments*. 2nd edn. Englewood Cliffs, NJ: Prentice-Hall Inc.

Gastineau, G., Holterman, G. and Beighley, S. (1993) *Equity Investment Across Borders: Cutting the Costs*. SBC Research, Swiss Bank Corp. Inc. (January), 24.

Heston, S. and Rouwenhorst, G. (1994) 'Does industrial structure explain the benefits of international diversification?', *Journal of Financial Economics*, August.

Holland, J. (1993) *International Financial Management*. 2nd edn. Oxford: Blackwell.

Melton, P. (1996) *The Investor's Guide to Going Global with Equities*. London: FT/Pitman Publishing.

Pitelis, C.N. and Sugden, R. (eds) (1991) *The Nature of the Transnational Firm*. London: Routledge.

Price Waterhouse (1997) *Converging Cultures: Trends in European Corporate Governance*. London: Price Waterhouse Europe (April).

Simmonds, A. and Azières, O. (1989) *Accounting for Europe – Success by 2000AD?* London: Touche Ross.

Solnik, B. (1974) 'Why not diversify internationally?', *Financial Analysts Journal*, July/August, 48–54.

Index